# SHORT STORY INDEX

Supplement 1969-1973

# SHORT STORY INDEX

Supplement 1969-1973

AN INDEX TO 11,561 STORIES IN
805 COLLECTIONS

Edited by
ESTELLE A. FIDELL

NEW YORK
THE H. W. WILSON COMPANY
1974

Copyright © 1974

By The H. W. Wilson Company

Printed in the United States of America

International Standard Book Number 0-8242-0497-2

Library of Congress Card Number (53-8991)

# Preface

The fifth supplement of SHORT STORY INDEX indexes 11,561 stories in 805 collections published during the five-year period 1969-1973. As in previous volumes, the arrangement is alphabetical by author, title, and subject. The author entry, which mentions the collection in which a story can be found, is the most complete entry. A List of Collections Indexed and a Directory of Publishers and Distributors complete the volume.

The H. W. Wilson Company is grateful to those publishers who provided copies of their books for indexing.

# Contents

# Directions for Use

Part I of this Index is in dictionary form with author, title, and subject entries in one alphabet. Part II is a List of the Collections Indexed. Part III is a Directory of Publishers and Distributors. The following directions apply to Part I.

**Author entry.** This entry gives the name of the author, title of the story, and author and title of the collection or collections in which the story is found. It may be recognized by the boldface type, *not* in capital letters.

Sample entry:

**Yglesias, José**
    The guns in the closet
        The Best American short stories, 1972

This means that the short story by José Yglesias, "The guns in the closet" appears in the collection entitled The Best American short stories, 1972. For fuller information about The Best American short stories, 1972 consult the "List of Collections Indexed" under The Best American short stories, 1972.

**Title entry.** This entry is used primarily to identify the author under whose name the full information is given. Only the first word (not an article) of each title entry is in boldface type.

Sample entry:

    The **guns** in the closet. Yglesias, J.

**Subject entry.** All stories in this Index dealing in whole or in part with a particular subject are listed under that subject. Such entries are in capital letters, in boldface type.

Sample entry:

**FATHERS AND SONS**
    Yglesias, J. The guns in the closet

# SHORT STORY INDEX, 1969-1973

## PART I

### Author, Title, and Subject Index

About the miraculous fritter of Frat' Agostino of the Cappuccini. Corvo, F. Baron

About the original fritter of Sangiuseppe. Corvo, F. Baron

About the preface of Fra Cherubino. Corvo, F. Baron

About the rooster and his children. Leskov, N.

About the witch's head and Santignazio of Loyola. Corvo, F. Baron

Abroad. Gordimer, N.

Absence. Kampmann, C.

Absence. Soto, P. J.

The absent-minded coterie. Barr, R.

**ABSENT-MINDEDNESS**
Barr, R. The absent-minded coterie

Absent without leave. Böll, H.

Absolutely elsewhere. Sayers, D. L.

Absolutely inflexible. Silverberg, R.

**ABSTINENCE.** *See* Fasting

The Absurd One. Bullins, E.

Acacias. Stewart, N.

**ACADIANS IN LOUISIANA**
Chopin, K. Azélie
Chopin. K. A night in Acadie

**ACAPULCO.** *See* Mexico—Acapulco

Access to the children. Trevor, W.

Accessories after the fact. Gilbert, M.

The accident. Dorris, J. R.

The accident. McElroy, J.

The accident. Wiesel, E.

Accident vertigo. Elmslie, K.

**ACCIDENTAL DEATH.** *See* Accidents

**ACCIDENTAL SHOOTING.** See Accidents; Hunting—Accidents

**ACCIDENTS**
Angell, R. In an early winter
Arthur, E. Cal always said
Beckett, S. Walking out
Bierce, A. George Thurston
Böll, H. Lohengrin's death
Borchert, W. From the other side to the other side
Churchill, W. Man overboard
Clement, H. Lecture demonstration
Cornish, M. Superstitious ignorance
Di Donato, P. The broken scaffold
Elmslie, K. Accident vertigo
García Márquez, G. Nabo
Gottlieb, K. The gun
Greene, G. The basement room
Greene, G. A shocking accident
Hoffman, C. F. The man in the reservoir
Hopkinson, T. Mountain madness
Hopper, W. O. Where the immortal are
James, H. My friend Bingham
Joensen, M. The "man" on board
Kaplan, B. Eddie Angel
Kipling, R. At the pit's mouth
Lavin, M. A pure accident
Madden, D. The pale horse of fear
Marshall, E. The flying lion
Michaels, L. Isaac
Mitchison, N. After the accident
Nedreaas, T. Music from a blue well
Oates, J. C. Demons
O'Hara, J. Flight

O'Hara, J. Grief
Phillifent, J. T. Aim for the heel
Reynolds, M. Prone
Terry, W. S. The bottomless well
Tindall, G. The secret of a joyful life
Tuohy, F. Fingers in the door
Wilson, A. A sad fall

See also Aeronautics—Accidents; Automobiles—Accidents; Drowning; Hunting—Accidents; Mine accidents; Motorcycles—Accidents; Mountaineering—Accidents; Shooting; Trucks—Accidents

**Accioly, Breno**
João Urso
Cohen, J. M. ed. Latin American writing today

An accommodation. Cotterill, A.

Accomplished desires. Oates, J. C.

**ACCOUNTANTS**
Cather, W. The bookkeeper's wife
Hunter, E. The sharers
Kaupas, J. The organ of Kurkliškés
Kipling, R. A gift for numbers
Maupassant, G. de. A little walk
Nourse, A. E. A gift for numbers

Accusing eyes of vengeance. Williamson, G.

**Achebe, Chinua**
Akueke
Achebe, C. Girls at war, and other stories
Chike's school days
Achebe, C. Girls at war, and other stories
Civil peace
Achebe, C. Girls at war, and other stories
Dead men's path
Achebe, C. Girls at war, and other stories
Girls at war
Achebe, C. Girls at war, and other stories
The madman
Achebe, C. Girls at war, and other stories
Marriage is a private affair
Achebe, C. Girls at war, and other stories
The sacrificial egg
Achebe, C. Girls at war, and other stories
Sugar Baby
Achebe, C. Girls at war, and other stories
Uncle Ben's choice
Achebe, C. Girls at war, and other stories
Vengeful creditor
Achebe, C. Girls at war, and other stories
The voter
Achebe, C. Girls at war, and other stories

**ACHESON, DEAN GOODERHAM**
Russell, B. Dean Acheson's nightmare

Achilles' heel. O'Connor, F.

Acme Rooms and sweet Marjorie Russell. Hunt, H. A.

ACOLYTES. *See* Altar boys
ACROBATS AND ACROBATICS. *See*
   Jugglers and juggling
**Across** Neahkahnie. Berry, D.
**Across** the bar. Reed, K.
**Across** the bridge. Böll, H.
**Across** the bridge. Greene, G.
**Across** the plains. Sienkiewicz, H.
An **act** of admiration. Dorr, L.
An **act** of charity. O'Connor, F.
An **act** of prostitution. McPherson, J. A.
ACTING. *See* Actors; Actresses; Theater
   and stage life
**Acton, Harold**
   The gift horse
      Winter's tales 17
ACTORS
   Aiken, J. Furry night
   Aldiss, B. W. The young soldier's horo-
      scope
   Allingham, M. Publicity
   Ayton, M. A performance of Saint Joan
   Biggle, L. Leading man
   Bloch, R. The play's the thing
   Brown, F. Ten percenter
   Bukowski, C. The murder of Ramon Vas-
      quez
   Collier, J. Gavin O'Leary
   Cortázar, J. Instructions for John Howell
   Crane, S. Manacled
   Eklund, G. Lovemaker
   Ellin, S. The house party
   Ellison, H. All the sounds of fear
   Fast, H. The interval
   Hoffman, E. T. A. Princess Brambilla
   Hudson, J. How does that make you feel?
   Kanin, G. The Cavalier collar
   Kanin, G. The he-she chemistry
   Kaplan, B. How revolutionaries are made
   Maloney, R. Intimacy
   O'Hara, J. Conversation at lunch
   Onetti, J. C. A dream come true
   Paley, G. Goodbye and good luck
   Silverberg, R. Counterpart
   Singer, I. B. A friend of Kafka
   Wain, J. A sample of the ocean
   Williams, G. The yellow brick road
     *See also* Actresses; Moving picture
     actors and actresses; Strolling players
ACTORS, MOVING PICTURE. *See* Mov-
   ing picture actors and actresses
The **actress**. Zobarskas, S.
The **actress** Olenina. Linklater, E.
ACTRESSES
   Bambara, T. C. The survivor
   Cabrera Infante, G. At the great 'Ecbo'
   Charyn, J. Sing, Shaindele, sing
   Cheever, J. The fourth alarm
   Chekhov, A. A dreary story
   Chekhov, A. A stage manager under the
      sofa
   Colette. The victim
   Collier, J. Gavin O'Leary
   Collier, J. Pictures in the fire
   Collier, J. Youth from Vienna
   Eklund, G. Lovemaker
   Gallant, M. The old friends
   Goulart, R. Subject to change
   Henry, O. The memento

   Hoffman, E. T. A. Princess Brambilla
   Hudson, J. How does that make you feel?
   Kanin, G. Don't forget
   Kanin, G. There goes my other phone
   Kanin, G. Who to who
   Kaplan, B. How revolutionaries are made
   Lessing, D. Side benefits of an honourable
      profession
   Lessing, D. An unposted love letter
   Linklater, E. The actress Olenina
   McGahern, J. Peaches
   Moravia, A. You're all right
   Mudrick, M. Cleopatra
   Oates, J. C. You
   Onetti, J. C. Dreaded hell
   Parker, D. Glory in the daytime
   Pritchett, V. S. The chain-smoker
   Queen, E. No parking
   Rushmore, R. The trumpets of Épignon
   Zobarskas, S. The actress
     *See also* Actors; Entertainers; Mov-
     ing picture actors and actresses
ACTRESSES, MOVING PICTURE. *See*
   Moving picture actors and actresses
ADAM (FIRST MAN)
   Boulle, P. When the serpent failed
**Adam** and Eve. Kazakov, Y.
**Adam** and his sons. Steinbeck, J.
**Adam** and no Eve. Bester, A.
**Adams, Alice**
   Gift of grass
      Prize stories, 1971: The O. Henry
        Awards
   Ripped off
      Prize stories, 1972: The O. Henry
        Awards
   The swastika on our door
      Prize stories, 1973: the O. Henry
        Awards
**Adams, Clifton**
   Hell command
      Western Writers of America. A West-
      ern bonanza
**Adams, Thomas E.**
   Sled
      Lytle, A. ed. Craft and vision
ADAPTATION (BIOLOGY)
   Russell, R. The Darwin sampler
   Zelazny, R. The keys to December
**Adcock, Arthur St John**
   At the dock gate
      Keating, P. J. ed. Working-class stories
      of the 1890s
ADDICTS. *See* Narcotic habit
ADDITIVES, FOOD. *See* Food additives
**Address** unknown. Taylor, K.
ADIRONDACK MOUNTAINS
   Heald, H. The man of stone
**Administrative** grace. Leskov, N.
ADOLESCENCE
   Adams, A. Gift of grass
   Aguallo, T. Doing well
   Ahlin, L. Polluted zone
   Ansell, J. Thought of love on a summer
      afternoon
   Arkanov, A. The high jump
   Baldwin, J. The outing
   Bambara, T. C. Sweet town
   Beneš, J. My greatest love

**ADOLESCENCE**—*Continued*

Rindfleisch, N. The summer of his discontent

Rodgers, C. Blackbird in a cage

Savitz, H. M. Peter

Savitz, H. M. The road to anywhere

Savitz, H. M. Why, Bo? Why?

Schecktor, M. C. Glow, little glowworm

Schultz, J. Witness

Schwartz, J. The deep end

Shepherd, J. The star-crossed romance of Josephine Cosnowski

Shepherd, J. Wanda Hickey's night of golden memories

Silverberg, R. Push no more

Slesinger, T. White on black

Street, P. The magic apple

Sturgeon, T. Jorry's gap

Taylor, P. Daphne's lover

Taylor, P. Venus, Cupid, folly and time

Trevor, W. An evening with John Joe Dempsey

Tuohy, F. The licence

Tuohy, F. The Palladian Bridge

Turgenev, I. The watch

Updike, J.  A sense of shelter

Vargas Llosa, M. Sunday, Sunday

West, J. Crimson Ramblers of the world, farewell

Williamson, J. N. They never even see me

Wolfe, G. The death of Doctor Island

Yellen, S. The four sides of a triangle

Zebrowski, G. First love, first fear

  *See also* Boys; Children; Gangs; Girls; Juvenile delinquency; Youth

**ADOLESCENTS.** *See* Adolescence

The **adopted** child. *See* Maupassant, G. de. The adoption

**ADOPTED CHILDREN.** *See* Adoption; Foster children

**ADOPTION**

Bates, P. The enemy

Parker, D. Little Curtis

Reed, K. Winston

Tindall, G. One of the family

  *See also* Foster children

The **adoption.** Maupassant, G. de

**Adrift** on the freeway. Bryant, E.

The **adult** education class. Bradbury, M.

**ADULTERY.** *See* Marriage problems

**ADVENTURE.** *See* Manhunts

The **adventure.** Sirof, H.

**ADVENTURE AND ADVENTURERS**

Carpentier, A. The Highroad of Saint James

Christie, A. The manhood of Edward Robinson

Geeraerts, J. Indian summer

Green, R. L. ed. Ten tales of adventure; 10 stories

Lamb, H. The White Khan

Lamb, H. The winged rider

Maclagan, D. Dr Black's castle

Maclagan, D. Journey to Enog

Maclagan, D. Three falling stars

Nye, R. Captain Rufus Coate

Ottley, R. Brumbie running

Ottley, R. Bush camels

Sindbad, the sailor. The second voyage of Sindbad the Seaman

Smith, C. A. The Ampoi giant

  *See also* Brigands and robbers; Interplanetary voyages; Science fiction; Sea stories; Spies; Western stories

An **adventure** at Brownville. Bierce, A.

An **adventure** from a work in progress. Thomas, D.

An **adventure** in futurity. Smith, C. A.

An **adventure** in the Yolla Bolly Middle Eel Wilderness. Aandahl, V.

The **adventure** of a desperate man. Prévost, A.

The **adventure** of Abraham Lincoln's clue. Queen, E.

An **adventure** of Francesco Sforza. Straparola

The **adventure** of Prince Florizel and a detective. Stevenson, R. L.

The **adventure** of the dog in the knight. Fish, R. L.

The **adventure** of the double-bogey man. Fish, R. L.

**Adventure** of the Grice-Paterson curse. Derleth, A.

The **adventure** of the hansom cab. Stevenson, R. L.

The **adventure** of the mantises. Chatain, R.

The **adventure** of the President's half disme. Queen, E.

The **adventure** of the red leech, Derleth, A.

The **adventure** of the seven black cats. Queen, E.

The **adventure** of the speckled band. *See* Doyle, Sir A. C. The speckled band

The **adventure** of Walter Schnaffs. Maupassant, G. de

**ADVENTURERS.** *See* Adventure and adventurers

**Adventures** of a novelist. Crane, S.

**Adventures** of a people buff. De Vries, P.

The **adventures** of Chichikov. Bulgakov, M.

The **adventures** of Shamrock Jolnes. Henry, O.

The **adventures** of the Adam bomb. Fish, R. L.

The **adventurous** exploit of the cave of Ali Baba. Sayers, D. L.

**ADVERTISING**

Ansell, J.  I passed for Yankee

Auchincloss, L. Second chance

Ballard, J. G. The sublimal man

Davidson, A. The sources of the Nile

Garrett, R. After a few words

Kanin, G. Buddy buddy

Moravia, A. Imitation

  *See also* Publicity; Sales promotion; Television advertising

**ADVERTISING, OUTDOOR.** *See* Skywriting

**ADVERTISING AGENCIES.** *See* Advertising

**Aelurophobe.** Brown, F.

**AENEUS SYLVIUS.** *See* Pius II, Pope

**Aepyornis** Island. Wells, H. G.

**Aerial** tracks. Pasternak, B.

**Aerial** ways. *See* Pasternak, B. Aerial tracks

**AERONAUTICS**
Cassill, R. V. The invention of the airplane

**Accidents**
Aldridge, J. The unfinished soldiers
Clarke, A. C. The wind from the sun
Cortázar, J. The island at noon
Ellison, R. Flying home
Emshwiller, C. Al
Heller, J. Snowden
Hughes, T. Snow
Norman, J. No rescue
Silverberg, R. One-way journey
Wolfe, G. Continuing westward

**Flights**
Bryant, E. No. 2 plain tank
Cheever, J. Three stories: III
De Ford, M. A. A case for the U.N.
Greene, G. The over-night bag

**AERONAUTICS, COMMERCIAL**
**Hijacking**
See Hijacking of airplanes
The **Aesculapians**. Mandell, M.
The **affair** at Coulter's Notch. Bierce, A.
The **affair** at Grover Station. Cather, W.
The **Affair** at 7, rue de M——. Steinbeck, J.
An **affair** of honor. Nabokov, V.
An **affair** of outposts. Bierce, A.
The **affair** of the 'Avalanche Bicycle and Tyre Co., Limited'. Morrison, A.
The **affair** of the German Dispatch-Box. Whitechurch, V. L.
The **affair** of the reluctant witness. Gardner, E. S.
The **affair** of the stolen mice. Kimberly, G.
**AFGHAN HOUNDS**
Sturgeon, T. The girl who knew what they meant
**Aflame**; in flower. Casper, L.
**AFRICA**
Chester, A. Safari
Freeman, R. A. Indoro Bush College
Gbadamossi, R. A. Bats and babies
Gordimer, N. Livingstone's companions
Gordimer, N. Livingstone's companions; 16 stories
Green, L. G. Virgin peak
Heald, H. Winged death
Hemingway, E. The short happy life of Francis Macomber
Jones, E. Show me first your penny
Larson, C. R. ed. African short stories; 12 stories
Naipaul, V. S. In a free state
Njoku, M. C. The python's dilemma
Nolen, B. ed. Africa is thunder and wonder; 10 stories
Obudo, N. They stole our cattle
Richter, J. The prisoner of Zemu Island
Ruoro, P. End of month
Waiguru, J. The untilled field
See also countries of Africa, e.g. Sierra Leone
**Farm life**
See Farm life—Africa
**Native races**
Laurence, M. The tomorrow-tamer

Lawrence, M. The dogs of Pemba
Mérimée, P. Tamango
Smith, C. A. The Venus of Azombeii
Stern, J. The cloud
See also names of countries or areas with subdivision Native races; and names of African people or tribes, e.g. Zulus
**Race problems**
Hughes, L. African morning
Nicol, A. As the night, the day
**School life**
See School life—Africa
**AFRICA, CENTRAL**
Lispector, C. The smallest woman in the world
**Native races**
Humphreys, L. G. Tanya
**AFRICA, EAST**
Richter, J. Only so much to reveal
Waugh, E. Incident in Azania
See also countries in this area, e.g. Kenya
**Native races**
Oliver, C. Far from this earth
**AFRICA, NORTH**
Reynolds, M. Black sheep astray
See also Algeria
**Politics**
See Politics—Africa, North
**AFRICA, SOUTH**
Gordimer, N. The defeated
Gordimer, N. A satisfactory settlement
Lessing, D. The story of a non-marrying man
See also English in Africa, South
**Native races**
Mphalele, E. Mrs Plum
See also Kafirs (African people)
**Race problems**
Essa, A. The prisoner
Gordimer, N. Africa emergent
Gordimer, N. Inkalamu's place
Gordimer, N. Open house
Gordimer, N. Which new era would that be?
La Guma, A. Coffee for the road
Mphalele, E. Mrs Plum
Rive, R. Resurrection
Starke, R. The day
**AFRICA, WEST**
Nesvadba, J. The death of an apeman
Ogot, G. Tekayo
See also countries in this area, e.g. Mauritania
**Africa** emergent. Gordimer, N.
**African** morning. Hughes, L.
The **African** tree beavers. Gilbert, M.
**AFRICAN TRIBES.** See names of tribes and peoples
**AFRICANS**
Larson, C. R. Up from slavery
**AFRICANS IN ENGLAND**
Thereaux, A. The wife of God

**AFRICANS IN THE UNITED STATES**
　Aidoo, A. A. Other versions
　Davis, O. The roof garden
**After** a few words. Garrett, R.
**After** all I did for Israel. Levin, M.
**After** Saturday nite comes Sunday. San-
　　chez, S.
**After** seventeen years. Kim, Y. I.
**After** the accident. Mitchison, N.
**After** the ball. Colter, C.
**After** the ball. Tolstoi, L.
**After** the battle. West, J.
**After** the lights are out. Downer, M. L.
**After** the parrot. Fielding, G.
**After** the party. Slesinger, T.
**After** the show. Wilson, A.
**After** the sirens. Hood, H.
**After** the theatre. Chekhov, A.
**After** the war. Lewis, C. W.
**After** twenty years. Henry, O.
The **afternoon.** Fast, H.
**Afternoon** in the jungle. Maltz, A.
**Afternoon** of a faun. De Vries, P.
**Afternoon** waltz. O'Hara, J.
**Afterward.** Wharton, E.
**Against** the Lafayette Escadrille. Wolfe, G.
**AGAPITUS, SAINT**
　Corvo, F. Baron. About doubles in gener-
　　al: and Sanvenanzio and Santaga-
　　pito, in particular.
　Corvo, F. Baron. About Sanvenanzio, San-
　　tagapito, and Padre Dotto Vagheg-
　　gino, S.J.
**Agathe.** Keeling, N.
The **age** of gold. Yurick, S.
**AGED.** See Old Age
**Agenda** for tomorrow. Deutsch, A. H.
**AGENTS, THEATRICAL**
　Brown, F. Ten percenter
　Roth, P. On the air
**Agnes.** Hayes, A. H.
**Agnon, S. Y.**
　Agunot
　　Agnon, S. Y. Twenty-one stories
　At the outset of the day
　　Agnon, S. Y. Twenty-one stories
　The doctor's divorce
　　Agnon, S. Y. Twenty-one stories
　The document
　　Agnon, S. Y. Twenty-one stories
　Fable of the goat
　　Agnon, S. Y. Twenty-one stories
　The face and the image
　　Agnon, S. Y. Twenty-one stories
　　Foff, A. and Knapp, D. eds. Story
　Fernheim
　　Agnon, S. Y. Twenty-one stories
　First kiss
　　Agnon, S. Y. Twenty-one stories
　Friendship
　　Agnon, S. Y. Twenty-one stories
　From lodging to lodging
　　Agnon, S. Y. Twenty-one stories
　The kerchief
　　Agnon, S. Y. Twenty-one stories
　　Same as: Story of the kerchief of my
　　mother, listed in 1955-1958 supple-
　　ment

The lady and the pedlar
　Agnon, S. Y. Twenty-one stories
The letter
　Agnon, S. Y. Twenty-one stories
Metamorphosis
　Agnon, S. Y. Twenty-one stories
The night
　Agnon, S. Y. Twenty-one stories
On the road
　Agnon, S. Y. Twenty-one stories
The orchestra
　Agnon, S. Y. Twenty-one stories
Out of the depths
　Goodman, P. ed. The Yom Kippur an-
　　thology
A Passover courting
　Decker, C. R. and Angoff, C. eds. Mod-
　　ern stories from many lands
The tale of the scribe
　Agnon, S. Y. Twenty-one stories
Tehilah
　Michener, J. A. ed. First fruits
To father's house
　Agnon, S. Y. Twenty-one stories
To the doctor
　Agnon, S. Y. Twenty-one stories
A whole loaf
　Agnon, S. Y. Twenty-one stories
**Agnon, Samuel Joseph.** See Agnon, S. Y.
**Agnon, Shmuel Yosef.** See Agnon, S. Y.
**Agony** column. Malzberg, B. N.
The **agony** of A. Boscas. Boyle, P.
**Agostino.** Moravia, A.
**AGRICULTURAL LABORERS**
　Dumas, H.　A boll of roses
　Francis, H. E. The fence
　Himes, C. Cotton gonna kill me yet
　Steinbeck, J. Breakfast
　Steinbeck, J. Breakfast and work
　Stern, J. Mister and Miss
　Stuart, J. Little giant
　　　See also Migrant labor
**AGRICULTURAL MACHINERY**
　Hignett, S. Allotment
**AGRICULTURAL WORKERS.** See Agri-
　　cultural laborers
**AGRICULTURALISTS**
　Clement, H. Halo
　Stafford, J. The lippia lawn
**AGRICULTURE**
　McCaffrey, A. Daughter
　　　**Economic aspects**
　Stuart, J. Appalachian patriarch
　Stuart, J. Eighty-one summers
**Aguallo, Thomaline**
　Doing well
　　Rosmond, B. comp. Today's stories from
　　Seventeen
**Agunot.** Agnon, S. Y.
**Ah** Ao. Sun, Hsi-chen
**Ah,** the family! Moravia, A.
**Ah,** the university! Collier, J.
**Ahlin, Lars**
　Polluted zone
　　Angoff, C. ed. Stories from The Literary
　　Review

AIR PILOTS—*Continued*
  Ballard, J. G. The cloud-sculptors of Coral D
  Brister, B. El papa sabalo
  Brunner, J. Puzzle for spacemen
  Buck, P. S. The courtyards of peace
  Ellison, R. Flying home
  Forester, C. S. Eagle Squadron
  Galouye, D. F. Prometheus rebound
  Grau, S. A. Sea change
  Lem, S. The patrol
  McLaughlin, D. Hawk among the sparrows
  Smith, C. A. The dimension of chance
    *See also* Astronauts; United States. Army Air Forces
AIR PIRACY. *See* Hijacking of airplanes
AIR POLLUTION. *See* Air—Pollution
AIR RAID SHELTERS
  Cheever, J. The brigadier and the golf widow
  Stanton, W. As long as you're here
AIR RAIDS
  Dorr, L. The binge
Air trails. Dawson, F.
AIR TRAVEL. *See* Aeronautics—Flights
Airforce wife. Zobarskas, S.
AIRPLANE ACCIDENTS. *See* Aeronautics—Accidents
AIRPLANES
  Keefauver, J. The Great Three-Month Super Supersonic Transport Stack-Up of 1999
  Marlowe, S. Drum beat
    *See also* Helicopters; Jet planes
        **Accidents**
    *See* Aeronautics—Accidents
        **Hijacking**
    *See* Hijacking of airplanes
        **Models**
  De Vries, P. Adventures of a people buff
        **Piloting**
    *See* Air pilots
        **Testing**
  Keller, D. H. Air lines
AIRPLANES, MILITARY
  Wolfe, G. Against the Lafayette Escadrille
AIRPORTS
  Emshwiller, C. Woman waiting
  Gordimer, N. No place like
The airtight case. Strong, P. N.
Airy persiflage on the heaving deep. Algren, N.
Aitken, James
  Lederer's legacy
    Karlin, W.; Paquet, B. T. and Rottman, L. eds. Free fire zone
AKANS (AFRICAN PEOPLE) *See* Fantis
The akeda. Ayrton, M.
Akens, Helen Morgan
  Call me ma
    Alabama prize stories, 1970
Akihi-san: a contemplation. Sherwin, J. J.
Akinari. *See* Uyeda, Akinari
Akroterion. Hermann, J.

Aksyenov, Vasily
  Samson and Samsoness
    Whitney, T. P. ed. The young Russians
Akueke. Achebe, C.
Akutagawa, Ryunosuke
  In a grove
    Shimer, D. B. ed. Voices of modern Asia
Al. Emshwiller, C.
ALABAMA
  Bierce, A. Incident at Owl Creek
  Ford, J. H. The trout
  Warren, R. P. Goodwood comes back
  Windham, B. The death of Uncle Edward Tabb
        **Farm life**
    *See* Farm life—Alabama
Alan, A. J.
  Coincidence
    Dickinson, S. ed. The usurping ghost, and other encounters and experiences
Alarcón, Pedro A. de
  The nun
    Hall, J. B. ed. The realm of fiction
Alas, poor Maling. Greene, G.
ALASKA
  Madden, D. Love makes nothing happen
The albatross. Bolitho, H.
Albatrosses
  Bolitho, H. The albatross
Albee, George Sumner
  The top
    Fitz Gerald, G. ed. Modern satiric stories
Albergo Empedocle. Forster, E. M.
Albert. Gilliatt, P.
ALBERTA. *See* Canada—Alberta
Alberts, A.
  The swamp
    Angoff, C. ed. Stories from The Literary Review
Alchemists. *See* Alchemy
ALCHEMY
  Davidson, A. The vat
  Day, J. W. Sung to his death by dead men
  Rohmer, S. The master of Hollow Grange
ALCOHOLICS. *See* Alcoholism; Drunkards
ALCOHOLISM
  Bontemps, A. The cure
  Cather, W. On the Divide
  Chekhov, A. Anna on the neck
  Gilliatt, P. Albert
  Hershman, M. Let there be night!
  Hughes, L. Minnie again
  Leskov, N. How it is not good to condemn weaknesses
  Maloney, R. The best man
  Maloney, R. The help comes in bottles
  Munro, A. An ounce of cure
  Naylor, P. R. Day after tomorrow
  Nemerov, H. The native in the world
  O'Connor, P. F. The gift bearer
  O'Connor, P. F. A San Francisco woman
  Olsen, T. Hey sailor, what ship?
  Pansing, N. P. The visitation
  Parker, D. Big blonde
  Runyon, D. Lillian
  Wilson, A. Raspberry jam
  Yatskiv, M. Cedar wood will grow
    *See also* Drunkards

Algren, Nelson—*Continued*
　The passion of upside-down-Emil
　　Algren, N. The last carousel
　Police and Mama-sans get it all
　　Algren, N. The last carousel
　Poor girls of Kowloon
　　Algren, N. The last carousel
　Previous days
　　Algren, N. The last carousel
　The ryebread trees of spring
　　Algren, N. The last carousel
　A ticket on Skoronski
　　Algren, N. The last carousel
　Tinkle Hinkle and the footnote king
　　Algren, N. The last carousel
　Watch out for Daddy
　　Algren, N. The last carousel
　What country do you think you're in?
　　Algren, N. The last carousel
**ALIBIS**
　Blackhurst, W. E. People change—alibis
　　don't
Alice and the Cheshire Cat. *See* Carroll, L.
　The Cheshire Cat
An alien flower. Gallant, M.
Alien stones. Wolfe, G.
**ALIENATION (SOCIAL PSYCHOLOGY)**
　Ascher, S. and Strauss, D. Even after a
　　machine is dismantled, it continues
　　to operate, with or without purpose
　Bullins, E. The enemy
　Graham, W. The island
　Hesse, H. Klein and Wagner
　Lispector, C. Preciousness
　Malamud, B. My son the murderer
　Nemerov, H. The escapist
　Nemerov, H. The native in the world
　Rascoe, J. Twice plighted, once removed
　Ribnikar, J.　I
　Weaver, G. The entombed man of Thule
　　*See also* Social isolation
**ALIENATION OF AFFECTIONS**
　Cecil, H. Operation enticement
The aliens. McCullers, C.
**ALIMONY**
　DeFord, M. A. The moment of time
Alive and real. West, J.
**AL KERAK.** *See* El Kerak
All around the mulberry tree. Hunter, K.
All but empty. Greene, G.
All but the words. Lafferty, R. A.
All cats are gray. Norton, A.
All fires the fire. Cortázar, J.
All for love. Goulart, R.
All God's children need radios. Sexton, A.
All God's chillun got pride. Himes, C.
All he needs is feet. Himes, C.
All horse players die broke. Runyon, D.
All I've tried to be. O'Hara, J.
All my bones. Weston, J.
All of a summer's day. Curley, D.
All of God's children got shoes. Schoen-
　feld, H.
All our yesterdays. Beekman, A.
All our yesterdays. Vuyk, B.
All pieces of a river shore. Lafferty, R. A.
All-seeing. Moravia, A.
All Souls'. Wharton, E.

All Souls' Day. Pelin, E.
All that the eye can see. Berne, S.
All the assholes in the world and mine.
　Bukowski, C.
All the carnivals in the world. Francis, H. E.
All the devils in hell. Brunner, J.
All the great writers. Bukowski, C.
All the last wars at once. Effinger, G. A.
All the lonely people. McPherson, J. A.
All the myriad ways. Niven, L.
All the people I never had. Francis, H. E.
All the pussy we want. Bukowski, C.
All the sounds of fear. Ellison, H.
All the traps of earth. Simak, C. D.
All the way home. Sandaval, J.
All the young men. La Farge, O.
All through the house. Kanin, G.
All you can eat. Bilker, H. L. and Bilker, A. L.
"All you zombies—" Heinlein, R. A.
All you've ever wanted. Aiken, J.
Allah will understand. Ruskay, S.
**ALLEGORIES**
　Agnon, S. Y.　A whole leaf
　Anderson, P. Goat song
　Bichsel, P. The earth is round
　Bichsel, P. The man who didn't want to
　　know any more
　Bierce, A. Haïta the shepherd
　Brownstein, M. The plot to save the world
　Brownstein, M. Who knows where the
　　time goes?
　Bryant, E. Dune's edge
　Bulatović, M.　A fable
　Bulwer-Lytton, E. Chairolas
　Chamisso, A. von. The strange story of
　　Peter Schlemihl
　Elliott, G. P. In a hole
　Ellison, H.　I have no mouth, and I must
　　scream
　Ellison, H. The Silver Corridor
　Forster, E. M. The other side of the hedge
　France, A. Putois
　Freemann, R. A. Indoro Bush College
　Gbadamossi, R. A. In the beginning
　Gide, A. The return of the prodigal son
　Hayes, R. E. The stigmata of the Rainy-
　　Day Sun
　Hesse, H. Augustus
　Hesse, H. The city
　Hesse, H. Faldum
　Hesse, H. Flute dream
　Hesse, H. The hard passage
　Hesse, H. Harry, the Steppenwolf
　Hesse, H. Iris
　Hunter, E. Inferiority complex
　Ionesco, E. Rhinoceros
　Kafka, F. Description of a struggle
　Kafka, F. Eleven sons
　Kafka, F. The hunter Gracchus: a frag-
　　ment
　Kafka, F. Josephine the singer
　Kafka, F. The knock at the manor gate
　Kafka, F. The refusal
　Kafka, F.　A report to an Academy
　Kafka, F.　A report to an Academy: two
　　fragments
　Kafka, F. Unhappiness
　Kafka, F. The village schoolmaster

**ALLEGORIES**—*Continued*

Kafka, F. Wedding preparations in the country

Kenyatta, J. The man who shared his hut

Lagerkvist, P. The myth of mankind

Lawrence, D. H. The man who loved islands

Liyong, T. L. The old man of Usumbura and his misery

McConnell, J. V. Learning theory

Myrivilis, S. The chronicle of an old rose-tree

Nemerov, H. The Twelve and the one

Nesvadba, J. The lost face

Njoku, M. C. The python's dilemma

P'u, Sung-ling. The Rakshas and the sea market

Silverberg, R. Sundance

Stevenson, R. L. The House of Eld

Sturgeon, T. Crate

Unamuno y Jugo, M. de. Abel Sanchez

Updike, J. The invention of the horse collar

Wolfe, G. Peritonitis

Wu, Ch'eng-en. The temptation of Saint Pigsy

Yehoshua, A. B. Flood tide

See also Fables; Fantasies; Parables; Symbolism

**Allen, Elizabeth**

The wrong road

Rosmond, B. comp. Today's stories from Seventeen

**Allen, Grant**

The episode of the diamond links

Greene, H. ed. Cosmopolitan crimes

The episode of the Mexican seer

Greene, H. ed. Cosmopolitan crimes

**Allen, Henry.** *See* Fisher, Clay

**Allen, John Houghton**

Tales of Diego

The Best little magazine fiction, 1971

**Allen, William Henry.** *See* Henry, Will

The **alligator** war. Quiroga, H.

**ALLIGATORS**

Hoagland, E. The final fate of the alligators

Quiroga, H. The alligator war

Silverberg, R. The calibrated alligator

See also Crocodiles

**Allingham, Margery**

The barbarian

Allingham, M. The Allingham minibus

Bird thou never wert

Allingham, M. The Allingham minibus

The border-line case

Allingham, M. The Allingham Case-book

The correspondents

Allingham, M. The Allingham minibus

Evidence in camera

Allingham, M. The Allingham Case-book

Face value

Allingham, M. The Allingham Case-book

Family affair

Manley, S. and Lewis, G. eds. Grande dames of detection

He preferred them sad

Allingham, M. The Allingham minibus

He was asking after you

Allingham, M. The Allingham minibus

Is there a doctor in the house?

Allingham, M. The Allingham Case-book

Joke over

Allingham, M. The Allingham Case-book

The lieabout

Allingham, M. The Allingham Case-book

Little Miss Know-All

Allingham, M. The Allingham Case-book

The lying-in-state

Allingham, M. The Allingham Case-book

Ellery Queen's Mystery Magazine. Ellery Queen's Grand slam

The man with the sack

Allingham, M. The Allingham minibus

The mind's eye mystery

Allingham, M. The Allingham Case-book

Mr Campion's lucky day

Allingham, M. The Allingham minibus

Mum knows best

Allingham, M. The Allingham Case-book

One morning they'll hang him

Allingham, M. The Allingham Case-book

The perfect butler

Allingham, M. The Allingham minibus

The pioneers

Allingham, M. The Allingham minibus

The pro and the con

Allingham, M. The Allingham Case-book

The psychologist

Allingham, M. The Allingham Case-book

Publicity

Allingham, M. The Allingham minibus

A quarter of a million

Allingham, M. The Allingham minibus

The same to us

Allingham, M. The Allingham minibus

The secret

Allingham, M. The Allingham minibus

The sexton's wife

Allingham, M. The Allingham minibus

She heard it on the radio

Allingham, M. The Allingham minibus

The snapdragon and the C.I.D.

Allingham, M. The Allingham Case-book

Tall story

Allingham, M. The Allingham Case-book

They never get caught

Allingham, M. The Allingham Case-book

Three is a lucky number

Allingham, M. The Allingham Case-book

'Tis not hereafter

Allingham, M. The Allingham minibus

**Allingham, Margery**—*Continued*
The unseen door
Allingham, M. The Allingham minibus
The Villa Marie Celeste
Allingham, M. The Allingham Case-
book
A Treasury of modern mysteries v 1
The wink
Allingham, M. The Allingham minibus
**Allison.** Henderson, D.
**Allonym.** McClatchy, J. D.
**Allotment.** Hignett, S.
The **allotted** period of time. Berne, A.
**Almighty** voice. Prebble, J.
**Almos'** a man. Wright, R.
**Almost** caught. Marshall, L.
**Almost** in Iowa. Irving, J.
The **almost** white boy. Motley, W.
**ALMSHOUSES AND WORKHOUSES**
Freeman, M. E. W. Sister Liddy
Goulart, R. Terminal
Hale, L. P. The Peterkins at the farm
Stafford, J. Life is no abyss
**Along** came a spider. Blackwood, A.
**Along** the long long road. Borchert, W.
**Alonso, Dora**
Cotton candy
Katz, N. and Milton, N. eds. Fragment
from a lost diary, and other stories
Times gone by
Katz, N. and Milton, N. eds. Fragment
from a lost diary, and other stories
**Aloys.** Lafferty, R. A.
**ALOYSIUS GONZAGA, SAINT**
Corvo, F. Baron. About the lilies of
Sanluigi
**Alper, Gerald Arthur**
The mechanical sweetheart
Scortia, T. N. ed. Strange bedfellows
**Alpha** Ralpha Boulevard. Smith, C.
The **alphabet** of mathematics. Friedman, P.
An **Alpine** idyll. Hemingway, E.
**ALPS**
Forster, E. M. The eternal moment
Maupassant, G. de. At the mountain inn
**ALPS, SWISS**
Alexander, D. Love will find a way
Graham, W. At the Chalet Lartrec
**ALTAR BOYS**
Rindfleisch, N. Of streetcars, drunks,
chestnuts and childhood
Ulibarri, S. R. The stuffing of the Lord
The **altar** of the dead. James, H.
The **altar** of the random gods. Rogoz, A.
The **Altdorf** syndrome. Powell, J.
**Altele.** Singer, I. B.
**Alter, Robert Edmond**
Man hunt on Dead Yank Creek
Fenner, P. S. comp. Consider the evi-
dence
The **alternative.** Baraka, I. A.
**Altov, Genrikh.** *See* Altov, Henrik
**Altov, Henrik**
Icarus and Daedalus
Ginsburg, M. ed. The ultimate threshold
The Master Builder
Suvin, D. ed. Other worlds, other seas
**ALUMNI REUNIONS.** *See* College alumni

**Alvarez, A.**
Laughter
Winter's tales 17
**Am** I insane? Maupassant, G. de
**Am** Strande von Tanger. Salter, J.
**Amadís de Gaula.** *See* Montalvo, Garcia
Ordoñez de
**Amado, Jorge**
How Porciúncula the mulatto got the
corpse off his back
Howes, B. ed. The eye of the heart
**Amarkant**
Assassins
Roadarmel, G. C. ed. A death in Delhi
**Amaryllis.** Engel, M.
**Amateau, Rod, and Davis, David**
The tilt of death
Mystery Writers of America. Merchants
of menace
The **amateur.** Gilbert, M.
**Amateur** standing. Blanc, S.
**AMATEUR THEATRICALS**
Auchincloss, L. Black Shylock
Burton, H. The explosion
McNair, K. Birnam Wood comes to
Dunsinane
Rindfleisch, N. A children's play
Simak, C. Shadow show
Theroux, P. The South Malaysia Pine-
apple Growers' Association
**Amazing** grace. Cohen, M.
The **amazing** planet. Smith, C. A.
**AMAZON RIVER**
Usher, F. Amazonian horrors
**AMAZON VALLEY.** *See* Brazil—Amazon
Valley
**Amazonian** horrors. Usher, F.
**AMAZONS**
Herodotus. The Amazons
Montalvo, G. O. de. The Queen of Cali-
fornia
The **Amazons.** Herodotus
**AMBASSADORS.** *See* Diplomatic life
The **amber** beads. Hume, F.
The **amber** witch. Brontë, E. J.
The **amber** witch. Meinhold, W.
**AMBIGUITIES.** Moravia, A.
**AMBITION**
Anderson, S. The egg
Chekhov, A. Gooseberries
A Ghost of a head
Hughes, L. Rock, church
Lins, O. The transparent bird
Posner, R. Jacob's bug
**Ambler, Eric**
Belgrade 1926
Mystery Writers of America. Dear dead
days
Spy-haunts of the world
Mystery Writers of America. Crime
without murder
**Ambler's** inspiration. Lumley, B.
**Ambrose** his mark. Barth, J.
**AMBULANCE DRIVERS**
Huey, T. The Ambulance Driver's Ball
The **Ambulance** Driver's Ball. Huey, T.
**AMBULANCES**
Deming, R. The competitors
The **ambush.** Djilas, M.

Amena. Tolstoy, A.

## AMERICA

### Discovery and exploration

Bishop, Z. The mound

America the beautiful. Leiber, F.

The American. Dawson, F.

American autumn. Schneeman, P.

American dead. Harrison, H.

American Gothic. O'Connor, P. F.

An American marriage. Klein, N.

An American memory, 1966. Friedman, P.

An American organ. Burgess, A.

An American romance. Bergé, C.

**AMERICAN SOLDIERS.** *See* Soldiers, American

An American student in Paris. Farrell, J. T.

The American wife. O'Connor, F.

## AMERICANS IN AFRICA

Arden, W. The savage

Chester, A. Safari

Crane, S. The King's favor

Nair, S. Mrs Kimble

Richter, J. The prisoner of Zemu Island

## AMERICANS IN AFRICA, CENTRAL

Humphreys, L. G. Tanya

## AMERICANS IN AFRICA, SOUTH

Gordimer, N. Open house

## AMERICANS IN BARBADOS

Meriwether, L. M.   A happening in Barbados

## AMERICANS IN BULGARIA

Updike, J. The Bulgarian poetess

## AMERICANS IN CANADA

Blaise, C. The salesman's son grows older

Sandman, J. One for the road

## AMERICANS IN CHINA

Buck, P. S. The courtyards of peace

Buck, P. S. Letter home

Thomason, J. W. Mixed marriage

Thomason, J. W. The Sergeant and the siren

Thomason, J. W. The sergeant and the spy

Thomason, J. W. With a dust storm blowing

## AMERICANS IN CRETE

Du Maurier, D. Not after midnight

## AMERICANS IN CUBA

Di Donato, P. Tropic of Cuba

## AMERICANS IN EGYPT

Updike, J. I am dying, Egypt, dying

## AMERICANS IN ENGLAND

Collins, W. Miss Bertha and the Yankee

Curley, D. In the hands of our enemies

Curley, D. Station: you are here

Keefe, F. L. The bicycle rider

Kipling, R. An habitation enforced

Oates, J. C. The turn of the screw

Plath, S. Mothers

Price, R.   A dog's death

Price, R. The happiness of others

Price, R. Scars

Rascoe, J.  Small sounds and tilting shadows

Richler, M. Dinner with Ormsby-Fletcher

Sallis, J. Front & centaur

Schwartz, J. Corners

Scott, E. The twelve apostles

Updike, J. Bech swings?

Wilde, O. The Canterville ghost

## AMERICANS IN EUROPE

Berkson, T. Thirty-day leave

Blaise, C. Continent of strangers

James, H. Daisy Miller

McCarthy, M. The Cicerone

Maddow, B. You, Johann Sebastian Bach

Schulman, L. M. ed. Travelers; 10 stories

Sherwin, J. J. These actions shall be held proof

Stafford, J. The children's game

Stern, R. Gaps

## AMERICANS IN FRANCE

Algren, N. He couldn't boogie-woogie worth a damn

Baldwin, J. Equal in Paris

Birstein, A. When the wind blew

Cather, W. The namesake

Cather, W. The profile

Farrell, J. T. An American student in Paris

Farrell, J. T. Exiles

Gold, H. Young man, old days

Gordimer, N.   A meeting in space

Hershman, M. Proposal perilous

Hunter, E. Someone at the door

Maxwell, W. The gardens of Mont-Saint-Michel

Runyon, D.   A light in France

Schwartz, J. Dennicker's love story

Schwartz, J. Waiting

Shaw, I. God was here but He left early

Stafford, J. Maggie Meriwether's rich experience

Steegmuller, F. One round trip only

Steegmuller, F. Soirée à la chandelle

Steele, M. Color the daydream yellow

Stevenson, R. L. Story of the physician and the Saratoga trunk

Taylor, P. Je suis perdu

Wharton, E. Madame de Treymes

Woods, W. C.   A mirror of the waves

## AMERICANS IN GERMANY

Brodeur, P. Behind the moon

Curley, D.   A day in Hamburg

Dawson, F. The American

Dawson, F. The photograph

Keefe, F. L. The word of Otto Pichler

Matthews, J. Another story

Porter, K. A. The leaning tower

Price, R. Waiting at Dachau

Stafford, J. The echo and the nemesis

Stafford, J. The maiden

Stoker, B. The squaw

Weaver, G. The salesman from Hong Kong

## AMERICANS IN GREECE

Bromell, H. The slightest distance

Hermann, J. Akroterion

McCord, J. Every day is yesterday again

Vassilikos, V. The harpoon gun

**AMERICANS IN GUINEA.** *See* Negroes in Guinea

## AMERICANS IN INDIA

Aldiss, B. W. When I was very Jung

Bednarz, W. Bracelet of destruction

Blaise, C. Going to India

Bloch, R. Untouchable

Brunner, J. The Vitanuls

**Andersen, Hans Christian**
  The darning needle
    Howes, B. and Smith, G. J. eds. The
      sea-green horse
  The Emperor's new clothes
    Authors' choice
  The nightingale
    Fairy tales for computers
  The red shoes
    Foff, A. and Knapp, D. eds. Story

**Anderson, Alston**
  Comrade
    Howes, B. and Smith, G. J. eds. The
      sea-green horse

**Anderson, David**
  The oil murders
    Gottesman, L.; Obenzingen, H. and
      Senauke, A. eds. A cinch

**Anderson, Karen.** *See* Anderson, P. jt. auth.

**Anderson, Poul**
  Call me Joe
    The Astounding-Analog reader v2
    The Science fiction hall of fame v2A
  A chapter of revelation
    The Day the sun stood still
  Cold victory
    Anderson, P. Seven conquests
  Delenda est
    Silverberg, R. ed. Worlds of maybe
  Details
    Anderson, P. Seven conquests
  Elementary mistake
    Analog 7
  Epilogue
    Anderson, P. Tales of the flying moun-
      tains
    Silverberg, R. ed. The ends of time
  Escape the morning
    Harrison, H. ed. Worlds of wonder
  The fatal fulfillment
    Five fates
  Ghetto
    Nolan, W. F. ed. A wilderness of stars
  Goat song
    Nebula award stories 8
  Gypsy
    Silverberg, R. ed. To the stars
  I tell you, it's true
    Nova 2
  Inside straight
    Anderson, P. Seven conquests
  Interlude 1
    Anderson, P. Tales of the flying moun-
      tains
  Interlude 2
    Anderson, P. Tales of the flying moun-
      tains
  Interlude 3
    Anderson, P. Tales of the flying moun-
      tains
  Interlude 4
    Anderson, P. Tales of the flying moun-
      tains
  Interlude 5
    Anderson, P. Tales of the flying moun-
      tains
  Interlude 6
    Anderson, P. Tales of the flying moun-
      tains

Journey's end
  Knight, D. ed. A science fiction argosy
  McComas, J. F. ed. Special wonder
  Silverberg, R. ed. Mind to mind
Kings who die
  Anderson, P. Seven conquests
License
  Anderson, P. Seven conquests
A little knowledge
  Del Rey, L. ed. Best science fiction
    stories of the year [1972]
Lodestar
  Astounding
No truce with kings
  Asimov, I. ed. The Hugo winners v2
Nothing succeeds like failure
  Anderson, P. Tales of the flying moun-
    tains
The problem of pain
  The Best from Fantasy & Science Fic-
    tion; 20th ser.
Prologue
  Anderson, P. Tales of the flying moun-
    tains
Que donn'rez vous?
  Anderson, P. Tales of the flying moun-
    tains
The Queen of Air and Darkness
  Nebula award stories 7
Ramble with a gamblin' man
  Anderson, P. Tales of the flying moun-
    tains
Recruiting nation
  Anderson, P. Tales of the flying moun-
    tains
The rogue
  Anderson, P. Tales of the flying moun-
    tains
Say it with flowers
  Anderson, P. Tales of the flying moun-
    tains
The sharing of flesh
  Asimov, I. ed. The Hugo winners v2
  Galaxy Magazine. The eleventh Galaxy
    reader
Strange bedfellows
  Anderson, P. Seven conquests
Sunjammer
  Anderson, P. Tales of the flying moun-
    tains
Wildcat
  Anderson, P. Seven conquests
Windmill
  Elwood, R. and Kidd, V. eds. Saving
    worlds
Wingless on Avalon
  Elwood, R. ed. Children of infinity
**Anderson, Poul, and Anderson, Karen**
  Dead phone
    McComas, J. F. ed. Crimes and mis-
      fortunes
**Anderson, Poul, and Dickson, Gordon R.**
  The sheriff of Canyon Gulch
    Norton, A. and Donaldy, E. eds. Gates
      to tomorrow
    Silverberg, R. ed. The science fiction
      bestiary

**Anderson, S. E.**
  The contraband
    King, W. ed. Black short story anthology

**Anderson, Sherwood**
  Death in the woods
    Abrahams, W. ed. Fifty years of the American short story v 1
    Foff, A. and Knapp, D. eds. Story
    Taylor, J. C. ed. The short story: fiction in transition
  The egg
    Hall, J. B. ed. The realm of fiction
    Thune, E. and Prigozy, R. eds. Short stories: a critical anthology
    12 short story writers
  I want to know why
    Tytell, J. and Jaffe, H. eds. Affinities
  I'm a fool
    Matthews, J. ed. Archetypal themes in the modern story
  Sophistication
    12 short story writers
  The untold lie
    12 short story writers

**Anderson Imbert, Enrique**
  The General makes a lovely corpse
    Yates, D. A. ed. Latin blood

**Andrea. O'Hara, J.**

The **Andrech** samples. Gores, J.

**Andreshko. Pelin, E.**

**Andrevon, J. P.**
  Observation of Quadragnes
    Rottensteiner, F. ed. View from another shore

**Andrews, Frank Earl**
  Bushwhacked
    Andrews, F. E. and Dickens, A. eds. Voices from the big house
  A man called Cain
    Andrews, F. E. and Dickens, A. eds. Voices from the big house
  Ynnel eht naitram
    Andrews, F. E. and Dickens, A. eds. Voices from the big house

**Andreyev, Vesselin**
  One night, one day
    Kirilov, N. and Kirk, F. eds. Introduction to modern Bulgarian literature

**Andriušis, Pulgis**
  He wasn't allowed to see
    Decker, C. R. and Angoff, C. eds. Modern stories from many lands

**Androcles** and the army. O'Connor, F.

**ANDROIDS.** *See* Automata

**Anfilov, Gleb**
  Erem
    Best SF: 1970
    Ginsburg, M. ed. The ultimate threshold

**Angel**-face. Fremlin, C.

**Angel** Levine. Malamud, B.

**Angel** of death. Brodeur, P.

The **angel** of the church. Phillips, R.

**Angell, Roger**
  In an early winter
    Kahn, J. ed. Trial and terror

**ANGELS**
  Barthelme, D. On angels

Collier, J. Fallen star
Collier, J. Hell hath no fury
Fast, H. The general zapped an angel
Fogel, A. The turtle hunt
Henderson, Z. Three-cornered and secure
Malamud, B. Angel Levine
Pangborn, E. Angel's egg
Twain, M. Extract from Captain Stormfield's visit to heaven
  *See also* Heaven

**Angel's** egg. Pangborn, E.

**ANGER**
  Kotowska, M. Twelve feet to heaven
  Petry, A. Like a winding sheet

**Angioxyl**, a rare cure. Tammuz, B.

**ANGLICAN AND EPISCOPAL BISHOPS.**
  *See* Bishops, Anglican and Episcopal

**ANGLICAN PRIESTS.** *See* Clergy, Anglican and Episcopal

**ANGLING.** *See* Fishing

The **Anglo-Saxon.** Golding, W.

**ANGLO-SAXONS**
  Valdrwulf
  Walsh, J. P. Wordhoard; 8 stories
  Walsh, J. P. and Crossley-Holland, K. Wordhoard

**Angoff, Charles**
  Azriel and Yolanda
    Ribalow, H. U. ed. My name aloud
  The steamer
    Decker, C. R. and Angoff, C. eds. Modern stories from many lands
    *See also* Decker, C. R. jt. ed.

**Angouleme.** Disch, T. M.

The **angry** heart. Naylor, P. R.

The **angry** street. Chesterton, G. K.

**ANIMAL ACTS.** *See* Animals — Training; Circus

**Animal** crackers in my soup. Bukowski, C.

The **animal** fair. Bester, A.

The **animal** kingdom. Boles, P. D.

The **animal** lover. Bischel, P.

**ANIMAL MUTATION**
  Curtis, R. Zoo 2000

The **animal** trainer. Rothberg, A.

**ANIMAL TRAINERS.** *See* Animals—Training

**ANIMALS**
  Bukowski, C. Animal crackers in my soup
  Cather, W. The strategy of the Were-Wolf Dog
  Effinger, G. A. Two sadnesses
  Hemingway, E. Old man at the bridge
  Morrison, W. Country doctor
  Yolen, J. comp. Zoo 2000; 12 stories
    *See also* Domestic animals; Extinct animals; Fables; Pets; and names of animal classes, e.g. Dogs; Dolphins; etc.

  **Training**
  Hughes, L. Mysterious Madame Shanghai
  O'Connor, F. Androcles and the army

  **Treatment**
  Jepson, H. L. The blackbird
  Krause, E. D. The snake
  Sheckley, R. Doctor Zombie and his furry little friends

**Anthony, Robert**
The witch baiter
Haining, P. ed. The necromancers
**ANTHRAX**
Bryant, E. File on the plague
**ANTHROPOLOGISTS**
Delany, S. R. High Weir
Elliott, G. P. Among the Dangs
Wolfe, G.   V. R. T.
**ANTI-COMMUNIST MOVEMENTS**
Nowakowski, T. The liberty picnic
**ANTI-GRAVITATION.** See Gravitation
**ANTIQUARIANS.** See Archeologists
**ANTIQUE DEALERS**
Brennan, J. P. The mystery of Myrrh Lane
Purdy, J. Mr Evening
Spark, M. Miss Pinkerton's apocalypse
See also Art collectors; Art dealers
An **antique** love story. Gilliatt, P.
**ANTIQUES**
Bester, A. The Flowered Thundermug
Jacobs, H. The toy
Laumer, K. Mechanical advantage
Proulx, E. A. The baroque marble
Silverberg, R. The artifact business
See also Antique dealers; Art objects
**ANTISEMITISM**
Glanville, B. No Jews or dogs
Kotowska, M. The payment will be made
on Sunday
L'Heureux, J. Something missing
Maxwell, J. A. Strictly from the Missis-
sippi
O'Connor, P. F. Matter of ages
Ruskay, S. The ruby ring
Singer, I. B. Pigeons
See also Jews
**Antonov, Sergei**
The application form
Johnson, E. W. ed. Short stories inter-
national
**ANTONY, SAINT.** See Anthony, Saint,
251?-356?
**ANTS**
Calvino, I. The Argentine ant
Long, F. B. Green glory
**ANTWERP:** See Netherlands—Antwerp
**Anvil, Christopher**
Behind the sandrat hoax
Galaxy Magazine. The eleventh Galaxy
reader
**ANXIETY.** See Fear
The **anxiety** in the eyes of the cricket.
Sallis, J.
**Any** day now. Litvinov, I.
**Any** friend of Nicholas Nickleby's is a friend
of mine. Bradbury, R.
The **anybody** notes. Jones, A.
**Anything** box. Henderson, Z.
**Anyuta.** See Chekhov, A. Aniuta
**APACHE INDIANS**
Lucey, J. D. Hell at Helio Three
Prebble, J. The long hate
**Apartheid.** Litvinov, I.
**APARTMENT HOUSES**
Ballard, J. G. Billenium
Bilker, H. and Bilker, A. Apartment hunt-
ing

Bishop, M. The windows in Dante's hell
Bulgakov, M. Moonshine lake
Bulgakov, M. No. 13. The Elpit-Rabkom-
mun Building
Bulgakov, M.   A treatise on housing
Campbell, R. At first sight
Carver, R. Neighbors
Colette. The find
Disch, T. M. The empty room
Elkin, S. The condominium
Farrell, J. T. Mr Austin
Friedman, P. The arm of interchangeable
parts
Gascar, P. The cat
Gilliatt, P. An antique love story
Gilliatt, P. As we have learnt from Freud,
there are no jokes
Hunter, E. The intruder
Keller, D. H. The pent house
McCullers, C. Court in the west eighties
Marshall, J.   A private place
Maximov, V. House in the clouds
Midwood, B. The burglars
Naylor, C. We are dainty little people
Paley, G. In time which made a monkey
of us all
Steegmuller, F. In the lobby
Tertz, A. Pkhentz
Wolitzer, H. The sex maniac
**Apartment** hunting. Bilker, H. and Bilker, A.
**APARTMENTS.** See Apartment houses
The **ape.** Pritchett, V. S.
**Apel, Johann August**
The fatal marksman
Haining. P. ed. Gothic tales of terror
**APES**
Nesvadba, J. The death of an apeman
Pritchett, V. S. The ape
See also Chimpanzees; Man, Prehis-
toric; Monkeys
**APHRODISIACS**
Eisenberg, L. The irresistible Party Chair-
man
Eisenberg, L. The saga of DMM
**Aphrodite.** Platonov, A.
**Apocalypse.** Erbaum, J.
**Apocalypse** at the Plaza. Klein, N.
An **Apocalypse:** some scenes from European
life. Moorcock, M.
**Apology** to Inky. Green, R.M.
The **Apotheosis** of Ki. DeFord, M. A.
**APPALACHIAN MOUNTAINS**
Madden, D. The world's one breathing
**Appalachian** patriarch. Stuart, J.
**APPALACHIAN REGION**
Fox, J. A purple rhododendron, and other
stories; 16 stories
Farm Life
See Farm life—Appalachian region
**APPARENT DEATH.** See Death, Apparent
**Apparition** in the sun. Brennan, J. P.
**APPARITIONS.** See Ghosts; Hallucinations
and illusions
**Appearance** and reality. Maugham, W. S.
**APPENDECTOMIES.** See Appendicitis
**APPENDICITIS**
Costello, M. Murphy agonistes
Fremlin, C. The baby-sitter
Grau, S. A. The wind shifting west

**ARGENTINE REPUBLIC, PROVINCIAL AND RURAL**
Borges, J. L. The challenge
Borges, J. L. The intruder
Borges, J. L. The life of Tadeo Isidoro Cruz (1829-1874)
Borges, J. L. The meeting
**Arguedas, José María**
The ayla
    Carpenter, H. and Brof, J. eds. Doors and mirrors
Warma kuyay
    Howes, B. ed. The eye of the heart
**Arias-Misson, Alain**
Superfiction
    New directions in prose and poetry 24
**Aricha, Yosef**
Night scene
    Larson, C. R. ed. Prejudice: 20 tales of oppression and liberation
**Arienti, Sabadino Degli.** See Sabadino degli Arienti
**ARISTOCRACY**
Barthelme, D. Views of my father weeping
Landolfi, T.   The sword
Rushmore, R.   A life in the closet
Strindberg, A. Unnatural selection
Vance, J. The last castle
    See also Class distinction
#### England
Beerbohm, M. Hilary Maltby and Stephen Braxton
Brand, C. The wicked ghost
Crane, S. The squire's madness
Forster, E. M. Dr Woolacott
Garrett, R. The muddle of the woad
Maugham, W. S. Lord Mountdrago
Thomas, D. The end of the river
#### France
James, H. Gabrielle De Bergerac
#### Germany
Mitchell, E. P. An uncommon sort of spectre
#### Ireland
Bradbury, R. The terrible conflagration up at the place
#### Italy
Hildesheimer, W.   A world ends
#### Russia
Leskov, N. About the Rooster and his children
#### Spain
Alarcón, P. A. de. The nun
Balzac, H. de. El Verdugo
Maugham, W. S. The punctiliousness of Don Sebastian
#### Switzerland
Hoffmann, E. T. A. The doubles
**ARISTOCRATIC FAMILIES.** See Aristocracy
**ARITHMETIC**
Crane, S.   A ghoul's accountant
**ARIZONA**
Henderson, Z. Through a glass—darkly

Sturgeon, T. Cactus dance
Woolgar, J. The Roman Candle Affair
#### Frontier and pioneer life
See Frontier and pioneer life—Arizona
#### Tucson
Ogan, M. G. Scent of treason
**Ark, Noah's.** See Noah's ark
Ark of bones. Dumas, H.
**Arkanov, Arkady**
The high jump
    Whitney, T. P. ed. The young Russians
**ARKANSAS**
Casper, L. Drink to private gods
Johnson, C. Trespasser
#### Farm life
See Farm life—Arkansas
**Arkley, Gail**
Staff of life
    New American Review no. 13
**ARLES.** See Frances—Arles
Arlette. Farrell, J. T.
**Arlt, Roberto**
Esther Primavera
    Carpenter, H. and Brof, J. eds. Doors and mirrors
One Sunday afternoon
    Howes, B. ed. The eye of the heart
**ARM**
Kawabata, Y. One arm
The **arm** of interchangeable parts. Friedman, P.
**Armageddon.** Dickens, A.
Armaments race. Clarke, A. C.
**ARMENIANS IN THE UNITED STATES**
Saroyan, W. The pomegranate trees
Saroyan, W. The summer of the beautiful white horse
Armida and reality. Flaiano, E.
**ARMOR.** See Arms and armor
The **armored** car. Brautigan, R.
**ARMS AND ARMOR**
Barthelme, D. Report
Verne, J. The Begum's fortune
    See also Firearms
**Armstrong, Charlotte**
The enemy
    Queen, E. ed. Ellery Queen's The golden 13
From out of the garden
    Ellery Queen's Mystery Magazine. Ellery Queen's Murder menu
The splintered Monday
    Hitchcock, A. ed. Alfred Hitchcock presents: Stories to stay awake by
    Kahn, J. ed. Hanging by a thread
**Armstrong, Marion**
Communion
Intro #2
**Armstrong, Martin**
The fisherman
    Corodimas, P. ed. In trout country
**ARMY AIR FORCES.** See United States. Army Air Forces
**ARMY LIFE.** See Soldiers; Soldiers, American; Soldiers, French; etc.; and subhead Army, under names of individual countries, e.g. Bulgaria. Army
The **army** of the Callahan. Fox, J.

**ARTIFICIAL SATELLITES**
Bester, A. Something up there likes me
Bova, B. Test in orbit
Clarke, A. C. Dial F for Frankenstein
**ARTIFICIAL TEETH.** *See* Teeth, Artificial
**ARTIFICIAL WEATHER CONTROL.** *See* Weather control
**ARTISANS**
García Márquez, G. Balthazar's marvelous afternoon
The Jade Kuan-yin
Leskov, N. The steel flea
**ARTIST LIFE**
Bontly, T. Eight meetings
Bukowski, C. A popular man
Clarke, A. When he was free and young and he used to wear silks
Crane, S. Stories told by an artist
Emshwiller, C. Al
Fielding, G. The catch
Fielding, G. Figs in spring
Hesse, H. Klingsor's last summer
Hurlbut, K. Lilli
Midwood, B. Portrait of the policeman as a young artist
Stevenson, R. L. Providence and the guitar
*See also* Architects; Artists; Painters; Sculptors
The **artist** of the beautiful. Hawthorne, N.
**Artist** unknown. Broun, H.
**ARTISTS**
Aiken, J. Follow my fancy
Aldiss, B. W. As for our fatal continuity
Aldiss, B. W. Castle scene with penitents
Ayrton, M. The evil head
Ayrton, M. John Calder of Kelty
Barthelme, D. Engineer-private Paul Klee misplaces an aircraft between Milbertshofen and Cambrai, March 1916
Barthelme, D. The falling dog
Beneš, J. Expertise
Bergé, C. Huan
Brown, W. The scar
Buck, P. S. Going home
Collier, J. Night! Youth! Paris! And the moon!
Daniel, Y. Atonement
Davis, O. Sappho in Wales
Deming, B. An illness
Eastlake, W. Portrait of an artist with 26 horses
Fielding, G. The trip
Graham, W. The Medici earring
Kanin, G. Buddy buddy
Kaplan, B. Ben Early is raving
Levine, G. Every other bar but this one
Lins, O. The transparent bird
Malone, J. The fugitives
Malstrom, R. C. The great A
Marshall, L. Unknown artist
Nussbaum, A. The dead past
Oates, J. C. Bodies
O'Connor, P. F. Mastodon's box
Perowne, B. Papa Tral's harvest
Pritchett, V. S. The skeleton
Rosenthal, C. A specialist in still lifes
Roth, H. H. From image to expression
Rotsler, W. Patron of the arts
Sayers, D. L. The unsolved puzzle of the man with no face
Siegel, J. The man who believed in Christmas trees
Soto, P. J. Scribbles
Stern, R. Milius and Melanie
Stewart, J. I. M. A change of heart
Treat, L. Justice magnifique
Warner, S. T. A visionary gleam
Zelazny, R. A museum piece
*See also* Artist life; Architects; Illustrators; Negro artists; Painters; Sculptors
**ARTISTS, NEGRO.** *See* Negro artists
**ARTISTS' MODELS**
Franklin, E. Girl in a white dress
Hurlbut, K. Lilli
James, H. The real thing
Lieber, F. The girl with the hungry eyes
Sayers, D. L. The abominable history of the man with copper fingers
Stafford, J. The philosophy lesson
Wain, J. You could have fooled me
As for our fatal continuity. Aldiss, B. W.
As I am . . . as I was. Novás-Calvo, L.
As I was going up the stair. Chester, A.
As is. Silverberg, R.
As it is written. Rolf, F.
As long as you're here. Stanton, W.
As man to man. Patton, F. G.
As simple as that. Henderson, Z.
As the night, the day. Nicol, A.
As we have learnt from Freud, there are no jokes. Gilliatt, P.
**ASCENSION DAY**
Peterkin, J. Green Thursday
**Ascher, Sheila, and Straus, Dennis**
Even after a machine is dismantled, it continues to operate, with or without purpose
Voices of Brooklyn
**ASEXUAL REPRODUCTION.** *See* Reproduction, Asexual
**ASHANTIS.** *See* Fantis
**Ashby, Richard**
Master race
Furman, A. L. ed. Teen-age space adventures
**Ashdown, Clifford**
The Assyrian rejuvenator
Greene, H. ed. The rivals of Sherlock Holmes
The Chicago heiress
Best detective stories of the year [1969]
The submarine boat
Greene, H. ed. The rivals of Sherlock Holmes
Ashes. Peterkin, J.
**ASHTAROTH.** *See* Astarte (Goddess)
The **ashtray.** Moravia, A.
**Asia**
Buck, P. S. The good deed, and other stories of Asia; 10 stories
Shimer, D. B. ed. Voices of modern Asia; 18 stories
The **Asian** shore. Disch, T. M.
**Asigh.** Lavin, M.

**Asimov, Isaac**—*Continued*
  Victory unintentional
    Santesson, H. S. ed. The days after
      tomorrow
  The weapon too dreadful to use
    Asimov, I. The early Asimov
  What if—
    Asimov, I. Nightfall, and other stories
  What is this thing called love?
    Asimov, I. Nightfall, and other stories
**Asimov, Isaac, and MacCreigh, James**
  Legal rites
    Asimov, I. The early Asimov
  The little man on the subway
    Asimov, I. The early Asimov
The **Aska-Damn** dog. Spears, R. S.
**Askeland, Luthers**
  The Quest Sonata
    The Best little magazine fiction, 1971
**Aspects** of Langranak. Sheckley, R.
The **Aspern** papers. James, H.
The **assailant**. Oates, J. C.
**ASSASSINATION**
  Bradbury, R. Downwind from Gettysburg
  DeFord, M. A. The Peak Lords
  Dickson, G. R. Brothers
  Harrison, H. From fanaticism, or for re-
    ward
  Hoch, E. D. I'd know you anywhere
  McGerr, P. Selena robs the White House
  Malzberg, B. N. The union forever
  Moorcock, M. The tank trapeze
  Pilnyak, B. The death of the Army Com-
    mander: a tale of the unextinguished
    moon
  Purdy, K. W. The Dannold cheque
  Sturgeon, T.  The patterns of Dorne
  Thelwell, M. The organizer
  Vassilikos, V. Self-slaughter
  Walker, E. K. Harlem transfer
      *See also* Murder stories; Political
  crimes and offenses
**ASSASSINATION, ATTEMPTED.** *See* As-
  sassination
**Assassins.** Amarkant
The **Assassins.** Shelley, P. B.
**Assassins** of air. Zebrowski, G.
**ASSAULT AND BATTERY**
  Bullins, E. Travel from home
  Clarke, A. An invitation to join
  Hawkes, J. The universal fears
  Margaret of Navarre. The virtuous widow
  Michaels, L. The deal
  Michaels, L. Going places
  Oates, J. C. The assailant
  O'Connor, F. Revelation
  Pentecost, H. The man inside
  Stern, R. Ins and outs
  Williams, G. The yellow brick road
**Assault** and battery. Beekman, A.
**ASSEMBLY-LINE METHODS.** *See* Auto-
  mata; Factories
**Assenov, Dragomir**
  A strict upbringing
    Kirilov, N. and Kirk, F. eds. Introduc-
    tion to modern Bulgarian literature
**ASSER, BP. OF SHERBORNE**
  Walsh, J. P. and Crossley-Holland, K.
    Asser's book

**Asser's** book. Walsh, J. P. and Crossley-
  Holland, K.
**ASSES AND MULES**
  Brown, F. Puppet show
  Brown, R. One-man mule
  Crane, S. How the donkey lifted the hills
  Green, B. K. Fast mule buyer
  Green, B. K. Fence trouble
  Green, B. K. Foreign trade
  Green, B. K. Mule schoolin'
  Green, B. K. Watermelon hauler's mule
  Guthrie, A. B. The big it
  Philippe de Vigneulles. Modicum et
    bonum
  Stuart, J. Victory and the dream
  Verga, G. Story of the Saint Joseph's ass
**Assis, Machado de.** *See* Machado de Assis
**ASSISI, FRANCIS OF, SAINT.** *See* Francis
  of Assisi, Saint
The **Assyrian** rejuvenator. Ashdown, C.
**ASSYRO-BABYLONIAN INSCRIPTIONS.**
  *See* Cuneiform inscriptions
**ASTARTE (GODDESS)**
  Heinesen, W. The celestial journey
**ASTEROIDS.** *See* Planets, Minor
**ASTHMA**
  Costello, M. Punch & Judy
  Davis, O. Loss and chaos
**ASTIGMATISM**
  Anstey, F. The lights of Spencer Prim-
    mett's eyes
**ASTRAL PROJECTION.** *See* Supernatural
  phenomena
**ASTROLOGERS**
  Aldiss, B. W. The young soldier's horo-
    scope
The **Astrologer's** prediction; or The Maniac's
  fate
    Haining, P. ed. Gothic tales of terror
**ASTROLOGY**
  Gilliatt, P. The position of the planets
  Narayan, R. K. Seventh House
**ASTRONAUTS**
  Aldiss, B. W. Man in his time
  Anderson, P. Que donn'rez vous?
  Anderson, P. Say it with flowers
  Anderson, P. Sunjammer
  Asimov, I. Ring around the sun
  Biggle, L. Orphan of the void
  Bova, B. Fifteen miles
  Bova, B. Test in orbit
  Bova, B. Zero gee
  Bradbury, R. June 2001:-and the moon be
    still as bright
  Clarke, A. C. Maelstrom II
  Clement, H. Dust rag
  Cox, J. Fame
  Delany, S. R. Aye, and Gomorrah
  Dickson, G. R. Whatever gods there be
  Disch, T. M. Moondust, the smell of hay,
    and dialectical materialism
  Disch, T. M. The number you have
    reached
  Disch, T. M. Things lost
  Farmer, P. J. The blasphemers
  Laumer, K. Mind out of time
  Long, F. B. Filch
  Malzberg, B. N. Ups and downs
  Niven, L. Neutron Star

ASTRONAUTS—*Continued*
  O'Donnell, K. M. Still-life
  Shcherbakov, V. "We played under your
    window"
  Silverberg, R. The feast of St. Dionysus
  Silverberg, R. His head in the clouds
  Varshavsky, I. The Noneatrins
  Weiner, A. Empire of the sun
ASTRONOMERS
  Wells, H. G. The star
ASTRONOMICAL OBSERVATORIES
  Asimov, I. Nightfall
Asturias, Miguel Angel
  The mirror of Lida Sal
    Carpentier, H. and Brof, J. eds. Doors
      and mirrors
  Tatuana's tale
    Howes, B. ed. The eye of the heart
ASYLUM, RIGHT OF
  Carpentier, A. Right of sanctuary
ASYLUMS. *See* Mentally ill—Care and treat-
    ment
At arm's length. Gardner, E. S.
At Central. Reed, K.
At first sight. Campbell, R.
At home with the Colonel. Tuohy, F.
At last, the true story of Frankenstein. Har-
    rison, H.
At night all cats are grey. Boyle, P.
At old man Eckert's. Bierce, A.
At Sallygap. Lavin, M.
At sea. Chekhov, A.
At the bridge, Böll, H.
At the Chalet Lartrec. Graham, W.
At the Cothurnos Club. O'Hara, J.
At the depot. Bergelson, D.
At the dock gate. Adcock, A. St J.
At the drugstore. Taylor, P.
At the end of days. Silverberg, R.
At the end of the passage. Kipling, R.
At the fitting shop. Sallis, J.
At the Fort Flag. Sharp, M.
At the great 'Ecbo.' Cabrera Infante, G.
At the heart of it. Harrison, M.
At the lake. Davis, O.
At the mountain inn. Maupassant, G. de
At the outset of the day. Agnon, S. Y.
At the pit door. Crane, S.
At the pit's mouth. Kipling, R.
At the Silver Rail. Fields, R.
At the station. Landolfi, T.
At the stroke of twelve. Christie, A.
At the Tolstoy Museum. Barthelme, D.
Ata Bakhartaunu: thou hast chosen us.
    Blum-Alquit, E.
Athanas, Verne
  Royal elk
    Lucia, E. ed. This land around us
ATHEISM
  Steele, W. D. The man who saw through
    heaven
Atheism. Benes, J.
Athénaïse. Chopin, K.
ATHLETES
  Faust, I. The world's fastest human
  MacDonald, J. D. Half-past eternity
  Neugeboren, J.   Ebbets Field
    *See also* Sports; and names of specific
      athletic activity, e.g. Track athletics

Atkinson, Hugh
  The language of flowers
    Hamilton, A. ed. Splinters
ATLANTA. *See* Georgia—Atlanta
ATLANTIC CITY. *See* New Jersey—Atlantic
    City
ATLANTIS
  Tarkington, B. The veiled feminists of
    Atlantis
Atlantis on $5.00 a day. Haag, J.
ATOLLS
  Liggett, B. The cat man
ATOMIC BOMB
  Benét, S. V. By the waters of Babylon
  Buzzati, D.   A Siberian shepherd's report
    of the atom bomb
  Filer, B. K. Hot potato
  Spinrad, N. The big flash
            **Physiological effect**
    *See* Radioactivity—Physiological ef-
    fect
ATOMIC ENERGY
  Asimov, I. "Breeds there a man . . . ?"
  Asimov, I. Half-breed
    *See also* Atomic power plants
ATOMIC POWER PLANTS
  Del Rey, L. Nerves
ATOMIC WARFARE
  Anderson, P.   A chapter of revelation
  Disch, T. M. Casablanca
  Hood, H. After the sirens
  Pei, M. 1976
  Sallis, J. The anxiety in the eyes of the
    cricket
  Sallis, J. Jeremiad
  Sturgeon, T. Thunder and roses
  Vandeloo, J. The day of the dead God
    *See also* Atomic bomb
ATONEMENT
  Singer, I. B.   A crown of feathers
Atonement. Daniel, Y.
ATROCITIES
  Shaw, I. God was here but He left early
    *See also* names of wars with subdivi-
    sion Atrocities, e.g. World War, 1939-
    1945—Atrocities
The attacker. Wolson, M.
An attempt at reform. Strindberg, A.
ATTEMPTED ASSASSINATION. *See* As-
    sassination
ATTEMPTED MURDER. *See* Murder
    stories
ATTEMPTED SUICIDE. See Suicide
The attic. Blackwood, A.
The attic express. Hamilton, A.
The attic room. Fellowes-Gordon, I.
Attorney Street. Blum-Alquit, E.
ATTORNEYS. *See* Law and lawyers
Atwood, Margaret
  The grave of the famous poet
    New Canadian stories, 72
Auchincloss, Louis
  Black Shylock
    Auchincloss, L. Second chance
  The cathedral builder
    Auchincloss, L. Second chance
  The collector
    Auchincloss, L. Second chance

**Auchincloss, Louis**—*Continued*
Days of wrath
Auchincloss, L. Second chance
The double gap
Auchincloss, L. Second chance
The prince and the pauper
Auchincloss, L. Second chance
The prison window
Auchincloss, L. Second chance
Matthews, J. ed. Archetypal themes in
the modern story
Red light
Auchincloss, L. Second chance
The sacrifice
Auchincloss, L. Second chance
Second chance
Auchincloss, L. Second chance
Suttee
Auchincloss, L. Second chance
The waiver
Auchincloss, L. Second chance
The **auction**. Crane, S.
**AUCTIONS**
Crane, S. The auction
Fleming, I. The property of a lady
Lavin, M. The mock auction
Steegmuller, F. The credo
**AUDITORS**
Stanev, L.  A visitor
**Augury**. Ayrton, M.
**August** heat. Harvey, W. F.
**August 1999**: the Earth men. Bradbury, R.
**August 1999**: the summer night. Brad-
bury, R.
**August** ninth at Natural Bridge. Bingham, S.
**August 2001**: the settlers. Bradbury, R.
**August 2002**: night meeting. Bradbury, R.
**August 2005**: the old ones. Bradbury, R.
**August 2026**: there will come soft rains.
Bradbury, R.
**Augustus**. Hesse, H.
The **aunt**. Bichsel, P.
**Aunt** Agatha. Buck, D. P.
**Aunt** Mae Lewis comes home. Holmes, E. M.
**Aunt** Sally's life. Gatty, Mrs A.
**AUNTS**
Aiken, J. All you've ever wanted
Aiken, J. Summer by the sea
Blount, M. The right books
Böll, H. Christmas every day
Buck, D. P. Aunt Agatha
Burton, H. The Zenana Mission Bazaar
Cather, W. Uncle Valentine
Cather, W.  A Wagner's matinee
Cheever, J. Percy
Clarke, A. C. The reluctant orchid
Costello, M. Callahan's black Cadillacs
Donoso, J. Paseo
Fremlin, C. Something evil in the house
Friedman, B. J. The enemy
Friedman, B. J. The hero
Greene, G. Travel tips from Aunt Augusta
Grendon, S. The drifting snow
Hayes, A. H. Four days
Hughes, L.  Last whipping
Kipling, R. The gardener
Lavin, M. The small bequest
Leffland, E. The forest
Linn, M. L. Please listen, Aunt Viney

McEwan, I. Disguises
Petaja, E. Dark balcony
Rice, J. The willow tree
Singer, I. B. Guests on a winter night
Steinberg, B. The Nazi machine
Stern, J. Under the beech tree
Summers, H. Mister Joseph Botts
West, J. Mother's Day
Wilson, A. The wrong set
Yellen, S. The four sides of a triangle
*See also* Nephews; Nieces
**Aura**. Fuentes, C.
The **Austin** murder case. Breen, J. L.
**AUSTRALIA**
Atkinson, H. The language of flowers
Coburn, A. The tale of the fourth stranger
Ottley, R. Brumbie running
Ottley, R. Bush camels
Ottley, R. Bush secret
Ottley, R. Dusty deal
Ottley, R. Epitaph to Jones'y
Ottley, R. The last of the horsemen
Ottley, R. Stampede
**Native races**
Jennings, G. Sooner or later or never never
**New South Wales**
Ottley, R. Midnight
**AUSTRIA**
**Politics**
*See* Politics—Austria
**Vienna**
Doderer, H. von. The magician's art
Slesinger, T.  The times so unsettled are
**AUSTRIA, PROVINCIAL AND RURAL**
Doderer, H. von. Stepfield
Schnitzler, A. Fräulein Else
**AUSTRIANS IN THE UNITED STATES**
Wister, O. Hank's woman
The **austringer**. Rothschild, M.
**Author!** Author! Asimov, I.
**AUTHORITARIANISM.** *See* Totalitarianism
**AUTHORS**
Agnon, S. Y. The orchestra
Aprilov, B.  Blue
Asimov, I. Author! Author!
Babel, I.  Inspiration
Babel, I. The nine
Barth, J. Life-story
Beerbohm, M. Hilary Maltby and Stephen
Braxton
Bergé, C. In motion
Biggle, L. Well of the deep wish
Bingham, S. The facts of his life
Blecher, G. The death of the Russian
novel
Blish, J. More light
Blish, J. Statistician's day
Bloch, R. The shadow from the steeple
Bloch, R. The shambler from the stars
Bontly, T. Eight meetings
Borges, J. L. Pierre Menard, author of
Don Quixote
Bradbury, R. Any friend of Nicholas
Nickleby's is a friend of mine
Brautigan, R. The literary life in Califor-
nia/1964

AUTHORS—*Continued*

Brautigan, R. 1/3, 1/3, 1/3
Brennan, J. P. The way to the attic
Brown, G. M. The eye of the hurricane
Bukowski, C. All the great writers
Bukowski, C.　A shipping clerk with a red nose
Bukowski, C. Twelve flying monkeys who won't copulate properly
Bukowski, C. You can't write a love story
Bullins, E. Moonwriter
Bullins, E. The reason of why
Bullins, E. Support your local police
Campbell, R. The Franklyn paragraphs
Carpenter, D. Hollywood whore
Cather, W. The willing muse
Charyn, J. The man who grew younger
Collier, J. Collaboration
Collier, J. Pictures in the fire
Collier, J. Variation on a theme
Davidson, A. Selectra Six-Ten
Davidson, A. The sources of the Nile
De Vries, P. The irony of it all
Di Donato, P. Mask in the cage
Di Donato, P. Nude of an author
Di Donato, P. The overnight guest
Disch, T. M. The squirrel cage
Easmon, R. S. The human touch
Eaton, C. E. The case of the missing photographs
Eddy, C. M. Black moon
Eddy, C. M. Deaf, dumb and blind
Effinger, G. A. The ghost writer
Farmer, P. J. Father's in the basement
Farrell, J. T. Episodes of a return
Farrell, J. T. Exiles
Farrell, J. T. Jump to Chicago
Farrell, J. T. Native's return
Farrell, J. T.　A night in new Jerusalem
Farrell, J. T. Sunday evening
Fiedler, L. A.　An expense of spirit
Fiedler, L. A. The teeth
Forster, E. M. The eternal moment
Fremlin, C. The special gift
Friedman, P. The story of a story
Glaze, E. And bigger fools
Gold, H.　A death on the East Side
Goulart, R. Confessions
Goulart, R. Muscadine
Greene, G. May we borrow your husband?
Greene, G.　A visit to Morin
Helbemäe, G. Still life
Hemingway, E. On writing
Henry, O. Proof of the pudding
Henry, O. Sound and fury
Hill, R. Out in the garage
Himes, C. Da-da-dee
Holst, S. True confessions story
Jacobi, C. Round robin
James, H. The middle years
Katz, E. Reynold Stengrow's short story
Kipling, R. 'The finest story in the world'
Landolfi, T. Cancerqueen
Lavin, M. Trastevere
Law, W. The Harry Hastings Method
Lewis, S. The post-mortem murder
Liggett, B. The cat man
Linklater, E.　A sociable plover
Litvinov, I. Farewell to the dacha

Litvinov, I. To be a Daniel
Long, F. B. The space-eaters
Lowry, M. Ghostkeeper
Lu, Hsun.　A happy family
Lu, Hsun. Regret for the past
Lumley, B. Ambler's inspiration
Lumley, B. An item of supporting evidence
Lumley, B. The writer in the garret
McClatchy, J. D. Allonym
McCullers, C. Who has seen the wind?
McGahern, J. Peaches
Mailer, N. The man who studied yoga
Malamud, B. The last Mohican
Malamud, B. Man in the drawer
Maloney, R. The help comes in bottles
Maltz, A. The cop
Mandelstam, O. Fourth prose
Manners, M. The plot
Mansfield, K. Psychology
Matthews, J. The party
Mayhall, J. The enemy
Michaels, L. Storytellers, liars, and bores
Miłosz, C. Brognart
Moravia, A. Words and the body
Nabokov, V. Lips to lips
Oates, J. C. Accomplished desires
Oates, J. C. Loving }
　　　　Losing } a man
　　　　Loving }
Oates, J. C. The sacred marriage
O'Connor, F. The enduring chill
Osamu, D. Villon's wife
Ozick, C. Envy
Ozick, C. Yiddish in America
Paley, G.　A conversation with my father
Panshin, A. How can we sink when we can fly?
Peirce, J. F. The total portrait
Phillips, R. Obsession
Price, R. Scars
Rodriguez, B. The naked man
Sallis, J. Front & centaur
Sallis, J. Letter to a young poet
Salter, J. The destruction of the Goetheanum
Saltus, E. The grand duke's rubies
Saroyan, W. The daring young man on the flying trapeze
Schmitz, J. H. Where the time went
Schoenfeld, H. Built up logically
Schwartz, J. Corners
Shiina, R. The go-between
Singer, I. B. The beard
Singer, I. B. The cabalist of East Broadway
Singer, I. B. The cafeteria
Singer, I. B.　A day in Coney Island
Singer, I. B. Dr Beeber
Singer, I. B. The joke
Singer, I. B. The lecture
Singer, I. B. The mentor
Singer, I. B. Schloimele
Slesar, H.　A note on American literature by my uncle, Monroe Sanderson
Slesinger, T. After the party
Slesinger, T.　A life in the day of a writer
Smith, C. A. The resurrection of the rattlesnake

Babushka. Litvinov, I.
The baby. Kemal, Y.
Baby born in the field. Kemal, O.
Baby is three. Sturgeon, T.
Baby Perpetua. Dillon, M.
The baby-sitter. Fremlin, C.
BABY SITTERS
  Boles, P. D. The holiday rider
  Coover, R. The babysitter
  DeFord, M. A. Mrs Hinck
  Fremlin, C. The baby-sitter
  Hayes, A. H. Four days
  Kotzwinkle, W. Soldier in the blanket
  Marshall, L. The leaning tower
  Payes, R. C. Grandma was never like this
  Stafford, J. The darkening moon
  Tammuz, B. An enigma
  Warner, L. Melissa Savage
The baby tramp. Bierce, A.
The Babylon lottery. See Borges, J. L. The
  lottery in Babylon
A baby's mouth. Peterkin, J.
The babysitter. Coover, R.
BACCHUS. See Dionysus
The Bach Master. Goldberg, G. J.
BACHELORS
  Acton, H. The gift horse
  Cather, W. Consequences
  Drake, R. The music lover
  Drake, R. The single heart
  Drake, R.　A wreath for Ed Meachum
  Elkin, S. The condominium
  Elkin, S. The making of Ashenden
  Francis, H. E. One of the boys
  Friedman, P. The arm of interchangeable
    parts
  Henry, O.　A poor rule
  Henry, O. The ransom of Mack
  Jones, A. Hope should always
  Joyce, J.　A painful case
  Kafka, F. Blumfeld, an elderly bachelor
  Lavin, M.　A memory
  Litvinov, I. To be a Daniel
  Nowlan, A. The girl who went to Mexico
  O'Faolain, S. Brainsy
  O'Faolain, S. 'Our fearful innocence'
  O'Hara, J. Afternoon waltz
  Ozick, C. The dock-witch
  Ozick, C .The doctor's wife
  Reinbold, J. S. Mr Staal
  Shaber, D. Scotch sour
  Sié, Cheou-kang. The reward
  Steinbeck, J. Pat Humbert's
  Trevor, W. The forty-seventh Saturday
  Trevor, W.　A meeting in middle age
  Updike, J.　I am dying, Egypt, dying
  Yaari, Y. The wanderer and the blind man
Back for Christmas. Collier, J.
Back from that bourne. Mitchell, E. P.
Back into the present. Schwimmer, W.
Back to back. Spielberg, P.
Back to the tree. Bullock, M.
BACKACHE
  Busch, F. While Susan Hayward weeps
  Roth, P. Novotny's pain
BACKPACKING
  Gonik, V. Honeymoon in October
Backward, turn backward. Davis, D. S.

Bacon, Gertrude
  The Gorgon's head
    Manley, S. and Lewis, G. eds. Ladies of
    horror
BACTERIAL WARFARE. See Bacteriologi-
  cal warfare
Bad characters. Stafford, J.
A bad example. Maugham, W. S.
Bad luck. Strindberg, A.
Bad news. Spike, P.
Bad scene at Buffalo Jump. Fiedler, L. A.
A bad streak. Glanville, B.
A bad trip. Bukowski, C.
A bad woman. Jhabvala, R. P.
BADGERS
  Boyle, P. Meles vulgaris
Badges of rank. Marinković, R.
A baffled ambuscade. Bierce, A.
A bag of cherries. Metcalf, J.
The bagman's story. Dickens, C.
BAGPIPERS. See Musicians—Bagpipers
Bagrat-Ogley and the eyes of his bull.
  Babel, I.
BAHAISM
  Bergé, C. The Farm Woman
BAHAMAS
  Spike, P. The diary of Noel Wells
Bahr, Jerome
  The burning capital
    Bahr, J. The perishing republic
  Daniel and the boulder
    Bahr, J. The perishing republic
  Deedie and her lovers
    Bahr, J. The perishing republic
  Downfall of a general
    Bahr, J. The perishing republic
  Farewell to Fritzie
    Bahr, J. The perishing republic
  Flagged
    Bahr, J. The perishing republic
  Footnote to a famous peace march
    Bahr, J. The perishing republic
  The girl on the post
    Bahr, J. The perishing republic
  The great debate
    Bahr, J. The perishing republic
  Incident on Galiano Street
    Bahr, J. The perishing republic
  The man who wanted to give up
    Bahr, J. The perishing republic
  Old Tom's egg box
    Bahr, J. The perishing republic
  The perilous affirmative
    Bahr, J. The perishing republic
  The polite captain
    Bahr, J. The perishing republic
BAIL
  Elkin, S. The bailbondsman
The bailbondsman. Elkin, S.
Bailey, Don
  A bauble for Bernice
    New Canadian stories, 72
  A few notes for Orpheus
    Fourteen stories high
Bailey, Hilary
  Dogman of Islington
    Carr, T. ed. Into the unknown

The **bailiff** and the scrupulous curate. Nicolas de Troyes

**BAILIFFS**
Nicolas de Troyes. The bailiff and the scrupulous curate

**BAIT**
Davidson, J. A. The Black sons-of-bitches

**Baker, Denys Val**
Cat without a name
Necker, C. ed. Supernatural cats

**BAKERIES AND BAKERS**
Gorky, M. Twenty-six men and a girl
Kaplan, B. Rare and stinging days

**BAKERS.** *See* Bakeries and bakers

The **baker's** daughter. Blum-Alquit, E.

**Bakhnov, Vladlen**
Speaking of demonology
Magidoff, R. ed. Russian science fiction, 1969
Unique
Magidoff, R. ed. Russian science fiction, 1969

**BAKING.** *See* Bakeries and bakers; Bread; Pastry

**Bakshi, Ramesh**
Empty
Roadarmel, G. C. ed. A death in Delhi

**Balaam.** Boucher, A.

**BALANCE OF NATURE.** *See* Ecology

The **balancing** act. Casper, L.

**BALBO, ITALO**
Pei, M. The flight that failed

**BALDWIN IV, KING OF JERUSALEM**
Coolidge, O. The heir 1170

**Baldwin, Gulielmus**
Beware the cat
Parry, M. ed. Beware of the cat

**Baldwin, James**
Come out the wilderness
Abrahams, W. ed. Fifty years of the American short story v 1
James, C. L. ed. From the roots
King, W. ed. Black short story anthology
Equal in Paris
Schulman, L. M. ed. Travelers
The man child
Turner, D. T. ed. Black American literature
The outing
Margolies, E.   A native sons reader
Sonny's blues
Adoff, A. ed. Brothers and sisters
Burnett, W. ed. Black hands on a white face
Charyn, J. ed. The troubled vision
McKenzie, B. ed. The process of fiction
Matthews, J. ed. Archetypal themes in the modern story
Schulman, L. M. ed. The loners
This morning, this evening, so soon
Kissin, E. H. ed. Stories in black and white
McKenzie, B. ed. The process of fiction

**Baldwin, Michael**
The ice palace
Hamilton, A. ed. Splinters

**BALL GAMES**
Sheckley, R. Game: first schematic
*See also* names of specific ball games, e.g. Baseball; Basketball; Football; etc.

**Ball**-of-Fat. Maupassant, G. de

**Ball** of Tallow. *See* Maupassant, G. de. Ball-of-Fat

The **ballad** of Barney Cohen. Kaplan, B.

The **ballad** of lost C'mell. Smith, C.

The **ballad** of Rosabella. Di Donato, P.

**Ballard, J. G.**
Billenium
Ballard J. G. Chronopolis, and other stories
Build-up
Ballard, J. G. Chronopolis, and other stories
The cage of sand
Ballard, J. G. Chronopolis, and other stories
Disch, T. M. ed. The ruins of earth
Chronopolis
Ballard, J. G. Chronopolis, and other stories
The cloud-sculptors of Coral D
The Best from Fantasy and Science Fiction; 18th ser.
Deep end
Ballard, J. G. Chronopolis, and other stories
The drowned giant
Ballard, J. G. Chronopolis, and other stories
Carr, T. ed. Into the unknown
Same as: Souvenir, listed in 1964-1968 supplement
End game
Ballard, J. G. Chronopolis, and other stories
The garden of time
Ballard, J. G. Chronopolis, and other stories
The killing ground
Best SF: 1969
Manhole 69
Ballard, J. G. Chronopolis, and other stories
Now wakes the sea
Ballard, J. G. Chronopolis, and other stories
The screen game
Haining, P. ed. The Hollywood nightmare
The sound-sweep
Ballard, J. G. Chronopolis, and other stories
Knight, D. ed. Tomorrow and tomorrow
Storm-bird, storm-dreamer
Ballard, J. G. Chronopolis, and other stories
The subliminal man
Silverberg, R. ed. The mirror of infinity
The terminal beach
Ballard, J. G. Chronopolis, and other stories
Total Effect. Survival printout
Thirteen for Centaurus
Clareson, T. D. ed. A spectrum of worlds

BARS. *See* Hotels, taverns, etc.
**BARTENDERS**
  Böll, H. Dear old Renée
  Casper, L. Drink to private gods
  Di Donato, P. Mass for unknown soldiers
  Maloney, R.   A bird of gaudy plumage
  Maloney, R. Last stop before the carbarn
  Maloney, R. The way it all comes loose
**BARTER**
  Simak, C. D. The big front yard
  Steegmuller, F. The system
**Barth, John**
  Ambrose his mark
    Karl, F. R. and Hamalian, L. eds. The
      naked i
  Autobiography: a self-recorded fiction
    New American Review no. 2
    Oates, J. C. ed. Scenes from American
      life
  Dunyazadiad
    Lish, G. ed. The secret life of our times:
      new fiction from Esquire
  The law
    Charyn, J. ed. The single voice
  Life-story
    Stevick, P. ed. Anti-story
  Lost in the funhouse
    Abrahams, W. ed. Fifty years of the
      American short story v 1
    Prize stories, 1969: The O. Henry
      Awards
  Menelaiad
    Elkin, S. ed. Stories from the sixties
  Night-sea journey
    Gulassa, C. M. ed. The fact of fiction
    Minot, S. and Wilson, R. eds. Three
      stances of modern fiction
**Barthelme, Donald**
  Alexandria and Henrietta
    New American Review no. 12
  At the Tolstoy Museum
    Barthelme, D. City life
  The balloon
    Minot, S. and Wilson, R. eds. Three
      stances of modern fiction
  Bone bubbles
    Barthelme, D. City life
  Brain damage
    Barthelme, D. City life
  The catechist
    Barthelme, D. Sadness
  City life
    Barthelme, D. City life
    Disch, R. and Schwartz, B. eds. Killing
      time
  A city of churches
    Barthelme, D. Sadness
    The Best American short stories, 1973
  Critique de la vie quotidienne
    Barthelme, D. Sadness
  Daumier
    Barthelme, D. Sadness
  Departures
    Barthelme, D. Sadness
  Engineer-private Paul Klee misplaces an
    aircraft between Milbertshofen and
    Cambrai, March 1916
    Barthelme, D. Sadness

The explanation
    Barthelme, D. City life
The falling dog
    Barthelme, D. City life
A film
    Barthelme, D. Sadness
The flight of pigeons from the palace
    Barthelme, D. Sadness
Game
    Stevick, P. ed. Anti-story
The genius
    Barthelme, D. Sadness
    Best SF: 1971
The glass mountain
    Barthelme, D. City life
The Indian uprising
    Charyn, J. ed. The singing voice
    Foff, A. and Knapp, D. eds. Story
Kierkegaard unfair to Schlegel
    Barthelme, D. City life
Me and Miss Mandible
    Gulassa, C. M. ed. The fact of fiction
    Karl, F. R. The naked i
    Spinner, S. ed. Live and learn
On angels
    Barthelme, D. City life
Paraguay
    Barthelme, D. City life
The party
    Barthelme, D. Sadness
Perpetua
    Barthelme, D. Sadness
The Phantom of the Opera's friend
    Barthelme, D. City life
The Policemen's Ball
    Barthelme, D. City life
Report
    Schulman, L. M. ed. The cracked look-
      ing glass
    Thune, E. and Prigozy, R. eds. Short
      stories: a critical anthology
The rise of capitalism
    Barthelme, D. Sadness
Robert Kennedy saved from drowning
    New American Review no. 3
The sandman
    Barthelme, D. Sadness
See the moon?
    Abrahams, W. ed. Fifty years of the
      American short story v 1
    Roecker, W. A. ed. Stories that count
Sentence
    Barthelme, D. City life
Subpoena
    Barthelme, D. Sadness
    Prize stories, 1972: The O. Henry
      Awards
The temptation of St Anthony
    Barthelme, D. Sadness
Träumerei
    Barthelme, D. Sadness
Views of my father weeping
    Barthelme, D. City life
**Bartleby** the scrivener. Melville, H.
**Bartov, Hanoch**
  In a son's footsteps
    Michener, J. A. ed. First fruits
    Rabikovitz, D. ed. The new Israeli
      writers

**Barwin, Victor**
The call
    Goodman, P. ed. The Yom Kippur anthology
**Bar-Yosef, Yosef**
The window
    Rabikovitz, D. ed. The new Israeli writers
**BASEBALL**
Algren, N. Go! Go! Go! Forty years ago
Dawson, F. The next turn of the wheel
Farrell, J. T. Jump to Chicago
Farrell, J. T. Monologue of an old pitcher
Greenberg, A. The real meaning of the Faust legend
Highsmith, P. The barbarians
Keefe, F. L. Mama Drobek and the great American game
Malamud, B. Pre-game
Morris, H. Lillian
Neugeboren, J. Ebbets Field
Roth, H. H. The Cinderella Kid
Updike, J. The slump
Warren, R. P. Goodwood comes back
    See also Little league baseball
Basement. Bambara, T. C.
The basement. Lagerkvist, P.
The basement room. Greene, G.
**BASHFULNESS.** See Timidity
Basil and Cleopatra. Fitzgerald, F. S.
The basket chair. Graham, W.
A basket of apples. Faessler, S.
**BASKETBALL**
Breen, J. L. Frank Merriswell's greatest case
Greenlee, S. Sonny's not blue
McNear, R. Death's door
Neugeboren, J. Something is rotten in the Borough of Brooklyn
**BASQUES**
Lanier, S. Fraternity brother
**BASS.** See Bass fishing
**BASS FISHING**
Blackhurst, W. E. Business before bass
Brister, B.    A matter of rationale
**BASS PLAYERS.** See Musicians—Bass players
**Bassani, Giorgio**
The last years of Clelia Trotti
    Bassani, G. Five stories of Ferrara
Lida Mantovani
    Bassani, G. Five stories of Ferrara
A night in '43
    Bassani, G. Five stories of Ferrara
A plaque on Via Mazzini
    Bassani, G. Five stories of Ferrara
The walk before supper
    Bassani, G. Five stories of Ferrara
The bastard. Stanton, M.
The bastards of Thanos. Petrakis, H. M.
**Bastos, Augusto Roa.** See Roa Bastos, Augusto
**Bates, H. E.**
The small portion
    Zolotow, C. ed. An overpraised season
**Bates, Harry**
Farewell to the master
    The Astounding-Analog reader v 1

**Bates, Paulette**
The enemy
    Intro #2
The bath of acid. Usher, F.
**BATHING BEACHES.** See Seashore
**BATHING SUITS**
Crane, S. The reluctant voyagers
**Batki, John**
Strange-dreaming Charlie, cow-eyed Charlie
    Prize stories, 1972: The O. Henry Awards
**BATS**
Usher, F. The great white bat
Bats and babies. Gbadamossi, R. A.
Bat's belfry. Derleth, A.
The battered-earth syndrome. Malzberg, B. N.
**BATTLE OF CHICKAMAUGA.** See Chickamauga, Battle of, 1863
The battle of Forty Fort. Crane, S.
The battle of Klandurskot. Winther, M. A.
Battle sight. Thomason, J. W.
The battler. Hemingway, E.
**BATTLES**
Bierce, A. One officer, one man
Macpherson, J. Calthon and Colmal
    See also names of individual battles, e.g. Chickamauga, Battle of, 1863; Hastings, Battle of, 1066; Midway, Battle of, 1942
A bauble for Bernice. Bailey, D.
**Bauer, Gerard M.**
From all of us
    Elwood, R. ed. The new mind
Bauman's tale. Roosevelt, T.
**Baxter, John**
Apple
    Yolen, J. comp. Zoo 2000
Bayaminiña. Soto, P. J.
**Bayley, Barrington J.**
Mutation planet
    Elwood, R. ed. Tomorrow's alternatives
**BAZAARS.** See Fairs
Be a Wingdinger, earn big money. Petaja, E.
The beach. Dunn, P.
The beach of Falesá. Stevenson, R. L.
The beach umbrella. Colter, C.
**BEACH UMBRELLAS.** See Umbrellas
**Beachcroft, T. O.**
The eyes
    Lamb, H. ed. A tide of terror
**BEACHES.** See Seashore
Beachhead in Bohemia. Marsh, W.
Beads of brains. Veitch, T.
The beagle and the eagle. Delapp, T.
The beaked horror which sank a ship. Day, J. W.
**Beal, M. F.**
The end of days
    New American Review no. 7
Gold
    The Best American short stories, 1972
    New American Review no. 11
Survival
    Gulassa, C. M. ed. The fact of fiction
    New American Review no. 3

**Beale, Charles Willing**
The ghost of Guir House
Bleiler, E. F. ed. Five Victorian ghost novels
A **bear** for the F.B.I.; excerpt. Van Peebles, M.
**BEAR HUNTING**
Tendryakov, V. Justice
The **bear** with the knot on his tail. Tall, S.
**Beard, Henry**
The last recall
Best detective stories of the year, 1973
The **beard.** Singer, I. B.
**BEARS**
Cather, W. The strategy of the Were-Wolf Dog
Crane, S. Killing his bear
Crane, S.  A tent in agony
Elkin, S. The making of Ashenden
Sharp, M. Mr Hamble's bear
West, R. B. The last of the grizzly bears
Wolfe, G. An article about hunting
The **beast** from 20,000 fathoms. Bradbury, R.
The **beast** in the jungle. James, H.
The **beast** that shouted love at the heart of the world. Ellison, H.
The **beast** with five fingers. Harvey, W. F.
**Beasts** of the southern wild. Betts, D.
**BEAT GENERATION.** See Bohemianism
**BEATIFICATION.** See Canonization
**BEATNIKS.** See Hippies
**Beatrice** Trueblood's story. Stafford, J.
**Beaumont, Charles**
Free dirt
Ferman, E. L. and Mills, R. P. eds. Twenty years of The Magazine of Fantasy and Science Fiction
The new people
Haining, P. ed. The Hollywood nightmare
**BEAUTICIANS.** See Beauty shops
**BEAUTIFUL, THE.** See Esthetics
The **beautiful** fire. Kotowska, M.
The **beautiful** soul of Don Damián. Bosch, J.
**BEAUTY.** See Esthetics
**BEAUTY, PERSONAL**
Brautigan, R. The pretty office
Bukowski, C. The most beautiful woman in town
Delattre, P. Mrs Tibet
Drake, R. The ugliest white woman you ever saw in your life
García Márquez, G. The handsomest drowned man in the world
Stafford, J. The end of a career
Wharton, E. The looking glass
See also Ugliness
**Beauty.** Greene, G.
**BEAUTY CONTESTS**
Delattre, P. Mrs Tibet
Reed, K. In behalf of the product
The **beauty** in that house. Mayberry, F. V.
**BEAUTY SHOPS**
Rugel, M. Paper poppy
Seth, R. Scent of death
Starke, R. Lionel
Walker, A. Her sweet Jerome
Welty, E. Petrified man

**Employees**
O'Hara, J. The friends of Miss Julia
**Beautyland.** Wolfe, G.
**BEAUVOIR, SIMONE DE**
Algren, A. Brave bulls of Sidi Yahya
**Becalmed** in hell. Niven, L.
**Bech** in Rumania. Updike, J.
**Bech** panics. Updike, J.
**Bech** takes pot luck. Updike, J.
**Becker, Jürgen**
Margins
New Directions in prose and poetry 24
The **Becket** girls' tree. Jewett, S. O.
**Beckett, Samuel**
Dante and the lobster
Beckett, S. More pricks than kicks
Ding-dong
Beckett, S. More pricks than kicks
Draff
Beckett, S. More pricks than kicks
Fingal
Beckett, S. More pricks than kicks
Love and lethe
Beckett, S. More pricks than kicks
The Smeraldina's billet doux
Beckett, S. More pricks than kicks
Stories and texts for nothing, III
Hall, J. B. ed. The realm of fiction
Walking out
Beckett, S. More pricks than kicks
A wet night
Beckett, S. More pricks than kicks
What a misfortune
Beckett, S. More pricks than kicks
Yellow
Beckett, S. More pricks than kicks
**Beckford, William**
The Nymph of the Fountain
Haining, P. ed. Gothic tales of terror
**Becky.** Toomer, J.
**Bed** sheets are white. Lief, E.
**Bedlam's** rent. Sterling, T.
**Bednarz, Wilma**
Bracelet of destruction
Furman, A. L. ed. Teen-age secret agent stories
**BEDROOMS**
Bogan, L. Journey around my room
**BEDS**
Collins, W.  A terribly strange bed
A **bedtime** story. Marguerite de Navarre
**Beecher** Island. Overholser, W. D.
**Beeding, Francis**
Death by judicial hanging
Hitchcock, A. ed. Alfred Hitchcock presents: Stories to stay awake by
**BeeGee's** ghost. Hunter, K.
**Beekman, Allan**
All our yesterdays
Beekman, A. Hawaiian tales
Assault and battery
Beekman, A. Hawaiian tales
Behind every man
Beekman, A. Hawaiian tales
Dog spirit
Beekman, A. Hawaiian tales
The expert
Beekman, A. Hawaiian tales

**Beekman, Allan**—*Continued*
  Hawaiian hospitality
    Beekman, A. Hawaiian tales
  Mr Maki and the new order
    Beekman, A. Hawaiian tales
  No place beneath the rising sun
    Beekman, A. Hawaiian tales
  Ordeal by fire
    Beekman, A. Hawaiian tales
  Point of view
    Beekman, A. Hawaiian tales
  Those who walk the streets
    Beekman, A. Hawaiian tales
**Beekman, E. M.**
  Cornada
    New Directions in prose and poetry 24
**BEELZEBUB.** *See* Devil
**Beelzebub.** Bloch, R.
**Beer** and poets and talk, Bukowski, C.
**Beerbohm, Max**
  A. V. Laider
    Untermeyer, L. ed. Treasury of great
      humor
  Hilary Maltby and Stephen Braxton
    Auchincloss, L. ed. Fables of wit and
      elegance
**BEES**
  Barth, J. Ambrose his mark
  Brennan, M.   A large bee
  Ulibarri, S. R. Get that straight
**BEETHOVEN, LUDWIG VAN**
           **Parodies, travesties, etc.**
  Jones, L. Symphony no. 6 in C minor:
    The tragic, by Ludwig van Beeth-
    oven II
**BEETLES**
  Bulatović, M.   A fable
The **before** and after of Hymie Farbotnik.
  Yurick, S.
**Before** Eden. Clarke, A. C.
**Before** sunrise, Goryushkin, V.
**Before** the operation. Breslow, P.
**Before** the storm. Shapiro, L.
**Beggar** my neighbor. Jacobson, D.
**Beggarman,** thief. DeFord, M. A.
**BEGGARS**
  Blish, J. None so blind
  Bradbury, R. McGillahee's brat
  Francis, H. E. The itinerary of beggars
  Francis, H. E. The woman from Jujuy
  Hollander, J. In the creep block, one was
    observed . . .
  Jacobson, D. Beggar my neighbor
  Lagerkvist, P. The basement
  Moravia, A. Down and out
  Premchand.   A feast for the holy man
  Sallis, J. Les amis
  Singer, I. B. Her son
       *See also* Tramps
**BEGGING.** *See* Beggars
The **beginner.** Bukowski, C.
The **beginning** and the end. Stern, J.
The **beginning** of summer. Grau, S. A.
The **beginning** of the armadillos. Kipling, R.
The **beginning** of tomorrow. Turner, C. E.
The **beginnings** of a fortune. Lispector, C.
The **begonia.** Minkov, S.
The **Begum's** fortune. Verne, J.

**BEHAVIOR PROBLEMS (CHILDREN)**
  *See* Problem children
**Beheaded** in error
  Kahn, J. ed. Hanging by a thread
The **beheading.** Hunter, E.
**Behind** a mask. Ansky, S.
**Behind** every man. Beekman, A.
**Behind** our lines. *See* Hall, J. B. God cares,
  but waits: Behind our lines
**Behind** the moon. Brodeur, P.
**Behind** the sandrat hoax. Anvil, C.
**Behind** the Singer Tower. Cather, W.
**Behold** my servant. Simckes, L. S.
**Behold** the dreamer. Rosenak, M.
**Behold** the key. Malamud, B.
**Beidenbauer's** flea. Ellin, S.
**Being** an epick of Sangiorgio, protector of
  the kingdom. Corvo, F. Baron
**Belcher, C. Davis**
  The price
    Orbit 5
**BELGIAN SOLDIERS.** *See* Soldiers, Bel-
  gian
**BELGIUM**
    *See also* Flanders
           **Farm life**
    *See* Farm life—Belgium
**BELGIUM, PROVINCIAL AND RURAL**
  Streuvels, S. October
**BELGRADE.** *See* Yugoslavia—Belgrade
**Belgrade** 1926. Ambler, E.
**BELIEF AND DOUBT.** *See* Faith
The **believer.** Horler, S.
The **believing** child. Henderson, Z.
The **Belknap** apparatus. Hay, J.
**Bell, J. J.**
  The message on the sundial
    Dickinson, S. ed. The drugged cornet,
      and other mystery stories
The **bell.** Van Duyn, M.
**Bella** Napoli. Steegmuller, F.
**Bellamy, Edward**
  To whom this may come
    Bowman, J. S. ed. A book of islands
**Belle** of the ball. Aiken, J.
La **belle** Zoraïde. Chopin, K.
**Belles** lettres, 2272. Corwin, N.
**Bellflower.** Maupassant, G. de
**Belloc, Hilaire**
  A conversation with a cat
    Montgomery, J. ed. The world's best
      cat stories
**Bellow, Saul**
  A father-to-be
    Foff, A. and Knapp, D. eds. Story
  The Gonzaga manuscripts
    Abrahams, W. ed. Fifty years of the
      American short story v 1
  Looking for Mr Green
    Hall, J. B. ed. The realm of fiction
    Thune, E. and Prigozy, R. eds. Short
      stories: a critical anthology
  Mosby's memoirs
    Elkin, S. ed. Stories from the sixties
  Smolak
    Charyn, J. ed. The single voice
**BELLS AND BELL RINGERS**
  Aytoun, W. E. The man in the bell

Belphagor. Machiavelli, N.
**Bemba, Sylvain**
  The dark room
    Larson, C. R. ed. African short stories
**Ben.** Davis, G.
**Ben** [another story]. Davis, G.
**Ben.** Lester, J.
**Ben-Amotz, Dan**
  Parents' Day
    Rabikovitz, D. ed. The new Israeli writers
**Ben Blower's story.** Hoffman, C.
**Ben Early is raving.** Kaplan, B.
**Ben Hodges' last trip.** Estes, W. M.
**Benchley, Nathaniel**
  Fathers' Day
    Zolotow, C. ed. An overpraised season
**BENDORF.** *See* Germany—Bendorf
**Benedetti, Mario**
  The Iriartes
    Cohen, J. M. ed. Latin American writing today
**Benedict, Andrew**
  Pool party
    Hitchcock, A. ed. Alfred Hitchcock presents: A month of mystery
**Benefit** of clergy. Russell, B.
The **benefits** of American life. Farrell, J. T.
**Beneš, Jan**
  Atheism
    Beneš, J. The blind mirror
  Boy with a rose
    Beneš, J. The blind mirror
  The class enemy
    Beneš, J. The blind mirror
  Coming-out party
    Beneš, J. The blind mirror
  Expertise
    Beneš, J. The blind mirror
  The last possibility
    Beneš, J. The blind mirror
  Mood indigo: extracurricular thoughts between seven and nine a.m.
    Beneš, J. The blind mirror
  The mother of the regiment
    Beneš, J. The blind mirror
  My greatest love
    Beneš, J. The blind mirror
  On the spot
    Beneš, J. The blind mirror
  A pancake memory
    Beneš, J. The blind mirror
  The problem
    Beneš, J. The blind mirror
  A rainy night
    Beneš, J. The blind mirror
  The request
    Beneš, J. The blind mirror
  Stabbed Ophelia
    Beneš, J. The blind mirror
  State witness
    Beneš, J. The blind mirror
  Strength of will
    Beneš, J. The blind mirror
  What do you know of the Kaplan turbine?
    Beneš, J. The blind mirror
**Benét, Stephen Vincent**
  All that money can buy
    Haining, P. ed. The ghouls

Same as: The Devil and Daniel Webster
  By the waters of Babylon
    Clareson, T. D. ed. A spectrum of worlds
    Fitz Gerald, G. ed. Modern satiric stories
  The Devil and Daniel Webster
    Abrahams, W. ed. Fifty years of the American short story v 1
    Same as: All that money can buy
  Freedom's a hard-bought thing
    Fenner, P. R. comp. Desperate moments
  Jacob and the Indians
    Lewis, J. D. ed. Tales of our people
  The King of the Cats
    Knight, D. ed. The golden road
    Necker, C. ed. Supernatural cats
    Parry, M. ed. Beware of the cat
  The treasure of Vasco Gomez
    Fenner, P. R. comp. Finders keepers
**Benford, Gregory**
  And the sea like mirrors
    Ellison, H. ed. Again, dangerous visions
**Benford, Gregory, and Eklund, Gordon**
  West wind, falling
    Universe 1
**Benjamen** burning. Winslow, J. M.
**Benji's** pencil. McAllister, B.
**Ben-Ner, Yitzhak**
  The tower
    Rabikovitz, D. ed. The new Israeli writers
**Bennett, A. W.**
  The pram
    Hitchcock, A. comp. Alfred Hitchcock's Supernatural tales of terror and suspense
**Bennett, Arnold**
  A bracelet at Bruges
    Bennett, A. The loot of cities
    Greene, H. ed. Cosmopolitan crimes
  A comedy on the gold coast
    Bennett, A. The loot of cities
  The fire of London
    Bennett, A. The loot of cities
  In the capital of the Sahara
    Bennett, A. The loot of cities
  "Lo! 'Twas a gala night!"
    Bennett, A. The loot of cities
  The Sisters Qita
    Hall, J. B. ed. The realm of fiction
  A solution of the Algiers mystery
    Bennett, A. The loot of cities
**Bennett, D. B.**
  The Christmas spirit
    Hitchcock, A. comp. Alfred Hitchcock's Supernatural tales of terror and suspense
**Bennett, Hal**
  Dotson Gerber resurrected
    The Best American short stories, 1971
**Bennett, Lerone**
  The convert
    King, W. ed. Black short story anthology
**Benny.** Maloney, R.

**Benson, A. C.**
The closed window
  Lamb, H. ed.    A tide of terror
**Benson, E. F.**
'And no bird sings'
  Haining, P. ed. Vampires at midnight
The bus conductor
  Dickinson, S. ed. The usurping ghost,
  and other encounters and experiences
Expiation
  Tomlinson, D. ed. Walk in dread
Gavon's eve
  Haining, P. ed. The necromancers
The sanctuary
  Haining, P. ed. The Satanists
The step
  Lamb, H. ed.    A tide of terror
**Benson, Margaret**
The soul of a cat
  Montgomery, J. ed. The world's best
  cat stories
**Benson, R. H.**
Father Brent's tale
  Lamb, H. ed.    A tide of terror
**Benson Watts is dead and in Virginia.**
  Betts, D.
**Bentley, E. C.**
Greedy night
  Hitchcock, A. ed. Alfred Hitchcock pre-
  sents: A month of mystery
  Sayers, D. L. Lord Peter
**Bentley, Phyllis**
A midsummer night's crime
  Manley, S. and Lewis, G. eds. Grande
  dames of detection
The secret
  Ellergy Queen's Mystery Magazine.
  Ellery Queen's Murder menu
**BEQUESTS.** *See* Inheritance and succes-
  sion; Wills
**Beresford, Elisabeth**
Portrait of Henry
  Dickinson, S. ed. The drugged cornet,
  and other mystery stories
**Berg, Alan M.**
The defeat of the Nez Percé
  Voices of Brooklyn
**Bergé, Carol**
An American romance
  Bergé, C.    A couple called Moebius
And now, Alexandra . . .
  Bergé, C.    A couple called Moebius
Blue jump
  Bergé, C.    A couple called Moebius
The challenge
  Bergé, C.    A couple called Moebius
Events of a March night
  Bergé, C.    A couple called Moebius
The Farm Woman
  Bergé, C.    A couple called Moebius
Huan
  Bergé, C.    A couple called Moebius
In motion
  Bergé, C.    A couple called Moebius
The kitchen
  Bergé, C.    A couple called Moebius
Kou
  Bergé, C.    A couple called Moebius

The water ceremony
  Bergé, C.    A couple called Moebius
**Bergelson, David**
At the depot
  Wisse, R. R. ed.    A shtetl, and other
  Yiddish novellas
**Bergengruen, Werner**
Ordeal by fire
  Steinhauer, H. ed. Ten German novellas
**Bergerac, Cyrano de.** *See* Cyrano de
  Bergerac
**Berkeley, Elizabeth.** *See* Lovecraft, H. P.
  jt. auth.
**BERKELEY.** *See* California—Berkeley
**Berkman, Sylvia**
The saffron boat
Women
**Berkson, Terry**
Thirty-day leave
  Voices of Brooklyn
**BERLIN.** *See* Germany—Berlin
**BERLIOZ, HECTOR**
Ayrton, M. An episode in the life of a
  gambler
**Bermudez, Maria Elvira**
The puzzle of the broken watch
  Yates, D. A. ed. Latin blood
**Bernard, Kenneth**
The queen of moths
  American Review 16
Sister Francetta and the pig baby
  American Review 16
**Berne, Stanley**
All that the eye can see
  Berne, S. The unconscious victorious,
  and other stories
The allotted period of time
  Berne, S. The unconscious victorious,
  and other stories
The bandelier cave dwellers
  Berne, S. The unconscious victorious,
  and other stories
Brown earth as medium
  Berne, S. The unconscious victorious,
  and other stories
A connection of the legs
  Berne, S. The unconscious victorious,
  and other stories
The divided self
  Berne, S. The unconscious victorious,
  and other stories
Heaven above, hell below
  Berne, S. The unconscious victorious,
  and other stories
The Indian signs of hope
  Berne, S. The unconscious victorious,
  and other stories
The invention of God and heaven
  Berne, S. The unconscious victorious,
  and other stories
Now alone
  Berne, S. The unconscious victorious,
  and other stories
A recognizable message
  Berne, S. The unconscious victorious,
  and other stories
To leave the city to its own devices
  Berne, S. The unconscious victorious,
  and other stories

Berne, Stanley—*Continued*
  The unconscious victorious
    Berne, S. The unconscious victorious,
      and other stories
  The units that make up this moment
    Berne, S. The unconscious victorious,
      and other stories
Bernie the Faust. Tenn, W.
Bernott, Joan
  The test-tube creature, afterward
    Ellison, H. ed. Again, dangerous visions
Bernstein, Stephanie Eve
  Of women and other items
    Intro 4
Berriault, Gina
  The stone boy
    Simon, J. ed. Fourteen for now
Berry, Don
  Across Neahkahnie
    Lucia, E. ed. This land around us
Berryman, John
  The lovers
    Moss, H. ed. The poet's story
Beryl, the Croucher and the rest of England.
    Burke, T.
Beside the railroad track. Nalkowska, Z.
Best friend. Lightner, A. M.
The best man. Maloney, R.
The best of everything. Yates, R.
The best years of our lives. Stuart, J.
Bester, Alfred
  Adam and no Eve
    Silverberg, R. ed. Beyond control
  The animal fair
    The Best from Fantasy & Science Fic-
      tion; 20th ser.
  Disappearing act
    Silverberg, R. ed. Other dimensions
  5,271,009
    Ferman, E. L. and Mills, R. P. eds.
      Twenty years of the Magazine of
      Fantasy and Science Fiction
  The Flowered Thundermug
    Nolan, W. F. ed. The human equation
  Fondly Fahrenheit
    Science fiction hall of fame v 1
    Total Effect. Survival printout
  Hobson's choice
    Knight, D. ed.   Tomorrow and to-
      morrow
  The push of a finger
    The Astounding-Analog reader v 1
  Something up there likes me
    Astounding
  Will you wait?
    Knight, D. ed. The golden road
Bestiary. Cortazar, J.
A bet on marriage. Schwimmer, W.
BETHLEHEM
  Meek, F. M. The Bethlehem Inn
The Bethlehem Inn. Meek, F. M.
The betrayal. Fremlin, C.
The betrayed kingdom. Brautigan, R.
The betrayers. Boyle, P.
The betrothal of Yindi. Chang, E.
BETROTHALS
  Allingham, M. Publicity
  Babel, I.   A father
  Beckett, S. Walking out

  Bellow, S.   A father-to-be
  Boles, R. The engagement party
  Colette. Secrets
  Fremlin, C. The new house
  Goulart, R. Shandy
  Henry, O. The Count and the wedding
    guest
  James, H. The story of a masterpiece
  Kelley, W. M. Saint Paul and the monkeys
  Klein, N. Magic
  Leskov, N. On the harm that exists for
    many of reading worldly books
  MacMahon, B. Wedding eve
  Marshall, L. Almost caught
  O'Hara, J. The frozen face
  Rama Rau, S. Who cares?
  Schwartz, J.   A trip to Brooklyn
  Scott, D. C. The winning of Marie-Louise
  Sharp, M. The Lost Chapel picnic
  Thomason, J. W. The Sergeant runs away
  Trevisan, D. The fiancé
  Woiwode, L. The suitor
  Yates, R. The best of everything
  Zakin, L. P. The contract
  Zhurakhovich, S. Stubborn Nadya
    *See also* Courtship; Marriage
Bets. *See* Wagers
The better choice. Wright, S. F.
The better ending. Marshall, L.
The better man. Russell, R.
A better mousehole. Pangborn, E.
BETTING. *See* Gambling; Wagers
A betting man. Glanville, B.
BETTING ON NUMBERS. *See* Gambling
Betts, Doris
  Beasts of the southern wild
    Betts, D. Beasts of the southern wild,
      and other stories
  Benson Watts is dead and in Virginia
    Betts, D. Beasts of the southern wild,
      and other stories
  Burning the bed
    Betts, D. Beasts of the southern wild,
      and other stories
  The glory of his nostrils
    Betts, D. Beasts of the southern wild,
      and other stories
  Hitchhiker
    Betts, D. Beasts of the southern wild,
      and other stories
  The mother-in-law
    Betts, D. Beasts of the southern wild,
      and other stories
  The spider gardens of Madagascar
    Betts, D. Beasts of the southern wild,
      and other stories
  Still life with fruit
    The Best little magazine fiction, 1971
    Betts, D. Beasts of the southern wild,
      and other stories
  The sword
    Matthews, J. ed. Archetypal themes in
      the modern story
  The ugliest pilgrim
    Betts, D. Beasts of the southern wild,
      and other stories
Between fire & water. Ostaijen, P. van
Between the porch and the altar. Stafford, J.
Between trains in X. Böll, H.

Beware the cat. Baldwin, G.
Bewitched. Uyeda, A.
Bewitched. Wharton, E.
Beyond the bayou. Chopin, K.
Beyond the game. Aandahl, V.
Beyond the gates. Grekova, I.
Beyond the glass mountain. Stegner, W.
Beyond the pale. Kipling, R.
Beyond the threshold. Derleth, A.
Beyond the wall. Bierce, A.
'Beyondaril.' Metcalfe, J.
Bezhin Meadow. Turgenev, I.
**Bhatty, Margaret**
 The Resin-man
  Winter's tales 17
**BIAFRA.** *See* Nigeria
**BIBLE. OLD TESTAMENT**
 Lagerkvist, P. Paradise
**BIBLE. OLD TESTAMENT. GENESIS**
  Parodies, travesties, etc.
Bond, N. The cunning of the beast
**BIBLE STORIES.** *See* Bible; Biblical stories
**BIBLICAL STORIES**
 Chekhov, A. The student
  *See also* Adam (First man)
**BIBLIOMANIA.** *See* Book collecting
**BIBLIOPHILY.** *See* Book collecting
The bibulous business of a matter of taste.
 Sayers, D. L.
**Bichsel, Peter**
 The animal lover
  Bichsel, P. And really Frau Blum
  would very much like to meet the
  milkman
 The aunt
  Bichsel, P. And really Frau Blum
  would very much like to meet the
  milkman
 The daughter
  Bichsel, P. And really Frau Blum
  would very much like to meet the
  milkman
 The earth is round
  Bichsel, P. There is no such place as
  America
 Floors
  Bichsel, P. And really Frau Blum
  would very much like to meet the
  milkman
 Flowers
  Bichsel, P. And really Frau Blum
  would very much like to meet the
  milkman
 From the sea
  Bichsel, P. And really Frau Blum
  would very much like to meet the
  milkman
 The game of cards
  Bichsel, P. And really Frau Blum
  would very much like to meet the
  milkman
 Herr Gigon
  Bichsel, P. And really Frau Blum
  would very much like to meet the
  milkman
 His evening
  Bichsel, P. And really Frau Blum
  would very much like to meet the
  milkman

The inventor
 Bichsel, P. There is no such place as
 America
Jodok sends his love
 Bichsel, P. There is no such place as
 America
The knife
 Bichsel, P. And really Frau Blum
 would very much like to meet the
 milkman
The lions
 Bichsel, P. And really Frau Blum
 would very much like to meet the
 milkman
The man who didn't want to know any
 more
 Bichsel, P. There is no such place as
 America
The man with the memory
 Bichsel, P. There is no such place as
 America
The men
 Bichsel, P. And really Frau Blum
 would very much like to meet the
 milkman
The milkman
 Bichsel, P. And really Frau Blum
 would very much like to meet the
 milkman
Musical boxes
 Bichsel, P. And really Frau Blum
 would very much like to meet the
 milkman
Novel
 Bichsel, P. And really Frau Blum
 would very much like to meet the
 milkman
Peonies
 Bichsel, P. And really Frau Blum
 would very much like to meet the
 milkman
San Salvador
 Bichsel, P. And really Frau Blum
 would very much like to meet the
 milkman
A table is a table
 Bichsel, P. There is no such place as
 America
There is no such place as America
 Bichsel, P. There is no such place as
 America
Wood shavings
 Bichsel, P. And really Frau Blum
 would very much like to meet the
 milkman
**BICYCLE RACING**
 Aymé, M. The last
The bicycle rider. Keefe, F. L.
**BICYCLES AND BICYCLING**
 Morrison, A. The affair of the 'Avalanche
  Bicycle and Tyre Co., Limited'
 Saroyan, W. The rescue of the perishing
**BICYCLING.** *See* Bicycle racing; Bicycles
 and bicycling
**Bierce, Ambrose**
 An adventure at Brownville
  Bierce, A. The complete short stories of
  Ambrose Bierce

Bierce, Ambrose—*Continued*

Killed at Resaca
  Bierce, A. The complete short stories of Ambrose Bierce

A lady from Redhorse
  Bierce, A. The complete short stories of Ambrose Bierce

The little story
  Bierce, A. The complete short stories of Ambrose Bierce

The major's tale
  Bierce, A. The complete short stories of Ambrose Bierce

The man and the snake
  Bierce, A. The complete short stories of Ambrose Bierce

The man out of the nose
  Bierce, A. The complete short stories of Ambrose Bierce

The man overboard
  Bierce, A. The complete short stories of Ambrose Bierce

A man with two lives
  Bierce, A. The complete short stories of Ambrose Bierce

The middle toe of the right foot
  Bierce, A. The complete short stories of Ambrose Bierce
  Haining, P. ed. Nightfrights

Mr Masthead, journalist
  Bierce, A. The complete short stories of Ambrose Bierce

Mr Swiddler's flip-flap
  Bierce, A. The complete short stories of Ambrose Bierce

The mocking-bird
  Bierce, A. The complete short stories of Ambrose Bierce

The moonlit road
  Bierce, A. The complete short stories of Ambrose Bierce

Moxon's master
  Bierce, A. The complete short stories of Ambrose Bierce
  Elwood, R. and Ghidalia, V. eds. Androids, time machines and blue giraffes

My favorite murder
  Bierce, A. The complete short stories of Ambrose Bierce

The night-doings at "Deadman's"
  Bierce, A. The complete short stories of Ambrose Bierce

An occurrence at Owl Creek Bridge
  Bierce, A. The complete short stories of Ambrose Bierce
  Howes, B. and Smith, G. J. eds. The sea-green horse
  Knight, D. ed. Perchance to dream
  Stansbury, D. L. ed. Impact
  Tytell, J. and Jaffe, H. eds. Affinities
  Same as: Incident at Owl Creek

Oil of dog
  Bierce, A. The complete short stories of Ambrose Bierce

One kind of officer
  Bierce, A. The complete short stories of Ambrose Bierce
  Hale, J. B. ed. The realm of fiction

One of the missing
  Bierce, A. The complete short stories of Ambrose Bierce

One of twins
  Bierce, A. The complete short stories of Ambrose Bierce

One officer, one man
  Bierce, A. The complete short stories of Ambrose Bierce

The other lodgers
  Bierce, A. The complete short stories of Ambrose Bierce

Parker Adderson, philosopher
  Bierce, A. The complete short stories of Ambrose Bierce

Present at a hanging
  Bierce, A. The complete short stories of Ambrose Bierce

A providential intimation
  Bierce, A. The complete short stories of Ambrose Bierce

A psychological shipwreck
  Bierce, A. The complete short stories of Ambrose Bierce

The race at Left Bower
  Bierce, A. The complete short stories of Ambrose Bierce

The realm of the unreal
  Bierce, A. The complete short stories of Ambrose Bierce

A resumed identity
  Bierce, A. The complete short stories of Ambrose Bierce

A revolt of the gods
  Bierce, A. The complete short stories of Ambrose Bierce

The secret of Macarger's Gulch
  Bierce, A. The complete short stories of Ambrose Bierce

A shipwreckollection
  Bierce, A. The complete short stories of Ambrose Bierce

A son of the Gods
  Bierce, A. The complete short stories of Ambrose Bierce

The Spook House
  Bierce, A. The complete short stories of Ambrose Bierce

Staley Fleming's hallucination
  Bierce, A. The complete short stories of Ambrose Bierce

The story of a conscience
  Bierce, A. The complete short stories of Ambrose Bierce

The stranger
  Bierce, A. The complete short stories of Ambrose Bierce

The suitable surroundings
  Bierce, A. The complete short stories of Ambrose Bierce

The thing at Nolan
  Bierce, A. The complete short stories of Ambrose Bierce

Three and one are one
  Bierce, A. The complete short stories of Ambrose Bierce

A tough tussle
  Bierce, A. The complete short stories of Ambrose Bierce

**Bierce, Ambrose**—*Continued*

Two military executions
  Bierce, A. The complete short stories of
    Ambrose Bierce
An unfinished race
  Bierce, A. The complete short stories of
    Ambrose Bierce
A vine on a house
  Bierce, A. The complete short stories of
    Ambrose Bierce
A watcher by the dead
  Bierce, A. The complete short stories of
    Ambrose Bierce
Why I am not editing "The Stinger"
  Bierce, A. The complete short stories of
    Ambrose Bierce
The widower Turmore
  Bierce, A. The complete short stories of
    Ambrose Bierce
A wireless message
  Bierce, A. The complete short stories of
    Ambrose Bierce

**Big** Ada. Hayes, A. H.
**Big** Black good man. Wright, R.
**Big** blonde. Parker, D.
The **big** bounce. Tevis, W. S.
**Big** Boy leaves home. Wright, R.
**Big** brother. Joshi, S.
The **big** brown trout. Traver, R.
The **big** connection. Scott, R.
The **big** day. Bingham, S.
The **big** flash. Spinrad, N.
The **big** front yard. Simak, C. D.
**Big** game hunt. Clarke, A. C.
The **big** gleaming coach. O'Hara, J.
The **big** it. Guthrie, A. B.
The **big** light. Blum-Alquit, E.
**Big** old gold old thing. Weaver, G.
**Big** pebble, little pebble. Peak, E. F.
The **big** pencil. Bondarenko, W. C.
The **big** pot game. Bukowski, C.
**Big** Red's buffleheads. Brister, B.
**Big** Sam. Davidson, A.
**Big** Sam was my friend. Ellison, H.
The **big** space fuck. Vonnegut, K.
The **big** story. Dawson, F.
The **big** stretch. Matthews, C.
**Big** two-hearted river. Hemingway, E.
**Big** two-hearted river: part II. Heming-
    way, E.

**BIGAMY**

Bandello, M. Spanish revenge
Collins, W.  A marriage tragedy
Gissing, G. Lou and Liz
Hayes, A. H. Mail-order bride
Scott, Sir W. The tale of the mysterious
    mirror
Trevisan, D. João Nicolau
The **biggest** game. Brunner, J.
The **biggest** snowball in the world will melt
    if the sun is hot enough. McNair, K.
The **biggest** thing since Custer. Eastlake, W.

**Biggle, Lloyd**
The Botticelli horror
  Biggle, L. The metallic muse
In his own image
  The Best from Fantasy and Science Fic-
    tion; 18th ser.
  Biggle, L. The metallic muse

Leading man
  Biggle, L. The metallic muse
Orphan of the void
  Biggle, L. The metallic muse
Spare the rod
  Biggle, L. The metallic muse
The tunesmith
  Biggle, L. The metallic muse
Well of the deep wish
  Biggle, L. The metallic muse

**BIGOTRY.** *See* Prejudices and antipathies
**Bilker, Audrey L.** *See* Bilker, H. L. jt. auth.
**Bilker, Harvey L.**
Genetic faux pas
  Scortia, T. N. ed. Strange bedfellows
**Bilker, Harvey L. and Bilker, Audrey L.**
All you can eat
  Elwood, R. ed. Children of infinity
Apartment hunting
  Elwood, R. ed. Future city
The **bill.** Malamud, B.
The **bill** collector. Logan, L.
**BILL COLLECTORS.** *See* Debtor and cred-
    itor
**Billbrook.** Borchert, W.
**Billenium.** Ballard, J. G.

**BILLIARDS**
Carpenter, D. The crossroader
Hunter, K. The pool table caper
Soto, P. J. Champs

**BILLS.** *See* Debts
**Billy** the Snide. Rook, C.
**Billy's** Oak. Lumley, B.
**Binaries.** Sallis, J.
**Binder, Eando**
Son of the stars
  Elwood, R. and Ghidalia, V. eds. An-
    droids, time machines and blue gi-
    raffes
The **binge.** Dorr, L.
**Bingham, Sallie**
August ninth at natural bridge
  Bingham, S. The way it is now
The big day
  Bingham, S. The way it is now
Conversations
  Bingham, S. The way it is now
The facts of his life
  Bingham, S. The way it is now
Fear
  Bingham, S. The way it is now
The frog prince
  Bingham, S. The way it is now
Mourning
  Bingham, S. The way it is now
The need
  Bingham, S. The way it is now
A new life
  Bingham, S. The way it is now
The old woman
  Bingham, S. The way it is now
Please no eating no drinking
  Bingham, S. The way it is now
Rachel's island
  Bingham, S. The way it is now
The visit
  Bingham, S. The way it is now
The way it is now
  Bingham, S. The way it is now

**Bloch, Robert**—*Continued*
Forever and amen
  Elwood, R. ed. And walk now gently through the fire, and other science fiction stories
The funny farm
  Derleth, A. ed. Dark things
Girl from Mars
  Haining, P. ed. The freak show
A good imagination
  McComas, J. F. ed. Crimes and misfortunes
The head hunter
  Haining, P. ed. The nightmare reader
The living dead
  Haining, P. ed. Vampires at midnight
Notebook found in a deserted house
  Derleth, A. ed. Tales of Cthulhu Mythos
The play's the thing
  Best detective stories of the year, 1972
The plot is the thing
  Haining, P. ed. The Hollywood nightmare
The real bad friend
  Mystery Writers of America. Merchants of menace
The shadow from the steeple
  Derleth, A. ed. Tales of Cthulhu Mythos
The shambler from the stars
  Derleth, A. ed. Tales of Cthulhu Mythos
The skull
  Haining, P. ed. The ghouls
Space-born
  Elwood, R. ed. Children of infinity
Spawn of the dark one
  Haining, P. ed. The Satanists
That Hell-bound train
  Ferman, E. L. and Mills, R. P. eds. Twenty years of The Magazine of Fantasy and Science Fiction
  Same as: The Hell-bound train, listed in the 1959-1963 supplement
A toy for Juliette
  Ellison, H. Partners in wonder
Untouchable
  Mystery Writers of America. Mirror, mirror, fatal mirror
  *For another story by this author see* Fiske, Tarleton

**Blochman, Lawrence G.**
Red wine
  Hitchcock, A. ed. Alfred Hitchcock presents: Stories to stay awake by

**Block, Anita Rowe**
Sunday morning
  Ribalow, H. U. ed. My name aloud

**Block, Lawrence**
Death wish
  Hitchcock, A. ed. Alfred Hitchcock presents: A month of mystery
**Block.** De Vries, P.
The **blond** bat. Holst, S.
**BLOOD**
  Hearn, L. Haceldama
  Henderson, Z. The effectives
**Blood.** Singer, I. B.
**Blood**-burning moon. Toomer, J.
**Blood** harvest. Marsh, W.

**Blood** letting. Gerald, J. B.
**Blood** of tyrants. Bova, B.
**BLOOD TRANSFUSION**
  Francis, H. E. The transfusion man
**Bloodflowers.** Valgardson, W. D.
**Blood's** a rover. Oliver, C.
**Bloodstar.** Dawson, F.
**Blount, Margaret**
The right books
  Winter's tales 19
"**Blow** up with the brig!" Collins, W.
**Blue.** Aprilov, B.
A **blue** blonde in the sky over Pennsylvania. Lynds, D.
**Blue** boy. Bontemps, A.
**Blue** Eyes. Carpenter, D.
The **blue** film. Greene, G.
The **blue** giraffe. De Camp, L. S.
The **blue** halo. Bullock, M.
The **blue** hotel. Crane, S.
**BLUE JAY**
  Twain, M. Jim Baker's blue jay yarn
**Blue** jump. Bergé, C.
**Blue** lawns. Brodeur, P.
The **blue** mouse. Wolfe, G.
The **blue** of madness. Kemp, A.
The **blue** rug. Yamamoto, M.
The **blue** tambourine. Olson, D.
**Blues** ain't no mockin bird. Bambara, T. C.
**Blueskin** the pirate. Pyle, H.
**Blum, Ralph**
In the blue country
  New American Review no. 9
**Blum-Alquit, Eliezer**
Amerika, Amerika
  Blum-Alquit, E. Revolt of the apprentices, and other stories
Ata Bakhartaunu: thou hast chosen us
  Blum-Alquit, E. Revolt of the apprentices, and other stories
Attorney Street
  Blum-Alquit, E. Revolt of the apprentices, and other stories
The baker's daughter
  Blum-Alquit, E. Revolt of the apprentices, and other stories
The big light
  Blum-Alquit, E. Revolt of the apprentices, and other stories
The comet and the egg
  Blum-Alquit, E. Revolt of the apprentices, and other stories
Each spring
  Blum-Alquit, E. Revolt of the apprentices, and other stories
Gogol's ring
  Blum-Alquit, E. Revolt of the apprentices, and other stories
A highwayman in the woods of Chelm
  Blum-Alquit, E. Revolt of the apprentices, and other stories
In the light of Morris Rosenfeld
  Blum-Alquit, E. Revolt of the apprentices, and other stories
In the tall windows
  Blum-Alquit, E. Revolt of the apprentices, and other stories
One of the fiddlers two
  Blum-Alquit, E. Revolt of the apprentices, and other stories

**BOHEMIAN LIFE.** *See* Artist life; Bohemianism

**BOHEMIANISM**
  Brodeur, P. The spoiler
  Gold, H. Song of the first and last beatnik
  Gold, H. Waiting for the Forty-one Union
  Gold, H. Young man, old days
  Wilson, A.   A bit off the map
    *See also* Hippies

**BOHEMIANS IN ENGLAND**
  Gilliatt, P. The last to go

**BOHEMIANS IN THE UNITED STATES**
  Cather, W. The Bohemian girl
  Cather, W. Peter
The **bold** Dragoon. Irving, W.

**Boles, Paul Darcy**
  The animal kingdom
    Boles, P. D.   I thought you were a unicorn, and other stories
  Brother whistler
    Rosmond, B. comp. Today's stories from Seventeen
  The girl at the Plaza
    Boles, P. D.   I thought you were a unicorn, and other stories
  The holiday rider
    Boles, P. D.   I thought you were a unicorn, and other stories
  I thought you were a unicorn
    Boles, P. D.   I thought you were a unicorn, and other stories
  Lucas and Jake
    Boles, P. D.   I thought you were a unicorn, and other stories
  Miss Rose
    Boles, P. D.   I thought you were a unicorn, and other stories
  The somewhere music
    Boles, P. D.   I thought you were a unicorn, and other stories
  Summer candles
    Boles, P. D.   I thought you were a unicorn, and other stories
  The telephone artist
    Boles, P. D.   I thought you were a unicorn, and other stories
  Today is my sister's wedding
    Boles, P. D.   I thought you were a unicorn, and other stories
  A verray parfit gentil knight
    Boles, P. D.   I thought you were a unicorn, and other stories

**Boles, Robert**
  The engagement party
    Gulassa, C. M. ed. The fact of fiction

**Bolitho, Hector**
  The albatross
    Manley, S. and Lewis, G. eds. Shapes of the supernatural

**BOLÍVAR, SIMÓN**
  Borges, J. L. Guayaquil

**BOLIVIA**
           **20th century**
  Ocampo, R. The Indian Paulino
**Böll, Heinrich**
  Absent without leave
    Charyn, J. ed. The troubled vision

Across the bridge
  Böll, H. Children are civilians too
At the bridge
  Böll, H. Children are civilians too
Between trains in X
  Böll, H. Children are civilians too
Black sheep
  Böll, H. Children are civilians too
Breaking the news
  Böll, H. Children are civilians too
Broommakers
  Böll, H. Children are civilians too
Business is business
  Böll, H. Children are civilians too
Candles for the Madonna
  Böll, H. Children are civilians too
Children are civilians too
  Böll, H. Children are civilians too
Christmas every day
  Thune, E. and Prigozy, R. eds. Short stories: a critical anthology
Dear old Renée
  Böll, H. Children are civilians too
Drinking in Petöcki
  Böll, H. Children are civilians too
In the darkness
  Böll, H. Children are civilians too
Like a bad dream
  Hall, J. B. ed. The realm of fiction
Lohengrin's death
  Böll, H. Children are civilians too
The man with the knives
  Böll, H. Children are civilians too
Murke's collected silences
  Simon, J. ed. Fourteen for now
My expensive leg
  Böll, H. Children are civilians too
My pal with the long hair
  Böll, H. Children are civilians too
My sad face
  Böll, H. Children are civilians too
On the hook
  Böll, H. Children are civilians too
Pale Anna
  Johnson, E. W. ed. Short stories international
Parting
  Böll, H. Children are civilians too
The ration runners
  Böll, H. Children are civilians too
Reunion on the avenue
  Böll, H. Children are civilians too
Reunion with Drüng
  Böll, H. Children are civilians too
Rise, my love, rise
  Böll, H. Children are civilians too
The seventh trunk
  Stevick, P. ed. Anti-story
"Stranger, bear word to the Spartans we . . ."
  Böll, H. Children are civilians too
That time we were in Odessa
  Böll, H. Children are civilians too
What a racket
  Böll, H. Children are civilians too
A **boll** of roses. Dumas, H.

**BOLSHEVIKS.** *See* Communism—Russia
**BOLSHEVISM.** *See* Communism—Russia
The **bolt** behind the blue. Parker, D.

The **bomb**. Keen, M. L.
**Bomb** box. McGahern, J.
**BOMB SHELTERS.** *See* Air raid shelters
**Bombal, María-Luisa**
  The tree
    Howes, B. ed. The eye of the heart
**BOMBAY.** *See* India—Bombay
**BOMBS**
  Dempsey, H. The defensive bomber
  Keen, M. L. The bomb
  Marlowe, S. Drum beat
  Rathjen, C. H. Touch and blow!
  Ritchie, J. Ten minutes from now
**Bon** bons. Nemerov, H.
**Bonanza** 1972 in Toronto. Clarke, A.
**Bond, Nelson S.**
  The cunning of the beast
    Mohs, M. ed. Other worlds, other gods
  The priestess who rebelled
    Moskowitz, S. ed. When women rule
**Bond, Stephen**
  Chinatown evening
    Mystery Writers of America. Mirror, mirror, fatal mirror
**Bondarenko, W. C.**
  The big pencil
    New Directions in prose and poetry 19
  Knots untied
    New Directions in prose and poetry 19
**Bone** bubbles. Barthelme, D.
**BONES.** *See* Fractures
The **bones** of Charlemagne. Pei, M.
The **bones** of Louella Brown. Petry, A.
**Bonetti, Edward**
  Fever
    New American Review no. 13
The **bonfire**. O'Hara, J.
**BONFIRES.** *See* Fires
**Bonner, Paul Hyde**
  John Monahan
    Corodimas, P. ed. In trout country
**BONNETS.** *See* Hats
**Bontemps, Arna**
  Black thunder; excerpt
    Long, R. A. and Collier, E. W. eds. Afro-American writing v2
  Blue boy
    Bontemps, A. The Old South
  The cure
    Bontemps, A. The Old South
  The devil is a conjurer
    Bontemps, A. The Old South
  Heathen at home
    Bontemps, A. The Old South
  Hoppergrass man
    Bontemps, A. The Old South
  Let the church roll on
    Bontemps, A. The Old South
  Lonesome boy, silver trumpet
    Bontemps, A. The Old South
  Mr Kelso's lion
    Bontemps, A. The Old South
  Saturday night
    Bontemps, A. The Old South
  A summer tragedy
    Bontemps, A. The Old South
    James, C. L. ed. From the roots
  Talk to the music
    Bontemps, A. The Old South

3 pennies for luck
    Bontemps, A. The Old South
A woman with a mission
    Bontemps, A. The Old South
**Bontly, Thomas**
  Eight meetings
    Lish, G. ed. The secret life of our times: new fiction from Esquire
**Bontscha** the Silent. *See* Peretz, Y. L. Silent Bontsche
**Bontzye Shweig.** *See* Peretz, Y. L. Silent Bontsche
The **book**. Irwin, M.
The **book**. Margroff, R. E. and Offutt, A. J.
**BOOK COLLECTING**
  Auchincloss, L. The collector
**BOOK DEALERS.** *See* Booksellers and bookselling
The **book** of experience. Yashpal
The **book** of the machine. Butler, S.
The **book** of Thoth. Green, R. L.
**BOOK RARITIES**
  Ayrton, M. An imperfect copy of Antichrist
  Brennan, J. P. The mystery of Myrrh Lane
  Summers, M. The grimoire
**BOOK SALESMEN.** *See* Booksellers and bookselling
**BOOK SHOPS.** *See* Booksellers and bookselling
**Booked** solid. Russell, R.
**BOOKKEEPERS.** *See* Accountants
The **bookkeeper's** wife. Cather, W.
**BOOKMAKERS.** *See* Gambling
**BOOKS**
  Beresford, E. Portrait of Henry
  Padgett, L. Compliments of the author
  Sallis, J. Residue
  Wodehouse, P. G. Strychnine in the soup
    *See also* Manuscripts; Book rarities
    **Collectors and collecting**
  Russell, R. Quoth the raven
**BOOKS, RARE.** *See* Book rarities
**BOOKS AND READING**
  Bradbury, R. The mad wizards of Mars
  Campbell, J. R. Cold print
  Di Donato, P. I killed Maria Goretti
  Grahame, K. Its walls were as of jasper
  Leskov, N. On the harm that exists for many of reading worldly books
  Merwin, W. S. The inheritance
  Naylor, P. R. A change of plans
  Wolfe, G. The island of Doctor Death, and other stories
**BOOKSELLERS AND BOOKSELLING**
  Beresford, E. Portrait of Henry
  Brennan, J. P. Canavan's back yard
  Busch, F. While Susan Hayward weeps
  Campbell, J. R. Cold print
  Chekhov, A. The story of a commercial venture
  Cohen, F. C. The promise
  Francis, H. E. Where was my life before I died?
  Gor, G. The minotaur
  Harrison, M. At the heart of it
  Lagerkvist, P. God's little travelling salesman

**BOOKSELLERS AND BOOKSELLING—**
*Continued*
Rush, N. In late youth
Shaw, I. Small Saturday
Slesinger, T. Jobs in the sky
Warner, L. Sky in winter
**BOOKSHOPS.** *See* Booksellers and bookselling
**Boomerang.** Fleming, G.
**Boona** on Scancia. Henderson, Z.
**BOONE, DANIEL**
      **Parodies, travesties, etc.**
Stuart, J. Our Wiff and Daniel Boone
**Booth, P. H.**
The eyes of Mme Dupree
   Derleth, A. ed. Dark things
**Boothby, Guy**
The Duchess of Wiltshire's diamonds
   Greene, H. ed. The rivals of Sherlock Holmes
**BOOTLEGGING.** *See* Liquor traffic
The **boots.** Chekhov, A.
**BOOTS AND SHOES**
Andersen, H. C. The red shoes
Chekhov, A. The boots
Clarke, A. An Easter carol
Henry, O. Ships
Henry, O. Shoes
Kim, Y. I. The wedding shoes
Steegmuller, F. A ride with Ralph
**Bop** bop against that curtain. Bukowski, C.
**Borchert, Wolfgang**
Along the long long road
   Borchert, W. The man outside
Billbrook
   Borchert, W. The man outside
The bread
   Borchert, W. The man outside
The coffee is indefinable
   Borchert, W. The man outside
Conversation over the roofs
   Borchert, W. The man outside
The crows fly home at night
   Borchert, W. The man outside
The dandelion
   Borchert, W. The man outside
Do stay, Giraffe
   Borchert, W. The man outside
Done with, done with
   Borchert, W. The man outside
From the other side to the other side
   Borchert, W. The man outside
He too had a lot of trouble with the wars
   Borchert, W. The man outside
In May, in May cried the cuckoo
   Borchert, W. The man outside
Jesus won't play any more
   Borchert, W. The man outside
The kangaroo
   Borchert, W. The man outside
The kitchen clock
   Borchert, W. The man outside
Lots and lots of snow
   Borchert, W. The man outside
My paleface brother
   Borchert, W. The man outside
The nightingale sings
   Borchert, W. The man outside

On that Tuesday
   Borchert, W. The man outside
Our little Mozart
   Borchert, W. The man outside
Radi
   Borchert, W. The man outside
Rats do sleep at night
   Borchert, W. The man outside
There are voices in the air—at night
   Borchert, W. The man outside
Thithyphuth
   Borchert, W. The man outside
The three dark magi
   Borchert, W. The man outside
   Same as: The three dark kings, listed in the 1964-1968 supplement
The **border**-line case. Allingham, M.
A **border**-line case. Du Maurier, D.
**Bordered** in black. Niven, L.
**BOREDOM**
Brunner, J. Planetfall
Šoljan, A. Rain
   *See also* Alienation (Social psychology)
**BORES (PERSONS)**
Moravia, A. Bores
**Bores.** Moravia, A.
**Borger, Robert**
The other place
   Kahn, J. ed. Hanging by a thread
**Borges, Jorge Luis**
The Aleph
   Borges, J. L. The Aleph, and other stories, 1933-1969
The approach to al-Mu'tasim
   Borges, J. L. The Aleph, and other stories, 1933-1969
The challenge
   Borges, J. L. The Aleph, and other stories, 1933-1969
The circular ruins
   Borges, J. L. The Aleph, and other stories, 1933-1969
   Harrison, H. ed. The light fantastic
   Knight, D. ed. Perchance to dream
The dead man
   Borges, J. L. The Aleph, and other stories, 1933-1969
   Carpentier, H. and Brof, J. eds. Doors and mirrors
Death and the compass
   Best detective stories of the year, 1971
   Borges, J. L. The Aleph, and other stories, 1933-1969
   Taylor, J. C. ed. The short story: fiction in transition
   Yates, D. A. ed. Latin blood
Deutsches requiem
   Thune, E. and Prigozy, R. eds. Short stories: a critical anthology
Doctor Brodie's report
   Borges, J. L. Doctor Brodie's report
The duel
   Borges, J. L. Doctor Brodie's report
The elder lady
   Borges, J. L. Doctor Brodie's report
The end
   Kahn, J. ed. Hanging by a thread

Borges, Jorge Luis—*Continued*
  The end of the duel
    Borges, J. L. Doctor Brodie's report
  The garden of forking paths
    Davis, R. G. ed. Ten modern masters
    Schulman, L. M. ed. The cracked looking glass
    Yates, D. A. ed. Latin blood
  The Gospel according to Mark
    Borges, J. L. Doctor Brodie's report
  Guayaquil
    Borges, J. L. Doctor Brodie's report
    New American Review no. 13
  The handwriting of god
    Cohen, J. M. ed. Latin American writing today
    Same as: The god's script, listed in the 1964-1968 supplement
  Ibn Hakkan al-Bokhari, dead in his labyrinth
    Borges, J. L. The Aleph, and other stories, 1933-1969
  The immortals
    Borges, J. L. The Aleph, and other stories, 1933-1969
  The intruder
    Borges, J. L. The Aleph, and other stories, 1933-1969
    Borges, J. L. Doctor Brodie's report
    Davis, R. G. ed. Ten modern masters
  Juan Muraña
    Borges, J. L. Doctor Brodie's report
  The Library of Babel
    Silverberg, R. ed. The mirror of infinity
  The life of Tadeo Isidoro Cruz (1829-1874)
    Borges, J. L. The Aleph, and other stories, 1933-1969
  The lottery in Babylon
    Carr, T. ed. Into the unknown
    Karl, F. R. and Hamalian, L. eds. The naked i
    Same as: The Babylon lottery, listed in the 1959-1963 supplement
  The maker
    Borges, J. L. The Aleph, and other stories, 1933-1969
  The man on the threshold
    Borges, J. L. The Aleph, and other stories, 1933-1969
  The meeting
    Borges, J. L. The Aleph, and other stories, 1933-1969
    Borges, J. L. Doctor Brodie's report
  The other death
    Borges, J. L. The Aleph, and other stories, 1933-1969
    Howes, B. ed. The eye of the heart
  Pedro Salvadores
    Borges, J. L. The Aleph, and other stories, 1933-1969
  Pierre Menard, author of Don Quixote
    Charyn, J. ed. The single voice
    Davis, R. G. ed. Ten modern masters
    Stevick, P. ed. Anti-story
  Rosendo's tale
    Borges, J. L. The Aleph, and other stories, 1933-1969
    Borges, J. L. Doctor Brodie's report
  The secret miracle
    Hall, J. B. ed. The realm of fiction
    Konigsberg, I. ed. The classic short story
  The shape of the sword
    Johnson, E. W. ed. Short stories international
    Same as: The form of the sword, listed in 1959-1963 supplement
  Streetcorner man
    Borges, J. L. The Aleph, and other stories, 1933-1969
  Tlön, Uqbar, Orbis Tertius
    Konigsberg, I. ed. The classic short story
  The two kings and the two labyrinths
    Bernkopf, J. F. comp. Boucher's choicest
  The unworthy friend
    Borges, J. L. Doctor Brodie's report
  The widow Ching, lady pirate
    Lish, G. ed. The secret life of our times: new fiction from Esquire

**Parodies, travesties, etc.**
Greenberg, A. "Franz Kafka" by Jorge Luis Borges
**Borges, Jorge Luis, and Bioy Casares, Adolfo.** *See* Domecq, H. Bustos
**Borgese, Elisabeth Mann**
  The mongol
    New Directions in prose and poetry 19
  To whom it may concern
    Fitz Gerald, G. ed. Modern satiric stories
**BORMANN, MARTIN**
  Boulle, P. His last battle
A **born** farmer. Jewett, S. O.
A **born** homemaker. Warner, L.
**Born** of man and woman. Matheson, R.
**Born** to exile. Eisenstein, P.
**Borowski, Tadeusz**
  This way for the gas, ladies and gentlemen
    Charyn, J. ed. The single voice
**BORSTAL.** *See* Reformatories—England
**Bosch, Juan**
  The beautiful soul of Don Damián
    Howes, B. ed. The eye of the heart
**Bosem, Hedda**
  The third hill
    Michener, J. A. ed. First fruits
**BOSNIA AND HERZEGOVINA.** *See* Yugoslavia—Bosnia and Herzegovina
**BOSTON.** *See* Massachusetts—Boston
The **bo'sun's** body. Hardwick, M. and Hardwick, M.
**BOSWELL, JAMES**
  De La Torre, L. The Monbodda ape boy
**BOTANISTS**
  Fast, H. UFO
  Lightner, A. M. A great day for the Irish
    *See also* Naturalists
**BOTANY.** *See* Flowers
The **Botleas.** Carr, J.
The **Botticelli** horror. Biggle, L.
A **bottle** full of kismet. Davidson, A.
The **Bottle**-Imp. Musäus, J. K. A.
The **bottle** imp. Stevenson, R. L.

Bottle party. Collier, J.

A bottomless grave. Bierce, A.

The bottomless well. Terry, W. S.

Boucher, Anthony

Balaam

Mohs, M. ed. Other worlds, other gods

The compleat werewolf

Boucher, A. The compleat werewolf, and other stories of fantasy and science fiction

Expedition

Boucher, A. The compleat werewolf, and other stories of fantasy and science fiction

Hipolito, J. and McNelly, W. E. eds. Mars, we love you

The ghost of me

Boucher, A. The compleat werewolf, and other stories of fantasy and science fiction

Mr Lupescu

Boucher, A. The compleat werewolf, and other stories of fantasy and science fiction

The pink caterpillar

Boucher, A. The compleat werewolf, and other stories of fantasy and science fiction

Q. U. R.

Boucher, A. The compleat werewolf, and other stories of fantasy and science fiction

The quest for Saint Aquin

Mohs, M. ed. Other worlds, other gods

Science fiction hall of fame v 1

Robinc

Boucher, A. The compleat werewolf, and other stories of fantasy and science fiction

A shape in time

Nolan, W. F. ed. The future is now

Snulbug

Boucher, A. The compleat werewolf, and other stories of fantasy and science fiction

They bite

Boucher, A. The compleat werewolf, and other stories of fantasy and science fiction

We print the truth

Boucher, A. The compleat werewolf, and other stories of fantasy and science fiction

Bought and sold. Moravia, A.

Boule de Suif. See Maupassant, G. de. Ball-of-fat

Boulle, Pierre

The duck blind

Boulle, P. Because it is absurd

The heart and the galaxy

Boulle, P. Because it is absurd

His last battle

Boulle, P. Because it is absurd

The holy places

Boulle, P. Because it is absurd

Interferences

Boulle, P. Because it is absurd

The plumber

Boulle, P. Because it is absurd

When the serpent failed

Boulle, P. Because it is absurd

Bound by a spell; excerpt. Greene, L.

Bound for Taos. Fergusson, H.

The bound man. Aichinger, I.

Boundless time. Kirilov, N.

Bounty. Sherred, T. L.

The bourgeois king. Darío, R.

BOURGEOISIE. See Middle classes

Bova, Ben

Blood of tyrants

Bova, B. Forward in time

Fifteen miles

Bova, B. Forward in time

Knight, D. ed. A pocketful of stars

The man who saw Gunga Din thirty times

Elwood, R. ed. Showcase

Men of good will

Bova, B. Forward in time

The next logical step

Bova, B. Forward in time

The perfect warrior

Bova, B. Forward in time

The sightseers

Elwood, R. ed. Future city

A slight miscalculation

Bova, B. Forward in time

Stars, won't you hide me?

Bova, B. Forward in time

Test in orbit

Bova, B. Forward in time

The weathermakers

Bova, B. Forward in time

Zero Gee

Bova, B. Forward in time

Ellison, H. ed. Again, dangerous visions

Bova, Ben, and Ellison, Harlan

Brillo

Ellison, H. Partners in wonder

The Bowditch footnote. Goldberg, G. J.

BOWDLER, THOMAS

Russell, B. Mr Bowdler's nightmare

Bowen, Elizabeth

Coming home

Insights

The demon lover

Minot, S. and Wilson, R. eds. Three stances of modern fiction

Hand in glove

Manley, S. and Lewis, G. eds. Ladies of horror

Her table spread

Hall, J. B. ed. The realm of fiction

Parodies, travesties, etc.

De Vries, P. Touch and go

Bowen, Marjorie

Cambric tea

Kahn, J. ed. Hanging by a thread

Manley, S. and Lewis, G. eds. Mistresses of mystery

The Crown Derby plate

Manley, S. and Lewis, G. eds. Shapes of the supernatural

Bower, B. M.

Finders is keepers

Collier, N. ed. Great stories of the West

**Bowering, George**
  Apples
    Fourteen stories high
  Time and again
    Metcalf, J. ed. Sixteen by twelve
A **bowl** bigger than earth. Farmer, P. J.
A **bowl** of Biskies makes a growing boy.
  Jones, R. F.
**Bowles, Jane**
  A stick of green candy
    Simon, J. ed. Fourteen for now
**Bowles, Paul**
  The echo
    Abrahams, W. ed. Fifty years of the
      American short story v 1
  The hyena
    McCrindle, J. F. ed. Stories from the
      Transatlantic Review
  Pages from Cold Point
    Kraus, R. and Wiegand, E. eds. Stu-
      dent's choice
  The scorpion
    Taylor, J. C. ed. The short story: fic-
      tion in transition
  The time of friendship
    Spinner, S. ed. Live and learn
**BOWLS**
  Jewett, S. O. The green bowl
The **box.** Blish, J.
**Box** 456. Spike, P.
**BOXERS.** *See* Boxing
**BOXING**
  Algren, N. Dark came early in that coun-
    try
  Bukowski, C. Goodbye Watson
  Bukowski, C. You and your beer and how
    great you are
  Carter, R. Return of the Kid
  Di Donato, P. Mass for unknown soldiers
  Glanville, B. The twins
  Graham, W. Jacka's fight
  Hemingway, E. The battler
  Hemingway, E. Fifty grand
  Kaplan, B. Eddie Angel
  Lewis, H. The famous Dempsey crouch
  Queen, E. Mind over matter
  Symons, J. Eight minutes to kill
**Boy** and girl. Oates, J. C.
A **boy** and his dog. Ellison, H.
A **boy** hunting birds. Trevisan, D.
The **boy** in the green hat. Klein, N.
**BOY SCOUTS**
  Kotzwinkle, W. The bird watcher
  Weidman, J. Good man, bad man
The **boy** stood on the burning deck. For-
  ester, C. S.
The **boy** who painted Christ Black. Clarke,
  J. H.
The **boy** who was born again. Ford, C.
A **boy** with a gun. Clarke, D.
**Boy** with a rose, Beneš, J.
The **boy** with the violin. Vezhinov, P.
**Boyle, Kay**
  Black boy
    Hall, J. B. ed. The realm of fiction
  The white horses of Vienna
    Abrahams, W. ed. Fifty years of the
      American short story v 1

Your body is a jewel box
    Spinner, S. ed. Feminine plural
**Boyle, Patrick**
  The agony of A. Boscas
    Matthews, J. ed. Archetypal themes in
      the modern story
  At night all cats are grey
    Boyle, P. At night all cats are grey, and
      other stories
  The betrayers
    Boyle, P. At night all cats are grey, and
      other stories
  Go away, old man, go away
    Boyle, P. At night all cats are grey, and
      other stories
  Home again, home again, jigetty-jig
    Hamilton, A. ed. Splinters
  The lake
    Boyle, P. At night all cats are grey, and
      other stories
  Meles vulgaris
    Boyle, P. At night all cats are grey, and
      other stories
  The metal man
    Boyle, P. At night all cats are grey, and
      other stories
  Myko
    Boyle, P. At night all cats are grey, and
      other stories
  Odorous perfume her harbinger
    Boyle, P. At night all cats are grey, and
      other stories
  Oh, death where is thy sting-aling-aling?
    Boyle, P. At night all cats are grey, and
      other stories
  The pishogue
    Boyle, P. At night all cats are grey, and
      other stories
  The port wine stain
    Boyle, P. At night all cats are grey, and
      other stories
  Square dance
    Boyle, P. At night all cats are grey, and
      other stories
  Suburban idyll
    Boyle, P. At night all cats are grey, and
      other stories
  The window
    Boyle, P. At night all cats are grey, and
      other stories
**BOYS**
  Achebe, C. Chicke's school days
  Aldridge, J. Bush boy, poor boy
  Andrews, F. E. Bushwhacked
  Arason, S. The snowstorm
  Armstrong, C. The enemy
  Asimov, I. The ugly little boy
  Barth, J. Lost in the funhouse
  Blaise, C. Snow people
  Blum-Alquit, E. Revolt of the apprentices
  Bødker, C. The Deaf'un's door
  Boles, P. D. Lucas and Jake
  Boyle, P. The window
  Brautigan, R. Corporal
  Brautigan, R. The ghost children of
    Tacoma
  Brautigan, R. 1962 Cotton Mather news-
    reel

**Brackett, Leigh**
  Come sing the moons of Moravenn
    Elwood, R. ed. The other side of to-
      morrow
**Brackett, Leigh, and Bradbury, Ray**
  Lorelei of the red mist
    Nolan, W. F. ed. The human equation
**Bradbury, Malcolm**
  The adult education class
    McCrindle, J. F. ed. Stories from the
      Transatlantic Review
**Bradbury, Ray**
  Any friend of Nicholas Nickleby's is a
    friend of mine
    Bradbury, R. I sing the Body Electric!
  April 2000: the third expedition
    Bradbury, R. The Martian chronicles
    Same as: Mars is heaven!
  April 2003: the musicians
    Bradbury, R. The Martian chronicles
  April 2005: Usher II
    Bradbury, R. The Martian chronicles
  April 2026: the long years
    Bradbury, R. The Martian chronicles
  August 1999: the Earth men
    Bradbury, R. The Martian chronicles
    Same as: The Earth men, listed in
      earlier volumes
  August 1999: the summer night
    Bradbury, R. The Martian chronicles
  August 2001: the settlers
    Bradbury, R. The Martian chronicles
  August 2002: night meeting
    Bradbury, R. The Martian chronicles
    Same as: Night meeting, listed in the
      1950-1954 and the 1964-1968 sup-
      plements
  August 2005: the old ones
    Bradbury, R. The Martian chronicles
  August 2026: there will come soft rains
    Bradbury, R. The Martian chronicles
  The beast from 20,000 fathoms
    Haining, P. ed. The ghouls
    Same as: The Fog Horn
  The cold wind and the warm
    Bradbury, R. I sing the Body Electric!
  The crowd
    Stansbury, D. L. ed. Impact
  December 2001: the green morning
    Bradbury, R. The Martian chronicles
  December 2005: the silent towns
    Bradbury, R. The Martian chronicles
  Downwind from Gettysburg
    Bradbury, R. I sing the Body Electric!
  The dwarf
    Haining, P. ed. The freak show
  February 1999: Ylla
    Bradbury, R. The Martian chronicles
    Same as: Ylla, listed in the 1950-1954
      and the 1964-1968 supplements
  February 2002: the locusts
    Bradbury, R. The Martian chronicles
  February 2003: interim
    Bradbury, R. The Martian chronicles
  Fever dream
    Ball, J. E. ed. Designs for reading:
      short stories

A final sceptre, a lasting crown
  Ferman, E. L. and Mills, R. P. eds.
    Twenty years of The Magazine of
    Fantasy and Science Fiction
The fire balloons
  McComas, J. F. ed. Special wonder
  Same as: November 2002: the fire
    balloons
The Fog Horn
  Authors' choice
  Howes, B. and Smith, G. J. eds. The
    sea-green horse
  Same as: The beast from 20,000 fath-
    oms
The haunting of the new
  Bradbury, R. I sing the Body Electric!
  Haining, P. ed. The nightmare reader
Heavy-set
  Bradbury, R. I sing the Body Electric!
Henry the Ninth
  Bradbury, R. I sing the Body Electric!
I, Mars
  Nolan, W. F. ed. A wilderness of stars
I sing the Body Electric!
  Bradbury, R. I sing the Body Electric!
The Inspired Chicken Motel
  Bradbury, R. I sing the Body Electric!
Invisible boy
  Kahn, J. ed. Somethings fierce and fatal
January 1999: rocket summer
  Bradbury, R. The Martian chronicles
June 2001:—and the moon be still as
    bright
  Bradbury, R. The Martian chronicles
  Same as: And the moon be still as
    bright; listed in the basic volume and
    the 1950-1954 supplement
June 2003: way in the middle of the air
  Bradbury, R. The Martian chronicles
The Kilimanjaro device
  Bradbury, R. I sing the Body Electric!
The lost city of Mars
  Bradbury, R. I sing the Body Elec-
    tric!
  Hipolito, J. and McNelly, W. E. eds.
    Mars, we love you
McGillahee's brat
  Carr, T. ed. Into the unknown
The mad wizards of Mars
  Haining, P. ed. The witchcraft reader
The Man in the Rorschach Shirt
  Bradbury, R. I sing the Body Elec-
    tric!
March 2000: the taxpayer
  Bradbury, R. The Martian chronicles
Mars is heaven!
  Science fiction hall of fame v 1
  Same as: April 2000: the third expedi-
    tion
May 2003: the wilderness
  Bradbury, R. The Martian chronicles
  Same as: The wilderness, listed in the
    1950-1954 and the 1964-1968 sup-
    plements
The naming of names
  Norton, A. and Donaldy, E. eds. Gates
    to tomorrow
  Same as: 2004-05: the naming of
    names

**Bradbury, Ray—***Continued*
Night call, collect
  Bradbury, R.  I sing the Body Electric!
November 2002: the fire balloons
  Bradbury, R. The Martian chronicles
  Same as: The fire balloons
November 2005: the luggage store
  Bradbury, R. The Martian chronicles
November 2005: the off season
  Bradbury, R. The Martian chronicles
November 2005: the watchers
  Bradbury, R. The Martian chronicles
October 2002: the shore
  Bradbury, R. The Martian chronicles
October 2026: the million-year picnic
  Bradbury, R. The Martian chronicles
  Same as: The million-year picnic, listed
    in the 1950-1954 and the 1964-1968
    supplements
The one who waits
  Minot, S. and Wilson, R. eds. Three
    stances of modern fiction
The pendulum
  Moskowitz, S. ed. Horrors unknown
Pillar of fire
  Haining, P. ed. Vampires at midnight
The prehistoric producer
  Haining, P. ed. The Hollywood nightmare
September 2005: the Martian
  Bradbury, R. The Martian chronicles
The small assassin
  Haining, P. ed. Nightfrights
The terrible conflagration up at the place
  Bradbury, R.  I sing the Body Electric!
The Tombling day
  Bradbury, R.  I sing the Body Electric!
Tomorrow's child
  Bradbury, R.  I sing the Body Electric!
2004-05: the naming of names
  Bradbury, R. The Martian chronicles
  Same as: The naming of names
A wild night in Galway
  Haining, P. ed. The wild night company: Irish stories of fantasy and horror
The women
  Bradbury, R.  I sing the Body Electric!
Yes, we'll gather at the river
  Bradbury, R.  I sing the Body Electric!
  *See also* Brackett, L. jt. auth.
**Bradbury, Ray, and Hasse, Henry**
Pendulum [another version]
  Moskowitz, S. ed. Horrors unknown
**Braddon, Mary Elizabeth.** *See* Braddon, Mrs
**Braddon, Mrs**
Eveline's visitant
  Manley, S. and Lewis, G. eds. Ladies of horror
  Tomlinson, D. ed. Walk in dread
**BRADFORD, JOHN**
Green, W. C. Secrets of Cabalism
**Bradshaw, M. E.**
Rebel in the driver's seat
  Fenner, P. R. comp. Where speed is king

**Bragg, Melvyn**
The initiation
  Winter's tales 18
**BRAGGARTS.** *See* Pride and vanity
**BRAHMANS**
Kipling, R. The miracle of Purun Bhagat
Premchand.  A car-splashing
Premchand.  A coward
Premchand. Deliverance
Premchand.  A lesson in the holy life
Premchand. Man's highest duty
Premchand.  A moral victory
**BRAHMINS.** *See* Brahmans
The **Brahms** kick. Kanin, G.
**BRAIN**
Goldin, S. The last ghost
### Diseases
*See* Encephalitis
### Experiments
Mitchell, E. P. The professor's experiment
### Tumors
Ansell, J. Day of the prophets
**Brain** damage. Barthelme, D.
**BRAIN SURGERY.** *See* Surgery
**Brain** wipe. MacLean, K.
**Brainsy.** O'Faolain, S.
**BRAINWASHING**
Anderson, P.  I tell you, it's true
Hill, A. R. Omega
Rocklynne, R. Randy-Tandy man
**Braly, Malcolm**
An outline of history
  Disch, T. M. ed. Bad moon rising
**Bramah, Ernest**
The coin of Dionysius
  Bramah, E. Best Max Carrados detective stories
The disappearance of Marie Severe
  Bramah, E. Best Max Carrados detective stories
The game played in the dark
  Greene, H. ed. The rivals of Sherlock Holmes
The ghost at Massingham Mansions
  Bramah, E. Best Max Carrados detective stories
The Holloway flat tragedy
  Bramah, E. Best Max Carrados detective stories
The ingenious Mr Spinola
  Bramah, E. Best Max Carrados detective stories
The Knight's Cross signal problem
  Bramah, E. Best Max Carrados detective stories
The last exploit of Harry the actor
  Bramah, E. Best Max Carrados detective stories
The mystery of the poisoned dish of mushrooms
  Bramah, E. Best Max Carrados detective stories
  Same as: Who killed Charlie Winpole?
The mystery of the vanished Petition Crown
  Bramah, E. Best Max Carrados detective stories
  Same as: The vanished crown, listed in the basic volume

**Bramah, Ernest**—*Continued*
  The tragedy at Brookbend Cottage
    Bramah, E. Best Max Carrados detective stories
    Greene, Sir H. ed. The further rivals of Sherlock Holmes
  Who killed Charlie Winpole?
    Dickinson, S. ed. The drugged cornet, and other mystery stories
    Same as: The mystery of the poisoned dish of mushrooms
**Bramble** bush. Nourse, A. E.
**Brand, Christianna**
  King of the air
    Ellery Queen's Mystery Magazine. Ellery Queen's Murder menu
  Poison in the cup
    Ellery Queen's Mystery Magazine. Ellery Queen's Grand slam
  The scapegoat
    Ellery Queen's Mystery Magazine. Ellery Queen's Headliners
  The wicked ghost
    Ellery Queen's Mystery Magazine. Ellery Queen's Murder menu
**Brand, Max**
  Wine on the desert
    Taylor, J. G. ed. Great Western short stories
**Brand, Thomas**
  Don slow and his electric girl getter
    Elder, J. ed. Eros in orbit
The **Brand** X business. Littke, L. J.
**Brandão, Raul**
  The thief and his little daughter
    Satin, J. ed. Reading literature
**Brandenburg** Concerto. Dorr, L.
**BRANDING OF CATTLE.** *See* Cattle—Marking
**Brandt, Jørgen Gustava**
  The Finnish sailor
    Holm, S. ed. The devil's instrument, and other Danish stories
**Branson, Robert**
  The red-headed murderess
    Howes, B. and Smith, G. J. eds. The sea-green horse
**Brasher, Nell**
  The pink puppy
    Alabama prize stories, 1970
**Brautigan, Richard**
  The armored car
    Brautigan, R. Revenge of the lawn
  The betrayed kingdom
    Brautigan, R. Revenge of the lawn
  The Cleveland Wrecking Yard
    Corodimas, P. ed. In trout country
    Minot, S. and Wilson, R. eds. Three stances of modern fiction
  Coffee
    Brautigan, R. Revenge of the lawn
  Complicated banking problems
    Brautigan, R. Revenge of the lawn
  Corporal
    Brautigan, R. Revenge of the lawn
  Elmira
    Brautigan, R. Revenge of the lawn
  Forgiven
    Brautigan, R. Revenge of the lawn

44:40
    Brautigan, R. Revenge of the lawn
  Getting to know each other
    Brautigan, R. Revenge of the lawn
  The ghost children of Tacoma
    Brautigan, R. Revenge of the lawn
  Greyhound tragedy
    Brautigan, R. Revenge of the lawn
  Halloween in Denver
    Brautigan, R. Revenge of the lawn
  Holiday in Germany
    Brautigan, R. Revenge of the lawn
  Homage to the San Francisco YMCA
    Brautigan, R. Revenge of the lawn
  The hunchback trout
    Corodimas, P. ed. In trout country
  The literary life in California/1964
    Brautigan, R. Revenge of the lawn
  A long time ago people decided to live in America
    Brautigan, R. Revenge of the lawn
  The lost chapters of Trout fishing in America: "Rembrandt Creek" and "Carthage Sink"
    Brautigan, R. Revenge of the lawn
    Lish, G. ed. The secret life of our times: new fiction from Esquire
  1962 Cotton Mather newsreel
    Brautigan, R. Revenge of the lawn
  1/3, 1/3, 1/3
    Brautigan, R. Revenge of the lawn
  The post offices of Eastern Oregon
    Brautigan, R. Revenge of the lawn
  The pretty office
    Brautigan, R. Revenge of the lawn
  Revenge of the lawn
    Brautigan, R. Revenge of the lawn
  Sand castles
    Brautigan, R. Revenge of the lawn
  A short history of Oregon
    Brautigan, R. Revenge of the lawn
  A short history of religion in California
    Brautigan, R. Revenge of the lawn
  Trout fishing in America terrorists
    Foff, A. and Knapp, D. eds. Story
  "A trout fishing sampler"
    Charyn, J. ed. The troubled vision
  The wild birds of heaven
    Brautigan, R. Revenge of the lawn
  Winter rug
    Brautigan, R. Revenge of the lawn
  The World War I Los Angeles airplane
    The Best American short stories, 1972
    Brautigan, R. Revenge of the lawn
    New American Review no. 12
**Brave** bulls of Sidi Yahya. Algren, N.
**Brave** newer world. Harrison, H.
**BRAVERY.** *See* Courage
**Bravery.** Fielding, G.
**Brawley, Ernest**
  The chicken
    Gulassa, C. M. ed. The fact of fiction
The **brazen** locked room. Asimov, I.
**BRAZIL**
  Derry, V.  A date with a spider
  Lispector, C. The daydreams of a drunk woman
  Machado, A. M. The piano
  Trevisan, D. Death on the square

**BRAZIL**—*Continued*

**Amazon Valley**

Karlen, A. The guardian

**Curitiba**

Trevisan, D. Dear old girl

Trevisan, D. The elephants' graveyard

Trevisan, D. My dear husband

**Farm life**

*See* Farm life—Brazil

**Race problems**

Veiga, J. J. Holiday Sunday

**Ranch life**

*See* Ranch life—Brazil

**Rio de Janeiro**

Trevisan, D.   A visit to the teacher

**BRAZIL, PROVINCIAL AND RURAL**

Amado, J. How Porciúncula the mulatto got the corpse off his back

Machado de Assis. The psychiatrist

Maia, C. V. Sun

Veiga, J. J. Incident at Sumaúma

Veiga, J. J. Saturday afternoon and Sunday morning

Veiga, J. J. The ten-league journey

**BREAD**

Arkley, G. Staff of life

The **bread**. Borchert, W.

**Bread**. Strindberg, A.

The **bread**-winner. Strindberg, A.

The **breadman**. Heath, M.

A **break** in the weather. Jacobs, H.

**Breakfast**. Steinbeck, J.

**Breakfast** and work. Steinbeck, J.

**BREAKFAST FOODS**. *See* Cereals, Prepared

**Breaking** the news. Böll, H.

**Breaking** the news. Nabokov, V.

**Breakout** in Ecol 2. Bunch, D. R.

The **breakthrough**. Du Maurier, D.

**Breakthrough**. Warner, L.

**Breath** from the sky. McCullers, C.

A **breath** of Lucifer. Narayan, R. K.

**Breckenridge** and the continuum. Silverberg, R.

**Breeding** stock. Khamsing, S.

"**Breeds** there a man . . .?" Asimov, I.

**Breen, Jon L.**

The Austin murder case

    Mystery Writers of America. Dear dead days

The fortune cookie

    Ellery Queen's Mystery Magazine. Ellery Queen's Mystery bag

Frank Merriswell's greatest case; or, The daring one-hander

    Ellery Queen's Mystery Magazine. Ellery Queen's Murder menu

The Lithuanian eraser mystery

    Best detective stories of the year [1969]

**Brember**. Thomas, D.

**Brenda**

Victoria-Bess

    Victorian doll stories

**Brennan, Joseph Payne**

Apparition in the sun

    Brennan, J. P. The casebook of Lucius Leffing

Apprehension

    Brennan, J. P. Stories of darkness and dread

Black thing at midnight

    Brennan, J. P. Stories of darkness and dread

Canavan's back yard

    Hitchcock, A. ed. Alfred Hitchcock presents: Stories to stay awake by

The case of the uncut corpse

    Brennan, J. P. The casebook of Lucius Leffing

City of the Seven Winds

    Brennan, J. P. Stories of darkness and dread

Death at Draleman's Pond

    Brennan, J. P. The casebook of Lucius Leffing

Death mask

    Brennan, J. P. The casebook of Lucius Leffing

Death of a derelict

    Brennan, J. P. The casebook of Lucius Leffing

Delivery of Erdmore Street

    Brennan, J. P. Stories of darkness and dread

The Dismal Flats murder

    Brennan, J. P. The casebook of Lucius Leffing

The dump

    Brennan, J. P. Stories of darkness and dread

The enemy unknown

    Brennan, J. P. The casebook of Lucius Leffing

Episode on Cain Street

    Brennan, J. P. Stories of darkness and dread

Fingers of steel

    Brennan, J. P. The casebook of Lucius Leffing

The haunted housewife

    Brennan, J. P. The casebook of Lucius Leffing

The house at 1248

    Brennan, J. P. Stories of darkness and dread

The house on Hazel Street

    Brennan, J. P. Stories of darkness and dread

In death as in life

    Brennan, J. P. The casebook of Lucius Leffing

In the very stones

    Brennan, J. P. Stories of darkness and dread

The intangible threat

    Brennan, J. P. The casebook of Lucius Leffing

The Keeper of the Dust

    Brennan, J. P. Stories of darkness and dread

Killer cat

    Brennan, J. P. Stories of darkness and dread

The man in grey tweeds

    Brennan, J. P. Stories of darkness and dread

**Brennan, Joseph Payne**—*Continued*
  The Mantzen diamond mystery
    Brennan, J. P. The casebook of Lucius
      Leffing
  Mr Octbur
    Brennan, J. P. Stories of darkness and
      dread
  Monton
    Brennan, J. P. Stories of darkness and
      dread
  The mystery of Myrrh Lane
    Brennan, J. P. The casebook of Lucius
      Leffing
  The North Knoll
    Brennan, J. P. Stories of darkness and
      dread
  On the elevator
    Lamb, H. ed. A tide of terror
  "The peril that lurks among ruins"
    Derleth, A. ed. Dark things
  The ransacked room
    Brennan, J. P. The casebook of Lucius
      Leffing
  The rising man
    Haining, P. ed. The freak show
  The seventh incantation
    Brennan, J. P. Stories of darkness and
      dread
  The strange case of Peddler Phelps
    Brennan, J. P. The casebook of Lucius
      Leffing
  The Walford case
    Brennan, J. P. The casebook of Lucius
      Leffing
  The way to the attic
    Brennan, J. P. Stories of darkness and
      dread
  Whirlwind of blood
    Brennan, J. P. The casebook of Lucius
      Leffing
  Zombique
    Brennan, J. P. Stories of darkness and
      dread
**Brennan, Maeve**
  The barrel of rumors
    Brennan, M. In and out of never-never
      land
  The carpet with the big pink roses on it
    Brennan, M. In and out of never-never
      land
  The children are there, trying not to laugh
    Brennan, M. In and out of never-never
      land
  The children are very quiet when they are
      away
    Brennan, M. In and out of never-never
      land
  The clever one
    Brennan, M. In and out of never-never
      land
  The day we got our own back
    Brennan, M. In and out of never-never
      land
  The devil in us
    Brennan, M. In and out of never-never
      land
  The door on West Tenth Street
    Brennan, M. In and out of never-never
      land

The drowned man
    Brennan, M. In and out of never-never
      land
  The eldest child
    The Best American short stories, 1969
    Brennan, M. In and out of never-never
      land
  A free choice
    Brennan, M. In and out of never-never
      land
  I see you, Bianca
    Brennan, M. In and out of never-never
      land
  In and out of never-never land
    Brennan, M. In and out of never-never
      land
  A large bee
    Brennan, M. In and out of never-never
      land
  The lie
    Brennan, M. In and out of never-never
      land
  The morning after the big fire
    Brennan, M. In and out of never-never
      land
  The old man of the sea
    Brennan, M. In and out of never-never
      land
  The shadow of kindness
    Brennan, M. In and out of never-never
      land
  The sofa
    Brennan, M. In and out of never-never
      land
  Stories of Africa
    Brennan, M. In and out of never-never
      land
  The twelfth wedding anniversary
    Brennan, M. In and out of never-never
      land
  A young girl can spoil her chances
    Brennan, M. In and out of never-never
      land
**Brent, Joanna**
  A little trip through Griffley
    Intro #3
**Brent, Peter**
  Mewed up
    Hamilton, A. ed. Splinters
**Breslow, Paul**
  Before the operation
    McCrindle, J. F. ed. Stories from the
      Transatlantic Review
  Honey bee
    New Directions in prose and poetry 22
**Bretherton, Vivian**
  The rock and the wind; excerpt
    Lucia, E. ed. This land around us
**Brethren** horse traders. Green, B. K.
**Bretnor, R.**
  Dr Birdmouse
    Scortia, T. N. ed. Strange bedfellows
  Donoghan's wife
    McComas, J. F. ed. Crimes and misfor-
      tunes
  The gnurrs come from the voodvork out
    McComas, J. F. ed. Special wonder
    Silverberg, R. ed. The science fiction
      bestiary

Bretnor, R.—*Continued*

The Greatest of All Webley Collectors
  Ellery Queen's Mystery Magazine. El-
  lery Queen's Headliners
A matter of equine ballistics
  Best detective stories of the year, 1972
Paper tiger
  Ellery Queen's Mystery Magazine. El-
  lery Queen's Grand slam

**Bretnor, R. and, Neville, Kris**

Gratitude guaranteed
  Ferman, E. L. and Mills, R. P. eds.
  Twenty Years of The magazine of
  Fantasy and Science Fiction

**Breuer, Miles J.**

The captured cross-section
  Silverberg, R. ed. Other dimensions

**Brewster, Harry**

The Marquis and the crocodile
  Lytle, A. ed. Craft and vision

**BRIBERY**

Bierce, A. Corrupting the press
Ellin, S. Kindly dig your grave

**BRICKLAYERS**

Di Donato, P. The broken scaffold
The **bride** comes to Yellow Sky. Crane, S.
**Bride** in danger. Queen, E.
The **bride** of Christ. Gordimer, N.
The **bride** of the grave. Tieck, J. L.
**BRIDES.** *See* Honeymoons; Husband and
  wife; Weddings

**BRIDGE (GAME)**

Von Elsner, D. The man who played too
  well
The **bridge.** Blaise, C.
The **bridge.** Blish, J.
The **bridge.** Tabori, P.
The **bridge.** Takeda, T.
The **bridge** of magpies. Sié, Cheou-kang
**Bridge** of stone. Elizondo, S.
The **bridge** to the other side. Kotowska, M.

**Bridges, Thomas**

Music to lay eggs by
  McCrindle, J. F. ed. Stories from the
  Transatlantic Review

**BRIDGES**

Blish, J. The Bridge
Chekhov, A. The New Villa
Laurence, M. The tomorrow-tamer
  *See also* names of bridges, e.g. Brook-
  lyn Bridge
The **bridled** ass. Mathes, W.
A **brief** chronology of death and night.
  Greenberg, A.
**Brief** lives, from next door. Rascoe, J.
The **brief,** swinging career of Dan and Judy
  Smythe. Wilson, C.
**Brief** visit back. Naylor, P. R.
The **briefcase.** Singer, I. B.
The **brigadier.** Rosenfeld, I.
The **brigadier** and the golf widow.
  Cheever, J.
The **brigadier** general and the columnist's
  wife. Just, W.

**BRIGANDS AND ROBBERS**

Allen, J. H. Tales of Diego
Aricha, Y. Night scene

Blum-Alquit, E. A highwayman in the
  woods of Chelm
Corvo, F. Baron. About the insistence of
  Sangiuseppe
Corvo, F. Baron. About the preface of Fra
  Cherubino
Djilas, M. The ambush
Fitzgerald, F. S. Dalyrimple goes wrong
Jewett, S. O.  A dark night
Nesvadba, J. The lost face
Roberts, K. The Lady Margaret
Runyon, D. The hottest guy in the world
Russ, J. The man who could not see devils
Stoker, B. The burial of the rats
Strashimirov, A. Soura Bir
Thomason, J. W. The Sergeant and the
  bandits
Verga, G. Gramigna's mistress
Yovkov, Y. Shibil
  *See also* Outlaws

**Bright** an' mownin' star. Thelwell, M.
**Bright** and morning star. Wright R.
**Bright** eyes. Ellison, H.
**Bright** Shores. *See* Litvinov, I. Portrait of a
  lady; Flight from Bright Shores

The **bright** spade. Brown, G. M.

**Brightness** falls from the air. St Clair, M.

**Brigid.** Lavin, M.

**Briholme** in winter. Davis, O.

**Brillo.** Bova, B. and Ellison, H.

**Brindley.** Dorr, L.

**Bringing** home the dog. Blackhurst, W. E.

**Brinley, Bertrand**

The Great Gas Bag Race
  Fenner, P. R. comp. Where speed is
  king

**Brister, Ben**

The cry of the hen
  Brister, B. Moss, mallards and mules,
  and other hunting and fishing stories

**Brister, Bob**

Anatomy of a goose hunt
  Brister, B. Moss, mallards and mules,
  and other hunting and fishing stories
Big Red's buffleheads
  Brister, B. Moss, mallards and mules,
  and other hunting and fishing stories
The canvasback jury
  Brister, B. Moss, mallards and mules,
  and other hunting and fishing stories
A game of Gulf poker
  Brister, B. Moss, mallards and mules,
  and other hunting and fishing stories
The golden redfish
  Brister, B. Moss, mallards and mules,
  and other hunting and fishing stories
Grandfather's geese
  Brister, B. Moss, mallards and mules,
  and other hunting and fishing stories
The Holly Beach hurricane
  Brister, B. Moss, mallards and mules,
  and other hunting and fishing stories
The holy mackerel
  Brister, B. Moss, mallards and mules,
  and other hunting and fishing stories
The London gun
  Brister, B. Moss, mallards and mules,
  and other hunting and fishing stories

Brister, Bob—*Continued*
A matter of rationale
   Brister, B. Moss, mallards and mules,
    and other hunting and fishing stories
Moss, mallards and mules
   Brister, B. Moss, mallards and mules,
    and other hunting and fishing stories
The naming of Rattlesnake Road
   Brister, B. Moss, mallards and mules,
    and other hunting and fishing stories
The night of manhood
   Brister, B. Moss, mallards and mules,
    and other hunting and fishing stories
Of perches and pleasures
   Brister, B. Moss, mallards and mules,
    and other hunting and fishing stories
One very fine doe
   Brister, B. Moss, mallards and mules,
    and other hunting and fishing stories
El papa sabalo
   Brister, B. Moss, mallards and mules,
    and other hunting and fishing stories
The price of a pintail
   Brister, B. Moss, mallards and mules,
    and other hunting and fishing stories
Professor Tequila Joe
   Brister, B. Moss, mallards and mules,
    and other hunting and fishing stories
The sand trout seminar
   Brister, B. Moss, mallards and mules,
    and other hunting and fishing stories
The sharks
   Brister, B. Moss, mallards and mules,
    and other hunting and fishing stories
A small wager among gentlemen
   Brister, B. Moss, mallards and mules,
    and other hunting and fishing stories
Tiro al pichon!
   Brister, B. Moss, mallards and mules,
    and other hunting and fishing stories
The trial of Job
   Brister, B. Moss, mallards and mules,
    and other hunting and fishing stories
Two boys
   Brister, B. Moss, mallards and mules,
    and other hunting and fishing stories
The whitewing snow job
   Brister, B. Moss, mallards and mules,
    and other hunting and fishing stories
The wrong-way ambush
   Brister, B. Moss, mallards and mules,
    and other hunting and fishing stories
BRITISH COLUMBIA. *See* Canada—British
   Columbia
BRITISH IN AFRICA. *See* English in
   Africa
BRITISH IN AFRICA, SOUTH. *See* En-
   glish in Africa, South
BRITISH IN ARABIAN PENINSULA
   Lanier, S. The leftovers
BRITISH IN CARIBBEAN ISLANDS. *See*
   English in Caribbean Islands
BRITISH IN FRANCE. *See* English in
   France
BRITISH IN ITALY. *See* English in Italy
BRITISH IN PALESTINE. *See* English in
   Palestine

BRITISH IN THE CZECHOSLOVAK RE-
   PUBLIC. *See* English in the Czecho-
   slovak Republic
BRITISH SOLDIERS. *See* Soldiers, British
Brittain, William
   Falling object
    Ellery Queen's Mystery Magazine. El-
    lery Queen's Mystery bag
   The man who read Sir Arthur Conan
    Doyle
    Ellery Queen's Mystery Magazine. El-
    lery Queen's Murder menu
   Mr Strang finds the answers
    Gibson, W. ed. Rogues' gallery
BRITTANY. *See* France, Provincial and
   rural—Brittany
Broadway Joe. Spike, P.
Brockle-face. Foster, B.
Brodeur, Paul
   Angel of Death
    Brodeur, P. Downstream
   Behind the moon
    Brodeur, P. Downstream
   Blue lawns
    Brodeur, P. Downstream
   Hydrography
    Brodeur, P. Downstream
   The proposal
    Brodeur, P. Downstream
   The secret
    Brodeur, P. Downstream
    Rosmond, B. comp. Today's stories from
    Seventeen
   The sick fox
    Brodeur, P. Downstream
   The siphon
    Brodeur, P. Downstream
   The snow in Petrograd
    Brodeur, P. Downstream
   The spoiler
    Brodeur, P. Downstream
   The toll
    Brodeur, P. Downstream
   The turtle
    Brodeur, P. Downstream
   A war story
    Brodeur, P. Downstream
Brodkey, Harold
   Innocence
    American Review 16
   Play
    American Review 17
Brognart. Milosz, C.
Broke down engine. Goulart, R.
The **broken** bridge. Tuohy, F.
The **broken**-down van. Crane, S.
The **broken** globe. Kreisel, H.
The **broken** leg. Stern, J.
The **broken** lyre. MacMahon, B.
**Broken** pattern. Chesbro, G. C.
The **broken** scaffold. Di Donato, P.
The **broken** wings. Lardas, K.
Brokennosejob. Raffel, M.
BROKERS
   Case, R. O. Hard money
   Farrell, J. T. Mr Austin
   Henry, O. The romance of a busy broker
   Pudney, J. Kitty, Kitty, Kitty

BROTHERS AND SISTERS—*Continued*
Francis, H. E. One of the boys
Hemingway, E. The last good country
Hopper, W. O. Where the immortal are
Hubschman, T.   A woman of thirty
Jackson, C.   A night visitor
Lavin, M. Brigid
Marguerite de Navarre.   A love match
Munro, A. Boys and girls
Naylor, P. R. Dark side of the moon
Naylor, P. R. One of the gang
Nin, A. Under a glass bell
O'Connor, F. First confession
O'Connor, F. Sue
O'Hara, J. Your fah neefah neeface
Polidori, J. The vampyre
Porter, K. A. The grave
Richter, C. Early marriage
Rule, J. Brother and sister
Sargent, P. Clone sister
Sharp, M. Interlude at Spanish Harbour
Smith, L. The dying of Eunice LeBel
Taylor, P.   A spinster's tale
Taylor, P. Venus, Cupid, Folly and Time
Tindall, G. One of the family
Tuohy, F.   A reprieve
Ulibarri, S. R. The Frater family
Veiga, J. J. Dialogue on relativity
Verney, J. The drugged cornet
Vestdijk, S. My brown friend
Walker, A. The child who favored Daughter
Warner, L. The expectancy of my survival
Warner, L. The girl who liked Communists
Warner, S. T. Two children
Wilson, A.   A visit in bad taste
   *See also* Brothers; Family life; Sisters
The **brothers** and the girl. Djilas, M.
**BROTHERS-IN-LAW**
Drake, R. St Peter right in the eye
Glaze, E. The embrace
Grau, S. A. The wind shifting west
Olsen, T. V.   A kind of courage
Soto, P. J. Captive
**Brothers** of the bugle. Fowler, K.
**Broun, Heywood**
Artist unknown
   Knight, D. ed. The golden road
**Brown, Alice**
Farmer Eli's vacation
   Westbrook, P. D. ed. Seacoast and upland: a New England anthology
Number five
   Westbrook, P. D. ed. Seacoast and upland: a New England Anthology
**Brown, Cecil**
The life and loves of Mr Jiveass Nigger (Prologue)
   Chapman, A. ed. New Black voices
**Brown, Charles Brockden**
Memoirs of Carwin, the biloquist
   Haining, P. ed. Gothic tales of terror
**Brown, Frank London**
McDougal
   Margolies, E. A native sons reader

**Brown, Fredric**
Aelurophobe
   Brown, F. Paradox lost, and twelve other great science fiction stories
Arena
   Science fiction hall of fame v 1
Double standard
   Brown, F. Paradox lost, and twelve other great science fiction stories
Eine kleine Nachtmusik
   Brown, F. Paradox lost, and twelve other great science fiction stories
It didn't happen
   Brown, F. Paradox lost, and twelve other great science fiction stories
Knock
   Brown, F. Paradox lost, and twelve other great science fiction stories
The last train
   Brown, F. Paradox lost, and twelve other great science fiction stories
The new one
   Brown, F. Paradox lost, and twelve other great science fiction stories
Nothing Sirius
   Brown, F. Paradox lost, and twelve other great science fiction stories
Obedience
   Brown, F. Paradox lost, and twelve other great science fiction stories
Paradox lost
   Brown, F. Paradox lost, and twelve other great science fiction stories
Placet is a crazy place
   The Astounding-Analog reader v 1
Puppet show
   Brown, F. Paradox lost, and twelve other great science fiction stories
   McComas, J. F. ed. Special wonder
Something green
   Brown, F. Paradox lost, and twelve other great science fiction stories
Ten percenter
   Brown, F. Paradox lost, and twelve other great science fiction stories
Town wanted
   McComas, J. F. ed. Crimes and misfortunes
Witness in the dark
   Hitchcock, A. ed. Alfred Hitchcock presents: Stories to be read with the lights on
**Brown, George Mackay**
The bright spade
   Brown, G. M.   A time to keep, and other stories
A carrier of stones
   Brown, G. M.   A time to keep, and other stories
Celia
   Brown, G. M.   A time to keep, and other stories
The eye of the hurricane
   Brown, G. M.   A time to keep, and other stories
The five of spades
   Brown, G. M.   A time to keep, and other stories

Brown, George Mackay—*Continued*

Icarus

Brown, G. M.  A time to keep, and other stories

The story teller

Brown, G. M.  A time to keep, and other stories

Tartan

Brown, G. M.  A time to keep, and other stories

A time to keep

Brown, G. M.  A time to keep, and other stories

A treading of grapes

Brown, G. M.  A time to keep, and other stories

The whaler's return

Brown, G. M.  A time to keep, and other stories

The wireless set

Brown, G. M.  A time to keep, and other stories

Brown, Margery Finn

In the forests of Riga the beasts are very wild indeed

Prize stories, 1972: The O. Henry Awards

Brown, Rollin

One-man mule

Collier, N. ed. Great stories of the West

Brown, Rosellen

Good housekeeping

American Review 18

A letter to Ismael in the grave

New American Review no. 12

Prize stories, 1972: The O. Henry Awards

Mainlanders

Prize stories, 1973: The O. Henry Awards

Brown, Sterling

And/or

James, C. L. ed. From the roots

Brown, Wenzell

The scar

Mystery Writers of America. Mirror, mirror, fatal mirror

Brown, William Wells

Escape of Clotel

Long, R. A. and Collier, E. W. eds. Afro-American writing v 1

The **brown** coat. Futrelle, J.

**Brown** earth as medium. Berne, S.

The **Brownie** of the Black Haggs. Hogg, J.

**Brownshoes.** Sturgeon, T.

Brownstein, Michael

Footprints on the moon

Brownstein, M. Brainstorms

Jet set melodrama

Brownstein, M. Brainstorms

Joy and confusion

Brownstein, M. Brainstorms

An old story

Brownstein, M. Brainstorms

The plot to save the world

Brownstein, M. Brainstorms

Disch, T. M. ed. The ruins of earth

Minot, S. and Wilson, R. eds. Three stances of modern fiction

Psycho doesn't exist

Brownstein, M. Brainstorms

Resentment

Brownstein, M. Brainstorms

Some take cover

Brownstein, M. Brainstorms

Torture: a children's story

Brownstein, M. Brainstorms

What is vision?

Brownstein, M. Brainstorms

Who knows where the time goes?

Brownstein, M. Brainstorms

BRÚ, HEÒIN

Emanuel

Faroese short stories

Lice

Faroese short stories

The long darkness

Faroese short stories

Men of letters

Faroese short stories

Old Halgir

Faroese short stories

A summons for the blacksmith

Faroese short stories

The white church

Faroese short stories

**Bruised** reeds. Deutsch, A. H.

**Brumbie** running. Ottley, R.

BRUNELLESCHI, FILIPPO

Ayrton, M. The vanishing point

Brunner, John

All the devils in hell

Haining, P. ed. The witchcraft reader

The biggest game

Brunner, J. From this day forward

Hamilton, A. ed. Splinters

An elixir for the emperor

Brunner, J. From this day forward

Even chance

Brunner, J. From this day forward

Factsheet six

Brunner, J. From this day forward

Fairy tale

Brunner, J. From this day forward

Fifth Amendment

Brunner, J. From this day forward

The inception of the epoch of Mrs Be-donebyasyoudid

Brunner, J. From this day forward

Jack fell down

Santesson, H. S. ed. Crime prevention in the 30th century

Judas

Brunner, J. From this day forward

Mohs, M. ed. Other worlds, other gods

Planetfall

Brunner, J. From this day forward

Puzzle for spacemen

McComas, J. F. ed. Special wonder

Report on the nature of the lunar surface

Clement, H. ed. First flights to the moon

The trouble I see

Brunner, J. From this day forward

The Vitanuls

Brunner, J. From this day forward

Mohs, M. ed. Other worlds, other gods

Buck, Pearl S.—*Continued*
  The green sari
    Buck, P. S. The good deed, and other
      stories of Asia, past and present
  Letter home
    Buck, P. S. The good deed, and other
      stories of Asia, past and present
  The sacred skull
    Buck, P. S. The good deed, and other
      stories of Asia, past and present
    Tibbets, A. B. ed. Boys are boys
  Sunrise at Juhu
    Buck, P. S. The good deed, and other
      stories of Asia, past and present
The **bucket** rider. Kafka, F.
**Buckskin** and smoke. Hayes, A. H.
**BUDAPEST.** *See* Hungary—Budapest
**BUDDHA AND BUDDHISM**
  Wu, Ch'eng-en. The temptation of Saint
    Pigsy
**BUDDHIST PRIESTS**
  Takeda, T. The bridge
  Uyeda, A. Daydreams
  Uyeda, A. Demon
  Wu, Ch'eng-en. The temptation of Saint
    Pigsy
**Buddies.** Verga, G.
**Buddy** buddy. Kanin, G.
**Budget** planet. Sheckley, R.
**Budrys, Algis**
  The man who always knew
    Knight, D. ed. Tomorrow and tomorrow
  Now hear the word of the Lord
    Best SF: 1969
  The peasant girl
    Kahn, J. ed. Hanging by a thread
  Riya's foundling
    Silverberg, R. ed. Mind to mind
  Rogue moon
    The Science fiction hall of fame v2B
  The Weeblies
    Knight, D. ed. The golden road
**Budrys, Algis, and Ellison, Harlan**
  Wonderbird
    Ellison, H. Partners in wonder
**BUENOS AIRES.** *See* Argentine Republic—
    Buenos Aires
**BUFFALO, AMERICAN.** *See* Bison
The **buffalo.** Lispector, C.
The **buffalo** hunter. Elman, R.
**Build**-up. Ballard, J. G.
**Builder** of kingdoms. Deutsch, A. H.
**Builders.** Yates, R.
The **builders** and the dream. Stuart, J.
**BUILDING.** *See* Wrecking
**Building** on the line. Dickson, G. R.
**BUILDING SUPERINTENDENTS.** *See*
    Janitors
**BUILDINGS**
  Cather, W. Behind the Singer Tower
  Curley, D. The gingerbread man
  Fast, H. The vision of Milty Boil
  Laski, M. The tower
  Ostaijen, P. van. The city of builders
**Built** up logically. Schoenfeld, H.
**Bukowski, Charles**
  All the assholes in the world and mine
    Bukowski, C. South of no north

  All the great writers
    Bukowski, C. Erections, ejaculations,
      exhibitions and general tales of or-
      dinary madness
  All the pussy we want
    Bukowski, C. Erections, ejaculations,
      exhibitions and general tales of or-
      dinary madness
  Animal crackers in my soup
    Bukowski, C. Erections, ejaculations,
      exhibitions and general tales of or-
      dinary madness
  Another horse story
    Bukowski, C. Erections, ejaculations,
      exhibitions and general tales of or-
      dinary madness
  A bad trip
    Bukowski, C. Erections, ejaculations,
      exhibitions and general tales of or-
      dinary madness
  Beer and poets and talk
    Bukowski, C. Erections, ejaculations,
      exhibitions and general tales of or-
      dinary madness
  The beginner
    Bukowski, C. Erections, ejaculations,
      exhibitions and general tales of or-
      dinary madness
  The big pot game
    Bukowski, C. Erections, ejaculations,
      exhibitions and general tales of or-
      dinary madness
  The birth, life and death of an under-
      ground newspaper
    Bukowski, C. Erections, ejaculations,
      exhibitions and general tales of or-
      dinary madness
  The blanket
    Bukowski, C. Erections, ejaculations,
      exhibitions and general tales of or-
      dinary madness
  Bop bop against that curtain
    Bukowski, C. South of no north
  Christ on rollerskates
    Bukowski, C. South of no north
  Class
    Bukowski, C. South of no north
  Confessions of a man insane enough to
      live with beasts
    Bukowski, C. South of no north
  The copulating mermaid of Venice, Cali-
      fornia
    Bukowski, C. Erections, ejaculations,
      exhibitions and general tales of or-
      dinary madness
  A couple of winos
    Bukowski, C. South of no north
  Cunt and Kant and a happy home
    Bukowski, C. Erections, ejaculations,
      exhibitions and general tales of or-
      dinary madness
  The day we talked about James Thurber
    Bukowski, C. Erections, ejaculations,
      exhibitions and general tales of or-
      dinary madness
  The devil was hot
    Bukowski, C. South of no north
  Dr Nazi
    Bukowski, C. South of no north

Bulgakov, Mikhail—*Continued*
No. 13. The Elpit-Rabkommun Building
  Bulgakov, M. Diaboliad, and other stories
Psalm
  Bulgakov, M. Diaboliad, and other stories
The raid
  Bulgakov, M. Diaboliad, and other stories
A treatise on housing
  Bulgakov, M. Diaboliad, and other stories

**BULGARIA**
  *See also* Communism—Bulgaria
      **20th century**
  Groubeshlieva, M. Second-hand shop
  Manov, E. Vanya and the statuette
  Severnyak, S. The stone pigeons
  Stanev, L.  A visitor
  Updike, J. The Bulgarian poetess
  Vezhinov, P. Spanish cholera
      **Army**
  Neznakomov, P. The Painlevé case
      **Peasant life**
  *See* Peasant life—Bulgaria
**BULGARIA, PROVINCIAL AND RURAL**
  Andreyev, V. One night, one day
  Dastkalov, S. T.  A new attitude toward life
  Fouchedjiev, D. The woman who walked about the sky
  Haitov, N. Paths
  Karaslavov, G. The portrait
  Kirilov, N. Boundless time
  Kirilov, N. Radiant skies
  Mishev, G. The rabbit census
  Stanev, L. Youth
  Strashimirov, A. Soura Bir
  Vazov, I. Old Yotso is watching
  Yovkov, Y. Heroes' heads
  Yovkov, Y. Shibil
The **Bulgarian** poetess. Updike, J.
**BULGARIANS IN YUGOSLAVIA**
  Djilas, M. Under the yoke
The **bull** that thought. Kipling, R.
**BULLDOZERS**
  Stuart, J. Mad Davids and mechanical Goliath
**Bullet** for one. Stout, R.
**BULLFIGHTERS AND BULLFIGHTING**
  Beekman, E. M. Cornada
  Deck, J. One Sunday in Spain
  Kipling, R. The bull that thought
  Mistral, F. The complaint of the bulls of the Camargue
  Zelazny, R. Corrida
      *See also* Bulls
**BULLFIGHTING.** *See* Bullfighters and bullfighting
**BULLFINCH**
  Holst, S. Bullfinch & goblin
**Bullfinch** & goblin. Holst, S.
**Bullins, Ed**
  The Absurd One
    Bullins, E. The hungered one

An ancient one
  Bullins, E. The hungered one
Dandy; or Astride the funky finger of lust
  Bullins, E. The hungered one
  King, W. ed. Black short story anthology
The drive
  Bullins, E. The hungered one
The enemy
  Bullins, E. The hungered one
The excursion
  Bullins, E. The hungered one
He couldn't say sex
  Bullins, E. The hungered one
The helper
  Bullins, E. The hungered one
The hungered one
  Bullins, E. The hungered one
In New England winter
  Bullins, E. The hungered one
In the wine time
  Bullins, E. The hungered one
The messenger
  Bullins, E. The hungered one
Mister newcomer
  Bullins, E. The hungered one
Moonwriter
  Bullins, E. The hungered one
The rally; or, Dialect determinism
  Bullins, E. The hungered one
The real me
  Bullins, E. The hungered one
The reason of why
  Bullins, E. The hungered one
The reluctant voyage
  Bullins, E. The hungered one
The saviour
  Bullins, E. The hungered one
Support your local police
  Bullins, E. The hungered one
Travel from home
  Bullins, E. The hungered one
**Bullock, Michael**
Back to the tree
  Bullock, M. Sixteen stories as they happened
The bule halo
  Bullock, M. Sixteen stories as they happened
The expanding and contracting lake
  Bullock, M. Sixteen stories as they happened
The flight
  Bullock, M. Sixteen stories as they happened
A man, a girl and a door
  Bullock, M. Sixteen stories as they happened
The man who loved trees
  Bullock, M. Sixteen stories as they happened
The net
  Bullock, M. Sixteen stories as they happened
Noire's dialogues
  Bullock, M. Sixteen stories as they happened

**Bullock, Michael—***Continued*

The open gate
  Bullock, M. Sixteen stories as they happened

The railway station
  Bullock, M. Sixteen stories as they happened

Red Beard's quest
  Bullock, M. Sixteen stories as they happened

The return of Noire
  Bullock, M. Sixteen stories as they happened

Through the trees to the river
  Bullock, M. Sixteen stories as they happened

Tiger in the park
  Bullock, M. Sixteen stories as they happened

To the top of the tower
  Bullock, M. Sixteen stories as they happened

Two girls and a man coming and going
  Bullock, M. Sixteen stories as they happened

**Bullring** of the summer night. Algren, N.

**BULLS**

Ayrton, M. The paradise bull pen
Babel, I. Bagrat-Ogly and the eyes of his bull
Casely-Hayford, G. M. Shadow of darkness
Ibuse, M. Old Ushitora
Kim, Y. I. The sunny side after the harvest
Kipling, R. The bull that thought
Mistral, F. The complaint of the bulls of the Camargue
O'Connor, F. Greenleaf
Stuart, J. Give Charlie a little time
  *See also* Cattle

**Bulwer-Lytton, Edward**

Chairolas
  Bishop, M. ed. A Romantic storybook
The haunted and the haunters
  Kahn, J. ed. Hanging by a thread
  *For other titles by this author see* Lytton, Lord

**Bumpus, Jerry**

The conspiracy against Mister Mann
  The Best little magazine fiction, 1970
In Utica
  Lish, G. ed. The secret life of our times: new fiction from Esquire

**BUMS.** *See* Tramps

**Bunch, David R.**

Breakout in Ecol 2
  Nova 3
That high-up blue day that saw the black sky-train come spinning
  The Best from Fantasy and Science Fiction; 18th ser.

**Bunco** game. Deming, R.

**Bunin, Ivan**

The gentleman from San Francisco
  Kahn, J. ed. Trial and terror
  Proffer, C. R. ed. From Karamzin to Bunin: an anthology of Russian short stories

Sunstroke
  Johnson, E. W. ed. Short stories international

**Bunner** sisters. Wharton, E.

**Buntcheh** the Silent. *See* Peretz, Y. L. Silent Bontsche

**Burden** of proof. Shaw, B.

The **Bureau** d'Echange de Maux. Dunsany, Lord

**BUREAUCRACY**

Agnon, S. Y. The document
Antonov, S. The application form
Bulgakov, M. Diaboliad
Elman, R. A friend's story
Greenberg, J. Upon the waters
Just, W. Burns
Just, W. Slayton
Kafka, F. The nature Theatre of Oklahoma
Laumer, K. In the queue
Malzberg, B. N. Agony column
Solzhenitsyn, A. For the good of the cause
Sternberg, J. Fin de siècle
Tendryakov, V. Creature of a day

**Burger** Creature. Chapman, S.

**Burgess, Anthony**

An American organ
  Hamilton, A. ed. Splinters
The Muse
  Best Sf: 1969
  Harrison, H. ed. The light fantastic

The **burglar.** Colette

**BURGLAR-ALARMS**

Law, W. The Harry Hastings Method

The **burglars.** Midwood, B.

**BURGLARS.** *See* Thieves

The **burglar's** Christmas. Cather, W.

**BURGLARY PROTECTION.** *See* Burglar-alarms

**Burhoe, B. Alan**

Ornithanthropus
  Best Sf: 1971
  Del Rey, L. ed. Best science fiction stories of the year [1972]

**BURIAL.** *See* Cemeteries; Cremation; Cryonics; The dead; Exhumation; Funeral rites and ceremonies; Soldiers' bodies, Disposition of; Tombs

**BURIAL, PREMATURE**

Hardwick, M. and Hardwick, M. Rose: a Gothick tale
Poe, E. A. The premature burial
Smith, C. A. A tale of Sir John Maundeville
Woolrich, C. Graves for the living

The **burial.** Byron, Lord

A **burial** at Surabaya. Theroux, P.

**BURIAL GROUNDS.** *See* Cemeteries

**Burial** monuments three. Hoch, E. D.

The **burial** of the rats. Stoker, B.

**BURIED ALIVE.** *See* Burial, Premature

The **buried** city. Witton, D.

**BURIED TREASURE**

Benét, S. V. The treasure of Vasco Gomez
Coburn, A. The tale of the fourth stranger
Cottrell, D. The mysterious box
Drake, D. Lord of the depths
Hoch, E. D. The theft of the Coco loot
Kipling, R. The King's ankus

BUSINESS—*Continued*

Goulart, R. Junior partner
Hesse, H. The homecoming
Hesse, H. Walter Kömpff
Hoffman, L. and Toomey, R. E. Lost in the marigolds
O'Hara, J. The hardware man
Peirce, J. F. The hot tamales murder case
Simpson, L. The ferris wheel
Thurber, J. The catbird seat
Vonnegut, K. Deer in the works
> *See also* Businessmen; Merchants; Women in business

**Unscrupulous methods**

Brister, B. The golden redfish
Brister, B. One very fine doe
Pronzini, B. The snatch
> *See also* Business ethics

Business before bass. Blackhurst, W. E.

A business deal. Strindberg, A.

**BUSINESS DEPRESSION, 1929**

Bellow, S. Looking for Mr Green
Bradbury, R. The Inspired Chicken Motel
Bukowski, C. Bop bop against that curtain
Curley, D.   A story of love, etc.
Holmes, E. M. Not for hire
Taylor, P. The other times

**BUSINESS ESPIONAGE.** *See* Business intelligence

**BUSINESS ETHICS**

Böll, H. Like a bad dream
Bukowski, C. Christ on rollerskates
Cross, J. Pin money
Zuroy, M. The businessmen
> *See also* Business intelligence

**BUSINESS EXECUTIVES.** *See* Executives

**BUSINESS INTELLIGENCE**

Goulart, R. The trouble with machines
Business is business. Böll, H.
Business was a Jewish kid's business. Deutschman, B.

**BUSINESSMEN**

Bodelsen, A. Success
Drake, R. The ring-tail tooter
Phillips, R. Rise up singing
Stuart, J. Lost land of youth
> *See also* Self-made men

The businessmen. Zuroy, M.

**BUSINESSWOMEN.** *See* Women in business

Buster. Burns, A.

The busybody. O'Hara, J.

But at the stroke of midnight. Warner, S. T.

But for the grace of God. Graham, W.

But who can replace a man. *See* Aldiss, B. W. Who can replace a man?

Butch minds the baby. Runyon, D.

**BUTCHERING.** *See* Slaughtering and slaughterhouses

**BUTCHERS**

Corvo, F. Baron. About Our Lady of Dreams
Trevor, W.   A choice of butchers
> *See also* Slaughtering and slaughterhouses

Butenas, Naomi
The girl that had no face
> Intro 4

Butler, Gwendoline
The sisterhood
> Ellery Queen's Mystery Magazine. Ellery Queen's Murder menu

Butler, Samuel
The book of the machine
Fairy tales for computers

**BUTLERS.** *See* Servants—Butlers

Butor, Michel
Welcome to Utah
> Stevick, P. ed. Anti-story

**BUTTE.** *See* Montana—Butte

**BUTTERFLIES**

Kipling, R. The Butterfly that stamped
Sié, Cheou-kang.   A butterfly's dream

The butterfly. Chekhov, A.

The butterfly and the tank. Hemingway, E.

The butterfly and the traffic light. Ozick, C.

The Butterfly that stamped. Kipling, R.

A butterfly's dream. Sié, Cheou-kang

Butterworth, Michael
The front room
> Mystery Writers of America. Merchants of menace

"Buttons are made of animal blood." Dillon, M.

Buying the child. Kumin, M.

**BUZZARDS**

West, J. Up a tree

Buzzati, Dino
A Siberian shepherd's report of the atom bomb
> Decker, C. R. and Angoff, C. eds. Modern stories from lands

By a lake in the Bois. Stewart, N.

By an unknown hand. Sladek, J.

By child undone. Ritchie, J.

By his bootstraps. MacDonald, A.

By new hearth fires. Dickson, G. R.

By the Falls. Harrison, H.

By the river. Oates, J. C.

By the waters. Rose, C.

By the waters of Babylon. Benét, S. V.

Byrne, Donn
A manner of legacy
> Kahn, J. ed. Hanging by a thread

Byron, Lord
The burial
> Haining, P. ed. Gothic tales of terror

The bystander. Wharton, T. L.

# C

C-chute. Asimov, I.

**CIA.** *See* United States. Central Intelligence Agency

"Ça ne peut pas durer." Vassilikos, V.

**CAB DRIVERS**

Chekhov, A. Heartache
Farrell, J. T. Small town taxicab driver
Henry, O. From the cabby's seat
Jewett, S. O. The spur of the moment
Linklater, E. Joy as it flies
Malamud, B. Man in the drawer

**CAB DRIVERS**—*Continued*
> Tindall, G. The night driver, or an alternative life
> Yates, R. Builders
> Yurick, S. The passage

The **Cabala**. Di Donato, P.

The **cabalist** of East Broadway. Singer, I. B.

**Cabell, James Branch**
> Porcelain cups
>> Abrahams, W. ed. Fifty years of the American short story v 1

The **cabinet** of Kafru. Gohman, F.

**CABINETMAKERS.** *See* Carpenters

**CABLE-LAYING.** *See* Telephone cables

**CABLES, ELECTRIC.** *See* Telephone cables

**CABLES, SUBMARINE**
> Delany, S. R. Driftglass

**CABOT, SEBASTIAN**
> Kipling, R. Hal o' the Draft

**Cabrera Infante, Guillermo**
> At the great 'Ecbo'
>> Cohen, J. M. ed. Latin American writing today
> A nest of sparrows on the awning
>> Howes, B. ed. The eye of the heart

**Cactus** dance. Sturgeon, T.

A **caddy's** diary. Lardner, R.

**Cadillac** flambé. Ellison, R.

**Cadmus** Henry. Edmonds, W. D.

**Cady, Jack**
> The art of a lady
>> Cady, J. The burning, & other stories
> The burning
>> Cady, J. The burning, & other stories
>> Stansbury, D. L. ed. Impact
> The forest ranger
>> Cady, J. The burning, & other stories
> The girl in the orange hat
>> Cady, J. The burning, & other stories
> I take care of things
>> The Best American short stories, 1971
>> Cady, J. The burning, & other stories
> Land
>> Cady, J. The burning, & other stories
> Play like I'm sheriff
>> The Best American short stories, 1969
>> Cady, J. The burning, & other stories
> Ride the thunder
>> Cady, J. The burning, & other stories
> The shark
>> Cady, J. The burning, & other stories
> The sounds of silence
>> Cady, J. The burning, & other stories
> Texts and notes on a sermon preached in Harlan, Ky., Bluefield, West Va., Hamilton, Ohio, and elsewhere
>> Cady, J. The burning, & other stories
> Thermopylae
>> Cady, J. The burning, & other stories
> The troll
>> Cady, J. The burning, & other stories
> With no breeze
>> The Best American short stories, 1970
>> Cady, J. The burning, & other stories

**CAEDMON**
> Walsh, J. P. and Crossley-Holland, K. Caedmon

**Cædmon.** Walsh, J. P. and Crossley-Holland, K.

**Cafe** Nore. Summers, H.

**CAFÉS.** *See* Restaurants, lunchrooms, etc.

The **cafeteria.** Singer, I. B.

**CAFETERIAS.** *See* Restaurants, lunchrooms, etc.

**CAGE BIRDS**
> Khamsing, S. Dark glasses

The **cage birds.** Pritchett, V. S.

**Cage** of brass. Delany, S. R.

The **cage** of sand. Ballard, J. G.

**CAGES, BIRD.** *See* Birdcages

**Cain, Paul**
> Red 71
>> Kahn, J. ed. Trial and terror

**Cain's** mark. Pronzini, B.

**Cal** always said. Arthur, E.

A **calculated** risk. Moravia, A.

**CALCULATING-MACHINES**
> Asimov, I. The machine that won the war
> Asimov, I. Someday
> Clarke, A. C. The nine billion names of God
> Gallico, P. The terrible answer
> *See also* Electronic computers

The **calculation** of probability. Landolfi, T.

**CALCUTTA.** *See* India—Calcutta

**CALDER, JOHN**
> Ayrton, M. John Calder of Kelty

**Caldwell, Bruce**
> The members
>> New Directions in prose and poetry 27

**Caldwell, Erskine**
> Country full of Swedes
>> Abrahams, W. ed. Fifty years of the American short story v 1

**CALGARY.** *See* Canada—Calgary

**Caliban.** Silverberg, R.

The **calibrated** alligator. Silverberg, R.

**CALIFORNIA**
> Fuchs, D. Twilight in southern California
> Thomas, V. Where's your feathers?

#### 1846-1900
> Harte, B. The outcasts of Poker Flat
> Harte, B. Tennessee's partner
> Rathjen, C. H. Sacrifice spurs
> Sienkiewicz, H.   A comedy of errors

#### 20th century
> Granat, R. Prana
> Hill, R. To sport with Amaryllis
> Morris, W. Since when do they charge admission?
> Steinbeck, J. Breakfast
> Steinbeck, J. Breakfast and work
> Steinbeck, J. The chrysanthemums
> Steinbeck, J. Frog hunt
> Steinbeck, J.   A future we can't foresee
> Steinbeck, J. Life and death
> Steinbeck, J. Of mice and men
> Steinbeck, J. The red pony: The great mountains
> West, J. Alive and real

##### Anaheim
> Sienkiewicz, H. Circus!
> Sienkiewicz, H. The cranes

CALIFORNIA—*Continued*
**Berkeley**
Devine, R. Parenthesis
**Country life**
*See* Country life—California
**Farm life**
*See* Farm life—California
**Hollywood**
Algren, N. Otto Preminger's strange sus-
    penjers
Carpenter, D. New York to Los Angeles
Clarke, A. C. Armaments race
Kanin, G. All through the house
**Los Angeles**
Bryant, E. Tactics
Bullins, E. The drive
Carpenter, D. New York to Los Angeles
Cleaver, E. The flashlight
Goldberg, G. J. 126 days of continuous
    sunshine
Goulart, R. Broke down engine
Goulart, R. Lofthouse
Goulart, R. Nobody starves
Himes, C. Lunching at the Ritzmore
Hunter, E. The birthday party
Jacobs, H. The voyage of the peanut
Williams, J. A. Son in the afternoon
**Mariposa**
Sienkiewicz, H.  A legionary of Mieros-
    lawski
**Missions**
*See* Missions—California
**Monterey**
Steinbeck, J. Danny
Steinbeck, J. Pilon
Steinbeck, J. The pirate
Steinbeck, J. Tortillas and beans
Steinbeck, J. The treasure hunt
**Point Reyes National Seashore**
Brautigan, R. Sand castles
**Ranch life**
*See* Ranch life—California
**Sacramento**
Sienkiewicz, H. The horizon widens
**San Francisco**
Algren, N. I know they'll like me in
    Saigon
Anderson, P. The fatal fulfillment
Brautigan, R. The betrayed kingdom
Brautigan, R.  A long time ago people
    decided to live in America
Brawley, E. The chicken
Castro, A. de. The last test
Cather, W.  A son of the Celestial
Dillon, M. Destiny Canal and the private
    eye
Gold, H. Girl getting educated at noon
    on Sunday
Gold, H. The older woman
Gold, H. Song of the first and last beatnik
Gold, H. Waiting for the Forty-one Union
Gores, J. File #2: Stakeout on Page Street
Gores, J. N. Watch for it
Marsh, W. It always comes out dixie

O'Connor, P. F. American Gothic
O'Connor, P. F. My imaginary father
Pronzini, B. Death of a nobody
**Santa Barbara**
Rascoe, J. Yours, and mine
Stern, R. Veni, vidi . . . Wendt
**Santa Clara Valley**
Shipley, M. The tea bowl of Ninsei No-
    mura
**Santa Monica**
Nolan, W. F. Down the long night
A **California** novel. Lindholm, C.
**Caline.** Chopin, K.
**Calisher, Hortense**
    In the absence of angels
        Auchincloss, L. ed. Fables of wit and
            elegance
    The scream on 57th Street
        Elkin, S. ed. Stories from the sixties
The **call.** Barwin, V.
The **call.** Weston, J.
**Call** him Lord. Dickson, G. R.
**Call** it love. Litvinov, I.
**Call** me Joe. Anderson, P.
**Call** me ma. Akens, H. M.
The **call** of Cthulhu. Lovecraft, H. P.
The **call** of the hand. Golding, L.
The **call** of wings. Christie, A.
**Callaghan, Morley**
    All the years of her life
        Metcalf, J. ed. Sixteen by twelve
    Let me promise you
        Stephens, D. ed. Contemporary voices
    A sick call
        Metcalf, J. ed. Sixteen by twelve
**Callahan's** black Cadillacs. Costello, M.
**Callender, Timothy**
    Car drive
        Howes, B. and Smith, G. J. eds. The
            sea-green horse
The **caller** of The Black. Lumley, B.
**Callie.** Jay, B.
**Calling** all stars. Szilard, L.
**Calling** Dr Clockwork. Goulart, R.
**Calliope** and Gherkin and the Yankee
    Doodle thing. Smith, E. E.
The **Callistan** menace. Asimov, I.
**Calthon** and Colmal. Macpherson, J.
**CALVES.** *See* Cattle
**CALVINISM**
    De Vries, P. Good boy
    De Vries, P. Tulip
**Calvino, Italo**
    The Argentine ant
        Calvino, I. The watcher & other stories
    A sign in space
        Knight, D. ed. Tomorrow and tomorrow
    Smog
        Calvino, I. The watcher & other stories
    The watcher
        Calvino, I. The watcher & other stories
**Calvo, Lino Novás-** *See* Novás-Calvo, Lino
**Cambric** tea. Bowen, M.
**CAMBRIDGE, ENGLAND**
**University**
Day, J. W. The dead killed him in his
    own grave
Day, J. W. Sung to his death by dead men

Cambridge is sinking. Clayton, J. J.

**CAMELS**
Kipling, R. How the Camel got his hump
Ottley, R. Bush camels
Pei, M. From the further adventures of Sinbad the sailor

Camels and dromedaries, Clem. Lafferty, R. A.

**CAMERAS**
Clement, H. Sun spot

**CAMORRA**
Conrad, J. Il conde

Camp, L. Sprague de. *See* De Camp, L. Sprague

**CAMP FOLLOWERS**
Achebe, C. Girls at war

**CAMP-MEETINGS.** *See* Revivals

Campaign fever. McGerr, P.

The campaign of Hector Rodriguez. Neugeboren, J.

**CAMPAIGNS, POLITICAL.** *See* Politics—United States

**Campbell, J. F.**
The sea-maiden
Haining, P. ed. The clans of darkness

Campbell, J. Ramsey. *See* Campbell, Ramsey

**Campbell, John W.**
The machine
Elwood, R. and Ghidalia, V. eds. Androids, time machines and blue giraffes
Twilight
Science fiction hall of fame v 1
Silverberg, R. ed. The ends of time
Silverberg, R. ed. The mirror of infinity
*For other stories by this author see* Stuart, Don A.

**Campbell, Ramsey**
At first sight
Campbell, R. Demons by daylight
Cat and mouse
Parry, M. ed. Beware of the cat
Cold print
Derleth, A. ed. Tales of Cthulhu Mythos
Concussion
Campbell, R. Demons by daylight
The enchanted fruit
Campbell, R. Demons by daylight
The end of a summer's day
Campbell, R. Demons by daylight
The Franklyn paragraphs
Campbell, R. Demons by daylight
The guy
Campbell, R. Demons by daylight
The interloper
Campbell, R. Demons by daylight
The lost
Campbell, R. Demons by daylight
Made in Goatswood
Campbell, R. Demons by daylight
Napier Court
Derleth, A. ed. Dark things
The Old Horns
Campbell, R. Demons by daylight
Potential
Campbell, R. Demons by daylight

The second staircase
Campbell, R. Demons by daylight
The sentinels
Campbell, R. Demons by daylight
The stocking
Campbell, R. Demons by daylight

**Campert, Remco**
A trip to Zwolle
Krispyn, E. ed. Modern stories from Holland and Flanders

**CAMPING**
Brautigan, R. A short history of religion in California
Crane, S. The cry of a huckleberry pudding: a dim study of camping experiences
Crane, S. The holler tree
Crane, S. A tent in agony
Dorr, L. Once you were no people
Dorr, L. A slow, soft river
Hall, J. B. God cares, but waits: A transfiguration by vines
Hemingway, E. Big two-hearted river
Hemingway, E. Three shots
Hermann, J. Shebie
Maloney, R. Intimacy
Rinehart, M. R. Rock River fugitive
Thomas, T. The intruder
Welty, E. Moon Lake
*See also* Camps, Summer; Outdoor life

**Campo, Vincent**
Raymond, his wife, and his women
Voices of Brooklyn

**CAMPS, SUMMER**
Ahlin, L. Polluted zone
Ansell, J. Thought of love on a summer afternoon
Delapp, T. Escape from camp 9
Dillon, M. Baby Perpetua
Haimowitz, B. Zucker

**Camus, Albert**
The guest
Foff, A. and Knapp, D. eds. Story
Kahn, J. ed. Hanging by a thread
Larson, C. R. ed. Prejudice: 20 tales of oppression and liberation
Morton, M. ed. Voices from France
The stranger
Hamalian, L. and Volpe, E. L. eds. Eleven modern short novels

Can you explain love? Ribalow, H. U.

Can you feel anything when I do this? Sheckley, R.

**CANA, MARRIAGE IN.** *See* Marriage in Cana (Miracle)

**CANADA**
Bailey, D. A bauble for Bernice
Fourteen stories high; 14 stories
Hoch, E. D. The impossible "impossible crime"
Laurence, M. A bird in the house; 8 stories
MacEwen, G. House of the whale
MacFadden, D. Who can avoid a place?
Marriott, A. Stella
Sandman, J. One for the road
Wiebe, R. Where is the voice coming from?

**CANONIZATION**
Pangborn, E. My brother Leopold
**CANONS.** *See* Catholic priests; Clergy
**Can't** we come back yesterday? Ansell, J.
The **Canterville** ghost. Wilde, O.
**CANTORS**
Des Périers, B. The cantor's stew
Peretz, I. L. Neilah in Gehenna
The **cantor's** stew. Des Périers, B.
The **canvas** bag. Nourse, A. E.
The **canvasback** jury. Brister, B.
**Canzoneri, Robert**
Barbed wire
The Best American short stories, 1971
The Best little magazine fiction, 1971
Canzoneri, R. Barbed wire, and other stories
City of heaven
Canzoneri, R. Barbed wire, and other stories
The extended hand
Canzoneri, R. Barbed wire, and other stories
Freddy-bear
Canzoneri, R. Barbed wire, and other stories
The harp of the winds
Canzoneri, R. Barbed wire, and other stories
Moffett
Canzoneri, R. Barbed wire, and other stories
The peak of the ritual
Canzoneri, R. Barbed wire, and other stories
The poetess
Canzoneri, R. Barbed wire, and other stories
The prodigal uncle
Canzoneri, R. Barbed wire, and other stories
The shadow of death
Canzoneri, R. Barbed wire, and other stories
Sunday preacher
Canzoneri, R. Barbed wire, and other stories
Under the black umbrella
Canzoneri, R. Barbed wire, and other stories
A very pretty girl
Canzoneri, R. Barbed wire, and other stories
The weight of feathers
Canzoneri, R. Barbed wire, and other stories
**CAPE COD.** *See* Massachusetts—Cape Cod
**Cape** trip. Hemenway, R.
**Čapek, Karel**
The last judgment
Hall, J. B. ed. The realm of fiction
**CAPITAL PUNISHMENT.** *See* Executions and executioners
**CAPITALISM**
Barthelme, D. The rise of capitalism
**CAPITALISTS AND FINANCIERS**
Boulle, P. Interferences
Brunner, J. Factsheet six
Kanin, G. The money man

**Capote, Truman**
A diamond guitar
Fenner, P. R. comp. Desperate moments
Master Misery
Schulman, L. M. ed. The cracked looking glass
Miriam
Abrahams, W. ed. Fifty years of the American short story v 1
Haining, P. ed. The Lucifer society
**CAPS.** *See* Hats
The **Captain.** Crane, S.
**Captain** America. Dawson, F.
**Captain** Descalzo. Fuentes, N.
**Captain** Honario Harpplayer, R. N. Harrison, H.
**Captain** Nemo's last adventure. Nesvadba, J.
The **captain** of the "Camel." Bierce, A.
**Captain** Pink. Lang, A.
**Captain** Rufus Coate. Nye, R.
**CAPTAINS.** *See* Shipmasters; also subhead: Officers, under the branches of armed forces of various countries, e.g. U.S. Army—Officers
The **captain's** gift. Stafford, J.
**CAPTAINS OF SHIPS.** *See* Shipmasters
The **captive.** Singer, I. B.
**Captive.** Soto, P. J.
The **captured** cross-section. Breuer, M. J.
The **captured** shadow. Fitzgerald, F. S.
**CAR DEALERS.** *See* Automobile industry and trade
**Car** drive. Callender, T.
**CAR SALESMAN.** *See* Automobile industry and trade
**Car** sinister. Wolfe, G.
A **car**-splashing. Premchand
**CARACAS.** *See* Venezuela—Caracas
**CARAVAGGIO, MICHELANGELO MERISI DA**
Ayrton, M. Tenebroso
**CARAVANS**
Smith, C. A. Told in the desert
**CARD-SHARPERS.** *See* Gambling
The **cardboard** screen. Summers, H.
**CARDINALS.** *See* Catholic priests
**Cardoso, Onelio Jorge**
It's a long time ago
Cohen, J. M. ed. Latin American writing today
**CARDS**
Bichsel, P. The game of cards
*See also* names of card games, e.g. Bridge (Game); Poker (Game)
**Cards** with a stranger. Aldridge, H. R.
**Cardwell, Guy A.**
Did you once see Shelley?
Prize stories, 1971: The O. Henry Awards
A **cargo** of cat. Bierce, A.
**Cargo** of gold. Rawlings, C.
**CARHOPS.** *See* Servants—Waitresses
**CARIBBEAN AREA**
Bowles, P. Pages from Cold Point
Henry, O. The lotus and the bottle
Henry, O. Masters of arts
Henry, O. Ships
Henry, O. Shoes

Carr, Jess—*Continued*
Two for the show
　　Carr, J.　A creature was stirring, and other stories
Carr, John
The Botleas
　Intro #2
Carr, John Dickson
The footprint in the sky
　　Hitchcock, A.　Alfred Hitchcock's Daring detectives
　　Mystery Writers of America. Crime without murder
The gentleman from Paris
　　McComas, J. F. ed. Crimes and misfortunes
　　Queen, E. ed. Ellery Queen's The golden 13
The other hangman
　　Mystery Writers of America. Dear dead days
　　　*For another story by this author see* Dickson, Carter
Carr, Mary Jane
Traps of quicksand
　　Lucia, E. ed. This land around us
Carr, Terry
The answer
　　Elwood, R. ed. Tomorrow's alternatives
City of yesterday
　　Silverberg, R. ed. Beyond control
The Dance of the Changer and the Three
　　Nebula award stories 4
　　Silverberg, R. ed. Deep space
Hop-friend
　　Knight, D. ed.　A pocketful of stars
Ozymandias
　　Ellison, H. ed. Again, dangerous visions
Saving the world
　　Elwood, R. and Kidd, V. eds. Saving worlds
Stanley toothbrush
　　Silverberg, R. ed. Other dimensions
Touchstone
　　Carr, T. ed. Into the unknown
The winds at Starmont
No mind of man
Le carrefour. Spielberg, P.
CARRIAGES AND CARTS
Phanishwarnath "Renu." The third vow
CARRICK-ON-SHANNON.　*See* Ireland—Carrick-On-Shannon
Carrier, J. G.
A strangeness of habit, a twist of mind
　　New Canadian stories, 1973
Carrier. Sheckley, R.
A carrier of stones. Brown, G. M.
Carrighar, Sally
The cutthroat trout
　　Corodimas, P. ed.　In trout country
Carrion spring. Stegner, W.
Carroll, Lewis
The Cheshire Cat
　　Montgomery, J. ed. The world's best cat stories
　　Same as: Alice and the Cheshire Cat, listed in the 1959-1963 supplement
Pig and pepper

Minot, S. and Wilson, R. eds. Three stances of modern fiction
CARS (AUTOMOBILES) *See* Automobiles
Carskadon, T. R.
Nigger schoolhouse
　　Burnett, W. ed. Black hands on a white face
Carsten Curator. Storm, T.
Carter, Lin
The dweller in the tomb
　　Derleth, A. ed. Dark things
Shaggai
　　Derleth, A. ed. Dark things
Carter, Rubin
Return of the Kid
　　Andrews, F. E. and Dickens, A. eds. Voices from the big house
CARTER. *See* Truck drivers
CARTHAGE
Anderson, P. Delenda est
Cartmill, Cleve
The green cat
　　Necker, C. ed. Supernatural cats
No news today
　　Haining, P. ed. The Satanists
CARTOONISTS
Stout, R. The Squirt and the monkey
CARTOONS AND CARICATURES.　*See* Moving picture cartoons
CARTS. *See* Carriages and carts
The cartwheel. Skármeta, A.
Carver, Raymond
Neighbors
　　Lish, G. ed. The secret life of our times: new fiction from Esquire
A night out
　　The Best little magazine fiction, 1971
Sixty acres
　　The Best little magazine fiction, 1970
What is it?
　　Lish, G. ed. The secret life of our times: new fiction from Esquire
　　Prize stories, 1973: The O. Henry Awards
Cary, Joyce
The rebel
　　Fitz Gerald, G. ed. Modern satiric stories
A special occasion
　　Kraus, R. and Wiegand, W. eds. Student's choice
A caryatid. Brackenbury, R.
CASABLANCA. *See* Morocco—Casablanca
Casablanca. Disch, T. M.
Casares, Adolfo Bioy- *See* Bioy-Casares, Adolfo
Case, David
The cell
　　Case, D. The cell
The dead end
　　Case, D. The cell
The hunter
　　Case, D. The cell
Case, Robert Ormond
Hard money
　　Lucia, E. ed. This land around us
Case, Victoria
When the Indians came
　　Lucia, E. ed. This land around us

**Case.** Deck, J.
The **case** for the defence. Greene, G.
A **case** for the U.N. DeFord, M. A.
The **case** of Janissary. Morrison, A.
The **case** of Laker, absconded. Morrison, A.
A **case** of sacred and profane love. Margaret of Navarre
The **case** of the crimson kiss. Gardner, E. S.
The **case** of the crying swallow. Gardner, E. S.
The **case** of the double husband. Lawrence, M.
The **case** of the Dow twins. Mitchell, E. P.
The **case** of the flaming phantom. *See* Futrelle, J. The flaming phantom
The **case** of the irate witness. Gardner, E. S.
The **case** of the missing photographs. Eaton, C. E.
The **case** of the "Southern Arrow." Isla, L. A.
The **case** of the travelling corpse. Edwards, A.
The **case** of the uncut corpse. Brennan, J. P.
The **case** of the vanishing spinster. McLean, A. C.
**Casely-Hayford, Gladys Mae**
   Shadow of darkness
      Tibbets, A. B. ed. Boys are boys
**Casey** Agonistes. McKenna, R.
**CASHIERS.** *See* Banks and banking
The **cask** of Amantillado. Poe, E. A.
The **casket**-demon. Leiber, F.
**Casper, Leonard**
   Aflame; in flower
      Casper, L.    A lion unannounced
   The balancing act
      Casper, L.    A lion unannounced
   Deep country part
      Casper, L.    A lion unannounced
   Drink to private gods
      Casper, L.    A lion unannounced
   Face like an ikon
      Casper, L.    A lion unannounced
   The fifth wall
      Casper, L.    A lion unannounced
   Hard, in these fastnesses
      Casper, L.    A lion unannounced
   Least common denominator
      Casper, L.    A lion unannounced
   A lion unannounced
      Casper, L.    A lion unannounced
   A nest of boxes
      Casper, L.    A lion unannounced
   Sense of direction
      Casper, L.    A lion unannounced
   Silent outcry, sleep
      Casper, L.    A lion unannounced
   The tumbler
      Casper, L.    A lion unannounced
The **casquemoors.** Veiga, J. J.
**Cassill, R. V.**
   Happy marriage
      Hall, J. B. ed. The realm of fiction
   The invention of the airplane
      The Best little magazine fiction, 1971
   The rationing of love
      New American Review no. 3
**Cast** the first stone. Naylor, P. R.
The **castaway.** Fritch, C. E.

**CASTAWAYS.** *See* Shipwrecks and castaways
**CASTE**
   Asimov, I. Strikebreaker
                    **India**
      *See* Untouchables
**Castell, Daphne**
   Come up and see me
      McCaffrey, A. ed. Alchemy and academe
The **castle** on the crag. Wyal, P.
**Castle** scene wtih penitents. Aldiss, B. W.
**CASTLES**
   Aldiss, B. W. Castle scene with penitents
   Maclagen, D. Dr Black's castle
**CASTOR AND POLLUX**
   Ayrton, M. Enigma
**Castro, Adolphe de**
   The electric executioner
      Lovecraft, H. P. ed. The horror in the museum, and other revisions
   The last test
      Lovecraft, H. P. ed. The horror in the museum, and other revisions
**CASTS, PLASTER.** *See* Plaster casts
The **cat.** Gascar, P.
**Cat** and mouse. Campbell, R.
The **cat** and the child. Aberconway, C.
The **cat,** "I Am." Heard, G.
The **Cat** in the Hat for President. Coover, R.
The **cat** man. Liggett, B.
**Cat** people. King, F.
The **cat** that walked by himself. Kipling, R.
The **cat** that was fey. Riggs, A. S.
**Cat** without a name. Baker, D. V.
**CATACOMBS**
   Poe, E. A. The cask of Amontillado
A **catastrophe.** Premchand
**CATASTROPHES.** *See* Disasters
The **catbird** seat. Thurber, J.
The **catch.** Dickson, G. R.
The **catch.** Fielding, G.
**Catch** that Martian. Knight, D.
The **catechist.** Barthelme, D.
**Catfish.** Peterkin, J.
The **cathedral** builder. Auchincloss, L.
**CATHEDRALS**
                  **England**
   James, M. R. An episode of Cathedral history
              **New York (City)**
   Auchincloss, L. The cathedral builder
**Cather, Willa**
   The affair at Grover Station
      Cather, W. Willa Cather's Collected short fiction, 1892-1912
   Ardessa
      Cather, W. Uncle Valentine, and other stories
   Behind the Singer Tower
      Cather, W. Willa Cather's Collected short fiction, 1892-1912
   The Bohemian girl
      Cather, W. Willa Cather's Collected short fiction, 1892-1912
   The bookkeeper's wife
      Cather, W. Uncle Valentine, and other stories

Chang, Eileen—*Continued*
  The golden cangue
    Hsia, C. T. ed. Twentieth-century Chinese stories
Chang, T'ien-i
  Spring Breeze
    Hsia, C. T. ed. Twentieth-century Chinese stories
A change of air. Gold, I.
A change of heart. Jewett, S. O.
A change of heart. Stewart, J. I. M.
A change of plan. Purdy, K.
A change of plans. Naylor, P. R.
CHANGE OF SEX
  Delany, S. R. Aye, and Gomorrah
  Keller, D. H. The feminine metamorphosis
  Scortia, T. N. Flowering Narcissus
Change over. Goulart, R.
Changed. Meacock, N.
CHANTRAINE, ANNE DE
  Mallet-Joris, F. Anne
CHAPEL HILL. *See* North Carolina—Chapel Hill
Chapman, Steve
  Burger Creature
    Orbit 12
  Testing . . . one, two, three, four
    Analog 8
A chapter of revelation. Anderson, P.
CHARACTERS AND CHARACTERISTICS IN LITERATURE
  Asimov, I. Author! Author!
Charcoal. Scott, D. C.
The charge at Soissons. Thomason, J. W.
CHARITIES
  Crane, S. The men in the storm
  Deutsch, A. H. Mission to Ghana
  Holmes, E. M. Town office
  Kipling, R. The record of Badalia Herodsfoot
  Parker, D. Song of the shirt, 1941
  Weaver, G. Haskell hooked on the northern Cheyenne
CHARITY
  Grebanier, B. D. N. Life began today
  Jewett, S. O. The spur of the moment
  Schwimmer, W. Christmas on Rush Street
    *See also* Fund raising
Charity. Nissenson, H.
Charivari. Hawkes, J.
CHARLATANS. *See* Quacks and quackery
CHARLEMAGNE
  Pei, M. The bones of Charlemagne
Charles Ashmore's trail. Bierce, A.
Charles Axis. Cohen, L.
Charlotte. Phillips, P. R.
CHARMS
  De Valera, S. The fairies' revenge
  Gbadamossi, R. A. In the beginning
  The Vampire cat
Charney, David H.
  Mommy loves ya
    Elwood, R. ed. Tomorrow's alternatives
Charnock, Graham
  The Chinese boxes
    Orbit 8

Charteris, Leslie
  The wicked cousin
    Hitchcock, A. ed. Alfred Hitchcock's Daring detectives
CHARWOMEN. *See* Servants—Cleaning women
Charyn, Jerome
  Farewell! . . . Farewell! . . .
    Lewis, J. D. ed. Tales of our people
  The man who grew younger
    Charyn, J. ed. The single voice
    Ribalow, H. U. ed. My name aloud
  Sing, Shaindele, sing
    McCrindle, J. F. ed. Stories from the Transatlantic Review
Chase, Mary Ellen
  Hannah and Benjamin Stevens
    Westbrook, P. D. ed. Seacoast and upland: a New England anthology
Chase, Virginia
  The nut
    Rosmond, B. comp. Today's stories from Seventeen
The chase. Moravia, A.
The chaser. Collier, J.
Chasm of monsters. Keller, D. H.
CHASTITY
  Brautigan, R. The betrayed kingdom
  Leskov, N. Superfluous mother love
CHASTITY BELTS
  Linklater, E. The Crusader's key
Chatain, Robert
  The adventure of the mantises
    Gulassa, C. M. ed. The fact of fiction
    New American Review no. 7
  On the perimeter
    New American Review no. 13
CHATTERTON, THOMAS
  Nye, R. Mr Benjamin
The cheat. O'Connor, F.
Cheated. Strindberg, A.
CHEATING. *See* Swindlers and swindling
CHEATING (EDUCATION)
  Brittain, W. Mr Strang finds the answers
Check! Mrozek, S.
Cheesy, baby! Holmes, R. E.
Cheever, John
  Artemis, the honest well digger
    Cheever, J. The world of apples
  The brigadier and the golf widow
    Satin, J. ed. Reading literature
  The chimera
    Cheever, J. The world of apples
  The embarkment for Cythera
    Abrahams, W. ed. Fifty years of the American short story v 1
  The enormous radio
    Harrison, H. ed. The light fantastic
    Thune, E. and Prigozy, R. eds. Short stories: a critical anthology
  The fourth alarm
    Cheever, J. The world of apples
  The geometry of love
    Cheever, J. The world of apples
  The jewels of the Cabots
    The Best American short stories, 1973
    Cheever, J. The world of apples
    Prize stories, 1973: The O. Henry Awards

**Chekhov, Anton—***Continued*

The Princess
  Chekhov, A. The Oxford Chekhov v5
The sinner from Toledo
  Chekhov, A. The sinner from Toledo,
    and other stories
A stage manager under the sofa
  Chekhov, A. The sinner from Toledo,
    and other stories
The story of a commercial venture
  Chekhov, A. The Oxford Chekhov v6
The student
  Davis, R. G. ed. Ten modern masters
The Swedish match
  Chekhov, A. The sinner from Toledo,
    and other stories
A tale without a title
  Chekhov, A. The sinner from Toledo,
    and other stories
Tears the world does not see
  Chekhov, A. The sinner from Toledo,
    and other stories
  Same as: Tears the world sees not,
    listed in 1959-1963 supplement
Terror
  Chekhov, A. The Oxford Chekhov v6
Thieves
  Chekhov, A. The Oxford Chekhov v5
Three years
  Chekhov, A. Seven short novels
The trick
  Chekhov, A. The sinner from Toledo,
    and other stories
  Same as: The little trick, entered in
    1964-1968 supplement
A trifle from real life
  Davis, R. G. ed. Ten modern masters
  Same as: Trifle from life, listed in main
    volume; Trifling occurrence, listed in
    main volume
Volodya
  Chekhov, A. The sinner from Toledo,
    and other stories
Ward Number Six
  Chekhov, A. The Oxford Chekhov v6
  Chekhov, A. Seven short novels
The witch
  Chekhov, A. The sinner from Toledo,
    and other stories
The woman who had no prejudices
  Minot, S. and Wilson, R. eds. Three
    stances of modern fiction
A woman's kingdom
  Chekhov, A. Seven short novels
The women
  Chekhov, A. The sinner from Toledo,
    and other stories
**Chekkash.** Gorky, M.
**CHELM.** *See* Poland—Chelm
The **chemical** formula of destiny. Nes-
  vadba, J.
**CHEMICAL WARFARE**
  Barthelme, D. Report
    *See also* Gases, Asphyxiating and
    poisonous
**CHEMISTS**
  Allingham, M. They never get caught
  Asimov, I. The magnificent possession

Greene, G. When Greek meets Greek
Tushnet, L.    A plague of cars
Yamamoto, M. The blue rug
**CHEOPS, KING OF EGYPT**
  Mencken, H. L. The visionary
**Chernoff, Sanford**
  Not my animal
    New Directions in prose and poetry 21
The **cherries.** Durrell, L.
**Cherry, Kelly**
  Covenant
    The Best American short stories, 1972
**Chesbro, George C.**
  Broken pattern
    Best detective stories of the year, 1973
The **Cheshire** Cat. Carroll, L.
**Chestnutt, Charles W.**
  The goophered grapevine
    James, C. L. ed. From the roots
    Long, R. A. and Collier, E. W. eds.
      Afro-American writing v 1
  The gray wolf's ha'nt
    James, C. L. ed. From the roots
  Po' Sandy
    Margolies, E.    A native sons reader
    Turner, D. T. ed. Black American
      literature
  The sheriff's children
    Kissin, E. H. ed. Stories in black and
      white
  The web of circumstance
    Hall, J. B. ed. The realm of fiction
**CHESS**
  Ballard, J. G. End game
  Holst, S. Chess
  Mrozek, S. Check!
  Trevino, E. B. de. The secret of the wall
**Chess.** Holst, S.
**Chester, Alfred**
  As I was going up the stair
    Simon, J. ed. Fourteen for now
  The foot
    New American Review no. 9
  In praise of Vespasian
    Elkin, S. ed. Stories from the sixties
  Ismael
    McCrindle, J. F. ed. Stories from the
      Transatlantic Review
  Safari
    New American Review no. 15
**Chester** forgets himself. Wodehouse, P. G.
**Chesterton, G. K.**
  The angry street
    Haining, P. ed. The Lucifer society
  The invisible man
    Dickinson, S. ed. The drugged cornet,
      and other mystery stories
**CHESTS (FURNITURE)**
  Doyle, Sir A. C. The striped chest
**CHEWING-GUM**
  Bondarenko, W. C. The big pencil
  Steinbeck, J. The Affair at 7, rue de M—
**CHEYENNE INDIANS**
  Overholser, W. D. Beecher Island
        Treaties
  Prebble, J. My great aunt Appearing Day
**CHICAGO.** *See* Illinois—Chicago
The **Chicago** heiress. Ashdown, C.

Chickamauga. Bierce, A.
**CHICKAMAUGA, BATTLE OF, 1863**
 Bierce, A. Chickamauga
The **chicken.** Brawley, E.
The **Chicken.** Lispector, C.
**Chicken.** Sillitoe, A.
**Chicken** catchers. Ford, R.
The **chicken**-god. Yevtushenko, Y.
**Chicken** Hawk's dream. Young, A.
The **chicken** which became a rat. Drake, A.
**CHICKENS**
 Lispector, C. The chicken
 Phillips, P. R. Charlotte
  *See also* Eggs; Poultry; Roosters
**Chike's** school days. Achebe, C.
The **child.** Ivanov, V.
The **child.** Neugeboren, J.
The **child.** Strindberg, A.
**CHILD ABUSE.** *See* Cruelty to children
The **child** and the water-tap. Kassam, S.
The **Child-God** dance. Yurick, S.
**CHILD MARRIAGE**
 Toer, P. A. Inem
**CHILD MOLESTING**
 Wilson, A.   A visit in bad taste
**Child** of the century. West, J.
**CHILD PRODIGIES.** *See* Children, Gifted
The **child** watcher. Harrison, E.
The **child** who favored Daughter. Walker, A.
A **child** with a very old head. Deutsch-
 man, B.
**CHILDBIRTH**
 Aidoo, A. A. The message
 Anand, M. R. Birth
 Betts, D. Still life with fruit
 Casper, L. Least common denominator
 Dorman, S. The living end
 Ford, J. H. The bitter bread
 Jay, B. Callie
 Kemal, O. Baby born in the field
 Khamsing, S. The plank
 Landolfi, T. Stefano's two sons
 Lau, S. Grandma takes charge
 Laurence, M. To set our house in order
 Maltz, A. With laughter
 Mayer, T.   A birth in the Delta
 Orlav, O. My daughter
 Peterkin, J. Over the river
 Schoonover, S. The star blanket
 Stuart, J. Maybelle's first-born
 Suter, J. F. Doctor's orders
 Sutiasumarga, R. On the outskirts of the
  city
 Yurick, S. "And not in utter naked-
  ness . . ."
  *See also* Pregnancy
**Childe** Roland. Theroux, A.
**CHILDHOOD.** *See* Children
**Childhood** is not forever. Farrell, J. T.
**Childhood** memories. *See* Autobiographical
 stories
The **childhood** of the human hero. Emsh-
 willer, C.
**CHILDLESS COUPLES.** *See* Marriage,
 Childless
The **childmaster.** Walsh, J. P. and Crossley-
 Holland, K.

**CHILDREN**
 Bambara, T. C. The hammer man
 Bambara, T. C. Happy birthday
 Bambara, T. C. The lesson
 Böll, H. Lohengrin's death
 Bosem, H. The third hill
 Bradbury, R.   I sing the Body Electric!
 Brennan, M. The children are there, try-
  ing not to laugh
 Brennan, M. In and out of never-never
  land
 Bukowski, C. The fiend
 Bulgakov, M. Psalm
 Cary, J.   A special occasion
 Casper, L. The tumbler
 Cather, W. The way of the world
 Christie, A. The lamp
 Coover, R. The gingerbread house
 Cortázar, J. Silvia
 Crane, S.   A dark-brown dog
 Crane, S.   A great mistake
 Crane, S. An ominous baby
 Cullinan, E. The time of Adam
 DeFord, M. A. The monster
 De La Mare, W. The giant
 Enright, E.   A Christmas tree for Lydia
 Enright, E. The playground
 Etchison, D. Damechild
 Ewing, Mrs. Our field
 Farjeon, E. The glass peacock
 Faulkner, W. That evening sun
 Fielding, G. Bravery
 Gaines, E. J.   A long day in November
 Gaskell, E. The old nurse's story
 Grahame, K. Its walls were as of jasper
 Henderson, D. Allison
 Henderson, D. Christmas
 Henderson, D. Mother and the town
 Henderson, Z. Anything Box
 Hensley, J. L. and Ellison, H. Rodney
  Parish for hire
 Hoydal, K. Summer eve at "Rockall"
 Hunter, K. All around the mulberry tree
 Hunter, K. Mom Luby and the social
  worker
 Hutsalo, Y.   A sea story
 Jacobson, D. Beggar my neighbor
 Jewett, S. O. The Becket girls' tree
 Kim, Y. I. Till the candle blew out
 Kotowska, M. The bridge to the other side
 Kotowska, M. The city at night
 Kotowska, M. Everyone grows up
 Kotowska, M. The payment will be made
  on Sunday
 Kotowska, M. Still life with ice cream
 Kotowska, M. Test games
 Kotowska, M. Twelve feet to heaven
 Kotowska, M. Winning
 Kotowska, M. Words
 Lafferty, R. A. "Enfants terribles"
 Lafferty, R. A. The transcendent tigers
 Lagerkvist, P. The children's campaign
 Lardas, K. The broken wings
 Lavin, M. The sand castle
 Lavin, M. Tomb of an ancestor
 Litvinov, I. Apartheid
 McCarthy, M. The unspoiled reaction
 Mackenzie, C. No. 25 to be let or sold
 McKern, R. O. When my father died
 Mansfield, K. The doll's house

CHILE—*Continued*
### Ranch life
*See* Ranch life—Chile
## CHILE, PROVINCIAL AND RURAL
Vallejo, C. On the other side of life and death
## CHILEANS IN THE UNITED STATES
Skármeta, A. The cartwheel
**Chilson, Robert**
In his image
Analog 8
The **chimaera.** Moravia, A.
The **chimera.** Cheever, J.
The **chimney** sweep. Singer, I. B.
## CHIMNEY-SWEEPS
Landolfi, T. Wedding night
Singer, I. B. The chimney sweep
## CHIMPANZEES
Leinster, M. Keyhole
Lugones, L. Yzur
Ullian, R.   A snag in the harp
## CHINA
Birch, C. ed. Anthology of Chinese literature v2; 12 stories
Kotzwinkle, W. Tiger Bridge
Li, Ju-chen. In the country of women
P'u, Sung-ling. The Rakshas and the sea market
Sié, Cheou-kang. A butterfly's dream & other Chinese tales; 12 stories
Sié, Cheou-kang. Vinegar
Thomason, J. W. Sergeant Bridoon of the Horse Marines
   *See also* Mongolia
### Early to 1643
Ch'ü, Yu.   A record of the Land of the Blessed
Gulik, R. van. Judge Dee at work; 8 stories
The Jade Kuan-yin
Lamb, H. The White Khan
Ma, Chung-hsi. The wolf of Chung-shan
Wu, Ch'eng-en. The temptation of Saint Pigsy
### 1900-date
Branson, R. The red-headed murderess
Buck, P. S. The courtyards of peace
Buck, P. S. Dagger in the dark
Buck, P. S. Going home
Buck, P. S. Letter home
Lee, Yu-hwa. The last rite
Lu, Hsün. Benediction
Lu, Hsün. A happy family
Lu, Hsün, Selected stories of Lu Hsün; 18 stories
Shih, Ming. Fragment from a lost diary
Spinrad, N. The last hurrah of the Golden Horde
Wang, T'ieh. The smashing of the Dragon King
### Farm life
*See* Farm life—China
### Peasant life
*See* Peasant life—China
### Peking
Lu, Hsün. An incident

Lu, Hsün. Regret for the past
Thomason, J. W. Love story of a Marine
Thomason, J. W. Mixed marriage
Thomason, J. W. The Sergeant and the siren
Thomason, J. W. The Sergeant and the spy
### Shanghai
Chang, E. The bethrothal of Yindi
Chang, E. The golden cangue
## CHINA, PROVINCIAL AND RURAL
Chang, T'ien-i. Spring Breeze
Lao, H.   A country boy quits school
Lau, S. Grandma takes charge
Lu, Hsün. The divorce
Lu, Hsün. In the wine shop
Lu, Hsün. Kung I-Chi
Lu, Hsün. A madman's diary
Lu, Hsün. Medicine
Lu, Hsün. The misanthrope
Lu, Hsün. My old home
Lu, Hsün. The New Year's sacrifice
Lu, Hsün. Soap
Lu, Hsün. Storm in a teacup
Lu, Hsün. Tomorrow
Lu, Hsün. The true story of Ah Q
Mao, Tun. Spring silkworms
P'u, Sung-ling. Ying-ning
Shen, Ts'ung-wen. Daytime
Shen, Ts'ung-wen. Quiet
Sun, Hsi-chen. Ah Ao
Yüan, Mei. Three ghost stories
## CHINA (PORCELAIN) *See* Antique dealers
The **Chinaman.** Babel, I.
## CHINATOWN. *See* Chinese in the United States—New York (City); Chinese in the United States—San Francisco
**Chinatown** evening. Bond, S.
## CHINESE
Aldiss, B. W. Lambeth Blossom
Derry, V. The image of fear
Lusin. Our story of Ah Q
Malraux, A. March 21, 1927
The **Chinese** boxes. Charnock, G.
## CHINESE IN AFRICA
La Guma, A.   A matter of taste
## CHINESE IN BORNEO
Shui, Ching. Hi Lili hi Li . . .
## CHINESE IN ENGLAND
Burke, T. Beryl, the Croucher and the rest of England
Burke, T. The bird
Burke, T. The Chink and the child
Burke, T. The father of Yoto
Burke, T. Gracie Goodnight
Burke, T. Limehouse nights; 14 stories
Burke, T. The paw
Burke, T. The sign of the lamp
Burke, T. Tai Fu and Pansy Greers
Theroux, A. Mrs Proby gets hers
## CHINESE IN GERMANY
Weaver, G. The salesman from Hong Kong
## CHINESE IN JAPAN
Yü, Ta-fu. Sinking
## CHINESE IN NEW YORK (CITY) *See* Chinese in the United States—New York (City)

**CHINESE IN RUSSIA**
Babel, I. The Chinaman
Bulgakov, M.  A Chinese tale
**CHINESE IN SAN FRANCISCO.** *See Chi*-
nese in the United States—San Fran-
cisco
**CHINESE IN THE UNITED STATES**
Bierce, A. The haunted valley
Johnson, D. An apple, an orange
Maul, M. Pao-yu and the Grand Duchess
Sharp, M. The amethyst cat
      **New York (City)**
Bond, S. Chinatown evening
Buck, P. S. The good deed
Di Donato, P. New York Chinese world
Hoagland, E. Kwan's Coney Island
Pai, Hsien-yung. Li T'ung: a Chinese girl
   in New York
      **San Francisco**
Cather, W. The conversion of Sum Loo
Cather, W.  A son of the Celestial
Gardner, E. S. Fingers of Fong
**CHINESE LANGUAGE**
     **Study and teaching**
Maul, M. Pao-yu and the Grand Duchess
**CHINESE MERCENARIES**
Little, L. Out with the lions
**CHINESE OPERA.** *See* Opera, Chinese
**Chinese** puzzle. Wyndham, J.
A **Chinese** tale. Bulgakov, M.
**Ching Shui.** *See* Shui, Ching
**Ching** witch! Rocklynne, R.
The **Chink** and the child. Burke, T.
**Chinoiserie.** McCloy, H.
**CHIPPEWA INDIANS**
Swan, S. M. To Charley Iron Necklace
   (wherever he is)
**Chippings** with a chisel. Hawthorne, N.
**CHOCOLATE**
Nemerov, H. Bon bons
**Chocolate.** Tarasov-Rodyonov, A.
The **choice.** Deming, R.
**Choice** and responsibility. Steinbeck, J.
**Choice** grain. Leskov, N.
The **choice** of Amyntas. Maugham, W. S.
A **choice** of butchers. Trevor, W.
**CHOIRS (MUSIC)**
Clarke, A. An Easter carol
Phillips, R. Songs of three seasons
**CHOLERA**
Frishman, D. Three who ate
Kipling, R. The daughter of the regiment
Kipling, R. Without benefit of clergy
**Choosing.** Kotowska, M.
**Chopin, Kate**
Athénaïse
   Chopin, K. The awakening, and other
   stories
The awakening
   Chopin, K. The awakening, and other
   stories
Azélie
   Chopin, K. The awakening, and other
   stories
La belle Zoraïde
   Chopin, K. The awakening, and other
   stories

Beyond the bayou
   Chopin, K. The awakening, and other
   stories
Caline
   Chopin, K. The awakening, and other
   stories
Désirée's baby
   Chopin, K. The awakening, and other
   stories
The kiss
   Chopin, K. The awakening, and other
   stories
A lady of Bayou St John
   Chopin, K. The awakening, and other
   stories
Madame Célestin's divorce
   Chopin, K. The awakening, and other
   stories
The maid of Saint Philippe
   Chopin, K. The awakening, and other
   stories
Miss McEnders
   Chopin, K. The awakening, and other
   stories
Mrs Mobry's reason
   Chopin, K. The awakening, and other
   stories
Nég Créol
   Chopin, K. The awakening, and other
   stories
A night in Acadie
   Chopin, K. The awakening, and other
   stories
A no-account Creole
   Chopin, K. The awakening, and other
   stories
A respectable woman
   Chopin, K. The awakening, and other
   stories
A shameful affair
   Chopin, K. The awakening, and other
   stories
The story of an hour
   Chopin, K. The awakening, and other
   stories
A visit to Avoyelles
   Chopin, K. The awakening, and other
   stories
Wiser than a god
   Chopin, K. The awakening, and other
   stories
**Chopin.** Stewart, N.
**CHORAL MUSIC**
Greenberg, J. The Lucero requiem
**CHORAL SINGING.** *See* Choral music
The **chosen.** Carpentier, A.
The **chosen.** Wilhelm, K.
The **chosen** one. Davies, R.
**Chou, Shu-jên.** *See* Lu, Hsün
**Chozen** at four A.M. Whalen, T.
**Chrisoula.** Petrakis, H. M.
**Christ** on rollerskates. Bukowski, C.
**Christabel's** crystal. Wells, C.
**CHRISTENING**
Maupassant, G. de. The Christening
The **Christening.** Maupassant, G. de

CHRISTMAS—*Continued*
  O'Connor, F. Christmas morning
  O'Donnell, M. K.  A celebration of light
  Paley, G. The loudest voice
  Patton, F. G. First principles
  Roberts, K. Weihnachtabend
  Schwimmer, W. Christmas on Rush Street
  Scott, C. B. Far bella figura
  Siegel, J. The man who believed in Christmas trees
  West, J. Home for Christmas
  Wilson, A.  A flat country Christmas
  Witton, D. The miracle of the Kings
  Zobarskas, S. The night before Christmas
    *See also* Jesus Christ—Nativity
Christmas. McGahern, J.
Christmas at Fort Clatsop. Holm, D.
The Christmas cat. Montgomery, J.
Christmas Day in the workhouse. Wilson, A.
A Christmas dinner won in battle. Crane, S.
A Christmas encounter. Naylor, P. R.
Christmas Eve. Marshall, L.
Christmas Eve on Lonesome. Fox, J.
Christmas every day. Böll, H.
Christmas gift. Himes, C.
CHRISTMAS GIFTS. See Christmas; Gifts
A Christmas guest. Jewett, S. O.
Christmas morning. O'Connor, F.
Christmas on Ganymede. Asimov, I.
Christmas on Rush Street. Schwimmer, W.
The Christmas present. Dickson, G. R.
A Christmas present for Uncle Bob. Stuart, J.
CHRISTMAS PRESENTS. See Christmas; Gifts
Christmas song. Hughes, L.
The Christmas spirit. Bennett, D. B.
CHRISTMAS STORIES. See Christmas
A Christmas tale. Mauriac, F.
A Christmas tree and a wedding. Dostoevsky, F.
A Christmas tree for Lydia. Enright, E.
CHRISTMAS TREES
  Böll, H. Christmas every day
  Clingerman, M. The wild wood
  Enright, E.  A Christmas tree for Lydia
  Farjeon, E. The glass peacock
  Hayes, A. H. How a sagebrush became a Christmas tree
  Siegel, J. The man who believed in Christmas trees
  Wakefield, H. R. Lucky's grove
Christopher, John
  Rendezvous
    Burke, J. ed. Tales of unease
Christopher Frame. Swoboda, N. C.
Christopher K°a°p°l°a°n. Rosten, L.
The chronicle of an old rose-tree. Myriveles, S.
Chronicles of a comer. O'Donnell, K. M.
Chronoclasm. Wyndham, J.
Chronopolis. Ballard, J. G.
The chrysanthemums. Steinbeck, J.
Chu, Yo-sup
  My mother and the roomer
    Angoff, C. ed. Stories from The Literary Review

Ch'ü, Yu
  A record of the Land of the Blessed
    Birch, C. ed. Anthology of Chinese literature v2
Chuck Berry, won't you please come home. McCullough, K.
CHURCH ATTENDANCE
  Dawson, F. The vertical fields
  Jewett, S. O. The first Sunday in June
  Linn, M. L. Please listen, Aunt Viney
  Updike, J. The deacon
CHURCH ENTERTAINMENTS
  Blackhurst, W. E. The magic nickel
  Hubbard, L. R. He didn't like cats
  Plath, S. Mothers
CHURCH HISTORY
  **Primitive and early church**
  Walsh, J. P. and Crossley-Holland, K. Thurkell the Tall
Church militant. Greene, G.
CHURCH OF THE BRETHREN
  Drake, R. The stark naked Baptist
  Drake, R. Will the merchant prince's son come down the sawdust trail?
CHURCH SCHOOLS
  Carrier, J. G.  A strangeness of habit, a twist of mind
  Farrell, J. T. Sister
  McGahern, J. The recruiting officer
  O'Connor, P. F. Story hour
  O'Faolain, S. Brainsy
  Rascoe, J.  A line of order
CHURCH SOCIABLES. See Church entertainments
CHURCHES
  Barthelme, D.  A city of churches
  Boyle, P. The window
  Canzoneri, R. The prodigal uncle
  Corvo, F. Baron. About Sampietro and Sampaolo
  Kipling, R. Hal o' the Draft
  Lovecraft, H. P. The haunter of the dark
  Mabry, T. Lula Borrow
  West, J. The heavy stone
Churchill, Winston
  Man overboard
    Haining, P. ed. The Lucifer society
Chute, B. J.
  The legacy
  Insights
Ciao Fabrizio. Steegmuller, F.
The Cicerone. McCarthy, M.
La cigale. Chekhov, A.
CIGARETTES. See Smoking
CIGARS. See Smoking
Cil. Vance, J.
CINCINNATI. See Ohio—Cincinnati
The Cinderella Kid. Roth, H. H.
Cinderella up-to-date. Blackhurst, W. E.
Cindy. Green, B. K.
Čingo, Živko
  From's daughter
    Johnson, B. ed. New writing in Yugoslavia
Cinthio. See Giraldi, G. B.
CIPHER AND TELEGRAPH CODES
  Eisenberg, L. The Pirokin effect
  Harrison, H. The mothballed spaceship

**CIPHERS**
  Young, A. K. Ponsonby and the classic cipher
    *See also* Cryptography
**CIRCE**
  Welty, E. Circe
Circe. Welty, E.
The **circle**. Nabokov, V.
A **circle** in the fire. O'Connor, F.
The **circle** of affection. Scott, D. C.
**Circles**. Hemenway, R.
**Circles** in the sky. Winston, D.
The **circular** ruins. Borges, J. L.
**CIRCUMCISION**
  Babel, I. Karl Yankel
  Ellison, A.   A coupla scalped Indians
  Glanville, B. An enemy
**CIRCUMSTANTIAL EVIDENCE.** *See* Evidence, Circumstantial
**CIRCUS**
  Aichinger, I. The bound man
  Bennett, A. The Sisters Qita
  Böll, H. What a racket
  Brand, T. Don Slow and his electric girl getter
  Burke, T. The cue
  Coover, R. Romance of the thin man and the fat lady
  Coppard, A. E. Silver circus
  Ellen, S. Beidenbauer's flea
  Ellison, H. Big Sam was my friend
  Goldberg, G. J. The Bowditch footnote
  Malamud, B. Talking horse
  Maltz, A. Circus come to town
  O'Connor, F. Androcles and the army
  Robbins, T. Freaks
  Robbins, T. Spurs
  Sienkiewicz, H. Circus!
  Sienkiewicz, H. Sachem
    *See also* Carnival
**Circus!** Sienkiewicz, H.
**Circus** come to town. Maltz, A.
**CIRCUS ENTERTAINERS.** *See* Circus
**CIRCUS PERFORMERS.** *See* Circus
**CITIES AND TOWNS**
  Ambler, E. Spy-haunts of the world
  Barthelme, D. City life
  Blackwood, A. The destruction of Smith
  Hesse, H. The city
  Lafferty, R. A.   A special condition in Summit City
  Laumer, K. The Forbidden City
  Sheckley, R. Aspects of Langranak
  Simak, C. D. City; excerpt
  Spielberg, P. The architecture of the city
    *See also* Collective settlements; Ghost towns; Small town life
**CITIES AND TOWNS, RUINED, EXTINCT, ETC.**
  Bradbury, R. The lost city of Mars
  Reynolds, M. Among the bad baboons
The **city.** Hesse, H.
**City;** excerpt. Simak, C. D.
The **city** at night. Kotowska, M.
**City** boy. Michaels, L.
**CITY LIFE.** *See* Cities and towns
**City** life. Barthelme, D.
**City** lights, city nights. O'Donnell, K. M.

The **city** of builders. Ostaijen, P. van
A **city** of churches. Barthelme, D.
**City** of heaven. Canzoneri, R.
The **City** of Penetrating Light. Disch, T. M.
The **city** of refuge. Fisher, R.
The **City** of the Gone Away. Bierce, A.
**City** of the Seven Winds. Brennan, J. P.
**City** of yesterday. Carr, T.
**CITY TRAFFIC.** *See* Traffic engineering
**CIVIL DISORDERS.** *See* Riots
**CIVIL LIBERTY.** *See* Liberty
**Civil** peace. Achebe, C.
**CIVIL RIGHTS DEMONSTRATIONS.** *See* Negroes—Civil rights
**CIVIL SERVICE**
  Bulgakov, M. Diaboliad
  Chekhov, A. On official business
  Greene, G. Men at work
  Just, W. Three Washington stories: Slayton
  Kemal, Y. The drumming-out
  Yadav, R.   A reminder
  Yashpal. The book of experience
    *See also* Bureaucracy; United States —Officials and employees
**Civil** strife. Carr, E. A.
**CIVIL WAR.** *See* United States—19th century—Civil War
**CIVILIZATION.** *See* Society, Primitive
**Civilization** and its discontents. Roth, P.
**Claiborne, Sybil**
  The great western civilization caper
    Lish, G. ed. The secret life of our times: new fiction from Esquire
**Clair** de lune. *See* Maupassant, G. de. Moonlight
**CLAIRVOYANCE**
  Bierce, A.   A psychological shipwreck
  Brunner, J. Factsheet six
  Brunner, J. The trouble I see
  Cumberland, M. The voice
  Du Maurier, D. Don't look now
  Ellison, H. The very last day of a good woman
  Forester, C. S. The man who didn't ask why
  Nodier, C. Jean-François Bluestockings
  Riggs, A. S. The cat that was fey
  Singer, I. B. The chimney sweep
    *See also* Divination; Fortune-telling
The **clan** of no-name. Crane, S.
**CLANS AND CLAN SYSTEM**
  Linklater, E. The masks of purpose
    *See also* Family life
**CLARE.** *See* Ireland, Provincial and rural— Clare
**CLARINET PLAYERS.** *See* Musicians— Clarinet players
**Clark, Eleanor**
  Responsibility
    Howes, B. and Smith, G. J. eds. The sea-green horse
**Clark, Philip**
  Wheel to wheel
    Fenner, P. R. comp. Where speed is king

Clarke, Austin
  Bonanza 1972 in Toronto
    Clarke, A. When he was free and young
      and he used to wear silks
  The collector
    McCrindle, J. F. ed. Stories from the
      Transatlantic Review
  An Easter carol
    Clarke, A. When he was free and young
      and he used to wear silks
  Four stations in his circle
    Clarke, A. When he was free and young
      and he used to wear silks
  Griff!
    Clarke, A. When he was free and young
      and he used to wear silks
  Hammie and the Black dean
    Clarke, A. When he was free and young
      and he used to wear silks
    New American Review no. 14
  Her name was Reggina
    Clarke, A. When he was free and young
      and he used to wear silks
  An invitation to join
    Clarke, A. When he was free and young
      and he used to wear silks
  Leaving this island place
    Clarke, A. When he was free and young
      and he used to wear silks
  The motor car
    Clarke, A. When he was free and young
      and he used to wear silks
  One among them
    Clarke, A. When he was free and young
      and he used to wear silks
  What happened?
    Larson, C. R. ed. Prejudice: 20 tales of
      oppression and liberation
  When he was free and young and he used
    to wear silks
    Clarke, A. When he was free and young
      and he used to wear silks
Clarke, Desmond
  A boy with a gun
    Angoff, C. ed. Stories from The Literary
      Review
Clarke, James
  Sheriff's son
    Collier, N. ed. Great stories of the West
Clarke, John Henrik
  The boy who painted Christ Black
    Adoff, A. ed. Brothers and sisters
    Larson, C. R. ed. Prejudice: 20 tales of
      oppression and liberation
  Santa Claus is a white man
    James, C. L. ed. From the roots
Clash. Khamsing, S.
Clash by night. O'Donnell, L.
Class. Bukowski, C.
CLASS DISTINCTION
  Aidoo, A. A. For whom things did not
    change
  Chekhov, A.  A woman's kingdom
  Maloney, R.  Harry W. A. Davis, jr.
  Mansfield, K. The doll's house
  Petry, A. The bones of Louella Brown
  Shepherd, J. Daphne Bigelow and the
    spine-chilling saga of the snail-en-
    crusted tinfoil noose

  Slesinger, T. The Friedmans' Annie
  Stern, J. Mister and Miss
  Strindberg, A. The reward of virtue
  Wilson, A. Once a lady
      See also Snobs and snobbishness; So-
      cial status
The class enemy. Beneš, J.
A class of new Canadians. Blaise, C.
The classical annex. Forster, E. M.
Claus, Hugo
  The Black emperor
    Krispyn, E. ed. Modern stories from
      Holland and Flanders
Clay. Joyce, J.
The clay statues. Sié, Cheou-kang
The clay war. Targan, B.
Clayton, John J.
  Cambridge is sinking!
    The Best American short stories, 1973
The clean hands of Vose Millen. Holmes,
  E. M.
CLEANING. See House cleaning
CLEANING WOMEN. See Servants—Clean-
  ing women
CLEANLINESS
  Delattre, P.  A Confucian reprimand
Clearman, Mary
  Lambing out
    Prize stories, 1972: The O. Henry
      Awards
Cleaver, Eldridge
  The flashlight
    The Best American short stories, 1970
    Prize stories, 1971: The O. Henry
      Awards
The clemency of the court. Cather, W.
Clemens, Samuel Langhorne. See Twain,
  Mark
Clement, Hal
  Dust rag
    Asimov, I. ed. Where do we go from
      here?
    Clement, H. Small changes
  Fireproof
    Clement, H. Small changes
  The foundling stars
    Clement, H. Small changes
  Halo
    Clement, H. Small changes
  Lecture demonstration
    Astounding
  The mechanic
    Clement, H. Small changes
  Proof
    Asimov, I. ed. Where do we go from
      here?
  Raindrop
    Clement, H. Small changes
  Sun spot
    Clement, H. Small changes
  "Trojan fall"
    Clement, H. Small changes
  Uncommon sense
    Clement, H. Small changes
Clemons, Walter
  A different thing
    McCrindle, J. F. ed. Stories from the
      Transatlantic Review

## CLOCKS AND WATCHES
Anand, M. R. The gold watch
Ballard, J. G. Chronopolis
Bierce, A. John Bartine's watch
Borchert, W. The kitchen clock
Cecil, H. Perjury
Greenberg, J. Timekeeper
Groubeshlieva, M. Second-hand shop
Gunn, N. M. The clock
Hawthorne, N. The artist of the beautiful
Jones, L. The great clock
Lafferty, R. A. Barnaby's clock
Lumley, B. De Marigny's clock
Powell, J. Coins in the Frascati Fountain
Raphael. The magic watch
Turgenev, I. The watch

Cloete, Stuart
The second nail
Ellery Queen's Mystery Magazine. Ellery Queen's Murder menu

Clone sister. Sargent, P.

CLONES. See Reproduction, Asexual

Clonk clonk. Golding, W.

Close behind him. Wyndham, J.

The closed door. Marshall, L.

The closed window. Benson, A. C.

The closest school. Henderson, Z.

Closing with nature. Rush, N.

Clothe the naked. Parker, D.

Clothes make the man. Keller, G.

## CLOTHING AND DRESS
Andersen, H. The Emperor's new clothes
Cecil, H. Made to measure
Grossman, S. The happy ending
Pritchett, V. S. The cage birds
Singer, I. B. The primper
Stoker, B. Crooken sands
Woolf, V. The new dress

See also individual articles of apparel, e.g. Gloves; Hats; Jackets; Robes; Shirts; etc.

The cloud. Stern, J.
Cloud nine. Gordon, C.
The cloud-sculptors of Coral D. Ballard, J. G.
The clown. Mann, T.

## CLOWNS
Kim, Y. I. They won't crack it open
Klein, N. Pratfalls
The club. Rukeyser, M.

## CLUBS
Asimov, I. The man who never told a lie
Cohen, M. The Monday rhetoric of the Love Club
Crane, S. A night at The Millionaire's Club
Fielding, G. The young bloods
Hunter, K. Guests in the promised land
Jayme, W. N. I will please come to order
O'Hara, J. Pat Collins
Paley, G. In time which made a monkey of us all
Stevenson, R. L. Story of the young man with the cream tarts

Clute Boulay. Scott, D. C.

C'mon you. Wertheim, J.

COACHES. See Buses

## COACHING (ATHLETICS)
Glanville, B. The footballers
Glanville, B. The man behind the goal
Glanville, B. The prodigy

COAL MINERS. See Coal mines and mining

## COAL MINES AND MINING
Griffith, J. Black Goddess
The coal shoveller. Fort, K.

COAST GUARD. See United States. Coast Guard

COASTING. See Sleighing

Coates, Robert M.
In a foreign city
Kahn, J. ed. Trial and error
The law
Fitz Gerald, G. ed. Modern satiric stories

## COATS
Dorman, S. Harry the tailor
Gogol, N. The overcoat

Cobb, Irvin S.
Five hundred dollars reward
Fenner, P. R. comp. Consider the evidence

The cobbler. Shevchuk, V.

COBBLERS. See Shoemakers

## COBRAS
Kipling, R. 'Rikki-tikki-tavi'

Coburn, Anthony
The tale of the fourth stranger
Fenner, P. R. comp. Finders keepers

Coburn, Walt
Pud Ackley, cowboy
Collier, N. ed. Great stories of the West

COCAINE. See Drugs; Narcotic habit

The cock. Tao Kim Hai

## COCK-FIGHTING
Buck, P. S. The cockfight
Cockadoodledoo. Singer, I. B.
The cockfight. Buck, P. S.

COCKNEY DIALECT. See Dialect stories—English—Cockney

## COCKROACHES
Bryant, E. The human side of the village monster
Disch, T. M. The roaches
Kafka, F. The metamorphosis
Trevisan, D. Creatures of the night

Cockroaches. Moravia, A.

COCKS. See Roosters

COCKTAIL PARTIES. See Parties

A cocktail party. Tyrmand, L.

The cocomacaque. Jacobi, C.

The cocoon. Goodwin, J. B. L.

CODES. See Cryptography; Cyphers

COERCION. See Terrorism

Coffee. Brautigan, R.

Coffee for the road. La Guma, A.

The coffee is indefinable. Borchert, W.

A coffeehouse acquaintance. Templeton, E.

## COFFINS
Boyle, P. Myko
Cranch, C. P. A musical enigma
Poe, E. A. The oblong box

The coffins of the Emperor. Gulik, R. van

Cogswell, Ted, and Thomas, Ted. See Thomas, Cogswell

**Cogswell, Theodore R.**
The burning
  Knight, D. ed. A pocketful of stars
Probability zero! The population implosion
  Astounding
The spectre general
  The Science fiction hall of fame v2B
The wall around the world
  Harrison, H. ed. Worlds of wonder
**Cogswell, Theodore R. and Thomas, Theodore L.**
Early bird
  Astounding
**Cohen, Florence Chanock**
The promise
  Ribalow, H. U. ed. My name aloud
**Cohen, Keith**
Strands growing downward
  Gottesman, L.; Obenzinger, H. and Senauke, A. eds.   A cinch
You froze the light and flew
  Gottesman, L.; Obenzinger, H. and Senauke, A. eds.   A cinch
**Cohen, Leonard**
Charles Axis
  Charyn, J. ed. The single voice
"F."
  Charyn, J. ed. The troubled vision
"A long letter from F."
  Karl, F. R. and Hamalian, L. eds. The naked i
**Cohen, Marvin**
Josephine's literary choice
  New Directions in prose and poetry 23
Love by proxy of solitude
  New Directions in prose and poetry 21
The Monday rhetoric of the Love Club
  New Directions in prose and poetry 19
**Cohen, Matt**
Amazing grace
  New Canadian stories, 73
The **Cohen** Dog Exclusion Act. Schrader, S.
**COIN COLLECTING.** *See* Coins
**Coin** diver. Ekwensi, C.
The **coin** of Dionysius. Bramah, E.
**Coin** of the realm. Ellin, S.
**Coincidence.** Alan, A. J.
**COINS**
Bramah, E. The coin of Dionysius
Bramah, E. The mystery of the vanished Petition Crown
Harrison, M. Wit's end
**Coins** in the Frascati Foundation. Powell, J.
**Colby, Robert**
Shadows on the road
  Hitchcock, A. ed. Alfred Hitchcock presents: Stories to be read with the lights on
**COLD.** *See* Low temperatures
A **cold** dark night with snow. Wilhelm, K.
The **cold** equations. Goodwin, T.
A **cold** greeting. Bierce, A.
**Cold** print. Campbell, J. R.
**Cold** turkey. Padgett, R. and Gallup, D.
**Cold** victory. Anderson, P.
**Cold** war. Clarke, A. C.
The **Cold** War . . . continued. Reynolds, M.
The **cold** wind and the warm. Bradbury, R.

The **cold** winds of Adesta. Flanagan, T.
**Cole, Tom**
Familiar usage in Leningrad
  Schulman, L. M. ed. Travelers
Saint John of the Hershey Kisses: 1964
  Prize stories, 1970: The O. Henry Awards
**COLERIDGE, SAMUEL TAYLOR**
Aiken, J. The windshield weepers
**Colette**
The abduction
  Insights
The bracelet
  Colette. The other woman
The burglar
  Colette. The other woman
'Châ'
  Colette. The other woman
Dawn
  Colette. The other woman
The dead end
  Colette. The other woman
The find
  Colette. The other woman
The fox
  Colette. The other woman
Green sealing-wax
  Spinner, S. ed. Feminine plural
Habit
  Colette. The other woman
The hand
  Colette. The other woman
The judge
  Colette. The other woman
The landscape
  Colette. The other woman
Laughter
  Insights
Mirror-play
  Colette. The other woman
The murderer
  Colette. The other woman
My friend Valentine
  Colette. The other woman
One evening
  Colette. The other woman
The other wife
  Colette. The other woman
The portrait
  Colette. The other woman
The secret woman
  Colette. The other woman
Secrets
  Colette. The other woman
The victim
  Colette. The other woman
**Colette, Sidonie Gabrielle.** *See* Colette
**Colin, Vladimir**
The contact
  Suvin, D. ed. Other worlds, other seas
**Collaboration.** Collier, J.
**Collecting** team. Silverberg, R.
**COLLECTIVE FARMS**
       **Bulgaria**
Kirilov, N. Boundless time
       **Russia**
Yanovsky, Y.   A boat in the sea
Yashin, A. Lovers

Conlin, Joan
  The manhood of Neilly Sullivan
    Voices of Brooklyn
CONNECTICUT
  Brodeur, P. The siphon
        19th century
  Cooke, R. T. Mrs Flint's married experi-
    ence
        New Haven
  Mitchell, E. P. The legendary ship
        Putnam
  Steingass, D. Down in the eighth
        Westport
  De Vries, P. Split-level
A connection of the legs. Berne, S.
Connell, Evan S.
  The fisherman from Chihuahua
    Gulassa, C. M. ed. The fact of fiction
  I came from yonder mountain
    Abrahams, W. ed. Fifty years of the
      American short story v 1
Connell, Richard
  The most dangerous game
    Bell, J. E. ed. Designs for reading: short
      stories
    Bowman, J. S. ed. A book of islands
    Haining, P. ed. The ghouls
Connelly. Kahn, S.
Connolly, Cyril
  Year nine
    Fitz Gerald, G. ed. Modern satiric sto-
      ries
    Satin, J. ed. Reading literature
Conqueror. Eisenberg, L.
The conquerors 1096-1099. Coolidge, O.
Conquest. Malzberg, B. N.
The conquest of Mike. Thomason, J. W.
Conrad, Joseph
  Amy Foster
    Davis, R. G. ed. Ten modern masters
  Il conde
    Taylor, J. C. ed. The short story: fiction
      in transition
    Thune, E. and Prigozy, R. eds. Short
      stories: a critical anthology
  Heart of darkness
    Hamalian, L. and Volpe, E. L. eds.
      Eleven modern short novels
    Satin, J. ed. Reading literature
  The lagoon
    Foff, A. and Knapp, D. eds. Story
  An outpost of progress
    Hall, J. B. ed. The realm of fiction
  The secret sharer
    Davis, R. G. ed. Ten modern masters
    Schulman, L. M. ed. The loner
Conroy, Frank
  White days and red nights
    Charyn, J. ed. The single voice
CONSANGUINITY
  Davidson, A. The House the Blakeneys
    built
CONSCIENCE
  Burnett, W. Sherrel
  Poe, E. A. William Wilson
  Ruskay, S. The scar
  Stevenson, R. L. Markheim

Trevisan, D. The little goldfish
  Van Duyn, M. The bell
  Wharton, E. The touchstone
    See also Guilt
Conscience in art. Henry, O.
The conscience of the cop. Fay, W.
CONSCIENTIOUS OBJECTORS
  Babel, I. The Quaker
  Cady, J. The sounds of silence
  Gerald, J. B. Blood letting
The conscription of troops. Kafka, F.
Consequences. Cather, W.
CONSERVATION OF NATURE. See Na-
    ture conservation
CONSERVATION OF WILD LIFE. See
    Wild life—Conservation
CONSERVATISM
  Dickens, C. Lively turtle
Consider her ways. Wyndham, J.
Consolation. Verga, G.
CONSPIRACIES
  Djilas, M. The ambush
  Sáenz, D. A. Far South
  Van Vogt, A. E. Don't hold your breath
The conspiracy against Mister Mann. Bum-
    pus, J.
The conspirators. White, J.
CONSTABLES. See Police
Constance. Davis, O.
CONSTANTINOPLE. See Turkey—Istanbul
CONSTRUCTION. See Buildings
CONSTRUCTION CAMPS. See Labor
    camps
CONSTRUCTION INDUSTRY
  McGahern, J. Hearts of oak and bellies of
    brass
  Ostaijen, P. van. The city of builders
    See also Wrecking
CONSULS
  Abish, W. The Istanbul papers
  Galey, J. H. When you're 3,000 miles from
    home
  Henry, O. The lotus and the bottle
  Henry, O. Ships
  Henry, O. Shoes
Consumer goods. Moravia, A.
CONSUMER PROTECTION
  Brunner, J. Factsheet six
CONSUMERS
  Sheckley, R. Pas de trois of the chef and
    the waiter and the customer
CONSUMPTION. See Tuberculosis
CONSUMPTION (ECONOMICS)
  Pohl, F. The Midas plague
The contact. Colin, V.
Contact with the working class. Moravia, A.
CONTAGIOUS DISEASES. See Diseases
Contamination crew. Nourse, A. E.
CONTAMINATION OF THE ENVIRON-
    MENT. See Pollution
Contemplations of ecstasy on the day of my
    suicide. Francis, H. E.
CONTEMPT OF COURT
  Cecil, H. Contempt of court
Contempt of court. Cecil, H.
CONTENTMENT
  Stevenson, R. L. Will o' the Mill
The contents of the coffin. Fletcher, J. S.

COSMONAUTS
　Yemtsev, M. and Parnov, Y. He who leaves
　　no trace
　　　*See also* Astronauts
COSMOPOLITANISM. *See* Internationalism
A **cosmopolite** in a café. Henry, O.
COSSACKS
　Gogol, N. Black Sunday
　Kipling, R. The man who was
　Lamb, H. Khlit
　Lamb, H. Tal Taulai Khan
　Lamb, H. The White Khan
　Lamb, H. The winged rider
　Lamb, H. Wolf's war
COST AND STANDARD OF LIVING
　Mishima, Y. Three million yen
　Strindberg, A.　A business deal
　Strindberg, A. His servant
　Strindberg, A. Love and the price of grain
Costantini, Humberto
　In the beginning
　　Howes, B. ed. The eye of the heart
Costello, Mark
　Callahan's black Cadillacs
　　Costello, M. The Murphy stories
　Murphy Agonistes
　　Costello, M. The Murphy stories
　Murphy in Missouri
　　Costello, M. The Murphy stories
　Murphy's misogyny
　　Costello, M. The Murphy stories
　Murphy's Xmas
　　The Best American short stories, 1969
　　Costello, M. The Murphy stories
　Punch & Judy
　　Costello, M. The Murphy stories
　Strong is your hold O love
　　Costello, M. The Murphy stories
COSTERMONGERS. *See* Peddlers and ped-
　dling
The **cottage**. Long, F. B.
**Cottage** for August. Kyd, T.
Cotterill, Anne
　An accommodation
　Intro 4
Cottle, Thomas J.
　The place between living and dying
　　American Review 17
**Cotton** Alley. Crayton, P.
**Cotton** candy. Alonso, D.
**Cotton** gonna kill me yet. Himes, C.
COTTON MANUFACTURE
　Stewart, J. C. The last day
COTTON MILLS. *See* Cotton manufacture
COTTON PICKERS. *See* Agricultural la-
　borers
Cottrell, Dorothy
　The mysterious box
　　Fenner, P. R. comp. Finders keepers
**Cotty's** Cove. Graham, W.
Couch, Sir Arthur Quiller- *See* Quiller-
　Couch, Sir Arthur
**Could** World War I have been a mistake?
　Algren, N.
**Councillor** Krespel. Hoffmann, E. T. A.
Counselman, Mary Elizabeth
　The tree's wife
　　Manley, S. and Lewis, G. eds. Ladies of
　　horror

The **Count** and the wedding guest. Henry, O.
The **Count** of Crow's Nest. Cather, W.
**Counter** charm. St Clair, M.
**Counter** intelligence. Fish, R. L.
COUNTERFEITERS
　Allingham, M. The psychologist
　Ellin, S. Coin of the realm
　Henry, O. One dollar's worth
　Hershman, M.　A matter of pride
　Hershman, M. Willing victim
　Nabokov, V. The Leonardo
　Rook, C. Billy the Snide
**Counterpart**. Silverberg, R.
**Counterparts**. Joyce, J.
**Counterpoint**. Haldeman, J. W.
The **counterpoint** of view. Heidenry, J.
**Counterpunch**. Forester, C. S.
COUNTESSES. *See* Aristocracy
**Countries**. Harvor, B.
**Country**-born. Linklater, E.
A **country** boy quits school. Lao, H.
COUNTRY CLUBS. *See* Clubs
A **country** doctor, Kafka, F.
**Country** doctor. Morrison, W.
The **country** doctor. Turgenev, I.
A **country** excursion. Maupassant, G. de
**Country** full of Swedes. Caldwell, E.
COUNTRY LIFE
　Wilhelm, K. On the road to Honeyville
　　*See also* Small town life
**Austria**
　Doderer, H. von. Stepfield
**California**
　Steinbeck, J. Breakfast
　Steinbeck, J. Breakfast and work
　Steinbeck, J. Frog hunt
**Faeroe Islands**
　Brú, H. The long darkness
**Indiana**
　Crane, S. An Indiana campaign
**Maine**
　Holmes, E. M. Not for hire
　Holmes, E. M.　A part of the main
　Holmes, E. M. Restitution
　Jewett, S. O. The foreigner
　Jewett, S. O. The King of Folly Island
　Jewett, S. O. The Stage Tavern
　Pangborn, E. Longtooth
**Missouri**
　Schultz, J. Visit to my grandfather's grave
　alone
**New England**
　Jewett, S. O. The honey tree
　Jewett, S. O. In a country practice
　Jewett, S. O.　A landlocked sailor
　Jewett, S. O.　A village patriot
**New Hampshire**
　Jewett, S. O. An every-day girl
　Jewett, S. O. The girl with the cannon
　dresses
　Kumin, M. Buying the child
**Tennessee**
　Taylor, P. Two pilgrims
**United States**
　Cady, J. The troll

Crane, Stephen—*Continued*
  The shrapnel of their friends
    Crane, S. Tales of war
  The snake
    Crane, S. Tales, sketches, and reports
  The squire's madness
    Crane, S. Tales, sketches, and reports
  Stories told by an artist
    Crane, S. Tales, sketches, and reports
  The surrender of Forty Fort
    Crane, S. Tales, sketches, and reports
  A tale of mere chance
    Crane, S. Tales, sketches, and reports
  The "Tenderloin" as it really is
    Crane, S. Tales, sketches, and reports
  A tent in agony
    Crane, S. Tales, sketches, and reports
  This majestic lie
    Crane, S. Tales of war
  Three miraculous soldiers
    Crane, S. Tales of war
  Twelve o'clock
    Crane, S. Tales of adventure
  Uncle Jake and the bell-handle
    Crane, S. Tales, sketches, and reports
  The upturned face
    Crane, S. Tales of war
    Stansbury, D. L. ed. Impact
  The veteran
    Crane, S. The portable Stephen Crane
    Crane, S. Tales of war
  The victory of the moon
    Crane, S. Tales, sketches, and reports
  Virtue in war
    Crane, S. Tales of war
  The voice of the mountain
    Crane, S. Tales, sketches, and reports
  War memories
    Crane, S. Tales of war
  When man falls, a crowd gathers
    Crane, S. Tales, sketches, and reports
  Why did the young clerk swear? or, The
    unsatisfactory French
    Crane, S. Tales, sketches, and reports
  The wise men: a detail of American life
    in Mexico
    Crane, S. Tales of adventure
  Yen-Hock Bill and his sweetheart
    Crane, S. Tales, sketches, and reports
The **cranes.** Sienkiewicz, H.
**Crate.** Sturgeon, T.
Craven, Margaret
  Juan, the Basque shepherd boy
    Tibbets, A. B. ed. Boys are boys
**Crawfish.** Mayhar, A. F.
Crawford, Francis Marion
  The dead smile
    Haining, P. ed. The wild night com-
    pany: Irish stories of fantasy and
    horror
  Man overboard
    Kahn, J. ed. Some things dark and
    dangerous
    Tomlinson, D. ed. Walk in dread
  The screaming skull
    Manley, S. and Lewis, G. eds. A
    gathering of ghosts

Crawford, Margaret
  The real me
    Alabama prize stories, 1970
The **crawling** chaos. Lovecraft, H. P. and
    Berkeley, E.
Crayton, Pearl
  Cotton Alley
    Adoff, A. ed. Brothers and sisters
  The day the world almost came to an end
    Bambara, T. C. ed. Tales and stories
    for Black folks
**Crazy** crowd. Wilson, A.
The **crazy** old man. Nissenson, H.
A **crazy** way to make a living. Dumonte, E.
CREATION
  Lafferty, R. A. When all the lands pour
    out again
The **creation** of Bennie Good. Sallis, J.
**Creative** writing. Pritchett, V. S.
**Creature** of a day. Tendryakov, V.
**Creature** of the snows. Sambrot, W.
A **creature** was stirring. Carr, J.
**Creatures** of the night. Trevisan, D.
The **credibility** gap. Gordimer, N.
CREDIT
  Brautigan, R. The wild birds of heaven
  Malamud, B. The bill
    *See also* Debtor and creditor
**CREDITOR.** *See* Debtor and creditor
CREE INDIANS
  O'Brien, D. C. Pool number 37
  Prebble, J. Almighty voice
  Wiebe, R. Where is the voice coming
    from?
Creeley, Robert
  The boat
    Taylor, J. C. ed. The short story: fiction
    in transition
CREMATION
  Bradbury, R. Pillar of fire
  Thomas, D. The burning baby
The **Cremona** violin. Hoffmann, E. T. A.
CREOLES
  Chopin, K. Athénaïse
  Chopin, K. The awakening
  Chopin, K. La belle Zoraïde
  Chopin, K. Beyond the bayou
  Chopin, K. Caline
  Chopin, K. Madame Célestin's divorce
  Chopin, K. Nég Créol
  Chopin, K.  A night in Acadie
  Chopin, K.  A no-account Creole
  Chopin, K.  A visit to Avoyelles
  Henry, O. The renaissance at Charleroi
**Crêpes** flambées. Taylor, E.
CRESPEL, JOHANN BERNHARD
  Hoffmann, E. T. A. Councillor Krespel
  Hoffmann, E. T. A. The Cremona violin
**Cress** Delahanty. West, J.
**Crest** of fear. Holmes, E. M.
**CRETE.** *See* Americans in Crete; English in
    Crete; etc.
Crews, Harry
  The unattached smile
    Lytle, A. ed. Craft and vision
The **crib** circuit. DeFord, M. A.
Crichton, Michael
  The most powerful tailor in the world
    Best detective stories of the year, 1972
The **cricket** beneath the waterfall. Krleža, M.

# CRICKETS

Algren, N. What country do you think you're in?

**Criers** and kibitzers, kibitzers and criers. Elkin, S.

The **cries** of love. Highsmith, P.

# CRIME AND CRIMINALS

Aiken, C. Smith and Jones

Amores, A. F.   A scrap of tinfoil

Anderson, P. Recruiting nation

Anderson Imbert, E. The General makes a lovely corpse

Andrews, F. E.   A man called Cain

Bichsel, P. The knife

Blackhurst, W. E.   A rat's a rat

Böll, H. My sad face

Borchert, W. Our little Mozart

Borges, J. L. Juan Muraña

Borges, J. L. The unworthy friend

Brown, F. Town wanted

Brunner, J. Jack fell down

Burke, T. Ding-Dong-Dell

Burke, T. The gorilla and the girl

Burke, T. The knight-errant

Burke, T. The sign of the lamp

Čapek, K. The last judgment

Casper, L.   A nest of boxes

Clark, W. M. The supermen

Colette. The murderer

Cortázar, J. The other heaven

Crane, S.   A tale of mere chance

DeFord, M. A. No loose ends

Delany, S. R. Time considered as a helix of semi-precious stones

Dentinger, S. The future is ours

Dickson, G. R. The mousetrap

Di Donato, P.   I killed Maria Goretti

Elkin, S. The bailbondsman

Fast, H. Cephes 5

Fellowes-Gordon, I. The events at Schloss Heidiger

Fish, R. L. Double entry

Gores, J. File #2: Stakeout on Page Street

Grant, C. L. The summer of the Irish Sea

Haycox, E. McQuestion rides

Henry, O.   A retrieved reformation

Hensley, J. L. and Ellison, H. Rodney Parish for hire

Hoch, E. D. The Leopold locked room

Holding, J. Second talent

Kaplan, B. Diaspora

Laumer, K. Once there was a giant

Leiber, F. Ill met in Lankhmar

McAuliffe, F. The Iranian Farmer Commission

McGivern, W. P. Killer on the turnpike

Midwood, B. Portrait of the policeman as a young artist

Muller-Thym, T.   A word about justice

Nolan, W. F. Dark encounter

Pentecost, H. In the middle of nowhere

Phillifent, J. T. Aim for the heel

Phillips, R.   A teacher's rewards

Pronzini, B. Cain's mark

Reynolds, M. Criminal in Utopia

Ritchie, J. Dropout

Ruskay, S. The jack

Sayers, D. L. The adventurous exploit of the cave of Ali Baba

Sayers, D. L. The inspiration of Mr Budd

Schmitz, J. H. Lion loose

Scott, J. Out of the country

Sharp, M. Seal Tregarthen's cousin

Sherred, T. L. Bounty

Stevenson, R. L. The adventure of Prince Florizel and a detective

Stevenson, R. L. The adventure of the hansom cab

Stevenson, R. L. Story of the house with the green blinds

Stevenson, R. L. Story of the young man in holy orders

Sukenick, R. What's your story

Tenn, W. Party of the two parts

Ulyansky, A. The fleecy jacket

Usher, F. The Black Dahlia

Varshavsky, I.   A raid takes place at midnight

Wakefield, H. R. Appointment with fire

Warren, S. The March assize

Wilson, A.   A visit in bad taste

Wodhams, J. There is a crooked man

Woods, W. C. The viping hour

*See also* Arson; Blackmail; Brigands and robbers; Conspiracies; Convicts, Escaped; Counterfeiters; Gangsters; Juvenile delinquency; Mafia; Murder stories; Mystery and detective stories; Smuggling; Swindlers and swindling; Theft

### Identification

Shaw, B. Burden of proof

**Crime** and punishment. Laumer, K.

**Crime** in the Rue Sainte-Catherine. Simenon, G.

The **crime** of Ezechiele Coen. Ellin, S.

**CRIME OF PASSION.** *See* Crime passionel

The **crime** of the mathematics professor. Lispector, C.

# CRIME PASSIONEL

Woolrich, C. New York blues

Yamamoto, M. The blue rug

# CRIMEAN WAR, 1853-1856

Linklater, E. The Duke

The **criminal.** Gores, J.

**Criminal** in Utopia. Reynolds, M.

# CRIMINAL INVESTIGATION

Bond, S. Chinatown evening

Madsen, S. A. The judge

Malone, J. The fugitive

Pronzini, B. Death of a nobody

**CRIMINALS.** *See* Crime and criminals

The **Crimson** Island. Bulgakov, M.

**Crimson** Ramblers of the world, farewell. West, J.

**CRIPPLED CHILDREN.** *See* Cripples

# CRIPPLES

Betts, D. The mother-in-law

Burke, T. Old Joe

Carr, J.   A steelie for the King

Clarke, A. C. The cruel sky

Golding, W. Clonk clonk

Goryushkin, V. Before sunrise

Green, B. K. Cindy

Hensley, J. Shut the last door

Lagerkvist, P. The basement

**CRIPPLES**—*Continued*
McCord, J. Where the aurochs lingered
Madden, D. The pale horse of fear
Maloney, R. Gallantry
Maltz, A. The cop
Maupassant, G. de. Bellflower
Maupassant, G. de. Clochette
Rothschild, M. Dog in the manger
Vassilikos, V. Jingle Bells
Weaver, G. Finch the spastic speaks
Witton, D. Esteban and the marionettes
Witton, D. The miracle of the Kings
    *See also* Amputees; Hunchbacks
**CRIPPLES, WAR.** *See* Cripples
A **crisis.** Maupassant, G. de
A **crisis** for the Guard. Fox, J.
**Crisis** over. Abercrombie, N.
The **critic.** Stewart, N.
**Critical** angle. Chandler, A. B.
**Critical** mass. Clarke, A. C.
**CRITICS.** *See* Art critics; Dramatic critics;
    Literary critics; Music critics
**Critique** de la vie quotidienne. Barthel-
    me, D.
The **critters.** Long, F. B.
**CROATIA**
Krleža, M. Devil's island
Krleža, M. Dr Gregor and the Evil One
Krleža, M. The love of Marcel Faber-
    Fabriczy for Miss Laura Warronigg
**CROATS IN FRANCE.** *See* Yugoslavs in
    France
**CROATS IN THE UNITED STATES**
Maloney, R. Viva Caporetto!
**Crocker's** Hole. Blackmore, R. D.
The **crocodile.** Dostoevsky, F.
The **crocodile.** Hernández, F.
**CROCODILES**
Brewster, H. The marquis and the croco-
    dile
Dostoevsky, F. The crocodile
    *See also* Alligators
**Cronin, A. J.**
The strange meeting
    Haining, P. ed. The clans of darkness
**Crooked** bone. Kersh, G.
**Crooked** lightning. Gardner, E. S.
The **crooked** road. Gaby, A.
**Crooken** sands. Stoker, B.
The **crooks.** Okara, G.
The **crop.** O'Connor, F.
**Cross, James**
Pin money
    Hitchcock, A. ed. Alfred Hitchcock pre-
    sents: Stories to be read with the
    lights on
The weaker vessel
    Mystery Writers of America. Mirror,
    mirror, fatal mirror
**Cross, John Keir**
Music when soft voices die . . .
    Haining, P. ed. The clans of darkness
The **cross.** Shapiro, L.
The **cross.** Thurston, J.
**Cross**-country snow. Hemingway, E.
A **cross** of centuries. Kuttner, H.
**Crossbones.** Michaels, L.
The **crossing.** Dumas, H.
**Crossing** over. Elman, R.

**Crossing** the Mississippi. Hemingway, E.
**Crossley-Holland, Kevin.** *See* Walsh, J. P.
    jt. auth.
The **crossroader.** Carpenter, D.
The **crossroads** of history. Sax, F.
**CROW INDIANS**
Carr, M. J. Traps of quicksand
Johnson, D. M. The unbeliever
Lampman, E. S. A meeting with Dr
    McLoughlin
Wister, O. Little Big Horn medicine
The **crowded** bedchamber. Boccaccio, G.
**CROWDS**
Crane, S. When man falls, a crowd gathers
Kemp, A. The blue of madness
    *See also* Riots
**Crowley, Aleister**
The testament of Magdalen Blair
    Haining, P. ed. The nightmare reader
        **About**
Maugham, S. The magician
Wheatley, D. The black magician
The **crown** Derby plate. Bowen, M.
A **crown** of feathers. Singer, I. B.
**Crowning** glory. Henderson, Z.
**CROWNS**
James, M. R.   A warning to the curious
**CROWS**
Nemerov, H. Digressions around a crow
The **crows** fly home at night. Borchert, W.
**CRUCIFIXION**
Borges, J. L. The Gospel according to
    Mark
Yeats, W. B. The crucifixion of the out-
    cast
The **crucifixion** of the outcast. Yeats, W. B.
**Crucifixus** etiam. Miller, W. M.
"**Cruel** and barbarous treatment." McCar-
    thy, M.
The **cruel** equations. Sheckley, R.
The **cruel** sky. Clarke, A. C.
**CRUELTY**
Bødker, C. The Deaf'un's door
Bukowski, C. The murder of Ramon Vas-
    quez
Holmes, E. M. Not to the swift
Koontz, D. R.   A mouse in the walls of
    the Global Village
Rees, B. Sidney, oh Sidney
Tolstoi, L. After the ball
Trevisan, D. Hog-killing day
    *See also* Sadism; Torture
**Cruelty.** DeCles, J.
**CRUELTY TO ANIMALS.** *See* Animals—
    Treatment
**CRUELTY TO CHILDREN**
Bingham, S. Fear
Donoso, J. Ana María
**Cruise.** Waugh, E.
**Cruise** of the Lazy Lisa. Holmes, E. M.
The **cruise** of the Morwenna. Val Baker, D.
The **cruise** of the "Willing Mind." Mason,
    A. E. W.
**Crusade.** Clarke, A. C.
The **Crusader's** key. Linklater, E.
**CRUSADES**
Coolidge, O. Tales of the Crusades; 12
    stories

**Cuomo, George**—*Continued*
　The deliverance of the pure
　　Cuomo, G. Sing, choirs of angels
　Exactly, what do you want, lady?
　　Cuomo, G. Sing, choirs of angels
　Looking for a job
　　Cuomo, G. Sing, choirs of angels
　A man's crazy to want to go to Philadelphia
　　Cuomo, G. Sing, choirs of angels
　Oceans apart
　　Cuomo, G. Sing, choirs of angels
　A part of the bargain
　　Cuomo, G. Sing, choirs of angels
　A real good price
　　Cuomo, G. Sing, choirs of angels
　Sing, choirs of angels
　　Cuomo, G. Sing, choirs of angels
　Sophisticated lady
　　Cuomo, G. Sing, choirs of angels
　Tracy's brief slump
　　Cuomo, G. Sing, choirs of angels
　Twenty-two years and fifty cents
　　Cuomo, G. Sing, choirs of angels
　The unholy trio
　　Cuomo, G. Sing, choirs of angels
**Cupid** and the Vicar of Swale. Maugham, W. S.
The **cupid** mirror. Marsh, N.
The **cure**. Bontemps, A.
The **cure**. Kuttner, H. and Moore, C. L.
**Curfew.** Dorr, L.
**CURITIBA.** *See* Brazil—Curitiba
**Curley, Daniel**
　All of a summer's day
　　Curley, D. In the hands of our enemies
　A day in Hamburg
　　Curley, D. In the hands of our enemies
　The day of the equinox
　　Curley, D. In the hands of our enemies
　The gingerbread man
　　Curley, D. In the hands of our enemies
　In the hands of our enemies
　　Curley, D. In the hands of our enemies
　Look homeward, tourist
　　Curley, D. In the hands of our enemies
　Love in the winter
　　Elkin, S. ed. Stories from the sixties
　The man who was drafted
　　Curley, D. In the hands of our enemies
　The manhunt
　　Curley, D. In the hands of our enemies
　The moth, the bear, and the shivering stars
　　Curley, D. In the hands of our enemies
　A ride in the snow
　　Curley, D. In the hands of our enemies
　Station: you are here
　　Curley, D. In the hands of our enemies
　A story of love, etc.
　　Curley, D. In the hands of our enemies
　The tale of the peasant Osip
　　Curley, D. In the hands of our enemies
　A very small grove
　　Curley, D. In the hands of our enemies
　Where you wouldn't want to walk
　　Curley, D. In the hands of our enemies

**Currer, Barney**
　The Rabbi
　　Karlin, W.; Paquet, B. T. and Rottmann, L. eds. Free fire zone
**Curried** cow. Bierce, A.
The **curse**. Clarke, A. C.
The **curse** of Yig. Bishop, Z.
**CURSES**
　Arnim, A. von. The mad veteran of Fort Ratonneau
　Chesnutt, C. W. The goophered grapevine
　Chesnutt, C. W. The gray wolf's ha'nt
　Dunsany, Lord. Witch wood
　Heron-Maxwell, B. The Devil Stone
　Linklater, E. The abominable imprecation
　Moore, G. Julia Cahill's curse
　Mulisch, H. The horses' jump and the fresh sea
　　*See also* Superstition
**Curtis, Betsy**
　The key to out
　　McCaffrey, A. ed. Alchemy and academe
**Curtis, Julia Anne.** *See* Anne of Swansea
**Curtis, Richard**
　Zoo 2000
　　Yolen, J. comp. Zoo 2000
**Cururo** . . . sheep dog. Coloane, F. A.
The **custard** heart. Parker, D.
The **custodian**. Hill, S.
**Custom.** Schultz, J.
The **cutthroat** trout. Carrighar, S.
**Cutting** edge. Purdy, J.
**CYBERNETICS**
　Asimov, I. "Nobody here but—"
　Borgese, E. M. To whom it may concern
　Sheckley, R. The cruel equations
　Wolfe, B. Self portrait
　　*See also* Automata; Electronic computers
**CYBORGS.** *See* Automata
**Cycles.** Ruskay, S.
**CYCLING.** *See* Bicycles and tricycles
**Cyclists'** raid. Rooney, F.
The **cyclone**. Hesse, H.
**CYCLONES**
　Hesse, H. The cyclone
**CYPHERS**
　Brittain, W. The man who read Sir Arthur Conan Doyle
The **Cyprian** cat. Sayers, D. L.
**CYPRUS**
　Lumley, B. The pearl
The **cyprus** shell. Lumley, B.
**Cyrano De Bergerac**
　A journey to the moon; abridged
　　De Camp, L. S. and De Camp, C. C. eds. 3000 years of fantasy and science fiction
**CZECHOSLOVAK REPUBLIC**
　Beneš, J. The blind mirror; 18 stories
　Beneš, J. Coming-out party
　Nesvadba, J. The lost face
　　　**Prague**
　Templeton, E. A coffeehouse acquaintance

CZECHOSLOVAK REPUBLIC—*Continued*
**Intervention—1968-**
Moorcock, M. The tank trapeze
Theroux, P. A political romance
**Police**
*See* Police—Czechoslovak Republic
CZECHOSLOVAKIAN SOLDIERS. *See* Soldiers, Czechoslovakian
CZECHS IN ENGLAND
Nesvadba, J. Vampire ltd.
CZECHS IN THE UNITED STATES
Cather, W. Neighbour Rosicky
Czoe, Zông-Hùi
The memorial service on the mountain
Katz, N. and Milton, N. eds. Fragment from a lost diary, and other stories

# D

D. M. Z. Yu, H.
DACHAU (CONCENTRATION CAMP)
Price, R. Waiting at Dachau
DA-da-dee. Himes, C.
Daddy. Ober, H.
Daddy. Tindall, G.
Daddy Wolf. Purdy, J.
Dagerman, Stig
The games of night
Simon, J. ed. Fourteen for now
Dagger in the dark. Buck, P. S.
Daguio, Amador
Wedding dance
Katz, N. and Milton, N. eds. Fragment from a lost diary, and other stories
Dahl, Roald
The landlady
Hitchcock, A. ed. Alfred Hitchcock present: Stories to be read with the lights on
Poison
Stansbury, D. L. ed. Impact
The way up to heaven
Kahn, J. ed. Hanging by a thread
Daisy. Maugham, W. S.
Daisy and the changes. Midwood, B.
Daisy Miller. James, H.
DAKOTA INDIANS
Fisher, C. The skinning of black coyote
Garfield, B. The glory riders
Olsen, T. V. The strange valley
Ulyatt, K. Ghost riders of the Sioux
DALAI LAMA. *See* Lamas
Daley goes home. Schultz, J.
DALLAS. *See* Texas—Dallas
Dalsgaard, Hans
Nelson's last stand
Faroese short stories
Dalyrimple goes wrong. Fitzgerald, F. S.
Dam, Albert
The mandrake
Holm, S. ed. The devil's instrument, and other Danish stories
Dam nuisance. Laumer, K.
DAMASCUS. *See* Syria—Damascus
Damechild. Etchison, D.
The damned thing. Bierce, A.

DAMS
Laumer, K. Dam nuisance
*See also* Grand Coulee Dam
The dance. Fitzgerald, F. S.
The dance. Singer, I. B.
A dance and a hop. Singer, I. B.
The dance at Chevalier's. Cather, W.
DANCE BANDS. *See* Bands (Music)
DANCE CONTESTS. *See* Dance marathons; Dancing
DANCE HALLS
Trevor, W. The ballroom of romance
DANCE MARATHONS
Farrell, J. T. The benefits of American life
The Dance of the Changer and the Three. Carr, T.
The Dance of the Dead
Haining, P. ed. Gothic tales of terror
Dance of the happy shades. Munro, A.
DANCERS
Boles, P. D. The girl at the Plaza
Burke, T. Gina of the Chinatown
Colette. 'Châ'
Franklin, E. Girl in a white dress
Kawabata, Y. The Izu dancer
Maupassant, G. de. Minuet
Petry, A. Olaf and his girl friend
Pynchon, T. V. in love
*See also* Dancing
The dancers. Linklater, E.
The dancers. *See* Maupassant, G. de. Minuet
DANCES. *See* Dancing
DANCES (PARTIES) *See* Parties
DANCING
Brandt, J. G. The Finnish sailor
Cabrera Infante, G. At the great 'Ecbo'
Deck, J. Greased Samba
Delattre, P. The dancing master of Kung Fu
Fitzgerald, F. S. A woman with a past
Fraser, G. M. The general danced at dawn
Hunter, K. Two's enough of a crowd
Jones, L. The screamers
O'Hara, J. Afternoon waltz
Parker, D. The waltz
Woolrich, C. Dead on her feet
Yurick, S. The Child-God dance
The dancing boy. Eastlake, W.
The dancing man. Dawson, F.
The dancing master of Kung Fu. Delattre, P.
The dancing of Red Hershl with the withered hand. Fiedler, L. A.
The dandelion. Borchert, W.
Dandy; or Astride the funky finger of lust. Bullins, E.
DANES
Kipling, R. The knights of the joyous venture
DANES IN ENGLAND
Treece, H. The black longship
DANES IN THE UNITED STATES
Cather, W. Lou, the prophet
Hayes, A. H. The yellow teapot
Danger hole. Short, L.
Danger—human. Dickson, G. R.

**Daniel, Yuli**
Atonement
Daniel, Y. This is Moscow speaking, and other stories
Hands
Daniel, Y. This is Moscow speaking, and other stories
Tyrmand, L. ed. Explorations in freedom: prose, narrative, and poetry from Kultura
The man from MINAP
Daniel, Y. This is Moscow speaking, and other stories
This is Moscow speaking
Daniel, Y. This is Moscow speaking, and other stories
**Daniel** and the boulder. Bahr, J.
**Daniels, Harold R.**
Three ways to rob a bank
Hitchcock, A. ed. Alfred Hitchcock presents: Stories to be read with the lights on
**Dann, Jack M.**
The drum lollipop
Orbit 11
I'm with you in Rockland
Scortia, T. N. ed. Strange bedfellows
Whirl cage
Orbit 10
**Dannay, Frederic.** See Queen, Ellery
The **Dannold** cheque. Purdy, K. W.
**Danny.** Steinbeck, J.
**Dans** le vrai. Wright, S.
**Dante** and the lobster. Beckett, S.
**Daphne** Bigelow and the spine-chilling saga of the snail-encrusted tinfoil noose. Shepherd, J.
**Daphne's** lover. Taylor, P.
**Da Porto, Luigi.** See Porto, Luigi da
**Dare** to struggle, dare to win. Kempton, J.
The **daring** young man on the flying trapeze. Saroyan, W.
**Darío, Rubén**
The bourgeois king
Howes, B. ed. The eye of the heart
**Darius.** Panghorn, E.
**DARK AGES.** See Middle Ages; also names of countries with appropriate period subdivision, e.g. England—449-1066
**Dark** balcony. Petaja, E.
A **dark**-brown dog. Crane, S.
**Dark** came early in that country. Algren, N.
A **dark** carpet. Jewett, S. O.
**Dark** Dolores. Runyon, D.
**Dark** encounter. Nolan, W. F.
**Dark** glasses. Hood, H.
**Dark** glasses. Khamsing, S.
**Dark** hollow. Petaja, E.
**Dark** mission. Del Rey, L.
A **dark** night. Jewett, S. O.
The **dark** room. Bemba, S.
**Dark** side of the moon. Naylor, P. R.
The **dark** unfathomed caves. Neville, H.
The **darkening** moon. Stafford, J.
**Darkling** I listen. Marsh, W.
**DARKNESS.** See Light
**Darkness.** Carneiro, A.
The **darling.** Chekhov, A.

**D'Arnaud, François Baculard**
The Witch of Eye
Haining, P. ed. Gothic tales of terror
The **darning** needle. Anderson, H. C.
The **Darwin** sampler. Russell, R.
**Das, Manoj**
The mystery of the missing cap
Winter's tales 18
A **dashing** fellow. Nabokov, V.
**Daskalov, Stoyan T.**
A new attitude toward life
Kirilov, N. and Kirk, F. eds. Introduction to modern Bulgarian literature
A **date** with a spider. Derry, V.
**DATES.** See Dating (Social customs)
**DATING (SOCIAL CUSTOMS)**
Bahr, J. The girl on the post
Beneš, J. What do you know of the Kaplan turbine?
Boles, P. D. The animal kingdom
Boles, P. D. I thought you were a unicorn
Campbell, R. At first sight
Campbell, R. The stocking
Corrington, J. W. Old men dream dreams, young men see visions
Fitzgerald, F. S. First blood
Grau, S. A. Homecoming
Helwig, D. One evening
Hunter, K. Two's enough of a crowd
McNair, K. The legend of Carrie Marie
McNair, K. Milli's gentle summer
Morris, H. Lillian
Parker, D. The last tea
Petrakis, H. M. The sweet life
Shaw, I. Small Saturday
Stuart, J. The highest bidder
See also Parties
**Daugherty, Molly Gates**
The givers
Alabama prize stories, 1970
The **daughter.** Bichsel, P.
**Daughter.** McCaffrey, A.
The **daughter.** Naylor, P. R.
A **daughter** of the Germans. Fielding, G.
The **daughter** of the regiment. Kipling, R.
The **daughter** of the tree. DeFord, M. A.
**DAUGHTERS.** See Fathers and daughters; Mothers and daughters; Parent and child
**DAUGHTERS-IN-LAW**
Chekhov, A. In the ravine
Crawford, M. The real me
**Daughters** of Earth. Merril, J.
**Daumier.** Barthelme, D.
**Davenport, Guy**
Robot
The Best American short stories, 1973
**Davidson, Avram**
Amphora
Dickensheet, D. ed. Men and malice
Après nous
Davidson, A. Strange seas and shores
Big Sam
McCaffrey, A. ed. Alchemy and academe
A bottle full of kismet
Davidson, A. Strange seas and shores
The certificate
Davidson, A. Strange seas and shores

**Day, J. Wentworth**
  The beaked horror which sank a ship
    Canning, J. ed. 50 great horror stories
  The dead killed him in his own grave
    Canning, J. ed. 50 great horror stories
  The dog-man horror of the valley
    Canning, J. ed. 50 great horror stories
  The man who turned into a cat
    Canning, J. ed. 50 great horror stories
  Sung to his death by dead men
    Canning, J. ed. 50 great horror stories
  The tongueless woman of Glamis Castle
    Canning, J. ed. 50 great horror stories
  The vampire of Castle Furstenstein
    Canning, J. ed. 50 great horror stories
The **day.** Saxton, C.
The **day.** Starke, R.
The **day** after Saturday. Márquez, G. G.
**Day** after tomorrow. Naylor, P. R.
A **day** among the liars. Mitchell, E. P.
**Day** and night. Lipski, L.
**Day** and night. Thompson, R.
The **day** Beaumont became acquainted with his pain. LeClézio, J. M. G.
**Day** by day. Konstantinov, K.
A **day** in Coney Island. Singer, I. B.
A **day** in Hamburg. Curley, D.
A **day** in operations. Grinstead, D.
A **day** in the life of a debt-collector. Premchand
The **day** is done. Del Rey, L.
The **day** Jesus came. Holland, R.
**Day** Million. Pohl, F.
**DAY OF ATONEMENT (JEWISH HOLIDAY)** *See* Yom Kippur
A **day** of days. James, H.
The **day** of decisions. Rothgiesser, R.
The **day** of the bullet. Ellin, S.
**Day** of the butterfly. Munro, A.
The **day** of the dead God. Vandeloo, J.
The **day** of the dragon. Endore, G.
The **day** of the dying rabbit. Updike, J.
The **day** of the equinox. Curley, D.
The **day** of the hawk. West, J.
The **day** of the hunter. Holmes, E. M.
The **day** of the landslide. Rulfo, J.
**Day** of the prophets. Ansell, J.
The **day** of trials. Lebowitz, A.
A **day** off. Hokororo, A. M.
A **day** saved. Greene, G.
The **day** that went terribly wrong. Burton, H.
The **day** the children vanished. Pentecost, H.
The **day** the flowers came. Madden, D.
The **day** the world almost came to an end. Crayton, P.
The **day** we got our own back. Brennan, M.
The **day** we talked about James Thurber. Bukowski, C.
The **day** without forgiveness. Wiesel, E.
**DAYDREAMS.** *See* Dreams
The **daydreams** of a drunk woman. Lisspector, C.
**Days** of wrath. Auchincloss, L.
**Daytime.** Shen, Ts'ung-wen
The **deacon.** Updike, J.

**DEACONS**
  Chekhov, A. The duel
  Cooke, R. T. Mrs Flint's married experience
  Updike, J. The deacon
**THE DEAD**
  Bloch, R. The living dead
  Böll, H. Rise, my love, rise
  Bradbury, R. Pillar of fire
  Bradbury, R. The Tombling day
  Buck, D. P. Aunt Agatha
  Bukowski, C. The copulating mermaid of Venice, California
  Bullock, M. The return of Noire
  Collins, W. Mad Monkton
  Crane, S. A desertion
  Crowley, A. The testament of Magdalen Blair
  The Dance of the Dead
  Eastlake, W. The biggest thing since Custer
  Greene, S. Four o'clock
  Harrison, H. At last, the true story of Frankenstein
  Ionesco, E. Oriflamme
  Lagerkvist, P. The eternal smile
  Lavin, M. The living
  Matthews, J. On the shore of Chad Creek
  The Monk of horror
  Neugeboren J. A family trip
  Petry, A. The bones of Louella Brown
  Poe, E. A. King Pest
  Poe, E. A. Shadow—a parable
  Rigsby, H. Dead man's story
  Robbe-Grillet, A. The secret room
  Shamir, M. Next of kin
  Steegmuller, F. Ciao Fabrizio
  The Strange guests
  Summers, H. How they chose the dead
  Usher, F. The walking dead
    *See also* Death; Mummies; Resurrection

The **dead.** Joyce, J.
The **dead.** Oates, J. C.
A **dead** cert. O'Faolain, S.
The **dead** end. Case, D.
The **dead** end. Colette
**Dead** end. Hodous, M.
The **dead** finger. Pyle, H.
The **dead** hand. Collins, W.
The **dead** killed him in his own grave. Day, J. W.
**Dead** language Master. Aiken, J.
The **dead** man. Borges, J. L.
The **dead** man was a lively one. De La Vega, P. M.
**Dead** man's story. Rigsby, H.
**Dead** men walk. Hamilton, A.
**Dead** men's path. Achebe, C.
**Dead** on her feet. Woolrich, C.
The **dead** past. Asimov, I.
The **dead** past. Nussbaum, A.
**Dead** phone. Anderson, P. and Anderson, K.
The **dead** smile. Crawford, F. M.
The **dead** woman. Keller, D. H.
**DEAF**
  Bergé, C. Events of a March night
  Cullinan, E. The old priest
  Gbadamossi, R. A. The sexton's deaf son

DECK HANDS. *See* Longshoremen
DeCles, Jon
Cruelty
McComas, J. F. ed. Special wonder
The **decline** and fall of Officer Fergerson. Montgomery, M.
The **decline** and fall of the Boslowits family. Reve, G. K. van het
The **decline** of Sholem Waldman. Markfield, W.
The **decompensator** Lhasa. Delattre, P.
DECORATION DAY. *See* Memorial Day
DECORATIONS OF HONOR
Maupassant, G. de. How he got the Legion of Honor
A **deed** without a name. Theroux, P.
**Deedie** and her lovers. Bahr, J.
**Deep** country part. Casper, L.
**Deep** end. Ballard, J. G.
The **deep** end. Schwartz, J.
**Deep** in the interior and everything and all. Drake, R.
The **deep** ones. Wade, J.
The **deep** range. Clarke, A. C.
The **deep**-sea conch. Lumley, B.
**Deeper** than the darkness. Ellison, H.
The **deepest** blue in the world. Dorman, S.
The **deepest** chamber. Francis, H. E.
DEER HUNTING
Brister, B. One very fine doe
Holmes, E. M. The day of the hunter
Holmes, E. M. Island hunt
Jacobson, D. The game
**Deer** in the works. Vonnegut, K.
**Deerglen** Queen. Knox, B.
DEFAMATION. *See* Libel and slander
The **defeat** of the city. Henry, O.
The **defeat** of the Nez Percé. Berg, A. M.
The **defeated.** Gordimer, N.
**Defender** of the faith. Roth, P.
The **defenestration** of Ermintrude Inch. Clark, A. C.
The **defensive** bomber. Dempsey, H.
**Define** the word "wife." Kanin, G.
Defoe, Daniel
The friendly demon
Haining, P. ed. The wild night company: Irish stories of fantasy and horror
The magician
Haining, P. ed. The freak show
True relation of the apparition of one Mrs Veal
Thune, E. and Prigozy, R. eds. Short stories: a critical anthology
De Forbes
My sister Annabelle
Best of the Best detective stories
DeFord, Miriam Allen
The apotheosis of Ki
DeFord, M. A. Elsewhere, elsewhen, elsehow
McComas, J. F. ed. Special wonder
Beggarman, thief
Dickensheet, D. ed. Men and malice
A case for the U. N.
Bernkopf, J. F. comp. Boucher's choicest

The colony
DeFord, M. A. Elsewhere, elsewhen, elsehow
The crib circuit
DeFord, M. A. Elsewhere, elsewhen, elsehow
The daughter of the tree
Scortia, T. N. ed. Strange bedfellows
The eel
DeFord, M. A. Elsewhere, elsewhen, elsehow
Santesson, H. S. ed. Crime prevention in the 30th century
Farewell to the Faulkners
Mystery Writers of America. Merchants of menace
First dig
DeFord, M. A. Elsewhere, elsewhen, elsehow
5,000,000 A.D.
Elwood, R. ed. Future city
Freak show
DeFord, M. A. Elsewhere, elsewhen, elsehow
Lazarus II
New dimensions 2
The margenes
DeFord, M. A. Elsewhere, elsewhen, elsehow
Mrs Hinck
DeFord, M. A. Elsewhere, elsewhen, elsehow
The moment of time
Mystery Writers of America. Mirror, mirror, fatal mirror
The monster
DeFord, M. A. Elsewhere, elsewhen, elsehow
The 1980 president
DeFord, M. A. Elsewhere, elsewhen, elsehow
No loose ends
Hitchcock, A. ed. Alfred Hitchcock presents: Stories to be read with the lights on
Not snow nor rain
DeFord, M. A. Elsewhere, elsewhen, elsehow
The old bunch and Dusty Stiggins
DeFord, M. A. Elsewhere, elsewhen, elsehow
Old man Morgan's grave
DeFord, M. A. Elsewhere, elsewhen, elsehow
The old woman
DeFord, M. A. Elsewhere, elsewhen, elsehow
The Peak Lords
DeFord, M. A. Elsewhere, elsewhen, elsehow
Prison break
DeFord, M. A. Elsewhere, elsewhen, elsehow
The ptarmigan knife
Mystery Writers of America. Dear dead days
Slips take over
Silverberg, R. ed. Worlds of maybe

DETECTIVES, PRIVATE—*Continued*

Stevenson, R. L. The adventure of Prince Florizel and a detective

Vinge, V. The Science Fair

Wollheim, D. A. The embassy

Zelazny, R. The eve of Rumoko

**DETERGENTS**

Shaw, I. The Mannichon solution

**De Trevino, Elizabeth Borton.** *See* Trevino, Elizabeth Borton de

**Detritus.** Reid, R.

**De Unamuno y Jugo, Miguel.** *See* Unamuno y Jugo, Miguel de

**Deutsch, A. J.**

A subway named Mobius

Asimov, I. ed. Where do we go from here?

**Deutsch, Alfred H.**

Agenda for tomorrow

Deutsch, A. H. Bruised reeds, and other stories

Bruised reeds

Deutsch, A. H. Bruised reeds, and other stories

Builder of kingdoms

Deutsch, A. H. Bruised reeds, and other stories

Dubious winnings

Deutsch, A. H. Bruised reeds, and other stories

The last hour

Deutsch, A. H. Bruised reeds, and other stories

Mission to Ghana

Deutsch, A. H. Bruised reeds, and other stories

Obedience without delay

Deutsch, A. H. Bruised reeds, and other stories

The quality of reward

Deutsch, A. H. Bruised reeds, and other stories

Refining fire

Deutsch, A. H. Bruised reeds, and other stories

**Deutsches** requiem. Borges, J. L.

**Deutschman, Ben**

Business was a Jewish kid's business

Deutschman, B. In a small town a kid went to shul, and other stories

A child with a very old head

Deutschman, B. In a small town a kid went to shul, and other stories

Gittel Branfman the impossible

Deutschman, B. In a small town a kid went to shul, and other stories

Have you ever substituted for a dead horse?

Deutschman, B. In a small town a kid went to shul, and other stories

In a small town a kid went to shul

Deutschman, B. In a small town a kid went to shul, and other stories

A Jew a farmer?

Deutschman, B. In a small town a kid went to shul, and other stories

Mama's medicine made Jewish kids strong

Deutschman, B. In a small town a kid went to shul, and other stories

An only son

Deutschman, B. In a small town a kid went to shul, and other stories

The Rabbi had little angels

Deutschman, B. In a small town a kid went to shul, and other stories

Sam and Ben: deputy police officers

Deutschman, B. In a small town a kid went to shul, and other stories

So this is called success?

Deutschman, B. In a small town a kid went to shul, and other stories

Society . . . or who says they don't have a caste system in America

Deutschman, B. In a small town a kid went to shul, and other stories

Tante Sadie and the matches

Deutschman, B. In a small town a kid went to shul, and other stories

Uncle Gadalia and the chasseneh

Deutschman, B. In a small town a kid went to shul, and other stories

Women from seven to eleven and I don't mean p.m.

Deutschman, B. In a small town a kid went to shul, and other stories

You have to take music lessons

Deutschman, B. In a small town a kid went to shul, and other stories

**De Valera, Sinead**

The fairies' revenge

Haining, P. ed. The wild night company: Irish stories of fantasy and horror

The **devastating** boys. Taylor, E.

**De Vigny, Alfred.** *See* Vigny, Alfred de

**DEVIL**

Ainsworth, W. H. The spectre bride

Allingham, M. The wink

Anne of Swansea. The unknown!

Apel, J. A. The fatal marksman

Asimov, I. The brazen locked room

Benét, S. V. All that money can buy

Benét, S. V. The Devil and Daniel Webster

Bester, A. Will you wait?

The Black Spider

Bloch, R. Spawn of the dark one

Bloch, R. That Hell-bound train

Brown, F. Ten percenter

Bukowski, C. The devil was hot

Cartmill, C. No news today

Chamisso, A. von. The strange story of Peter Schlemihl

Collier, J. The Devil, George and Rosie

Collier, J. Fallen star

Collier, J. Hell hath no fury

Corvo, F. Baron. Beeing an epick of Sangiorgio, protector of the kingdom

Defoe, D. The friendly demon

De Quincey, T. The dice

Fast, H. Tomorrow's "Wall Street Journal"

Gallegos, R. The Devil's twilight

Hawthorne, N. The Salem Mass

Hawthorne, N. Young Goodman Brown

Heinlein, R. A. Magic, inc.

Hesse, H. An evening with Dr Faust

DIALECT STORIES—Negro—Continued

Peterkin, J. The merry-go-round
Peterkin, J. Missie
Peterkin, J. Missy's twins
Peterkin, J. Mount Pleasant
Peterkin, J. Plum blossoms
Peterkin, J.   A Sunday
Reeves, D.   A shonuff real man
Thelwell, M. Bright an' mownin' star
Wright, R. Almos' a man
Wright, R. Big Boy leaves home
Wright, R. Bright and morning star
Wright, R. Fire and cloud
Wright, R. The man who was almost a man
Yerby, F. Health card

### New England

Jewett, S. O. The honey tree
Macdougall, A. R. The sun stood still
Robinson, R. E. An old-time March meeting
Robinson, R. E. The purification of Cornbury

### Scotch

Fraser, G. M. Play up, play up and get tore in
Fraser, G. M. Silence in the ranks
Fraser, G. M. The whisky and the music
Hardwick, Michael, and Hardwick, Mollie. Double damnation
McGregor, M. W. Porkchops with whiskey and ice cream
Stevenson, R. L. Thrawn Janet

### Southern

Ansell, J.   I passed for Yankee
Faulkner, W. Barn burning
Faulkner, W. Two soldiers
Faulkner, W. Wash
Jay, B. Callie
Maltz, A. The way things are
Rigsby, H. Dead man's story

### West Indian

Clarke, A. Bonanza 1972 in Toronto
Walrond, E. The yellow one

### Western

Hayes, A. H. Mail-order bride
Dialogue on a cliff. Marshall, L.
Dialogue on relativity. Veiga, J. J.
A diamond guitar. Capote, T.
The diamond lens. O'Brien, F. J.
The diamond necklace. Maupassant, G. de
The diamond ring. Peterkin, J.

DIAMOND SMUGGLING

Easmon, R. S. Knave of diamonds

DIAMONDS

Allen, G. The episode of the diamond links
Bootby, G. The Duchess of Wiltshire's diamonds
Gardner, E. S. Crooked lightning
Griffith, G. Five hundred carats
Maupassant, G. de. The diamond necklace
Mergendahl, C.   A very fine deal
Powell, J. The Gobineau necklace
Richter, J. Only so much to reveal
Stevenson, R. L. The adventure of Prince Florizel and a detective

Stevenson, R. L. Story of the bandbox
Stevenson, R. L. Story of the house with the green blinds
Stevenson, R. L. Story of the young man in holy orders
Diamonds and diamonds. Crane, S.

DIARIES (STORIES IN DIARY FORM)

Barthelme, D.   Me and Miss Mandible
Beal, M. F. Gold
Bumpus, J. In Utica
Carter, L. The dweller in the tomb
Chester, A. Ismael
Collier, J. Evening primrose
Copper, B. The knocker at the portico
Disch, T. M. Things lost
Doyle, Sir A. C. The silver mirror
Farmer, P. J. Sketches among the ruins of my mind
Gide, A. The Pastoral Symphony
Green, J. Let my people go!
Heald, H. Winged death
Huey, T. The Ambulance Driver's Ball
Ibuse, M. Tajinko Village
Ionesco, E. Spring 1939
James, H.   A landscape painter
James, H.   A light man
Landolfi, T. Cancerqueen
Landolfi, T. Looking
Landolfi, T. Week of sun
Lardner, R.   A caddy's diary
Lumley, W. The diary of Alonzo Typer
McConnell, J. V. Learning theory
Maupassant, G. de. The Horla
Midwood, B. The Huntley Brinkley report
Oates, J. C. The turn of the screw
O'Donnell, K. M. Chronicles of a comer
Pangborn, E. Angel's egg
Papaleo, J. The diary of Gerald Xavier
Parker, D. From the diary of a New York lady
Payes, R. C.   . . . And the power . . .
Rodriguez, B. The naked man
Scortia, T. N. Judas fish
Scortia, T. N. The tower
Scott, D. C. Labrie's wife
Sexton, A. All God's children need radios
Shih, Ming. Fragment from a lost diary
Spielberg, P. Sickness unto death
Spike, P. The diary of Noel Wells
Steegmuller, F.   A real saint
Sternberg, J. Fin de siècle
Theroux, P. The prison diary of Jack Faust
Vance, J. Noise
West, J. The day of the hawk
Wolfe, B. Self portrait

DIARIES, STORIES ABOUT

Rothschild, M. Rhapsody of a hermit
Diary of a poltergeist. Duncan, R.
The diary of Alonzo Typer. Lumley, W.
The diary of an African nun. Walker, A.
The diary of Gerald Xavier. Papaleo, J.
The diary of Noel Wells. Spike, P.
Diary of Old Spots. Blackhurst, W. E.
Diaspora. Kaplan, B.
Díaz Alfaro, Abelardo
  The dogs
    Howes, B. ed. The eye of the heart
The dice. De Quincey, T.

The **dichotomy**. Greene, P. L.

**Dick, Philip K.**
Autofac
  Disch, T. M. ed. The ruins of earth
  Silverberg, R. ed. Beyond control
The electric ant
  Best SF: 1969
Impostor
  The Astounding-Analog reader v2
Novelty act
  Nolan, W. F. ed. The human equation
The Preserving Machine
  Silverberg, R. ed. The science fiction
    bestiary
Roog
  Silverberg, R. ed. Invaders from space
We can remember it for you wholesale
  Ferman, E. L. and Mills, R. P. eds.
    Twenty years of The Magazine of
    Fantasy and Science Fiction

**Dick** Baker's cat. Twain, M.

**Dickens, Albert**
Armageddon
  Andrews, F. E. and Dickens, A. eds.
    Voices from the big house
Let there be light
  Andrews, F. E. and Dickens, A. eds.
    Voices from the big house

**Dickens, Charles**
The bagman's story
  Manley, S. and Lewis, G. eds. Shapes
    of the supernatural
The father of the Marshalsea
  Kraus, R. and Wiegand, W. eds. Stu-
    dent's choice
The history of a self-tormentor
  Kraus, R. and Wiegand, W. eds. Stu-
    dent's choice
Horatio Sparkins
  Thune, E. and Prigozy, R. eds. Short
    stories: a critical anthology
Lively turtle
  Untermeyer, L. ed. Treasury of great
    humor
The young couple
  Untermeyer, L. ed. Treasury of great
    humor

**About**
Bradbury, R. Any friend of Nicholas
  Nickleby's is a friend of mine

**Dickens, Monica**
To reach the sea
  Manley, S. and Lewis, G. eds. Mis-
    tresses of mystery

**Dickinson, Marguerite**
A murderous slice
  Hitchcock, A. ed. Alfred Hitchcock
    presents: Stories to stay awake by

**Dickinson, William Croft**
His own number
  Dickinson, S. ed. The usurping ghost,
    and other encounters and experi-
    ences
The witch's bone
  Dickinson, S. ed. The usurping ghost,
    and other encounters and experi-
    ences

**Dickson, Carter**
The footprint in the sky
  Gibson, W. ed. Rogues' gallery
    *For other stories by this author see*
  Carr, John Dickson

**Dickson, Gordon R.**
And then there was peace
  Dickson, G. R. Danger—human
Black Charlie
  Dickson, G. R. Danger—human
Brothers
  Astounding
Building on the line
  Dickson, G. R. The star road
By new hearth fires
  Dickson, G. R. Mutants
Call him Lord
  Dickson, G. R. Danger—human
The catch
  Dickson, G. R. The star road
The Christmas present
  Dickson, G. R. The star road
Computers don't argue
  The Astounding-Analog reader v2
Danger—human
  Dickson, G. R. Danger—human
  Dickson, G. R. Mutants
Dolphin's Way
  Dickson, G. R. Danger—human
Flat tiger
  Dickson, G. R. Danger—human
Hilifter
  Dickson, G. R. The star road
Home from the shore
  Dickson, G. R. Mutants
An honorable death
  Dickson, G. R. Danger—human
  Knight, D. ed. A pocketful of stars
Idiot solvant
  Dickson, G. R. Mutants
The immortal
  Dickson, G. R. Mutants
Jackal's meal
  Dickson, G. R. The star road
James
  Dickson, G. R. Danger—human
Jean Duprès
  Nova 1
The Law-Twister Shorty
  Bova, B. ed. The many worlds of sci-
    ence fiction
Listen
  Dickson, G. R. Mutants
Lulungomeena
  Dickson, G. R. Danger—human
  Silverberg, R. ed. Deep space
The man from earth
  Dickson, G. R. Danger—human
Maverick
  Five fates
Miss Prinks
  Dickson, G. R. Mutants
The mousetrap
  Dickson, G. R. The star road
Of the people
  Dickson, G. R. Mutants
On Messenger Mountain
  Dickson, G. R. The star road

The **dimension** of chance. Smith, C. A.

**DiNapoli, Nan**
  Sam the sorry zebra
    Voices of Brooklyn

**Dinesen, Isak**
  The ring
    Howes, B. and Smith, G. J. eds. The
      sea-green horse
  The sailor-boy's tale
    Johnson, E. W. ed. Short stories inter-
      national
    Tytell, J. and Jaffe, H. eds. Affinities
**Ding**-dong. Beckett, S.
**Ding**-Dong-Dell. Burke, T.
**DINING.** *See* Dinners
The **dinner.** Lispector, C.
**Dinner.** Trevisan, D.
**Dinner** at Diop's. Fuller, H. W.
**Dinner** at Helen's. Carlson, W.
**DINNER PARTIES.** *See* Dinners
The **dinner** party. Vassilikos, V.
**Dinner** with Ormsbee-Fletcher. Richler, M.
**DINNERS**
  Algren, N. Tinkle Hinkle and the foot-
    note king
  Allingham, M. The same to us
  Bowen, E. Her table spread
  Colter, C. Black for dinner
  Dickens, C. Horatio Sparkins
  Goldman, W. The ice cream eat
  Graham, W. The Medici earring
  Harrison, W. Eating it
  Henry, O. The renaissance at Charleroi
  Huxley, A. The Tillotson banquet
  Katz, S.   A home-cooked meal for the as-
    tronaut
  Lispector, C. The dinner
  Malamud, B. Notes from a lady at a din-
    ner party
  Maugham, W. S. Cousin Amy
  Pei, M. The Huntsmen's Banquet
  Richler, M. Dinner with Ormsby-Fletcher
  Rulfo, J. The day of the landslide
  Runyon, D.   A piece of pie
  Silverberg, R. The Iron Chancellor
  Trevisan, D. Soup
    *See also* Food; Luncheons; Parties
**DINOSAURS**
  De Camp, L. S.   A gun for dinosaur
  Laumer, K. Giant killer
  Updike, J. During the Jurassic
**DIONYSUS**
  Ayrton, M. Rout
  Silverberg, R. The Feast of St Dionysus
**Diop, Birago**
  Sarzan
    Larson, C. R. ed. African short stories
  The wages of good
    Bambara, T. C. ed. Tales and stories
      for black folks
**DIPHTHERIA**
  Kipling, R.   A second-rate woman
**DIPLOMATIC LIFE**
  Carpentier, A. Right of sanctuary
  Collette. 'Châ'
  Dickson, G. R. Jackal's meal
  Goulart, R. Change over
  Green, J. L. The birdlover

Just, W. Burns
Just, W. Slayton
Laumer, K. Ballots and bandits
Laumer, K. Crime and punishment
Laumer, K. Dam nuisance
Laumer, K. The Forbidden City
Laumer, K. The forest in the sky
Laumer, K. Giant killer
Laumer, K. Internal affair
Laumer, K. Mechanical advantage
Laumer, K. The piecemakers
Laumer, K. Pime doesn't cray
Laumer, K. Retief: Ambassador to space;
  7 stories
Laumer, K. Retief of the CDT; 5 stories
Laumer, K. Trick or treaty
Laumer, K. Truce or consequences
Laumer, K. Ultimatum
Piper, H. B. He walked around the horses
Sallis, J. Kettle of stars
Taylor, P. There
Zobarskas, S. The wish
    *See also* Consuls
**DIPLOMATS.** *See* Diplomatic life
**Direct** action. Thelwell, M.
**Direction** of the road. Le Guin, U. K.
The **director's** wife. Glanville, B.
**Dirt** track decoy. Gault, W. C.
**Dirty** Ralphy. Fiedler, L. A.
A **dirty** story. Kemal, Y.
**DISABLED.** *See* Cripples
The **disappearance** of Marie Severe. Bra-
  mah, E.
The **disappearance** of Mr Davenheim.
  Christie, A.
**DISAPPEARANCES**
  Allingham, M. Family affair
  Allingham, M. Joke over
  Allingham, M. The Villa Marie Celeste
  Anderson Imbert, E. The General makes
    a lovely corpse
  Armstrong, C. From out of the garden
  Bierce, A. At old man Eckert's
  Bierce, A. Charles Ashmore's trail
  Bierce, A. The difficulty of crossing a
    field
  Bierce, A. An unfinished race
  Blount, M. The right books
  Campbell, R. The end of a summer's day
  Campbell, R. The Old Horns
  Carr, T. Stanley Toothbrush
  Cather, W. The willing muse
  Christie, A. The disappearance of Mr
    Davenheim
  Christie, A. The Listerdale mystery
  Cross, J. K. Music when soft voices die . . .
  DeFord, M. A. Farewell to the Faulkners
  Eisenberg, L. The vanishing borough
  Eisenberg, L. What happened to Auguste
    Clarot?
  Gardner, E. S. The case of the crying
    swallow
  Gardner, E. S. A man is missing
  Gilbert, A. Who cares about an old
    woman?
  Henry, O. The renaissance at Charleroi
  Holmes, E. M. Beyond Shadow Island
  Kipling, R. The return of Imray

**Dneprov, Anatoly**—*Continued*
 The island of the crabs
  Suvin, D. ed. Other worlds, other seas
  Same as: Crabs take over the island
 The S°T°A°P°L°E Farm
  Suvin, D. ed. Other worlds, other seas
 When questions are asked
  Ginsburg, M. ed. The ultimate threshold
**Do** androids dream of electric love? Leibscher, W.
**Do** it for Mama! Mundis, J. J.
**Do** not pass me by. Glaze, E.
**Do** re mi. Kanin, G.
**Do** stay, Giraffe. Borchert, W.
**Do** they talk about Genêt in Larchmont? Yurick, S.
**Do** you like it here? O'Hara, J.
**Doby's** gone. Petry, A.
The **dock**-witch. Ozick, C.
**DOCKERS.** *See* Longshoremen
The **Doctor.** Dubus, A.
**Dr** A. R. Broga. Ayrton, M.
The **doctor** and the doctor's wife. Hemingway, E.
The **doctor** and the eagle. Djilas, M.
**Dr** Beeber. Singer, I. B.
**Dr** Birdmouse. Bretnor, R.
**Dr** Black's castle. Maclagan, D.
**Dr** Blanke's first command. Forester, C. S.
**Doctor** Crombie. Greene, G.
**Dr** Gregor and the Evil One. Krleža, M.
**Doctor** Moreau's other island. Nesvadba, J.
**Dr** Morris Goldpepper returns. Davidson, A.
**Dr** Nazi. Bukowski, C.
**Dr** Ox will die at midnight. Kersh, G.
**Dr** Porthos. Copper, B.
The **Dr** Sherrock commission. McAuliffe, F.
**Dr** Southport Vulpes's nightmare. Russell, B.
**Dr** Woolacott. Forster, E. M.
**Doctor** Zombie and his furry little friends. Sheckley, R.
**Doctorow, E. L.**
 The songs of Billy Bathgate
  New American Review no. 2
**DOCTORS.** *See* Physicians
The **doctor's** divorce. Agnon, S. Y.
**Doctor's** orders. Suter, J. F.
The **doctor's** son. O'Hara, J.
The **doctor's** wife. Ozick, C.
The **doctor's** wife. Updike, J.
The **document.** Agnon, S. Y.
**Dodecagon** garden. Petaja, E.
**Doderer, Heimito von**
 The magician's art
  Decker, C. R. and Angoff, C. eds. Modern stories from many lands
 Sonatina
  Angoff, C. ed. Stories from the Literary Review
 Stepfield
  Angoff, C. ed. Stories from the Literary Review
**Dodgson, Charles Lutwidge.** *See* Carroll, Lewis
The **doe** and the gantlet. Stadley, P.
**Does** the Army always get its man? Stuart, J.
The **dog.** Annixter, P.

**Dog.** Deck, J.
The **dog.** Marshall, L.
The **dog** act. Kanin, G.
**Dog** days. Theroux, P.
**Dog** in a fisherman's net. Delany, S. R.
**Dog** in the manger. Rothschild, M.
The **dog**-man horror of the valley. Day, J. W.
**Dog** spirit. Beekman, A.
**Dogman** of Islington. Bailey, H.
**DOGS**
 Aiken, J. Summer by the sea
 Anderson, A. Comrade
 Anderson, S. Death in the woods
 Annixter, P. The dog
 Armstrong, C. The enemy
 Bahr, J. Deedie and her lovers
 Bailey, H. Dogman of Islington
 Barthelme, D. The falling dog
 Bichsel, P. The animal lover
 Bierce, A. Oil of dog
 Blackhurst, W. E. Bringing home the dog
 Brautigan, R. Winter rug
 Brennan, M. The children are very quiet when they are away
 Brennan, M. The door on West Tenth Street
 Brennan, M. In and out of never-never land
 Carpentier, A. The fugitives
 Christie, A. Next to a dog
 Collier, J. A dog's a dog
 Coloane, F. A. Cururo . . . sheep dog
 Crane, S. The black dog
 Crane, S. A dark-brown dog
 Deck, J. Dog
 Delapp, T. Escape from camp 9
 Delapp, T. Once upon a funeral
 Díaz Alfaro, A. The dogs
 Dick, P. K. Roog
 Dickson, G. R. By new hearth fires
 Donoso, J. Paseo
 Ellison, H. A boy and his dog
 Elman, R. On making friends
 Emshwiller, C. Pelt
 Ford, J. H. Foxy
 Goldman, W. The ice cream eat
 Goulart, R. Prez
 Greenberg, A. A brief chronology of death and night
 Heinesen, J. P. Gestur
 Henderson, Z. Boona on Scancia
 Holm, S. Miss Urst visits the Deer Park
 Hunter, K. BeeGee's ghost
 Karlin, W. The Vietnamese elections
 Kawabata, Y. Of birds and beasts
 Khamsing, S. The peasant and the white man
 Kim, Y. I. From below the bridge
 Kipling, R. Red Dog
 Kotzwinkle, W. Nippy
 Landolfi, T. Fable
 Landolfi, T. Hands
 Laurence, M. The half-husky
 Lightner, A. M. Best friend
 Lispector, C. The crime of the mathematics professor
 London, J. The devil-dog
 Madden, D. Love makes nothing happen
 Maltz, A. The farmer's dog

The **doors** of his face, the lamps of his mouth. Zelazny, R.

The **doors** of life. Hughes, L.

**Dorg.** Lafferty, R. A.

**Dorman, Sonya**
The deepest blue in the world
  SF: authors' choice 3
Harry the tailor
  Knight, D. ed. A pocketful of stars
The living end
  Orbit 7
Lunatic assignment
  The Best from Fantasy and Science Fiction; 18th ser.
A mess of porridge
  McCaffrey, A. ed. Alchemy and academe

**DORMITORIES**
Baraka, I. A. The alternative

**Dorr, Lawrence**
An act of admiration
  Dorr, L. A slow, soft river
The binge
  Dorr, L. A slow, soft river
Bradenburg Concerto
  Dorr, L. A slow, soft river
Brindley
  Dorr, L. A slow, soft river
Curfew
  Dorr, L. A slow, soft river
Once you were no people
  Dorr, L. A slow, soft river
A slow, soft river
  Dorr, L. A slow, soft river

**Dorris, James R.**
The accident
  Karlin, W.; Paquet, B. T. and Rottmann, L. eds. Free fire zone

**DORSETSHIRE.** *See* England, Provincial and rural—Dorsetshire

**Dostoevskii, F. M.** *See* Dostoevsky, Fyodor

**Dostoevsky, Fyodor**
A Christmas tree and a wedding
  Hall, J. B. ed. The realm of fiction
The crocodile
  Taylor, J. C. ed. The short story: fiction in transition
The dream of a ridiculous man
  Knight, D. ed. Perchance to dream
  Proffer, C. R. ed. From Karamzin to Bunin: an anthology of Russian short stories
The grand inquisitor
  Disch, R. and Schwartz, B. eds. Killing time
The peasant Marey
  Satin, J. ed. Reading literature

**Dotson** Gerber resurrected. Bennett, H.

**DOUBLE-BASS PLAYERS.** *See* Musicians —Violinists

**Double** birthday. Cather, W.

**Double** damnation. Hardwick, Michael, and Hardwick, Mollie

**Double** dare. Silverberg, R.

**Double** entry. Fish, R. L.

The **double** gap. Auchincloss, L.

**Double** image. Vickers, R.

**Double** Nigger. Dumas, H.

**Double** or nothing. De Vries, P.

**Double** people. Dawson, F.

**Double** standard. Brown, F.

**Doubled**-cross. Pechtel, C.

**DOUBLES.** *See* Impersonations

The **doubles.** Hoffmann, E. T. A.

**Doubles.** Moravia, A.

The **doubter.** Green, R. L.

**Doucement,** s'il vous plaît. Sallis, J.

**Dougherty's** eye-opener. Henry, O.

**DOVES.** *See* Pigeons

**Dowell, Coleman**
The birthmark
  New Directions in prose and poetry 27
The keepsake
  New Directions in prose and poetry 26

**Down** and out. Moravia, A.

**Down** by the old maelstrom. Wellen, E.

**Down** in the black gang. Farmer, P. J.

**Down** in the eighth. Steingass, D.

**Down** our way. Wain, J.

**Down** the digestive tract and into the cosmos with Mantra, Tantra, and Specklebang. Sheckley, R.

**Down** the long night. Nolan, W. F.

**Downer, Mary Louise**
After the lights are out
  Ellery Queen's Mystery Magazine. Ellery Queen's Mystery bag

**Downey, Harris**
The hunters
  Oates, J. C. ed. Scenes from American life

**Downfall** of a general. Bahr, J.

The **downward** path to wisdom. Porter, K. A.

**Downwind** from Gettysburg. Bradbury, R.

**Doyle, Sir Arthur Conan**
The fiend of the cooperage
  Bowman, J. S. ed. A book of islands
How the brigadier saved an army
  Green, R. L. ed. Ten tales of adventure
The secret of Goresthorpe Grange
  Manley, S. and Lewis, G. eds. Shapes of the supernatural
The silver mirror
  Haining, P. ed. The nightmare reader
The speckled band
  Dickinson, S. ed. The drugged cornet, and other mystery stories
  Same as: The adventure of the speckled band, entered in earlier volumes
The striped chest
  Green, R. L. ed. Thirteen uncanny tales
Through the veil
  Haining, P. ed. The clans of darkness
    **Parodies, travesties, etc.**
Brittain, W. The man who read Sir Arthur Conan Doyle
Fish, R. L. The adventure of the Adam bomb
Fish, R. L. The adventure of the dog in the knight
Fish, R. L. The adventure of the double-bogey man

**Dozois, Gardner R.**
Chains of the sea
  Chains of the sea

**Dozois, Gardner R.**—*Continued*
A dream at noonday
Orbit 7
Horse of air
Nebula award stories 7
Orbit 8
King harvest
New dimensions 2
A kingdom by the sea
Orbit 10
Machines of loving grace
Orbit 11
The man who waved hello
Universe 2
A special kind of morning
New dimensions 1
Where no sun shines
Orbit 6

**Drabble, Margaret**
The gifts of war
Winter's tales 16

**Dracula's** guest. Stoker, B.

**Draff.** Beckett, S.

**DRAFT, MILITARY.** *See* Military service, Compulsory

**DRAFT EVADERS.** *See* Military service, Compulsory

The **Dragon** masters. Vance, J.

**Dragonrider.** McCaffrey, A.

**DRAGONS**
Endore, G. The day of the dragon
Gardner, J. The song of Grendel
Grahame, K. The reluctant dragon
McCaffrey, A. Dragonrider
McCaffrey, A. Weyr search
Richards, D. Traveller's joy
Vance, J. The Dragon masters
Wyndham, J. Chinese puzzle
Zelazny, R. The monster and the maiden
*See also* Fantasies

**DRAGOONS.** *See* Soldiers

**Drake, Albert**
The chicken which became a rat
The Best American short stories, 1971

**Drake, David**
Lord of the depths
Derleth, A. ed. Dark things

**Drake, Nathan**
The Abbey of Clunedale
Haining, P. ed. Gothic tales of terror

**Drake, Robert**
The cook and the sheriff
Drake, R. The single heart
Cousin Hon
Drake, R. The single heart
Deep in the interior and everything and all
Drake, R. The single heart
Don't they look natural?
Drake, R. The single heart
The fifth wheel
Drake, R. The single heart
Maiden lady
Drake, R. The single heart
The music lover
Drake, R. The single heart
My own true love
Drake, R. The single heart

The pressure cooker
Drake, R. The single heart
Pretty boy
Drake, R. The single heart
The ring-tail tooter
Drake, R. The single heart
St Peter right in the eye
Drake, R. The single heart
She was strangely affected
Drake, R. The single heart
The single heart
Drake, R. The single heart
The stark naked Baptist
Drake, R. The single heart
They cut her open and then just sewed her back up
Drake, R. The single heart
The tower and the pear tree
Drake, R. The single heart
The trained nurse
Drake, R. The single heart
The ugliest white woman you ever saw in your life
Drake, R. The single heart
The voices of women at the back of my mind
Drake, R. The single heart
Where the hurt is
Drake, R. The single heart
Will the merchant prince's son come down the sawdust trail?
Drake, R. The single heart
A wreath for Ed Meachum
Drake, R. The single heart
The wrong element
Drake, R. The single heart
You scoundrel of a beast
Drake, R. The single heart

**Drake** feeds the buzzards. Kent, W. H. B.

**DRAMATIC CRITICS**
Kanin, G. Who to who

**DRAMATISTS**
Carpenter, D. New York to Los Angeles
Cather, W. The treasure of Far Island
Dennison, G. Interview with the author of Caryatids
Fenton, F. The perfect plot
Fitzgerald, F. S. A snobbish story
Gilliatt, P. Known for her frankness
Hunter, E. The beheading
Kanin, G. An echo of love
Kanin, G. The only game in town
Marsh, W. Mexican hayride
O'Hara, J. Conversation at lunch
O'Hara, J. Flight
Simak, C. Shadow show

**Drawing** room B. O'Hara, J.

**DRAWINGS.** *See* Cave drawings

**Dreaded** hell. Onetti, J. C.

The **dreadful** has already happened. Kagan, N.

The **dream.** Apuleius

**Dream.** Dawson, F.

A **dream.** Kafka, F.

**Dream.** Lafferty, R. A.

The **dream.** Shelley, M. W.

A **dream** at noonday. Dozois, G. R.

A **dream** come true. Onetti, J. C.

**Dream** journeys. Hesse, H.

**Du Fail, Noël**
A man's best friend
Cholakian, P. F. and Cholakian, R. C.
eds. The early French novella
**Du Gard, Roger Martin**
The reformatory
Morton, M. ed. Voices from France
The **Duke.** Linklater, E.
**Dumas, Henry**
Ark of bones
Dumas, H. Ark of bones, and other
stories
A boll of roses
Dumas, H. Ark of bones, and other
stories
The crossing
Dumas, H. Ark of bones, and other
stories
Double Nigger
Dumas, H. Ark of bones, and other
stories
Echo tree
Dumas, H. Ark of bones, and other
stories
Fon
Dumas, H. Ark of bones, and other
stories
A Harlem game
Dumas, H. Ark of bones, and other
stories
Rain god
Adoff, A. ed. Brothers and sisters
Strike and fade
Dumas, H. Ark of bones, and other
stories
Will the circle be unbroken?
Dumas, H. Ark of bones, and other
stories
**Du Maurier, Daphne**
The birds
Disch, T. M. ed. The ruins of earth
Manley, S. and Lewis, G. eds. Ladies of
horror
A border-line case
Du Maurier, D. Don't look now
The breakthrough
Du Maurier, D. Don't look now
Don't look now
Du Maurier, D. Don't look now
A Treasury of modern mysteries v 1
Not after midnight
Du Maurier, D. Don't look now
The Way of the Cross
Du Maurier, D. Don't look now
The **dumb** Dutchman. Forester, C. S.
**Dumbroviç.** Farrell, J. T.
**DUMMIES.** See Models, Fashion
The **dummy.** Matthews, C.
**Dumonte, Ed**
A crazy way to make a living
Ellery Queen's Mystery Magazine. El-
lery Queen's Grand slam
The **dump.** Brennan, J. P.
**Dunbar, Paul Laurence**
The ingrate
James, C. L. ed. From the roots
Jim's probation
James, C. L. ed. From the roots

The lynching of Jube Benson
Long, R. A. and Collier, E. W. eds.
Afro-American writing v 1
Mr Cornelius Johnson, office-seeker
Turner, D. T. ed. Black American liter-
ature
The mortification of the flesh
Turner, D. T. ed. Black American liter-
ature
The wisdom of silence
James, C. L. ed. From the roots
**Duncan, Ronald**
Diary of a poltergeist
Turner, J. ed. Unlikely ghosts
**Dunghill.** Khamsing, S.
**Dunn, Pat**
The beach
Intro #3
**Dunsany, Edward J. M. Drax Plunkett,
18th Baron.** See Dunsany, Lord
**Dunsany, Lord**
The Bureau d'Echange de Maux
Haining, P. ed. The nightmare reader
The hashish man
Kahn, J. ed. Hanging by a thread
Witch wood
Haining, P. ed. The wild night com-
pany: Irish stories of fantasy and
horror
**Duodu, Cameron**
The tax dodger
Larson, C. R. ed. African short stories
**DUPLICATING PROCESSES.** See Copy-
ing processes
**DURHAM.** See North Carolina—Durham
**During** the Jurassic. Updike, J.
**Durrell, Lawrence**
The cherries
Haining, P. ed. The Lucifer society
**Dusk** before fireworks. Parker, D.
A **dusk** of idols. Blish, J.
**Dusk** to dawn. Woolrich, C.
**DUST**
Clement, H. Dust rag
**Dust** in the house. Keller, D. H.
**Dust** rag. Clement, H.
**Dust** underfoot. Khamsing, S.
**Dusty** deal. Ottley, R.
The **dusty** drawer. Muheim, H.
**DUTCH IN NEW GUINEA**
Mulisch, H. What happened to Sergeant
Masuro?
**DUTCH IN SUMATRA**
Saltus, E.   A transient guest
**DUTCH IN THE UNITED STATES**
Irving, W. Guests from Gibbet Island
Irving, W. The legend of Sleepy Hollow
Johnson, D. An apple, an orange
**DUTCH SOLDIERS.** See Soldiers, Dutch
**DWARFS**
Bradbury, R. McGillahee's brat
Hoffmann, E. T. A. Little Zaches, sur-
named Zinnober
Huxley, A. Sir Hercules
Nabokov, V. The Potato-Elf
Robbins, T. Freaks
Robbins, T. Spurs
Shelley, M. The transformation
Smith, C. A. The amazing planet

The **dweller** in darkness, Derleth, A.

The **dweller** in the tomb. Carter, L.

**DWELLINGS.** *See* Houses

**DYING.** *See* Death

Dying. Oates, J. C.

The **dying** footballer. Glanville, B.

The **dying** of Eunice LeBel. Smith, L.

**DYING SCENES.** *See* Deathbed scenes

Dylath-leen. Lumley, B.

'**Dymchurch** Flit'. Kipling, R.

**DYNAMOS**
 Wells, H. G. The Lord of the Dynamos

Dzhan. Platonov, A.

# E

E for effort. Sherred, T. L.

**EPICAC.** Vonnegut, K.

**ESP.** *See* Extra-sensory perception

Each spring. Blum-Alquit, E.

Eagle Squadron. Forester, C. S.

**EAGLES**
 Blackhurst, W. E. Kindred souls
 Djilas, M. The doctor and the eagle
 Eastlake, W. The death of Sun

The **ear.** Ayrton, M.

The **ear** specialist. Des Périers, B.

**Earls, William**
 Jump
  Analog 8
 Traffic problem
  Best SF: 1970

**Early** Autumn. Hughes, L.

**Early** bird. Cogswell, T. R. and Thomas, T. L.

**EARLY CHRISTIANS.** *See* Christians, Early

**Early** in the morning. Dawson, F.

**Early** marriage. Richter, C.

**Early** morning murder. Ayala Gauna, V.

**EARRINGS**
 Graham, W. The Medici earring

**EARTH**
 Landolfi, T.   A family chat
  **Internal structure**
 Mitchell, E. P. The inside of the earth

**EARTH (PLANET)**
 Clarke, A. C. Reunion

**EARTH, DESTRUCTION OF**
 Aldiss, B. W. Heresies of the Huge God
 Asimov, I. Super-neutron
 Ballard, J. G. Deep end
 Bester, A. Adam and no Eve
 Blish, J. We all die naked
 Bradbury, R. October 2026: the million-year picnic
 Carr, T. The answer
 Clarke, A. C. The curse
 Clarke, A. C. If I forget thee, o Earth
 Clarke, A. C. The last command
 Ellison, H. Hindsight: 480 seconds
 Fast, H. Not with a bang
 Fast, H. Show cause
 Knight, D. Shall the dust praise thee?
 Lafferty, R. A. And walk now gently through the fire
 Lafferty, R. A. The transcendent tigers

Lafferty, R. A. When all the lands pour out again

Laumer, K. Prototaph

Leiber, F.   A pail of air

Long, F. B. Preview

Rocklynne, R. Ching witch!

Sheckley, R. Potential

Sheckley, R. Zirn left unguarded, the Jenghik Palace in flames, Jon Westerly dead

Silverberg, R. When we went to see the end of the world

Silverberg, R. The wind and the rain

Simak, C. D. Epilog

Slesar, H. and Ellison, H. Survivor #1

Tenn, W. The liberation of earth

Wilhelm, K. The chosen
  *See also* End of the world

The **earth** is round. Bichsel, P.

The **earth** men. *See* Bradbury, R. August 1999: the Earth men

**Earthcoming.** Meredith, R. C.

**Earthman,** come home. Blish, J.

**EARTHQUAKES**
 Bova, B.   A slight miscalculation
 De Vries, J. Journey to the center of the room
 Elliott, G. P. In a hole
 Le Guin, U. K. Nine lives
  *See also* Disasters

**Easmon, R. Sarif**
 The human touch
  Angoff, C. and Povey, J. eds. African writing today
 Knave of diamonds
  Angoff, C. and Povey, J. eds. African writing today

**EAST AND WEST**
 Forster, E. M. The life to come

**EAST INDIANS IN AFRICA**
 Richter, J. The prisoner of Zemu Island

**EAST INDIANS IN ENGLAND**
 Jhabvala, R. P.   A course in English studies
 Naipaul, V. S. Tell me who to kill
 Naipaul, S. The tenant
 Theroux, A. Childe Rowland

**EAST INDIANS IN THE UNITED STATES**
 Harter, E. The stone lovers
 Naipaul, V. S. One out of many
 Theroux, P.   A love knot
 White, R. Mixed relations

**EAST SIDE.** *See* New York (City)—Lower East Side

**East,** West . . . Midwest. Stern, R.

"**East** wind, west wind." Robinson, F. M.

**EASTER**
 Jewett, S. O. The green bonnet, a story of Easter day
 Solzhenitsyn, A. The Easter procession
 West, J. The heavy stone
  *See also* Jesus Christ—Resurrection

An **Easter** carol. Clarke, A.

**Easter** egg. Brookhouser, F.

The **Easter** procession. Solzhenitsyn, A.

**EASTERN ORTHODOX CHURCH.** *See* Orthodox Eastern Church

**Eisen, W. I.**
Checkmate in two moves
Yates, D. A. ed. Latin blood
**Eisenberg, Larry**
The chameleon
Eisenberg, L. The best laid schemes
Conqueror
Eisenberg, L. The best laid schemes
Duckworth's forever
Eisenberg, L. The best laid schemes
Duckworth's IQ soup
Eisenberg, L. The best laid schemes
Hold your fire!
Eisenberg, L. The best laid schemes
The irresistible Party Chairman
Eisenberg, L. The best laid schemes
Is there life in inner space?
Eisenberg, L. The best laid schemes
The marvelous Marshall
Eisenberg, L. The best laid schemes
A matter of recordings
Eisenberg, L. The best laid schemes
A matter of time and place
Eisenberg, L. The best laid schemes
The mighty Matterhorn
Eisenberg, L. The best laid schemes
The open secrets
Eisenberg, L. The best laid schemes
The Pirokin effect
Eisenberg, L. The best laid schemes
Project Amnion
Eisenberg, L. The best laid schemes
The saga of DMM
Eisenberg, L. The best laid schemes
The time of his life
Eisenberg, L. The best laid schemes
Too many Cooks
Eisenberg, L. The best laid schemes
The two lives of Ben Coulter
Eisenberg, L. The best laid schemes
Uncle Sam's children
Eisenberg, L. The best laid schemes
The vanishing borough
Eisenberg, L. The best laid schemes
What happened to Auguste Clarot?
Eisenberg, L. The best laid schemes
**EISENHOWER, DWIGHT DAVID, PRES-
IDENT U.S.**
Russell, B. Eisenhower's nightmare
**Eisenhower's** nightmare. Russell, B.
**Eisenstein, Alex, and Eisenstein, Phyllis**
The trouble with the past
New dimensions 1
**Eisenstein, Phyllis**
Born to exile
The Best from Fantasy & Science Fiction; 20th ser.
*See also* Eisenstein, A. jt. auth.
**Eklund, Gordon**
Examination day
Elwood, R. ed. The other side of tomorrow
Free City blues
Universe 3
Lovemaker
Elder, J. ed. Eros in orbit
The Shrine of Sebastian
Chains of the sea

Stalking the sun
Universe 2
Underbelly
Del Rey, L. ed. Best science fiction stories of the year [1973]
White summer in Memphis
New dimensions 2
*See also* Benford, G. jt. auth.
**Ekwensi, Cyprian**
Coin diver
Nolen, B. ed. Africa is thunder and wonder
**Ela, Jonathan**
From sea to shining sea
Best SF: 1972
**ELBA**
Glanville, B. Arrivederci, Elba
The **elder** lady. Borges, J. L.
The **eldest** child. Brennan, M.
**El Dorado:** a Kansas recessional. Cather, W.
**Eleanor's** house. Cather, W.
The **elect.** Taylor, P.
**ELECTIONS**
Achebe, C. The voter
Calvino, I. The watcher
Farrel, J. T. Native's return
Khamsing, S. The politician
The **electric** ant. Dick, P. K.
**ELECTRIC COMMUNICATION.** *See* Telecommunication
The **electric** executioner. Castro, A. de
**ELECTRIC POWER DISTRIBUTION**
Delany, S. R. We, in some strange power's employ, move on a rigorous line
Janifer, L. M. Thine alabaster cities gleam
Weaver, G. The entombed man of Thule
*See also* Electricity
**ELECTRICITY**
Nemerov, H. The outage
Smith, G. O. Lost art
Summers, H. The terrible death of Mister Vimont
**ELECTROMAGNETIC SCREENS.** *See* Shielding (Electricity)
**ELECTROMAGNETIC SHIELDS.** *See* Shielding (Electricity)
**ELECTRONIC COMPUTERS**
Anderson, P. Goat song
Asimov, I. The last question
Bakhnov, V. Unique
Bester, A. Something up there likes me
Bova, B. The next logical step
Bretnor, R. and Neville, K. Gratitude guaranteed
Chapman, S. Testing . . . one, two, three, four
Clarke, A. C. The pacifist
Corwin, N. Belles lettres, 2272
Dickinson, W. C. His own number
Dickson, G. R. Computers don't argue
Eisenberg, L. The open secrets
Ellison, H. I have no mouth, and I must scream
Gilliatt, P. An antique love story
Goldin, S. Sweet dreams, Melissa
Goulart, R. Broke down engine
Goulart, R. Looking into it
Green, J. Space to move

ENGLAND—*Continued*

**London**—12th century

Naipaul, V. S. Tell me who to kill

**London**—16th century

Burgess, A. The muse

**London**—19th century

Ashdown, C. The Assyrian rejuvenator

Ashdown, C. The submarine boat

Boothby, G. The Duchess of Wiltshire's diamonds

Bramah, E. The game played in the dark

Freeman, R. A. The Moabite cipher

Gissing, G. Lou and Liz

Hebel, J. P. The strange story of a young Englishman

Keating, P. J. ed. Working-class stories of the 1890s; 13 stories

Kipling, R. The record of Badalia Herodsfoot

Morrison, A. The case of Laker, absconded

Morrison, A. Lizerunt

Nevinson, H. Sissero's return

Orczy, Baroness. The mysterious death on the Underground Railway

Orczy, Baroness. The woman in the big hat

Pain, B. The grey cat

Pemberton, M. The ripening rubies

Pugh, E.  A small talk exchange

Riddell, Mrs J. H. The uninhabited house

Rook, C. Billy the Snide

Rook, C. Concerning hooligans

Rook, C. Young Alf

**London**—20th century

Alvarez, A. Laughter

Bailey, H. Dogman of Islington

Bragg, M. The initiation

Bramah, E. The Holloway flat tragedy

Bromhead, F.  A winter evening

Burke, T. Beryl, the Croucher and the rest of England

Burke, T. The bird

Burke, T. The Chink and the child

Burke, T. The cue

Burke, T. Ding-Dong-Dell

Burke, T. The father of Yoto

Burke, T. Gina of the Chinatown

Burke, T. The gorilla and the girl

Burke, T. Gracie Goodnight

Burke, T. The knight-errant

Burke, T. Limehouse nights; 14 stories

Burke, T. Old Joe

Burke, T. The paw

Burke, T. The sign of the lamp

Burke, T. Tai Fu and Pansy Greers

Cortázar, J. Instructions for John Howell

Curley, D. In the hands of our enemies

Curley, D. Station: you are here

Farjeon, E. The glass peacock

Glanville, B. Everything laid on

Glanville, B. Hanger-on

Goudge, E. Lost—one angel

Graham, W.  I had known Sam Taylor for years

Greene, G. Jubilee

Greene, G. Special duties

Kersh, G. Mr Tomorrow

Lessing, D. Notes for a case history

Lessing, D. An old woman and her cat

Linklater, E. The actress Olenina

Litvinov, I. Call it love

Litvinov, I. To be a Daniel

Manning, O. The Banana House

Moorcock, M. An apocalypse: some scenes from European life

Mordaunt, E. The yellow cat

Nabokov, V. The Potato Elf

Pritchett, V. S. The cage birds

Pudney, J. Kitty, Kitty, Kitty

Rees, B. Poor Margaret

Symons, J. Eight minutes to kill

Taylor, E. Tall boy

Theroux, A. Childe Roland

Theroux, A. Mrs Proby gets hers

Theroux, A. Three wogs; 3 stories

Tindall, G. An end in Great Russell Street

Tindall, G. Fiona

Tuohy, F.  A life membership

Tuohy, F. The trap

Updike, J. Bech swings?

Wain, J.  A man in a million

Wain, J. You could have fooled me

Warner, S. T. But at the stroke of midnight

Warner, S. T. The green torso

**London**—Streets

Morrison, A.  A street

**Norfolk**

*See* England, Provincial and rural—Norfolk

**Nottingham**—20th century

Sillitoe, A. Canals

Sillitoe, A. Guzman, go home, and other stories; 7 stories

Sillitoe, A. The rope trick

**Politics**

*See* Politics—England

**Radicalism**

*See* Radicalism—England

**School life**

*See* School life—England

**Stratford-upon-Avon**

Bentley, P.  A midsummer night's crime

**Suffolk**

*See* England, Provincial and rural—Suffolk

**Wiltshire**

*See* England, Provincial and rural—Wiltshire

**Yorkshire**

*See* England, Provincial and rural—Yorkshire

**ENGLAND, PROVINCIAL AND RURAL**

Aberconway, C. The cat and the child

Aiken, J. The apple of trouble

Blish, J. Statistician's day

Bowen, M. The Crown Derby plate

Brackenbury, R. Horsemen

Brand, C. King of the air

Burton, H. Not the end of the world

Campbell, R. The Sentinels

**ENGLISH IN INDIA**
Aldiss, B. W. Orgy of the living and the dying
Borges, J. L. The man on the threshold
Buck, P. S. The green sari
Hesse, H. Robert Aghion
Jhabvala, R. P. A star and two girls
Kipling, R. At the end of the passage
Kipling, R. At the pit's mouth
Kipling, R. A bank fraud
Kipling, R. Beyond the pale
Kipling, R. The daughter of the regiment
Kipling, R. The man who would be king
Kipling, R. The mark of the beast
Kipling, R. My own true ghost story
Kipling, R. The phantom 'rickshaw
Kipling, R. The return of Imray
Kipling, R. A second-rate woman
Kipling, R. The story of Muhammad Din
Kipling, R. The strange ride of Morrowbie Jukes
Kipling, R. Wee Willie Winkie
Kipling, R. Without benefit of clergy
Middleton, J. A. Black magic
Singh, K. Karma
Theroux, P. What have you done to our Leo?

**ENGLISH IN IRELAND**
Fielding, G. The young bloods

**ENGLISH IN ISRAEL**
Silk, D. Montefiore

**ENGLISH IN ITALY**
Bates, H. E. The small portion
Du Maurier, D. Don't look now
Glanville, B. The footballers
Glanville, B. The prodigy
Lavin, M. Trastevere
Rees, B. Mrs Wall, Mrs Wall

**ENGLISH IN JAMAICA**
West, P. The season of the single women

**ENGLISH IN MOROCCO**
Haylock, J. A different party

**ENGLISH IN PALESTINE**
Wiesel, E. Dawn

**ENGLISH IN PORTUGAL**
Fielding, G. Figs in spring

**ENGLISH IN RUSSIA**
Leskov, N. The archbishop and the Englishman
Litvinov, I. Farewall to the dacha
Litvinov, I. Portrait of a lady

**ENGLISH IN SCOTLAND**
Stoker, B. Crooken sands

**ENGLISH IN SICILY**
Forster, E. M. Albergo Empedocle

**ENGLISH IN SIERRA LEONE**
Johnson, L. Melon flowers

**ENGLISH IN SINGAPORE**
Theroux, P. A deed without a name
Theroux, P. You make me mad

**ENGLISH IN SPAIN**
Sillitoe, A. Guzman, go home

**ENGLISH IN SWEDEN**
Greene, G. Minty's day

**ENGLISH IN SWITZERLAND**
Graham, W. At the Chalet Lartrec

**ENGLISH IN SYRIA**
Jones, R. Cuisine bourgeoise

**ENGLISH IN THE ARCTIC REGIONS**
Lütgen, K. Umanarsuak

**ENGLISH IN THE AZORES**
Glanville, B. A bad streak

**ENGLISH IN THE CZECHOSLOVAK REPUBLIC**
Templeton, E. A coffeehouse acquaintance

**ENGLISH IN THE UNITED STATES**
Forester, C. S. "You are welcome!"
Gilliatt, P. Frank
Godwin, G. An intermediate stop
Gordimer, N. Why haven't you written?
Graham, W. Jacka's fight
Lanier, S. His coat so gay
Leiber, F. America the beautiful
Maloney, R. Gallantry
Tuohy, F. Windows

**ENGLISH IN TUNISIA**
Taylor, E. Crépes flambées

**ENGLISH IN VIETNAM**
Greene, G. A small affair

**ENGLISH IN WALES**
Johnson, B. S. Sheela-na-gig

**ENGLISH LANGUAGE**
Sentences
Locke, D. M. The power of the sentence
Slang
*See* Slang

**ENGLISH LITERATURE**
Study and teaching
Dillon, M. Ladies' logic

**ENGLISH SCHOLARS.** *See* Scholars, English

**ENGLISH SOLDIERS.** *See* Soldiers, British

Enigma. Ayrton, M.

An enigma. Tammuz, B.

**ENLISTMENT.** *See* under individual armies of specific countries, with subdivision recruiting, enlistment, etc. Great Britain. Army—Recruiting, enlistment, etc.

Enoch. Bloch, R.

Enoch and the gorilla. O'Connor, F.

Enrica Baile. Moravia, A.

**Enright, Elizabeth**
A Christmas tree for Lydia
Authors' choice
The playground
Zolotow, C. ed. An overpraised season

The ensouled violin. Blavatsky, Madame

**ENTERTAINERS**
Anmar, F. Jenny among the zeebs
Bryant, E. Their thousandth season
Carpenter, D. Road show
Dick, P. K. Novelty act
Effinger, G. A. The ghost writer
Goulart, R. Princess #22
Metcalf, J. The strange aberration of Mr Ken Smythe
Nabokov, V. The Potato Elf
Phanishwarnath "Renu." The third vow
Priest, C. The head and the hand
Runyon, D. Lillian
Spinrad, N. The big flash
Stopa, J. Kiddy-Lib

Estes, Winston M.—*Continued*
> Myrtle McAfee Dunlap's concern with culture
>> Estes, W. M.   A streetful of people
> The natural talents of Merlin Hancock
>> Estes, W. M.   A streetful of people
> Purdy Robinson's parade
>> Estes, W. M.   A streetful of people
> Willis Shumaker's resignation
>> Estes, W. M.   A streetful of people

Esther Primavera. Arlt, R.

**ESTHETICS**
> Hawthorne, N. The artist of the beautiful
> Marshall, L. Dialogue on a cliff
> Vynnychenko, V.   A strange episode

**ESTONIA**
> Seth, R. The recluse of Kotka Veski

The estuary. Metcalf, J.

Et Dona Ferentes. Wilson, A.

Et tu, Uncle Tom. Sax, F.

**ETCHINGS**
> Broun, H. Artist unknown

**Etchison, Dennis**
> Damechild
>> Nolan, W. F. ed. The future is now

The eternal amateur. Compton, D. G.

**ETERNAL LIFE.** *See* Immortality

Eternal longing. Trevisan, D.

The eternal moment. Forster, E. M.

**ETERNAL PUNISHMENT.** *See* Hell

The eternal smile. Lagerkvist, P.

The eternal wanderer. Blackhurst, W. E.

The eternal woman. Hippius, Z.

**ETHICS**
> Chopin, K. Miss McEnders
> O'Connor, F. The lame shall enter first
> Ritchie, J. For all the rude people
> Scortia, T. N. Final exam
> Strindberg, A. The reward of virtue
> Tendryakov, V. Justice
> Wharton, E. Sanctuary
>> *See also* Christian ethics

**ETHICS, CHRISTIAN.** *See* Christian ethics

**ETHNOLOGISTS**
> Bishop, Z. The mound
> Lovecraft, H. P. White ape

**ETIQUETTE**
> Bendello, M. Savoir-vivre in a courtesan's parlor
> Sié, Cheou-kang. Fetal education

Etta's mind. Gant, L.

Eugene V. Deb's last mackintosh. Elmslie, K.

**EUGENICS.** *See* Genetics; Heredity

**EULOGIES.** *See* Funeral orations; Funeral rites and ceremonies

Euphoria in the rootcellar. Segal, L.

Eurema's dam. Lafferty, R. A.

Europe. James, H.

Europe after the rain; excerpt. Burns, A.

**EUROPEAN WAR, 1914-1918**
> Di Donato, P. Mass for unknown soldiers
> Hemingway, E. Night before landing

**Aerial operations**
> McLaughlin, D. Hawk among the sparrows

**Casualties**
> Hemingway, E. In another country

**England**
> Linklater, E. The actress Olenina

**France**
> Babel, I. On the field of honor
> Rolland, R. Pierre and Luce
> Thomason, J. W. Battle sight
> Thomason, J. W. The charge at Soissons
> Thomason, J. W. Marines at Blanc Mont
> Thomason, J. W. Monkey-meat
> Thomason, J. W. Red pants
> Thomason, J. W. Woman's reason

**Germany**
> Barthelme, D. Engineer-private Paul Klee misplaces an aircraft between Milbertshofen and Cambrai, March 1916
> Thomason, J. W. The Rhine

**Italy**
> Hemingway, E. Now I lay me
> Hemingway, E.   A way you'll never be
> Maugham, W. S. The Greek

**Naval operations**
> Thomason, J. W. Mutiny

**Russia**
> Hippius, Z. The strange law

**Yugoslavia**
> Djilas, M. Under the yoke

**EUROPEANS IN AFRICA**
> Stern, J. The cloud

**EUROPEANS IN INDIA**
> Jhabvala, R. P. An experience of India

**EUROPEANS IN THE UNITED STATES**
> Rushmore, R.   A life in the closet

**Eustace, Robert.** *See* Jepson, E. jt. auth.; Meade, L. T. jt. auth.

**Eustis, Helen**
> A winter's tale
>> Kahn, J. ed. Hanging by a thread

**EUTHANASIA**
> Goldin, S. and Hensel, C. F. Harriet
> Herbert, F. Murder will in
> Kaplan, B. Mercy
> Silverberg, R. Neighbor

Evacuation. Ford, C. H.

**EVANGELISTS**
> Fast, H. The price
> O'Connor, F. The peeler
> Shipley, M. The tea bowl of Ninsei Nomura
> Stafford, J.   A reading problem
> Warren, R. P. Statement of Ashby Wyndham
>> *See also* Revivals

**EVE**
> Boulle, P. When the serpent failed

The eve of Rumoko. Zelazny, R.

Eveline's visitant. Braddon, Mrs

Even after a machine is dismantled, it continues to operate, with or without purpose. Ascher, S. and Straus, D.

Even chance. Brunner, J.

**EVENING AND CONTINUATION SCHOOLS**
> Rosten, L. Christopher K*A*P*L*A*N

An evening at the Empress's. Babel, I.

An evening of fun. Friedman, P.

Evening primrose. Collier, J.

An **evening** with Dr Faust. Hesse, H.
An **evening** with John Joe Dempsey. Trevor, W.
**Evenings** down under. Rascoe, J.
**Evensong.** Del Rey, L.
The **events** at Schloss Heidiger. Fellowes-Gordon, I.
**Events** of a March night. Bergé, C.
**Ever** been to Braden? Roberts, J. B.
**EVEREST, MOUNT**
  Clarke, A. C. The cruel sky
**Everett, Mrs H. D.**
  A water witch
    Haining, P. ed. A circle of witches
**EVERGLADES.** *See* Florida
**EVERLASTING PUNISHMENT.** *See* Hell
The **everlasting** witness. Shedd, M.
An **every**-day girl. Jewett, S. O.
**Every** day is yesterday again. McCord, J.
**Every** girl has a mother somewhere. Warner, L.
**Every** leave that falls. De Vries, P.
**Every** other bar but this one. Levine, G.
**Everyday** life in the later Roman Empire. Disch, T. M.
**Everyday** use. Walker, A.
**Everyone** grows up. Kotowska, M.
**Everything** a man needs. Blythe, R.
**Everything** counts. Aidoo, A. A.
**Everything** inside is a penny. Algren, N.
**Everything** is good at the end of the world. Móricz, Z.
**Everything** laid on. Glanville, B.
**Everything** today. Naylor, P. R.
**Everything** was perfect but . . . Schwimmer, W.
**EVIDENCE, CIRCUMSTANTIAL**
  Hardwick, Michael, and Hardwick, Mollie. The bo'sun's body
  Pentecost, H. The man inside
  Post, M. D.   A twilight adventure
  Tolstoy, L. God sees the truth, but waits
**Evidence** in camera. Allingham, M.
**EVIL.** *See* Devil; Good and evil
The **evil** clergyman. Lovecraft, H. P.
**Evil** eye. Stewart, N.
The **evil** head. Ayrton, M.
An **evil** town. Bukowski, C.
**EVOLUTION**
  Blish, J. How beautiful with banners
  Harrison, H.   A tale of the ending
  Pangborn, E. Mount Charity
**Evtushenko, Evgenii Aleksandrovich.** *See* Yevtushenko, Yevgeny
**Ewing, Mrs**
  Our field
    Authors' choice
The **exact** science of matrimony. Henry, O.
**Exactly.** Moravia, A.
**Exactly,** what do you want, lady? Cuomo, G.
**Examination** day. Eklund, G.
**EXAMINATIONS**
  Scortia, T. N. Final exam
**EXAMINATIONS, MEDICAL.** *See* Diagnosis
**EXCAVATIONS (ARCHAEOLOGY)**
  Doyle, Sir A. C. Through the veil
**Excelsior.** Wodehouse, P. G.

**EXCEPTIONAL CHILDREN.** *See* Children, Gifted; Problem children
An **exceptional** Sunday. Kotowska, M.
**Exchanging** their souls. Mitchell, E. P.
**EX-CONVICTS**
  Andrews, F. E.   A man called Cain
  Blackhurst, W. E. Kindred souls
  Borchert, W. From the other side to the other side
  Bukowski, C.   A .45 to pay the rent
  Hall, J. B. God cares, but waits: Outside the cave
  Himes, C. Pork chop paradise
  Hunter, K. Hero's return
  Lane, R. W.   A spool of thread
  Pronzini, B. It's a lousy world
  Shiina, R. The lukewarm one
  Sillitoe, A. The rope trick
    *See also* Tramps
The **excursion.** Bullins, E.
The **excursion** ticket. Crane, S.
The **excursion** to the source. Taylor, E.
**EXECUTION.** *See* Executions and executioners; Hanging
The **executioner.** Lagerkvist, P.
**EXECUTIONERS.** *See* Executions and executioners
**EXECUTIONS AND EXECUTIONERS**
  Balzac, H. de. El Verdugo
  Bloch, R. The head hunter
  Borges, J. L. The end of the duel
  Borges, J. L. The man on the threshold
  Borges, J. L. The secret miracle
  Boyle, P. The lake
  Castro, A. de. The electric executioner
  Daniel, Y. Hands
  Djilas, M. The girl with the gold tooth
  Djilas, M. The stone and the violets
  Ellin, S. The question
  Fitzsimmons, P. M. The green house
  Gores, J. The second coming
  Hoch, E. D. Howdunit: every fifth man
  Isaković, A. April Fool's Day
  Kafka, F. In the penal colony
  Khvylovy, M. My being
  Lagerkvist, P. The executioner
  Maupassant, G. de. A fishing excursion
  O'Connor, F. Guests of the nation
  Watson, E. The revolution and Mister Wilson
  Wiesel, E. Dawn
    *See also* Hanging
The **executive.** Nemerov, H.
**EXECUTIVES**
  Friedman, B. H. Whispers
  Gold, H.   A death on the East Side
**EXERCISE.** *See* Physical fitness
The **exhibition.** Edelstein, S.
**EXHUMATION**
  Blum-Alquit, E. Gogol's ring
  Hawkes, J. Death of an airman
**Exiled.** Uyeda, A.
**EXILES**
  Chekhox, A. In exile
  Dickson, G. R. The mousetrap
  Schmitz, J. H. The end of the line
    *See also* Refugees
**Exiles.** Farrell, J. T.

The **existentialist's** nightmare. Russell, B.

**Exit** Mr. Smith. Jacobi, C.

**EXOBIOLOGY.** *See* Space biology

The **exorcising** of the restless monk. Seth, R.

**EXORCISM**

Brennan, J. P. In death as in life

Cuddon, J. A. Isabo

Hamilton, A. Under the eildon tree

Miłosz, C. Magdalena

Seth, R. The exorcising of the restless monk

Seth, R. Scent of death

Telfair, D. In a quart of water

**Exorcism.** Sax, F.

The **expanding** and contracting lake. Bullock, M.

**EXPATRIATES.** *See* Expatriation

**EXPATRIATION**

Marsh, W. Honor bright

The **expectancy** of my survival. Warner, L.

**Expedition.** Boucher, A.

**Expedition** in the opposite direction. Nesvadba, J.

**Expedition** Polychrome. Winter, J. A.

The **expedition** to Hell. Hogg, J.

**EXPEDITIONS, SCIENTIFIC.** *See* Scientific expeditions

An **expense** of spirit. Fiedler, L. A.

The **expensive** delicate ship. Aldiss, B. W.

An **experience** of India. Jhabvala, R. P.

An **experiment** in luxury. Crane, S.

An **experiment** in misery. Crane, S.

**Experiment** in personality. Symons, J.

**EXPERIMENTAL STORIES**

Ayrton, M. The autobiography of Lameich Trojan

Barthelme, D. At the Tolstoy Museum

Barthelme, D. Bone bubbles

Barthelme, D. Brain damage

Barthelme, D. The explanation

Barthelme, D. Game

Barthelme, D. The glass mountain

Barthelme, D. Kierkegaard unfair to Schlegel

Barthelme, D. Paraguay

Barthelme, D. Sentence

Barthelme, D. Views of my father weeping

Becker, J. Margins

Beckett, D. More pricks than kicks; 10 stories

Beckett, S. Stories and texts for nothing, III

Beckett, S. What a misfortune

Berne, S. All that the eye can see

Berne, S. The allotted period of time

Berne, S. The bandelier cave dwellers

Berne, S. Brown earth as medium

Berne, S. A connection of the legs

Berne, S. The divided self

Berne, S. Heaven above, hell below

Berne, S. The Indian signs of hope

Berne, S. The invention of God and heaven

Berne, S. Now alone

Berne, S. A recognizable message

Berne, S. To leave the city to its own devices

Berne, S. The unconscious victorious

Berne, S. The units that make up this moment

Brautigan, R. "A trout fishing sampler"

Bukowski, C. Confessions of a man insane enough to live with beasts

Bukowski, C. No neck and bad as hell

Bullins, E. The Absurd One

Bullock, M. The expanding and contracting lake

Bullock, M. A man, a girl and a door

Bullock, M. The net

Bullock, M. Noire's dialogues

Bullock, M. The open gate

Bullock, M. Red Beard's quest

Bullock, M. The return of Noire

Bullock, M. Through the trees to the river

Bullock, M. To the top of the tower

Bullock, M. Two girls and a man coming and going

Burns, A. Buster

Burns, A. Europe after the rain; excerpt

Butor, M. Welcome to Utah

Caldwell, B. The members

Campbell, R. Potential

Cohen, L. "F."

Cohen, M. Amazing grace

Coover, R. The babysitter

Coover, R. The door: a prologue of sorts

Coover, R. The gingerbread house

Coover, R. The hat act

Coover, R. Lucky Pierre and the music lesson

Coover, R. The magic poker

Dawson, F. The unborn

Dixon, S. Love and will

Dixon, T. Hate is a sandpaper ice cube with polka dots of love on it

Effinger, G. A. Wednesday, November 15, 1967

Ellison, H. At the mouse circus

Elman, R. Chamber music

Elman, R. Crossing over

Elman, R. Old old friends

Elman, R. On making friends

Elmslie, K. Accident vertigo

Elmslie, K. Eugene V. Debs' last mackintosh

Elmslie, K. Fauteuil

Elmslie, K. Moon canal morning

Elmslie, K. Mooning

Elmslie, K. My Holy City geography book

Elmslie, K. Native innards

Elmslie, K. Streetcar

Elmslie, K. Sunshine revelations

Elmslie, K. Waking up

Elmslie, K. Zoroaster

Fields, R. At the Silver Rail

Ford, C. H. Evacuation

Francis, H. E. Running

Gerrold, D. With a finger in my I

Gildner, G. Shake the dew

Harrison, M. J. Lamia mutable

Hawkes, J. Charivari

Hawkes, J. The goose on the grave

Jones, L. The coming of the sun

Kotzwinkle, W. The jewel of Amitaba

Kremer, R. The list

Lief, E. Bed sheets are white

EXPERIMENTAL STORIES—*Continued*

Lord, P. Friday night at the project and tenuous relationships reaching to Long Island
MacBeth, G. The ski murders
Malzberg, B. N. The battered-earth syndrome
Malzberg, B. N. Gehenna
Midwood, B. # [Tic tac toe]
Pelieu, C. Medleys & abraca-caha
Raffel, M. Brokennosejob
Raffel, M. Snailsfeet
Randall, M. The impossible film strip
Ribnikar, J.  I
Sallis, J. Bubbles
Sallis, J. The creation of Bennie Good
Sallis, J. Kazoo
Sallis, J. Only the words are different
Sarduy, S. From Cuba with a song
Sax, F. Exorcism
Sax, F. Nouveaux riches
Sax, F. On borrowed time
Schneeman, P. American autumn
Schoenfeld, H. Built up logically
Silk, D. Montefiore
Smith, R. Colours
Sontag, S. Debriefing
Spike, P.  A.B. Dick
Spike, P. Multi
Stein, G.  G. M. P.
Stein, G.  A long gay book
Stein, G. Many many women
Stevick, P. ed. Anti-story; 23 stories
Sukenick, R. The birds
Sukenick, R. Roast beef: a slice of life
Weiner, A. Empire of the sun
White, E. B. The door
Wulffson, D. You too can be a floorwax that even your husband could apply
Yurick, S. The age of gold
Yurick, S. "And not in utter nakedness . . ."
Yurick, S. Someone just like me . . .
Zinnes, H. Entropisms
Zoline, P. A. The heat death of the universe

EXPERIMENTS, SCIENTIFIC

Anvil, C. Behind the sandrat hoax
Blish, J. Getting along
Budrys, A. Rogue moon
Budrys, A. The Weeblies
Charnock, G. The Chinese boxes
Clement, H. The foundling stars
Dickson, G. R. Danger—human
Dnieprov, A. Crabs take over the island
Dnieprov, A. The island of the crabs
Du Maurier, D. The breakthrough
Effinger, G. A. $f(x) = (11/15/67)$ $x =$ her, $f(x) \neq 0$
Eisenberg, L. The chameleon
Eisenberg, L. Duckworth's forever
Eisenberg, L. Duckworth's IQ soup
Eisenberg, L. Hold your fire!
Eisenberg, L. Uncle Sam's children
Eisenberg, L. The vanishing borough
Farmer, P. J. How deep the grooves
Fast, H. The hoop
Jacobi, C. The random quantity
Jewett, S. O. The New Methuselah

Jones, R. F. Noise level
Kevles, B. Mars-station
Kimberly, G. The affair of the stolen mice
Lightner, A. M. The Mars jar
Lugones, L. Yzur
McConnell, J. V. Learning theory
Meade, L. T. and Halifax, C.  A race with the sun
Mitchell, E. P. The soul spectroscope
Paley, G. In time which made a monkey of us all
Scortia, T. N. Final exam
Shaw, I. The Mannichon solution
Silverberg, R. The calibrated alligator
Varshavsky, I. Preliminary research
Voiskunsky, Y. and Lukodyanov, I.  A farewell on the shore
Wade, J. The deep ones
Wilhelm, K. The planners
Wilhelm, K. Somerset dreams
   *See also* fields of scientific experimentation, e.g. Skin grafting

The **expert.** Beekman, A.
**Expertise.** Beneš, J.
**Expiation.** Benson, E. F.
**Expiation.** Scott, D. C.
The **explanation.** Barthelme, D.

EXPLORATION

Outer space
   *See* Outer space—Exploration
**Exploration.** Malzberg, B. N.

EXPLORATIONS. *See* Explorers; Scientific expeditions

EXPLORERS

Lispector, C. The smallest woman in the world
Long, F. B. Cones
Russell, E. F. The Waitabits
Winn, P. Right off the map
Wodehouse, P. G. Strychnine in the soup
The **explosion.** Burton, H.
**Explosion.** Raes, H.
An **explosion** of seven babies. Crane, S.

EXPLOSIONS

Algren, N. The leak that defied the books
Burton, H. The explosion

EXPLOSIVES

Kersh, G. The unsafe deposit box

EX-SHERIFFS. *See* Sheriffs
The **extended** hand. Canzoneri, R.
**Extending** the holdings. Grinnell, D.

EXTERMINATION. *See* Pest control
**Exterminator.** Burroughs, W.
The **exterminator.** Laumer, K.

EXTINCT ANIMALS

Farmer, P. J. The King of beasts

EXTINCT CITIES. *See* Cities and towns, Ruined, extinct, etc.

EXTORTION. *See* Blackmail
**Extract.** Karlin, W.
**Extract** from Captain Stormfield's visit to heaven. Twain, M.
**Extractions** and contractions. Blaise, C.

EXTRADITION

Henry, O. The theory and the hound
**Extraordinary** popular delusions. Oates, J. C.
An **extraordinary** wedding. Mitchell, E. P.

**EXTRASENSORY PERCEPTION**
    Hardwick, Michael, and Hardwick, Mollie. The eyes of Thomas Bolter
    Kersh, G. Dr Ox will die at midnight
    Long, F. B. The flame midget
    McCaffrey, A. Apple
    O'Neil, D. Report on a broken bridge
    Peirce, J. F. The total portrait
      *See also* Thought transference

**EXTRATERRESTRIAL LIFE.** *See* Space biology

**EYE**
    Elman, R. Eyes
    Gerrold, D. With a finger in my I
    Stanton, M. The bastard
    Wharton, E. The eyes
      *See also* Vision

        **Diseases**
    DeFord, M. A. The voyage of the "Deborah Pratt"
    Henderson, Z. Through a glass—darkly
      *See also* Astigmatism

The **eye**. Bødker, C.
An **eye** for an eye. Djilas, M.
**Eye** of the beholder. Filer, B. K.
The **eye** of the hurricane. Brown, G. M.
The **eye** of the hurricane. Walsh, J. P. and Crossley-Holland, K.
The **eye** of the lens. Jones, L.
An **eye** to the West. Delattre, P.
**Eyebem**. Wolfe, G.

**EYEGLASSES**
    Anstey, F. The lights of Spencer Primmett's eyes

**EYES.** *See* Eye
**Eyes.** Blaise, C.
**Eyes.** Elman, R.
The **eyes.** Wharton, E.
**Eyes** do more than see. Asimov, I.
**Eyes** like the sky. Bukowski, C.
**Eyes** of dust. Ellison, H.
The **eyes** of Mme Dupree. Booth, P. H.
The **eyes** of the panther. Bierce, A.
The **eyes** of Thomas Bolter. Hardwick, Michael, and Hardwick, Mollie
**Eyes** that miss nothing. Gilbert, M.


# F

"**F.**" Cohen, L.
**F.** Herrmann, J.
**FBI.** *See* United States. Federal Bureau of Investigation
$f(x) = (11/15/67) \ x = her, \ f(x) \neq 0.$ Effinger, G. A.
A **fable.** Bulatović, M.
A **fable.** Fox, R.
**Fable.** Landolfi, T.
**Fable** of the goat. Agnon, S. Y.
**FABLES**
    Agnon, S. Y. Fable of the goat
    Crane, S. How the donkey lifted the hills
    Crane, S. The victory of the moon
    Crane, S. The voice of the mountain
    Des Périers, B. The too clever fox

    DiNapoli, N. Sam the sorry zebra
    Diop, B. The wages of good
    Holst, S. Another impostor
    Holst, S. The blond bat
    Holst, S. Bullfinch & goblin
    Holst, S. Chess
    Holst, S.   A following
    Holst, S. The language of cats
    Holst, S. The man who was always wishing
    Holst, S. The mirror story
    Holst, S. Miss lady
    Holst, S. The Monroe Street monster
    Holst, S. The music copyist
    Holst, S. On hope
    Holst, S. The Santa Claus murderer
    Holst, S. 10,000 reflections
    Holst, S. True confessions story
    Holst, S. The zebra storyteller
    Ibuse, M. Salamander
    Kenyatta, J. The man who shared his hut
    Kipling, R. The beginning of the Armadillos
    Kipling, R. The Butterfly that stamped
    Kipling, R. The Cat that walked by himself
    Kipling, R. The Crab that played with the sea
    Kipling, R. The Elephant's Child
    Kipling, R. How the Camel got his hump
    Kipling, R. How the Leopard got his spots
    Kipling, R. How the Rhinoceros got his skin
    Kipling, R. How the Whale got his throat
    Kipling, R. The sing-song of Old Man Kangaroo
    Ma, Chung-hsi. The wolf of Chung-shan
    Quiroga, H. The alligator war
    Sarduy, S. From Cuba with a song
      *See also* Allegories

**FACE**
    **Abnormities and deformities**
    Ansell, J. The first sip of the second martini
    Barthelme, D. The Phantom of the Opera's friend
    Boyle, P. The port wine stain
    Cather, W. The profile
    Clemons, W.   A different thing
    Dowell, C. The birthmark
    Ellison, H. Nothing for my noon meal
The **face** and the image. Agnon, S. Y.
The **face** behind the bar. Stern, J.
The **face** in the mirror. Val Baker, D.
**Face** like an ikon. Casper, L.
The **face** of Mrs Cartwright. Fellowes-Gordon, I.
**Face** value. Allingham, M.
**Faces** & hands. Sallis, J.
**Facing** the forests. Yehoshua, A. B.
**FACTORIES**
    Baldwin, M. The ice palace
    Barker, M. Payday
    Beekman, A. Behind every man
    Dick, P. K. Autofac
    Holmes, E. M. Mitch
    Mitchison, N. The factory
    O'Donnell, E. P. Arrangement in Black

# 174

**FACTORIES**—*Continued*
Petrakis, H. M. The witness
Petry, A. Like a winding sheet
Phillips, R. Rise up singing
Swados, H. Joe, the vanishing American
> *See also* Cotton manufacture; Mill towns

The **factory**. Mitchison, N.
**FACTORY WORKERS.** *See* Factories; Labor and laboring classes; Mill towns
The **facts** in the case of M. Valdemar. Poe, E. A.
The **facts** in the Ratcliff case. Mitchell, E. P.
The **facts** of his life. Bingham, S.
**Factsheet** six. Brunner, J.
**Faed-out.** Davidson, A.
**FAEROE ISLANDS**
Dalsgaard, H. Nelson's last stand
Faroese short stories; 25 stories
Heinesen, W. Gamaliel's bewitchment
Poulsen, V. The huntsman
> **Country life**
> *See* Country life—Faeroe Islands
> **Farm life**
> *See* Farm life—Faeroe Islands
> **Police**
> *See* Police—Faeroe Islands
> **Religion**
> *See* Religion—Faeroe Islands

**Faessler, Shirley**
A basket of apples
Metcalf, J. ed. Sixteen by twelve
**FAILURE**
Burns, A. Buster
Lusin. Our story of Ah Q
Weaver, G. Porch fixing
West, J. Child of the century
The **failure** of Hope & Wandel. Bierce, A.
**Fair, Ronald L.**
We who came after
Chapman, A. ed. New Black voices
The **fair** of San Gennaro. McPhee, J.
The **fair** singer. Steegmuller, F.
**FAIRIES**
Beckford, W. The Nymph of the Fountain
Brunner, J. Fairy tale
Collier, J. Bottle party
De Valera, S. The fairies' revenge
Goethe, J. W. von. The new Melusina
Hoffmann, E. T. A. Little Zaches, surnamed Zinnober
Holst, S. Bullfinch & goblin
Kipling, R. 'Dymchurch Flit'
Kipling, R. Weland's sword
La Motte Fouqué, F. Baron de. The Field of Terror
Linklater, E. The dancers
Schreiber, A. W. The Devil's ladder
Singer, I. B. The lantuch
The **fairies'** revenge. De Valera, S.
**Fairman, Paul W.**
The missing symbol
Clement, H. ed. First flights to the moon
**FAIRS**
Burton, H. The Zenana Mission Bazaar
Clarke, A. An invitation to join

Fisher, D. C. The heydey of the blood
Fitzgerald, F. S. A night at the fair
Hesse, H. Faldum
Jewett, S. O. Paper roses
Joyce, J. Araby
McPhee, J. The fair of San Gennaro
Shepherd, J. County fair!
**Fair's** fair. Speed, J.
**Fairview.** Selzer, R. A.
**Fairy** tale. Brunner, J.
**FAIRY TALES.** *See* Fairies; Fantasies; Legends and folk tales
**FAITH**
Anderson, P. A chapter of revelation
Anderson, P. The problem of pain
Ayrton, M. The akeda
Carr, J. A steelie for the King
Corvo, F. Baron. About Our Lady of Dreams
The Day the sun stood still; 3 stories
Dickson, G. R. Things which are Caesar's
Fast, H. The pragmatic seed
Fast, H. Show cause
Lessing, D. The temptation of Jack Orkney
Maugham, W. S. Faith
Mauriac, F. A Christmas tale
Meek, F. M. The fourth wise man's detour
Melville, H. The lightning-rod man
Oates, J. C. Shame
O'Connor, F. Parker's back
Petaja, E. Pattern for plunder
Petrakis, H. M. The waves of night
Rugel, M. The flower
Sié, Cheou-kang. Old Man Stupidity
Silverberg, R. Thomas the proclaimer
Singer, I. B. The blasphemer
Singer, I. B. Something is there
> *See also* Catholic faith; Judaism

**Faith.** Maugham, W. S.
**Faith** and mountains. Russell, B.
**FAITH CURE**
García Márquez, G. Blacamán the Good, vendor of miracles
Landolfi, T. At the station
Malzberg, B. N. The men inside
Payes, R. C. . . . And the power . . .
Pritchett, V. S. Blind love
Selph, W. The miracle worker
Wade, R. Shepherd, show me . . .
**FAITH HEALERS.** *See* Faith cure
**Faith:** in a tree. Paley, G.
**FAITHFULNESS**
Linklater, E. Escape forever
Marmontel, J. F. The shepherdess of the Alps
Sharp, M. Driving home
The **falcon** and the falconeer. Malzberg, B.
**FALCONRY.** *See* Falcons; Hawks
**FALCONS**
Delapp, T. The beagle and the eagle
**Faldum.** Hesse, H.
**FALL.** *See* Autumn
**Fall** fire. Holmes, E. M.
**Fall** guy. De Vries, P.
The **fall** of the high-flying Dutchman. Simenon, G.
**Fallen** star. Collier, J.
The **falling** dog. Barthelme, D.
The **falling** leaves. Patton, F. G.

**Falling** object. Brittain, W.
**FALLS.** *See* Accidents
**FALSE ACCUSATION**
  Bierce, A. The man out of the nose
  Blake, G.  A modern development
  Dillon, M. Rape
  Ellin, S. The crime of Ezechiele Coen
  Isaković, A. April Fool's Day
  Lewis, M. G. The anaconda
  L'Heureux, J. Something missing
  Maupassant, G. de. The piece of string
  Meinhold, W. The amber witch
  Phillips, R. The lost child
  Spofford, H. P. The ray of displacement
  Tolstoy, L. God sees the truth, but waits
  Treat L. The verdict
  Warren, S. The March assize
**False** dawn. Yarbro, C. Q.
The **false** gems. Maupassant, G. de
**FALSE TEETH.** *See* Teeth, Artificial
**FALSEHOOD.** *See* Truthfulness and false-hood
**FALUN.** *See* Sweden—Falun
**Fame.** Cox, J.
**Familiar** usage in Leningrad. Cole, T.
**FAMILY.** *See* Brothers; Brothers and sisters; Family chronicles; Family life; Family reunions; Fathers; Fathers and daughters; Fathers and sons; Husband and wife; Marriage problems; Mothers; Mothers and daughters; Mothers and sons; Parent and child

A **family.** Maupassant, G. de
**Family** affair. Allingham, M.
A **family** argument. West, J.
A **family** chat. Landolfi, T.
**FAMILY CHRONICLES**
  Bromell, H. Photographs
  Casper, L. The fifth wall
  García Márquez, G. Leaf storm
  Holmes, E. M. Island hunt
  Le Fanu, J. S. The white cat of Drumgun-niol
  Rivera, E. Antecedentes
    *See also* Family life

**Family** evening. O'Hara, J.
**FAMILY HISTORIES.** *See* Family chronicles
**FAMILY LIFE**
  Alexander, R. W. When it really counts
  Angell, R. In an early winter
  Ansell, J. One day is pretty much like another
  Bailey, H. Dogman of Islington
  Baldwin, J. The man child
  Barth, J. Ambrose his mark
  Bergé, C. The kitchen
  Betts, D. The mother-in-law
  Birstein, A. How I spent my summer vacation
  Boles, P. D. The somewhere music
  Böll, H. Christmas every day
  Boyle, P. Home again, home again, jigetty-jig
  Brackenbury, R. Horsemen
  Brennan, M. The twelfth wedding anniversary

Brennan, M.  A young girl can spoil her chances
Brodeur, P. The secret
Brown, A. Farmer Eli's vacation
Brown, G. M.  A time to keep
Buck, P.  A certain star
Buck, P. Death and the dawn
Bukowski, C.  A .45 to pay the rent
Bukowski, C. One for Walter Lowenfels
Burton, H. The day that went terribly wrong
Burton, H. The explosion
Burton, H. Not the end of the world
Burton, H. The Zenana Mission Bazaar
Cady, J. The troll
Casper, L. Silent outcry, sleep
Cather, W. The Bohemian girl
Cather, W. The sentimentality of William Tavener
Cather, W. Uncle Valentine
Chang, E. The golden cangue
Cheever, J. Percy
Chekhov, A.  A dreary story
Chekhov, A. In the ravine
Chekhov, A. Three years
Chopin, K. Mrs Mobry's reason
Conlin, J. The manhood of Neilly Sullivan
Costello, M. Murphy's Xmas
Cullinan, E. The ablutions
Cullinan, E. Le petit déjeuner
Cullinan, E. The reunion
Curley, D. Look homeward, tourist
Curley, D.  A very small grove
Dann, J. M. The drum lollipop
Daugherty, M. G. The givers
Davidson, A. The House the Blakeneys built
Davis, O. The lodge pin
Davis, O. The scent of apples
Deck, J. The rite of Latin hips
De La Mare, W. In the forest
Delapp, T. Once upon a funeral
Delapp, T.  A puppy for baby
De Vries, P. Fall guy
Distler, A. White and fast water
Donohue, H. E. F. Joe College
Dorr, L. Brindley
Drake, R. Maiden lady
Engberg, S. Lambs of God
Faessler, S.  A basket of apples
Farmer, P. J. Down in the black gang
Ferber, E. The fast
Francis, H. E. The moment of fish
Fremlin, C. The hated house
Friedman, B. J. The enemy
Friedman, P. An evening of fun
Gaines, E. J.  A long day in November
Gass, W. H. The Pedersen kid
Gide, A. The return of the prodigal son
Gilbert, M. The system
Gillespie, A. Tonight at nine thirty-six
Gilliatt, P. Foreigners
Gilliatt, P. Frank
Gilliatt, P. The tactics of hunger
Godwin, G.  A sorrowful woman
Gottlieb, E. The lizard
Granit, A. Come into the hallway, for 5 cents!
Grau, S. A. The land and the water

## FAMILY LIFE—*Continued*

**FAMILY LIFE**—*Continued*

Shevchuk, V. The cobbler
Shiina, R. The go-between
Shore, W. Is it the end of the world?
Silverberg, R. The mutant season
Singer, I. B. Guests on a winter night
Sirof, H. The adventure
Smith, E. E. Calliope and Gherkin and the
    Yankee Doodle thing
Stafford, J. The tea time of stouthearted
    ladies
Stein, G. The making of Americans
Steinberg, J. Forgiven
Stern, J. The beginning and the end
Stewart, N. By a lake in the Bois
Stuart, J. Two worlds
Summers, H. Love
Summers, H. The third ocean
Taylor, P. Dean of men
Taylor, P. Heads of houses
Taylor, P. Je suis perdu
Trevisan, D. Soup
Trevor, W.   A happy family
Trilling, L. The other Margaret
Tsonev, V. Let's go vacationing
Tuohy, F. Fingers in the door
Ullian, R. A snag in the harp
Updike, J. The day of the dying rabbit
Updike, J. Incest
Updike, J. Sublimating
Vaižgantas. Aleksiukas' father and mother
Van Duyn, M. The bell
Verga, G. Black bread
Verga, G. Consolation
Vonnegut, K. The big space fuck
Warner, L. How sweet my daughter, how
    deep my anger
Weisbrod, R. The ninth cold day
West, J. Home for Christmas
Willard, N. The tailor who told the truth
Wilson, A. Et Dona Ferentes
Windham, B. The death of Uncle Edward
    Tabb
Wolkers, J. Minister in a straw hat
Wright, S.   A shark-infested rice pudding
Yanovsky, Y.   A boat in the sea
Yashpal. One cigarette
Yehoshua, A. B.   A long hot day
Yehoshua, A. B.   A long hot day, his de-
    spair, his wife and his daughter
    *See also* Brothers; Brothers and sis-
    ters; Family chronicles; Family re-
    unions; Fathers; Fathers and daughters;
    Fathers and sons; Husband and wife;
    Marriage problems; Mothers; Mothers
    and daughters; Mothers and sons; Par-
    ent and child

**Family** matters. Schwartz, J.

The **family** of a Vourdalak. Tolstoy, A.

**Family** portrait. Lardner, S.

**Family** portrait. Reinbold, J. S.

**FAMILY REUNIONS**

Bingham, S. Mourning
Edwards, J. Mother Dear and Daddy
Greenberg, J. To the members of the
    D.A.R.
Hawkes, J. The grandmother
Hippius, Z. There is no return
Jones, A. Emancipation day

Lispector, C. Happy birthday
Marsh, W. My house is yours
Marsh, W.   A sentimental journey
O'Donnell, M. K.   A celebration of light
O'Hara, J. The big gleaming coach
Wilson, A. Union reunion

**Family** soliloquy. Naylor, P. R.

**Family** ties. Lispector, C.

A **family** trip. Neugeboren, J.

**FAMINES**

Chekhov, A. My wife
    *See also* Hunger

The **famous** Dempsey crouch. Lewis, H.

The **famous** Gilson bequest. Bierce, A.

**Fan** village. Wu, Tsu-hsiang

**FANATICISM**

Aymé, M. The last
Baldwin, M. The ice palace
Lagerkvist, P. Saviour John

The **fancy** woman. Taylor, P.

The **fangs** of the trees. Silverberg, R.

**FANS**

De Camp, L. S. The Emperor's fan

**FANTASIES**

Aandahl, V. Beyond the game
Agnon, S. Y.   A whole loaf
Aiken, J. All you've ever wanted
Aiken, J. Follow my fancy
Aiken, J. Mrs Considine
Aldiss, B. W. Serpent burning on an altar
Aldiss, B. W. The serpent of Kundalini
Aldiss, B. W. Swastika!
Andersen, H. C. The darning needle
Andersen, H. C. The red shoes
Anouilh, J. The moment is near
Anthony, P. In the barn
Asimov, I. Legal rites
Asimov, I. Sally
Asimov, I. Time pussy
Asimov, I. Unto the fourth generation
Asimov, I. The up-to-date sorcerer
Asimov, I. What if—
Asimov, I. and MacCreigh, J. The little
    man on the subway
Asturias, M. A. Tatuana's tale
Bailey, H. Dogman of Islington
Ballard, J. G. The drowned giant
Ballard, J. G. The garden of time
Ballard, J. G. Now wakes the sea
Barthelme, D. The balloon
Barthelme, D. Daumier
Barthelme, D. The glass mountain
Barthelme, D. The Indian uprising
Barthelme, D. Report
Beaumont, C. Free dirt
Beerbohm, M.   A. V. Laider
Benét, S. V. By the waters of Babylon
Benét, S. V. The King of the Cats
Berg, A. M. The defeat of the Nez Percé
Bester, A. The animal fair
Bloch, R. The funny farm
Borchert, W. Radi
Borges, J. L. The Aleph
Borges, J. L. The approach to al-Mu'tasim
Boucher, A. Mr Lupescu
Boucher, A.   A shape in time
Boulle, P. The holy places
Bova, B. The man who saw Gunga Din
    thirty times

FANTASIES—*Continued*

Goulart, R. The peppermint-striped good-bye
Goulart, R. Please stand by
Goulart, R. Subject to change
Grahame, K. The reluctant dragon
Green, R. M. Apology to Inky
Greene, G. Alas, poor Maling
Grubb, D. The rabbit prince
Hamilton, A. The attic express
Hamilton, A. Words of warning
Harrison, W. Eating it
Heinesen, W. The knife
Hemesath, J. B. Harry the Hare
Henderson, Z. Anything Box
Henderson, Z. The believing child
Henderson, Z. Incident after
Henderson, Z. J-line to nowhere
Henderson, Z. Three cornered and secure
Hesse, H. An evening with Dr Faust
Hesse, H. Harry, the Steppenwolf
Hesse, H. A man by the name of Ziegler
Hill, A. R. Omega
Hoffmann, E. T. A. Master Flea
Hoffmann, E. T. A. Princess Brambilla
Holst, K. The pumpkins
Ionesco, E. Oriflamme
Ionesco, E. The stroller in the air
Jackson, S. One ordinary day, with peanuts
Jansson, T. The fillyjonk who believed in disasters
Jones, L. The coming of the sun
Kawabata, Y. One arm
Kersh, G. The unsafe deposit box
Knight, D. Mary
Kotowska, M. My good ladies
Kotzwinkle, W. The magician
Kotzwinkle, W. A most incredible meal
Kuttner, H. A cross of centuries
Lafferty, R. A. All pieces of a river shore
Lafferty, R. A. Camels and dromedaries, Clem
Lafferty, R. A. Dream
Lafferty, R. A. Four sides of infinity
Lafferty, R. A. Groaning hinges of the world
Lafferty, R. A. Rainbird
Lafferty, R. A. A special condition in Summit City
Lagerkvist, P. The lift that went down into hell
Landolfi, T. Gogol's wife
Laumer, K. The devil you don't
Le Guin, U. K. Direction of the road
Le Guin, U. K. The word of unbinding
Leiber, F. One station of the way
Leiber, F. The secret songs
Leiber, F. Space-time for springers
Lewis, C. S. The Shoddy Lands
Linklater, E. The abominable imprecation
Linklater, E. God likes them plain
Linklater, E. The goose girl
Linklater, E. Sealskin trousers
Littke, L. J. A feline felony
Locke, D. M. The power of the sentence
Long, F. B. The cottage
Lovecraft, H. P. and Berkeley, E. The green meadow

Lumley, B. The Cyprus shell
Lumley, B. Dylath-Leen
Lumley, B. In the vaults beneath
McAllister, B. Prime-time teaser
McCaffrey, A. Dragonrider
Machen, A. The soldier's rest
McKenna, R. The secret place
Malamud, B. The Jewbird
Malamud, B. Rembrandt's hat
Malzberg, B. N. The battered-earth syndrome
Margroff, R. E. and Offutt, A. J. The book
Marshall, E. The flying lion
Maugham, W. S. The choice of Amyntas
Midwood, B. One's ship
Mitchell, E. P. The cave of the Splurgles
Mitchell, E. P. The wonderful Corot
Moore, C. L. and others. The challenge from beyond
Moravia, A. Celestina
Nabokov, V. The visit to the museum
Nemerov, H. The Twelve and the one
Nesbit, E. The egg
Neville, K. Dominant species
Nye, R. The amber witch
Nye, R. Howell
Nye, R. Mr Benjamin
Nye, R. A Portuguese person
Nye, R. Sdeath and Northangerland
Nye, R. The wandering Jew
O'Brien, F. From hand to mouth
Ozick, C. The dock-witch
Pangborn, E. A better mousehole
Pangborn, E. Maxwell's monkey
Pangborn, E. Pickup for Olympus
Pangborn, E. Tiger boy
Pangborn, E. Wogglebeast
Pangborn, E. The wrens in Grampa's whiskers
Panshin, A. The destiny of Milton Gomrath
Peretz, I. L. Neilah in Gehenna
Piserchia, D. Half the kingdom
Platt, C. New York Times
Pohl, F. Day Million
Pritchett, V. S. The ape
P'u, Sung-ling. The Rakshas and the sea market
Pudney, J. Kitty, Kitty, Kitty
Pynchon, T. Low-lands
Raes, H. Explosion
Reyes, A. Major Aranda's hand
Roberts, K. The Lady Margaret
Rocklynne, R. Find the face
Runyon, C. W. Sweet Helen
Russell, B. Faith and mountains
Russell, B. The right will prevail
Russell, B. Zahatopolk
Russell, E. F. Mutants for sale
Saki. Tobermory
Sallis, J. Doucement, s'il vous plaît
Sallis, J. Front & centaur
Sallis, J. Only the words are different
Scortia, T. N. When you hear the tone
Shaw, B. Light of other days
Shui, Ching. Hi Lili hi Li . . .
Silverberg, R. As is

## FANTASIES—Continued

Silverberg, R. Breckenridge and the continuum
Silverberg, R. The fangs of the trees
Silverberg, R. Going down smooth
Skues, G. E. M. Mr Theodore Castwell
Slater, E. The Sooey pill
Slesar, H. My father, the cat
Smith, C. A. A tale of Sir John Maundeville
Smith, C. A. Ubbo-Sathla
Smith, W. A patchwork hog in the petunia world
Spike, P. Bad news
Spike, P. Broadway Joe
Spike, P. Specks saga
Spinrad, N. No direction home
Staunton, W. As long as you're here
Stockton, F. R. The Griffin and the Minor Canon
Stubbs, J. Are you there?
Sturgeon, T. And now the news
Sturgeon, T. One foot and the grave
Sturgeon, T. The Silken-swift . . .
Sturgeon, T. To here and the easel
Sturgeon, T. A touch of strange
Svevo, I. The mother
Tenn, W. Bernie the Faust
Tertz, A. Pkhentz
Thomas, D. An adventure from a work in progress
Thomas, D. The Holy Six
Thomas, D. The horse's ha
Thurston, R. Good-bye, Shelley, Shirley, Charlotte, Charlene
Tieck, J. L. The Runenberg
Twain, M. Jim Baker's bluejay yarn
Twain, M. Sold to Satan
Twohy, R. Routine investigation
Updike, J. The Baluchitherium
Vance, J. Green magic
Vance, J. Rumfuddle
Wain, J. Master Richard
Wellen, E. Down by the old maelstrom
Wilhelm, K. Jenny with wings
Williamson, J. The metal man
Wilson, G. M-1
Wilson, R. The apple
Wolfe, G. Car sinister
Wolfe, G. The death of Doctor Island
Wolfe, G. The headless man
Wolfe, G. The island of Doctor Death, and other stories
Wolfe, G. Peritonitis
Wyal, P. The castle on the crag
Wyndam, J. Jizzle
Wyndham, J. Technical slip
Zelazny, R. Love is an imaginary number
Zelazny, R. The man who loved the Faioli
  See also Allegories; Angels; Devil; Dragons; Dreams; Fables; Fairies; Future, Stories of the; Ghosts; Hallucinations and illusions; Improbable stories; Jinn; Science fiction; Supernatural phenomena; Time, Travels in

**FANTASTIC FICTION.** See Fantasies

The **fantastic** horror of the cat in the bag. Sayers, D. L.

**FANTASTIC STORIES.** See Fantasies

Fantastico. Weaver, G.

## FANTIS

Aidoo, A. A. A gift from somewhere
Aidoo, A. A. No sweetness here

**Fanu, Joseph Sheridan Le.** See Le Fanu, Joseph Sheridan

Far bella figura. Scott, C. B.
Far Centaurus. Van Vogt, A. E.
Far from this earth. Oliver, C.
Far South. Sáenz, D. A.

**Farber, Jerry**
  Gorman
    Best SF: 1970

The **fare** to Crown Point. Myers, W.
Farewell! . . . Farewell! . . . Charyn, J.
The **Farewell** murder. Hammett, D.
A **farewell** on the shore. Voiskunsky, Y. and Lukodyanov, I.
Farewell to Brahms. Di Donato, P.
Farewell to Cuba. Cozzens, J. G.
Farewell to Fritzie. Bahr, J.
Farewell to Legs. Wodehouse, P. G.
Farewell to the dacha. Litvinov, I.
Farewell to the Faulkners. DeFord, M. A.
Farewell to the master. Bates, H.

**FAREWELLS.** See Leave-takings

**Farjeon, Eleanor**
  The glass peacock
    Authors' choice

**Farley, Ralph Milmer**
  Time for sale
    Elwood, R. and Ghidalia, V. eds. Androids, time machines and blue giraffes

**FARM ANIMALS.** See Domestic animals

**FARM HOUSES.** See Houses

## FARM LIFE

Davidson, A. Rite of spring
Perkins, L. A. The hidden ears
Simak, C. D. Neighbor
Wright, W. C. The green fly and the box
  See also Agricultural laborers; Country life; Milkmaids

### Africa
Stern, J. The cloud

### Alabama
Akens, H. M. Call me ma
Richey, G. The legacy

### Appalachian region
Stuart, J. Victory and the dream

### Arkansas
Caspar, L. Drink to private gods

### Belgium
Streuvels, S. October

### Brazil
Veiga, J. J. On the road to Daybreak

### California
Steinbeck, J. A future we can't foresee
Steinbeck, J. The harness
Steinbeck, J. Pat Humbert's

### Canada
Garner, H. Red racer

### China
Wang, T'ieh. The smashing of the Dragon King

**Fast, Howard**—*Continued*
　The mouse
　　Fast, H. The general zapped an angel
　　Yolen, J. comp. Zoo 2000
　The movie house
　　Fast, H. The general zapped an angel
　Not with a bang
　　Fast, H.　A touch of infinity
　The pragmatic seed
　　Fast, H.　A touch of infinity
　The price
　　Fast, H.　A touch of infinity
　Show cause
　　Fast, H.　A touch of infinity
　The talent of Harvey
　　Fast, H.　A touch of infinity
　Tomorrow's "Wall Street Journal"
　　Fast, H. The general zapped an angel
　UFO
　　Fast, H.　A touch of infinity
　The vision of Milty Boil
　　Fast, H. The general zapped an angel
　The wound
　　Fast, H. The general zapped an angel
The **fast.** Ferber, E.
The **fast.** Singer, I. B.
**Fast** horseflesh. West, J.
**Fast** mule buyer. Green, B. K.
**Fast**-Train Ike. Stuart, J.
**FASTING**
　Premchand.　A moral victory
　Singer, I. B. The fast
**FAT.** *See* Corpulence
The **fat** cat. Patrick, Q.
**Fat** chance. Bloch, R.
**Fat** girl. Gill, B.
The **fatal** cipher. Futrelle, J.
The **fatal** eggs. Bulgakov, M.
The **fatal** fulfillment. Anderson, P.
The **fatal** marksmen. Apel, J. A.
A **fatal** success. Van Dyke, H.
**FATALISM.** *See* Fate and fatalism
**Fate.** Hippius, Z.
**Fate.** Singer, I. B.
**FATE AND FATALISM**
　Harvey, W. F. August heat
　Henry, O. Roads of destiny
　James, H. De Grey: a romance
　Lessing, D. Out of the fountain
　Singer, I. B. Fate
The **fated** interview. Fremlin, C.
**Fateful** first day on Xene. Tofte, A.
A **father.** Babel, I.
The **father.** Maupassant, G. de
**Father** and I. Lagerkvist, P.
**Father** Brent's tale. Benson, R. H.
**Father** Buh Buh Boo. Sweat, J.
**FATHER CHRISTMAS.** *See* Santa Claus
**Father** Kelly. Henderson, D.
The **father** of the Marshalsea. Dickens, C.
The **father** of Yoto. Burke, T.
A **father**-to-be. Bellow, S.
**FATHERS**
　Agnon, S. Y. To father's house
　Anderson, S. The egg
　Blaise, C. Extractions and contractions
　Burke, T. The father of Yoto
　Canzoneri, R. Barbed wire

　Cullinan, E. The power of prayer
　Dagerman, S. The games of night
　DeFord, M. A. The Peak Lords
　Drake, R. The trained nurse
　Karchmer, S. His father's evening
　Kemal, Y. The baby
　Khamsing, S. The gold-legged frog
　Kiš, D. Garden, ashes
　Lavin, M. The new gardener
　Maupassant, G. de. The father
　Minot, S. Mars revisited
　Neugeboren, J.　A family trip
　Petrakis, H. M. The witness
　Putnam, C. The news from Troy
　Stuart, J. Pa's a man's man all right
　Terry, W. S. The bottomless well
　Thurston, J. The cross
　Warner, L. An insubstantial father
　Weidman, J. My father sits in the dark
　　*See also* Fathers and daughters; Fathers and sons; Illegitimacy; Parent and child; Stepfathers
**FATHERS AND DAUGHTERS**
　Agnon, S. Y. Agunot
　Agnon, S. Y. At the outset of the day
　Babel, I.　A father
　Betts, D. Burning the bed
　Bingham, S. August ninth at Natural Bridge
　Blackwood, A. The tarn of sacrifice
　Brandão, R. The thief and his little daughter
　Brautigan, R. Getting to know each other
　Brautigan, R.　A short history of religion in California
　Burke, T. The Chink and the child
　Burke, T. The gorilla and the girl
　Burke, T. The paw
　Busch, F. How does that garden grow
　Butenas, N. The girl that had no face
　Canzoneri, R. The shadow of death
　Carr, A. H. Z. The black kitten
　Cather, W. The Count of Crow's Nest
　Chute, B. J. The legacy
　Čingo, Ž. From's daughter
　Colter, C. After the ball
　Crane, S.　A desertion
　Dawson, F. The highwayman
　Deck, J. The preface to Anonymous Max
　Du Maurier, D.　A border-line case
　Farmer, P. J. Father's in the basement
　Francis, H. E. Don't stay away too long
　Glaze, E. Silver grapes
　Gold, H. "I want a Sunday kind of love"
　Gold, H. Love and like
　Grau, S. A. Pillow of stone
　Hawthorne, N. Rappaccini's daughter
　Hemenway, R. Take it easy, Edna
　Henderson, D. Ditch Valley
　Hermann, J. Penates
　Hoffmann, E. T. A. The Cremona violin
　Holmes, E. M. Drums again
　Hughes, M. G. The foreigner in the blood
　Jones, A. In black and white
　Koch, C. F.　A matter of family
　Latimer, O. The secret of Raccoon Ridge
　Lavin, M. Asigh
　Lavin, M. One summer
　Linklater, E. The redundant miracle

**FATHERS AND SONS—***Continued*

Lynch, J. The visit
McCord, J. Sunshine yellow and red
McGahern, J. Bomb box
McGahern, J. Korea
McGahern, J. Wheels
McGerr, P. This one's a beauty
Malamud, B. My son the murderer
Maloney, R. Intimacy
Mérimée, P. Mateo Falcone
Minot, S. Mars revisited
Mitchell, E. P. An uncommon sort of spectre
Moravia, A. The Judas tree
Nagibin, Y. The green bird with the red head
Naylor, P. R. The candidate
Naylor, P. R. Second son
Oates, J. C. Extraordinary popular delusions
Oates, J. C. Love and death
Oates, J. C. Wild Saturday
O'Connor, F. The lame shall enter first
O'Connor, F. An out-and-out free gift
O'Connor, P. F. My imaginary father
O'Hara, J. The frozen face
O'Hara, J. Interior with figures
Ozick, C. The suitcase
Panduro, L. 'Rosslein auf der Heide'
Patrick, Q. Portrait of a murderer
Patton, F. G. As man to man
Peterkin, J. Teaching Jim
Prebble, J. The regulator
Prebble, J. Spanish stirrup
Purdy, J. Cutting edge
Ramkumar. Sailor
Reynolds, M. Black sheep astray
Rosa, J. G. The third bank of the river
Rush, N. In late youth
Rushmore, R. Open water
Rushmore, R. The winning game
Saltus, E. Fausta
Schwartz, J. The project
Schwartz, J. A trip to Brooklyn
Schwimmer, W. The goodest son in the world
Shcherbakov, V. "We played under your window"
Shevchuk, V. My father decided to plant orchards
Singer, I. B. The son
Spielberg, P. Radix malorum
Steegmuller, F. A real saint
Steinbeck, J. Adam and his sons
Steinbeck, J. Choice and responsibility
Steinbeck, J. Timshel
Stevenson, R. L. The story of a lie
Storm, T. Carsten Curator
Tedlock, E. W. 'Tis a fond ambush
Thompson, T. Son of a King
Tottenham, J. 'Go on, Johnny, go on!'
Trevisan, D. Dinner
Trevisan, D. The girl from normal school
Trevisan, D. The little goldfish
Tucci, N. Strong man
Tuohy, F. The licence
Ulibarri, S. R. Man without a name
Vaižgantas. Aleksiukas' father and mother
Vaižgantas. The misfit
Van Peebles, M. A bear for the F.B.I.; excerpt
Veiga, J. J. The ten-league journey
Vestdijk, S. The stone face
Vezhinov, P. The boy with the violin
Weaver, G. Oskar Hansen, Jr., speaks to his son
Wiesel, E. Night
Winters, E. God's agents have beards
Wister, O. Little Big Horn medicine
Wolfe, G. The fifth head of Cerberus
Yehoshua, A. B. A poet's continuing silence
Yglesias, J. The guns in the closet
    *See also* Conflict of generations; Family life; Fathers; Parent and child

**Fathers** and sons. Hemingway, E.

**Fathers'** Day. Benchley, N.

The **father's** father. Delattre, P.

**FATHERS-IN-LAW**

Brautigan, R. The World War I Los Angeles airplane
Maddow, B. "To hell the rabbis"
Ozick, C. The suitcase
Scott, D. C. The winning of Marie-Louise

**Father's** in the basement. Farmer, P. J.

**Fatimas** and kisses. O'Hara, J.

**Faulkner, William**

Barn burning
    Abrahams, W. ed. Fifty years of the American short story v 1
    Konigsberg, I. ed. The classic short story
    Schulman, L. M. ed. The loners
    12 short story writers
A courtship
    Lytle, A. ed. Craft and vision
Death drag
    Thune, E. and Prigozy, R. eds. Short stories: a critical anthology
Dry September
    Davis, R. G. ed. The modern masters
    Kissin, E. H. ed. Stories in black and white
    12 short story writers
Old man
    Hamalian, L. and Volpe, E. L. eds. Eleven modern short novels
The old people
    Davis, R. G. ed. Ten modern masters
Red leaves
    Roecker, W. A. ed. Stories that count
    Tytell, J. and Jaffe, H. eds. Affinities
A rose for Emily
    Disch, R. and Schwartz, B. eds. Killing time
    Haining, P. ed. The Lucifer society
    Konigsberg, I. ed. The classic short story
    Taylor, J. C. ed. The short story: fiction in transition
Shingles for the Lord
    Davis, R. G. ed. Ten modern masters
Sunset
    Howes, B. and Smith, G. J. eds. The sea-green horse

**Faulkner, William**—*Continued*

That evening sun
> Foff, A. and Knapp, D. eds. Story
> Same as: That evening sun go down

That evening sun go down
> Burnett, W. ed. Black hands on a white face
> Same as: That evening sun

Two soldiers
> Insights

Wash
> Konigsberg, I. ed. The classic short story
> 12 short story writers

> **Parodies, travesties, etc.**
> De Vries, P. Requiem for a noun

**Fauntleroy.** Collins, W.

**Faust, Frederick.** *See* Brand, Max

**Faust, Irvin**

Into the green night
> Simon, J. ed. Fourteen for now

Philco baby
> Schulman, L. M. ed. The loners

Wobbillobby Mobbays
> Charyn, J. ed. The single voice

The world's fastest human
> McCrindle, J. F. ed. Stories from the Transatlantic Review

**FAUST LEGEND**

Bakhnov, V. Speaking of demonology
The History of the damnable life and deserved death of Dr John Faustus
> *See also* Devil

**Fausta.** Saltus, E.

**Fauteuil.** Elmslie, K.

The **favor.** O'Hara, J.

**Fay, William**

The conscience of the cop
> Best of the Best detective stories

**FEAR**

Ansell, J. Can't we come back yesterday?
Ballard, J. G. Zone of terror
Banville, J. Summer voices
Beneš, J. The last possibility
Bierce, A. The man and the snake
Bierce, A.  A watcher by the dead
Brautigan, R. 1962 Cotton Mather newsreel
Brodeur, P. The spoiler
Burke, T. The gorilla and the girl
Chekhov, A. Nerves
Chesbro, G. C. Broken pattern
Chopin, K. Beyond the bayou
De La Mare, W. The giant
Derleth, A. The lonesome place
Faulkner, W. That evening sun
Gardner, E. A. Wide O—
Goldberg, G. J. 126 days of continuous sunshine
Greene, G. The end of the party
Hemingway, E. The short happy life of Francis Macomber
Hemingway, E. Three shots
Henderson, Z. Swept and garnished
Jansson, T. The fillyjonk who believed in disasters
Kaplan, B. Diaspora
Keller, D. H. The thing in the cellar

Kimberly, G. Peace, love, and food for the hungry
Kipling, R. At the end of the passage
Le Guin, U. K. Vaster than empires and more slow
Long, F. B. The Man from Time
McKimmey, J. Keep us safe
Maupassant, G. de. The duel
Maupassant, G. de. The Horla
Michaels, L. Going places
Olsen, T.   O yes
Paton, A. The waste land
Randall, F. E. The watchers
Spielberg, P. Hide-and-seek
Thomas, D. In the garden
Trevisan, D. Three o'clock in the morning
Tucci, N. Strong man
Walton, R. The siege of Brooklyn Bridge
Wharton, E. All Souls'

**Fear.** Bingham, S.

The **fear** of innocence. Fiedler, L. A.

"The **fear** that walks by noonday." Cather, W.

A **feast** for the holy man. Premchand

The **Feast** of St Dionysus. Silverberg, R.

The **featherbedders.** Herbert, F.

**Feathertop:** a moralized legend. *See* Hawthorne, N. Puritan passions

**February 1999:** Ylla. Bradbury, R.

**February 2002:** the locusts. Bradbury, R.

**February 2003:** interim. Bradbury, R.

**FEDERAL BUREAU OF INVESTIGATION.** *See* United States. Federal Bureau of Investigation

**FEDERAL GOVERNMENT**

Silverberg, R. Point of focus

**FEEBLE-MINDED**

Babel, I. On the field of honor
Conroy, F. White days and red nights
Dalsgaard, H. Nelson's last stand
Dickson, G. R. Rehabilitated
Francis, H. E. 3
Grau, S. A. The lovely April
Hitchens, D. If you see this woman
Kotzwinkle, W. The doorman
Maupassant, G. de. The rabbit
Pentecost, H. The monster of Lakeview
Phillips, R. The lost child
Steinbeck, J. Of mice and men
> *See also* Children, Abnormal and backward; Mentally handicapped; Mongolism

**Feed** my lambs. O'Faolain, S.

**Feel** free. Garner, A.

The **feel** of it. Mayer, T.

**FEET.** *See* Foot

**Feet** foremost. Hartley, L. P.

**Feet** of clay. Glanville, B.

**Feet** of clay. Wodehouse, P. G.

**Fejes, Endre**

Engagement
> Decker, C. R. and Angoff, C. eds. Modern stories from many lands

**Feldman, Alan**

Living in the sea
> Ribalow, H. U. ed. My name aloud

Rian's story
> Gottesman, L.; Obenzinger, H. and Senauke, A. eds. A cinch

A **feline** felony. Littke, L. J.

**Fellowes-Gordon, Ian**
  The attic room
    Canning, J. ed. 50 great horror stories
  The birthday gift
    Canning, J. ed. 50 great horror stories
  Donovan's Drop
    Canning, J. ed. 50 great horror stories
  The events at Schloss Heidiger
    Canning, J. ed. 50 great horror stories
  The face of Mrs Cartwright
    Canning, J. ed. 50 great horror stories
  The girl in the flame-red dress
    Canning, J. ed. 50 great horror stories
  The girl in the train
    Canning, J. ed. 50 great horror stories

**Feminine** intuition. Asimov, I.

A **feminine** jurisdiction. Lanier, S.

The **feminine** metamorphosis. Keller, D. H.

The **fence.** Francis, H. E.

**Fence** trouble. Green, B. K.

**Fences.** Hooper, H. G.

**Fenimore, W.**
  The pool of the stone god
    Moskowitz, S. ed. Horrors unknown

**Fenton, Frank**
  The perfect plot
    Haining, P. ed. The Hollywood nightmare

**Ferber, Edna**
  The fast
    Lewis, J. D. ed. Tales of our people

**Ferdinand, Val**
  Second line/cutting the body loose
    Coombs, O. ed. What we must see: young Black storytellers

**Ferguson, Dale**
  The island of the endangered
    Yolen, J. comp. Zoo 2000

**Ferguson, J. M.**
  Spending the day
    The Best little magazine fiction, 1970

**Ferguson, John**
  The white line
    Dickinson, S. ed. The drugged cornet, and other mystery stories

**Fergusson, Harvey**
  Bound for Taos
    Taylor, J. G. ed. Great Western short stories

**Ferlinghetti, Lawrence**
  Where is Vietnam?
    New Directions in prose and poetry 19

**Fernheim.** Agnon, S. Y.

**Fernhurst.** Stein, G.

**FERRARA.** *See* Italy—Ferrara

**FERRETS**
  Saki. Sredni Vashtar

**FERRIES**
  Gonzalez, N. V. M. On the ferry

The **ferris** wheel. Simpson, L.

**FERTILIZERS AND MANURES.** *See* Compost

**Fessier, Michael**
  That's what happened to me
    Burnett, W. ed. That's what happened to me

The **festival.** Lovecraft, H. P.

**FESTIVALS**
  Kanin, G. The grand illumination
  O'Connor, F. The Partridge festival
  Verga, G. War between saints
  Witton, D. The potter's wheel

**Fetal** education. Sié, Cheou-kang

**Fetler, Andrew**
  To Byzantium
    New American Review no. 12

**FEUDS**
  Cobb, I. S. Five hundred dollars reward
  Fox, J. The pardon of Becky Day
  Haycox, E. Lin of Pistol Gap
  Henry, O. A blackjack bargainer
  Henry, O. Squaring the circle
  Hershman, M. A matter of pride
  Highsmith, P. The barbarians
  Jewett, S. O. The lost turkey
  Saki. The interlopers
  Sansom, W. A last word
  Scott, D. C. Clute Boulay
  Silverberg, R. The outbreeders
  Stuart, J. The old law wasn't strong enough

**FEVER**
  West, J. 99.6

**Fever.** Bonetti, E.

**Fever** dream. Bradbury, R.

A **few** last words. Sallis, J.

A **few** miles. Farmer, P. J.

A **few** notes for Orpheus. Bailey, D.

The **fiancé.** Trevisan, D.

**FICTITIOUS ANIMALS.** *See* Animals, Fictitious; Animals, Mythical

**FICTITIOUS NAMES.** *See* Pseudonyms

**FIDDLE.** *See* Violin

**Fiddler's** green. McKenna, R.

**Fiedler, Leslie A.**
  Bad scene at Buffalo Jump
    Fiedler, L. A. Nude croquet
  The dancing of Reb Hershl with the withered hand
    Fiedler, L. A. Nude croquet
  Dirty Ralphy
    Fiedler, L. A. Nude croquet
  An expense of spirit
    Fiedler, L. A. Nude croquet
  The fear of innocence
    Fiedler, L. A. Dirty Ralphy
  The girl in the black raincoat
    Fiedler, L. A. Nude croquet
  Let nothing you dismay
    Fiedler, L. A. Nude croquet
  Nobody ever died from it
    Fiedler, L. A. Nude croquet
  Nude croquet
    Fiedler, L. A. Nude croquet
  Pull down vanity!
    Fiedler, L. A. Nude croquet
  The stain
    Fiedler, L. A. Nude croquet
  The teeth
    Fiedler, L. A. Nude croquet

The **field** devil. Hesse, H.

**FIELD-GLASSES**
  Keefe, F. L. The field glasses
  Koš, E. The man who knew where the north was and where the south

The **field** glasses. Keefe, F. L.

The **field** of mustard. Coppard, A. E.

The **Field** of Terror. La Motte Fouqué, F. Baron de
**Fielding, Gabriel**
  After the parrot
    Fielding, G. New queens for old
  Bravery
    Fielding, G. New queens for old
  The catch
    Fielding, G. New queens for old
  A daughter of the Germans
    Fielding, G. New queens for old
  The dear demesne
    Fielding, G. New queens for old
  Figs in spring
    Fielding, G. New queens for old
  New queens for old
    Fielding, G. New queens for old
  The treat
    Fielding, G. New queens for old
  The trip
    Fielding, G. New queens for old
  The young bloods
    Fielding, G. New queens for old
**Fields, Julia**
  Not your singing, dancing spade
    King, W. ed. Black short story anthology
**Fields, Richard**
  At the Silver Rail
    New Directions in prose and poetry 20
The **fiend**. Bukowski, C.
The **fiend** of the cooperage. Doyle, Sir A. C.
The **fierce** and beautiful world. Platonov, A.
**Fiesta** brava. Reynolds, M.
**FIESTAS.** See Festivals
**Fifteen** miles. Bova, B.
The **Fifteenth** joy of marriage
  Cholakian, P. F. and Cholakian, R. C. eds. The early French novella
**Fifth** commandment. Brunner, J.
The **fifth** head of Cerberus. Wolfe, G.
The **fifth** wall. Casper, L.
The **fifth** wheel. Drake, R.
**Fifty** grand. Hemingway, E.
**53rd** American dream. Sallis, J.
The **fifty** yard dash. Saroyan, W.
**FIGHTING.** See Boxing; Dueling; Fighting, Hand-to-hand; Wrestling
**FIGHTING, HAND-TO-HAND**
  Blum-Alquit, E. Each spring
  Burhoe, B. A. Ornithanthropus
  Crane, S. The blue hotel
  Desnica, V. Justice
  De Vries, P. The irony of it all
  Kotzwinkle, W. Turning point
  MacMahon, B. The broken lyre
  Mihajlović, D. When the pumpkins blossomed
  Neugeboren, J. The application
  Preda, M. Encounter in the fields
  Sturgeon, T. Take care of Joey
    See also Boxing
**Fighting** fascism. Rush, N.
**Figs** in spring. Fielding, G.
**Figueredo, Parra y.** See Parra, A.
**Figúra.** Leskov, N.
The **figure** eight. Williams, J. A.
**FIGUREHEADS OF SHIPS**
  Ozick, C. The dock-witch

**Filch.** Long, F. B.
**File #1:** The Mayfield case. Gores, J.
**File #2:** Stakeout on Page Street. Gores, J.
**File #4:** Lincoln sedan deadline. Gores, J.
**File** on the plague. Bryant, E.
**Filer, Burt K.**
  Eye of the beholder
    Ellison, H. ed. Again, dangerous visions
  Hot potato
    Bova, B. ed. The many worlds of science fiction
    Del Rey, L. ed. Best science fiction stories of the year [1972]
  Sun
    Knight, D. ed. A pocketful of stars
  The time trawlers
    Galaxy Magazine. The eleventh Galaxy reader
The **fillyjonk** who believed in disasters. Jansson, T.
A **film.** Barthelme, D.
**Filomena** & Greg & Rikki-Tikki & Barlow & the alien. Tiptree, J.
**Fin** de siècle. Sternberg, J.
**Final** exam. Scortia, T. N.
The **final** fate of the alligators. Hoagland, E.
A **final** sceptre, a lasting crown. Bradbury, R.
**Final** war. O'Donnel, K. M.
**Final** warning. Trevisan, D.
**FINANCE, PERSONAL**
  Henry, O. An unfinished story
A **financial** failure: the story of a New England wooing. Jewett, S. O.
**FINANCIERS.** See Capitalists and financiers
**Finch** the spastic speaks. Weaver, G.
The **find.** Colette
**Find** the face. Rocklynne, R.
**Find** the woman. Macdonald, R.
**Finders** is keepers. Bower, B. M.
**Finding** peace. Peterkin, J.
**Fine, Warren**
  The mousechildren and the famous collector
    New American Review no. 9
The **fine** white mist of winter. Oates, J. C.
The **finer** points. Grover, W.
The **finer** things of life. Patton, F. G.
'The **finest** story in the world'. Kipling, R.
**Fingal.** Beckett, S.
**Finger**-nails. Moravia, A.
**Fingerprints** don't lie. Palmer, S.
**Fingers** and toes. Michaels, L.
**Fingers** in the door. Tuohy, F.
**Fingers** in the sky. Keller, D. H.
**Fingers** of Fong. Gardner, E. S.
**Fingers** of steel. Brennan, J. P.
**Finkel.** Neugeboren, J.
**FINLAND**
  Blum, R. In the blue country
**Finley, Drew H.**
  One little candle
  Intro #3
**Finn.** Michaels, L.
**Finney, Jack**
  Such interesting neighbors
    Stern, P. V. ed. The other side of the clock
  The third level
    Knight, D. ed. A science fiction argosy

**Flesh.** Taylor, E.
**Flesh** and the devil. De Vries, P.
**Fletcher, J. S.**
    The contents of the coffin
        Greene, Sir H. ed. The further rivals of Sherlock Holmes
    The convict and the clerics
        Dickinson, S. ed. The drugged cornet, and other mystery stories
A **flicker** of the torch. Carr, J.
**FLIES**
    Asimov, I. Flies
    Bloch, R. Beelzebub
    Langelaan, G. The fly
**Flies.** Asimov, I.
**Flies.** Silverberg, R.
**FLIGHT**
    Carr, T. The winds at Starmont
The **flight.** Bullock, M.
**Flight.** Lessing, D.
**Flight.** O'Hara, J.
**Flight.** Steinbeck, J.
**Flight** from Bright Shores. Litvinov, I.
The **flight** of pigeons from the palace. Barthelme, D.
The **flight** that failed. Pei, M.
The **flight** to the moon. Lu, Hsun
**Flight** useless, inexorable the pursuit. Disch, T. M.
The **flirt.** Elman, R.
**Flirtation.** Maugham, W. S.
The **flogging.** Milner, R.
The **flood.** Steinbeck, J.
The **flood.** Zelver, P.
**Flood** tide. Yehoshua, A. B.
**FLOODS**
    Aldiss, B. W. Orgy of the living and the dying
    Coover, R. The brother
    Faulkner, W. Old man
    García Márquez, G. Monologue of Isabel watching it rain in Macondo
    Harte, B. High-water mark
    Heard, H. F. The President of the United States, detective
    Pentecost, H. In the middle of nowhere
    Steinbeck, J. The flood
    Warner, S. T. Truth in the cup
    Williamson, G. Trapped in a flooded tunnel
    Yehoshua, A. B. Flood tides
    Zelver, P. The flood
**FLOORS**
    Bichsel, P. Floors
The **floors** of his heart. Sallis, J.
**Flora, Fletcher**
    In the shade of the old apple tree
        McComas, J. F. ed. Crimes and misfortunes
**Floral** tribute. Bloch, R.
A **floral** tribute. Tuohy, F.
**FLORENCE.** See Italy—Florence
**FLORICULTURE.** See Gardens and gardening
**FLORIDA**
    Amft, M. J. When the two hands are up
    Ballard, J. G. The cage of sand
    Deming, B. The rattler
    Garrett, G. The satyr shall cry

    Gunn, J. E. The old folks
    Rigsby, H. Dead man's story
        **Dialect stories**
        See Dialect stories—Florida
        **Fort Lauderdale**
    Blaise, C. The bridge
        **Miami**
    Brodeur, P. Blue lawns
    Gold, H. Death in Miami Beach
    Miller, J. Sondra / Miami
    Wylie, P. The old crawdad
**FLORISTS**
    Moravia, A.    A middling type
The **flower.** Rugel, M.
**FLOWER ARRANGEMENT**
    West, J. The heavy stone
**FLOWER GARDENING.** See Gardens and gardening
**Flower** horse. Bukowski, C.
The **Flowered** Thundermug. Bester, A.
**Flowering** Judas. Porter, K. A.
**Flowering** Narcissus. Scortia, T. N.
The **flowering** of the strange orchid. Wells, H. G.
**FLOWERS**
    Bichsel, P. Flowers
    Kantor, M. The purple moccasin
        See also Flower arrangements; also names of specific flowers, e.g. Orchids
The **flowers.** Walker, A.
**Flowers** for Algernon. Keyes, D.
The **flowers** of friendship. Kanin, G.
**Fluffy.** Sturgeon, T.
**Flute** dream. Hesse, H.
**FLUTISTS.** See Musicians—Flutists
The **fly.** Langelaan, G.
The **fly.** Mansfield, K.
The **fly-paper.** Taylor, E.
**Flying** home. Ellison, R.
The **flying** lion. Marshall, E.
**FLYING SAUCERS**
    Spark, M. Miss Pinkerton's apocalypse
        See also Interplanetary visitors
The **flying** weathercock. Mitchell, E. P.
The **Flyman.** Woolf, D.
**Flythe, Starkey**
    Point of conversion
        Prize stories, 1972: The O. Henry Awards
**FOG**
    Anthony, P. Phog
The **Fog** Horn. Bradbury, R.
**FOG HORNS**
    Bradbury, R. The beast from 20,000 fathoms
    Bradbury, R. The Fog Horn
**Fogel, Aaron**
    The turtle hunt
        Gottesman, L.; Obenzinger, H. and Senauke, A. eds. A cinch
**FOGHORNS.** See Fog horns
**FOLK-LORE, MEDICAL.** See Folk Medicine
**FOLK MEDICINE**
    Deutschman, B. Mama's medicine made Jewish kids strong
    Henderson, Z. Love every third stir

**FOREIGN LEGION.** *See* France. Army.
  Foreign Legion
**FOREIGN SERVICE.** *See* Civil service;
  Diplomatic life
**Foreign** trade. Green, B. K.
**FOREIGN VISITORS.** *See* Tourist trade;
  Visitors, Foreign
The **foreigner.** Jewett, S. O.
The **foreigner** in the blood. Hughes, M. G.
**FOREIGNERS.** *See* Visitors, Foreign
**Foreigners.** Gilliatt, P.
The **foreman.** Peterkin, J.
**FOREMEN**
  Stewart, J. C. The last day
**Forerunner.** Sutton, J.
The **forest.** Leffland, E.
**FOREST FIRES**
  Deck, J. The way the wind blows
  Garner, H. Red racer
  Holmes, E. M. Fall fire
  Yehoshua, A. B. Facing the forests
    *See also* Fires; Forests and forestry
The **forest** in the sky. Laumer, K.
The **forest** path to the spring. Lowry, M.
The **forest** ranger. Cady, J.
**Forester, C. S.**
  The boy stood on the burning deck
    Forester, C. S. The man in the yellow
    raft
  Counterpunch
    Forester, C. S. The man in the yellow
    raft
  Dawn attack
    Forester, C. S. Gold from Crete
  December 6th
    Forester, C. S. The man in the yellow
    raft
  Depth charge!
    Forester, C. S. Gold from Crete
  Dr Blanke's first command
    Forester, C. S. The man in the yellow
    raft
  The dumb Dutchman
    Forester, C. S. Gold from Crete
  Eagle Squadron
    Forester, C. S. Gold from Crete
  An egg for the major
    Forester, C. S. Gold from Crete
  Gold from Crete
    Forester, C. S. Gold from Crete
  If Hitler had invaded England
    Forester, C. S. Gold from Crete
  Intelligence
    Forester, C. S. Gold from Crete
  The man in the yellow raft
    Forester, C. S. The man in the yellow
    raft
  The man who didn't ask why
    Haining, P. ed. The Lucifer society
  Night stalk
    Forester, C. S. Gold from Crete
  Rendezvous
    Forester, C. S. The man in the yellow
    raft
  Triumph of the Boon
    Forester, C. S. The man in the yellow
    raft

The turn of the tide
  Kahn, J. ed. Some things fierce and
  fatal
U.S.S. Cornucopia
  Forester, C. S. The man in the yellow
  raft
"You are welcome!"
  Forester, C. S. Gold from Crete
  **Parodies, travesties, etc.**
  Harrison, H. Captain Honario Harpplay-
  er, R.N.
**FORESTERS**
  Saki. The interlopers
  Yehoshua, A. B. Facing the forests
    *See also* Forests and forestry
**FORESTS AND FORESTRY**
  De La Mare, W. In the forest
  Derleth, A. The dweller in darkness
  Le Guin, U. K. The word for world is for-
  est
**Forever** and amen. Bloch, R.
**Forever** panting. De Vries, P.
**Forge** without fire. Ulibarri, S. R.
**FORGERIES, LITERARY.** *See* Literary
  forgeries and mystifications
**FORGERY**
  Collins, W. Fauntleroy
  Pentecost, H. Hector is willin'
**FORGERY OF WORKS OF ART**
  Goulart, R. Granny
  Kersh, G. The Pettifer collection
  Ritchie, J. Who's got the lady?
  Sandaval, J. Art for money's sake
  Silverberg, R. The artifact business
**Forgetfulness.** Stuart, D. A.
**Forging** ahead. Fitzgerald, F. S.
**Forging** the swords. Lu, Hsun
**Forgiven.** Brautigan, R.
**Forgiven.** Steinberg, J.
**FORGIVENESS**
  Leskov, N. Figúra
  Rosenthal, E. D. Yom Kippur
  Steinberg, J. Forgiven
The **forks.** Powers, J. F.
The **form** of the sword. *See* Borges, J. L.
  The shape of the sword
**FORMOSA**
  Nieh, Hua-ling. The several blessings of
  Wang Ta-nien
**Forms** of things unknown. Lewis, C. S.
**Formula** of immortality. Dneprov, A.
**Forster, E. M.**
  Albergo Empedocle
    Forster, E. M. The life to come, and
    other short stories
  Ansell
    Forster, E. M. The life to come, and
    other short stories
  Arthur Snatchfold
    Forster, E. M. The life to come, and
    other short stories
  The classical annex
    Forster, E. M. The life to come, and
    other short stories
  Dr Woolacott
    Forster, E. M. The life to come, and
    other short stories

FRANCE—18th century—*Continued*

Tolstoy, A. The reunion after three hundred years

**18th century—1789-1799**

Balzac, H. de. An episode of the terror
Holst, S. 10,000 reflections
Nodier, C. Jean-François Bluestockings
Orczy, Baroness.  A question of passports

**19th century**

James, H.  A tragedy of error
Maupassant, G. de. French tales of love and passion; 20 stories
Maupassant, G. de. The horseman

**Commune, 1871**

*See* France—Paris—Commune, 1871

**1945-**

Woods, W. C.  A mirror of the waves

**Arles**

Mistral, F. The immaculate Arlésiennes

**Army**

Doyle, Sir A. C. How the brigadier saved an army

**Army. Foreign Legion**

Gallant, M. Ernst in civilian clothes

**Army—Officers**

Balzac, H. de.  El Verdugo
Fitzgerald, F. S. Emotional bankruptcy

**Brittany**

*See* France, Provincial and rural—Brittany

**Farm life**

*See* Farm life—France

**Le Havre**

Maupassant, G. de. My Uncle Jules

**Lourdes**

O'Faolain, S. Feed my lambs

**Marseilles**

Arnim, A. von. The mad veteran of Fort Ratonneau
Collier, J. If youth knew, if age could

**Normandy**

*See* France, Provincial and rural—Normandy

**Paris—15th century**

Stevenson, R. L.  A lodging for the night

**Paris—17th century**

Hoffmann, E. T. A. Mademoiselle de Scudéri

**Paris—18th century**

Prévost, A. The adventure of a desperate man

**Paris—19th century**

Collins, W. The story of a terribly strange bed
Collins, W.  A terribly strange bed
France, A. Crainquebille
Maupassant, G. de. The diamond necklace
Maupassant, G. de. The father
Maupassant, G. de. Mademoiselle Perle
Maupassant, G. de.  A man of influence
Maupassant, G. de. The two friends

Moorcock, M. An apocalypse: some scenes from European life
Stoker, B. The burial of the rats

**1815-1848**

Vigny, A. de. The Malacca Cane

**Paris—20th century**

Anouilh, J. The moment is near
Colette. The find
Colette. The fox
Cortázar, J. The other heaven
Cortázar, J. The southern thruway
Ellin, S. Kindly dig your grave
Farrell, J. T. Arlette
Gold, H. Young man, old days
Greene, G. Brother
Greene, G. Two gentle people
Kevles, B. Georgie in the middle
Krleža, M. Hodorlahomor the Great
Maugham, W. S. Appearance and reality
Rainov, B. Rush hour
Rolland, R. Pierre and Luce
Sackville-West, V. Thirty clocks strike the hour
Schwartz, J. Dennicker's love story
Taylor, P. Je suis perdu

**Peasant life**

*See* Peasant life—France

**Provence**

*See* France, Provincial and rural—Provence

**Pyrénées-Orientales**

*See* France, Provincial and rural—Pyrénées-Orientales

**Riviera**

*See* Riviera

**Verdun**

Björneboe, J. Moment of freedom

**FRANCE, PROVINCIAL AND RURAL**

Blackwood, A. Ancient sorceries
Du Gard, R. M. The reformatory
Ionesco, E. Spring 1939
James, H. Gabrielle De Bergerac
Kipling, R. The bull that thought
Maupassant, G. de. The adoption
Maupassant, G. de. The homecoming
Maupassant, G. de.  A piece of string
Maupassant, G. de. Simon's papa
Maxwell, W. The gardens of Mont-Saint-Michel
Runyon, D.  A light in France
Rushmore, R. The trumpets of Épignon
Simenon, G. Crime in the Rue Sainte-Catherine
Stevenson, R. L. Providence and the guitar

**Brittany**

Maupassant, G. de. For sale
Treat, L. Justice magnifique
Wharton, E. Kerfol

**Normandy**

Maupassant, G. de. The farmer

**Provence**

Greene, G. Beauty
Mistral, F. The complaint of the bulls of the Camargue

**FRANCE, PROVINCIAL AND RURAL—**
*Continued*

**Pyrénées-Orientales**

Collier, J. Witch's money

**FRANCESCO DE ASSISI, SAINT.** *See* Francis of Assisi, Saint

**FRANCIS OF ASSISI, SAINT**
Corvo, F. Baron. About Sodom, Gomorrah, and the two admirable Jesuits
Goudge, E. Giovanni
Hesse, H. From the childhood of Saint Francis of Assisi

**Francis, Elaine Fiske**
The sissy señor
Tibbets, A. B. ed. Boys are boys

**Francis, H. E.**
All the carnivals in the world
Francis, H. E. The itinerary of beggars
All the people I never had
Francis, H. E. The itinerary of beggars
Contemplations of ecstasy on the day of my suicide
Francis, H. E. The itinerary of beggars
The deepest chamber
Francis, H. E. The itinerary of beggars
Don't stay away too long
Francis, H. E. The itinerary of beggars
The fence
Francis, H. E. The itinerary of beggars
The frog lady
Francis, H. E. The itinerary of beggars
The game
Francis, H. E. The itinerary of beggars
Going West
Alabama prize stories, 1970
Francis, H. E. The itinerary of beggars
The itinerary of beggars
Francis, H. E. The itinerary of beggars
The man who made people
Francis, H. E. The itinerary of beggars
The moment of fish
Francis, H. E. The itinerary of beggars
One of the boys
Francis, H. E. The itinerary of beggars
The rate of decomposition in a cold climate
Francis, H. E. The itinerary of beggars
Running
Francis, H. E. The itinerary of beggars
3
Francis, H. E. The itinerary of beggars
The transfusion man
Francis, H. E. The itinerary of beggars
Where was my life before I died?
Francis, H. E. The itinerary of beggars
The woman from Jujuy
Francis, H. E. The itinerary of beggars

**FRANCISCANS**
Marguerite de Navarre. The tonsured husband
Powers, J. F. Lions, harts, leaping does

**FRANCO-GERMAN WAR, 1870-1871**
Maupassant, G. de. The adventure of Walter Schnaffs
Maupassant, G. de. Ball-of-Fat
Maupassant, G. de. The duel
Maupassant, G. de. A fishing excursion

**FRANCO-PRUSSIAN WAR.** *See* Franco-German War, 1870-1871

François Yattend. Van Itallie, J. C.

Frank. Gilliatt, P.

Frank Merriswell's greatest case. Breen, J. L.

Frank Reade Jr's Air wonder. Senarens, L. P.

Frank Reade, Jr's, Air wonder fights the Klamath Indians. *See* Senarens, L. P. Frank Reade Jr's Air wonder

**Franke, Herbert W.**
Slum
Rottensteiner, F. ed. View from another shore

Frankie Mae. Smith J. W.

**Franklin, Edward**
Girl in a white dress
McCrindle, J. F. ed. Stories from the Transatlantic Review

**Franklin, J. E.**
The enemy
King, W. ed. Black short story anthology

The **Franklyn** paragraphs. Campbell, R.

"**Franz Kafka**" by Jorge Luis Borges. Greenberg, A.

**Franzos, Karl Emil**
A savior of the people
Goodman, P. ed. The Yom Kippur anthology

**Fraser, George MacDonald**
The general danced at dawn
Fraser, G. M. The general danced at dawn, and other stories
Guard at the castle
Fraser, G. M. The general danced at dawn, and other stories
McAuslan's court-martial
Fraser, G. M. The general danced at dawn, and other stories
Monsoon Selection Board
Fraser, G. M. The general danced at dawn, and other stories
Night run to Palestine
Fraser, G. M. The general danced at dawn, and other stories
Play up, play up and get tore in
Fraser, G. M. The general danced at dawn, and other stories
Silence in the ranks
Fraser, G. M. The general danced at dawn, and other stories
Wee Wullie
Fraser, G. M. The general danced at dawn, and other stories
The whiskey and the music
Fraser, G. M. The general danced at dawn, and other stories

**Fraser, Mrs Hugh**
The Satanist
Haining, P. ed. A circle of witches

The **Frater** family. Ulibarri, S. R.

Fraternity brother. Lanier, S.

**FRATRICIDE**
Golding, L. The call of the hand
Maturin, C. Leixlip Castle
Smith, C. A. The return of the sorcerer
Steinbeck, J. Timshel
Vos, H. The sons of Pepe Gimenez

A **fratricide**. Kafka, F.

**FRAUD**

Aldiss, B. W. The young soldier's horoscope

Amateau, R. and Davis, D. The tilt of death

Ashdown, C. The Assyrian rejuvenator

Cecil, H. The hidden money

Collier, J. Sleeping beauty

Das, M. The mystery of the missing cap

DeFord, M. A. The moment of time

Hardwick, Michael, and Hardwick, Mollie. The princess of Thebes

Jepsen, H. L. The blackbird

Malamud, B. The silver crown

Singer, I. B. The bishop's robe

Singer, I. B. The captive

Singer, I. B. The séance

Sturgeon, T. Well spiced

   *See also* Hoaxes; Impersonations; Impersonators, Male; Impostors and imposture; Quacks and quackery; Swinders and swindling; Trials (Fraud)

**Fräulein** Else. Schnitzler, A.

**Frazee, Steve**

My brother down there

   Queen, E. ed. Ellery Queen's The golden 13

**Frazer, Chris**

Zydeco

   Burnett, W. ed. Black hands on a white face

**Freak** show. DeFord, M. A.

**FREAKS.** *See* Deformities; Dwarfs; Monsters

**Freaks.** Robbins, T.

**Fred** and Arthur. Gilliatt, P.

**Freddy**-bear. Canzoneri, R.

**Free** Agent. Nourse, A. E.

A **free** choice. Brennan, M.

**Free** City blues. Eklund, G.

**Free** dirt. Beaumont, C.

**Free** for all. Cecil, H.

**Free** vacation. Macfarlane, W.

**FREEDOM.** *See* Liberty

**Freedom.** Cosić, D.

**Freedom.** O'Connor, F.

**Freedom.** Verga, G.

**Freedom** fighter. Collins, M.

**FREEDOM MARCHES.** *See* Negroes—Civil rights

**Freedom** now. Heyman, A.

**Freedom's** a hard-bought thing. Benét, S. V.

**Freeman, Anne Hobson**

Whatever became of Agnes Mason

   Brown, E. P. ed. Twice fifteen

**Freeman, Mary E. Wilkins**

A conflict ended

   Westbrook, P. D. ed. Seacoast and upland: a New England anthology

An honest soul

   Westbrook, P. D. ed. Seacoast and upland: a New England anthology

Old Woman Magoun

   Westbrook, P. D. ed. Seacoast and upland: a New England anthology

A poetess

   Westbrook, P. D. ed. Seacoast and upland: a New England anthology

Sister Liddy

   Westbrook, P. D. ed. Seacoast and upland: a New England anthology

The wind in the rose-bush

   Manley, S. and Lewis, G. eds. Ladies of horror

**Freeman, Michael**

The scapegoat

   The Times of London Anthology of detective stories

**Freeman, R. Austin**

The Moabite cipher

   Greene, H. ed. The rivals of Sherlock Holmes

**Freemann, Richard A.**

Indoro Bush College

   Angoff, C. ed. Stories from the Literary Review

   Angoff, C. and Povey, J. eds. African writing today

**FREETOWN.** *See* Sierre Leone—Freetown

**Freeway** to wherever. Ogden, M.

**FREEZING OF HUMAN BODIES.** *See* Cryonics

**FREIGHT AND FREIGHTAGE**

Guthrie, A. B. Bargain

Silverberg, R. Delivery guaranteed

A **freight** car incident. Crane, S.

**Freitag, George H.**

An old man and his hat

   Foff, A. and Knapp, D. eds. Story

**Fremlin, Celia**

Angel-face

   Fremlin, C. Don't go to sleep in the dark

The baby-sitter

   Fremlin, C. Don't go to sleep in the dark

The betrayal

   Ellery Queen's Mystery Magazine. Ellery Queen's Murder menu

   Fremlin, C. Don't go to sleep in the dark

Don't be frightened

   Ellery Queen's Mystery Magazine. Ellery Queen's Headliners

   Same as: "The hated house"

The fated interview

   Fremlin, C. Don't go to sleep in the dark

For ever fair

   Fremlin, C. Don't go to sleep in the dark

The hated house

   Fremlin, C. Don't go to sleep in the dark

   Same as: "Don't be frightened"

The irony of fate

   Fremlin, C. Don't go to sleep in the dark

Last day of spring

   Fremlin, C. Don't go to sleep in the dark

The locked room

   Fremlin, C. Don't go to sleep in the dark

The new house

   Fremlin, C. Don't go to sleep in the dark

**Fremlin, Celia**—*Continued*
   Old Daniel's treasure
      Fremlin, C. Don't go to sleep in the dark
   The quiet game
      Fremlin, C. Don't go to sleep in the dark
   Something evil in the house
      Kahn, J. ed. Some things fierce and fatal
      Mystery Writers of America. Merchants of menace
   The special gift
      Fremlin, C. Don't go to sleep in the dark
**FRENCH AND INDIAN WAR.** *See* United States— 18th century—French and Indian War
**FRENCH CANADIANS**
   Laurence, M. The loons
   London, J. The devil-dog
   Murphy, R. There was a bigger one
   Scott, D. C. Spirit River
**FRENCH CANADIANS IN THE UNITED STATES**
   Blaise, C. Snow people
**FRENCH IN AFRICA**
   Balzac, H. de. A passion in the desert
**FRENCH IN CANADA**
   Scott, D. C. Paul Farlotte
**FRENCH IN EGYPT**
   Fielding, G. New queens for old
**FRENCH IN ENGLAND**
   Ionesco, E. The stroller in the air
   Lang, A. Captain Pink
**FRENCH IN GERMANY**
   Edwards, A. B. Monsieur Maurice
**FRENCH IN ITALY**
   Ely, D. The gourmet hunt
**FRENCH IN RUSSIA**
   Hebel, J. P. Monsieur Charles
   Nabokov, V. Mademoiselle O
**FRENCH IN SPAIN**
   Balzac, H. de. El Verdugo
**FRENCH IN THE UNITED STATES**
   Cather, W. The Count of Crow's Nest
   Cather, W.   A night at Greenway Court
   Chopin, K.   A lady of Bayou St John
   Chopin, K. The maid of Saint Philippe
   Stafford, J. Caveat emptor
   Stewart, N. What sadness
**FRENCH REVOLUTION.** *See* France— 18th century—1789-1799
**FRENCH SOLDIERS.** *See* Soldiers, French
**Friar** Stefano's resurrection. Parabosco, G.
**FRIARS.** *See* Monks
**FRIARS, GRAY.** *See* Franciscans
**Friday** night at the project and tenuous relationships reaching to Long Island. Lord, P.
**Friedman, Alan**
   The tell-tale hearse
      New American Review no. 9
   Willy-nilly
      New American Review no. 2
**Friedman, B. H.**
   Drinking smoke
      New American Review no. 15
   Whispers
      New American Review no. 5

**Friedman, Bruce Jay**
   The enemy
      McCrindle, J. F. ed. Stories from the Transatlantic Review
   The hero
      Simon, J. ed. Fourteen for now
   Lady
      Lish, G. ed. The secret life of our times: new fiction from Esquire
   Yes, we have no Ritchard
      Ferman, E. L. and Mills, R. P. eds. Twenty years of The Magazine of Fantasy and Science Fiction
**Friedman, Paul**
   The alphabet of mathematics
      Friedman, P. And if defeated allege fraud
   An American memory, 1966
      Friedman, P. And if defeated allege fraud
   The arm of interchangeable parts
      Friedman, P. And if defeated allege fraud
   An evening of fun
      Friedman, P. And if defeated allege fraud
   The forecast
      Friedman, P. And if defeated allege fraud
   In equal parts
      Friedman, P. And if defeated allege fraud
   The inheritance editor
      Friedman, P. And if defeated allege fraud
   A matter of survival
      Friedman, P. And if defeated allege fraud
   Never lose your cool
      Friedman, P. And if defeated allege fraud
   Portrait: my American man, fall, 1966
      Friedman, P. And if defeated allege fraud
      New Directions in prose and poetry 20
   The story of a story
      Friedman, P. And if defeated allege fraud
      New Directions in prose and poetry 22
The **Friedmans'** Annie. Slesinger, T.
**Friedrich, Baron de la Motte Fouqué.** *See* La Motte Fouqué, Friedrich, Baron de
A **friend** of Don Juan. Mulkerns, V.
A **friend** of Kafka. Singer, I. B.
A **friend** of the court. Patton, F. G.
The **friend** of the family. McCarthy, M.
A **friend** to Alexander. Thurber, J.
The **friendly** call. Henry, O.
The **friendly** demon. Defoe, D.
**FRIENDS.** *See* Friendship
**FRIENDS, SOCIETY OF**
   Babel, I. The Quaker
   Nissenson, H. Grace
   Russell, B. Stalin's nightmare
   West, J. Except for me and thee; 11 stories
   West, J.   A family argument
   West, J. Fast horseflesh
   West, J. First loss

**FROGS**—*Continued*

Twain, M. The celebrated jumping frog of Calaveras County

**From** all of us. Bauer, G. M.

**From** below the bridge. Kim, Y. I.

**From** Cuba with a song. Sarduy, S.

**From** fanaticism, or for reward. Harrison, H.

**From** hand to mouth. O'Brien, F.

**From** here to eternity. Stanton, J.

**From** image to expression. Roth, H. H.

**From** lodging to lodging. Agnon, S. Y.

**From** out of the garden. Armstrong, C.

**From** Proust to dada. Gold, H.

**From** rags to riches. Roditi, E.

**From** sea to shining sea. Ela, J.

**From** shadowed places. Matheson, R.

**From** the cabby's seat. Henry, O.

**From** the childhood of Saint Francis of Assisi. Hesse, H.

**From** the darkness. Mrozek, S.

**From** the diary of a New York lady. Parker, D.

**From** the further adventures of Sinbad the sailor. Pei, M.

**From** the mouse to the hawk. Henderson, D.

**From** the other side to the other side. Borchert, W.

**From** the sea. Bichsel, P.

**From** there to infinity. De Vries, P.

**From** your evil ways. Heeresma, H.

**From's** daughter. Čingo, Ž.

**Front** & centaur. Sallis, J.

The **front** room. Butterworth, M.

**FRONTIER AND PIONEER LIFE**

Rothschild, M. The price of pine

*See* also Homesteading; Western stories

**Arizona**

Wister, O.   A pilgrim on the Gila

**Canada**

Prebble, J. Almighty voice

Scott, D. C. Expiation

Scott, D. C. Labrie's wife

**Colorado**

White, S. E.   A corner in horses

**Idaho**

Gulick, B. Something in the air

Hayes, A. H. The first wedding

Hayes, A. H. Mail-order bride

Hayes, A. H. Pioneer wife

Wister, O. The Second Missouri Compromise

**Montana**

Guthrie, A. B. Rendezvous

**Nebraska**

Cather, W.   A Wagner matinee

**New York (State)**

Edmonds, W. D. The matchlock gun

Edmonds, W. D. Wilderness clearing

**Ohio**

Bierce, A. The boarded window

**Oklahoma**

Bishop, Z. The curse of Yig

**Oregon**

Bretherton, V. The rock and the wind; excerpt

Haycox, E. Into the deep gorge

Henry, W. Lapwai winter

James, D. The thin thread

Jones, N. The arrival of Jane Barnes

McGraw, E. J. Moccasin trail; excerpt

Moore, L. Homestead in the valley

Stone, N. B. The long trail

**Southwest, New**

Richter, C. Early marriage

**Washington**

DeFord, M. A. The daughter of the tree

**The West**

Berry, D. Across Neahkahnie

Case, V. When the Indians came

Johnson, D. M. The unbeliever

Prebble, J. The long hate

*See also* Western stories

**Wyoming**

Parkman, F. Scenes at Fort Laramie

Prebble, J. My great-aunt Appearing Day

**Yukon Territory**

Hendryx, J. B. The parson

The **frozen** face. O'Hara, J.

**FRUIT**

Crane, S.   A great mistake

A **fruitful** Sunday. Christie, A.

A **fruitless** assignment. Bierce, A.

**Fuchs, Daniel**

Twilight in southern California

Abrahams, W. ed. Fifty years of the American short story v 1

The **fuck** machine. Bukowski, C.

**FUEL**

Forester, C. S. Rendezvous

**Fuentes, Carlos**

Aura

Cohen, J. M. ed. Latin American writing today

Karl, F. R. and Hamalian, L. eds. The naked i

Holy place

Triple cross

The two Elenas

Howes, B. ed. The eye of the heart

**Fuentes, Norberto**

Captain Descalzo

Carpentier, H. and Brof, J. eds. Doors and mirrors

For the night

Carpentier, H. and Brof, J. eds. Doors and mirrors

**FUGITIVES**

Alter, R. E. Man hunt on Dead Yank Creek

Babel, I. Sulak

Fuentes, N. Captain Descalzo

Gbadamossi, R. A. Bats and babies

Goulart, R. All for love

Greene, G. Across the bridge

Steinbeck, J. Flight

Steinbeck, J. Ma and Tom

Wright, R. Big Boy leaves home

# G

GHOSTS—*Continued*

Hamilton-Paterson, J. Salpingogram
Hardwick, Michael, and Hardwick, Mollie. Let sleeping bones lie
Hardwick, Michael, and Hardwick, Mollie. Lullaby for the dead
Hardwick, Michael, and Hardwick, Mollie. Ole rockin' chair
Hartley, L. P. Feet foremost
Heald, H. The horror in the burying ground
Heriot, C. D. The trapdoor
Hodgson, W. H. The house among the laurels
Howard, R. E. The house in the oaks
Hunt, L.   A tale for a chimney corner
Hunter, K. BeeGee's ghost
Irving, W. Guests from Gibbet Island
Irving, W. The legend of Sleepy Hollow
The Jade Kuan-yin
James, H. Henry James: stories of the supernatural; 18 stories
James, H. The romance of certain old clothes
James, M. R. The haunted doll's house
James, M. R. Lost hearts
James, M. R. The stalls of Barchester Cathedral
James, M. R.   A warning to the curious
Johnson, P. H. The empty schoolroom
Kipling, R. The house surgeon
Kipling, R. My own true ghost story
Kipling, R. The phantom 'rickshaw
Kipling, R. "They"
Kneale, N. Minuke
Lafferty, R. A. Cliffs that laughed
Landolfi, T. Shadows
Landon, P. Thurnley Abbey
Lang, A. The House of Strange Stories
Lathom, F. The water spectre
Lee, V.   A phantom lover
Le Fanu, J. S. The ghost and the bonesetter
Le Fanu, J. S. Madam Crowl's ghost
Le Fanu, J. S. Wicked Captain Walshawe
Lovecraft, H. P. The evil clergyman
Maclagan, D. Dr Black's castle
Maclagan, D. Journey to Enog
Manley, S. and Lewis, G. eds. A gathering of ghosts; 9 stories
Maugham, W. S.   A man from Glasgow
Mitchell, E. P. Back from that bourne
Mitchell, E. P. An uncommon sort of spectre
Milosz, C. Magdalena
Nesbit, E. John Charrington's wedding
Nin, A. Under a glass bell
O'Donnell, E. The haunted spinney
Oliphant, Mrs. The library window
Olsen, T. V. The strange valley
Padgett, R. and Gallup, D. Cold turkey
Page, T. N. "No Haid Pawn"
Palmer, E. Post-obit
Phillips, P. Manna
Pliny the Younger. The haunted house
Poe, E. A. King Pest
P'u, Sung-ling. Ying-ning
Quiller-Couch, Sir A.   A pair of hands
Radcliffe, A. The haunted chamber

Riddell, Mrs J. H. The uninhabited house
Russ, J. Poor man, beggar man
Schiller, J. F. von. The ghost-seer
Scott, E. The twelve apostles
Scott, Sir W. The tapestried chamber
Sentongo, N. Mulyankota
Seth, R. Footprints in the dust
Seth, R. Scent of death
Seymour, W. K.   A tale in a club
Shannon, D. The practical joke
Silverberg, R. Push no more
Smith, C. A. The ghost of Mohammed Din
The Spectre barber
Stockton, F. R. The transferred ghost
Stoker, B. The Judge's House
The Story of Glam
Tabori, P. The bridge
Talman, W. B. Two black bottles
Thurber, J. The night the ghost got in
Tomlinson, D. ed. Walk in dread; 12 stories
Turgenev, I. Bezhin Meadow
Ulyatt, K. Ghost riders of the Sioux
Urquhart, F. The ghostess with the mostest
Uyeda, A. Exiled
Uyeda, A. Prophesy
Uyeda, A. Wealth
Vallejo, C. On the other side of life and death
Vance, J. Guyal of Sfere
Wade, R. Shepherd, show me . . .
Wakefield, H. R. Mr Ash's studio
Wakefield, H. R. The triumph of death
Walpole, Sir H. Mrs Lunt
Wharton, E. Afterward
Wharton, E. All Souls'
Wharton, E. The ghost stories of Edith Wharton; 11 stories
Wharton, E. Kerfol
Wharton, E. The lady's maid's bell
Wharton, E. Miss Mary Pask
Wharton, E. Mr Jones
Wharton, E. Pomegranate seed
Wharton, E. The triumph of night
Wilde, O. The Canterville ghost
Wright, W. C. The green fly and the box
Yüan, Mei. Three ghost stories
   *See also* Hallucinations and illusions; Horror stories; Poltergeists; Spiritualism; Supernatural phenomena

The **ghosts** at Iron River. Yarbro, C. Q.

The **ghoul**. Smith, C. A.

A **ghoul's** accountant. Crane, S.

**GHOULS AND OGRES**

DeFord, M. A. The old bunch and Dusty Stiggins
Lovecraft, H. P. The dream quest of unknown Kadath
Smith, C. A. The ghoul

**GIACOMETTI, ALBERTO**

Ayrton, M.   A problem of space

The **giant**. De La Mare, W.

**Giant** killer. Chandler, A. B.

**Giant** killer. Laumer, K.

The **giant** mole. *See* Kafka, F. The village schoolmaster

**GIANTS**

Ballard, J. G. The drowned giant

GIRLS—*Continued*
  *See also* Adolescence; Children; Youth
Girls at war. Achebe, C.
Girls together. Manning, O.
Gissing, George
 Lou and Liz
  Keating, P. J. ed. Working-class stories of the 1890s
Gittel Branfman the impossible. Deutschman, B.
Gittin' even. Green, B. K.
Give Charlie a little time. Stuart, J.
Give her hell. Wollheim, D. A.
The givers. Daugherty, M. G.
GLACIAL EPOCH. *See* Ice Age
GLADIATORS
 Cortázar, J. All fires the fire
Gladius Dei. Mann, T.
Gladys's Gregory. West, J. A.
Glanville, Brian
 Arrivederci, Elba
  Glanville, B. A betting man, and other stories
 A bad streak
  Glanville, B. A betting man, and other stories
 A betting man
  Glanville, B. A betting man, and other stories
 The director's wife
  Glanville, B. A betting man, and other stories
 The dying footballer
  Glanville, B. A betting man, and other stories
 An enemy
  Glanville, B. A betting man, and other stories
 Everything laid on
  Glanville, B. A betting man, and other stories
 Feet of clay
  Glanville, B. A betting man, and other stories
 The footballers
  Glanville, B. A betting man, and other stories
 Goalkeepers are crazy
  Glanville, B. A betting man, and other stories
 Hanger-on
  Glanville, B. A betting man, and other stories
 If he's good enough, he's big enough
  Glanville, B. A betting man, and other stories
 The king of Hackney Marshes
  Glanville, B. A betting man, and other stories
 The man behind the goal
  Glanville, B. A betting man, and other stories
 The men on the GI bill
  Glanville, B. A betting man, and other stories

 Miss Lawrence will be at home
  Glanville, B. A betting man, and other stories
 No Jews or dogs
  Glanville, B. A betting man, and other stories
 The prodigy
  Glanville, B. A betting man, and other stories
 Roses in burnt oak
  Glanville, B. A betting man, and other stories
 The survivor
  Glanville, B. A betting man, and other stories
 The twins
  Glanville, B. A betting man, and other stories
GLASGOW. *See* Scotland—Glasgow
Glass, Dick
 The ultimate end
  Nova 3
GLASS EYES. *See* Eye
The glass mountain. Barthelme, D.
GLASS PAINTING AND STAINING
 Ruskay, S. Allah will understand
The glass peacock. Farjeon, E.
Glassgold, Peter
 Omelets were his specialty
  New Directions in prose and poetry 27
Glaze, Eleanor
 And bigger fools
  Glaze, E. The embrace, and stories
 Do not pass me by
  Glaze, E. The embrace, and stories
 The embrace
  Glaze, E. The embrace, and stories
 Madeira
  Glaze, E. The embrace, and stories
 Shadows
  Glaze, E. The embrace, and stories
 Silver grapes
  Glaze, E. The embrace, and stories
 Sisters
  Glaze, E. The embrace, and stories
 A strolling brink
  Glaze, E. The embrace, and stories
 The telephone
  Glaze, E. The embrace, and stories
 This certainly day
  Glaze, E. The embrace, and stories
 The window
  Glaze, E. The embrace, and stories
 You're at my island
  Glaze, E. The embrace, and stories
Gleepsite. Russ, J.
Glenallan. Lytton, Lord
GLENCOE MASSACRE, 1692
 Linklater, E. The masks of purpose
Glidden, Frank. *See* Short, Luke
GLOCKENSPIEL
 Moore, A. The great glockenspiel gimmick
Gloeckner, C. N.
 Miscount
  Del Rey, L. ed. Best science fiction stories of the year [1973]
Glory in the daytime. Parker, D.
The glory of his nostrils. Betts, D.
The glory riders. Garfield, B.

**GLOUCESTER, ELEANOR (COBHAM) DUCHESS OF**
D'Arnaud, F. B. The Witch of Eye
**Glover.** Henderson, D.
**GLOVES**
Bowen, E. Hand in glove
Brooke-Rose, C. Red rubber gloves
**Glow,** little glowworm. Shecktor, M. C.
**GLUCK, CHRISTOPH WILLIBALD, RITTER VON**
Hoffmann, E. T. A. Ritter Gluck
**GLUTTONY**
Bilker, H. L. and Bilker, A. L. All you can eat
Gill, B. Fat girl
Harrison, W. Eating it
Sentongo, N. Mulyankota
**Glynn, Thomas**
Luz
    Voices of Brooklyn
**The gnarly** man. De Camp, L. A.
**The gnurrs** come from the voodvork out. Bretnor, R.
**Go** away, old man, go away. Boyle, P.
**The go-between.** Shiina. R.
**Go! Go! Go!** Forty years ago. Algren, N.
**'Go on,** Johnny, go on!' Tottenham, J.
**Go tell** it on the mountain. Naylor, P. R.
**Goalkeepers** are crazy. Glanville, B.
**Goat song.** Anderson, P.
**Goat songs.** Weston, J.
**GOATHERDS**
Hauptmann, G. The heretic of Soana
Narayan, R. K.   A horse and two goats
    *See also* Shepherds
**GOATS**
Agnon, S. Y. Fable of the goat
Hall, J. B. Us he devours
Singer, I. B. Zlateh the goat
**The Gobineau** necklace. Powell, J.
**GOBLINS.** *See* Fairies
**GOD**
Brunner, J. Judas
Del Rey, L. Evensong
Knight, D. Shall the dust praise thee?
Lagerkvist, P. The eternal smile
Lagerkvist, P. Paradise
Winters, E. God's agents have beards
    *See also* Religion
**God** cares, but waits: A transfiguration by vines. Hall, J. B.
**God** cares, but waits: Behind our lines. Hall, J. B.
**God** cares, but waits: Outside the cave. Hall, J. B.
**God** in Harlem. Soto, P. J.
**God** likes them plain, Linklater, E.
**God** of many names. Schneeman, P.
**God** proud. Madden, D.
**"God** rest ye, merry gentlemen." Crane, S.
**God** sees the truth but is in no hurry to reveal it. *See* Tolstoy, L. God sees the truth, but waits
**God** sees the truth, but waits. Tolstoy, L.
**God** speaks. Updike, J.
**God** takes care of his own. Blackhurst, W. E.
**God** was here but He left early. Shaw, I.
**The goddess.** Dawson, F.

**The goddess** of the cats. Scortia, T. N.
**Godfrey, Dave**
Kwame Bird Lady Day
    Stephens, D. ed. Contemporary voices
**GODMOTHERS**
Di Donato, P. The Cabala
**GODRIC**
Walsh, J. P. and Crossley-Holland, K. The horseman
**GODS**
Asimov, I. and MacCreigh, J. The little man on the subway
Golding, W. The scorpion god
Gordon, C. Cloud nine
Harrison, H. Wife to the Lord
Leiber, F. When the last gods die
Mathes, W. The bridled ass
**God's** agents have beards. Winters, E.
**God's** little travelling salesman. Lagerkvist, P.
**The god's** script. *See* Borges, J. L. The handwriting of god
**God's** wrath. Malamud, B.
**Godwin, Gail**
An intermediate stop
    Minot, S. and Wilson, R. eds. Three stances of modern fiction
A sorrowful woman
    Lish, G. ed. The secret life of our times: new fiction from Esquire
    Oates, J. C. ed. Scenes from American life
**Godwin, Tom**
The cold equations
    The Astounding-Analog reader v2
    De Camp, L. S. and De Camp, C. C. eds. 3000 years of fantasy and science fiction
    Science fiction hall of fame v 1
**Goethe, Johann Wolfgang von**
The new Melusina
    Haining, P. ed. Gothic tales of terror
**Goff, Paula**
Blind in August
Intro 4
**Gogarty, Oliver St John**
Mr Satterthwaite's conversion
    Decker, C. R. and Angoff, C. eds. Modern stories from many lands
**Gogol, Nikolai**
Black Sunday
    Haining, P. ed. The ghouls
    Same as: The Viy, entered in earlier volumes
The nose
    Konigsberg, I. ed. The classic short story
The overcoat
    Konigsberg, I. ed. The classic short story
    Proffer, C. R. ed. From Karamzin to Bunin: an anthology of Russian short stories
    Same as: The cloak, entered in main volume
    **About**
Blum-Alquit, E. Gogol's ring
    **Parodies, travesties, etc.**
Bulgakov, M. The adventures of Chichikov
**Gogol's** ring. Blum-Alquit, E.
**Gogol's** wife. Landolfi, T.

**Gohman, Fred**
The cabinet of Kafru
Gohman, F. Spider Webb mysteries
The copy boy caper
Gohman, F. Spider Webb mysteries
The phantom fiddler
Gohman, F. Spider Webb mysteries
The tortoise and the hair
Gohman, F. Spider Webb mysteries
A trunkful of treasure
Gohman, F. Spider Webb mysteries
Vanishing act
Gohman, F. Spider Webb mysteries
**Going.** Silverberg, R.
**Going** down smooth. Silverberg, R.
**Going** home. Buck, P. S.
**Going** home. Kenary, J. S.
**Going** home. Trevor, W.
**Going** places. Michaels, L.
**GOING STEADY.** *See* Dating (Social customs)
**Going** to India. Blaise, C.
**Going** up. Nissenson, H.
**Going** west. Francis, H. E.
**Gold, Herbert**
Death in Miami Beach
Charyn, J. ed. The single voice
A death on the East Side
The Best American short stories, 1972
Gold, H. The magic will
Prize stories, 1972: The O. Henry Awards
From Proust to dada
Gold, H. The magic will
Girl getting educated at noon on Sunday
Gulassa, C. M. ed. The fact of fiction
A Haitian gentleman
Gold, H. The magic will
"I want a Sunday kind of love"
Gold, H. The magic will
Love and like
McKenzie, B. ed. The process of fiction
Max and the pacemaker
Gold, H. The magic will
The older woman
Gold, H. The magic will
A selfish story
Gold, H. The magic will
Song of the first and last beatnik
Gold, H. The magic will
Matthews, J. ed. Archetypal themes in the modern story
Waiting for the Forty-one Union
Gold, H. The magic will
The witch
McKenzie, B. ed. The process of fiction
Young man, old days
Gold, H. The magic will
**Gold, Ivan**
All you faceless voyagers
Schulman, L. M. ed. Travelers
A change of air
Charyn, J. ed. The single voice
The nickel misery of George Washington Carver Brown
Abrahams, W. ed. Fifty years of the American short story v 1
**GOLD**
Beal, M. F. Gold

Forester, C. S. Gold from Crete
Henderson, D. From the mouse to the hawk
Kipling, R. Harp song of the Dane women
Kipling, R. The knights of the joyous venture
Kipling, R. The Treasure and the Law
Rawlings, C. Cargo of gold
**Gold.** Beal, M. F.
**Gold** Coast. McPherson, J. A.
**Gold** from Crete. Forester, C. S.
The **gold**-legged frog. Khamsing, S.
**GOLD MINES AND MINING**
Bierce, A.   A holy terror
Sienkiewicz, H. The horizon widens
Wister, O. Hank's woman
The **gold** watch. Anand, M. R.
**Goldberg, Gerald Jay**
The Bach Master
Goldberg, G. J. 126 days of continuous sunshine
The Bowditch footnote
Goldberg, G. J. 126 days of continuous sunshine
The death of Los Angeles
Goldberg, G. J. 126 days of continuous sunshine
The education of Martin Fogle
Goldberg, G. J. 126 days of continuous sunshine
Kappleman in the Diaspora
Goldberg, G. J. 126 days of continuous sunshine
The loving tongue
Goldberg, G. J. 126 days of continuous sunshine
The mowers
Goldberg, G. J. 126 days of continuous sunshine
126 days of continuous sunshine
Goldberg, G. J. 126 days of continuous sunshine
A sign of favor
Goldberg, G. J. 126 days of continuous sunshine
Thursday
Goldberg, G. J. 126 days of continuous sunshine
Tyme
Goldberg, G. J. 126 days of continuous sunshine
**Golden** Acres. Reed, K.
The **golden** ball. Christie, A.
The **golden** cangue. Chang, E.
The **golden** key. Keller, D. H.
The **golden** pot. Hoffmann, E. T. A.
The **golden** redfish. Brister, B.
**Goldin, Stephen**
The last ghost
Nebula award stories 7
Sweet dreams, Melissa
Best SF: 1968
Galaxy Magazine. The eleventh Galaxy reader
**Goldin, Stephen, and Hensel, C. F.**
Harriet
Elwood, R. ed. Tomorrow's alternatives

Good night, Sophie. Aldani, L.

The **good** old days. Blackhurst, W. E.

The **good** professor who murdered the bad little girl. Gould, A.

A **good** revolution. Spike, P.

The **good** ring. Madsen, S. Å.

A **good** season. Williams, J. A.

**Good** to be a Martian. Long, F. B.

**Goodbye.** Schultz, J.

**Goodbye** and good luck. Paley, G.

**Goodbye**, Pops. Gores, J.

**Goodbye** to Francie. Twohy, R.

**Goodbye** Watson. Bukowski, C.

The **goodest** son in the world. Schwimmer, W.

**Goodman, Paul**
 The architect from New York
  McKenzie, B. ed. The process of fiction
 A lifeguard
  McKenzie, B. ed. The process of fiction

**Goodnight**, sweetheart. Purdy, J.

**Goodwin, John B. L.**
 The cocoon
  Kahn, J. ed. Some things strange and sinister

**Goodwin, Stephen**
 Sole surviving son
  The Best little magazine fiction, 1971

**Goodwood** comes back. Warren, R. P.

The **goophered** grapevine. Chestnutt, C. W.

The **goose** girl. Linklater, E.

The **goose** on the grave. Hawkes, J.

**Gooseberries.** Chekhov, A.

**Gor, Gennady**
 The garden
  Magidoff, R. ed. Russian science fiction, 1969
 The minotaur
  Magidoff, R. ed. Russian science fiction, 1969

**Gordimer, Nadine**
 Abroad
  Gordimer, N. Livingstone's companions
 Africa emergent
  Gordimer, N. Livingstone's companions
 The bride of Christ
  Gordimer, N. Livingstone's companions
 The credibility gap
  Gordimer, N. Livingstone's companions
 The defeated
  Johnson, E. W. ed. Short stories international
 Inkalamu's place
  Gordimer, N. Livingstone's companions
 An intruder
  Gordimer, N. Livingstone's companions
 The life of the imagination
  Gordimer, N. Livingstone's companions
 Livingstone's companions
  Gordimer, N. Livingstone's companions
 A meeting in space
  Gordimer, N. Livingstone's companions
 No place like
  Gordimer, N. Livingstone's companions
 Open house
  Gordimer, N. Livingstone's companions
 Otherwise birds fly in
  Gordimer, N. Livingstone's companions
 Rain-queen
  Gordimer, N. Livingstone's companions
 A satisfactory settlement
  Gordimer, N. Livingstone's companions
 A third presence
  Gordimer, N. Livingstone's companions
 Which new era would that be?
  Kissin, E. H. ed. Stories in black and white
 Why haven't you written?
  Gordimer, N. Livingstone's companions

**Gordon, Arthur**
 The sea devil
  Stansbury, D. L. ed. Impact

**Gordon, Caroline**
 Cloud nine
  Lytle, A. ed. Craft and vision
 Old Red
  Abrahams, W. ed. Fifty years of the American short story v 1

**Gordon, Ian Fellowes-** *See* Fellowes-Gordon, Ian

**Gores, Joe**
 The Andrech samples
  Best detective stories of the year, 1971
 The criminal
  Scortia, T. N. ed. Strange bedfellows
 File #1: The Mayfield case
  Bernkopf, J. F. comp. Boucher's choicest
 File #2: Stakeout on Page Street
  Ellery Queen's Mystery Magazine. Ellery Queen's Murder menu
 File #4: Lincoln sedan deadline
  McComas, J. F. ed. Crimes and misfortunes
 Goodbye, Pops
  Ellery Queen's Mystery Magazine. Ellery Queen's Grand slam
  Hitchcock, A. ed. Alfred Hitchcock presents: Stories to be read with the lights on
 O black and unknown bard
  Best detective stories of the year, 1973
 The O'Bannon blarney file
  Dickensheet, D. ed. Men and malice
 Odendahl
  Mystery Writers of America. Murder most foul
 A sad and bloody hour
  Mystery Writers of America. Dear dead days
 The second coming
  Hitchcock, A. ed. Alfred Hitchcock presents: Stories to stay awake by
 South of Market
  Hitchcock, A. ed. Alfred Hitchcock presents: A month of mystery
 Watch for it
  Mystery Writers of America. Mirror, mirror, fatal mirror

**Gores, Joseph N.** *See* Gores, Joe

**GORGONS**
 Bacon, G. The Gorgon's head
 Bishop, Z. Medusa's coil
 Lewis, C. S. Forms of things unknown

The **Gorgon's** head. Bacon, G.

The **gorilla** and the girl. Burke, T.

**GORILLAS**
 Collier, J. Variation on a theme
 Goulart, R. The whole round world

**GRANDSONS**
Canzoneri, R. Freddy-bear
Ford, J. H. The trout
Francis, H. E. The deepest chamber
Marshall, L. The leaning tower
O'Connor, F. The artificial nigger
Standish, L. Gremblins
    *See also* Grandfathers; Grandmothers
The **grandstand** complex. McCoy, H.
The **grandstand** passion play of Delbert and
    the Bumpus hounds. Shepherd, J.
**Granger, Peter**
    Hearse of the Speedway
        Fenner, P. R. comp. Where speed is
        king
**Granit, Arthur**
    Come into the hallway, for 5 cents!
        Ribalow, H. U. ed. My name aloud
**Granny.** Goulart, R.
The **granny** woman. Hughes, D. B.
**Grant, C. L.**
    The magic child
        Elwood, R. ed. The new mind
    The summer of the Irish Sea
        Orbit 11
**GRAPES**
    Chestnutt, C. W. The goophered grape-
    vine
The **grapes.** Trevisan, D.
The **grass** widows. Trevor, W.
**GRASSES.** *See* Grazing
**GRATITUDE**
    Sié, Cheou-kang. Gratitude
**Gratitude.** Sié, Cheou-kang
**Gratitude** guaranteed. Bretnor, R. and Ne-
    ville, K.
**Grau, Shirley Ann**
    The beach party
        Grau, S. A. The wind shifting west
    The beginning of summer
        Burnett, W. ed. That's what happened
        to me
    Eight o'clock one morning
        Grau, S. A. The wind shifting west
    Homecoming
        Grau, S. A. The wind shifting west
    The householder
        Grau, S. A. The wind shifting west
    The land and the water
        Grau, S. A. The wind shifting west
    The last gas station
        Grau, S. A. The wind shifting west
    The long afternoon
        Grau, S. A. The wind shifting west
    The lovely April
        Grau, S. A. The wind shifting west
    The man outside
        Grau, S. A. The wind shifting west
    Miss Yellow Eyes
        Spinner, S. ed. Feminine plural
    The other way
        Grau, S. A. The wind shifting west
    The patriarch
        Grau, S. A. The wind shifting west
    Pillow of stone
        Grau, S. A. The wind shifting west
    Sea change
        Grau, S. A. The wind shifting west

Stanley
    Grau, S. A. The wind shifting west
The thieves
    Grau, S. A. The wind shifting west
Three
    Grau, S. A. The wind shifting west
The way back
    Grau, S. A. The wind shifting west
The wind shifting west
    Grau, S. A. The wind shifting west
The **grave.** Porter, K. A.
The **grave** grass quivers. Kantor, M.
The **grave** of the famous poet. Atwood, M.
**GRAVE ROBBERS**
    Bierce, A. The City of the Gone Away
    Ibuse, M. Yosaku the settler
    Stevenson, R. L. The body-snatcher
    Stuart, J. Word and the flesh
**GRAVEDIGGERS**
    Borchert, W. Jesus won't play any more
    Brown, G. M. The bright spade
    Hawkes, J. Death of an airman
**Graves, Robert**
    Earth to earth
        Haining, P. ed. The Lucifer society
    The shout
        Harrison, H. ed. The light fantastic
**GRAVES.** *See* Cemeteries; Tombs
**GRAVES, MILITARY.** *See* Soldiers' bodies,
    Disposition of
**Graves** for the living. Woolrich, C.
**GRAVEYARDS.** *See* Cemeteries
**GRAVITATION**
    Anderson, P. Nothing succeeds like failure
    Clarke, A. C. What goes up
    Jameson, M. Tricky tonnage
    Jones, R. F. Noise level
    Lafferty, R. A. The man with the speckled
    eyes
    Niven, L. Neutron star
    Stuart, D. A. Night
        *See also* Levitation
**GRAVITY.** *See* Gravitation; Levitation
**Gray, Len**
    The little old lady from Cricket Creek
        Best detective stories of the year [1969]
The **gray** man. Jewett, S. O.
The **gray** mills of Farley. Jewett, S. O.
The **gray** wolf's ha'nt. Chesnutt, C. W.
**Grayson's** baby. Fox, J.
**GRAZING**
    Davis, H. L. Open winter
**Greased** Samba. Deck, J.
The **great** A.   Malstrom, R. C.
**GREAT BRITAIN**
    *See also* England; Ireland; Scotland;
    Wales
                    **Army**
    Fraser, G. M. Guard at the castle
    Fraser, G. M. McAuslan's court-martial
    Frazer, G. M. Monsoon Selection Board
    Fraser, G. M. Silence in the ranks
    Kipling, R. The daughter of the regiment
    Kipling, R. Wee Willie Winkie
                **Army. Cavalry**
    Kipling, R. The rout of the White Hussars
                **Army—Officers**
    Forester, C. S. An egg for the major

**Greene, Graham**—*Continued*
  The blessing
    Greene, G. Collected stories
    Greene, G. The portable Graham Greene
  The blue film
    Greene, G. Collected stories
  Brother
    Greene, G. Collected stories
    Hall, J. B. ed. The realm of fiction
  The case for the defence
    Greene, G. Collected stories
  Chagrin in three parts
    Greene, G. Collected stories
  A chance for Mr Lever
    Greene, G. Collected stories
  Cheap in August
    Greene, G. Collected stories
    Greene, G. The portable Graham Greene
  Church militant
    Greene, G. Collected stories
  A day saved
    Greene, G. Collected stories
  Dear Dr Falkenheim
    Greene, G. Collected stories
  The destructors
    Greene, G. Collected stories
    Greene, G. The portable Graham Greene
  A discovery in the woods
    Greene, G. Collected stories
  Doctor Crombie
    Greene, G. Collected stories
  Dream of a strange land
    Greene, G. Collected stories
  A drive in the country
    Greene, G. Collected stories
  The end of the party
    Greene, G. Collected stories
    Greene, G. The portable Graham Greene
    Harrison, H. ed. The light fantastic
    Knight, D. ed. Perchance to dream
  The hint of an explanation
    Greene, G. Collected stories
  I spy
    Greene, G. Collected stories
    Howes, B. and Smith, G. J. eds. The
      sea-green horse
  The innocent
    Greene, G. Collected stories
    Greene, G. The portable Graham Greene
    Johnson, E. W. ed. Short stories inter-
      national
  The invisible Japanese gentlemen
    Greene, G. Collected stories
  Jubilee
    Greene, G. Collected stories
  A little place off the Edgware Road
    Greene, G. Collected stories
  A marriage proposal
    Greene, G. The portable Graham Greene
  May we borrow your husband?
    Greene, G. Collected stories
  Men at work
    Greene, G. Collected stories
  Minty's day
    Greene, G. The portable Graham Greene
  Mortmain
    Greene, G. Collected stories
  The over-night bag
    Greene, G. Collected stories
  The prison cell
    Greene, G. The portable Graham Greene
  Proof positive
    Greene, G. Collected stories
  The root of all evil
    Greene, G. Collected stories
  The second death
    Greene, G. Collected stories
  A shocking accident
    Greene, G. Collected stories
    Greene, G. The portable Graham Greene
  The signing-up of 59200/5
    Greene, G. The portable Graham Greene
  A small affair
    Greene, G. The portable Graham Greene
  Special duties
    Greene, G. Collected stories
  Travel tips from Aunt Augusta
    Greene, G. The portable Graham Greene
  Two gentle people
    Greene, G. Collected stories
  Under the garden
    Greene, G. Collected stories
  A visit to Morin
    Greene, G. Collected stories
  When Greek meets Greek
    Greene, G. Collected stories
**Greene, Louisa**
  Bound by a spell; excerpt
    Haining, P. ed. A circle of witches
**Greene, Philip L.**
  The dichotomy
    Prize stories, 1971; The O. Henry
      Awards
**Greene, Sonia**
  Four o'clock
    Lovecraft, H. P. ed. The horror in the
      museum, and other revisions
  The invisible monster
    Lovecraft, H. P. ed. The horror in the
      museum, and other revisions
**Greenface.** Schmitz, J. H.
**Greenleaf.** O'Connor, F.
**Greenlee, Sam**
  Sonny's not blue
    King, W. ed. Black short story anthol-
      ogy
**GREENWICH VILLAGE.** *See* New York
    (City)—Greenwich Village
**Grekova, Irina**
  Beyond the gates
    Whitney, T. P. ed. The young Russians
**Gremblins.** Standish, L.
**Grendon, Stephen**
  The drifting snow
    Haining, P. ed. Vampires at midnight
    *For other stories by this author see*
    Derleth, August
**GRETTIR ASMUNDARSON**
  The Story of Glam
**Grettir** at Thorhall-stead. Norris, F.
**GRETTIR THE STRONG.** *See* Grettir As-
    mundarson; Grettis Saga
**GRETTIS SAGA**
  Norris, F. Grettir at Thorhall-stead
The **grey** cat. Pain, B.
The **grey** ones. Priestley, J. B.
A **grey** sleeve. Crane, S.
**Greyhound** tragedy. Brautigan, R.

# H

H as in homicide. Treat, L.
Haag, John
    Atlantis on $5.00 a day
        New American Review no. 13
Habit. Colette
An habitation enforced. Kipling, R.
The habits of the animals: the progress of
    the seasons. Higgins, G. V.
Haceldama. Hearn, L.
Haggard, H. Rider
    Magepa the Buck
        Green, R. L. ed. Ten tales of adventure
Hai, Tao Kim. See Tao Kim Hai
HAIDA INDIANS
    MacEwen, G. House of the whale
HAIGHT-ASHBURY. See California—San
    Francisco
Haimowitz, Benjamin
    Zucker
        New Directions in prose and poetry 24
HAIR
    Colette. The judge
    Henderson, Z. Crowning glory
    Marsh, R. The man who cut off my hair
    Midwood, B.   A thief in the temples
    Sayers, D. L. The inspiration of Mr Budd
    Stafford, J. The captain's gift
    Stafford, J. Cops and robbers
    Stoker, B. The secret of the growing gold
HAIRDRESSERS. See Beauty shops
HAIRPIECES. See Wigs
Hai's well. Barash, A.
Haïta the shepherd. Bierce, A.
HAITI
    Thomason, J. W. Hanneken
    Usher, F. The walking dead
                **Port-au-Prince**
Gold, H.   A Haitian gentleman
Gold, H. Max and the pacemaker
A Haitian gentleman. Gold, H.
Haitov, Nikolai
    Paths
        Kirilov, N. and Kirk, F. eds. Introduc-
            tion to modern Bulgarian literature
Hal o' the Draft. Kipling, R.
Haldeman, Jack C.
    Watchdøg
        Del Rey, L. ed. Best science fiction
            stories of the year [1973]
Haldeman, Jay. See Haldeman, Jack C.
Haldeman, Joe W.
    Counterpoint
        Orbit 11
    Hero
        Best SF: 1972
    John's other life
        Elwood, R. ed. Showcase
Hale, Lucretia P.
    The Peterkins at the farm
        Howes, B. and Smith, G. J. eds. The
            sea-green horse
Hale, Nancy
    The most elegant drawing room in Europe
        Abrahams, W. ed. Fifty years of the
            American short story v 1
Half-breed. Asimov, I.

HALF-BREEDS. See Half-castes
Half-breeds on Venus. Asimov, I.
HALF-BROTHERS
    Roberts, R. E. The New Jerusalem
HALF-CASTES
    Asimov, I. Half-breed
    Asimov, I. Half-breeds on Venus
    Buck, P. S. Duet in Asia
    Burke, T. The cue
    Carpenter, D. Blue Eyes
    Forster, E. M. The other boat
    Linklater, E. Country-born
The half-husky. Laurence, M.
Half life. Payes, R. C.
Half-past eternity. MacDonald, J. D.
Half the kingdom. Piserchia, D.
Halfway house. Silverberg, R.
Halfway to Hell. Collier, J.
Halifax, Clifford. See Meade, L. T. jt. auth.
Hall, Andrew
    The other woman
        Burke, J. ed. Tales of unease
Hall, James B.
    God cares, but waits: A transfiguration by
        vines
        New Directions in prose and poetry 22
    God cares, but waits: Behind our lines
        New Directions in prose and poetry 22
    God cares, but waits: Outside the cave
        New Directions in prose and poetry 22
    The other kingdom
        The Best little magazine fiction, 1970
    Triumph of the Omophagists
        New Directions in prose and poetry 21
    Us he devours
        Hall, J. B. ed. The realm of fiction
        Roecker, W. A. ed. Stories that count
Hall, Lawrence Sargent
    The ledge
        Roecker, W. A. ed. Stories that count
        Stansbury, D. L. ed. Impact
The Hall of Blood. Von Kramer, Professor
The hall of machines. Jones, L.
Halliday, Brett
    Human interest stuff
        Gibson, W. ed. Rogues' gallery
HALLOWEEN
    Brautigan, R. Halloween in Denver
    Layefsky, V. Moonlight—starlight
Halloween in Denver. Brautigan, R.
Hallowell's pretty sister, Jewett, S. O.
HALLUCINATIONS AND ILLUSIONS
    Aldiss, B. W. The serpent of Kundalini
    Anderson, P. and Anderson, K. Dead
        phone
    Ansell, J. Love, Mother
    Ayrton, M. The vanishing point
    Ballard, J. G. Manhole 69
    Ballard, J. G. The terminal beach
    Ballard, J. G. The watchtowers
    Ballard, J. G. Zone of terror
    Beerbohm, M. Hilary Maltby and Stephen
        Braxton
    Bierce, A. Staley Fleming's hallucination
    Blaise, C. Eyes
    Borges, J. L. The circular ruins
    Brooke-Rose, C. Red rubber gloves
    Brown, F. It didn't happen
    Bukowski, C. The blanket

**HAND-TO-HAND FIGHTING.** *See* Fighting, Hand-to-hand

The **handbook** of Hymen. Henry, O.

**Handel, Yehudit**
Zili and my friend Shaul
Rabikovitz, D. ed. The new Israeli writers

**HANDICAPPED.** *See* Mentally handicapped; Physically handicapped

**Hands.** Daniel, Y.

**Hands.** Landolfi, T.

The **handsomest** drowned man in the world. García Márquez, G.

The **handwriting** of god. Borges, J. L.

The **hanged** man. Bryant, E.

**Hanger**-on. Glanville, B.

**HANGING**
Bierce, A. Incident at Owl Creek
Bryant, E. The hanged man
Carr, J. D. The other hangman
Crane, S. Moonlight on the snow
Harte, B. Tennessee's partner
Hawkes, J. The owl
Hebel, J. P. The strange story of a young Englishman
Leach, P. Black Jesus
McGrath, R. L. Payment received
Schultz, J. Witness
Stoker, B. The Judge's House
Ware, E.   A lady comes to Paradise
*See also* Lynching

**HANGINGS (EXECUTIONS)** *See* Hanging

The **hangman** luck. De La Mare, W.

**HANGMEN.** *See* Executions and executioners; Hanging

**Hangover.** MacDonald, J. D.

**HANGOVERS.** *See* Drunkards

**Hankins, Paula**
Testimonial
King, W. ed. Black short story anthology

**Hank's** woman. Wister, O.

**Hannah** and Benjamin Stevens. Chase, M. E.

**Hanneken.** Thomason, J. W.

**Haply** the soul of my grandmother. Wilson, E.

A **happening** in Barbados. Meriwether, L. M.

**Happily** ever after. Nolan, W. F.

**HAPPINESS**
Bloch, R. That Hell-bound train
Disch, T. M. The City of Penetrating Light
Hesse, H. Augustus
Kotowska, M. Still life with ice cream
Lem, S. In hot pursuit of happiness
Platonov, A. Dzhan
*See also* Contentment; Joy and sorrow

**Happiness.** Lavin, M.

The **happiness** of others. Price, R.

**Happy** August the 10th. Williams, T.

**Happy** birthday, Bambara, T. C.

**Happy** birthday. Lispector, C.

The **happy** couple. Maugham, W. S.

A **happy** day in 2381. Silverberg, R.

A **happy** death. Lavin, M.

The **happy** ending. Grossman, S.

A **happy** family. Lu, Hsun

A **happy** family. Trevor, W.

**Happy** marriage. Cassill, R. V.

**Happy** Onion. Oates, J. C.

The **harbinger.** McWhirter, G.

**HARBORS.** *See* New York (City)—Harbor

A **hard** day at the office. De Vries, P.

**Hard,** in these fastnesses. Casper, L.

**Hard** money. Case, R. O.

The **hard** passage. Hesse, H.

**Hard** sell. Rice, C.

**Hard** times. Rostopchin, V.

A **hard**-working woman. Babel, I.

**Hardcastle.** Goulart, R.

The **hardware** man. O'Hara, J.

**Hardwick, Michael, and Hardwick, Mollie**
The bo'sun's body
Canning, J. ed. 50 great horror stories
Double damnation
Canning, J. ed. 50 great horror stories
The eyes of Thomas Bolter
Canning, J. ed. 50 great horror stories
The hand of Father Arrowsmith
Canning, J. ed. 50 great horror stories
Let sleeping bones lie
Canning, J. ed. 50 great horror stories
Lullaby for the dead
Canning, J. ed. 50 great horror stories
The man who hated cats
Canning, J. ed. 50 great horror stories
The mate of the Squando
Canning, J. ed. 50 great horror stories
Ole rockin' chair
Canning, J. ed. 50 great horror stories
The princess of Thebes
Canning, J. ed. 50 great horror stories
Ripe Stilton
Canning, J. ed. 50 great horror stories
Rose: a Gothick tale
Canning, J. ed. 50 great horror stories
The ruff
Canning, J. ed. 50 great horror stories
The vampire of Croglin
Canning, J. ed. 50 great horror stories
A warning to sceptics
Canning, J. ed. 50 great horror stories
With this ring
Canning, J. ed. 50 great horror stories

**Hardwick, Mollie.** *See* Hardwick, Michael, jt. auth.

The **hare** and the tortoise. Jewett, S. O.

**HARELIP**
Kim, Y. I. Love in winter

**HAREM LIFE**
Maupassant, G. de. Châli
Roditi, E. The Sultan's Little Harum-scarum
Smith, C. A. The kiss of Zoraida

**Hark:** 1831, Virginia. Styron, W.

**HARLEM.** *See* New York (City)—Harlem

A **Harlem** game. Dumas, H.

A **Harlem** tragedy. Henry, O.

**Harlem** transfer. Walker, E. K.

**Harnack, Curtis**
Voice of the town
The Best little magazine fiction, 1970

**Harness, Charles L.**
An ornament to his profession
Knight, D. ed. A science fiction argosy

The **harness.** Steinbeck, J.

**HAROLD, KING OF ENGLAND**
Walsh, J. P. and Crossley-Holland, K. The eye of the hurricane
**HAROLD II.** *See* Harold, King of England
The **harp.** Körner, K. T.
The **harp** of the winds. Canzoneri, R.
The **harpoon** gun. Vassilikos, V.
**Harriet.** Goldin, S. and Hensel, C. F.
**Harris, John Beynon.** *See* Wyndham, John
**Harrison, Ernest**
The child watcher
Parry, M. ed. Beware of the cat
**Harrison, Harry**
American dead
Harrison, H. ed. The year 2000
At last, the true story of Frankenstein
Haining, P. ed. The freak show
Brave newer world
Four futures
By the Falls
Nebula award stories 6
SF: authors' choice 3
Captain Honario Harpplayer, R.N.
Clareson, T. D. ed. A spectrum of worlds
From fanaticism, or for reward
Harrison, H. One step from earth
Heavy duty
Harrison, H. One step from earth
I always do what Teddy says
Santesson, H. S. ed. The days after tomorrow
I have my vigil
The Best from Fantasy and Science Fiction; 18th ser.
If
Harrison, H. ed. Worlds of wonder
The life preservers
Harrison, H. One step from earth
The mothballed spaceship
Astounding
No war, or battle's sound
Harrison, H. One step from earth
One step from earth
Harrison, H. One step from earth
Hipolito, J. and McNelly, W. E. eds. Mars, we love you
The powers of observation
Analog 8
Pressure
Harrison, H. One step from earth
Silverberg, R. ed. Tomorrow's worlds
Rescue operation
The Astounding-Analog reader v2
Roommates
Disch, T. M. ed. The ruins of earth
A tale of the ending
Harrison, H. One step from earth
Velvet glove
Santesson, H. S. ed. Crime prevention in the 30th century
Waiting place
Harrison, H. One step from earth
The wicked flee
Del Rey, L. ed. Best science fiction stories of the year 1972
New dimensions 1
Wife to the Lord
Harrison, H. One step from earth

**Harrison, M. John**
Lamia mutable
Ellison, H. ed. Again, dangerous visions
**Harrison, Michael**
At the heart of it
Haining, P. ed. The necromancers
Whatever happened to young Russell?
Ellery Queen's Mystery Magazine. Ellery Queen's Headliners
Wit's end
Best detective stories of the year, 1971
**Harrison, William**
Eating it
Lish, G. ed. The secret life of our times: new fiction from Esquire
The warrior
Lish, G. ed. The secret life of our times: new fiction from Esquire
**Harry** Belten and the Mendelssohn Violin Concerto. Targan, B.
The **Harry** Hastings Method. Law, W.
**Harry** the Hare. Hemesath, J. B.
**Harry,** the Steppenwolf. Hesse, H.
**Harry** the tailor. Dorman, S.
**Harry** W. A. Davis, Jr. Maloney, R.
**Harte, Bret**
High-water mark
Kahn, J. ed. Some things fierce and fatal
The outcasts of Poker Flat
Taylor, J. G. ed. Great Western short stories
Tennessee's partner
Tytell, J. and Jaffee, H. eds. Affinities
**Harter, Evelyn**
The stone lovers
Prize stories, 1971: The O. Henry Awards
**Hartley, L. P.**
Feet foremost
Dickinson, S. ed. The usurping ghost, and other encounters and experiences
**Hartridge, Jon**
Like father
Best SF: 1969
**HARVARD UNIVERSITY**
Updike, J. The Christian roommates
**Harvey, William Fryer**
August heat
Dickinson, S. ed. The usurping ghost, and other encounters and experiences
Stern, P. V. ed. The other side of the clock
The beast with five fingers
Haining, P. ed. The ghouls
**HARVILLIERS, JEANNE**
Mallet-Joris, F. Jeanne
**Harvor, Beth**
Countries
New Canadian stories, 73
Magicians
New Canadian stories, 72
Pain was my portion
The Best American short stories, 1971
**HARZ MOUNTAINS.** *See* Germany—Harz Mountains
**Has** anybody seen Miss Dora Dean? Petry, A.
**HASHISH**
Dunsany, Lord. The hashish man

The **hashish** man. Dunsany, Lord
**HASIDISM.** *See* Jews in Poland
**HASKALAH.** *See* Jews—Intellectual life
**Haskell** hooked on the northern Cheyenne. Weaver, G.
**Hasse, Henry.** *See* Bradbury, R. jt. auth.
**HASTINGS, BATTLE OF, 1066**
   Walsh, J. P. and Crossley-Holland, K. Wordhoard
The **hat** act. Coover, R.
**HATE**
   Auchincloss, L. The sacrifice
   Borges, J. L. The end of the duel
   Brown, W. The scar
   De Camp, L. S. Judgment day
   Fraser, Mrs H. The Satanist
   Hensley, J. Shut the last door
   Keeling, N. Agathe
   Knight, D. The country of the kind
   Lavin, M. At Sallygap
   Lispector, C. The buffalo
   London, J. The devil-dog
   Long, F. B. The cottage
   Lyon, D. The woman in the stone house
   Neugeboren, J. The application
   Prebble, J. The long hate
   Rocklynne, R. Randy-Tandy man
   Williams, J. A. Son in the afternoon
      *See also* Feuds
**Hate** is a sandpaper ice cube with polka dots of love on it. Dixon, T.
The **hated** house. Fremlin, C.
**HATRED.** *See* Hate
**HATS**
   Bukowski, C.   A lovely love affair
   Das, M. The mystery of the missing cap
   Jewett, S. O. The green bonnet: a story of Easter day
   Malamud, B. Rembrandt's hat
The **haunted** and the haunters. Bulwer-Lytton, E.
The **haunted** boy. McCullers, C.
The **haunted** chamber. Radcliffe, A.
The **haunted** doll's house. James, M. R.
The **haunted** future. Leiber, F.
The **haunted** house. Pliny the Younger
**HAUNTED HOUSES.** *See* Ghosts; Houses
The **haunted** housewife. Brennan, J. P.
A **haunted** island. Blackwood, A.
The **haunted** policeman. Sayers, D. L.
The **haunted** spinney. O'Donnell, E.
The **haunted** valley. Bierce, A.
The **haunter** of the dark. Lovecraft, H. P.
The **haunter** of the graveyard. Shea, J. V.
The **haunting** of the new. Bradbury, R.
**Haupt, Zygmunt**
   Lili Marlene
      Tyrmand, L. ed. Explorations in freedom: prose, narrative, and poetry from Kultura
**Hauptmann, Gerhart**
   The heretic of Soana
      Steinhauer, H. ed. Ten German novellas
**HAVANA.** *See* Cuba—Havana
**Have** a good time. Elman, R.
**Have** you ever substituted for a dead horse? Deutschman, B.

**HAWAII**
   Beekman, A. Hawaiian tales; 11 stories
   Beekman, A. Ordeal by fire
   Stern, J. Traveller's tears
   Stevenson, R. L. The bottle imp
   Stevenson, R. L. The Isle of Voices
      **Maui**
   Casper, L. Aflame; in flower
**Hawaiian** hospitality. Beekman, A.
**Hawaiian Islands.** *See* Hawaii
**Hawk** among the sparrows. McLaughlin, D.
**Hawkes, John**
   Charivari
      Hawkes J. Lunar landscapes
   Death of an airman
      Hawkes, J. Lunar landscapes
   The goose on the grave
      Hawkes, J. Lunar landscapes
   The grandmother
      Hawkes, J. Lunar landscapes
   Hencher
      Charyn, J. ed. The single voice
   A little bit of the old slap and tickle
      Hawkes, J. Lunar landscapes
   The nearest cemetery
      Hawkes, J. Lunar landscapes
   The owl
      Hawkes, J. Lunar landscapes
   A song outside
      Hawkes, J. Lunar landscapes
   The traveler
      Hawkes, J. Lunar landscapes
   The universal fears
      American Review 16
**HAWKS**
   Clark, W. V. Hook
   Pangborn, E. Mount Charity
   Rothschild, M. The austringer
**Hawthorne, Nathaniel**
   The artist of the beautiful
      Taylor, J. C. ed. The short story: fiction in transition
   The birthmark
      Disch, R. and Schwartz, B. eds. Killing time
   Chippings with a chisel
      Westbrook, P. D. ed. Seacoast and upland: a New England anthology
   The Christmas banquet
      Haining, P. ed. Gothic tales of terror
   The minister's Black Veil
      Konigsberg, I. ed. The classic short story
   My kinsman, Major Molineux
      Matthews, J. ed. Archetypal themes in the modern story
      Tytell, J. and Jaffe, H. eds. Affinities
   The prophetic pictures
      Bishop, M. ed. A Romantic storybook
   Puritan passions
      Haining, P. ed. The ghouls
      Same as: Feathertop: a moralized legend, entered in earlier volumes
   Rappaccini's daughter
      Manley, S. and Lewis, G. eds. Shapes of the supernatural
   Roger Malvin's burial
      Thune, E. and Prigozy, R. eds. Short stories: a critical anthology

**Healey, Rose Million**
Guessing game
  Hitchcock, A. ed. Alfred Hitchcock presents: Stories to be read with the lights on
**Health** card. Yerby, F.
The **health** of the sick. Cortázar, J.
**HEALTH RESORTS, WATERING PLACES, ETC.**
Beerbohm, M. A. V. Laider
Vezhinov, P. Spanish cholera
  *See also* Labor rest homes
**Heard, Gerald**
The cat, "I Am"
  Necker, C. ed. Supernatural cats
**Heard, H. F.**
The President of the United States, detective
  Queen, E. ed. Ellery Queen's The golden 13
**HEARING.** *See* Deaf
**Hearn, Lafcadio**
Haceldama
  Haining, P. ed. The nightmare reader
The reconciliation
  Tytell, J. and Jaffe, H. eds. Affinities
**Hearse** of the Speedway. Granger, P.
**HEARSES.** *See* Automobiles; Funeral rites and ceremonies
**HEART**

### Diseases

Brown, M. F. In the forests of Riga the beasts are very wild indeed
Cather, W. Neighbour Rosicky
Cather, W. On the gulls' road
Chopin, K. The story of an hour
Farrell, J. T. Mr Austin
Fast, H. The price
Gold, H. Max and the pacemaker
Nolan, W. F. He kilt it with a stick
Patton, F. G. The homunculus
Salpeter, S. . . . thicker than water
Stewart, J. C. The last day
Stuart, J. Old Jackson was my teacher
**Heart.** De Vries, P.
The **heart** and the galaxy. Boulle, P.
**HEART ATTACK.** *See* Heart—Diseases
**Heart** leaves. Peterkin, J.
The **heart** of a goof. Wodehouse, P. G.
**Heart** of darkness. Conrad, J.
**Heart** of gold. Lavin, M.
The **heart** of Lee W. Lee. O'Hara, J.
The **heart** of the park. O'Connor, F.
**Heartache.** Chekhov, A.
**Hearts** and crosses. Henry, O.
**Hearts** and hands. Henry, O.
**Hearts** of oak and bellies of brass. McGahern, J.
**Heat.** Schwartz, J.
The **heat** death of the universe. Zoline, P. A.
**Heath, Mary**
The breadman
  The Best American short stories, 1972
**Heathen** at home. Bontemps, A.
**Heathen** god. Zebrowski, G.
**HEATHENISM.** *See* Paganism

**HEAVEN**
Corvo, F. Baron. About doubles in general: and Sanvenanzio and Santagapito, in particular
Crane, S. Greed rampant
Himes, C. Heaven has changed
Khamsing, S. Owners of Paradise
Linkletter, E. Kind Kitty
Machen, A. The soldier's rest
Peretz, Y. L. Silent Bontsche
Sié, Cheou-kang. The bridge of magpies
Twain, M. Extract from Captain Stormfield's visit to heaven
**Heaven** above, hell below. Berne, S.
**Heaven** has changed. Himes, C.
**Heavenly** words. Hippius, Z.
**Heavy** duty. Harrison, H.
**Heavy** planet. Rothman, M. A.
**Heavy-set.** Bradbury, R.
The **heavy** sorrow of the body. Oates, J. C.
The **heavy** stone. West, J.
**Heavyplanet.** Rothman, M. A.
**Hebel, Johann Peter**
Monsieur Charles
  Bishop, M. ed. A Romantic storybook
The strange story of a young Englishman
  Bishop, M. ed. A Romantic storybook
An unexpected reunion
  Bishop, M. ed. A Romantic storybook
**Hecht, Florence M.**
Twin bed bridge
  Prize stories, 1971: The O. Henry Awards
**Heckelmann, Charles N.**
Death trap for an iron horse rebel
  Western Writers of America. A Western bonanza
**Hector** is willin'. Pentecost, H.
The **heel** of Achilles. Wodehouse, P. G.
**Heeresma, Heere**
From your evil ways
  Krispyn, E. ed. Modern stories from Holland and Flanders
**Heidenry, John**
The counterpoint of view
  Ellison, H. ed. Again, dangerous visions
**HEINE, HEINRICH**
Pasternak, B. Il tratto di Apelle
**Heinesen, Jens Pauli**
Gestur
  Faroese short stories
Little Frants Vilhelm
  Faroese short stories
**Heinesen, William**
The celestial journey
  Faroese short stories
Gamaliel's bewitchment
  Faroese short stories
In the madman's garden
  Faroese short stories
The knife
  Faroese short stories
The night of the storm
  Faroese short stories
The smoking mirror
  Faroese short stories

**Heinlein, Robert A.**
"All you zombies—"
  Silverberg, R. ed. The mirror of infinity
  Total Effect. Survival printout
"—And he built a crooked house—"
  Asimov, I. ed. Where de we go from here?
  Silverberg, R. ed. Other dimensions
  Stern, P. V. ed. The other side of the clock
The black pits of Luna
  Silverberg, R. ed. Tomorrow's worlds
Magic, inc.
  Knight, D. ed. The golden road
The man who sold the moon
  Knight, D. comp. Dimension X
The roads must roll
  Science fiction hall of fame v 1
Universe
  The Science fiction hall of fame v2A
    *For another story by this author see*
  MacDonald, Anson
**Heir** apparent. Nourse, E. A.
The **heir** 1170. Coolidge, O.
**HEIRS.** *See* Inheritance and succession
**Helbemäe, Gerd**
Still life
  Angoff, C. ed. Stories from The Literary Review
**HELEN OF TROY**
      Parodies, travesties, etc.
Barth, J. Menelaiad
**Helen** O'Loy. Del Rey, L.
**HELICOPTERS**
Rawlings, C. Cargo of gold
**Helix** the cat. Sturgeon, T.
**HELL**
Asimov, I. The brazen locked room
Collier, J. The Devil, George and Rosie
Corvo, F. Baron. About a vegetable purgatory
Hogg, J. The expedition to Hell
Joyce, J. Hell fire
Lagerkvist, P. The lift that went down into Hell
Littke, L. J. Mrs Twiller takes a trip
Peretz, I. L. Neilah in Gehenna
Rascoe, J. Evenings down under
Russell, B. The metaphysician's nightmare
Stevenson, R. L. The bottle imp
The **Hell**-bound train. *See* Bloch, R. That Hell-bound train
**Hell** command. Adams, C.
**Hell** fire. Joyce, J.
**Hell** has no limits. Donoso, J.
**Hell** hath no fury. Collier, J.
**Heller, Joseph**
Snowden
  Charyn, J. ed. The single voice
The **help** comes in bottles. Maloney, R.
The **helper.** Bullins, E.
The **helping** hand. Forster, E. M.
**Helú, Antonio**
Piropos at midnight
  Yates, D. A. ed. Latin blood
**Helvick, James**
Total recall
  Best of the Best detective stories

**Helwig, David**
One evening
  Metcalf, J. ed. Sixteen by twelve
Something for Olivia's scrapbook I guess
  Stephens, D. ed. Contemporary voices
**Hemenway, Robert**
Cape trip
  Hemenway, R. The girl who sang with the Beatles, and other stories
Circles
  Hemenway, R. The girl who sang with the Beatles, and other stories
The girl who sang with the Beatles
  Abrahams, W. ed. Fifty years of the American short story v 1
  Disch, R. and Schwartz, B. eds. Killing time
  Hemenway, R. The girl who sang with the Beatles, and other stories
  Prize stories, 1970: The O. Henry Awards
I am waiting
  Hemenway, R. The girl who sang with the Beatles, and other stories
Late Show
  Hemenway, R. The girl who sang with the Beatles, and other stories
The Old Glory
  Hemenway, R. The girl who sang with the Beatles, and other stories
One of the famous days
  Hemenway, R. The girl who sang with the Beatles, and other stories
Stories
  Hemenway, R. The girl who sang with the Beatles, and other stories
Take it easy, Edna
  Hemenway, R. The girl who sang with the Beatles, and other stories
**Hemesath, James B.**
Harry the Hare
  Ellison, H. ed. Again, dangerous visions
**Hemingway, Ernest**
An Alpine idyll
  Hemingway, E. The Nick Adams stories
The battler
  Hemingway, E. The Nick Adams stories
Big two-hearted river
  Hemingway, E. The Nick Adams stories
Big two-hearted river: part II
  Corodimas, P. ed. In trout country
The butterfly and the tank
  Hemingway, E. The fifth column, and four stories of the Spanish Civil War
Cross-country snow
  Hemingway, E. The Nick Adams stories
Crossing the Mississippi
  Hemingway, E. The Nick Adams stories
The denunciation
  Hemingway, E. The fifth column, and four stories of the Spanish Civil War
The doctor and the doctor's wife
  Hemingway, E. The Nick Adams stories
The end of something
  Hemingway, E. The Nick Adams stories
Fathers and sons
  Hemingway, E. The Nick Adams stories
Fifty grand
  Foff, A. and Knapp, D. eds. Story

**Hershman, Morris**
Let there be night!
Santesson, H. S. ed. Crime prevention in the 30th century
Letter to the editor
Hitchcock, A. ed. Alfred Hitchcock presents: Stories to stay awake by
A matter of pride
Mystery Writers of America. Crime without murder
Murder in Eden
Mystery Writers of America. Mirror, mirror, fatal mirror
Proposal perilous
Mystery Writers of America. Dear dead days
Willing victim
Best detective stories of the year, 1972
**HERTFORDSHIRE.** See England, Provincial and rural—Hertfordshire
**HERZEGOVINA.** See Yugoslavia—Bosnia and Herzegovina
**Hesse, Hermann**
Augustus
Hesse, H. Strange news from another star, and other tales
Chagrin d'amour
Hesse, H. Stories of five decades
A child's heart
Hesse, H. Klingsor's last summer
The city
Hesse, H. Stories of five decades
The cyclone
Hesse, H. Stories of five decades
Dream journeys
Hesse, H. Stories of five decades
A dream sequence
Hesse, H. Strange news from another star, and other tales
Edmund
Hesse, H. Stories of five decades
An evening with Dr Faust
Hesse, H. Stories of five decades
Faldum
Hesse, H. Strange news from another star, and other tales
The field devil
Hesse, H. Stories of five decades
Flute dream
Hesse, H. Strange news from another star, and other tales
From the childhood of Saint Francis of Assisi
Hesse, H. Stories of five decades
The hard passage
Hesse, H. Strange news from another star, and other tales
Harry, the Steppenwolf
Hesse, H. Stories of five decades
The homecoming
Hesse, H. Stories of five decades
Incipit vita nova
Hesse, H. Stories of five decades
Inside and outside
Hesse, H. Stories of five decades
Same as: Within and without, entered in 1950-1954 and 1959-1963 supplements

The interrupted class
Hesse, H. Stories of five decades
Iris
Hesse, H. Strange news from another star, and other tales
The island dream
Hesse, H. Stories of five decades
Klein and Wagner
Hesse, H. Klingsor's last summer
Klingsor's last summer
Hesse, H. Klingsor's last summer
The Latin scholar
Hesse, H. Stories of five decades
A man by the name of Ziegler
Hesse, H. Stories of five decades
The marble works
Hesse, H. Stories of five decades
November night
Hesse, H. Stories of five decades
The poet
Hall, J. B. ed. The realm of fiction
Hesse, H. Strange news from another star, and other tales
Robert Aghion
Hesse, H. Stories of five decades
Strange news from another star
Hesse, H. Strange news from another star, and other tales
To Frau Gertrud
Hesse, H. Stories of five decades
Tragic
Hesse, H. Stories of five decades
Walter Kompff
Hesse, H. Stories of five decades
The wolf
Hesse, H. Stories of five decades
**Het Reve, Gerard Kornelis van.** See Reve, Gerard Kornelis van het
**Hewat, Alan V.**
Men against the sea
Lish, G. ed. The secret life of our times: new fiction from Esquire
**Hexamnion.** Davis, C.
A **hexed** rifle. Gulick, B.
**Hey** sailor, what ship? Olsen, T.
**Hey** you down there. Rolseth, H.
The **heyday** of the blood. Fisher, D. C.
**Heyman, Arlene**
Freedom now
New American Review no. 5
Strains of Iris
New American Review no. 2
**Hi** diddle diddle. Silverberg, R.
**Hi** Lili hi Li. . . . Shui, Ching
**HIBERNATION (HUMAN)** See Sleep, Prolonged
The **hickory** stick rider. Schultz, J.
The **hidden** ears. Perkins, L. A.
The **hidden** money. Cecil, H.
**Hide** and seek. Clarke, A. C.
**Hide**-and-seek. Spielberg, P.
**HIDING-PLACES (SECRET CHAMBERS, ETC.)**
Borges, J. L. Pedro Salvadores
Derleth, A. The house in the valley
Dinesen, I. The ring
Queen, E. Miser's gold
Tedlock, E. W. 'Tis a fond ambush

Higgins, Anne
    Horses and crosses
        American Review 17
    In search of a missing IUD
        New American Review no. 15
Higgins, George V.
    The habits of the animals: the progress of
        the seasons
        The Best American short stories, 1973
Higgins, Robert J.
    Social climber
        Hitchcock, A. ed. Alfred Hitchcock pre-
            sents: Stories to be read with the
            lights on
The high ground. De Vries, P.
The high jump. Arkanov, A.
HIGH JUMPING. See Track athletics
HIGH SCHOOL LIFE. See School life
High stakes. Wodehouse, P. G.
High tide, low tide. Kaplan, B.
High victory. Lavender, D.
High-water mark. Harte, B.
High Weir. Delany, S. R.
Higher standards. Wilson, A.
The higher things. Pierce, J. R.
The highest bidder. Stuart, J.
HIGHJACKING OF AIRPLANES.  See
    Hijacking of airplanes
The highroad of Saint James. Carpentier, A.
Highsmith, Patricia
    Another bridge to cross
        Highsmith, P. The snail-watcher, and
            other stories
    The barbarians
        Highsmith, P. The snail-watcher, and
            other stories
    The birds poised to fly
        Highsmith, P. The snail-watcher, and
            other stories
    The cries of love
        Highsmith, P. The snail-watcher, and
            other stories
        Mystery Writers of America. Merchants
            of menace
    The empty birdhouse
        Highsmith, P. The snail-watcher, and
            other stories
    The gracious, pleasant life of Mrs Afton
        Bernkopf, J. F. comp. Boucher's choicest
    The heroine
        Highsmith, P. The snail-watcher, and
            other stories
    Mrs Afton, among thy green braes
        Highsmith, P. The snail-watcher, and
            other stories
    The quest for "Blank Claveringi"
        Highsmith, P. The snail-watcher, and
            other stories
        Hitchcock, A. comp. Alfred Hitchcock's
            Supernatural tales of terror and sus-
            pense
    The snail watcher
        Haining, P. ed. The Lucifer society
        Highsmith, P. The snail-watcher, and
            other stories
    The terrapin
        Highsmith, P. The snail-watcher, and
            other stories

When the fleet was in at Mobile
    Highsmith, P. The snail-watcher, and
        other stories
HIGHWAY ACCIDENTS. See Automobiles
    —Accidents; Trucks—Accidents
The highwayman. Dawson, F.
A highwayman in the woods of Chelm.
    Blum-Alquit, E.
HIGHWAYMEN. See Brigands and robbers
HIGHWAYS. See Roads
Hignett, Sean
    Allotment
        Winter's tales 16
Hijack. Fish, R. L.
HIJACKING OF AIRPLANES
    Fish, R. L. Hijack
    Oates, J. C. Did you ever slip on red
        blood?
Hijo de puta. Morriën, A.
HIKING. See Backpacking; Walking
Hilary Maltby and Stephen Braxton. Beer-
    bohm, M.
Hildesheimer, Wolfgang
    A world ends
        Hall, J. B. ed. The realm of fiction
        Karl, F. R. and Hamalian, L. eds. The
            naked i
        Stevick, P. ed. Anti-story
Hilifter. Dickson, G. R.
Hill, Alice R.
    Omega
        Derleth, A. Dark things
Hill, Richard
    Moth race
        Ellison, H. ed. Again, dangerous visions
    Out in the garage
        American Review 17
    To sport with Amaryllis
        Orbit 7
Hill, Susan
    The custodian
        Winter's tales 18
The hillies. Updike, J.
Hills like white elephants. Hemingway, E.
HIMALAYAN MOUNTAINS
    Kipling, R. Namgay Doola
    Sambrot, W. Creature of the snows
    Ullman, J. R. Top man
Himes, Chester
    All God's chillun got pride
        Himes, C. Black on Black
    All he needs is feet
        Himes, C. Black on Black
    Black laughter
        Himes, C. Black on Black
    Christmas gift
        Himes, C. Black on Black
    Cotton gonna kill me yet
        Himes, C. Black on Black
    Da-da-dee
        Himes, C. Black on Black
    Headwaiter
        Himes, C. Black on Black
    Heaven has changed
        Himes, C. Black on Black
    In the night
        Himes, C. Black on Black
    Lunching at the Ritzmore
        Himes, C. Black on Black

The **hitch**-hikers. Welty, E.

**Hitchens, Dolores**
If you see this woman
Mystery Writers of America. Crime without murder

**Hitchhiker.** Betts, D.

**HITCHHIKERS**
Abish, W. More by George
Bullins, E. Support your local police
Effinger, G. A. Things go better
Garner, H. The yellow sweater
Granat, R. Prana
Montross, D. Rape
Stone, A. The traveler
Welty, E. The hitch-hikers

**HITLER, ADOLF**
Aldiss, B. W. Swastika!
Boulle, P. His last battle
Bukowski, C. 卐 [Swastika]

**Hoag, M. de Koning**
Thursday's child
Rosmond, B. comp. Today's stories from Seventeen

**Hoagland, Edward**
The Colonel's power
New American Review no. 2
The final fate of the alligators
Prize stories, 1971: The O. Henry Awards
Kwan's Coney Island
New American Review no. 5

**HOAXES**
Adams, T. E. Sled
Allen, G. The episode of the diamond links
Allen, G. The episode of the Mexican seer
Allingham, M. 'Tis not hereafter
Babel, I. Shabos Nahamu
Bierce, A. A lady from Redhorse
Bowles, P. The hyena
Chilson, R. In his image
Compton, D. G. The eternal amateur
Cortázar, J. The health of the sick
Des Périers, B. The ear specialist
Fellowes-Gordon, I. The attic room
Himes, C. Cotton gonna kill me yet
Landolfi, T. Shadows
Masuccio. Fra Ieronimo and the miraculous arm
Nissenson, H. Forcing the end
Pritchett, V. S. The chain-smoker
Reed, K. At Central
Ruyslinck, W. The Madonna with the lump
Saltus, E. The grand duke's rubies
Scott, D. C. No. 68 Rue Alfred de Musset
Slesar, H. and Ellison, H. Survivor #1
Sørensen, V. In strange country
Stuart, J. Powderday's red hen
Sturgeon, T. Occam's scalpel
Taylor, P. Venus, Cupid, Folly and Time
Wain, J. The life guard
Wharton, E. Miss Mary Pask
White, S. E. A corner in horses

**HOBBIES**
Naylor, P. R. Mrs Perry becomes a person

**Hobo** jungle. Goulart, R.

**HOBOES.** *See* Tramps

**Hobson's** choice. Bester, A.

**Hoch, Edward D.**
Burial monuments three
Best detective stories of the year, 1973
Computer cops
Santesson, H. S. ed. Crime prevention in the 30th century
End of the day
Best detective stories of the year, 1972
Howdunit: every fifth man
Ellery Queen's Mystery Magazine. Ellery Queen's Grand slam
I'd know you anywhere
Hitchcock, A. ed. Alfred Hitchcock presents: Stories to be read with the lights on
The impossible "impossible crime"
Ellery Queen's Mystery Magazine. Ellery Queen's Murder menu
The Leopold locked room
Ellery Queen's Mystery Magazine. Ellery Queen's Mystery bag
The magic bullet
Best detective stories of the year [1969]
Night of the millennium
Elwood, R. ed. The other side of tomorrow
The oblong room
Bernkopf, J. F. comp. Boucher's choicest
Hitchcock, A. ed. Alfred Hitchcock presents: A month of mystery
Mystery Writers of America. Mirror, mirror, fatal mirror
Reunion
McComas, J. F. ed. Crimes and misfortunes
The ripper of Storyville
Mystery Writers of America. Dear dead days
The spy who came to the brink
Hitchcock, A. ed. Alfred Hitchcock presents: Stories to stay awake by
The spy who worked for peace
Gibson, W. ed. Rogues' gallery
The theft of the brazen letters
Mystery Writers of America. Crime without murder
The theft of the Coco loot
Best detective stories of the year, 1971
The theft of the laughing lions
Ellery Queen's Mystery Magazine. Ellery Queen's Headliners
Whodunit: murder offstage
Ellery Queen's Mystery Magazine. Ellery Queen's Grand slam
Whydunit: the Nile cat
Ellery Queen's Mystery Magazine. Ellery Queen's Grand slam
*For another story by this author see* Dentinger, Stephen

**HOCKEY**
Freeman, A. H. Whatever became of Agnes Mason

**Hodgson, S.**
Slip stream
Hitchcock, A. comp. Alfred Hitchcock's Supernatural tales of terror and suspense

**Hodgson, William Hope**
The horse of the invisible
Greene, H. ed. The rivals of Sherlock Holmes
The house among the laurels
Haining, P. ed. The wild night company: Irish stories of fantasy and horror

**Hodorlahomor** the Great. Krleza, M.

**Hodous, Mike**
Dead end
Analog 7

**Hoffman, Charles Fenno**
Ben Blower's story
Haining, P. ed. Gothic tales of terror
The man in the reservoir
Haining, P. ed. The nightmare reader

**Hoffman, Lee**
Soundless evening
Ellison, H. ed. Again, dangerous visions

**Hoffman, Lee, and Toomey, Robert E.**
Lost in the marigolds
Orbit 9

**Hoffmann, E. T. A.**
Councillor Krespel
Hoffmann, E. T. A. Selected writings of E. T. A. Hoffmann
Same as: The Cremona violin; Rath Krespel, entered in 1964-1968 supplement
The Cremona violin
Haining, P. ed. Gothic tales of terror
Same as: Councillor Krespel; Rath Krespel, entered in 1964-1968 supplement
The doubles
Hoffmann, E. T. A. Selected writings of E. T. A. Hoffmann
The golden pot
Hoffmann, E. T. A. Selected writings of E. T. A. Hoffmann
Little Zaches, surnamed Zinnober
Hoffmann, E. T. A. Three Märchen of E. T. A. Hoffmann
Mademoiselle de Scudéri
Hoffmann, E. T. A. Selected writings of E. T. A. Hoffmann
Master Flea
Hoffmann, E. T. A. Three Märchen of E. T. A. Hoffmann
The mines of Falun
Hoffmann, E. T. A. Selected writings of E. T. A. Hoffmann
Princess Brambilla
Hoffmann, E. T. A. Three Märchen of E. T. A. Hoffmann
Ritter Gluck
Hall, J. B. ed. The realm of fiction
Hoffmann, E. T. A. Selected writings of E. T. A. Hoffmann
The sandman
Bishop, M. ed. A Romantic storybook
Hoffmann, E. T. A. Selected writings of E. T. A. Hoffmann
Kahn, J. ed. Trial and terror

**Hog**-killing day. Trevisan, D.

**Hogan, David**
The leaping trout
Kahn, J. ed. Some things fierce and fatal

**Hogan, Ray.** See Grady, Gwynn, jt. auth.

**Hogg, James**
The Brownie of the Black Haggs
Haining, P. ed. The clans of darkness
The expedition to Hell
Haining, P. ed. Gothic tales of terror

**Hokororo, Anthony M.**
A day off
Nolen, B. ed. Africa is thunder and wonder

**Hold** 'em Yale. Runyon, D.

**Hold** your fire! Eisenberg, L.

**Holding, James**
The queen's jewel
Hitchcock, A. ed. Alfred Hitchcock presents: A month of mystery
Second talent
Hitchcock, A. ed. Alfred Hitchcock presents: Stories to stay awake by
A Treasury of modern mysteries v2

**HOLDUPS.** See Robberies

A **hole** in the ceiling. Koolhaas, A.

The **hole** in the floor. Fast, H.

The **holes** around Mars. Bixby, J.

**Holiday.** Porter, K. A.

**Holiday** Home. Litvinov, I.

**Holiday** in Germany. Brautigan, R.

The **holiday** man. Matheson, R.

The **holiday** rider. Boles, P. D.

**Holiday** Sunday. Veiga, J. J.

**Holiday** with the Larks. Stuart, J.

**HOLIDAYS.** See Vacations; also names of individual holidays, e.g. Halloween

**HOLIDAYS, JEWISH.** See Yom Kippur

**Holland, Kevin Crossley.** See Crossley-Holland, Kevin

**Holland, Ray**
The day Jesus came
Winter's tales 18

**HOLLAND.** See Netherlands

**Hollander, John**
In the creep block, one was observed . . .
Moss, H. ed. The poet's story

The **holler** tree. Crane, S.

**Hollis, H. H.**
Stoned counsel
Ellison, H. ed. Again, dangerous visions
Sword game
Nebula award stories 4

The **Holloway** flat tragedy. Bramah, E.

**Holly, J. Hunter**
The others
Elwood, R. ed. The other side of tomorrow

**Holly, Joan C.**
The gift of nothing
Elwood, R. ed. And walk now gently through the fire, and other science fiction stories

The **Holly** Beach hurricane. Brister, B.

**HOLLYWOOD.** See California—Hollywood

**Hollywood** heart. Carpenter, D.

**Hollywood** whore. Carpenter, D.

**Holm, Don**
Christmas at Fort Clatsop
Lucia, E. ed. This land around us

**HORROR STORIES—**_Continued_

Brennan, J. P. Killer cat
Brennan, J. P. Monton
Brennan, J. P. The North Knoll
Brennan, J. P. The rising man
Brennan, J. P. Stories of darkness and dread; 18 stories
Brown, F. Eine kleine Nachtmusik
Brunner, J. The biggest game
Bryant, E. The human side of the village monster
Bullins, E. The hungered one
Burke, J. ed. Tales of unease; 21 stories
Burke, T. The bird
Butterworth, M. The front room
Byron, Lord. The burial
Cady, J. Ride the thunder
Campbell, J. R. Cold print
Campbell, R. The guy
Campbell, R. The interloper
Campbell, R. The Sentinels
Canning, J. ed. 50 great horror stories; 50 stories
Carter, L. The dweller in the tomb
Case, D. The cell
Case, D. The cell; 3 stories
Case, D. The dead end
Case, D. The hunter
Churchill, W. Man overboard
Clarke, A. C.　A walk in the dark
Clingerman, M. The gay deceiver
Collier, J. Green thoughts
Collins, W. The story of a terribly strange bed
Cornish, M. Superstitious ignorance
Crawford, F. M. The dead smile
Crawford, F. M. The screaming skull
Dahl, R. The landlady
Dahl, R. The way up to heaven
Day, J. W. The tongueless woman of Glamis Castle
De Forbes. My sister Annabelle
De La Mare, W.　A: B: O.
De La Mare, W. Eight tales; 8 stories
De La Mare, W. The hangman luck
De La Mare, W. The Village of Old Age
Derleth, A. Beyond the threshold
Derleth, A. Carousel
Derleth, A. ed. Dark things; 24 stories
Derleth, A. The dweller in darkness
Derleth, A. The house in the valley
Derleth, A. The panelled room
Derleth, A. The slayers and the slain
Derleth, A. The watcher from the sky
Derleth, A.　A wig for Miss DeVore
Derry, V. The image of fear
Disch, T. M. Descending
Disch, T. M. The roaches
Doyle, Sir A. C. The fiend of the cooper-age
Du Maurier, D. The birds
Eddy, C. M. The loved dead
Ellison, H. The whimper of whipped dogs
Faulkner, W.　A rose for Emily
Fellowes-Gordon, I. Donovan's drop
Fenimore, W. The pool of the stone god
Fremlin, C. Don't go to sleep in the dark; 13 stories
Fremlin, C. The locked room

Fremlin, C. Something evil in the house
Fremlin, C. The special gift
Gardner, E. A. Wide O-
Gaskell, J. Jane
Gawsworth, J. The shifting growth
Gilman, C. P. The yellow wall paper
Goodwin, J. B. L. The cocoon
Grant, C. L. The summer of the Irish Sea
Graves, R. The shout
Greene, S. The invisible monster
Haining, P. ed. The clans of darkness; 19 stories
Haining, P. ed. The freak show; 19 stories
Haining, P. ed. The ghouls; 18 stories
Haining, P. ed. The Hollywood nightmare; 16 stories
Haining, P. ed. The Lucifer society; 24 stories
Haining, P. ed. Nightfrights; 18 stories
Haining, P. ed. The nightmare reader; 23 stories
Hamilton, A. ed. Splinters; 14 stories
Harrison, E. The child watcher
Harrison, H. At last, the true story of Frankenstein
Harvey, W. F. August heat
Harvey, W. F. The beast with five fingers
Heald, H. The horror in the museum
Heald, H. Out of the eons
Healey, R. M. Guessing game
Highsmith, P. The empty birdhouse
Highsmith, P. The snail watcher
Hitchcock, A. ed. Alfred Hitchcock presents: Stories to be read with the lights on; 37 stories
Hitchcock, A. comp. Alfred Hitchcock's Supernatural tales of terror and suspense; 11 stories
Hoffman, C. Ben Blower's story
Howard, R. E. The black stone
The Iron Shroud
Jackson, S. The lovely house
Jacobi, C. The aquarium
Jacobi, C. The cocomacaque
Jacobi, C. The Singleton barrier
Jacobi, C. The unpleasantness at Carver House
Kipling, R. The mark of the beast
Kuttner, H. The Salem horror
Lafferty, R. A. Ishmael into the Barrens
Lamb, H. ed. A tide of terror; 16 stories
Laski, M. The tower
Leiber, F. The casket-demon
Leiber, F. The girl with the hungry eyes
Leiber, F. The power of the puppets
Leroux, G. Phantom of the Opera
Lewis, M. G. The anaconda
Long, F. B. The hounds of Tindalos
Long, F. B. The man with a thousand legs
Long, F. B. The space-eaters
Lovecraft, H. P. The call of Cthulhu
Lovecraft, H. P. The cats of Ulthar
Lovecraft, H. P. Cool air
Lovecraft, H. P. The horror in the museum, and other revisions; 20 stories
Lovecraft, H. P. Monster of terror
Lovecraft, H. P. White ape
Lumley, B. Ambler's inspiration

## HORROR STORIES—*Continued*

Lumley, B. The caller of The Black; 14 stories
Lumley, B. Cement surroundings
Lumley, B. The deep-sea conch
Lumley, B. The Mirror of Nitocris
Lumley, B. The sister city
Lumley, B.   A thing about cars!
Lumley, B. The thing from the blasted heath
Lumley, W. The diary of Alonzo Typer
McAllister, B. The arrangement
McKimmey, J. Run with the wind
Maine, C. E. Short circuit
Manley, S. and Lewis, G. eds. Ladies of horror; 13 stories
Matheson, R. Duel
Maupassant, G. de. The Horla
Maupassant, G. de. Nerves
May, D. Grace note
May, F. Company in the orchard
Mergendahl, C. Secret recipe
The Monk of horror
Moore, C. L. Werewoman
Moskowitz, S. ed. Horrors unknown; 11 stories
Mulisch, H. What happened to Sergeant Masuro?
Nesbit, E. Man-size in marble
Newman, A. Such a good idea
Niland, D. The sound and the silence
Niven, L. Bordered in black
Nolan, W. F. Down the long night
Partington, C. The Manterfield inheritance
Peake, M. Same time, same place
Poe, E. A. The lunatics
Poe, E. A. MS found in a bottle
Poe, E. A. Morella
Poe, E. A. The oblong box
Poe, E. A. The pit and the pendulum
Poe, E. A. The tell-tale heart
Poe, E. A. William Wilson
Polidori, J. The vampyre
Priest, C. The head and the hand
Roa Bastos, A. The living tomb
St Clair, M. Counter charm
St Clair, M. Horrer howce
Sallis, J. 53rd American dream
Schmitz, J. H. Greenface
Scortia, T. N. The goddess of the cats
Shea, J. V. The haunter of the graveyard
Silverberg, R. Road to nightfall
Smith, C. A. The ghoul
Smith, C. A. The necromantic tale
Smith, C. A. The resurrection of the rattle-snake
Smith, C. A. The return of the sorcerer
Stevens, F. Unseen—unfeared
Stevenson, R. L. The body-snatcher
Stevenson, R. L. Strange case of Dr Jekyll and Mr Hyde
Stevenson, R. L. Thrawn Janet
Stoker, B. The Bram Stoker Bedside companion; 10 stories
Stoker, B. Dracula's guest
Stoker, B. The Judge's House
Stoker, B. The secret of the growing gold
Stoker, B. The squaw
Tabori, P. Janus
Taylor, E. R. Jujitsu
Tieck, J. L. The bride of the grave
Toonder, J. G. The spider
Val Baker, D. Passenger to Liverpool
Wade, J. The deep ones
Wells, H. G. The flowering of the strange orchid
Williamson, G. Accusing eyes of vengeance
Wilson, A. Animals or human beings
Wilson, A. Raspberry jam
Wilson, C. The return of the Lloigor
Wilson, G. The spot
Wintle, W. The black cat
Young, R. F. The ogress
Zelazny, R. Corrida

See also Cannibalism; Death; Ghosts; Gothic romances; Massacres; Murder stories; Supernatural phenomena; Vampires; Werewolves; Witchcraft

A **horse** and two goats. Narayan, R. K.

**HORSE BREAKING.** *See* Horses—Training

A **horse** of a different color. Kanin, G.

**Horse** of air. Dozois, G. R.

The **horse** of the invisible. Hodgson, W. H.

## HORSE RACING

Algren, N. Bullring of the summer night
Algren, N.   I never hollered cheezit the cops
Anderson, S.   I want to know why
Bierce, A. The race at Left Bower
Bradshaw, M. E. Rebel in the driver's seat
Bukowski, C. Another horse story
Bukowski, C. The beginner
Bukowski, C. Cunt and Kant and a happy home
Bukowski, C. Flower horse
Bukowski, C. Non-horseshit horse advice
Bukowski, C. Pittsburgh Phil & Co.
Bukowski, C. 25 bums in rags
Horn, H. The old man
Jesby, E. Ogre!
Lawrence, D. H. The rocking-horse winner
Malzberg, B. N. Notes just prior to the fall
Morrison, A. The case of Janissary
Runyon, D. All horse players die broke
Runyon, D.   A story goes with it
Watkins, R. H. The turf and the dirt
West, J. Fast horseflesh

See also Gambling; Jockeys

**Horse** thief. *See* Opatoshu, J. Romance of a horse thief

## HORSE THIEVES

Grove, F. War path
Newton, D. B. Chain of command
Opatoshu, J. Romance of a horse thief

## HORSE TRADING

Green, B. K. Brethren horse traders
Green, B. K. Fence trouble
Green, B. K. Foreign trade
Green, B. K. Gittin' even
Green, B. K. The last trail drive through downtown Dallas
Green, B. K. Mr Undertaker and the Cleveland Bay horse
Green, B. K. Runaway!
Green, B. K. Saddle marks

**Hoydal, Karsten**
Summer eve at "Rockall"
Faroese short stories
**Hsi, Yu Chi.** *See* Wu, Ch'eng-en
**Hsiang Lao.** *See* Lao, Hsiang
**Hsien-yung Pai.** *See* Pai, Hsien-yung
**Hsün Lu.** *See* Lu, Hsün
**Hua-ling Nieh.** *See* Nieh, Hua-ling
**Huan.** Bergé, C.
**Hubbard, L. Ron**
He didn't like cats
Necker, C. ed. Supernatural cats
**Hubly, Erlene**
In Sherwood Forest
The Best little magazine fiction, 1971
**Hubschman, Thomas**
A woman of thirty
Voices of Brooklyn
**Huddle, David**
The interrogation of the prisoner Bung by
Mister Hawkins and Sergeant Tree
Karlin, W.; Paquet, B. T. and Rott-
mann, L. eds. Free fire zone
Lish, G. ed. The secret life of our times:
new fiction from Esquire
**Huddling** place. Simak, C. D.
**Hudson, Jeffery**
How does that make you feel?
Mystery Writers of America. Crime
without murder
**HUDSON RIVER**
Irving, W. The legend of Sleepy Hollow
**Hue** and cry. McPherson, J. A.
**Huey, Tommy**
The Ambulance Driver's Ball; or, The
stabilization of Henry Aldrich Alias
Thornton
Intro 4
**Hufford, Liz**
Tablets of stone
Orbit 8
**Hughes, Dorothy B.**
The Granny woman
Mystery Writers of America. Crime
without murder
**Hughes, Langston**
African morning
Adoff, A. ed. Brothers and sisters
Christmas song
Turner, D. T. ed. Black American litera-
ture
Cora unashamed
James, C. L. ed. From the roots
The doors of life
Long, R. A. and Collier, E. W. eds.
Afro-American writing v2
Early Autumn
King, W. ed. Black short story anthology
Last whipping
Turner, D. T. ed. Black American
literature
Minnie again
Long, R. A. and Collier, E. W. eds.
Afro-American writing v2
Mysterious Madame Shanghai
Howes, B. and Smith, G. J. eds. The
sea-green horse

On the road
Minot, S. and Wilson, R. eds. Three
stances of modern fiction
Stansbury, D. L. ed. Impact
On the way home
Burnett, W. ed. Black hands on a white
face
Poor little Black fellow
Hall, J. B. ed. The realm of fiction
Rock, church
Margolies, E. A native sons reader
Thank you m'am
Bambara, T. C. ed. Tales and stories
for Black folks
Turner, D. T. ed. Black American
literature
Why, you reckon?
James, C. L. ed. From the roots
**Hughes, Mary Gray**
The foreigner in the blood
The Best American short stories, 1969
The Judge
The Best American short stories, 1972
**Hughes, Ted**
The rain horse
Stansbury, D. L. ed. Impact
Snow
Hall, J. B. ed. The realm of fiction
Karl, F. R. and Hamalian, L. eds. The
naked i
Taylor, J. C. ed. The short story: fiction
in transition
**Hugues,** the wer-wolf. Menzies, S.
**HUMAN COLD STORAGE.** *See* Cryonics
**Human** frailty. Xlebnikov, A.
**Human** interest stuff. Halliday, B.
The **human** operators. Ellison, H. and Van
Vogt, A. E.
The **human** operators. Van Vogt, A. E. and
Ellison, H.
**HUMAN RACE.** *See* Man
**HUMAN SACRIFICE.** *See* Sacrifice, Human
The **human** side of the village monster.
Bryant, E.
The **human** touch. Easmon, R. S.
A **humanist.** Gary, R.
**HUMANOIDS.** *See* Life on other planets
**Hume, Fergus**
The amber beads
Greene, Sir H. ed. The further rivals of
Sherlock Holmes
**Humility.** Hippius, Z.
**HUMOR**
Algren, N. The leak that defied the books
Asimov, I. Christmas on Ganymede
Ayrton, M. A problem of space
Babel, I. The awakening
Babel, I. Shabos Nahamu
Barthelme, D. Brain damage
Barthelme, D. Daumier
Barthelme, D. The falling dog
Bennett, H. Dotson Gerber resurrected
Bierce, A. The failure of Hope & Wandel
Bierce, A. The little story
Bierce, A. A providential intimation
Bierce, A. The race at Left Bower
Bierce, A. Why I am not editing "The
Stinger"

HUMOR—*Continued*

Maloney, R. Viva Caporetto!

Manoff, E. Mama and the spy

Maupassant, G. de. The adventure of Walter Schnaffs

Maupassant, G. de. A sale

Mitchell, E. P. A day among the liars

Mitchell, E. P. The terrible voyage of the Toad

Nesvadba, J. Captain Nemo's last adventure

O'Brien, F. "The little chest"

O'Donnell, K. M. Getting around

O'Hara, J. At the Cothurnos Club

Pangborn, E. The Ponsonby case

Perelmen, S. J. The idol's eye

Pierce, J. Miss Paisley on a diet

Powell, J. The Stollmeyer sonnets

Roditi, E. The Sultan's Little Harum-scarum

Rosenberg, E. Julius Pasternak and the Einstein letter

Rosten, L. Christopher K°A°P°L°A°N

Roth, P. Civilization and its discontents

Roth, P. The Jewish blues

Roth, P. On the air

Runyon, D. The hottest guy in the world

Russell, R. The better man

Saki. The interlopers

Sallis, J. Kazoo

Saroyan, W. The fifty yard dash

Scott, R. The big connection

Sheckley, R. The same to you doubled

Shepherd, J. County fair!

Shepherd, J. Daphne Bigelow and the spine-chilling saga of the snail-encrusted tinfoil noose

Shepherd, J. Ollie Hopnoddle's haven of bliss

Shepherd, J. The return of the smiling Wimpy doll

Shepherd, J. Scut Farkus and the murderous Mariah

Shepherd, J. The star-crossed romance of Josephine Cosnowski

Shepherd, J. Wanda Hickey's night of golden memories

Shulman, M. The unlucky winner

Singer, I. B. Cockadoodledoo

Smith, E. E. Calliope and Gherkin and the Yankee Doodle thing

Snyder, G. The Smokey the Bear Sutra

Standish, L. Gremblins

Stockton, F. R. The transferred ghost

Thackeray, W. M. The Devil's wager

Thurber, J. The catbird seat

Thurber, J. The greatest man in the world

Thurber, J. The night the ghost got in

Thurber, J. The secret life of Walter Mitty

Thurber, J. The unicorn in the garden

Tsonev, V. Let's go vacationing

Twain, M. The celebrated jumping frog of Calaveras County

Twain, M. Jim Baker's bluejay yarn

Untermeyer, L. ed. Treasury of great humor; 14 stories

Updike, J. The Baluchitherium

Varshavsky, I. Biocurrents, biocurrents . . .

Varshavsky, I. SOMP

Welty, E. The wide net

Wilde, O. The Canterville ghost

Wodehouse, P. G. Archibald's benefit

Wodehouse, P. G. The awakening of Rollo Podmarsh

Wodehouse, P. G. The clicking of Cuthbert

Wodehouse, P. G. The coming of Gowf

Wodehouse, P. G. Excelsior

Wodehouse, P. G. Farewell to Legs

Wodehouse, P. G. Feet of clay

Wodehouse, P. G. The golf omnibus

Wodehouse, P. G. The golf omnibus; 31 stories

Wodehouse, P. G. The heart of a goof

Wodehouse, P. G. The heel of Achilles

Wodehouse, P. G. High stakes

Wodehouse, P. G. Jane gets off the fairway

Wodehouse, P. G. Keeping in with Vosper

Wodehouse, P. G. The letter of the law

Wodehouse, P. G. The long hole

Wodehouse, P. G. The magic plus fours

Wodehouse, P. G. A mixed threesome

Wodehouse, P. G. Ordeal by golf

Wodehouse, P. G. The purification of Rodney Spelvin

Wodehouse, P. G. Rodney fails to qualify

Wodehouse, P. G. Rodney has a relapse

Wodehouse, P. G. The rough stuff

Wodehouse, P. G. The salvation of George Mackintosh

Wodehouse, P. G. Scratch man

Wodehouse, P. G. Sleepy time

Wodehouse, P. G. The story of Webster

Wodehouse, P. G. Strychnine in the soup

Wodehouse, P. G. Sundered hearts

Wodehouse, P. G. Tangled hearts

Wodehouse, P. G. There's always golf

Wodehouse, P. G. Those in peril on the tee

Wodehouse, P. G. Up from the depths

Wodehouse, P. G. A woman is only a woman

Zern, E. Something was fishy about Stonehenge

*See also* Improbable stories; Puns and punning; Satire

**Practical jokes**

Bierce, A. The baptism of Dobsho

Bierce, A. The major's tale

Brautigan, R. Trout fishing in America terrorists

Brú, H. A summons for the blacksmith

Deutschman, B. In a small town a kid went to shul

Duncan, R. Diary of a poltergeist

Edwards, A. The case of the travelling corpse

Fielding, G. The treat

Maupassant, G. de. A practical joke

Mishima, Y. The pearl

Porges, A. The reason

Saki. The lull

Sayers, D. L. The haunted policeman

Shannon, D. The practical joke

Singer, I. B. The wager

Taylor, P. There

Thurston, R. Stop me before I tell more

HUMOROUS STORIES. *See* Humor
Humphreys, Larry G.
  Tanya
    Story: the yearbook of discovery/1969
Humpty Dumpty had a great fall.
  Long, F. B.
The hunchback trout. Brautigan, R.
HUNCHBACKS
  Brackenbury, R.   A caryatid
  Mann, T. Litttle Herr Friedemann
  Stone, A. The traveler
  Tertz, A. Pkhentz
HUNGARIAN SOLDIERS. *See* Soldiers, Hungarian
HUNGARIANS IN ENGLAND
  Gilbert, A. The quiet man
HUNGARIANS IN SWITZERLAND
  Graham, W. At the Chalet Lartrec
HUNGARIANS IN THE UNITED STATES
  Collins, M. Freedom fighter
  Goldberg, G. J. The Bowditch footnote
  Inman, R. I'll call you
HUNGARIANS IN YUGOSLAVIA
  Djilas, M. An eye for an eye
HUNGARY
              14th century
  Von Kramer, Professor. The Hall of Blood
              20th century
  Örkény, I.   A prayer
        World War, 1939-1945
    *See* World War, 1939-1945—Hungary
          Army—Officers
  Krleža, M.   A funeral in Teresienburg
              Budapest
  Dorr, L. Brandenburg Concerto
HUNGARY, PROVINCIAL AND RURAL
  Barlay, K. The visitation of Aunt Clara
  Móricz, Z. Everything is good at the end of the world
HUNGER
  Borchert, W. The bread
  Bullins, E. The hungered one
  Charney, D. H. Mommy loves ya
  Goulart, R. Nobody starves
  Maupassant, G. de.   A vagabond
  Maupassant, G. de. The vagrant
      *See also* Fasting; Starvation
Hunger. Petaja, E.
Hunger. Winther, M. A.
The hungered one. Bullins, E.
Hunt, Hugh Allyn
  Acme Rooms and sweet Marjorie Russell
    McCrindle, J. F. ed. Stories from the Transatlantic Review
Hunt, Leigh
  A tale for a chimney corner
    Haining, P. ed. Gothic tales of terror
Hunt and destroy. Richie, M.
Hunter, Evan
  The beheading
    Hunter, E. The Easter Man (a play) and six stories
  The birthday party
    Hunter, E. The Easter Man (a play) and six stories

Inferiority complex
  Haining, P. ed. The Lucifer society
The interview
  Hunter, E. The Easter Man (a play) and six stories
The intruder
  Hunter, E. The Easter Man (a play) and six stories
The last spin
  Best of the Best detective stories
The sharers
  Hunter, E. The Easter Man (a play) and six stories
Someone at the door
  Ellery Queen's Mystery Magazine, Ellery Queen's Mystery bag
Terminal misunderstanding
  Hunter, E. The Easter Man (a play) and six stories
Hunter, Kristin
  All around the mulberry tree
    Hunter, K. Guests in the promised land
  BeeGee's ghost
    Hunter, K. Guests in the promised land
  Come out of that corner
    Hunter, K. Guests in the promised land
  Debut
    Hunter, K. Guests in the promised land
    Stansbury, D. L. ed. Impact
    Turner, D. T. ed. Black American literature
  Guests in the promised land
    Hunter, K. Guests in the promised land
  Hero's return
    Hunter, K. Guests in the promised land
  Mom Luby and the social worker
    Hunter, K. Guests in the promised land
  The pool table caper
    Hunter, K. Guests in the promised land
  The scribe
    Hunter, K. Guests in the promised land
  Two's enough of a crowd
    Hunter, K. Guests in the promised land
  You rap, I'll reap
    Hunter, K. Guests in the promised land
The hunter. Case, D.
The hunter at his ease. Aldiss, B. W.
Hunter, come home. McKenna, R.
The Hunter Gracchus: a fragment. Kafka, F.
HUNTERS. *See* Hunting
Hunter's gold. Holmes, E. M.
HUNTING
  Aldridge, J. Bush boy, poor boy
  Apel, J. A. The fatal marksman
  Athanas, V. Royal elk
  Brautigan, R. The post offices of Eastern Oregon
  Brautigan, A.   A short history of Oregon
  Brister, B. Anatomy of a goose hunt
  Brister, B. Grandfather's geese
  Brister, B. Moss, mallards and mules
  Brister, B. Moss, mallards and mules, and other hunting and fishing stories; 27 stories
  Brister, B. The naming of Rattlesnake Road
  Brister, B. The whitewing snow job
  Brister, B. The wrong-way ambush
  Connell, R. The most dangerous game
  Crane, S. Killing his bear

I guarantee: you are my man. Busch, F.

I guess you fellows just don't want me. Algren, N.

I had known Sam Taylor for years. Graham, W.

I have my vigil. Harrison, H.

I have no mouth, and I must scream. Ellison, H.

I haven't time. Moravia, A.

"I killed John Harrington." Walsh, T.

I killed Maria Goretti. Di Donato, P.

I know they'll like me in Saigon. Algren, N.

I live on your visits. Parker, D.

I love someone. Stafford, J.

I love you, Ricky. Wain, J.

I, Mars. Bradbury, R.

I never hollered cheezit the cops. Algen, N.

I passed for Yankee. Ansell, J.

I remember a winter. Pohl, F.

I see a man sitting on a chair, and the chair is biting his leg. Sheckley, R. and Ellison, H.

I see you, Bianca. Brennan, M.

I shot a man in Reno. Bukowski, C.

I sing the Body Electric! Bradbury, R.

I spy. Greene, G.

I take care of things. Cady, J.

I tell you, it's true. Anderson, P.

I thought about this girl. Weidman, J.

I thought you were a unicorn. Boles, P. D.

"I want a Sunday kind of love." Gold, H.

I want to know why. Anderson, S.

I was in love, Oates, J. C.

I will not let thee go, except thou bless me. Updike, J.

I will please come to order. Jayme, W. N.

Ibn Hakkan al-Bokhari, dead in his labyrinth. Borges, J. L.

**Ibuse, Masuji**
  Carp
    Ibuse, M. Lieutenant Lookeast, and other stories
  Lieutenant Lookeast
    Ibuse, M. Lieutenant Lookeast, and other stories
  Life at Mr Tange's
    Ibuse, M. Lieutenant Lookeast, and other stories
  Old Ushitora
    Ibuse, M. Lieutenant Lookeast, and other stories
  Pilgrims' Inn
    Ibuse, M. Lieutenant Lookeast, and other stories
  Plum blossom by night
    Ibuse, M. Lieutenant Lookeast, and other stories
  Salamander
    Ibuse, M. Lieutenant Lookeast, and other stories
  Savan on the roof
    Ibuse, M. Lieutenant Lookeast, and other stories
  Tajinko Village
    Ibuse, M. Lieutenant Lookeast, and other stories
  Yosaku the settler
    Ibuse, M. Lieutenant Lookeast, and other stories

**ICARIA.** See Greece, Modern—Icaria

**Icarus.** Brown, G. M.

**Icarus** and Daedalus. Altov, H.

**ICE AGE**
  Bradbury, R.   A final sceptre, a lasting crown

The **ice** cream eat. Goldman, W.

**ICE INDUSTRY**
  Bierce, A. The failure of Hope & Wandel

The **ice** palace. Baldwin, M.

**ICE SKATING.** See Skating

**ICEBERGS**
  Clarke, A. C. Cold War

The **icebox** blonde. Scortia, T. N.

**ICELAND**
  Norris, F. Grettir at Thorhall-stead
  The Story of Glam
  Thórdarson, A. If your sword is short

**ICONS**
  Theroux, P.   A real Russian ikon

**I'd** know you anywhere. Hoch, E. D.

**IDAHO**
  Hayes, A. H. Buckskin and smoke; 14 stories

       **Farm life**
    See Farm life—Idaho

    **Frontier and pioneer life**
    See Frontier and pioneer life—Idaho

    **Indians of North America**
    See Indians of North America—Idaho

       **Ranch life**
    See Ranch life—Idaho

       **Twin Falls**
  Hayes, A. H. How a Sagebrush became a Christmas tree
  Hayes, A. H. Wah-Tis-Kee—Little Flame

The **idea** of a university. Nemerov, H.

**IDEALISM**
  Asimov, I. "In a good cause—"
    See also Honesty

**Idealistic** demands. Strindberg, A.

**Ideas** die hard. Asimov, I.

**IDENTITY**
  Biggle, L. Orphan of the void
  Sherwin, J. J. The life of riot in one Luis Casas

**IDIOCY**
  Francis, H. E. The frog lady
  Petaja, E. Hunger
  Rulfo, J. Macario
  Wilson, A. Mummy to the rescue
    See also Feeble-minded

**Idiot** solvant. Dickson, G. R.

**IDIOTS.** See Idiocy

**IDOLS AND IMAGES**
  Drake, D. Lord of the depths
  Fenimore, W. The pool of the stone god
  Heald, H. The horror in the museum
  Pain, B. The grey cat
  Traven, B. When the priest is not at home

The **idol's** eye. Perelman, S. J.

**Idylls** of Dugan and Strunk. Stern, R.

**Ieli.** Verga, G.

**If.** Harrison, H.

**If** all the world were listening. Jones, A.

If he's good enough, he's big enough. Glanville, B.

If Hitler had invaded England. Forester, C. S.

If I forget thee, O Earth. Clarke, A. C.

If they knew Yvonne. Dubus, A.

If you don't go out the way you came in. Summers, H.

If you see this woman. Hitchens, D.

If your sword is short. Thórdarson, A.

If youth knew, if age could. Collier, J.

**IGNACIO DE LOYOLA, SAINT.** *See* Loyola, Ignacio de, Saint

**Ignatz.** Goulart, R.

**Ik, Kim Yong.** *See* Kim, Yong Ik

**Ika** Loch's brothel. Ostaijen, P. van

I'll ask him to come sooner. West, J.

I'll be waiting for you when the swimming pool is empty. Tiptree, J.

I'll call you. Inman, R.

Ill met in Lankhmar. Leiber, F.

**ILLEGITIMACY**

Aidoo, A. A. Something to talk about on the way to the funeral

Babel, I. The sin of Jesus

Burton, H. Not the end of the world

Faulkner, W. Wash

Lafferty, R. A. Ishmael into the Barrens

Maupassant, G. de. Abandoned

Maupassant, G. de. Simon's papa

The Miracle of the snow child

Oates, J. C. Stray children

O'Connor, F. Music when soft voices die

O'Connor, F. A set of variations on a borrowed theme

O'Connor, F. The weeping children

Pangborn, E. Tiger Boy

Pasternak, B. Aerial tracks

Petrakis, H. M. The bastards of Thanos

Sandaval, J. All the way home

Soto, P. J. God in Harlem

Stewart, J. I. M. Cucumber sandwiches

Undset, S. Simonsen

Weaver, G. Big old gold old thing

Weaver, G. Fantastico

Zobarskas, S. The night before Christmas

*See also* Unmarried mothers

**ILLICIT AFFAIRS.** *See* Marriage problems

**ILLICIT DISTILLING.** *See* Distilling, Illicit

**ILLINOIS**

**19th century**

Casper, L. The fifth wall

**Chicago**

Algren, N. Different clowns for different towns

Algren, N. The ryebread trees of spring

Bellow, S. Looking for Mr Green

Boles, P. D. Miss Rose

Daugherty, M. G. The givers

Drake, R. The tower and the pear tree

Elkin, S. The condominium

Farrell, J. T. Episodes of a return

Farrell, J. T. Native's return

Fitzgerald, F. S. First blood

Fitzgerald, F. S. A snobbish story

Greenberg, J. Timekeeper

Kaplan, B. One of the seas is called Tranquillity

McGivern, W. P. Old Willie

Monteleone, T. F. Chicago

Pechtel, C. Double-cross

Schwimmer, W. Christmas on Rush Street

Schwimmer, W. A full and happy life

Schwimmer, W. It happened on Rush Street; 14 stories

Schwimmer, W. The luckiest day in history

Schwimmer, W. The social event of the season for Rush Street

Schwimmer, W. Very unique for Rush Street

Schwimmer, W. Within the touch of a hand

Stern, R. East, West . . . Midwest

Stern, R. Idylls of Dugan and Strunk

Stern, R. Ins and outs

Wright, R. The man who went to Chicago

**Lake Forest**

Fitzgerald, F. S. A snobbish story

**ILLITERACY**

Hunter, K. The scribe

**ILLNESS**

Agnon, S. Y. The document

Agnon, S. Y. From lodging to lodging

Agnon, S. Y. To the doctor

Bukowski, C. Dr Nazi

Bukowski, C. A popular man

Callaghan, M. A sick call

Campbell, R. The enchanted fruit

Chekhov, A. A dreary story

Cortázar, J. The health of the sick

Cortázar, J. Nurse Cora

Forster, E. M. Dr Wollacott

Goldberg, G. J. The mowers

Hippius, Z. He is white

Ionesco, E. The slough

Kemal, Y. Green onions

Landolfi, T. At the station

McCord, J. Trial by summer

McGahern, J. Bomb box

McGregor, M. W. Porkchops with whiskey and ice cream

Narayan, R. K. Seventh House

Neville, L. and Neville, K. The quality of the product

Oates, J. C. Loving
Losing } a man
Loving

Peterkin, J. The foreman

Saxton, J. Elouise and the doctors of the planet Pergamon

Sexton, A. All God's children need radios

Solzhenitsyn, A. The right hand

Spielberg, P. Morning sickness

Spielberg, P. Sickness unto death

Stern, J. Next door to death

Stuart, J. The best years of our lives

Tolstoy, L. The death of Iván Ilych

Trevisan, D. The corpse in the parlor

Trevisan, D. Three o'clock in the morning

West, J. First loss

Yehoshua, A. B. A long hot day

Yovkov, Y. The white swallow

*See also* Children, Sick; Invalids; and names of specific illness or disease, e.g. Asthma; Cancer (Disease); Heart—Diseases; etc.

In his own image. Biggle, L.
In hot pursuit of happiness. Lem, S.
In late youth. Rush, N.
In lonely lands. Ellison, H.
In May, in May cried the cuckoo. Borchert, W.
In motion. Bergé, C.
In New England winter. Bullins, E.
In outraged stone. Lafferty, R. A.
In praise of Vespasian. Chester, A.
In prison. Bishop, E.
In Quebec city. Levine, N.
In re Glover. Tushnet, L.
In retirement. Malamud, B.
In search of a missing IUD. Higgins, A.
In seclusion. Jacobs, H.
In sheep's clothing. Nourse, A. E.
In Sherwood Forest. Hubly, E.
In shock. Litwak, L.
In strange country. Sørensen, V.
In the absence of angels. Calisher, H.
In the abyss. Pirandello, L.
In the barn. Anthony, P.
In the basement. Babel, I.
In the beginning. Constantini, H.
In the beginning. Gbadamossi, R. A.
In the blue country. Blum, R.
In the camp of the enemy. O'Neill, J.
In the capital of the Sahara. Bennett, A.
In the cards. Collier, J.
In the corridors of the underground: the escalator. Robbe-Grillet, A.
In the country of women. Li, Ju-chen
In the creep block, one was observed . . . Hollander, J.
In the cutting of a drink. Aidoo, A. A.
In the dark. Chekhov, A.
In the darkness. Böll, H.
In the flesh. Wolitzer, H.
In the footsteps of the Abominable Snowman. Nesvadba, J.
In the forest. De La Mare, W.
In the forests of Riga the beasts are very wild indeed. Brown, M. F.
In the garden. Thomas, D.
In the grainfields. Kosynka, H.
In the group. Silverberg, R.
In the hands of our enemies. Curley, D.
In the heart of the heart of the country. Gass, W. H.
In the land of the morning calm, déjà vu. Siegel, J.
In the light of Morris Rosenfeld. Blum-Alquit, E.
In the lobby. Steegmuller, F.
In loveless clarity. Rindfleisch, N.
In the madman's garden. Heinesen, W.
In the matter of the assassin Merefirs. Purdy, K. W.
In the men's room of the sixteenth century. DeLillo, D.
In the middle of nowhere. Pentecost, H.
In the middle of the fields. Lavin, M.
In the moonlight. See Maupassant, G. de. Moonlight.
In the night. Himes, C.
In the penal colony. Kafka, F.
In the pocket. O'Donnell, K. M.
In the queue. Laumer, K.

In the ravine. Chekhov, A.
In the region of ice. Oates, J. C.
In the reign of peace. Nissenson, H.
In the shade of the old apple tree. Flora, F.
In the tall windows. Blum-Alquit, E.
In the teeth of the evidence. Sayers, D. L.
In the Tenderloin: a duel between an alarm clock and a suicidal purpose. Crane, S.
In the twilight. Stegner, W.
In the vaults beneath. Lumley, B.
In the very stones. Brennan, J. P.
In the wide waste. Di Donato, P.
In the wine shop. Lu, Hsün
In the wine time. Bullins, E.
In the words of. Hayden, J.
In the zoo. Stafford, J.
In time which made a monkey of us all. Paley, G.
In trouble. Roth, P.
In Utica. Bumpus, J.
INBREEDING. See Consanguinity
The incarnation of Krishna Mulvaney. Kipling, R.
INCAS
  Russell, B. Zahatopolk
Incased in ancient rind. Lafferty, R. A.
The inception of the epoch of Mrs. Bedonebyasyoudid. Brunner, J.
INCEST
  Hauptmann, G. The heretic of Soana
  McEwan, I. Homemade
  Maupassant, G. de. The hermit
  Sargent, P. Clone sister
  Thomas, D. The burning baby
Incest. Updike, J.
An incident. Lu, Hsün
Incident after. Henderson, Z.
An incident at Krechetovka Station. Solzhenitsyn, A.
Incident at Owl Creek. Bierce, A.
Incident at Sumauma. Veiga, J. J.
Incident in a store. Trevisan, D.
Incident in Azania. Waugh, E.
Incident on a lake. Collier, J.
Incident on Galiano Street. Bahr, J.
Incipit vita nova. Hesse, H.
The incredible elopement of Lord Peter Wimsey. Sayers, D. L.
The incubus. Guerard, A. J.
The indelible kind. Henderson, Z.
The independent voter at twilight. De Vries, P.
The indestructible Sarah B. at the age of eighty. Ruskay, S.
INDIA
  Brunner, J. The Vitanuls
  Jhabvala, R. P. An experience of India; 7 stories
  Yashpal. Short stories of Yashpal; 9 stories
    British occupation, 1765-1947
  Anand, M. R. The gold watch
  Hesse, H. Robert Aghion
  Kipling, R. At the end of the passage
  Kipling, R. A bank fraud
  Kipling, R. Beyond the pale
  Kipling, R. The incarnation of Krishna Mulvaney
  Kipling, R. The Maltese Cat
  Kipling, R. The man who was

INDIA—British occupation, 1765-1947—*Continued*

Kipling, R. The man who would be king
Kipling, R. The mark of the beast
Kipling, R. The miracle of Purun Bhagat
Kipling, R. Moti Guj—mutineer
Kipling, R. My own true ghost story
Kipling, R. The phantom 'rickshaw
Kipling, R. The return of Imray
Kipling, R.   A second-rate woman
Kipling, R. The story of Muhammad Din
Kipling, R. The strange ride of Morrowbie Jukes
Kipling, R. Wee Willie Winkie
Kipling, R. Without benefit of clergy
Linklater, E. Country-born
Linklater, E. The prison of Cooch Perwanee
Maupassant, G. de. Châli
Morrow, W. C. His unconquerable enemy
Premchand. Intoxication
Premchand.   A little trick
Premchand.   A moral victory
Premchand. My big brother
Premchand. Penalty
Singh, K. Karma
Smith, C. A. The ghost of Mohammed Din
Smith, C. A. The mahout
Smith, C. A. The Raja and the tiger
Yashpal. The Emperor's justice
Yashpal. Sāg

### 1947-

Amarkant. Assassins
Bednarz, W. Bracelet of destruction
Bloch, R. Untouchable
Buck, P. S. The sacred skull
Gyanranjan. Our side of the fence and theirs
Jhabvala, R. P. An experience of India
Jhabvala, R. P. The housewife
Jhabvala, R. P. Rose petals
Jhabvala, R. P.   A star and two girls
Joshi, S. Big brother
Kishore, G. Relationship
Miller, C. T. Where they burn the dead
Naipaul, V. S. Tell me who to kill
Ramu Rau, S. Who cares?
Ramkumar. Sailor

#### Bombay

Buck, P. S. Sunrise at Juhu
Jhabvala, R. P.   A bad woman
Rama Rau, S. Who cares

#### Calcutta

Bakshi, R. Empty

#### Caste

*See* Brahmans

#### Daspur

Kotzwinkle, W. Elephant's graveyard

#### Delhi

Kamleshwar.   A death in Delhi
Theroux, P. Sinning with Annie
Yadav, R.   A reminder

#### Farm life

*See* Farm life—India

#### Lahore

Yashpal. The essence of love
Yashpal. To uphold righteousness

#### Marriage customs and rites

*See* Marriage customs and rites—India

#### New Delhi

Jhabvala, R. P. My first marriage

#### Politics

*See* Politics—India

#### Race problems

Kipling, R. Beyond the pale

#### Religion

Premchand.   A day in the life of a debt-collector
Premchand.   A feast for the holy man
White, R. First voice
Yashpal. To uphold righteousness
*See also* Brahmans

#### Simla

Kipling, R. At the pit's mouth

## INDIA, PROVINCIAL AND RURAL

Ahmad, I. Grandma
Aldiss, B. W. Orgy of the living and the dying
Anand, M. R. Birth
Anand, M. R. The man who loved monkeys more than human beings
Bhatty, M. The Resin-man
Dhumketu. The letter
Kipling, R. Letting in the jungle
Kipling, R. The spring running
Kipling, R. 'Tiger! Tiger!'
Linklater, E. Pathans
Middleton, J. A. Black magic
Narayan, R. K. Annamalai
Narayan, R. K.   A breath of Lucifer
Narayan, R. K.   A horse and two goats
Narayan, R. K. Seventh House
Narayan, R. K. Uncle
Phanishwarnath "Renu." The third vow
Premchand.   A catastrophe
Premchand.   A coward
Premchand.   A day in the life of a debt-collector
Premchand. Deliverance
Premchand.   A desperate case
Premchand.   A feast for the holy man
Premchand. January night
Premchand.   A lesson in the holy life
Premchand. Man's highest duty
Premchand. Neyur
Premchand. The power of a curse
Premchand. The price of milk
Premchand. The road to hell
Premchand. The road to salvation
Premchand. The shroud
Premchand. The Thakur's well
Pritam, A. The weed
Rajagopalachari, C. The nose jewel
Rakesh, M. Miss Pall
Shahu, M. N. The sun of the blind night
Smith, C. A. The justice of the elephant
Yashpal. The book of experience
Yashpal. A name for the painting
Yashpal. One cigarette
Yashpal. Purchased happiness
Yashpal. Two desperate souls

The **inn**. Turgenev, I.

**Innes, Michael**
  Comedy of discomfiture
    Ellery Queen's Mystery Magazine. El-
    lery Queen's Mystery bag
    *For other stories by this author see*
    Stewart, J. I. M.

**INNKEEPERS.** *See* Hotels, taverns, etc.

**Innocence.** Brodkey, H.

**Innocence.** O'Faoláin, S.

The **innocent**. Greene, G.

The **innocent**. Wain, J.

The **innocents**. Soto, P. J.

The **innocents** 1218. Coolidge, O.

**INNS.** *See* Hotels, taverns, etc.

**Innsmouth** clay. Lovecraft, H. P.

**INQUISITION**
  Poe, E. A. The pit and the pendulum
  Reynolds, G. W. M. The tribunal of the
    inquisition

**Ins** and outs. Stern, R.

**INSANE.** *See* Insanity

**INSANE ASYLUMS.** *See* Mentally ill—Care
  and treatment

**INSANE HOSPITALS.** *See* Mentally ill—
  Care and treatment

**INSANITY**
  Aldiss, B.  A pleasure shared
  Algren, N. The mad laundress of Ding-
    dong-Daddyland
  Arnim, A. von. The mad veteran of Fort
    Ratonneau
  The Astrologer's prediction
  Betts, D. The glory of his nostrils
  Bierce, A. The man out of the nose
  Bloch, R. Beelzebub
  Boyle, K. Your body is a jewel box
  Bradbury, R. August 1999: the Earth men
  Brown, F. Something green
  Brú, H. The long darkness
  Bryant, E. The hanged man
  Bukowski, C. Night streets of madness
  Cassill, R. V. The invention of the air-
    plane
  Collier, J. Special delivery
  Collins, W. Mad Monkton
  Copper, B. The knocker at the portico
  Crane, S. The squire's madness
  Durrell, L. The cherries
  Ellison, H. The beast that shouted love
    at the heart of the world
  Friedman, B. J. The enemy
  Garshin, V. The red flower
  Graham, W. The Cornish farm
  Greene, G.  A little place off the Edg-
    ware Road
  Hamilton, A. End of the road
  Hecht, F. M. Twin bed bridge
  Herlihy, J. L. Love and the buffalo
  Hesse, H.  A man by the name of Ziegler
  Ibuse, M. Lieutenant Lookeast
  Jacobi, C. The unpleasantness at Carver
    House
  Kaplan, B. Ben Early is raving
  Kuttner, H. Dream's end
  Landolfi, T. Cancerqueen
  Landolfi, T. Week of sun
  Lee, V.  A phantom lover

Leiber, F. The haunted future

Lu, Hsün.  A madman's diary

Maupassant, G. de. At the mountain inn

Mergendahl, C. Secret recipe

Millay, E. St V. The murder in the Fishing Cat

Mitchell, E. P. Exchanging their souls

Nesin, A. There is a nut on the roof

Newman, A. Such a good idea

Niland, D. The sound and the silence

O'Donnell, E. The haunted spinney

O'Hara, J. The decision

Olson, D. The blue tambourine

Pirandello, L. In the abyss

Powell, J. Maze in the elevator

Priestley, J. B. The grey ones

Ribnikar, J. You

Sartre, J. P. The room

Singer, I. B. The slaughterer

Smith, C. A. The supernumerary corpse

Stevenson, R. L. The merry men

Val Baker, D. The face in the mirror
    *See also* Hallucinations and illusions;
    Mental illness; Mentally ill—Care and
    treatment; Personality, Disorders of

**INSCRIPTIONS, ASSYRIAN.** *See* Cuneiform inscriptions

**INSCRIPTIONS, CUNEIFORM.** *See* Cuneiform inscriptions

**INSECTS**
  Bretnor, R. The gnurrs come from the
    voodvork out
  Clarke, A. C. The awakening
  Heald, H. Winged death
  Long, F. B. The last men
  Sheckley, R. Down the digestive tract and
    into the cosmos with Mantra, Tantra,
    and Specklebang
  White, T. Stella
    *See also* names of specific insects, e.g.
    Cockroaches; Flies; Praying mantis; etc.

The **insects**. Fast, H.

**Inside.** Carr, C.

**Inside** and outside. Hesse, H.

The **inside** of the earth. Mitchell, E. P.

**Inside** straight. Anderson, P.

An **inside** straight. Blanc, S.

**INSOMNIA**
  Ballard, J. G. Manhole 69
  Bukowski, C. The blanket
  Costello, M. Strong is your hold O love
  Hemingway, E. Now I lay me
  Parker, D. The little hours
  Svevo, I. Generous wine
  Trevisan, D. Creatures of the night

**Inspector** Maigret hesitates. Simenon, G.

**Inspector** Maigret's war of nerves. Simenon, G.

**Inspiration.** Babel, I.

The **inspiration** of Mr Budd. Sayers, D. L.

The **Inspired** Chicken Motel. Bradbury, R.

**Instant** of the hour after. McCullers, C.

The **institute.** Emshwiller, C.

**INSTITUTIONAL CARE.** *See* Children—
  Institutional care

**Instructions** for John Howell. Cortázar, J.

**INSTRUCTORS.** *See* Teachers

An **insubstantial** father. Warner, L.

Irving, Washington—*Continued*
 Guests from Gibbet Island
  Bowman, J. S. ed.  A book of islands
 The legend of Sleepy Hollow
  Green, R. L. ed. Thirteen uncanny tales
Irwin, Margaret
 The book
  Haining, P. ed. The Satanists
  Kahn, J. ed. Some things strange and
   sinister
Is it the end of the world? Shore, W.
Is there a doctor in the house? Allingham, M.
Is there life in inner space? Eisenberg, L.
Isaac. Michaels, L.
Isaac Starbuck. Sillitoe, A.
Isabo. Cuddon, J. A.
Isakovic, Antonije
 April Fool's Day
  Johnson, B. ed. New writing in Yugo-
   slavia
Ishmael in love. Silverberg, R.
Ishmael into the Barrens. Lafferty, R. A.
Isla, L. A.
 The case of the "Southern Arrow"
  Yates, D. A. ed. Latin blood
The island. Graham, W.
The island at noon. Cortázar, J.
The island dream. Hesse, H.
Island hunt. Holmes, E. M.
The island of Doctor Death, and other
  stories. Wolfe, G.
The island of the crabs. Dneprov, A.
The island of the endangered. Ferguson, D.
ISLANDS
 Aldiss, B. W. The hunter at his ease
 Bergé, C. The water ceremony
 Blackwood, A.  A haunted island
 Bryant, E. Shark
 Bulgakov, M. The Crimson Island
 Connell, R. The most dangerous game
 Coover, R. The magic poker
 Coover, R. Quenby and Ola, Swede and
  Carl
 Grau, S. A. Pillow of stone
 Holmes, E. M. Beyond Shadow Island
 Holmes, E. M. Fall fire
 Holmes, E. M. Island hunt
 Jacobsen, J. On the island
 Kazakov, Y. Adam and Eve
 Kazakov, Y. On the island
 Lafferty, R. A. Cliffs that laughed
 Lawrence, D. H. The man who loved
  islands
 Lovecraft, H. P. and Berkeley, E. The
  green meadow
 Maugham, W. S. German Harry
 Munson, G. Old Raccoon
 Nesvadba, J. Doctor Moreau's other island
 Sharp, M. The girl in the leopard-skin
  pants
 Sharp, M. Interlude at Spanish Harbour
 Sharp, M. Seal Tregarthen's cousin
 The Shipwrecked sailor
 Sindbad the Sailor. The first voyage of
  Sindbad the Sailor
 Smith, C. A. The uncharted isle
 Smith, Lady E. No ships pass
 Wilhelm, K. The fusion bomb

Wolfe, G. The death of Doctor Island
Yehoshua, A. B. Flood tide
  *See also* Atolls; Seashore; also names
   of islands or groups of islands, e.g. Aran
   Islands; Black Island, Labrador; St Paul
   Island; etc.
ISLANDS OF THE PACIFIC
 Ballard, J. G. The terminal beach
 Osbourne, L.  A son of empire
 Stern, J. Next door to death
 Stevenson, R. L. The beach of Falesá
  *See also* Aroe Islands
The Isle of Pines. Bierce, A.
The Isle of Voices. Stevenson, R. L.
ISLES DERNIERES. *See* Louisiana—Isles
 Dernieres
Ismael. Chester, A.
ISRAEL
 Aricha, Y. Night scene
 Ben-Amotz, D. Parents' Day
 Ben-Ner, Y. The tower
 Handel, Y. Zili and my friend Shaul
 Megged, A. An unusual deed
 Nissenson, H. Forcing the end
 Oz, A. The Trappist monastery
 Rabikovitz, D. ed. The new Israeli writers;
  14 stories
 Rabikovitz, D. Uri and Rachel
 Richler, M. This year at the Arabian
  Nights Hotel
 Shaham, N. Seven of them
 Singer, I. B. The mentor
 Tindall, G. Daddy
 Yehoshua, A. B. Facing the forests
 Yehoshua, A. B.  A poet's continuing
  silence
  *See also* Palestine
             **Army**
 Megged, A. The white city
 Raz, A. Oded Yarkoni's private war
        **Collective settlements**
  *See* Collective settlements—Israel
            **Farm life**
  *See* Farm life—Israel
            **Jerusalem**
 Agnon, S. Y. The letter
 Agnon, S. Y. The night
 Agnon, S. Y. Tehilah
 Bar-Yosef, Y. The window
 Boulle, P. The holy places
 Nissenson, H. The crazy old man
 Orlav, O. My daughter
 Robertson, J. W. She went to buy yarn
 Silk, D. Montefiore
 Silk, D. Porfiri and Esthalina
 Yaari, Y. The wanderer and the blind man
 Yehoshua, A. B.  A long hot day
 Yehoshua, A. B. Three days and a child
            **Kibbutzim**
  *See* Collective settlements—Israel
            **Tel-Aviv**
 Kaniuk, Y. The parched earth
 Nissenson, H. The throne of good
 Shamir, M. Mother of the oleanders
ISRAEL, PROVINCIAL AND RURAL
 Orpaz, Y. The wild plant

## ITALY, PROVINCIAL AND RURAL
Cheever, J. Montraldo
Di Donato, P. I killed Maria Goretti
McCarthy, M. The hounds of summer
Moravia, A. Contact with the working class
Verga, G. The last day
Verga, G. Stinkpot
Verga, G. Temptation
An **item** of supporting evidence. Lumley, B.
The **itinerary** of beggars. Francis, H. E.
**It's** a good life. Bixby, J.
**It's** a long time ago. Cardoso, O. J.
**It's** a lousy world. Pronzini, B.
**It's** all for the worse. Hippius, Z.
**It's** cold out there. Buchan, P.
**It's** not enough. Strindberg, A.
**It's** such a beautiful day. Asimov, I.
**Its** walls were as of jasper. Grahame, K.
**It's** you! Sturgeon, T.
**Itsikl** the mamzer. Shapiro, L.
**Ivanov, Vsevolod**
The child
Pomorski, K. ed. Fifty years of Russian prose: from Pasternak to Solzhenitsyn v 1
Same as: The kid, entered in 1950-1954 and 1955-1958 supplements
Sisyphus, the son of Aeolus
Rottensteiner, F. ed. View from another shore
The **ivory** comb. Sang, N.
**Ivy** day in the Committee Room. Joyce, J.
The **Izu** dancer. Kawabata, Y.

# J

**J**-line to nowhere. Henderson, Z.
**J.** / sleep. Miller, J.
**J's** marriage. Coover, R.
The **jack.** Ruskay, S.
**Jack**-a-Boy. Cather, W.
**Jack** and the beanstalk. Spencer, E.
**Jack** fell down. Brunner, J.
The **Jack** Gang. Moravia, A.
**Jack** of Newbury and the widow. Deloney, T.
**JACK THE RIPPER**
Bloch, R. A toy for Juliette
Ellison, H. The prowler in the city at the edge of the world
**JACKALS**
Kafka, F. Jackals and Arabs
**Jackals** and Arabs. Kafka, F.
**Jackal's** meal. Dickson, G. R.
**Jacka's** fight. Graham, W.
**JACKETS**
Ulyansky, A. The fleecy jacket
**Jackson, C. R.** *See* Jackson, Charles
**Jackson, Charles**
A night visitor
Insights
**Jackson, Shirley**
The lottery
Abrahams, W. ed. Fifty years of the American short story v 1
Hall, J. B. ed. The realm of fiction
Minot, S. and Wilson, R. eds. Three stances of modern fiction

The lovely house
Manley, S. and Lewis, G. eds. Ladies of horror
One ordinary day, with peanuts
Knight, D. ed. A science fiction argosy
The possibility of evil
Bernkopf, J. F. comp. Boucher's choicest
The witch
Taylor, J. C. ed. The short story: fiction in transition
**Jacob** and the Indians. Benét, S. V.
**Jacob** and the other. Onetti, J. C.
**Jacobi, Carl**
The aquarium
Jacobi, C. Disclosures in scarlet
The cocomacaque
Jacobi, C. Disclosures in scarlet
Exit Mr Smith
Jacobi, C. Disclosures in scarlet
The gentleman is an Epwa
Jacobi, C. Disclosures in scarlet
Gentlemen, the scavengers
Jacobi, C. Disclosures in scarlet
Kincaid's car
Jacobi, C. Disclosures in scarlet
Mr Iper of Hamilton
Jacobi, C. Disclosures in scarlet
The player at Yellow Silence
Jacobi, C. Disclosures in scarlet
The random quantity
Jacobi, C. Disclosures in scarlet
Round Robin
Jacobi, C. Disclosures in scarlet
The royal opera house
Jacobi, C. Disclosures in scarlet
Sequence
Jacobi, C. Disclosures in scarlet
The Singleton barrier
Derleth, A. ed. Dark things
Jacobi, C. Disclosures in scarlet
Strangers to Straba
Jacobi, C. Disclosures in scarlet
The unpleasantness at Carver House
Jacobi, C. Disclosures in scarlet
The war of the weeds
Jacobi, C. Disclosures in scarlet
The white pinnacle
Jacobi, C. Disclosures in scarlet
**Jacobs, Harvey**
A break in the weather
Jacobs, H. The egg of the Glak, and other stories
A disturbance of the peace
Jacobs, H. The egg of the Glak, and other stories
The egg of the Glak
The Best from Fantasy and Science Fiction; 18th ser.
Jacobs, H. The egg of the Glak, and other stories
Epilogue
Jacobs, H. The egg of the Glak, and other stories
The girl who drew the gods
Jacobs, H. The egg of the Glak, and other stories

**James, Henry, 1843-1916**—*Continued*
Osborne's revenge
 James, H. The tales of Henry James v 1
Owen Wingrave
 James, H. Henry James: stories of the
   supernatural
Poor Richard
 James, H. The tales of Henry James v 1
The private life
 James, H. Henry James: stories of the
   supernatural
A problem
 James, H. The tales of Henry James v 1
The pupil
 Spinner, S. ed. Live and learn
The real thing
 Foff, A. and Knapp, D. eds. Story
The real right thing
 James, H. Henry James: stories of the
   supernatural
The romance of certain old clothes
 James, H. Henry James: stories of the
   supernatural
 James, H. The tales of Henry James v 1
Sir Dominick Ferrand
 James, H. Henry James: stories of the
   supernatural
Sir Edmund Orme
 James, H. Henry James: stories of the
   supernatural
The story of a masterpiece
 James, H. The tales of Henry James v 1
The story of a year
 James, H. The tales of Henry James v 1
The third person
 James, H. Henry James: stories of the
   supernatural
A tragedy of error
 James, H. The tales of Henry James v 1
The turn of the screw
 James, H. Henry James: stories of the
   supernatural
 James, H. The spoils of Poynton, and
   other stories

**James, M. R.**
An episode of Cathedral history
 Haining, P. ed. Vampires at midnight
The haunted dolls' house
 Dickinson, S. ed. The usurping ghost,
   and other encounters and experiences
 Green, R. L. ed. Thirteen uncanny tales
 Haining, P. ed. Nightfrights
Lost hearts
 Kahn, J. ed. Hanging by a thread
The mezzotint
 Howes, B. and Smith, G. J. eds. The
   sea-green horse
A school story
 Haining, P. ed. The nightmare reader
The stalls of Barchester Cathedral
 Montgomery, J. ed. The world's best
   cat stories
 Necker, C. ed. Supernatural cats
A warning to the curious
 Manley, S. and Lewis, G. eds. Shapes
   of the supernatural

**James, P. D.**
Moment of power
 Ellery Queen's Mystery Magazine. El-
   lery Queen's Murder menu
**James.** Dickson, G. R.
**Jameson, Malcolm**
Tricky tonnage
 Harrison, H. ed. Worlds of wonder
Jan Schalken's three wishes
 Haining, P. ed. Gothic tales of terror
**Jane,** Gaskell, J.
**Jane.** Sitati, P.
**Jane crying.** Sallis, J.
**Jane gets off the fairway.** Wodehouse, P. G.
**Jane in search of a job.** Christie, A.
**Janifer, Laurence M.**
Thine alabaster cities gleam
 Elwood, R. ed. Future city
The **Janissaries** of Emilion. Cooper, B.
**JANITORS**
Curley, D. The day of the equinox
Disch, T. M. Now is forever
McPherson, J. A. Gold Coast
Malamud, B. The bill
Neugeboren, J. Finkel
**Jansson, Tove**
The fillyjonk who believed in disasters
 Authors' choice
**January night.** Premchand
**January 1999: rocket summer.** Bradbury, R.
**Janus.** Tabori, P.
**JAPAN**
Uyeda, A. Tales of moonlight and rain;
 9 stories
 **15th century**
Uyeda, A. Homecoming
Uyeda, A. Prophesy
 **17th century**
Ibuse, M. Yosaku the settler
 **19th-20th century**
Buck, P. S. The enemy
Ibuse, M. Carp
Ibuse, M. Life at Mr Tange's
Kawabata, Y. House of the sleeping beau-
 ties
Kawabata, Y. The Izu dancer
Kawabata, Y. Of birds and beasts
Mishima, Y. Death in midsummer
Mishima, Y. The pearl
Mishima, Y. Three million yen
Noma, H.  A red moon in her face
Shiina, R. The go-between
Shiina, R. Midnight banquet
Shūsei, T. Order of the White Paulownia
Stover, L. E. What we have here is too
 much communication
 **College life**
 *See* College life—Japan
 **Kyōto**
Hearn, L. The reconciliation
 **Legends and folk tales**
 *See* Legends and folk tales—Japan
 **Marriage customs and rites**
 *See* Marriage customs and rites—
Japan

JAPAN—*Continued*

**Politics**

*See* Politics—Japan

**School life**

*See* School life—Japan

**Tokyo**

Algren, N. No cumshaw no rickshaw

Ibuse, M. Plum blossom by night

Osamu, D. Villon's wife

Tuohy, F. The broken bridge

**JAPAN, PROVINCIAL AND RURAL**

Ibuse, M. Lieutenant Lookeast

Ibuse, M. Old Ushitora

Ibuse, M. Pilgrims' Inn

Ibuse, M. Tajinko Village

The **Japanese** girl. Graham, W.

**JAPANESE IN ENGLAND**

Graham, W. The Japanese girl

**JAPANESE IN HAWAII**

Beekman, A. All our yesterdays

Beekman, A. Dog spirit

Beekman, A. Mr Maki and the new order

Beekman, A. No place beneath the rising sun

Beekman, A. Ordeal by fire

Beekman, A. Point of view

**JAPANESE IN THE UNITED STATES**

Drake, A. The chicken which became a rat

Roth, H. H. From image to expression

**JAPANESE LEGENDS AND FOLK TALES.** *See* Legends and folk tales —Japan

**JAPANESE QUINCE.** *See* Quince

The **Japanese** quince. Galsworthy, J.

**JAPANESE SOLDIERS.** *See* Soldiers, Japanese

**Jarley's.** Thomas, D.

The **jawbone.** Galey, J. H.

**Jay, B.**

Callie

Alabama prize stories, 1970

**Jayme, William North**

I will please come to order

Bernkopf, J. F. comp. Boucher's choicest

**JAZZ MUSIC**

Baldwin, J. Sonny's blues

Brown, F. L. McDougal

McPherson, J. A. Private domain

Marsh, W. Mending wall

Tilley, R. J. Something else

**Je** suis perdu. Taylor, P.

**JEALOUSY**

Agnon, S. Y. The doctor's divorce

Aldiss, B. W. The young soldier's horoscope

Babel, I. Begrat, Ogly and the eyes of his bull

Bahr, J. Daniel and the boulder

Borges, J. L. The intruder

Bowles, P. The echo

Branson, R. The red-headed murderess

Brautigan, R. The literary life in California/1964

Brennan, J. P. Death at Draleman's Pond

Bridges, T. Music to lay eggs by

Colette. The dead end

Colter, C. A gift

Colter, C. The lookout

Corvo, F. Baron. About Our Lady of Dreams

Drake, N. The Abbey of Clunedale

Gill, B. Fat girl

Giraldi, G. B. The Moor of Venice

Heinesen, W. The night of the storm

Himes, C. The night's for cryin'

James, H. The romance of certain old clothes

Maupassant, G. de. Am I insane?

Maupassant, G. de. A wife's confession

Mayberry, F. V. The beauty in that house

O'Hara, J. The favor

Orpaz, Y. The wild plant

Parker, D. Cousin Larry

Parker, D. Just a little one

Parker, D. The last tea

Parker, D. The sexes

Peterkin, J. Plum blossoms

Sié, Cheou-kang. Vinegar

Singer, I. B. The prodigy

Stein, G. Q.E.D.

Unamuno y Jugo, M. de. Abel Sanchez

Vos, H. The sons of Pepe Gimenez

Wyndham, J. Jizzle

**Jean** Duprès. Dickson, G. R.

**Jean-Francois** Bluestockings. Nodier, C.

**Jeanne.** Mallet-Joris, F.

**JEFFERSON, THOMAS, PRESIDENT U.S.**

Butor, M. Welcome to Utah

**Jeffrey, William**

Shell game

Best detective stories of the year, 1973

The **jelly** woman. Ruskay, S.

**Jenkins, Will F.** *See* Leinster, Murray

**Jennings, Gary**

Sooner or later or never never

The Best from Fantasy & Science Fiction; 20th ser.

**Jenny** among the zeebs. Anmar, F.

**Jenny** Garrow's lovers. Jewett, S. O.

**Jenny** with wings. Wilhelm, K.

**Jepsen, Hans Lyngby**

The blackbird

Holm, S. ed. The Devil's instrument, and other Danish stories

**Jepson, Edgar, and Eustace, Robert**

The tea-leaf

Dickinson, S. ed. The drugged cornet, and other mystery stories

**Jeremey,** his arrangements. Zieroth, D.

**Jeremiad.** Sallis, J.

**Jericho's** brick battlements. Laurence, M.

**Jerry** Horn: man of steel. Fowler, D.

**JERUSALEM.** *See* Israel—Jerusalem; Palestine—Jerusalem

**Jesby, Ed**

Ogre!

The Best from Fantasy and Science Fiction; 18th ser.

Sea wrack

Knight, D. ed. A science fiction argosy

**Jesse, F. Tennyson**

The black veil

Kahn, J. ed. Trial and terror

**Jesse** had a wife. Schultz, J.
**Jessica** / tenderly. Miller, J.
**JESTERS.** *See* Fools and jesters
The **jesting** inquisitor. Sabadino degli Arienti
**JESUITS**
    Corvo, F. Baron. About Sanvenanzio, Santagapito, and Padre Dotto Vagheggino, S.J.
    Corvo, F. Baron. About Sodom, Gomorrah, and the two admirable Jesuits
    Meyer, C. F. The sufferings of a boy
    Sanders, W. P. The word to space
**JESUS CHRIST**
    Babel, I. The sin of Jesus
    Clarke, J. H. The boy who painted Christ Black
    Meek, F. M. The fourth wise man's detour
    Meek, F. M. He gave more than he knew
    Meek, F. M. Mary and the seven birthdays
    Pekić, B. The miracle in Cana
    Sarduy, S. From Cuba with a song
    Updike, J. Jesus on Honshu
### Crucifixion
    Graham, W. But for the grace of God
    Robertson, J. W. She went to buy yarn
### Nativity
    Goudge, E. The two caves
    Meek, F. M. The Bethlehem Inn
    Meek, F. M. The little shepherd
    Meek, F. M. The soldier and the census
    Meek, F. M. Tell me His name
    Meek, F. M. They see, but they do not understand
    Montgomery, J. The Christmas cat
### Resurrection
    Goudge, E. John
    Goudge, E. The two caves
**JESUS COLLEGE.** *See* Cambridge, England. University
**Jesus** on Honshu. Updike, J.
**Jesus** won't play any more. Borchert, W.
**JET PLANES**
    McLaughlin, D. Hawk among the sparrows
**Jet** set melodrama. Brownstein, M.
**Jetsam.** Chandler, A. B.
A **Jew** a farmer? Deutschman, B.
The **Jewbird.** Malamud, B.
The **jewel** of Amitaba. Kotzwinkle, W.
**JEWEL THIEVES**
    Allingham, M. The Allingham Case-book
    Allingham, M. The lieabout
    Allingham, M. Mum knows best
The **jeweled** butterfly. Gardner, E. S.
**JEWELERS**
    Naipaul, S. The tenant
    Woolf, V. The Duchess and the jeweller
The **jewelled** garden. Delattre, P.
**JEWELRY**
    Eisenberg, L. Is there life in inner space?
    Futrelle, J. The flaming phantom
    Lessing, D. Out of the fountain
    Maupassant, G. de. The false gems
    Pemberton, M. The ripening rubies
        *See also* jewelry items, e.g. Brooches; Earrings; Necklaces; Rings; etc.

**JEWELS.** *See* Jewelry; Precious stones; also types of jewels, e.g. Diamonds; Emeralds; Pearls; etc.
The **jewels.** *See* Maupassant, G. de. The false gems
The **jewels** of the Cabots. Cheever, J.
The **Jewess.** Babel, I.
**Jewett, Sarah Orne**
    The Becket girls' tree
        Jewett, S. O. The uncollected short stories of Sarah Orne Jewett
    A born farmer
        Jewett, S. O. The uncollected short stories of Sarah Orne Jewett
    A change of heart
        Jewett, S. O. The uncollected short stories of Sarah Orne Jewett
    A Christmas guest
        Jewett, S. O. The uncollected short stories of Sarah Orne Jewett
    A dark carpet
        Jewett, S. O. The uncollected short stories of Sarah Orne Jewett
    A dark night
        Jewett, S. O. The uncollected short stories of Sarah Orne Jewett
    Elleneen
        Jewett, S. O. The uncollected short stories of Sarah Orne Jewett
    An empty purse
        Jewett, S. O. The uncollected short stories of Sarah Orne Jewett
    An every-day girl
        Jewett, S. O. The uncollected short stories of Sarah Orne Jewett
    A financial failure: the story of a New England wooing
        Jewett, S. O. The uncollected short stories of Sarah Orne Jewett
    The first Sunday in June
        Jewett, S. O. The uncollected short stories of Sarah Orne Jewett
    The foreigner
        Jewett, S. O. The uncollected short stories of Sarah Orne Jewett
    A garden story
        Jewett, S. O.    A visit next door
    The girl with the cannon dresses
        Jewett, S. O. The uncollected short stories of Sarah Orne Jewett
    The gray man
        Westbrook, P. D. ed. Seacoast and upland: a New England anthology
    The gray mills of Farley
        Jewett, S. O. The uncollected short stories of Sarah Orne Jewett
        Westbrook, P. D. ed. Seacoast and upland: a New England anthology
    The green bonnet: a story of Easter day
        Jewett, S. O. The uncollected short stories of Sarah Orne Jewett
    The green bowl
        Jewett, S. O. The uncollected short stories of Sarah Orne Jewett
    The Growtown "Bugle"
        Jewett, S. O. The uncollected short stories of Sarah Orne Jewett

## JEWS IN THE UNITED STATES—*Continued*

### Boston
Mirsky, M. J. Mourner's Kaddish
Sara. So I'm not Lady Chatterley so better I should know it now
### Bridgeport
Butenas, N. The girl that had no face
### Chicago
Elkin, S. The condominium
### Cleveland
Sinclair, J. The medal
### Connecticut
Zeldis, C. The golem
### Long Island
Deutschman, B. So this is called success?
### Louisiana
Ansell, J. Blackberry winter
Ansell, J. The only one in town
### Middle West
Ferber, E. The fast
### New Jersey
Granit, A. Come into the hallway, for 5 cents!
Roth, P. The Jewish blues
### New York (City)
Block, A. R. Sunday morning
Blum-Alquit, E. Amerika, Amerika
Blum-Alquit, E. Ata Bakhartaunu: thou hast chosen us
Blum-Alquit, E. Attorney Street
Blum-Alquit, E. In the light of Morris Rosenfeld
Blum-Alquit, E. One of the fiddlers two
Charyn, J. The man who grew younger
Charyn, J. Sing, Shaindele, sing
Elman, R. Timmy
Elman, R. M. Tit for tat
Friedman, P. An evening of fun
Hayes, R. E. The stigmata of the Rainy-Day Sun
Heyman, A. Strains of Iris
Horwitz, J. The strudel
Jacobs, H. The lion's share
Kobak, D. The winter soldiers
Malamud, B. Black is my favorite color
Malamud, B. God's wrath
Malamud, B. The Jewbird
Manoff, E. Mama and the spy
Markfield, W. The decline of Sholem Waldman
Michaels, L. Isaac
Neugeboren, J. Ebbets Field
Nissenson, H. Charity
Ozick, C. Envy
Ozick, C. Yiddish in America
Paley, G. Goodbye and good luck
Rees, B. Sidney, oh Sidney
Ribalow, H. U. Can you explain love?
Roth, P. Civilization and its discontents
Roth, P. Marriage à la mode
Ruskay, S. Allah will understand
Ruskay, S. The indestructible Sarah B. at the age of eighty
Ruskay, S. Why bother with Solly?

Salpeter, S. . . . thicker than water
Schiller, M. Mr Princeton
Singer, I. B. The cabalist of East Broadway
Singer, I. B. The cafeteria
Singer, I. B. Fate
Singer, I. B. A friend of Kafka
Singer, I. B. The joke
Singer, I. B. The key
Singer, I. B. Property
Singer, I. B. Schloimele
Singer, I. B. The séance
Singer, I. B. The son
Singer, I. B. A wedding in Brownsville
Taube, M. Epstein
Winslow, J. M. Benjamen burning
Zakin, L. P. The contract
### New York (City)—Bronx
Charyn, J. Farewell! . . . Farewell! . . .
### New York (City)—Brooklyn
Neugeboren, J. Elijah
Neugeboren, J. Something is rotten in the Borough of Brooklyn
### New York (City)—Manhattan
Neugeboren, J. Finkel
### Pennsylvania
Deutschman, B. In a small town a kid went to shul
### Southern States
Adams, A. The swastika on our door
### Virginia
Updike, J. Bech: a book

**JEWS IN VIRGINIA.** *See* Jews in the United States—Virginia

**JEWS OF TRENT.** *See* Jews—Persecutions

**Jhabvala, R. Prawer**
A bad woman
    Jhabvala, R. P. An experience of India
A course of English studies
    Jhabvala, R. P. An experience of India
An experience of India
    Jhabvala, R. P. An experience of India
The housewife
    Jhabvala, R. P. An experience of India
My first marriage
    Spinner, S. ed. Feminine plural
Rose petals
    Jhabvala, R. P. An experience of India
A star and two girls
    Jhabvala, R. P. An experience of India
Suffering women
    Jhabvala, R. P. An experience of India

**JILTING**
Lavin, M. The mouse
Saltus, E. Fausta
The **jilting** of Granny Wetherall. Porter, K. A.
**Jim** and Mary G. Sallis, J.
**Jim** Baker's bluejay yarn. Twain, M.
**Jim** Blaine and his grandfather's ram. Twain, M.
**Jimmy** Hayes and Muriel. Henry, O.
**Jim's** probation. Dunbar, P. L.
**Jingle** Bells. Vassilikos, V.
**JINN**
Collier, J. Bottle party
Davidson, A. A bottle full of kismet

Jinn. Green, J.
**JIUJITSU**
Deming, R. Black belt
**Jizzle.** Wyndham, J.
**João** Nicolau. Trevisan, D.
**João** Urso. Accioly, B.
**JOB INTERVIEWS.** *See* Employment interviewing
**JOBLESS.** *See* Unemployed
**JOBS.** *See* Occupations
**Jobs** in the sky. Slesinger, T.
The **jockey.** McCullers, C.
**JOCKEYS**
Algren, N. Bullring of the summer night
Algren, N. Moon of the arfy darfy
Hemingway, E. My old man
McCullers, C. The jockey
Watkins, R. H. The turf and the dirt
**Jodok** sends his love. Bichsel, P.
**Jody** after the war. Bryant, E.
**Jody** rolled the bones. Yates, R.
**Joe.** Neugeboren, J.
**Joe** College. Donohue, H. E. F.
**Joe,** the vanishing American. Swados, H.
**Joensen, Martin**
The "man" on board
Faroese short stories
To be a dentist
Faroese short stories
**JOHN, SAINT, APOSTLE**
Goudge, E. John
**John.** Goudge, E.
**John.** Henderson, D.
**John** Bartine's watch. Bierce, A.
**JOHN BIRCH SOCIETY**
Bullins, E. Support your local police
**John** Calder of Kelty. Ayrton, M.
**John** Charrington's wedding. Nesbit, E.
**John** Monahan. Bonner, P. H.
**John** Mortonson's funeral. Bierce, A.
**Johnny** Dio and the sugar plum burglars. Miller, H. D.
**Johnny** Panic and the Bible of Dreams. Plath, S.
**John's** other life. Haldeman, J.
**Johnson, B. S.**
Sheela-na-gig
Burke, J. ed. Tales of unease
**Johnson, Curt**
Trespasser
Prize stories, 1973: The O. Henry Awards
**Johnson, Denis**
The taking of our own lives
Minot, S. and Wilson, R. eds. Three stances of modern fiction
**Johnson, Diane**
An apple, an orange
Prize stories, 1973: The O. Henry Awards
**Johnson, Dorothy M.**
Lost sister
Lucia, E. ed. This land around us
The unbeliever
Taylor, J. G. ed. Great Western short stories
**Johnson, Evelyn, and Palmer, Gretta**
Finger prints can't lie
Manley, S. and Lewis, G. eds. Grande dames of detection

**Johnson, Lemuel**
Melon flowers
Angoff, C. and Povey, J. eds. African writing today
**JOHNSON, LYNDON BAINES, PRESIDENT U.S.**
Parodies, travesties, etc.
Ferlinghetti, L. Where is Vietnam?
**Johnson, Myra Crawford**
Wild bouquet
Alabama prize stories, 1970
**Johnson, Pamela Hansford**
The empty schoolroom
Kahn, J. ed. Some things strange and sinister
**JOHNSON, SAMUEL**
De La Torre, L. The Monbodda ape boy
The **Johnson** girls. Bambara, T. C.
**JOINVILLE, JEAN, SIRE DE**
Collidge, O. The Saint 1298
The **joke.** Singer, I. B.
**Joke** over. Allingham, M.
**Joker** for hire. Goulart, R.
**JOKES.** *See* Humor
**JOKES, PRACTICAL.** *See* Humor—Practical jokes
The **jolly** corner. James, H.
**Jonas, Gerald**
The Shaker revival
Disch, T. M. ed. The ruins of earth
**Jones, Ann**
The anybody notes
Jones, A. Hope should always
In black and white
The Best American short stories, 1972
A dream of singing
Jones, A. Hope should always
Emancipation day
Jones, A. Hope should always
Hope should always
Jones, A. Hope should always
If all the world were listening
Jones, A. Hope should always
The phantom of Pear Tree Heights
Jones, A. Hope should always
The sixth age is ascribed to Jupiter
Jones, A. Hope should always
The very special dead people
Jones, A. Hope should always
**Jones, Buster Lloyd-** *See* Lloyd-Jones, Buster
**Jones, Eldred**
Show me first your penny
Angoff, C. and Povey, J. eds. African writing today
**JONES, JAMES**
Parodies, travesties, etc.
De Vries, P. From there to infinity
**Jones, John J.**
The passing of Big Joe
Andrews, F. E. and Dickens, A. eds. Voices from the big house
**Jones, Langdon**
The coming of the sun
Jones, L. The eye of the lens
SF: authors' choice 3
The eye of the lens
Jones, L. The eye of the lens

JOURNALISTS—*Continued*
O'Hara, J. The first day
O'Hara, J. The lady takes an interest
O'Hara, J. Pilgrimage
O'Hara, J. The skipper
Roditi, E. The vampires of Istanbul: a study in modern communications methods
Russell, E. F. Mutants for sale
St Clair, M. Counter charm
Schwimmer, W. No story
Simak, C. D. Neighbor
Stern, R. East, West . . . Midwest
Stern, R. Ins and outs
Theridion, P. Obituary
Tyrmand, L.  A cocktail party
Wain, J.  A man in a million
Ward, J. Three Washington stories: The brigadier general and the columnist's wife
West, N. "Shrike and Mrs Shrike"
Wolfe, B. The bisquit position
*See also* Authors; Editors; Women as journalists

JOURNALS. *See* Diaries (Stories in diary form)

Journey around my room. Bogan, L.
Journey back to the source. Carpentier, A.
Journey through the night. Lind, J.
Journey to Enog. Maclagan, D.
Journey to Ocean Grove. Minot, S.
Journey to the center of the room. De Vries, P.
A journey to the moon; abridged. Cyrano de Bergerac
Journey to the seed. Carpentier, A.
A journey with a nihilist. Leskov, N.

JOURNEYS. *See* Ocean travel

Journeys end. Anderson, P.

JOVIANS. *See* Jupiter (Planet)

Joy and confusion. Brownstein, M.

JOY AND SORROW
Böll, H. My sad face
Böll, H. Rise, my love, rise
Brodeur, P. Hydrography
Cather, W. Eleanor's house
Chekhov, A. Heartache
Hippius, Z. The pilgrim
Keeling, N. The year
Mishima, Y. Death in midsummer
Oates, J. C. The heavy sorrow of the body
Price, R. The happiness of others
Shaw, I. Where all things wise and fair descend
Stewart, N. Grief
Washington, J. It only happens once
Joy as it flies, Linklater, E.
The joy of Nelly Deane. Cather, W.
Joyce, James
Araby
Davis, R. G. ed. Ten modern masters
Foff, A. and Knapp, D. eds. Story
Konigsberg, I. ed. The classic short story
12 short story writers
The boarding house
Konigsberg, I. ed. The classic short story
12 short story writers

Clay
Satin, J. ed. Reading literature
Counterparts
Davis, R. G. eds. Ten modern masters
Foff, A. and Knapp, D. eds. Story
Taylor, J. C. ed. The short story: fiction in transition
Thune, E. and Prigozy, R. eds. Short stories: a critical anthology
The dead
Davis, R. G. ed. Ten modern masters
12 short story writers
An encounter
Insights
Hell fire
Haining, P. ed. The wild night company: Irish stories of fantasy and horror
Ivy day in the Committee Room
Konigsberg, I. ed. The classic short story
A little cloud
Foff, A. and Knapp, D. eds. Story
A painful case
Tytell, J. and Jaffe, H. eds. Affinities
The sisters
Hall, J. B. ed. The realm of fiction
Joyce, William
Rats
Story: the yearbook of discovery/1969
Juan Muraña. Borges, J. L.
Juan, the Basque shepherd boy. Craven, M.
Jubilee. Greene, G.
JUDAISM
Agnon, S. Y. The tale of the scribe
Agnon, S. Y. Tehilah
Barwin, V. The call
Nissenson, H. Charity
Nissenson, H. Going up
Nissenson, H. In the reign of peace
Nissenson, H. Lamentations
Roth, P. The conversion of the Jews
Wiesel, E. The day without forgiveness
Winslow, J. M. Benjamen burning
*See also* Jews; Rabbis

Judas. Brunner, J.
Judas fish. Scortia, T. N.
The Judas tree. Moravia, A.
The judge. Colette
The Judge. Hughes, M. G.
The judge. Madsen, S. A.
Judge Crawford and his friends, including the governor. Estes, W. M.
Judgement Day. O'Connor, F.
JUDGES. *See* Law and lawyers
The Judge's House. Stoker, B.
The judgment. Kafka, F.
JUDGMENT DAY
Knight, D. Shall the dust praise thee?
Korolenko, V. Makar's dream
O'Donnell, K. M. Chronicles of a comer
Judgment day. De Camp, S. L.
JUDICIAL ERROR. *See* Miscarriage of justice
Judith. Farrell, J. T.
JUG BANDS. *See* Entertainers
A jug of sirup. Bierce, A.
JUGGLERS AND JUGGLING
Sié, Cheou-kang. The reward

JUJITSU. *See* Jiujitsu
Jujitsu. Taylor, E. R.
JUKE BOXES. *See* Jukeboxes
JUKEBOXES
Kanin, G. Do re mi
Julia Cahill's curse. Moore, G.
Julien, or not Julien? Hippius, Z.
Juliet and the magician. Peyrou, M.
Julius Pasternak and the Einstein letter. Rosenberg, E.
JULY REVOLUTION, 1830. *See* France—1815-1848
Jump. Earls, W.
Jump job. Rathjen, C. H.
Jump to Chicago. Farrell, J. T.
June 6, 2016. England, G. A.
June 2001:- and the moon be still as bright. Bradbury, R.
June 2003: way in the middle of the air. Bradbury, R.
The jungle of Lord Lion. Jacobsen, J.
JUNGLES
Conrad, J. Heart of darkness
Dickson, G. R. Jean Duprès
Goulart, R. The whole round world
Kersh, G. Crooked bone
Kipling, R. How fear came
Kipling, R. Kaa's hunting
Kipling, R. The King's ankus
Kipling, R. Letting in the jungle
Kipling, R. Mowgli's brothers
Kipling, R. Red Dog
Kipling, R. The spring running
Mrozek, S. The Ugupu bird
Thomas, J. W. Air Patrol
Junior partner. Goulart, R.
JUNK ART. *See* Found objects (Art)
JUNK DEALERS. *See* Junk trade
JUNK TRADE
Brautigan, R. The Cleveland Wrecking Yard
Petry, A. Mother Africa
JUPITER (GREEK GOD) *See* Zeus
JUPITER (PLANET)
Anderson, P. Call me Joe
Anderson, P. Que donn'rez vous?
Asimov, I. Not final!
Asimov, I. Victory unintentional
Blish, J. The Bridge
Clarke, A. C.  A meeting with Medusa
Malzberg, B. N. Making it through
Simak, C. D. Desertion
Jupiter Doke, Brigadier-General. Bierce, A.
JURY DUTY. *See* Trials
Just, Ward
The brigadier general and the columnist's wife
Just, W. The Congressman who loved Flaubert, and other Washington stories
Same as: Three Washington stories: The brigadier general and the columnist's wife
Burns
The Best American short stories, 1973
Just, W. The Congressman who loved Flaubert, and other Washington stories

The Congressman who loved Flaubert
Just, W. The Congressman who loved Flaubert, and other Washington stories
A guide to the architecture of Washington, D.C.
Just, W. The Congressman who loved Flaubert, and other Washington stories
Noone
Just, W. The Congressman who loved Flaubert, and other Washington stories
Same as: Three Washington stories: Noone
Nora
Just, W. The Congressman who loved Flaubert, and other Washington stories
Prime evening time
Just, W. The Congressman who loved Flaubert, and other Washington stories
Simpson's wife
Just, W. The Congressman who loved Flaubert, and other Washington stories
Slayton
Just, W. The Congressman who loved Flaubert, and other Washington stories
Same as: Three Washington stories: Slayton
Three Washington stories: Noone
The Best American short stories, 1972
Same as: Noone
Three Washington stories: Slayton
The Best American short stories, 1972
Same as: Slayton
Three Washington stories: The brigadier general and the columnist's wife
The Best American short stories, 1972
Same as: The brigadier general and the columnist's wife
Just a little one. Parker, D.
Just lather, that's all. Téllez, H.
Just like a tree. Gaines, E.
Just one small part of living. Naylor, P. R.
Just to be married. Strindberg, A.
Justice, Donald
The lady
Moss, H. ed. The poet's story
JUSTICE
Cather, W. El Dorado: a Kansas recessional
Chesnutt, C. W. The web of circumstance
France, A. Crainquebille
Kleist, H. von. Michael Kohlhaas
Meyer, C. F. The sufferings of a boy
Silverberg, R. Precedent
Tendryakov, V. Justice
See also Law and lawyers; Trials
JUSTICE, MISCARRIAGE OF. *See* Miscarriage of justice
Justice. Desnica, V.
Justice. Tendryakov, V.
Justice has a high price. McGeer, P.
Justice has no murder. Segre, A.
Justice, inc. Phillips, R.

Justice magnifique. Treat, L.
The justice of the elephant. Smith, C. A.
**JUVENILE DELINQUENCY**
Bloch, R. Spawn of the dark one
Bova, B. Blood of tyrants
Cather, W. Paul's case
Colter, C. Mary's convert
Frazer, C. Zydeco
Friedman, P. Never lose your cool
Glanville, B.   A bad streak
Greene, G.   A marriage proposal
Hawkes, J. The universal fears
Helwig, D. Something for Olivia's scrapbook I guess
Hemingway, E. The last good country
Hunter, K. Hero's return
Neugeboren, J. Luther
Oates, J. C. How I contemplated the world from the Detroit House of Correction and began my life over again
Oates, J. C. Norman and the killer
O'Connor, F. The comforts of home
O'Connor, F. The lame shall enter first
O'Connor, P. F. American Gothic
O'Connor, P. F. Matter of ages
Petry, A. The witness
Purdom, T. Toys
Queen, E. Object lesson
Rook, C. Billy the Snide
Rook, C. Concerning hooligans
Rook, C. Young Alf
Santiago, D. The somebody
Sillitoe, A. The loneliness of the long-distance runner
Stiles, G. Lines from the quick
Sturgeon, T. Jorry's gap
Tofte, A. The speeders
Trevor, W. Going home
Vezhinov, P. The boy with the violin
Waller, L. The restless ones
Weesner, T. Stealing cars
Zebrowski, G. Assassins of air
   See also Gangs; Malicious mischief

# K

Kaa's hunting. Kipling, R.
**KAFFIRS.** See Kafirs (African people)
**KAFIRS (AFRICAN PEOPLE)**
Jacobson, D. Beggar my neighbor
   See also Zulus

**Kafka, Franz**
Blumfeld, an elderly bachelor
   Kafka, F. The complete stories
The bucket rider
   Disch, R. and Schwartz, B. eds. Killing time
   Kafka, F. The complete stories
The burrow
   Kafka, F. The complete stories
Children on a country road
   Kafka, F. The complete stories
The conscription of troops
   Kafka, F. The complete stories

A country doctor
   Kafka, F. The complete stories
   Karl, F. R. and Hamalian, L. eds. The naked i
   Minot, S. and Wilson, R. eds. Three stances of modern fiction
   Thune, E. and Prigozy, R. eds. Short stories: a critical anthology
   Tytell, J. and Jaffe, H. eds. Affinities
Description of a struggle
   Kafka, F. The complete stories
A dream
   Kafka, F. The complete stories
Eleven sons
   Kafka, F. The complete stories
First sorrow
   Kafka, F. The complete stories
A fratricide
   Kafka, F. The complete stories
The Great Wall of China
   Kafka, F. The complete stories
A hunger artist
   Foff, A. and Knapp, D. eds. Story
   Kafka, F. The complete stories
   Minot, S. and Wilson, R. eds. Three stances of modern fiction
The Hunter Gracchus
   Davis, R. G. ed. Ten modern masters
   Kafka, F. The complete stories
The Hunter Gracchus: a fragment
   Kafka, F. The complete stories
In the penal colony
   Kafka, F. The complete stories
   Schulman, L. M. ed. The cracked looking glass
   Taylor, J. C. ed. The short story: fiction in transition
Investigations of a dog
   Kafka, F. The complete stories
Jackals and Arabs
   Hall, J. B. ed. The realm of fiction
   Kafka, F. The complete stories
Josephine the singer
   Kafka, F. The complete stories
The judgment
   Kafka, F. The complete stories
The knock at the manor gate
   Kahn, J. ed. Trial and terror
A little woman
   Kafka, F. The complete stories
The married couple
   Kafka, F. The complete stories
   Satin, J. ed. Reading literature
The metamorphosis
   Hamalian, L. and Volpe, E. L. eds. Eleven modern short novels
   Kafka, F. The complete stories
The nature Theatre of Oklahoma
   Fairy tales for computers
An old manuscript
   Kafka, F. The complete stories
   Same as: Old page, entered in 1950-1954 supplement
The refusal
   Kafka, F. The complete stories
A report to an Academy
   Kafka, F. The complete stories
A report to an Academy: two fragments
   Kafka, F. The complete stories

Kempton, Mike
Survivors
New American Review no. 14
Kenary, James S.
Going home
The Best American short stories, 1973
KENNEDY, JOHN FITZGERALD, PRES-
IDENT U.S.
Di Donato, P. Lunch with President Ken-
nedy
Assassination
O'Donnell, K. M. City lights, city nights
Kennedy, Milward
Death in the kitchen
Dickinson, S. ed. The drugged cornet,
and other mystery stories
Kennedy, Raymond
Room temperature
Lish, G. ed. The secret life of our times:
new fiction from Esquire
Kent, W. H. B.
Drake feeds the buzzards
Collier, N. ed. Great stories of the West
KENT. See England, Provincial and rural—
Kent
Kentfield, Calvin
The last one
Three: 1971
KENTUCKY
Fox, J. The army of the Callahan
Fox, J. Courtin' on Cutshin
Fox, J.  A crisis for the Guard
Fox, J. The pardon of Becky Day
Fox, J. The Senator's last trade
Madden, D. The singer
Stuart, J. Dawn of remembered spring
Stuart, J. King of the hills
Stuart, J. Maybelle's first-born
Stuart, J. Uncle Mel comes to the aid of
his clan
Stuart, J. Wild plums
Summers, H. Love
Farm life
See Farm life—Kentucky
KENYA
Arden, W. The savage
Gores, J. Odendahl
Ngugi, J.  A meeting in the dark
Oliver, C. Far from this earth
Nairobi
Sitati, P. Jane
KENYA COLONY AND PROTECTOR-
ATE. See Kenya
Kenyatta, Jomo
The man who shared his hut
Nolen, B. ed. Africa is thunder and
wonder
The kept hotel key. Ostaijen, P. van
KERAK, EL. See El Kerak
The kerchief. Agnon, S. Y.
KERCHIEFS. See Scarves
Kerfol. Wharton, E.
Kerr, David
Epiphany for aliens
Ellison, H. ed. Again, dangerous visions

Kersh, Gerald
Crooked bone
Hitchcock, A. ed. Alfred Hitchcock pre-
sents: A month of mystery
Dr Ox will die at midnight
Best detective stories of the year, 1971
Mr Tomorrow
Ellery Queen's Mystery Magazine. El-
lery Queen's Headliners
The Pettifer collection
Ellery Queen's Mystery Magazine. El-
lery Queen's Murder menu
The unsafe deposit box
Harrison, H. ed. The light fantastic
Kesey, Ken
Winter is here
Lucia, E. ed. This land around us
Kessel, Joseph
The escape
Kahn, J. ed. Trial and terror
Kessler, Jascha
The dowry
Ribalow, H. U. ed. My name aloud
Kessler, the inside man. Fox, G.
Kettle of stars. Sallis, J.
Kevles, Bettyann
Georgie in the middle
Furman, A. L. ed. Teen-age secret
agent stories
Mars-station
Furman, A. L. ed. Teen-age space ad-
ventures
The key. Singer, I. B.
The key to out. Curtis, B.
Keyes, Daniel
Flowers for Algernon
Science fiction hall of fame v 1
Keyhole. Leinster, M.
KEYS. See Locks and keys
The keys to December. Zelazny, R.
Khamhawm, Lao. See Khamsing, Srinawk
Khamsing, Srinawk
Breeding stock
Khamsing, S. The politician, and other
stories
Clash
Khamsing, S. The politician, and other
stories
Dark glasses
Khamsing, S. The politician, and other
stories
Dunghill
Khamsing, S. The politician, and other
stories
Dust underfoot
Khamsing, S. The politician, and other
stories
The gold-legged frog
Khamsing, S. The politician, and other
stories
Owners of Paradise
Khamsing, S. The politician, and other
stories
The peasant and the white man
Khamsing, S. The politician, and other
stories
The plank
Khamsing, S. The politician, and other
stories

Khamsing, Srinawk—*Continued*
The politician
  Khamsing, S. The politician, and other stories
Quack doctor
  Khamsing, S. The politician, and other stories
Sales reps for the underworld
  Khamsing, S. The politician, and other stories
Khlit. Lamb, H.
Kholendro, Dmitry
Barmalei
  Whitney, T. P. ed. The young Russians
Khvylovy, Mykola
My being
  Luckyj, G. S. N. ed. Modern Ukrainian short stories
  Same as: My self (Romantica), listed in 1959-1963 supplement
KIBBUTZ. *See* Collective settlements—Israel; Farm life—Israel
Kick. Molyneux, T. W.
The Kicking Twelfth. Crane, S.
The kid. *See* Ivanov, V. The child
Kid Stardust on the porterhouse. Bukowski, C.
Kiddy-Lib. Stopa, J.
Kidnapped Baby Blake, millionaire. Futrelle, J.
KIDNAPPING
Allingham, M.  A quarter of a million
Anderson, P. License
Anderson, P. The Queen of Air and Darkness
Brent, P. Mewed up
Bukowski, C. ⚔ [Swastika]
Christie, A. At the stroke of twelve
Francis, H. E. The itinerary of beggars
Gilbert, M. The amateur
Henry, O. The ransom of Red Chief
Hitchens, D. If you see this woman
Littke, L. J. The Brand X business
Morrison, A. The loss of Sammy Throckett
O'Neill, J. In the camp of the enemy
Pentecost, H. The day the children vanished
Pronzini, B. The snatch
Pugh, E. The inevitable thing
Runyon, D. The snatching of Bookie Bob
Vasillikos, V. The harpoon gun
Wallman, J. M. Ransom demand
Waugh, E. Incident in Azania
Woolrich, C. Mamie 'n' me
KIDNEY

### Diseases

Sherwin, J. J. Love in the human heart
The kids. O'Hara, J.
KIERKEGAARD, SØREN AABYE
Ayrton, M. The akeda
Kierkegaard unfair to Schlegel. Barthelme, D.
The Kilimanjaro device. Bradbury, R.
The kill-joy. Phillips, R.
Killed at Resaca. Bierce, A.
The killer. Meri, V.
Killer cat. Brennan, J. P.
Killer on the turnpike. McGivern, W. P.

Killer out of work. Leavitt, J.
The killers. Bukowski, C.
The killers. Hemingway, E.
The killing ground. Ballard, J. G.
Killing his bear. Crane, S.
Kim, Yong Ik
After seventeen years
  Kim, Y. I. Love in winter
From below the bridge
  Kim, Y. I. Love in winter
  Johnson, E. W. ed. Short stories international
From here you can see the moon
  Kim, Y. I. Love in winter
Love in winter
  Kim, Y. I. Love in winter
Mother's birthday
  Kim, Y. I. Love in winter
The nun's advice
  Kim, Y. I. Love in winter
The sea girl
  Kim, Y. I. Love in winter
The seed money
  Kim, Y. I. Love in winter
The sunny side after the harvest
  Kim, Y. I. Love in winter
The taste of salt
  Kim, Y. I. Love in winter
They won't crack it open
  Kim, Y. I. Love in winter
Till the candle blew out
  Kim, Y. I. Love in winter
The wedding shoes
  Kim, Y. I. Love in winter
Kimberly, Gail
The affair of the stolen mice
  Furman, A. L. ed. Teen-age secret agent stories
Peace, love, and food for the hungry
  Elwood, R. ed. The other side of tomorrow
Kimenye, Barbara
The winner
  Larson, C. R. ed. African short stories
  Nolen, B. ed. Africa is thunder and wonder
Kimpel, John M.
And even beautiful hands cry
  Karlin, W.; Paquet, B. T. and Rottmann, L. eds. Free fire zone
Kincaid's car. Jacobi, C.
Kind Kitty. Linklater, E.
A kind of courage. Olsen, T. V.
A kind of light. Ansell, J.
Kindly dig your grave. Ellin, S.
Kindred souls. Blackhurst, W. E.
King, Francis
Cat people
  Kahn, J. ed. Trial and terror
The love game
  Winter's tales 17
King, Woodie
The game
  King, W. ed. Black short story anthology
The King. Babel, I.
The King. Peterson, E. L.
The king and the burning boy. Dawson, F.
KING ARTHUR. *See* Arthur, King

King harvest. Dozois, G. R.

The **King** of beasts. Farmer, P. J.

The **King** of Folly Island. Jewett, S. O.

The **king** of Hackney Marshes. Glanville, B.

**King** of the air. Brand, C.

**King** of the bingo game. Ellison, R.

The **King** of the Cats. Benét, S. V.

**King** of the hill. Oliver, C.

The **king** of the poets. Cosić, B.

**King** Pest. Poe, E. A.

A **kingdom** by the sea. Dozois, G. R.

**KINGS AND RULERS**
> Borges, J. L. The two kings and the two labyrinths
> Brunner, J. An elixir for the emperor
> Darío, R. The bourgeois king
> De Camp, L. S. The Emperor's fan
> Golding, W. Envoy extraordinary
> Golding, W. The scorpion god
> Goulart, R. Change over
> The Jade Kuan-yin
> Kipling, R. The man who would be king
> Kipling, R. Namgay Doola
> Lagerkvist, P. The princess and all the kingdom
> LeGuin, U. K. Winter's king
> Lem, S. The computer that fought a dragon
> Nabokov, V. Solus Rex
> Sié, Cheou-kang. Spring water
> Updike, J. God speaks
> Yashpal. The Emperor's justice
> Zelazny, R. The great slow kings
>> *See also* names of Kings and rulers, e.g. Sutoku, Emperor of Japan

The **King's** ankus. Kipling, R.

**King's** evil. Davidson, A.

The **King's** favor. Crane, S.

The **kings** of the sea. Lanier, S.

The **king's** stratagem. Weyman, S.

**Kings** think. Dawson, F.

**Kings** who die. Anderson, P.

**Kinkies.** Trevor, W.

**KINSHIP.** *See* Consanguinity

**Kipling, Rudyard**
> At the end of the passage
>> Konigsberg, I. ed. The classic short story
> At the pit's mouth
>> Kipling, R. A selection of his stories and poems v2
> A bank fraud
>> Kipling, R. A selection of his stories and poems v2
> The beginning of the Armadillos
>> Kipling, R. A selection of his stories and poems v 1
> Beyond the pale
>> Kipling, R. A selection of his stories and poems v2
>> Konigsberg, I. ed. The classic short story
> The brushwood boy
>> Knight, D. ed. Perchance to dream
> The bull that thought
>> Kipling, R. A selection of his stories and poems v2

> The Butterfly that stamped
>> Kipling, R. A selection of his stories and poems v 1
> The Cat that walked by himself
>> Kipling, R. A selection of his stories and poems v 1
> A Centurion of the Thirtieth
>> Kipling, R. A selection of his stories and poems v 1
> The Crab that played with the sea
>> Kipling, R. A selection of his stories and poems v 1
> The daughter of the regiment
>> Kipling, R. A selection of his stories and poems v2
> 'Dymchurch Flit'
>> Kipling, R. A selection of his stories and poems v 1
> The Elephant's Child
>> Kipling, R. A selection of his stories and poems v 1
> The finest story in the world
>> Harrison, H. ed. The light fantastic
>> Kipling, R. A selection of his stories and poems v2
> The gardener
>> Davis, R. G. ed. Ten modern masters
>> Thune, E. and Prigozy, R. eds. Short stories: a critical anthology
> An habitation enforced
>> Kipling, R. A selection of his stories and poems v2
> Hal o' the Draft
>> Kipling, R. A selection of his stories and poems v 1
> The house surgeon
>> Kipling, R. A selection of his stories and poems v2
> How fear came
>> Kipling, R. A selection of his stories and poems v 1
> How the Camel got his hump
>> Kipling, R. A selection of his stories and poems v 1
> How the Leopard got his spots
>> Kipling, R. A selection of his stories and poems v 1
> How the Rhinoceros got his skin
>> Kipling, R. A selection of his stories and poems v 1
> How the Whale got his throat
>> Kipling, R. A selection of his stories and poems v 1
> The incarnation of Krishna Mulvaney
>> Kipling, R. A selection of his stories and poems v2
> Kaa's hunting
>> Kipling, R. A selection of his stories and poems v 1
> The King's ankus
>> Kipling, R. A selection of his stories and poems v 1
> The knights of the joyous venture
>> Kipling, R. A selection of his stories and poems v 1
> Letting in the jungle
>> Kipling, R. A selection of his stories and poems v 1

KITES (BIRDS)
Brand, C. King of the air
**Kites.** Delattre, P.
**KITTENS.** *See* Cats
**Kittredge, William A.**
The waterfowl tree
Roecker, W. A. ed. Stories that count
**Kitty,** Kitty, Kitty. Pudney, J.
**Kizer, Carolyn**
A slight mechanical failure
Moss, H. ed. The poet's story
**Kjelgaard, J. A.** *See* Kjelgaard, Jim
**Kjelgaard, Jim**
The tiger's heart
Stansbury, D. L. ed. Impact
**'Kjwalll'kje'k'koothaïlll'kje'k.** Zelazny, R.
**KLAMATH INDIANS**
Senarens, L. P. Frank Reade Jr's Air wonder
**Klass, Philip.** *See* Tenn, William
The **Klausners.** Tushnet, L.
**Kleber** on murder in 30 volumes. Powell, J.
**Klee** dead. Coover, R.
**Klein, Gérard**
The valley of echoes
Rottensteiner, F. ed. View from another shore
**Klein, Norma**
An American marriage
Klein, N. Love and other euphemisms
Apocalypse at the Plaza
Klein, N. Love and other euphemisms
The boy in the green hat
The Best American short stories, 1969
Klein, N. Love and other euphemisms
Magic
Klein, N. Love and other euphemisms
Pratfalls
Klein, N. Love and other euphemisms
A sense of ritual
Klein, N. Love and other euphemisms
**Klein** and Wagner. Hesse, H.
**Kleist, Heinrich von**
Michael Kohlhaas
Steinhauser, H. ed. Ten German novellas
**KLEPTOMANIA**
Goulart, R. Subject to change
Warner, L. The girl who liked Communists
**Klingsor's** last summer. Hesse, H.
**Knave** of diamonds. Easmon, R. S.
**Kneale, Nigel**
Minuke
Dickinson, S. ed. The usurping ghost, and other encounters and experiences
**Kneel** down. Holmes, E. M.
The **knife.** Bichsel, P.
The **knife.** Crane, S.
The **knife.** Heinesen, W.
**KNIFE-THROWING**
Böll, H. The man with the knives
**Knight, Damon**
Catch that Martian
Hipolito, J. and McNelly, W. E. eds. Mars, we love you
Silverberg, R. ed. Invaders from space
The country of the kind
Science fiction hall of fame v 1

Four in one
Silverberg, R. ed. To the stars
Mary
Dozois, G. R. ed. A day in the life
Masks
Knight, D. ed. A pocketful of stars
On the wheel
Nova 2
Shall the dust praise thee?
Mohs, M. ed. Other worlds, other gods
Ticket to anywhere
Silverberg, R. ed. Deep space
You're another
McComas, J. F. ed. Special wonder
**Knight, Eric**
Never come Monday
Minot, S. and Wilson, R. eds. Three stances of modern fiction
**Knight, Etheridge**
A time to mourn
Chapman, A. ed. New Black voices
**Knight, Wallace E.**
The way we went
The Best American short stories, 1973
The **knight**-errant. Burke, T.
The **knight,** the lady, and the Abbot. La Sale, A. de
**KNIGHTS AND KNIGHTHOOD**
Anne of Swansea. The unknown!
Barbauld, A. L. Sir Bertrand
Beckford, W. The Nymph of the Fountain
Coolidge, O. The conquerors 1096-1099
Coolidge, O. The money-makers 1204
Hesse, H. Chagrin d'amour
Kipling, R. The knights of the joyous venture
Kipling, R. Old men at Pevensey
Kipling, R. Young men at the Manor
La Sale, A. de. Little Jehan de Saintré
The Lovers' tragedy
Schreiber, A. W. The Devil's ladder
The Self-made cuckold

*See also* Middle Ages

The **Knight's** Cross signal problem. Bramah, E.
The **knights** of the joyous venture. Kipling, R.
**KNIGHTS TEMPLARS (MONASTIC AND MILITARY ORDER)** *See* Templars
**KNIVES**
Borges, J. L. The meeting
Heinesen, W. The knife
Smith, C. A. The Malay krise
**Knock.** Brown, F.
The **knock** at the manor gate. Kafka, F.
The **knocker** at the portico. Copper, B.
**Knots** untied. Bondarenko, W. C.
**Knowles, John**
A turn with the sun
Burnett, W. ed. That's what happened to me
**Knowlton, Don**
The letter of the law
Fenner, P. R. comp. Desperate moments
Murderer on the mountain
Fenner, P. R. comp. Perilous ascent
**Known** for her frankness. Gilliatt, P.

**Knox, Bill**
Deerglen Queen
Mystery Writers of America. Crime without murder
**Knox, E .V.**
The murder at the Towers
Kahn, J. ed. Hanging by a thread
**KNOXVILLE.** *See* Tennessee—Knoxville
**Kobak, Dorothy**
The winter soldiers
Ribalow, H. U. ed. My name aloud
**Koch, Claude F.**
A matter of family
Lytle, A. ed. Craft and vision
**Koch, Kenneth**
The postcard collection
Moss, H. ed. The poet's story
**Kolpacoff, Victor**
The room
New American Review no. 1
**Konstantinov, Konstantin**
Day by day
Kirilov, N. and Kirk, F. eds. Introduction to modern Bulgarian literature
**Koolhaas, Anton**
A hole in the ceiling
Krispyn, E. ed. Modern stories from Holland and Flanders
**Koontz, Dean R.**
A mouse in the walls of the Global Village
Ellison, H. ed. Again, dangerous visions
Terra phobia
Elwood, R. and Ghidalia, V. eds. Androids, time machines and blue giraffes
The Undercity
Elwood, R. ed. Future city
Wake up to Thunder
Elwood, R. ed. Children of infinity
**KOREA**
Chu, Yo-sup. My mother and the roomer
Kim, Y. I. Mother's birthday
Kim, Y. I. The sea girl
Kim, Y. I. The seed money
Son, S. The poppy
**Pusan**
Kim, Y. I. From below the bridge
Kim, Y. I. From here you can see the moon
Kim, Y. I. Love in winter
Kim, Y. I. The nun's advice
Kim, Y. I. The wedding shoes
**Korea.** McGahern, J.
**KOREA, PROVINCIAL AND RURAL**
An, Su-Gil. The green chrysanthemum
Czoe, Zông-Hûi. The memorial service on the mountain
Kim, Y. I. After seventeen years
Kim, Y. I. The sunny side after the harvest
Kim, Y. I. The taste of salt
Kim, Y. I. Till the candle blew out
O, Yong-su. Nami and the taffyman
**KOREAN SOLDIERS.** *See* Soldiers, Korean
**KOREAN WAR, 1950-1953**
Buck, P. S. Duet in Asia
Deck, J. Sailors at their mourning: a memory

Schultz, J. Daley goes home
Schultz, J. Morgan
Siegel, J. In the land of the morning calm, déjà vu
Yu, H. D. M. Z.
**KOREANS IN THE UNITED STATES**
Kim, Y. I. They won't crack it open
**Kornbluth, C. M.**
Gomez
Knight, D. ed. Tomorrow and tomorrow
The little black bag
The Astounding-Analog reader v2
Science fiction hall of fame v 1
The marching morons
Knight, D. comp. Dimension X
The Science fiction hall of fame v2A
The mindworm
Silverberg, R. ed. Mind to mind
The silly season
Ferman, E. L. and Mills, R. P. eds. Twenty years of The Magazine of Fantasy and Science Fiction
Silverberg, R. ed. Invaders from space
The words of Guru
Knight, D. ed. The golden road
*See also* Pohl, F. jt auth.
**Körner, Karl Theodor**
The harp
Haining, P. ed. Gothic tales of terror
**Korolenko, Vladimir**
Makar's dreem
Proffer, C. R. ed. From Karamzin to Gunin: an anthology of Russian short stories
**Kos, Erih**
The man who knew where the north was and where the south
Johnson, B. ed. New writing in Yugoslavia
**Kosinski, Jerzy**
Steps; excerpt
Karl, F. R. and Hamalian, L. eds. The naked i
**Kosynka, Hryhoriy**
Black night
Luckyj, G. S. N. ed. Modern Ukrainian short stories
In the grainfields
Luckyj, G. S. N. ed. Modern Ukrainian short stories
**Kotowska, Monika**
The beautiful fire
Kotowska, M. The bridge to the other side
The bridge to the other side
Kotowska, M. The bridge to the other side
Choosing
Kotowska, M. The bridge to the other side
The city at night
Kotowska, M. The bridge to the other side
The enchanted street
Kotowska, M. The bridge to the other side
The end of the war
Kotowska, M. The bridge to the other side

**Kotowska, Monika**—*Continued*
Everyone grows up
Kotowska, M. The bridge to the other side
An exceptional Sunday
Kotowska, M. The bridge to the other side
My good ladies
Kotowska, M. The bridge to the other side
The old man with the bread
Kotowska, M. The bridge to the other side
The payment will be made on Sunday
Kotowska, M. The bridge to the other side
Sadness
Kotowska, M. The bridge to the other side
Still life with ice cream
Kotowska, M. The bridge to the other side
Test games
Kotowska, M. The bridge to the other side
Twelve feet to heaven
Kotowska, M. The bridge to the other side
The voyage inside the shell
Kotowska, M. The bridge to the other side
When the stars fall
Kotowska, M. The bridge to the other side
Winning
Kotowska, M. The bridge to the other side
Words
Kotowska, M. The bridge to the other side

**Kotsyubynsky, Mykhaylo**
On the rock
Luckyj, G. S. N. ed. Modern Ukrainian short stories

**Kotzwinkle, William**
The bird watcher
Kotzwinkle, W. Elephant bangs train
The doorman
Kotzwinkle, W. Elephant bangs train
Elephant bangs train
Kotzwinkle, W. Elephant bangs train
Elephant's graveyard
Kotzwinkle, W. Elephant bangs train
Follow the Eagle
Kotzwinkle, W. Elephant bangs train
The great liar
Kotzwinkle, W. Elephant bangs train
The jewel of Amitaba
Kotzwinkle, W. Elephant bangs train
The magician
Kotzwinkle, W. Elephant bangs train
Marie
Kotzwinkle, W. Elephant bangs train
A most incredible meal
Kotzwinkle, W. Elephant bangs train
Nippy
Kotzwinkle, W. Elephant bangs train
Soldier in the blanket
Kotzwinkle, W. Elephant bangs train

Stroke of good luck
Kotzwinkle, W. Elephant bangs train
Tiger Bridge
Kotzwinkle, W. Elephant bangs train
The trap
Kotzwinkle, W. Elephant bangs train
Turning point
Kotzwinkle, W. Elephant bangs train
**Kou.** Bergé, C.
**Kovac, Mirko**
Uncle Donato's death
Johnson, B. ed. New writing in Yugoslavia
**Kovacic, Lojze**
Messages from dreams: God
Johnson, B. ed. New writing in Yugoslavia
Twilight is falling on the earth
Decker, C. R. and Angoff, C. eds. Modern stories from many lands
**Kovalevska, Margarita**
The vision from the tower
Decker, C. R. and Angoff, C. eds. Modern stories from many lands
**KRAKEN.** *See* Sea monsters
The **Kraken.** Engelhardt, F.
**Kranes, David**
Dealer
Lish G. ed. The secret life of our times: new fiction from Esquire
**Krause, Ervin D.**
The snake
Stansbury, D. L. ed. Impact
**Krazy Kat.** Dawson, F.
**Kreisel, Henry**
The broken globe
Angoff, C. ed. Stories from The Literary Review
**Kremer, Rüdiger**
The list
New Directions in prose and poetry 27
**Krleza, Miroslav**
The cricket beneath the waterfall
Krleža, M. The cricket beneath the waterfall, and other stories
Devil's island
Krleža, M. The cricket beneath the waterfall, and other stories
Dr Gregor and the Evil One
Krleža, M. The cricket beneath the waterfall, and other stories
A funeral in Teresienburg
Krleža, M. The cricket beneath the waterfall, and other stories
Hodorlahomor the Great
Krleža, M. The cricket beneath the waterfall, and other stories
The love of Marcel Faber-Fabriczy for Miss Laura Warronigg
Krleža, M. The cricket beneath the waterfall, and other stories
**Ktorova, Alla**
My sister's applegarth
Scammell, M. ed. Russia's other writers
**KULIKOVO, BATTLE OF, 1380**
Solzhenitsyn, A. Zakhar-the-Pouch
**Kumin, Maxine**
Buying the child
American Review 16

Kung I-Chi. Lu, Hsun
**Kuprin, Alexander**
The garnet bracelet
Proffer, C. R. ed. From Karamzin to
Bunin: an anthology of Russian short
stories
**Kurahashi, Yumiko**
Partei
New Directions in prose and poetry 26
The ugly devils
New Directions in prose and poetry 24
**Kurland, Michael**
A matter of taste
Dickensheet, D. ed. Men and malice
**Kuttner, Henry**
A cross of centuries
Mohs, M. ed. Other worlds, other gods
Dream's end
Knight, D. ed. Perchance to dream
The Salem horror
Derleth, A. ed. Tales of Cthulhu Mythos
The shadow on the screen
Haining, P. ed. The Hollywood night-
mare
*For other stories by this author see*
O'Donnell, Lawrence; Padgett, Lewis;
Vance, Jack
**Kuttner, Henry, and Moore, C. L.**
The cure
Knight, D. ed. A science fiction argosy
**Kuykendall, Roger**
We didn't do anything wrong, hardly
Harrison, H. ed. Worlds of wonder
**Kwame** Bird Lady Day. Godfrey, D.
**Kwan's** Coney Island. Hoagland, E.
**Kyd, Thomas**
Cottage for August
A Treasury of modern mysteries v 1

# L

**L** as in loot. Treat, L.
**LSD.** *See* Lysergic acid diethylamide
**LABOR AND LABORING CLASSES**
Bukowski, C.   A couple of winos
Bukowski, C. The gut-wringing machine
Bukowski, C. Kid Stardust on the porter-
house
Chekhov, A. My life
Farrell, J. T. Only tomorrow and tomorrow
Mencken, H. L. The visionary
Morrison, A.   A street
Petry, A. Like a winding sheet
Weissenberg, I. M.   A shtetl
*See also* Labor camps; Labor unions;
Migrant labor; Strikes and lockouts
**LABOR CAMPS**
Gallant, M. My heart is broken
Lipski, L. Day and night
Maltz, A. The farmer's dog
**LABOR DEMONSTRATIONS.** *See* Strikes
and lockouts
**LABOR ORGANIZATIONS.** *See* Gilds
**LABOR REST HOMES**
### Russia
Nagibin, Y.   A light in the window

**LABOR UNIONS**
Kaplan, B. Rare and stinging days
*See also* Gilds; Strikes and lockouts
**LABORATORIES**
### Russia
Grekova, I. Beyond the gates
**LABORATORY ANIMALS**
Neville, K. Dominant species
**LABORERS.** *See* Labor and laboring classes
**Labrie's** wife. Scott, D. C.
**LABYRINTHS**
Borges, J. L. Ibn Hakkan al-Bokhari, dead
in his labyrinth
**LACENAIRE, PIERRE FRANÇOIS**
Ayrton, M. An episode in the life of a
gambler
**Ladies'** logic. Dillon, M.
**Lady.** Friedman, B. J.
The **lady.** Justice, D.
A **lady** and the masters of history. Farrell, J. T.
The **lady** and the pedlar. Agnon, S. Y.
A **lady** comes to Paradise. Ware, E.
A **lady** from Redhorse. Bierce, A.
**Lady** Habart. Maugham, W. S.
**Lady** Macbeth of the Mtsensk District. Les-
kov, N.
The **Lady** Margaret. Roberts, K.
A **lady** of Bayou St John. Chopin, K.
A **lady** of fashion. Phillips, R.
The **lady** of Glenwith Grange. Collins, W.
The **lady** on the gray. Collier, J.
The **lady** or the salmon? Lang, A.
The **lady** takes an interest. O'Hara, J.
The **Lady** Violante. Pei, M.
**Lady** with a lamp. Parker, D.
The **lady** with the dog. Chekhov, A.
The **lady** with the pet dog. Oates, J. C.
The **lady's** maid. Kanin, G.
The **lady's** maid's bell. Wharton, E.
**La Farge, Oliver**
All the young men
Taylor, J. G. ed. Great Western short
stories
**LAFAYETTE, MARIE JOSEPH PAUL
YVES ROCH GILBERT DU MO-
TIER, MARQUIS DE**
Jewett, S. Peg's little chair
**Lafferty, R. A.**
All but the words
Lafferty, R. A. Strange doings
All pieces of a river shore
Orbit 8
Aloys
Lafferty, R. A. Strange doings
And walk now gently through the fire
Elwood, R. ed. And walk now gently
through the fire, and other science
fiction stories
Barnaby's clock
Elwood, R. ed. Showcase
Camels and dromedaries, Clem
Lafferty, R. A. Strange doings
Cliffs that laughed
Lafferty, R. A. Strange doings
Condillac's statue
McCaffrey, A. ed. Alchemy and aca-
deme

The last cruise of the Judas Iscariot. Mitchell, E. P.
The last crusader 1464. Coolidge, O.
The last day. Stewart, J. C.
The last day. Verga, G.
The last day of all. Stanley, F. G.
Last day of spring. Fremlin, C.
The last day of winter. Spielberg, P.
The last exploit of Harry the actor. Bramah, E.
The last gas station. Grau, S. A.
The last ghost. Goldin, S.
The last good country. Hemingway, E.
The last hour. Deutsch, A. H.
The last house call. Nourse, A. E.
The last hurrah of the Golden Horde. Spinrad, N.
The last judgment. Čapek, K.
The last laugh. Hayes, A. H.
The last laugh. Val Baker, D.
The last leaf. Henry, O.
The last leaf. Macfarlane, W.
The last man. West, W. G.
The last men. Long, F. B.
The last Mohican. Malamud, B.
The last of Haley. O'Hara, J.
The last of the bluenoses. De Vries, P.
The last of the grizzly bears. West, R. B.
The last of the horsemen. Ottley, R.
The last of the Troubadours. Henry, O.
The last of the Valerii. James, H.
The last one. Kentfield, C.
The last operation. Mayer, T.
The last possibility. Beneš, J.
The last question. Asimov, I.
The last recall. Beard, H.
Last respects. O'Hara, J.
The last rite. Lee, Yu-hwa
The last round up. Stuart, J.
The last seance. Christie, A.
The last spin. Hunter, E.
Last stop before the carbarn. Maloney, R.
The last tea. Parker, D.
The last test. Castro, A. de
The last to go. Gilliatt, P.
The last trail drive through downtown Dallas. Green, B. K.
The last train. Brown, F.
Last train to Kankakee. Scott, R.
The last voyage of the ghost ship. García Márquez, G.
Last whipping. Hughes, L.
The last woman. Gardner, T. S.
A last word. Sansom, W.
The last years of Clelia Trotti. Bassani, G.
Lasting love. Maupassant, G. de
LAS VEGAS. See Nevada—Las Vegas
The late bud. Aidoo, A. A.
The late man. Schroeder, A.
Late Show. Hemenway, R.
Latham, Philip
    The Rose Bowl-Pluto hypothesis
        Orbit 5
Lathom, Francis
    The water spectre
        Haining, P. ed. Gothic tales of terror
Latimer, Olene
    The secret of Raccoon Ridge
        Alabama prize stories, 1970

LATIN AMERICA
    See also South America; also countries in this region, e.g. Nicaragua
        Politics
    See Politics—Latin America
The Latin scholar. Hesse, H.
La Torre, Lillian de. See De La Torre, Lillian
LATVIA
    Kovalevska, M. The vision from the tower
Lau, Shaw
    Grandma takes charge
        Shimer, D. B. ed. Voices of modern Asia
LAUGHTER
    Accioly, B. João Urso
    P'u, Sung-ling. Ying-ning
Laughter. Alvarez, A.
Laughter. Colette
Laughter in Ramonia. Monkov, S.
Laughter in the basement. De Vries, P.
Laumer, Keith
    Ballots and bandits
        Laumer, K. Retief of the CDT
    Crime and punishment
        Laumer, K. Retief: ambassador to space
    Dam nuisance
        Laumer, K. Retief: ambassador to space
    The devil you don't
        McCaffrey, A. ed. Alchemy and academe
    The exterminator
        Laumer, K. Once there was a giant
    The Forbidden City
        Laumer, K. Retief: ambassador to space
    The forest in the sky
        Laumer, K. Retief: ambassador to space
    Founder's day
        Laumer, K. Once there was a giant
    Giant killer
        Laumer, K. Retief: ambassador to space
    In the queue
        Nebula award stories 6
        Orbit 7
    Internal affair
        Laumer, K. Retief of the CDT
    The last command
        Analog 7
        Knight, D. ed. A pocketful of stars
        Laumer, K. Once there was a giant
    The lawgiver
        Harrison, H. ed. The year 2000
        Laumer, K. Once there was a giant
    Mechanical advantage
        Laumer, K. Retief of the CDT
    Mind out of time
        Laumer, K. Once there was a giant
    Of death what dreams
        Five fates
    Once there was a giant
        Laumer, K. Once there was a giant
    The piecemakers
        Laumer, K. Retief of the CDT
    Pime doesn't cray
        Laumer, K. Retief of the CDT
    The plague
        Norton, A. and Donaldy, E. eds. Gates to tomorrow

## LEGENDS AND FOLK TALES
Hesse, H. The field devil

    *See also* Fables; Fairies; Wandering Jew

### Arabia
Sindbad the Sailor. The first voyage of Sindbad the Sailor

Sindbad, the Sailor. The second voyage of Sindbad the Seaman

### China
Lu, Hsün. The flight to the moon

Lu, Hsün. Forging the swords

Takeda, T. The bridge

### Faroe Islands
Heinesen, W. The smoking mirror

### France
Perrault, C. The Master Cat

Weyman, S. The king's stratagem

### Germany
Beckford, W. The Nymph of the Fountain

Borchert, W. The three dark magi

The Dance of the Dead

### Greece
Barth, J. Menelaiad

Buchan, J. The Lemnian

Gordon, C. Cloud nine

Lanier, S.   A feminine jurisdiction

    *See also* Circe; Sisyphus

### Indians
    *See* Indians—Legends; Indians of North America—Legends

### Japan
Updike, J. Jesus on Honshu

Uyeda, A. Bewitched

Uyeda, A. Birdcall

Uyeda, A. Daydream

Uyeda, A. Exiled

Uyeda, A. Reunion

The Vampire cat

### Netherlands
Mulisch, H. The horses' jump and the fresh sea

### Nigeria
Freeman, R. A. Indoro Bush College

### Russia
Ransome, A. The tale of the silver saucer and the transparent apple

Tolstoy, L. The story of Yemilyan and the empty drum

### Scandinavia
Andersen, H. The Emperor's new clothes

### Scotland
Campbell, J. F. The sea-maiden

Thomas the Rhymer

Wilson, J. M. The doom of Soulis

### Siberia
Buzzati, D.   A Siberian shepherd's report of the atom bomb

### United States
Irving, W. Rip Van Winkle

**LEGERDEMAIN.** *See* Magic

**LEGION OF HONOR.** *See* Decorations of honor

A **legionary** of Mieroslawski. Sienkiewicz, H.

## LEGISLATION
Brister, B. The sand trout seminar

**Le Guin, Ursula K.**
Direction of the road
    Orbit 12
The end
    Orbit 6
Nine lives
    Best SF: 1969
    Nebula award stories 5
Vaster than empires and more slow
    New dimensions 1
Winter's king
    Orbit 5
The word for world is forest
    Ellison, H. ed. Again, dangerous visions
The word of unbinding
    Knight, D. ed. The golden road

**LE HAVRE.** *See* France—Le Havre

**Lehrman, Herb**
The ancient last
    Silverberg, B. ed. Phoenix feathers

**Leiber, Fritz**
America the beautiful
    Disch, T. M. ed. The ruins of earth
    Harrison, H. ed. The year 2000
The casket-demon
    Haining, P. ed. The Hollywood nightmare
Coming attraction
    Science fiction hall of fame v 1
The girl with the hungry eyes
    Haining, P. ed. Vampires at midnight
Gonna roll the bones
    Asimov, I. ed. The Hugo winners v2
The haunted future
    Dozois, G. R. ed. A day in the life
Ill met in Lankhmar
    Nebula award stories 6
Last
    Silverberg, R. ed. The ends of time
One station of the way
    Best SF: 1968
    Galaxy Magazine. The eleventh Galaxy reader
A pail of air
    Harrison, H. eds. Worlds of wonder
    Norton, A. and Donaldy, E. eds. Gates to tomorrow
The power of the puppets
    Haining, P. ed. The freak show
Rump-titty-titty-tum-tah-tee
    Knight, D. ed. A science fiction argosy
The secret songs
    Knight, D. ed. Perchance to dream
    Total Effect. Survival printout
Space-time for springers
    Necker, C. ed. Supernatural cats
237 talking statues, etc.
    Ferman, E. L. and Mills, R. P. eds. Twenty years of The Magazine of Fantasy and Science Fiction
The warlock
    Haining, P. ed. The witchcraft reader
When the last gods die
    Silverberg, R. ed. The ends of time

Leiber, Fritz—*Continued*
  The winter flies
    Knight, D. ed. A pocketful of stars
Leibscher, Walt
  Do androids dream of electric love?
    Scortia, T. N. ed. Strange bedfellows
Leinster, Murray
  First contact
    The Astounding-Analog reader v 1
    Science fiction hall of fame v 1
  Keyhole
    Harrison, H. ed. Worlds of wonder
  Nobody saw the ship
    Silverberg, R. ed. Invaders from space
  Sidewise in time
    Silverberg, R. ed. Worlds of maybe
LEISURE. *See* Hobbies; Retirement
Leixlip Castle. Maturin, C.
Lelchuk, Alan
  Of our time
    New American Review no. 4
Lem, Stanislaw
  The computer that fought a dragon
    Suvin, D. ed. Other worlds, other seas
  In hot pursuit of happiness
    Rottensteiner, F. ed. View from another
      shore
  The patrol
    Suvin, D. ed. Other worlds, other seas
  The thirteenth journey of Ion Tichy
    Suvin, D. ed. Other worlds, other seas
  The twenty-fourth journey of Ion Tichy
    Suvin, D. ed. Other worlds, other seas
LEMMINGS
  Thurber, J. Interview with a lemming
The lemnian. Buchan, J.
LENINGRAD. *See* Russia—Leningrad
Lennon, John
  Randolf's party
    Charyn, J. ed. The single voice
Lenny. Asimov, I.
Lentini, A.
  Autumntime
    Del Rey, L. ed. Best science stories of
      the year [1972]
Leof's leavetaking. Walsh, J. P. and Crossley-
  Holland, K.
León, Adriano González. *See* González
  León, Adriano
The Leonardo. Nabokov, V.
The leopard lady. Sayers, D. L.
LEOPARDS
  Balzac, H. de.  A passion in the desert
  Bierce, A. The eyes of the panther
  Grajewski, J. The meeting
  Kipling, R. How the Leopard got his
    spots
The Leopold locked room. Hoch, E. D.
The leper. Moravia, A.
LEPERS. *See* Leprosy
The leper's helix. Coover, R.
LEPROSY
  Collidge, O. The heir 1170
  Coover, R. The leper's helix
  Disch, T. M. Flight useless, inexorable the
    pursuit
  Greene, G. Dream of a strange land

  Kipling, R. The mark of the beast
  Masuccio. The lovers among the lepers
Le Queux, William
  The secret of the fox hunter
    Greene, H. ed. The rivals of Sherlock
      Holmes
Leroux, Gaston
  Phantom of the Opera
    Haining, P. ed. The ghouls
LESBIANISM
  Barthelme, D. Alexandria and Henrietta
  Betts, D. Burning the bed
  Breslow, P. Honey bee
  Davis, O. Sappho in Wales
  Greene, G. Chagrin in three parts
  Haylock, J.   A different party
  Meacock, N. Changed
  Pynchon, T.   V. in love
  Stein, G.   Q.E.D.
  Tuohy, F. At home with the Colonel
  Tuohy, F.   A reprieve
  Tuohy, F. Windows
  Zelazny, R. and Ellison, H. Come to me
    not in winter's white
Leskov, Nikolai
  About the folly of a certain prince
    Leskov, N. Satirical stories of Nikolai
      Leskov
  About the Rooster and his children
    Leskov, N. Satirical stories of Nikolai
      Leskov
  Administrative grace
    Leskov, N. Satirical stories of Nikolai
      Leskov
  The archbishop and the Englishman
    Leskov, N. Satirical stories of Nikolai
      Leskov
  Choice grain
    Leskov, N. Satirical stories of Nikolai
      Leskov
  Deception
    Leskov, N. Satirical stories of Nikolai
      Leskov
  Figúra
    Leskov, N. Satirical stories of Nikolai
      Leskov
  Fish soup without fish
    Leskov, N. Satirical stories of Nikolai
      Leskov
  How it is not good to condemn weaknesses
    Leskov, N. Satirical stories of Nikolai
      Leskov
  A journey with a nihilist
    Leskov, N. Satirical stories of Nikolai
      Leskov
  Lady Macbeth of the Mtsensk District
    Proffer, C. R. ed. From Karamzin to
      Bunin: an anthology of Russian short
      stories
  Night owls
    Leskov, N. Satirical stories of Nikolai
      Leskov
  On the harm that exists for many of read-
    ing worldly books
    Leskov, N. Satirical stories of Nikolai
      Leskov
  A product of nature
    Leskov, N. Satirical stories of Nikolai
      Leskov

**Leskov, Nikolai**—*Continued*
Singlethought
  Leskov, N. Satirical stories of Nikolai Leskov
The steel flea
  Leskov, N. Satirical stories of Nikolai Leskov
  Same as: The tale of the squint-eyed, left-handed Smith of Tula and the steel flea, listed in 1964-68 supplement
Superfluous mother love
  Leskov, N. Satirical stories of Nikolai Leskov
A winter day
  Leskov, N. Satirical stories of Nikolai Leskov

**Lessing, Doris**
Flight
  Zolotow, C. ed. An overpraised season
Lions, leaves, roses
  Lessing, D. The temptation of Jack Orkney, and other stories
Mrs Fortescue
  Lessing, D. The temptation of Jack Orkney, and other stories
Not a very nice story
  Lessing, D. The temptation of Jack Orkney, and other stories
Notes for a case history
  Spinner, S. ed. Feminine plural
An old woman and her cat
  Lessing, D. The temptation of Jack Orkney, and other stories
  New American Review no. 14
One off the short list
  Disch, R. and Schwartz, B. eds. Killing time
  Gulassa, C. M. ed. The fact of fiction
The other garden
  Lessing, D. The temptation of Jack Orkney, and other stories
Out of the fountain
  Lessing, D. The temptation of Jack Orkney, and other stories
Report on the threatened city
  Lessing, D. The temptation of Jack Orkney, and other stories
Side benefits of an honourable profession
  Lessing, D. The temptation of Jack Orkney, and other stories
Spies I have known
  Lessing, D. The temptation of Jack Orkney, and other stories
The story of a non-marrying man
  Lessing, D. The temptation of Jack Orkney, and other stories
The temptation of Jack Orkney
  Lessing, D. The temptation of Jack Orkney, and other stories
An unposted love letter
  Lessing, D. The temptation of Jack Orkney, and other stories
A year in Regent's Park
  Lessing, D. The temptation of Jack Orkney, and other stories
The lesson. Bambara, T. C.
Lesson in survival. Long, F. B.
A lesson in the holy life. Premchand

A lesson to errant wives. Margaret of Navarre
**Lester, Julius**
Ben
  Lester, J. Long journey home
Long journey home
  Lester, J. Long journey home
Louis
  Lester, J. Long journey home
The man who was a horse
  Lester, J. Long journey home
Satan on my track
  Lester, J. Long journey home
When freedom came
  Lester, J. Long journey home
**Le Sueur, Meridel**
Annunciation
  Le Sueur, M. Corn village
Corn village
  Le Sueur, M. Corn village
Gone home
  Le Sueur, M. Corn village
Persephone
  Le Sueur, M. Corn village
Let fall no burning leaf. James, B. P.
Let me hang loose. Howard, V.
Let me promise you. Callaghan, M.
Let my people go! Green, J.
Let no man put asunder. Farrell, J. T.
Let nothing you dismay. Fiedler, L. A.
Let sleeping bones lie. Hardwick, Michael, and Hardwick, Mollie
Let the church roll on. Bontemps, A.
Let there be light. Dickens, A.
Let there be night! Hershman, M.
Let's go vacationing. Tsonev, V.
The letter. Agnon, S. Y.
The letter. Dhumketu
The letter. Malamud, B.
Letter found on a drowned man. Maupassant, G. de
Letter from a very worried man. Slesar, H.
Letter home. Buck, P. S.
The letter of the law. Knowlton, D.
The letter of the law. Wodehouse, P. G.
Letter to a young poet. Sallis, J.
A letter to Ismael in the grave. Brown, R.
Letter to the editor. Hershman, M.
**LETTERS (STORIES IN LETTER FORM)**
Algren, N. I know they'll like me in Saigon
Anvil, C. Behind the sandrat hoax
Ayrton, M. The pyramid of counterpoint
Beckett, S. The Smeraldina's billet doux
Bierce, A. A lady from Redhorse
Blackhurst, W. E. God takes care of his own
Blish, J. Getting along
Borgese, E. M. To whom it may concern
Brunner, J. Fairy tale
Carr, J. D. The gentleman from Paris
Clarke, A. C. Loophole
Collins, W. The biter bit
Cortazar, J. Bestiary
Corwin, N. Belles lettres, 2272
Davidson, A. Selectra Six-Ten
Dawson, F. Dear Max
Deck, J. An offering
Delattre, P. A Confucian reprimand
Dickson, G. R. Computers don't argue

**Lewis, Matthew Gregory**
  The anaconda
    Haining, P. ed. Gothic tales of terror
  The midnight embrace
    Haining, P. ed. The nightmare reader
**Lewis, Sinclair**
  The post-mortem murder
    Haining, P. ed. The Lucifer society
**LEWIS AND CLARK EXPEDITION**
  Fisher, V. Trek through the mountains
  Holm, D. Christmas at Fort Clatsop
**LEYDEN.** *See* Netherlands—Leyden
**L'Heureux, John**
  Fox and swan
    The Best American short stories, 1972
  Something missing
    Gulassa, C. M. ed. The fact of fiction
**Li, Ju-chen**
  In the country of women
    Birch, C. ed. Anthology of Chinese literature v2
**Liar!** Asimov, I.
**LIARS**
  Kotzwinkle, W. The great liar
  Mitchell, E. P. A day among the liars
  Pritchett, V. S. The liars
The **liars.** Pritchett, V. S.
**Liars** don't qualify. Edwards, J.
**LIBEL AND SLANDER**
  Leskov, N. Administrative grace
The **liberation.** Stafford, J.
The **liberation** of Earth. Tenn, W.
**LIBERTY**
  Disch, T. M. Thesis on social forms and social controls in the U.S.A.
  Hood, H. Dark glasses
  Kotowska, M. The city at night
  O'Connor, F. Freedom
  Ostaijen, P. van. The prison in heaven
  Russell, E. F. . . . and then there were none
  Scott, D. C. The bobolink
  Smith, C. The ballad of lost C'mell
  Verga, G. Freedom
**Liberty.** Verga, G.
The **liberty** picnic. Nowakowski, T.
**LIBRARIANS**
  Campbell, R. The enchanted fruit
  Lewis, L. The man who talked with books
  West, J. The condemned librarian
**LIBRARIES**
  Babel, I. The public library
  Derleth, A. The slayers and the slain
  Fiedler, L. A. An expense of spirit
The **library.** Giovanni, N.
The **library** window. Oliphant, Mrs
**LICE**
  Brú, H. Lice
  Leskov, N. A product of nature
**Lice.** Brú, H.
**License.** Anderson, P.
The **license.** Tuohy, F.
A **lickpenny** lover. Henry, O.
**Lida** Mantovani. Bassani, G.
The **lie.** Brennan, M.
The **lie.** Vonnegut, K.
The **lieabout.** Allingham, M.

**Lieber, Joel**
  Eat a sour grape
    Ribalow, H. U. ed. My name aloud
**Lief, Evelyn**
  Bed sheets are white
    Ellison, H. ed. Again, dangerous visions
**LIES.** *See* Liars; Truthfulness and falsehood
**Lieutenant** Lookeast. Ibuse, M.
**LIEUTENANTS, RUSSIAN.** *See* Russia. Army—Officers
**LIFE (BIOLOGY)**
  Ballard, J. G. The voices of time
  Davis, H. To plant a Seed
  Eisenberg, L. Uncle Sam's children
  Fast, H. The pragmatic seed
**LIFE (PHILOSOPHY OF LIFE)**
  Bahr, J. The perilous affirmative
  Barth, J. Night-sea journey
  Blecher, G. The death of the Russian novel
  Delattre, P. A bubbling brook
  Hesse, H. Iris
  Hippius, Z. It's all for the worse
  Montgomery, M. The decline and fall of Officer Fergerson
  Peretz, Y. L. Silent Bontsche
  Petaja, E. Only gone before
  Russell, B. The perplexities of John Forstice
  Sheckley, R. Cordle to onion to carrot
  Wiesel, E. The accident
**LIFE, ARTIFICIAL.** *See* Artificial life
**Life** and death. Steinbeck, J.
**Life** and death in the charity ward. Bukowski, C.
The **life** and loves of Mr Jiveass Nigger (Prologue) Brown, C.
**Life** at Mr Tange's. Ibuse, M.
**Life** began today. Grebanier, B. D. N.
**Life,** death and other dreams. Schuyler, J.
A **life** for a life. Wheatley, D.
The **life** guard. Wain, J.
**LIFE GUARDS.** *See* Lifesaving
**Life** hutch. Ellison, H.
**Life** in a Texas whorehouse. Bukowski, C.
A **life** in the closet. Rushmore, R.
A **life** in the day of a writer. Slesinger, T.
**LIFE INSURANCE.** *See* Insurance, Life
**Life** is no abyss. Stafford, J.
**Life** is weird sometimes. Woolrich, C.
A **life** membership. Tuohy, F.
The **life** of riot in one Luis Casas. Sherwin, J. J.
The **life** of Tadeo Isidoro Cruz (1829-1874). Borges, J. L.
The **life** of the imagination. Gordimer, N.
A **life** of your own. O'Connor, F.
**LIFE ON OTHER PLANETS**
  Altov, G. The Master Builder
  Anderson, P. Lodestar
  Anderson, P. The Queen of Air and Darkness
  Asimov, I. Blind alley
  Asimov, I. The Callistan menace
  Asimov, I. Christmas on Ganymede
  Asimov, I. Green patches
  Asimov, I. Half-breeds on Venus
  Asimov, I. The hazing
  Asimov, I. Homo Sol

**LIFE ON OTHER PLANETS**—*Continued*

Asimov, I. Living space
Asimov, I. Strikebreaker
Asimov, I. What is this thing called love?
Bayley, B. J. Mutation planet
Blish, J. Earthman, come home
Blish, J. Surface tension
Bloch, R. Broomstick ride
Brackett, L. Come sing the moons of Moravenn
Bretnor, R. Dr Birdmouse
Brown, F. Knock
Brown, F. Nothing Sirius
Brown, F. Obedience
Brown, F. Placet is a crazy place
Budrys, A. and Ellison, H. Wonderbird
Burroughs, E. R.  A princess of Mars
Carr, T. The Dance of the Changer and the Three
Carr, T. The winds at Starmont
Clarke, A. C. Before Eden
Clarke, A. C. Crusade
Clarke, A. C.  A meeting with Medusa
Clarke, A. C.  A walk in the dark
Clement, H. Halo
Clement, H. Lecture demonstration
Clement, H. Uncommon sense
Colin, V. The contact
Cyrano de Bergerac.  A journey to the moon; abridged
Davis, R. L. Teratohippus
Delaney, S. R. The star pit
Delaney, S. R. and Ellison, H. The power of the nail
Dickson, G. R. Black Charlie
Dickson, G. R. Brothers
Dickson, G. R. Building on the line
Dickson, G. R. The catch
Dickson, G. R. The Christmas present
Dickson, G. R. Danger—human
Dickson, G. R. Jackal's meal
Dickson, G. R. The Law-Twister Shorty
Dickson, G. R. Listen
Dickson, G. R. The man from earth
Dickson, G. R. The mousetrap
Dickson, G. R. On Messenger Mountain
Dickson, G. R. 3-part puzzle
Eisenberg, L. Conqueror
Ellison, H. Blind lightning
Farmer, P. J. The blasphemers
Farmer, P. J.  A bowl bigger than earth
Farmer, P. J. Mother
Gilden, M. What's the matter with Herbie?
Gotlieb, P. Planetoid idiot
Goulart, R. Hobo jungle
Goulart, R. The romance of Dr Tanner
Goulart, R. Shandy
Green, J. The birdlover
Green, J. Space to move
Harrison, H. Heavy duty
Harrison, H. The life preservers
Harrison, H. Wife to the Lord
Holly, J. C. The gift of nothing
Kimberly, G. Peace, love, and food for the hungry
Knight, D. Four in one
Lafferty, R. A. In outraged stone
Laumer, K. Ballots and bandits
Laumer, K. Crime and punishment
Laumer, K. Dam nuisance
Laumer, K. The Forbidden City
Laumer, K. The forest in the sky
Laumer, K. Giant Killer
Laumer, K. Mechanical advantage
Laumer, K. Once there was a giant
Laumer, K. The piecemakers
Laumer, K. The plague
Laumer, K. Trick or treaty
Laumer, K. Truce or consequences
Le Guin, U. K. Nine lives
Lem, S. The thirteenth journey of Ion Tichy
Lem, S. The twenty-fourth journey of Ion Tichy
Long, F. B. The spiral intelligence
Macfarlane, W. Free vacation
Macfarlane, W. The last leaf
McKenna, R. Hunter, come home
McKenna, R. Mine own ways
MacLennan, P. Thus love betrays us
Malzberg, B. The falcon and the falconeer
Malzberg, B. N. Opening fire
Miller, P. S. The cave
Miller, P. S. Trouble on Tantalus
Miller, W. M. The lineman
Morphett, T. Litterbug
Niven, L. Bordered in black
Nourse, A. E. Rx
Oliver, C. Blood's a rover
Oliver, C. North wind
Panshin, A.  A sense of direction
Petaja, E. Dodecagon garden
Petaja, E. Moon fever
Rocklynne, R. Ching witch!
Runyon, C. W. Sweet Helen
Russ, J. Useful phrases for the tourist
Russell, E. F.  . . . and then there were none
Russell, E. F. The Waitabits
Sallis, J. The floors of his heart
Sallis, J. The history makers
Sallis, J. Kettle of stars
Sallis, J. Letter to a young poet
Schmitz, J. H. Grandpa
Schmitz, J. H. Novice
Schmitz, J. H. The witches of Karres
Sheckley, R. Aspects of Langranak
Sheckley, R. Untouched by human hands
Sheckley, R. Welcome to the standard nightmare
Silverberg, R. Blaze of glory
Silverberg, R. Flies
Silverberg, R. Ozymandias
Silverberg, R. Point of focus
Silverberg, R. Precedent
Smith, C. A. The immeasurable horror
Smith, C. A. Marooned in Andromeda
Sternberg, J. The ephemera
Sternberg, J. Very sincerely yours
Stuart, D. A. Forgetfulness
Szilard, L. Calling all stars
Tall, S. The bear with the knot on his tail
Thomas, C. Paradise regained
Tiptree, J. The milk of Paradise
Tofte, A. Fateful first day on Xene
Tofte, A. Terrafied
Vance, J. The moon moth
Varshavsky, I. The Noneatrins

**LIFE ON OTHER PLANETS**—*Continued*
Williams, J. Somebody to play with
Wolfe, G. The fifth head of Cerberus
Yep, L. Looking-glass sea
Zebrowski, G. First love, first fear
Zelazny, R. Collector's fever
Zelazny, R. The great slow kings
Zelazny, R. The keys to December
    *See also* Interplanetary visitors; Interplanetary voyages; Martians; Space colonies; Venusians
The **life** preservers. Harrison, H.
**LIFE-SAVING.** *See* Lifesaving
**Life**-story. Barth, J.
The **life** to come. Forster, E. M.
The **life** you save. Kelley, W. M.
The **life** you save may be your own. O'Connor, F.
A **lifeguard.** Goodman, P.
**LIFESAVING**
Davis, O. The other child
Goodman, P. A lifeguard
Wain, J. The life guard
The **lift** that went down into hell. Lagerkvist, P.
**Liggett, Byron**
The cat man
Parry, M. ed. Beware of the cat
**LIGHT**
Carneiro, A. Darkness
**LIGHT-HOUSES.** *See* Lighthouses
A **light** in France. Runyon, D.
A **light** in the window. Nagibin, Y.
A **light** man. James, H.
The **light** of darkness. Clarke, A. C.
**Light** of other days. Shaw, B.
The **light** of the world. Hemingway, E.
**LIGHTHOUSES**
Bradbury, R. The beast from 20,000 fathoms
Bradbury, R. The Fog Horn
Vance, J. When the five moons rise
**Lightner, A. M.**
Best friend
    Furman, A. L. ed. Teen-age space adventures
A great day for the Irish
    Furman, A. L. ed. Teen-age space adventures
The Mars jar
    Furman, A. L. ed. Teen-age space adventures
The stone monster
    Fenner, P. R. comp. Perilous ascent
**LIGHTNING**
Bramah, E. The tragedy at Brookbend Cottage
**LIGHTNING CONDUCTORS**
Melville, H. The lightning-rod man
The **lightning**-rod man. Melville, H.
**LIGHTNING-RODS.** *See* Lightning conductors
The **lights** of Algeciras. Starke, R.
The **lights** of Spencer Primmett's eyes. Anstey, F.
**Lihn, Enrique**
Rice water
    Carpenter, H. and Brof, J. eds. Doors and mirrors

**Like.** Drexler, R.
**Like** a bad dream. Böll, H.
**Like** a piece of blues. Davis, G.
**Like** a winding sheet. Petry, A.
**Like** doves. Strindberg, A.
**Like** father. Hartridge, J.
**Like** that. McCullers, C.
**Like** the night. Carpentier, A.
**Like** visitant of air. West, J.
**Lili** Marlene. Haupt, Z.
**LILIES**
Corvo, F. Baron. About the lilies of Sanluigi
**Lilli.** Hurlbut, K.
**Lillian.** Morris, H.
**Lillian.** Runyon, D.
The **Lily** of St Pierre. Runyon, D.
**Limbo.** Carpenter, D.
**LIMBS, ARTIFICIAL.** *See* Artificial limbs
**Limehouse** nights. Burke, T.
**Lin** of Pistol Gap. Haycox, E.
**LINCOLN, ABRAHAM, PRESIDENT U.S.**
Bradbury, R. Downwind from Gettysburg
**Lind, Jakov**
Journey through the night
    Johnson, E. W. ed. Short stories international
**Linda** and Daniel and Spike. Disch, T. M.
**Lindholm, Charles**
A California novel
    Gottesman, L.; Obenzinger, H. and Senauke, A. eds. A cinch
**Lindsay, Cressida**
Watch your step
    Burke, J. ed. Tales of unease
A **line** of order. Rascoe, J.
**Line!** Style! Moravia, A.
**Linebarger, Paul.** *See* Smith, Cordwainer
The **lineman.** Miller, W. M.
**Lines** from the quick. Stiles, G.
**Link** in the chain. Gilbert, E. L.
**Linklater, Eric**
The abominable imprecation
    Linklater, E. The stories of Eric Linklater
The actress Olenina
    Linklater, E. The stories of Eric Linklater
Country-born
    Linklater, E. The stories of Eric Linklater
The Crusader's key
    Linklater, E. The stories of Eric Linklater
The dancers
    Linklater, E. The stories of Eric Linklater
The duke
    Linklater, E. The stories of Eric Linklater
Escape forever
    Linklater, E. The stories of Eric Linklater
God likes them plain
    Linklater, E. The stories of Eric Linklater
The goose girl
    Linklater, E. The stories of Eric Linklater

The **lizard.** Gottlieb, E.
**LIZARDS**
  Goulart, R. Hobo jungle
  Goulart, R. The romance of Dr Tanner
**Lizerunt.** Morrison, A.
**Llosa, Mario Vargas.** *See* Vargas Llosa, Mario
**Lloyd-Jones, Buster**
  My cats
    Montgomery, J. ed. The world's best cat stories
**"Lo! 'Twas a gala night!"** Bennett, A.
**LOANS**
  Svevo, I. Traitorously
**LOANS, PERSONAL.** *See* Money-lenders
**LOCAL GOVERNMENT**
  Holmes, E. M. First selectman
  Holmes, E. M. Town office
**Locke, David, M.**
  The power of the sentence
    Del Rey, L. ed. Best science fiction stories of the year [1972]
The **locked** house. Barr, S.
The **locked** room. Fremlin, C.
The **locker** room. Merwin, W. S.
**Locklin, Gerald**
  The monopoly story
    The Best little magazine fiction, 1970
**LOCKS AND KEYS**
  Malamud, B. Behold the key
**LOCOMOTIVES**
  Platonov, A. The fierce and beautiful world
**Locust** gleanings. Elmslie, K.
**Lodestar.** Anderson, P.
The **lodge** pin. Davis, O.
A **lodging** for the night. Stevenson, R. L.
**LODGING HOUSES.** *See* Boarding houses
**Lofthouse.** Goulart, R.
**Logan, John**
  The success
    Moss, H. ed. The poet's story
**Logan, Louis**
  The bill collector
    Gulassa, C. M. ed. The fact of fiction
**LOGGERS.** *See* Lumber industry
**LOGGING.** *See* Lumber industry
**LOGIC**
  Kemelman, H. The nine mile walk
  Stevenson, R. L. The sinking ship
The **logic** of flesh. Rindfleisch, N.
**Lohengrin's** death. Böll, H.
**Loimos.** White, E.
**L'Olam** and White Shell Woman. Greenberg, J.
**Lolita.** Parker, D.
**London, Jack**
  The devil-dog
    Hitchcock, A. ed. Alfred Hitchcock presents: Stories to stay awake by
    Same as: Diable, a dog, listed in 1959-1963 supplement
  Love of life
    Tytell, J. and Jaffe, H. eds. Affinities
  The Red One
    Clareson, T. D. ed. A spectrum of worlds

To build a fire
  Ball, J. E. ed. Designs for reading: short stories
  Howes, B. and Smith, G. J. eds. The seagreen horse
To the man on trail
  Taylor, J. G. ed. Great Western short stories
**LONDON**
  *See also* England—London
            **Parks**
  *See* Regent's Park, London
            **Police**
  Allingham, M. Mum knows best
  Futrelle, J. The missing necklace
  Collins, W. Mr Policeman and the cook
The **London** gun. Brister, B.
The **lone** charge of William B. Perkins. Crane, S.
**Lone** riding. Madden, D.
**LONELINESS**
  Ansell, J. Love, Mother
  Blake, G.  A modern development
  Boyle, P. The port wine stain
  Brennan, M. The shadow of kindness
  Butenas, N. The girl that had no face
  Cady, J. Land
  Cady, J. Play like I'm sheriff
  Calisher, H. The scream on 57th Street
  Carpenter, D. One of those big-city girls
  Cather, W. Nanette: an aside
  Chekhov, A. Misery
  Christie, A. The lamp
  Clemons, W.  A different thing
  Colter, C. The beach umbrella
  Colter, C. Rapport
  Farrell, J. T. Only tomorrow and tomorrow
  Farrell, J. T. Sunday evening
  Franklin, E. Girl in a white dress
  Grau, S. A. The other way
  Grau, S. A. Sea change
  Hayden, J. In the words of
  Jewett, S. O. The King of Folly Island
  Levine, N.  A true story
  Moravia, A. He and I
  Nemerov, H. Bon bons
  O'Hara, J. The friends of Miss Julia
  Peterkin, J. Maum Lou
  Rascoe, J. Small sounds and tilting shadows
  Rascoe, J. Twice plighted, once removed
  Roth, P. The love vessel
  Sallis, J. Les amis
  Stafford, J. The bleeding heart
  Stafford, J. Children are bored on Sunday
  Stafford, J. The hope chest
  Steinbeck, J. Pat Humbert's
  Stern, J. The force
  Strindberg, A. Needs must
  Taylor, E. Tall boy
  Wain, J. Master Richard
  Wright, S. Dans le vrai
  Yurick, S. Not with a whimper, but . . .
    *See also* Solitude
**Loneliness.** Bukowski, C.
The **loneliness** of the long-distance runner. Sillitoe, A.

## LOVE STORIES—*Continued*

The **lovers**. Berryman, J.
The **lovers** among the lepers. Masuccio
The **Lovers'** tragedy
    Cholakian, P. F. and Cholakian, R. C. eds. The early French novella
**Loving** hands at home. Patton, F. G.
**Loving**
**Losing** } a man. Oates, J. C.
**Loving**
The **loving** tongue. Goldberg, G. J.
The **low** blow. Ayrton, M.
**LOW COUNTRIES.** *See* Flanders
**Low**-lands. Pynchon, T.
**LOW TEMPERATURES**
    Asimov, I. Ring around the sun
**LOWER EAST SIDE.** *See* New York (City) —Lower East Side
**Lowry, Malcolm**
    The forest path to the spring
        Stephens, D. ed. Contemporary voices
    Ghostkeeper
        American Review 17
**LOYALTY.** *See* Faithfulness
**LOYOLA, IGNACIO DE, SAINT**
    Corvo, F. Baron. About the witch's head and Santignazio of Loyola
**Lu, Hsün**
    Benediction
        Birch, C. ed. Anthology of Chinese literature v2
        Katz, N. and Milton, N. eds. Fragment from a lost diary, and other stories
    The divorce
        Lu, Hsün. Selected stories of Lu Hsün
        Shimer, D. B. ed. Voices of modern Asia
    The flight to the moon
        Lu, Hsün. Selected stories of Lu Hsün
    Forging the swords
        Lu, Hsün. Selected stories of Lu Hsün
    A happy family
        Lu, Hsün. Selected stories of Lu Hsün
    In the wine shop
        Lu, Hsün. Selected stories of Lu Hsün
    An incident
        Lu, Hsün. Selected stories of Lu Hsün
    Kung, I-Chi
        Lu, Hsün. Selected stories of Lu Hsün
    A madman's diary
        Lu, Hsün. Selected stories of Lu Hsün
    Medicine
        Lu, Hsün. Selected stories of Lu Hsün
    The misanthrope
        Lu, Hsün. Selected stories of Lu Hsün
    My old home
        Lu, Hsün. Selected stories of Lu Hsün
    The New Year's sacrifice
        Lu, Hsün. Selected stories of Lu Hsün
    Regret for the past
        Lu, Hsün. Selected stories of Lu Hsün
    Soap
        Lu, Hsün. Selected stories of Lu Hsün
    Storm in a teacup
        Lu, Hsün. Selected stories of Lu Hsün
    Tomorrow
        Lu, Hsün. Selected stories of Lu Hsün
    The true story of Ah Q
        Lu, Hsün. Selected stories of Lu Hsün

Village opera
    Lu, Hsün. Selected stories of Lu Hsün
    *For another story by this author see* Lusin
**Lu, Siun.** *See* Lu, Hsün.
**Lucas** and Jake. Boles, P. D.
The **Lucero** requiem. Greenberg, J.
**Lucey, James D.**
    Hell at Helio Three
        Western Writers of America. With Guidons flying
**LUCIFER.** *See* Devil
**Lucifer.** Zelazny, R.
**LUCK.** *See* Chance
The **luckiest** day in history. Schwimmer, W.
The **lucky** pair. Lavin, M.
**Lucky** Pierre and the music lesson. Coover, R.
**Lucky's** Grove. Wakefield, H. R.
**Ludmila.** Montross, D.
The **lug** wrench. Roueché, B.
**Lugones, Leopoldo**
    Yzur
        Howes, B. ed. The eye of the heart
**Lu-hsün.** *See* Lu, Hsün
**LUIGI, SAINT.** *See* Aloysius Gonzaga, Saint
The **lukewarm** one. Shiina, R.
**Lukodyanov, Isai.** *See* Voiskunsky, Y. jt. auth.
**Lula** Borrow. Mabry, T.
**Lull, Roderick**
    Footnote to American history
        Lucia, E. ed. This land around us
The **lull.** Saki
**Lullaby** for the dead. Hardwick, Michael, and Hardwick, Mollie
**Lulu.** Simak, C. D.
**Lulungomeena.** Dickson, G. R.
**LUMBER CAMPS.** *See* Lumber industry
**LUMBER INDUSTRY**
    Blackhurst, W. E. The planting of "Pruny" O'Lanney
    Blackhurst, W. E. Vengeance is mine
    Kesey, K. Winter is here
    Khamsing, S. Dust underfoot
    Tendryakov, V. Three, seven, ace
**LUMBERING.** *See* Lumber industry
**LUMBERJACKS.** *See* Lumber industry
**LUMBERMEN**
    Coover, R. The door: a prologue of sorts
**Lumley, Brian**
    Ambler's inspiration
        Lumley, B. The caller of The Black
    Billy's Oak
        Lumley, B. The caller of The Black
    The caller of The Black
        Lumley, B. The caller of The Black
    Cement surroundings
        Derleth, A. ed. Tales of Cthulhu Mythos
    The Cyprus shell
        Lumley, B. The caller of The Black
    The deep-sea conch
        Derleth, A. ed. Dark things
    De Marigny's clock
        Lumley, B. The caller of The Black
    Dylath-Leen
        Lumley, B. The caller of The Black
    In the vaults beneath
        Lumley, B. The caller of The Black

# M

Ma and Tom. Steinbeck, J.

**Mabry, Thomas**
Lula Borrow
Lytle, A. ed. Craft and vision

**MACABRE TALES.** *See* Horror stories

**McAllister, Bruce**
The arrangement
Elwood, R. ed. Showcase
Benji's pencil
The Best from Fantasy and Science
Fiction; 19th ser.
The man inside
Best SF: 1969
Prime-time teaser
Ferman, E. L. and Mills, R. P. eds.
Twenty years of The Magazine of
Fantasy and Science Fiction
World of the wars
Hipolito, J. and McNelly, W. E. eds.
Mars, we love you

**Macario.** Rulfo, J.

**Macaulay, Rose**
Whitewash
Manley, S. and Lewis, G. eds. Ladies
of horror

**McAuliffe, Frank**
The Dr Sherrock commission
Bernkopf, J. F. comp. Boucher's choicest
The Iranian Farmer Commission
McComas, J. F. ed. Crimes and misfortunes
The Maltese Falcon Commission
Dickensheet, D. ed. Men and malice

**McAuslan's** court martial. Fraser, G. M.

**MACAWS.** *See* Parrots

**MacBeth, George**
The ski murders
New Directions in prose and poetry 19

**McCaffrey, Anne**
Apple
Santesson, H. S. ed. Crime prevention
in the 30th century
Daughter
Bova, B. ed. The many worlds of science fiction
Dragonrider
Nebula award stories 4
Weyr search
Analog 7
Asimov, I. ed. The Hugo winners v2

**McCarthy, Mary**
The Cicerone
McKenzie, B. ed. The process of fiction
"Cruel and barbarous treatment"
Fitz Gerald, G. ed. Modern satiric stories
The friend of the family
Auchincloss, L. ed. Fables of wit and
elegance
The hounds of summer
Abrahams, W. ed. Fifty years of the
American short story v 1
The man in the Brooks Brothers shirt
Foff, A. and Knapp, D. eds. Story
The unspoiled reaction
McKenzie, B. ed. The process of fiction

**McClatchy, J. D.**
Allonym
Prize stories, 1972: The O. Henry
Awards

**McCloud, Richard**
The widening circle
Scortia, T. N. ed. Strange bedfellows

**McCloy, Helen**
Chinoiserie
Hitchcock, A. ed. Alfred Hitchcock presents: A month of mystery
Mystery Writers of America. Dear dead
days

**McCluskey, John**
The pilgrims
Coombs, O. ed. What we must see:
young Black storytellers

**McConnell, James V.**
Learning theory
Fitz Gerald, G. ed. Modern satiric stories

**McCord, Jean**
Bitter is the hawk's path
McCord, J. Bitter is the hawk's path
Every day is yesterday again
McCord, J. Bitter is the hawk's path
Images of loss
McCord, J. Bitter is the hawk's path
The lonely price of victory
McCord, J. Bitter is the hawk's path
Sunshine yellow and red
McCord, J. Bitter is the hawk's path
Tell me not . . . unaware
McCord, J. Bitter is the hawk's path
Trial by summer
McCord, J. Bitter is the hawk's path
Trying to lick the licks
McCord, J. Bitter is the hawk's path
The watching
McCord, J. Bitter is the hawk's path
Where the aurochs lingered
McCord, J. Bitter is the hawk's path

**McCormick, James**
Mr Twohands among the rune stones
New American Review no. 2

**McCourt, James**
Mawrdew Czgowchwz
New American Review no. 13

**McCoy, Horace**
The grandstand complex
Kahn, J. ed. Hanging by a thread

**MacCreigh, James.** *See* Asimov, I. jt. auth.

**McCullers, Carson**
The aliens
McCullers, C. The mortgaged heart
Art and Mr Mahoney
McCullers, C. The mortgaged heart
Breath from the sky
McCullers, C. The mortgaged heart
Correspondence
McCullers, C. The mortgaged heart
Court in the west eighties
McCullers, C. The mortgaged heart
The haunted boy
McCullers, C. The mortgaged heart
Instant of the hour after
McCullers, C. The mortgaged heart

**McCullers, Carson—***Continued*
The jockey
    Abrahams, W. ed. Fifty years of the American short story v 1
Like that
    McCullers, C. The mortgaged heart
Madame Zilensky and the King of Finland
    Taylor, J. C. ed. The short story: fiction in transition
The orphanage
    McCullers, C. The mortgaged heart
Poldi
    McCullers, C. The mortgaged heart
Sucker
    McCullers, C. The mortgaged heart
    Stansbury, D. L. ed. Impact
A tree. A rock. A cloud
    Satin, J. ed. Reading literature
    Schulman, L. M. ed. The loners
Untitled piece
    McCullers, C. The mortgaged heart
Who has seen the wind?
    McCullers, C. The mortgaged heart
Wunderkind
    McCullers, C. The mortgaged heart
    Spinner, S. ed. Feminine plural

**McCullough, Ken**
Chuck Berry, won't you please come home
    Ellison, H. ed. Again, dangerous visions

**MacDiarmid, Hugh**
Tam Mackie's trial
    Haining, P. ed. The clans of darkness

**MacDonald, Anson**
By his bootstraps
    The Astounding-Analog reader v 1
    *For other titles by this author see*
    Heinlein, Robert A.

**MacDonald, John D.**
The annex
    Best SF: 1968
Funny the way things work out
    Kahn, J. ed. Hanging by a thread
Half-past eternity
    Nolan, W. F. ed. The human equation
Hangover
    McComas, J. F. ed. Crimes and misfortunes
Hit and run
    Gibson, W. ed. Rogues' gallery
    A Treasury of modern mysteries v2
The homesick Buick
    Hitchcock, A. ed. Alfred Hitchcock presents: Stories to stay awake by
The legend of Joe Lee
    Hitchcock, A. ed. Alfred Hitchcock presents: A month of mystery

**Macdonald, Philip**
Private—keep out!
    Ferman, E. L. and Mills, R. P. eds. Twenty years of The Magazine of Fantasy and Science Fiction

**Macdonald, Ross**
Find the woman
    McComas, J. F. ed. Crimes and misfortunes

Gone girl
    Mystery Writers of America. Merchants of menace
    Mystery Writers of America. Murder most foul
The singing pigeon
    Hitchcock, A. ed. Alfred Hitchcock presents: A month of mystery

**McDougal. Brown, F. L.**

**Macdougall, Arthur R.**
The sun stood still
    Corodimas, P. ed. In trout country

**McElroy, Joseph**
The accident
    New American Review no. 2

**McEwan, Ian**
Disguises
    American Review 18
Homemade
    New American Review no. 15

**MacEwen, Gwendolyn**
House of the whale
    Fourteen stories high

**McFadden, David**
Who can avoid a place?
    New Canadian stories, 72

**Macfarlane, W.**
Free vacation
    Analog 7
The last leaf
    Orbit 9
To make a new Neanderthal
    Del Rey, L. ed. Best science fiction stories of the year [1972]

**McGahern, John**
Bomb box
    McGahern, J. Nightlines
Christmas
    McGahern, J. Nightlines
Coming into his kingdom
    McGahern, J. Nightlines
Hearts of oak and bellies of brass
    McGahern, J. Nightlines
Korea
    McGahern, J. Nightlines
Lavin
    McGahern, J. Nightlines
My love, my umbrella
    McGahern, J. Nightlines
Peaches
    McGahern, J. Nightlines
The recruiting officer
    McGahern, J. Nightlines
Strandhill, the sea
    McGahern, J. Nightlines
Wheels
    McGahern, J. Nightlines
Why we're here
    McGahern, J. Nightlines

**McGeer, Patricia**
Campaign fever
    Hitchcock, A. ed. Alfred Hitchcock presents: Stories to stay awake by
Justice has a high price
    Mystery Writers of America. Mirror, mirror, fatal mirror

The **magnificent** possession. Asimov, I.
**Magnolia** blossom. Christie, A.
The **mahout.** Smith, C. A.

**MAHOUTS**
Kipling, R. Moti Guj—mutineer

**Maia, C. Vasconcelos**
Sun
Cohen, J. M. ed. Latin American writing today

The **maid** and I. Vassilikos, V.
A **maid** of modern Athens. Saltus, E.
The **maid** of Saint Philippe. Chopin, K.
The **maiden.** Stafford, J.
**Maiden** lady. Drake, R.

**MAIDS.** *See* Servants—Maids
**Maids** and mistresses. Vassilikos, V.
**Maigret** and the lazy burglar. Simenon, G.
**Maigret** in society. Simenon, G.
**Maigret's** failure. Simenon, G.

**MAIL CARRIERS.** *See* Postal service
**Mail** day. Thomason, J. W.
**Mail**-order bride. Hayes, A. H.

**MAIL ORDER BUSINESS**
Hayes, A. H. Mail-order bride

**Mailer, Norman**
The man who studied yoga
Charyn, J. ed. The troubled vision

**MAILMEN.** *See* Postal service
**Mainchance.** Tate, P.

**Maine, Charles Eric**
Short circuit
Burke, J. ed. Tales of unease

**MAINE**
Brodeur, P. The proposal
Chase, M. E. Hannah and Benjamin Stevens
Curley, D. Look homeward, tourist
Holmes, E. M. A part of the main; 27 stories
Naylor, P. R. Brief visit back
Pearlman, E. Which Eleanor am I?
Theroux, P. Hayseed
Warner, L. Melissa Savage

**Country life**
*See* Country life—Maine

**Farm life**
*See* Farm life—Maine

**Mainlanders.** Brown, R.
**Maja** Thurup. Bukowski, C.
The **majesty** of the law. O'Connor, F.
**Major** Aranda's hand. Reyes, A.

**MAJORCA**
Curley, D. The gingerbread man

The **major's** tale. Bierce, A.
**Makar's** dream. Korolenko, V.
The **maker.** Borges, J. L.
**Makes** the whole world kin. Henry, O.
**Making** changes. Michaels, L.
**Making** it through. Malzberg, B. N.
The **making** of a New Yorker. Henry, O.
The **making** of Americans. Stein, G.
The **making** of Ashenden. Elkin, S.
The **Malacca** Cane. Vigny, A. de

**MALADJUSTED CHILDREN.** *See* Problem children

**Malamud, Bernard**
Angel Levine
Foff, A. and Knapp, D. eds. Story
Schulman, L. M. ed. The cracked looking glass
Behold the key
Davis, R. G. ed. Ten modern masters
The bill
Davis, R. G. ed. Ten modern masters
Black is my favorite color
Gulassa, C. M. ed. The fact of fiction
Kissin, E. H. ed. Stories in black and white
McKenzie, B. ed. The process of fiction
The death of me
Simon, J. ed. Fourteen for now
The German refugee
Ribalow, H. U. ed. My name aloud
Spinner, S. ed. Live and learn
God's wrath
The Best American short stories, 1973
In retirement
Malamud, B. Rembrandt's hat
The Jewbird
Disch, R. and Schwartz, B. eds. Killing time
Hall, J. B. ed. The realm of fiction
Howes, B. and Smith, G. J. eds. The sea-green horse
Larson, C. R. ed. Prejudice: 20 tales of oppression and liberation
Roecker, W. A. ed. Stories that count
The last Mohican
Schulman, L. M. ed. Travelers
Thune, E. and Prigozy, R. eds. Short stories: a critical anthology
The letter
Malamud, B. Rembrandt's hat
The magic barrel
Davis, R. G. ed. Ten modern masters
Johnson, E. W. ed. Short stories international
McKenzie, B. ed. The process of fiction
Man in the drawer
Abrahams, W. ed. Fifty years of the American short story v 1
Malamud, B. Rembrandt's hat
Prize stories, 1969: The O. Henry Awards
Winter's tales 15
My son the murderer
Malamud, B. Rembrandt's hat
Oates, J. C. ed. Scenes from American life
Prize stories, 1970: The O. Henry Awards
Notes from a lady at a dinner party
Malamud, B. Rembrandt's hat
Pictures of Fidelman
The Best American short stories, 1969
Pre-game
Charyn, J. ed. The troubled vision
Rembrandt's hat
Malamud, B. Rembrandt's hat
The silver crown
Malamud, B. Rembrandt's hat

Malamud, Bernard—*Continued*
  Talking horse
    Malamud, B. Rembrandt's hat
    Prize stories, 1973: The O. Henry
      Awards
MALARIA
  Verga, G. Malaria
Malaria. Verga, G.
The Malay krise. Smith, C. A.
MALAYA
  Theroux, P. The South Malaysia Pineapple
    Growers' Association
MALAYSIA. *See* Malaya
MALDON, BATTLE OF, 991
  Walsh, J. P. and Crossley-Holland, K.
    Wordhoard
MALICIOUS MISCHIEF
  Auchincloss, L. The prison window
  Brennan, J. P. The mystery of Myrrh Lane
  Brennan, J. P. The ransacked room
  Irving, J. Almost in Iowa
  Jackson, S. The possibility of evil
  Lyon, D. "Silence!"
  Theroux, P.    A deed without a name
Malleson, Lucy Beatrice. *See* Gilbert, An-
    thony
Mallet-Joris, Françoise
  Anne
    Mallet-Joris, F. The witches
  Elizabeth
    Mallet-Joris, F. The witches
  Jeanne
    Mallet-Joris, F. The witches
Malone, John
  The fugitives
    Prize stories, 1973: The O. Henry
      Awards
  Ground glass
    New American Review no. 3
Maloney, Ralph
  Benny
    Maloney, R. Fish in a stream in a cave
  The best man
    Maloney, R. Fish in a stream in a cave
  A bird of gaudy plumage
    Maloney, R. Fish in a stream in a cave
  Gallantry
    Maloney, R. Fish in a stream in a cave
  Harry W. A. Davis, jr.
    Maloney, R. Fish in a stream in a cave
  The help comes in bottles
    Maloney, R. Fish in a stream in a cave
  Intimacy
    The Best American short stories, 1972
    Maloney, R. Fish in a stream in a cave
  Last stop before the carbarn
    Maloney, R. Fish in a stream in a cave
  Natalie
    Maloney, R. Fish in a stream in a cave
  Viva Caporetto!
    Maloney, R. Fish in a stream in a cave
  The way it all comes loose
    Maloney, R. Fish in a stream in a cave
  What I need don't come in suitcases
    Maloney, R. Fish in a stream in a cave
  Yankee go home
    Maloney, R. Fish in a stream in a cave

Malraux, André
  March 21, 1927
    Kraus, R. and Wiegand, W. eds. Stu-
      dent's choice
Malstrom, Robert C.
  The great A
    New dimensions 1
The Maltese Cat. Kipling, R.
The Maltese Falcon Commission. McAu-
    liffe, F.
Maltz, Albert
  Afternoon in the jungle
    Maltz, A. Afternoon in the jungle
  Circus come to town
    Maltz, A. Afternoon in the jungle
  The cop
    Maltz, A. Afternoon in the jungle
  The farmer's dog
    Maltz, A. Afternoon in the jungle
  The happiest man on earth
    Maltz, A. Afternoon in the jungle
  Man on a road
    Maltz, A. Afternoon in the jungle
  Sunday morning on Twentieth Street
    Maltz, A. Afternoon in the jungle
  The way things are
    Maltz, A. Afternoon in the jungle
  With laughter
    Maltz, A. Afternoon in the jungle
Malzberg, Barry N.
  Agony column
    Hitchcock, A. ed. Alfred Hitchcock pre-
      sents: Stories to be read with the
      lights on
  The battered-earth syndrome
    Elwood, R. and Kidd, V. eds. Saving
      worlds
  Conquest
    Best SF: 1971
    New dimensions 1
  Conversations at Lothar's
    Elwood, R. ed. Children of infinity
  Culture lock
    Elwood, R. ed. Future city
  Dreaming and conversions: two rules by
      by which to live
    Nova 3
  Exploration
    Hipolito, J. and McNelly, W. E. eds.
      Mars, we love you
  The falcon and the falconeer
    SF: authors' choice 3
  Gehenna
    Best SF: 1971
  The interceptor
    Best detective stories of the year, 1973
  Making it through
    Elwood, R. ed. And walk now gently
      through the fire, and other science
      fiction stories
  The men inside
    New dimensions 2
  Notes for a novel about the first ship ever
      to Venus
    Universe 1
  Notes just prior to the fall
    The Best from Fantasy and Science Fic-
      tion; 19th ser.

The man who loved monkeys more than human beings. Anand, M. R.

The man who loved the Faioli. Zelazny, R.

The man who loved trees. Bullock, M.

The man who made people. Francis, H. E.

The man who never forgot. Silverberg, R.

The man who never told a lie. Asimov, I.

The man who played too well. Von Elsner, D.

The man who ploughed the sea. Clarke, A. C.

The man who read Sir Arthur Conan Doyle. Brittain, W.

The man who read Waugh. De Vries, P.

The man who saw Gunga Din thirty times. Bova, B.

The man who saw through heaven. Steele, W. D.

The man who shared his hut. Kenyatta, J.

The man who sold the moon. Heinlein, R. A.

The man who studied yoga. Mailer, N.

The man who talked with books. Lewis, L.

The man who turned into a cat. Day, J. W.

The man who walked home. Tiptree, J.

The man who wanted to be in the movies. Jakes, J.

The man who wanted to give up. Bahr, J.

The man who was. Kipling, R.

The man who was a horse. Lester, J.

The man who was almost a man. Wright, R.

The man who was always wishing. Holst, S.

The man who was drafted. Curley, D.

The man who was left behind. Ingalls, R.

The man who was loved. Stern, J.

The man who waved hello. Dozois, G. R.

The man who went to Chicago. Wright, R.

The man who would be king. Kipling, R.

The man with a thousand legs. Long, F. B.

The man with nerve. White, S. E.

A man with the bagpipes. Zobarskas, S.

The man with the knives. Böll, H.

The man with the memory. Bichsel, P.

The man with the sack. Allingham, M.

The man with the speckled eyes. Lafferty, R. A.

A man with two lives. Bierce, A.

The man without a body. Mitchell, E. P.

Man without a name. Ulibarri, S. R.

Manacled. Crane, S.

Management. Lamb, M.

The manager. O'Hara, J.

**Manchester, William**
Record run
Fenner, P. R. comp. Where speed is king

**Mandell, Marvin**
The Aesculapians
The Best American short stories, 1972

**Mandelstam, Osip**
Fourth prose
Scammell, M. ed. Russia's other writers

**MANDEVILLE, SIR JOHN**
Smith, C. A. A tale of Sir John Maundeville

**MANDOLIN PLAYERS.** *See* Musicians—Mandolin players

**MANDRAKE**
Dam, A. The mandrake

The mandrake. Dam, A.

The mandrakes. Smith, C. A.

**MANHATTAN.** *See* New York (City)—Manhattan

Manhole 69. Ballard, J. G.

The manhood of Edward Robinson. Christie, A.

The manhood of Neilly Sullivan. Conlin, J.

The manhunt. Curley, D.

**MANHUNTS**
Anderson, S. E. The contraband
Borges, J. L. The life of Tadeo Isidoro Cruz (1829-1874)
Connell, R. The most dangerous game
Curley, D. The manhunt
Faulkner, W. Red leaves
Fox, J. Man-hunting in the Pound
Frazee, S. My brother down there
Grant, C. L. The summer of the Irish Sea
Harrison, H. The wicked flee
Lanier, S. His only safari
McGivern, W. P. Killer on the turnpike
Scott, D. C. Charcoal
Woolrich, C. New York blues
*See also* Convicts, Escaped; Fugitives

Manikin. Michaels, L.

**MANILA.** *See* Philippine Islands—Manila

**MANITOBA.** *See* Canada—Manitoba

**Mann, Francis Oscar**
The devil in a convent
Haining, P. ed. The ghouls

**Mann, Thomas**
The clown
Steinhauer, H. ed. Ten German novellas
Disorder and early sorrow
Davis, R. G. ed. Ten modern masters
Insights
Gladius Dei
Hall, J. B. ed. The realm of fiction
The infant prodigy
Davis, R. G. ed. Ten modern masters
Little Herr Friedemann
Davis, R. G. ed. Ten modern masters
Thune, E. and Prigozy, R. eds. Short stories: a critical anthology
Mario and the magician
Foff, A. and Knapp, D. eds. Story
Hamalian, L. and Volpe, E. L. eds. Eleven modern short novels

Manna. Phillips, P.

**MANNED UNDERSEA RESEARCH STATIONS**
Lee, W. M. Sea home

A manner of legacy. Byrne, D.

**Manners, Margaret**
The plot
Mystery Writers of America. Crime without murder
Squeakie's second case
Hitchcock, A. ed. Alfred Hitchcock presents: Stories to stay awake by

**MANNERS.** *See* Etiquette

Manners. Peterkin, J.

The Mannichon solution. Shaw, I.

**Manning, Olivia**
The Banana House
Winter's tales 17
Girls together
Winter's tales 15

**Manning, Robert**
 Don't fish while I'm talking
  Corodimas, P. ed. In trout country
**Manoff, Eva**
 Mama and the spy
  Ribalow, H. U. ed. My name aloud
**Manov, Emil**
 Vanya and the statuette
  Kirilov, N. and Kirk, F. eds. Introduction to modern Bulgarian literature
A **man's** best friend. Du Fail, N.
**Man's** best friend. Stuart, D.
A **man's** crazy to want to go to Philadelphia. Cuomo, G.
**Man's** highest duty. Premchand
**Mansfield, Katherine**
 Bliss
  Foff, A. and Knapp, D. eds. Story
  12 short story writers
 A dill pickle
  Konigsberg, I. ed. The classic short story
  Thune, E. and Prigozy, R. eds. Short stories: a critical anthology
 The doll's house
  Authors' choice
  Konigsberg, I. ed. The classic short story
 The fly
  Taylor, J. C. ed. The short story: fiction in transition
 The garden-party
  12 short story writers
 Psychology
  12 short story writers
**MANSIONS.** See Houses
**MANSLAUGHTER.** See Assassination; Crime and criminals; Murder stories; Mystery and detective stories
**MANTA RAY.** See Ray (Fishes)
**Mantage.** Matheson, R.
The **Manterfield** inheritance. Partington, C.
The **Mantzen** diamond mystery. Brennan, J. P.
**MS.** found in a bottle. Poe, E. A.
**Manuscript** found in a police state. Aldiss, B.
**MANUSCRIPTS**
 Bellow, S. The Ganzaga manuscripts
 Borges, J. L. The immortals
 Forster, E. M. Ansell
 Greenberg, A. "Franz Kafka" by Jorge Luis Borges
 Malamud, B. Man in the drawer
 Pasternak, B. Il tratto di Apelle
 Wilson, C. The return of the Lloigor
**Many** mansions. Silverberg, R.
**Many** many women. Stein, G.
**Mao, Tun**
 Spring silkworms
  Birch, C. ed. Anthology of Chinese literature v2
The **marble** works. Hesse, H.
**MARBLES (GAME)**
 Carr, J. A steelie for the King
 Proulx, E. A. The baroque marble
The **March** assize. Warren, S.
**March** 21, 1927. Malraux, A.
**March** 2000: the taxpayer. Bradbury, R.
**Marchenko, Irena**
 Gaily but sadly
  Whitney, T. P. ed. The young Russians

**MARCHES (DEMONSTRATIONS)** See Demonstrations; Dissenters
**MARCHES FOR CIVIL RIGHTS.** See Negroes—Civil rights
The **marching** morons. Kornbluth, C. M.
**Marching** through Boston. Updike, J.
**Mare, Walter de la.** See De La Mare, Walter
**Maredata** and Giulio; or, The Ocean spirit
  Haining, P. ed. Gothic tales of terror
**Margaret** of Navarre. See Marguerite de Navarre
The **margenes.** DeFord, M. A.
**Margins.** Becker, J.
**Margroff, Robert E. and Offutt, Andrew, J.**
 The book
  Orbit 8
**Marguérite d' Angoulême, Queen of Navarre.** See Marguerite de Navarre
**Marguerite de Navarre**
 A bedtime story
  Cholakian, P. F. and Cholakian, R. C. eds. The early French novella
 A case of sacred and profane love
  Bishop, M. ed. A Renaissance storybook
 A lesson to errant wives
  Bishop, M. ed. A Renaissance storybook
 A love match
  Cholakian, P. F. and Cholakian, R. C. eds. The early French novella
 The priest and the plowman
  Cholakian, P. F. and Cholakian, R. C. eds. The early French novella
 The tonsured husband
  Cholakian, P. F. and Cholakian, R. C. eds. The early French novella
 The virtuous widow
  Bishop, M. ed. A Renaissance storybook
 The wise and foolish ladies
  Cholakian, P. F. and Cholakian, R. C. eds. The early French novella
**Maria** painted silver. Trevisan, D.
The **Marias.** Trevisan, D.
**Marie.** Kotzwinkle, W.
**Marigolds.** Collier, E.
**MARIHUANA**
 Bukowski, C. The big pot game
 Updike, J. Bech takes pot luck
**Marihuana** and a pistol. Himes, C. B.
**MARIJUANA.** See Marihuana
**MARINE CORPS.** See United States. Marine Corps
**MARINE RESOURCES**
 Clarke, A. C. The man who ploughed the sea
 Sheckley, R. and Ellison, H. I see a man sitting on a chair, and the chair is biting his leg
**MARINES.** See United States. Marine Corps
**Marines** at Blanc Mont. Thomason, J. W.
**Marines** see the Revolution. Thomason, J. W.
**Marines** signaling under fire at Guantanamo. Crane, S.
**Marinković, Ranko**
 Badges of rank
  Johnson, B. ed. New writing in Yugoslavia
**Marino, John**
 Little violin
  Voices of Brooklyn

**MARRIAGE PROBLEMS**—*Continued*

An, Su-Gil. The green chrysanthemum
Ansell, J. Night out
Ard, J. M.    A la mode
Atwood, M. The grave of the famous poet
Auchincloss, L. Days of wrath
Auchincloss, L. Second chance
Auchincloss, L. The waiver
Bahr, J. Deedie and her lovers
Bahr, J. The polite captain
Bambara, T. C. The survivor
Banks, R. The drive home
Barlay, K.    A mistake of creation
Barthelme, D. Critique de la vie quotidienne
Barthelme, D. Perpetua
Bassani, G.    A night in '43
Beal, M. F. Survival
Beekman, A. Behind every man
Beekman, A. The expert
Beneš, J. The mother of the regiment
Bergé, C. The challenge
Bergé, C. Events of a March night
Bergé, C. In motion
Bergengruen, W. Ordeal by fire
Bingham, S. Rachel's island
Blanc, S. An inside straight
Bloch, R. Fat chance
Borgese, E. M. The mongol
Boulle, P. Interferences
Brewster, H. The marquis and the crocodile
Brister, B. The canvasback jury
Brister, B. The sharks
Brown, F. Witness in the dark
Burke, J. Don't you dare
Burke, T. Ding-Dong-Dell
Burke, T. The paw
Campo, V. Raymond, his wife, and his women
Canzoneri, R. The weight of feathers
Casper, L. Aflame; in flower
Casper, L.    A lion unannounced
Cather, W. The Bohemian girl
Cather, W. The bookkeeper's wife
Cather, W. Eleanor's house
Cather, W. Flavia and her artists
Cather, W. The marriage of Phaedra
Cather, W. The profile
Cather, W. The willing muse
Cervantes. Marriage à la mode
Cheever, J. The brigadier and the golf widow
Cheever, J. The chimera
Cheever, J. The fourth alarm
Cheever, J. The geometry of love
Chekhov, A. An anonymous story
Chekhov, A. The butterfly
Chekhov, A. La cigale
Chekhov, A. The lady with the dog
Chekhov, A.    A little crime
Chekhov, A. My wife
Chekhov, A. Neighbours
Chekhov, A. Ninochka
Chekhov, A. Peasant women
Chekhov, A. Terror
Childress, W. Uncle Roman
Chopin, K. Athénaïse

Clarke, A. C. What happened?
Cohen, M. Josephine's literary choice
Colette. Dawn
Collier, J.    A dog's a dog
Collier, J. Without benefit of Galsworthy
Colter, C. Overnight trip
Cooke, R. T. Mrs Flint's married experience
Costello, M. Murphy in Missouri
Costello, M. Murphy's misogyny
Crawford, M. The real me
Cullinan, E. The power of prayer
Curley, D. Love in the winter
Czoe, Zông-Hûi. The memorial service on the mountain
Daguio, A. Wedding dance
Davis, O. Constance
Davis, O. Loss and chaos
Deck, J. An offering
Deck, J. One Sunday in Spain
De Vries, P. Double or nothing
De Vries, P. Forever panting
De Vries, P. Heart
De Vries, P. You and who else?
Di Donato, P. And your sister too!
Di Donato, P. The Cabala
Di Donato, P. Farewell to Brahms
Di Donato, P. The fireplace
Di Donato, P. The overnight guest
Dillon, M. Induce
Disch, T. M. Emancipation: a romance of the times to come
Drake, R. The pressure cooker
Drake, R. The wrong element
Ellin, S. The last bottle in the world
Elman, R.    I O U
Engel, M. Amaryllis
Everett, Mrs H. D.    A water witch
Farrell, J. T. Tom Carroll
Fiedler, L. A. Pull down vanity!
Fielding, G. The trip
The Fifteenth joy of marriage
Forster, E. M. The obelisk
Francis, H. E. One of the boys
Francis, H. E. The transfusion man
Fremlin, C. For ever fair
Fremlin, C. The irony of fate
Friedman, P. The arm of interchangeable parts
Friedman, P. An evening of fun
Friedman, P. In equal parts
Friedman, P. The inheritance editor
Fuchs, D. Twilight in southern California
Fuentes, C. The two Elenas
Gaines, E. J.    A long day in November
Gallant, M. An alien flower
Gilliatt, P. Albert
Gilliatt, P. Come back if it doesn't get better
Gilliatt, P. Foreigners
Gilliatt, P. Nobody's business
Glanville, B. The director's wife
Glaze, E. Madeira
Goldberg, G. J. Thursday
Gordimer, N. The life of the imagination
Gordimer, N. Why haven't you written?
Goulart, R. Keeping an eye on Janey
Graham, W. The Japanese girl
Graham, W. The Wigwam

**MARRIAGE PROBLEMS—***Continued*

Sillitoe, A. Isaac Starbuck
Sillitoe, A. Revenge
Sillitoe, A. The road
Singer, I. B. Altele
Singer, I. B. Blood
Singer, I. B. Dr Beeber
Singer, I. B. Gimpel the fool
Singer, I. B. Her son
Singer, I. B. The mentor
Singer, I. B. On a wagon
Singer, I. B. The prodigy
Singer, I. B. The riddle
Singer, I. B. The third one
Singer, I. B. The unseen
Sisskind, M. The dawn of a new day
Slesinger, T. On being told that her second husband has taken his first lover
Smith, P. C. Osborn and Sabrina
Spielberg, P. Back to back
Spielberg, P. The last day of winter
Spielberg, P.  A visit to the doctor's wife
Stafford, J. Cops and robbers
Stafford, J.  A country love story
Starke, R. The lights of Algeciras
Stephens, R. Horses
Stern, J. Our father
Stoker, B.  A star trap
Strindberg, A. Bad luck
Strindberg, A. Bread
Strindberg, A. The bread-winner
Strindberg, A.  A business deal
Strindberg, A. Cheated
Strindberg, A. The child
Strindberg, A.  A doll's house
Strindberg, A. Duel
Strindberg, A. His poem
Strindberg, A. Just to be married
Strindberg, A. Like doves
Strindberg, A. Misfits
Strindberg, A. Natural obstacles
Strindberg, A. With or without the ceremony of marriage
Stuart, J. Little giant
Summers, H. The cardboard screen
Thomason, J. W. Love story of a Marine
Thompson, K. Still life composition: Woman's clothes
Tišma, A. Personality
Toonder, J. G. The spider
Trevisan, D. Death on the square
Trevisan, D. Hotel room
Trevisan, D. Maria painted silver
Trevisan, D. My dear husband
Trevisan, D. Nausea
Trevisan, D. Penelope
Trevisan, D. The perfect crime
Trevisan, D. Skinned alive
Trevisan, D. Thirty-seven nights of passion
Trevisan, D. This bed which is mine which is thine
Trevor, W. The Mark-2 wife
Turgenev, I. The inn
Updike, J. Eros rampant
Updike, J. Solitaire
Updike, J. Sublimating
Updike, J. The witnesses
Vaižgantas. Sin at Easter
Verga, G. Donna Santa's sin
Verga, G. Ieli
Verga, G. Stinkpot
The Voice from on high
Walker, A. Her sweet Jerome
Walker, A. "Really, doesn't crime pay?"
Ward, J. Three Washington stories: The brigadier general and the columnist's wife
Warren, R. P. Meet me in the green glen
West, J. Mother's Day
Wieland, C. M. Love and friendship tested
Wilson, A. After the show
Wilson, A. Once a lady
Wodehouse, P. G. Jane gets off the fairway
Wolitzer, H. Ending
Wolitzer, H. In the flesh
Woolrich, C. For the rest of her life
Yashpal. The book of experience
Yatskiv, M. Cedar wood will grow
Yellen, S. The four sides of a triangle
Zieroth, D. Jeremey, his arrangements
Zobarskas, S. The actress
   *See also* Bigamy; Desertion and non-support; Divorce; Husband and wife; Love affairs; Sex problems

A **marriage** proposal. Greene, G.

**MARRIAGE PROPOSALS**

Brodeur, P. The proposal
Greene, G.  A marriage proposal
Maugham, W. S. Cupid and the Vicar of Swale
Maugham, W. S. Flirtation
Maugham, W. S. Lady Habart
Sturgeon, T. and Ward, D. The waiting thing inside

A **marriage** tragedy. Collins, W.

**Marriott, Anne**

Stella
   Winter's tales 18

**Marriott-Watson, Ethel**

The witch of the marsh
   Haining, P. ed. A circle of witches

**Marryat, H. B.**

The werewolf
   Manley, S. and Lewis, G. eds. Shapes of the supernatural

**MARS (PLANET)**

Asimov, I. Heredity
Asimov, I. The Martian way
Bixby, J. The holes around Mars
Blish, J. No jokes on Mars
Boucher, A. Balaam
Bradbury, R. April 2003: the musicians
Bradbury, R. April 2005: Usher II
Bradbury, R. April 2026: the long years
Bradbury, R. August 1999: the summer night
Bradbury, R. August 2001: the settlers
Bradbury, R. August 2002: night meeting
Bradbury, R. August 2005: the old ones
Bradbury, R. August 2026: there will come soft rains
Bradbury, R. December 2001: the green morning
Bradbury, R. December 2005: the silent towns
Bradbury, R. February 2002: the locusts
Bradbury, R. February 2003: interim

MARS (PLANET)—*Continued*
  Bradbury, R. The fire balloons
  Bradbury, R. January 1999: rocket summer
  Bradbury, R. June 2001:—and the moon be still as bright
  Bradbury, R. June 2003: way in the middle of the air
  Bradbury, R. The lost city of Mars
  Bradbury, R.  I, Mars
  Bradbury, R. Mars is heaven!
  Bradbury, R. The Martian chronicles; 28 stories
  Bradbury, R. May 2003: the wilderness
  Bradbury, R. The naming of names
  Bradbury, R. Night call, collect
  Bradbury, R. November 2002: the fire balloons
  Bradbury, R. November 2005: the luggage store
  Bradbury, R. November 2005: the off season
  Bradbury, R. November 2005: the watchers
  Bradbury, R. October 2002: the shore
  Bradbury, R. October 2026: the million-year picnic
  Bradbury, R. The one who waits
  Bradbury, R. September 2005: the Martian
  Bradbury, R. 2004-05: the naming of names
  Burroughs, E. R.   A princess of Mars
  Clarke, A. C. Loophole
  Clarke, A. C. Transit of Earth
  Delany, S. R. High Weir
  Del Rey, L. Dark mission
  Dick, P. K. We can remember it for you wholesale
  Dickson, G. R. Whatever gods there be
  Harrison, H. One step from earth
  Hipolito, J. comp. Mars, we love you; 16 stories
  Klein, G. The valley of echoes
  Long, F. B. Good to be a Martian
  Long, F. B. Mr Caxton draws a Martian bird
  McAllister, B. World of the wars
  Malzberg, B. N. Exploration
  Miller, P. S. The cave
  Miller, W. M. Crucifixus etiam
  Piper, H. B. Omnilingual
  Smith, G. O. Lost art
  Weinbaum, S. G.   A Martian odyssey
  Wells, H. G. War of the worlds
  Wollheim, D. A. The embassy
      *See also* Interplanetary voyages; Martians

Mars is heaven! Bradbury, R.
The Mars jar. Lightner, A. M.
Mars revisited. Minot, S.
Mars-station. Kevles, B.
Marse Chan. Page, T. N.
MARSEILLES. *See* France—Marseilles
Marsh, Anthony
  Loaded with money
      Mystery Writers of America. Crime without murder

Marsh, John
  The appointment
      Burke, J. ed. Tales of unease
Marsh, Ngaio
  The cupid mirror
      Dickinson, S. ed. The drugged cornet, and other mystery stories
  Death on the air
      Manley, S. and Lewis, G. eds. Grande dames of detection
Marsh, Richard
  The man who cut off my hair
      Greene, Sir H. ed. The further rivals of Sherlock Holmes
Marsh, Willard
  Beachhead in Bohemia
      Marsh, W. Beachhead in Bohemia
  Blood harvest
      Marsh, W. Beachhead in Bohemia
  Darkling I listen
      Marsh, W. Beachhead in Bohemia
  Forwarding service
      Marsh, W. Beachhead in Bohemia
  Honor bright
      Marsh, W. Beachhead in Bohemia
  It always comes out dixie
      Marsh, W. Beachhead in Bohemia
  Mending wall
      Oates, J. C. ed. Scenes from American life
  Mexican hayride
      Marsh, W. Beachhead in Bohemia
  My house is yours
      Marsh, W. Beachhead in Bohemia
  On Jordan's stormy banks
      Marsh, W. Beachhead in Bohemia
  A sentimental journey
      Marsh, W. Beachhead in Bohemia
  The vigil
      Marsh, W. Beachhead in Bohemia
  A winter's tale
      Marsh, W. Beachhead in Bohemia
The Marsha Summers song book, part I. Miller, J.
The Marsha Summers song book, part II. Miller, J.
The Marsha Summers song book, part III. Miller, J.
Marshal for Las Moras. Barker, E.
Marshall, Edison
  The flying lion
      Moskowitz, S. ed. Horrors unknown
Marshall, Joyce
  A private place
      New Canadian stories, 73
Marshall, Lenore
  Almost caught
      Marshall, L. The confrontation, and other stories
  The better ending
      Marshall, L. The confrontation, and other stories
  Christmas Eve
      Marshall, L. The confrontation, and other stories
  The closed door
      Marshall, L. The confrontation, and other stories

Marshall, Lenore—*Continued*

The confrontation
    Marshall, L. The confrontation, and other stories
Dialogue on a cliff
    Marshall, L. The confrontation, and other stories
The dog
    Marshall, L. The confrontation, and other stories
Eclipse
    Marshall, L. The confrontation, and other stories
Flashlight
    Marshall, L. The confrontation, and other stories
A gift of love
    Marshall, L. The confrontation, and other stories
Grandfather's nude swim
    Marshall, L. The confrontation, and other stories
The leaning tower
    Marshall, L. The confrontation, and other stories
A matter of taste
    Marshall, L. The confrontation, and other stories
The meteor boy
    Marshall, L. The confrontation, and other stories
The segregated hearts
    Marshall, L. The confrontation, and other stories
Unknown artist
    Marshall, L. The confrontation, and other stories

Marshall, Paule
To Da-duh, in memoriam
    Long, R. A. and Collier, E. W. eds. Afro-American writing v2

MARSHALS. *See* Sheriffs
MARSHES
Alberts, A. The swamp
Alter, R. E. Man hunt on Dead Yank Creek
Brister, B. Grandfather's geese
Hamelink, J. A pause in the thunder
Lovecraft, H. P. The moon bog
MARTHA'S VINEYARD. *See* Massachusetts —Martha's Vineyard
A Martian odyssey. Weinbaum, S. G.
The Martian way. Asimov, I.
MARTIANS
Andrevon, J. P. Observation of Quadragnes
Anmar, F. Jenny among the zeebs
Asimov, I. History
Asimov, I. The secret sense
Boucher, A. Expedition
Bradbury, R. August 1999: the Earth men
Bradbury, R. February 1999: Ylla
Bradbury, R. September 2005: the Martian
Burroughs, E. R. A princess of Mars
Carr, T. Hop-friend
Clarke, A. C. Loophole
Del Rey, L. Dark mission
Knight, D. Catch that Martian

Long, F. B. Man of distinction
Miller, P. S. The cave
Smith, C. A. An adventure in futurity
Weinbaum, S. G. A Martian odyssey
Wells, H. G. War of the worlds
Zelazny, R. A rose for Ecclesiastes
    *See also* Interplanetary visitors
The martyr. O'Connor, F.
MARTYRS
Pangborn, E. My brother Leopold
The marvelous Marshall. Eisenberg, L.
MARY, VIRGIN
Corvo, F. Baron. About the original fritter of Sangiuseppe
Delany, S. R. The unicorn tapestry
Meek, F. M. Mary and the seven birthdays
Traven, B. When the priest is not at home
Mary. Collier, J.
Mary. Knight, D.
Mary and Joe. Mitchison, N.
Mary and Norma. O'Hara, J.
Mary and the seven birthdays. Meek, F. M.
Mary Murder. Nye, R.
MARYLAND

Ocean City
Barth, J. Lost in the funhouse
Mary's convert. Colter, C.
Mask in the cage. Di Donato, P.
The mask of the bear. Laurence, M.
Masks. Knight, D.
The masks of purpose. Linklater, E.
MASOCHISM
Smith, C. A. Something new
Mason, A. E. W.
The cruise of the "Willing Mind"
    Green, R. L. ed. Ten tales of adventure
The masque of the Red Death. Poe, E. A.
The masquerade of souls. Lagerkvist, P.
MASQUERADES
Colette. The secret woman
O'Connor, F. Enoch and the gorilla
Poe, E. A. The masque of the Red Death
Sayers, D. L. The queen's square
MASS
O'Connor, F. The teacher's mass
Stafford, J. Between the porch and the altar
Mass for unknown soldiers. Di Donato, P.
The Mass Island. O'Connor, F.
MASS MEDIA
Kaplan, B. Media scare
MASSACHUSETTS

17th century
Hawthorne, N. My kinsman, Major Molineux

20th century
Cheever, J. The jewels of the Cabots
Cheever, J. Percy
Updike, J. The hillies

Boston
Jewett, S. O. A born farmer
Jewett, S. O. The hare and the tortoise
McPherson, J. A. Gold Coast
O'Faolain, S. The planets of the years
Theroux, P. A love knot
Warner, L. The girl who liked Communists

A **matter** of need. Toole, W.
A **matter** of pride. Hershman, M.
A **matter** of rationale. Brister, B.
A **matter** of recordings. Eisenberg, L.
A **matter** of size. Fast, H.
A **matter** of survival. Friedman, P.
A **matter** of taste. Collier, J.
A **matter** of taste. Kurland, M.
A **matter** of taste. La Guma, A.
A **matter** of taste. Marshall, L.
A **matter** of time and place. Eisenberg, L.
A **matter** of vocabulary. McPherson, J. A.

**Matthews, Clayton**
The big stretch
  Best detective stories of the year, 1971
The dummy
  Best detective stories of the year [1969]
The legacy
  Mystery Writers of America. Dear dead
  days

**Matthews, Jack**
Another story
  The Best American short stories, 1970
The girl at the window
  Matthews, J. ed. Archetypal themes in
  the modern story
On the shore of Chad Creek
  Prize stories, 1972: The O. Henry
  Awards

**Matthews, James**
The party
  Larson, C. R. ed. African short stories
  Larson, C. R. ed. Prejudice: 20 tales of
  oppression and liberation

**Maturin, Charles Robert**
Leixlip Castle
  Haining, P. ed. Gothic tales of terror
The parricide's tale
  Haining, P. ed. The wild night com-
  pany: Irish stories of fantasy and
  horror

Maud-Evelyn. James, H.

Maud Martha and New York. Brooks, G.

**Maugham, W. Somerset**
Appearance and reality
  Fitz Gerald, G. ed. Modern satiric
  stories
A bad example
  Maugham, W. S. Seventeen lost stories
The choice of Amyntas
  Maugham, W. S. Seventeen lost stories
The Colonel's lady
  Untermeyer, L. ed. Treasury of great
  humor
Cousin Amy
  Maugham, W. S. Seventeen lost stories
Cupid and the Vicar of Swale
  Maugham, W. S. Seventeen lost stories
Daisy
  Maugham, W. S. Seventeen lost stories
De amicitia
  Maugham, W. S. Seventeen lost stories
Faith
  Maugham, W. S. Seventeen lost stories
Flirtation
  Maugham, W. S. Seventeen lost stories
The fortunate painter
  Maugham, W. S. Seventeen lost stories

German Harry
  Bowman, J. S. ed.   A book of islands
Good manners
  Maugham, W. S. Seventeen lost stories
The Greek
  Gibson, W. ed. Rogues' gallery
The happy couple
  Maugham, W. S. Seventeen lost stories
An Irish gentleman
  Maugham, W. S. Seventeen lost stories
Lady Habart
  Maugham, W. S. Seventeen lost stories
Lord Mountdrago
  Knight, D. ed. Perchance to dream
The magician
  Haining, P. ed. The ghouls
A man from Glasgow
  Haining, P. ed. The Lucifer society
A marriage of convenience
  Maugham, W. S. Seventeen lost stories
A point of law
  Maugham, W. S. Seventeen lost stories
Pro patria
  Maugham, W. S. Seventeen lost stories
The punctiliousness of Don Sebastian
  Maugham, W. S. Seventeen lost stories

**MAUI.** *See* Hawaii—Maui

**Maul, Michael**
Pao-yu and the Grand Duchess
  Intro 4

**Maum** Lou. Peterkin, J.

**MAUNDEVILLE, SIR JOHN.** *See* Mandeville, Sir John

**Maupassant, Guy de**
Abandoned
  Maupassant, G. de. French tales of love
  and passion
The adoption
  Maupassant, G. de. Fifteen by Maupas-
  sant
  Same as: The adopted child, listed in
  1964-1968 supplement
The adventure of Walter Schnaffs
  Maupassant, G. de. Fifteen by Maupas-
  sant
Am I insane?
  Maupassant, G. de. Selected short stories
At the mountain inn
  Maupassant, G. de. Fifteen by Maupas-
  sant
Ball-of-Fat
  Maupassant, G. de. Selected short stories
  Same as: Ball of Tallow and Boule de
  Suif, both listed in basic volume; The
  cocotte; Tallow Ball
Bellflower
  Maupassant, G. de. The cocotte, and
  three other stories
  Maupassant, G. de. Selected short stories
  Same as: Clochette
Châli
  Maupassant, G. de. Selected short stories
The Christening
  Maupassant, G. de. French tales of love
  and passion
Clochette
  Maupassant, G. de. French tales of love
  and passion
  Same as: Bellflower

**Maupassant, Guy de**—*Continued*
The cocotte
  Maupassant, G. de. The cocotte, and
    three other stories
  Same as: Ball-of-Fat; Ball of Tallow
    and Boule de Suif, both listed in
    basic volume; Tallow Ball
A country excursion
  Konigsberg, I. ed. The classic short
    story
  Maupassant, G. de. Selected short stories
A crisis
  Maupassant, G. de. Selected short stories
The diamond necklace
  Maupassant, G. de. Selected short stories
  Same as: The necklace
The duel
  Konigsberg, I. ed. The classic short
    story
  Same as: A coward, listed in earlier
    volumes
The false gems
  Foff, A. and Knapp, D. eds. Story
  Maupassant, G. de. The cocotte, and
    three other stories
  Maupassant, G. de. Selected short stories
  Same as: The jewels, listed in earlier
    volumes
A family
  Maupassant, G. de. French tales of love
    and passion
The farmer
  Maupassant, G. de. French tales of love
    and passion
  Same as: Farmer's wife, listed in earlier
    volumes
The father
  Maupassant, G. de. Selected short stories
A fishing excursion
  Lyons, N. ed. Fisherman's bounty
  Same as: Fishing party, listed in basic
    volume
For sale
  Maupassant, G. de. French tales of love
    and passion
The guardian
  Maupassant, G. de. Fifteen by Maupas-
    sant
The hermit
  Maupassant, G. de. French tales of love
    and passion
The homecoming
  Maupassant, G. de. Fifteen by Maupas-
    sant
The Horla
  Elwood, R. and Ghidalia, V. eds. An-
    droids, time machines and blue
    giraffes
The horseman
  Maupassant, G. de. Fifteen by Maupas-
    sant
How he got the Legion of Honor
  Maupassant, G. de. Selected short stories
Lasting love
  Maupassant, G. de. French tales of love
    and passion
Letter found on a drowned man
  Maupassant, G. de. French tales of love
    and passion

A little walk
  Maupassant, G. de. Am I insane?
Love: three pages from a sportsman's book
  Maupassant, G. de. Fifteen by Maupas-
    sant
  Satin, J. ed. Reading literature
  12 short story writers
  Tytell, J. and Jaffe, H. eds. Affinities
Madame Tellier's establishment
  Maupassant, G. de. French tales of love
    and passion
  Same as: Mme Tellier's excursion
Mme Tellier's excursion
  Maupassant, G. de. Selected short stories
  Same as: Madame Tellier's establish-
    ment
Mademoiselle Fifi
  Maupassant, G. de. French tales of love
    and passion
Mademoiselle Perle
  Maupassant, G. de. Fifteen by Maupas-
    sant
  Same as: Mademoiselle Pearl, listed in
    earlier volumes
A man of influence
  Maupassant, G. de. Fifteen by Maupas-
    sant
Minuet
  Taylor, J. C. ed. The short story: fiction
    in transition
  Same as: The dancers, listed in earlier
    volumes
Miss Harriet
  Maupassant, G. de. Selected short stories
Moonlight
  Maupassant, G. de. Selected short stories
  Same as: Clair de lune, listed in basic
    volume; In the moonlight, listed in
    earlier volumes
My Uncle Jules
  Maupassant, G. de. Fifteen by Maupas-
    sant
The necklace
  Ball, J. E. ed. Designs for reading: short
    stories
  Same as: The diamond necklace
Nerves
  Kahn, J. ed. Some things strange and
    sinister
A Normandy joke
  Maupassant, G. de. Selected short stories
On the river
  Manley, S. and Lewis, G. eds. Shapes of
    the supernatural
  Maupassant, G. de. Fifteen by Maupas-
    sant
Our letters
  Maupassant, G. de. French tales of love
    and passion
The piece of string
  Hall, J. B. ed. The realm of fiction
  Maupassant, G. de. Selected short stories
  Same as: The string, listed in earlier
    volumes
A practical joke
  Maupassant, G. de. Selected short stories
The rabbit
  Maupassant, G. de. French tales of love
    and passion

**Maupassant, Guy de**—*Continued*
Room number eleven
    Maupassant, G. de. French tales of love and passion
    Maupassant, G. de. Selected short stories
A sale
    Maupassant, G. de. French tales of love and passion
Semillante
    Bowman, J. S. ed. A book of islands
    Same as: The vendetta, listed in earlier volumes
Simon's papa
    Maupassant, G. de. The cocotte, and three other stories
    Maupassant, G. de. Fifteen by Maupassant
    Maupassant, G. de. Selected short stories
The story of a farm girl
    Konigsberg, I. ed. The classic short story
    Maupassant, G. de. Selected short stories
The Tallow Ball
    Maupassant, G. de. French tales of love and passion
    12 short story writers
    Same as: Ball-of-Fat; Ball of Tallow and Boule de Suif, both listed in basic volume; The cocotte
The two friends
    Maupassant, G. de. Fifteen by Maupassant
Two little soldiers
    12 short story writers
    Same as: Little soldier, listed in basic volume
Ugly
    Maupassant, G. de. French tales of love and passion
Under the yoke
    Maupassant, G. de. French tales of love and passion
Useless beauty
    Thune, E. and Prigozy, R. eds. Short stories: a critical anthology
    Same as: Vain beauty, listed in earlier volumes
A vagabond
    Maupassant, G. de. Selected short stories
    Same as: The tramp, entered in basic volume; The vagrant
The vagrant
    Maupassant, G. de. Fifteen by Maupassant
    Same as: The tramp, entered in basic volume; A vagabond
Waiter, a bock!
    Maupassant, G. de. Selected short stories
A wife's confession
    Maupassant, G. de. French tales of love and passion
The wreck
    Maupassant, G. de. Fifteen by Maupassant

**Maura's** friends. Cullinan, E.

**Mauriac, François**
A Christmas tale
    Morton, M. ed. Voices from France

**MAURITANIA**
Godfrey, D. Kwame Bird Lady Day

**Maurois, André**
The house
    Kahn, J. ed. Some things strange and sinister

**Maverick.** Dickson, G. R.

**Mawrdew** Czgowchwz. McCourt, J.

**Max** and the pacemaker. Gold, H.

**Maximov, Herman**
The ultimate threshold
    Ginsburg, M. ed. The ultimate threshold

**Maximov, Vladimir**
House in the clouds
    Scammell, M. ed. Russia's other writers

**MAXIMUS, MAGNUS CLEMENS, EMPEROR OF ROME**
Kipling, R.   A Centurion of the Thirtieth
Kipling, R. On the Great Wall
Kipling, R. The Winged Hats

**Maxwell, Beatrice Heron-** *See* Heron-Maxwell, Beatrice

**Maxwell, James A.**
Strictly from the Mississippi
    Lewis, J. D. ed. Tales of our people

**Maxwell, William**
The gardens of Mont-Saint-Michel
    The Best American short stories, 1970
What every boy should know
    Schulman, L. M. ed. The loners

**Maxwell's** monkey. Pangborn, E.

**May, Derwent**
Grace note
    Hamilton, A. ed. Splinters

**May, Frances**
Company in the orchard
    Derleth, A. ed. Dark things

**MAY DAY**
Barrett, M. Death out of season

**May 2003**: the wilderness. Bradbury, R.

**May** we borrow your husband? Greene, G.

**Maybe** Jean-Baptiste Pierre Antoine de Monet, Chevalier de Lamarck, was a little bit right. Scott, R.

**Maybelle's** first-born. Stuart, J.

**Mayberry, Florence V.**
The beauty in that house
    Ellery Queen's Mystery Magazine. Ellery Queen's Mystery bag

**Mayer, Tom**
A birth in the Delta
    Mayer, T. The weary Falcon
The feel of it
    Kraus, R. and Wiegand, W. eds. Student's choice
Kafka for President
    Mayer, T. The weary Falcon
The last operation
    Mayer, T. The weary Falcon
A walk in the rain
    Mayer, T. The weary Falcon
The weary Falcon
    Mayer, T. The weary Falcon

**Mayhall, Jane**
The Enemy
    Prize stories, 1973: The O. Henry Awards

**MEETINGS**
 Farber, J. Gorman
 Fremlin, C. The special gift
**MEETINGS, PUBLIC.** *See* Public meetings
**Megged, Aharon**
 An unusual deed
  Rabikovitz, D. ed. The new Israeli writers
 The white city
  Michener, J. A. ed. First fruits
**Meh** Lady: a story of the war. Page, T. N.
**Meighan, Astrid**
 Shoe the horse and shoe the mare
 Insights
**Meinhold, Wilhelm**
 The amber witch
  Bleiler, E. F. ed. Five Victorian ghost novels
  Haining, P. ed. A circle of witches
**MELANCHOLIA.** *See* Depression, Mental
**Meles** vulgaris. Boyle, P.
**Melissa** Savage. Warner, L.
**Melon** flowers. Johnson, L.
**Melville, Herman**
 Bartleby
  Foff, A. and Knapp, D. eds. Story
  Same as: Bartleby the scrivener
 Bartleby the scrivener
  Disch, R. and Schwartz, B. eds. Killing time
  Matthews, J. ed. Archetypal themes in the modern story
  Taylor, J. C. ed. The short story: fiction in transition
  Tytell, J. and Jaffe, H. eds. Affinities
  Same as: Bartleby
 The lightning-rod man
  Stansbury, D. L. ed. Impact
The **members.** Caldwell, B.
The **memento.** Henry, O.
**Memento.** Thompson, T.
**Memoirs** of Carwin, the biloquist. Brown, C. B.
A **memorable** murder. Thaxter, C.
**MEMORIAL DAY**
 Jewett, S. O. The Parshley celebration
**Memorial** Fund. O'Hara, J.
The **memorial** service on the mountain. Czoe, Zông-Hûi
**Memories** of a curfew. Theroux, P.
**MEMORY**
 Barthelme, D. Träumeri
 Bichsel, P. The man with the memory
 Bryant, E. The legend of Cougar Lou Landis
 Carpentier, A. Journey back to the source
 Conway, G. F. Funeral service
 Dick, P. K. We can remember it for you wholesale
 Dozois, G. R. A dream at noonday
 Drake, R. The voices of women at the back of my mind
 Drake, R. You scoundrel of a beast
 Elmslie, K. Waking up
 Farmer, P. J. Sketches among the ruins of my mind
 Kanin, G. Sign that boy!
 Kawabata, Y. House of the sleeping beauties

Maxwell, W. The gardens of Mont-Saint-Michel
Nye, R. Axel
Sheckley, R. The Mnemone
Silverberg, R. The man who never forgot
Sternig, L. Total recall
Stewart, N. Acacias
**MEMORY, LOSS OF.** *See* Amnesia
A **memory.** Lavin, M.
**MEMPHIS.** *See* Tennessee—Memphis
The **men.** Bichsel, P.
The **men.** Stewart, J. I. M.
**Men** against the sea. Hewat, A. V.
**Men** at work. Greene, G.
The **men** in the storm. Crane, S.
The **men** inside. Malzberg, B. N.
**Men** of good will. Bova, B.
**Men** of letters. Brú, H.
The **men** on the GI bill. Glanville, B.
The **men** return. Vance, J.
**Mencken, H. L.**
 The visionary
  Fitz Gerald, G. ed. Modern satiric stories
**Mending** wall. Marsh, W.
**Mene,** Mene, Tekel, Upharsin. Cheever, J.
**Menelaiad.** Barth, J.
**MENOPAUSE**
 Carpenter, D. One of those big-city girls
**MENSERVANTS.** *See* Servants—Menservants
**MENTAL DEFECTIVES.** *See* Feebleminded; Mentally handicapped
**MENTAL DEPRESSION.** *See* Depression, Mental
**MENTAL HOSPITALS.** *See* Mentally ill—Care and treatment
**MENTAL ILLNESS**
 Accioly, B. João Urso
 Andersen, B. The passage
 Ansell, J. Eating out
 Betts, D. The spider gardens of Madagascar
 Bingham, S. The wedding
 Bloch, R. The plot is the thing
 Bukowski, C. Nut ward just east of Hollywood
 Bumpus, J. In Utica
 Chopin, K. La belle Zoraïde
 Dann, J. M. The drum lollipop
 Drake, R. She was strangely affected
 Feldman, A. Rian's story
 Forster, E. M. Albergo Empedocle
 Francis, H. E. Contemplations of ecstasy on the day of my suicide
 Fremlin, C. The quiet game
 Friedman, B. J. The hero
 García Márquez, G. Nabo
 Garrett, G. A game of catch
 Garshin, V. The red flower
 Gaskell, J. Jane
 Gilbert, A. Sleep is the enemy
 Gilbert, S. M. Weeping
 Godfrey, D. Kwame Bird Lady Day
 Godwin, G. A sorrowful woman
 Goldberg, G. J. The death of Los Angeles
 Goldberg, G. J. Tyme
 Heard, G. The cat, "I Am"
 Henderson, Z. Swept and garnished

Metamorphosis. Agnon, S. Y.
Metamorphosis. Hippius, Z.
The metamorphosis. Kafka, F.
The metamorphosis. Oates, J. C.
The metamorphosis of Earth. Smith, C. A.
The metaphysician's nightmare. Russell, B.
Metcalf, John
  A bag of cherries
    Metcalf, J. ed. Sixteen by twelve
  The estuary
    Metcalf, J. ed. Sixteen by twelve
  The strange aberration of Mr Ken Smythe
    New Canadian stories, 73
Metcalfe, John
  'Beyondaril'
    Derleth, A. ed. Dark things
METEMPSYCHOSIS. See Transmigration
The meteor boy. Marshall, L.
Meter, measure or catalogue raisonné. Rascoe, J.
A method bit in "B". Wolfe, G.
METHODIST CHURCH
  Henderson, D. Caroline and the nuns
Mewed up. Brent, P.
Mexican hayride. Marsh, W.
MEXICANS IN CALIFORNIA
  Cleaver, E. The flashlight
  Scortia, T. N. The goddess of the cats
  Steinbeck, J. Flight
MEXICANS IN THE UNITED STATES
  Cather, W. The dance at Chevalier's
  Crane, S.  A man and some others
  Gault, W. C. The murder car
  Hughes, M. G. The Judge
  McKimmey, J. Runners in the park
  Peirce, J. F. The hot tamales murder case
  Santiago, D. The somebody
MEXICO
  Weil, A. Four silver pitchers
  Witton, D. Teen-age Mexican stories; 6
    stories
### 20th century
  Allen, J. H. Tales of Diego
  Bellow, S. Mosby's memoirs
  Fuentes, C. Holy place
  Fuentes, C. The two Elenas
  Galey, J. H. The jawbone
  Greene, G. Across the bridge
  Marsh, W. Mexican hayride
  Marsh, W. My house is yours
  Nussbaum, A. The one who got away
  Porter, K. A. Flowering Judas
  Porter, K. A. Virgin Violeta
  Stone, R. Porque no tiene, porque le falta
### Acapulco
  Petaja, E.  A dog's best friend
### Cuernavaca
  Witton, D. The miracle of the Kings
### Guanajuato
  Trevino, E. B. de. The secret of the wall
### Mexico City
  Crane, S. The five white mice
  Crane, S. The wise men: a detail of American life in Mexico
  Sheckley, R. Doctor Zombie and his furry little friends
  Witton, D. The quarrel

### Police
  See Police—Mexico
### Religion
  Castro, A. de. The electric executioner
### Teotihuacán
  Witton, D. The buried city
### Tijuana
  Ellison, H.   O ye of little faith
MEXICO, GULF OF
  Grau, S. A. Pillow of stone
MEXICO, PROVINCIAL AND RURAL
  García Márquez, G. The day after Saturday
  Green, B. K. Saddle marks
  Marsh, W. Blood harvest
  Marsh, W. Honor bright
  Marsh, W. The vigil
  Marsh, W.   A winter's tale
  Rulfo, J. The day of the landslide
  Rulfo, J. They gave us the land
  Witton, D. The potter's wheel
  Woolrich, C. The moon of Montezuma
MEXICO CITY. See Mexico—Mexico City
Meyer, Conrad Ferdinand
  The sufferings of a boy
    Steinhauer, H. ed. Ten German novellas
The mezzotint. James, M. R.
MIAMI. See Florida—Miami
MICE
  Collier, J. The steel cat
  Fast, H. The mouse
  Fine, W. The mousechildren and the famous collector
  Hunter, E. Inferiority complex
  Kafka, F. Josephine the singer
  Landolfi, T. Hands
  Shapiro, L. Pals
Michael Kohlhaas. Kleist, H. von
Michaels, Leonard
  City boy
    Charyn, J. ed. The single voice
    Elkin, S. ed. Stories from the sixties
    Michaels, L. Going places
  Crossbones
    Michaels, L. Going places
    New American Review no. 3
  The deal
    Michaels, L. Going places
  Fingers and toes
    Michaels, L. Going places
  Finn
    Michaels, L. Going places
  Getting lucky
    New American Review no. 10
  Going places
    Michaels, L. Going places
  A green thought
    Michaels, L. Going places
  Intimations
    Michaels, L. Going places
  Isaac
    Michaels, L. Going places
  Making changes
    McCrindle, J. F. ed. Stories from the Transatlantic Review
    Michaels, L. Going places

**Milner, Ron**
The flogging
  King, W. ed. Black short story anthology
The ray
  King, W. ed. Black short story anthology

**Miłosz, Czesław**
Brognart
  Tyrmand, L. ed. Explorations in freedom: prose, narrative, and poetry from Kultura
Magdalena
  Tyrmand, L. ed. Explorations in freedom: prose, narrative, and poetry from Kultura

**Milton, John R.**
The inheritance of Emmy One Horse
  The Best American short stories, 1969

**Mimic.** Sillitoe, A.

The **mimosa** blight. Patton, F. G.

**Mimsy** were the borogoves. Padgett, L.

**MIND AND BODY**
  Moravia, A. Words and the body

**Mind** is how you go. Shewan, I.

The **mind** of God. Fast, H.

**Mind** out of time. Laumer, K.

**Mind** over matter. Queen, E.

**MIND READING**
  Bellamy, E. To whom this may come
  Hoffmann, E. T. A. Master Flea
  Kornbluth, C. M. The mindworm
  Shaw, I. Whispers in Bedlam
    *See also* Thought transference

**Minding** their own business. Spears, R. S.

The **mind's** eye mystery. Allingham, M.

**Mindship.** Conway, G. F.

The **mindworm.** Kornbluth, C. M.

**MINE ACCIDENTS**
  Beneš, J. The last possibility
  Griffith, J. Black Goddess

**Mine** own ways. McKenna, R.

**Mine,** yet not mine. Shecktor, M. C.

**MINERS.** *See* Mines and mining; and specific types of mines and mining, e.g. Coal mines and mining; Gold mines and mining; etc.

**MINES AND MINING**
  Castro, A. de. The electric executioner
  Hebel, J. P. An unexpected reunion
  Hoffmann, E. T. A. The mines of Falun
  Kafka, F. A visit to a mine
  Le Guin, U. K. Nine lives
  Twain, M. Dick Baker's cat
    *See also* Coal mines and mining; Gold mines and mining; Silver mines and mining

The **mines** of Falun. Hoffmann, E. T. A.

**Minette.** Aiken, J.

**Ming, Shih.** *See* Shih, Ming

**MINING TOWNS**
  Sienkiewicz, H. A legionary of Mieroslawski

**Minister** in a straw hat. Wolkers, J.

**MINISTERS.** *See* Clergy

The **minister's** Black Veil. Hawthorne, N.

**Minkov, Svetoslav**
The begonia
  Kirilov, N. and Kirk, F. eds. Introduction to modern Bulgarian literature
Laughter in Ramonia
  Kirilov, N. and Kirk, F. eds. Introduction to modern Bulgarian literature

**Minna** Minna Mowbray. Joseph, M.

**MINNESOTA**

**St Paul**
  Fitzgerald, F. S. He thinks he's wonderful
  Rindfleisch, N. In loveless clarity

**Minnie** again. Hughes, L.

The **minocorn.** Ayrton, M.

**Minor, William**
The anniversary
  The Best little magazine fiction, 1970

The **minor** repairs of life. Warner, L.

**MINORITIES.** *See* names of races or peoples living within a country dominated by another nationality, e.g. Mexicans in the U. S.

A **minority.** O'Connor, F.

**Minot, Stephen**
Journey to Ocean Grove
  Minot, S. and Wilson, R. eds. Three stances of modern fiction
Mars revisited
  Gulassa, C. M. ed. The fact of fiction
  Prize stories, 1971: The O. Henry Awards

The **minotaur.** Gor, G.

**MINSTRELS**
  Coolidge, O. The politicians 1192-1193
  Crane, S. At the pit door
  Eisenstein, P. Born to exile
  Yeats, W. B. The crucifixion of the outcast

**Minty's** day. Greene, G.

**Minuet.** Maupassant, G. de

**Minuke.** Kneale, N.

The **miracle** in Cana. Pekić, B.

The **miracle** of Purun Bhagat. Kipling, R.

The **miracle** of the Kings. Witton, D.

The **Miracle** of the snow child
  Cholakian, P. F. and Cholakian, R. C. eds. The early French novella

The **miracle** on the sea. Peretz, I. L.

The **miracle** worker. Selph, W.

The **miracle** workers. Vance, J.

**MIRACLES**
  Anderson, P. A chapter of revelation
  Bergengruen, W. Ordeal by fire
  Borges, J. L. The secret miracle
  The Day the sun stood still; 3 stories
  Dickson, G. R. Things which are Caesar's
  Kipling, R. The miracle of Purun Bhagat
  Peretz, I. L. The miracle on the sea
  Queiroz, D. S. de. Tarciso
  Robertson, J. W. She went to buy yarn
  Ruyslinck, W. The Madonna with the lump
  Silverberg, R. Thomas the proclaimer
    *See also* Mary, Virgin; Marriage in Cana (Miracle)

**Miracles** cannot be recovered. Bioy-Casares, A.

**MIRAGES**
  Smith, C. A. Told in the desert

**Miriam.** Capote, T.

The **mirror**. Singer, I. B.
**Mirror** of ice. Wright, G.
The **mirror** of Lida Sal. Asturias, M. A.
The **Mirror** of Nitocris. Lumley, B.
A **mirror** of the waves. Woods, W. C.
**Mirror**-play. Colette
The **mirror** story. Holst, S.
**MIRRORS**
  Kippax, J. Reflection of the truth
  Lindsay, C. Watch your step
  Lumley, B. The Mirror of Nitocris
  Shaw, B. Light of other days
  Singer, I. B. The mirror
**Mirsky, Mark**
  Mourner's Kaddish
    New Directions in prose and poetry 22
  Simcha
    Charyn, J. ed. The single voice
The **misanthrope**. Lu, Hsun
**Misbegotten** missionary. *See* Asimov, I.
  Green patches
**MISCARRIAGE.** *See* Abortion
**MISCARRIAGE OF JUSTICE**
  Hardwick, Michael, and Hardwick, Mollie.
    The bo'sun's body
**MISCEGENATION.** *See* Inter-racial mar-
  riage
**Miscount.** Gloeckner, C. N.
**Miscreant** from Murania. Eddy, C. M.
**Misdeal.** Landolfi, T.
**MISERS**
  Cooke, R. T. Mrs Flint's married expe-
    rience
  Henry, O. The enchanted profile
  Jewett, S. O. The Growtown "Bugle"
  Jewett, S. O. Mrs Parkins's Christmas Eve
  Verga, G. Property
**Miser's** gold. Queen, E.
**Misery.** Chekhov, A.
The **misfit**. Vaižgantas
**Misfits.** Strindberg, A.
**Mishev, Georgi**
  The rabbit census
    Kirilov, N. and Kirk, F. eds. Introduc-
      tion to modern Bulgarian literature
**Mishima, Yukio**
  Death in midsummer
    Johnson, E. W. ed. Short stories inter-
      national
  Patriotism
    Tytell, J. and Jaffe, H. eds. Affinities
  The pearl
    Thune, E. and Prigozy, R. eds. Short
      stories: a critical anthology
  Three million yen
    Hall, J. B. ed. The realm of fiction
    Shimer, D. B. ed. Voices of modern
      Asia
The **misplaced** machine. Veiga, J. J.
**Miss** A. and Miss M. Taylor, E.
**Miss** Bertha and the Yankee. Collins, W.
**Miss** Emeline. Lee, M.
**Miss** Harriet. Maupassant, G. de
**Miss** Kemper comes home in the dark.
  Yamamoto, M.
**Miss** Lace. Ansell, J.
**Miss** lady. Holst, S.
**Miss** Lawrance will be at home. Glan-
  ville, B.

**Miss** Leonora when last seen. Taylor, P.
**Miss** McEnders. Chopin, K.
**Miss** Manning's minister. Jewett, S. O.
**Miss** Mary Pask. Wharton, E.
**Miss** Muriel. Petry, A.
**Miss** Nora. Patterson, L.
**Miss** Omega Raven. Mitchison, N.
**Miss** Paisley on a diet. Pierce, J.
**Miss** Pall. Rakesh, M.
**Miss** Pinkerton's apocalpyse. Spark, M.
**Miss** Prinks. Dickson, G. R.
**Miss** Rose. Boles, P. D.
**Miss** Smith. Trevor, W.
**Miss** Urst visits the Deer Park. Holm, S.
**Miss** Yellow Eyes. Grau, S. A.
**Missie.** Peterkin, J.
**MISSING ARTICLES**
  Rajagopalachari, C. The nose jewel
  Singer, I. B. The briefcase
The **missing** man. MacLean, K.
The **missing** necklace. Futrelle, J.
**MISSING PERSONS.** *See* Disappearances
The **missing** symbol. Fairman, P. W.
**Mission** to Ghana. Deutsch, A. H.
**MISSIONARIES**
  Borges, J. L. Doctor Brodie's report
  Bradbury, R. The fire balloons
  Bradbury, R. November 2002: the fire
    balloons
  Branson, R. The red-headed murderess
  Forster, E. M. The life to come
  Hesse, H. Robert Aghion
  Jennings, G. Sooner or later or never never
  Steele, W. D. The man who saw through
    heaven
  Stevenson, R. L. The beach of Falesá
**MISSIONARIES, MEDICAL**
  Thomason, J. W. The Sergeant runs away
**MISSIONS**

### Africa
  Greene, G. Church militant

### California
  Cather, W. The conversion of Sum Loo
  Wister, O. Padre Ignazio

### India
  White, R. First voice

### Montana
  Weaver, G. Haskell hooked on the north-
    ern Cheyenne
**Missis** Flinders. Slesinger, T.
**MISSISSIPPI**
  Canzoneri, R. City of heaven
  Canzoneri, R. The harp of the winds
  Canzoneri, R. Sunday preacher
  Faulkner, W. Old man
  Thelwell, M. The organizer
  Welty, E. Moon Lake
**Mississippi** Ham Rider. Bambara, T. C.
**MISSISSIPPI RIVER**
  Hemingway, E. Crossing the Mississippi
**MISSOURI**
  Schultz, J. Eenie meenie minie mo
  Thelwell, M. Direct action

### Country life
  *See* Country life—Missouri

### Politics
  *See* Politics—Missouri

The **Monk** of horror; or, The Conclave of corpses
    Haining, P. ed. Gothic tales of terror
**Monkey**-meat. Thomason, J. W.
**MONKEYS**
    Anand, M. R. The man who loved monkeys more than human beings
    Davidson, A. Sacheverell
    Des Périers, B. The sagacious monkey
    Forester, C. S. Depth charge!
    Kipling, R. Kaa's hunting
    Lispector, C. Marmosets
    Marsh, W. The vigil
    Wilhelm, K. The planners
    Wyndham, J. Jizzle
        *See also* Apes
**MONKS**
    Agnon, S. Y. First kiss
    Chekhov, A. The Black Monk
    Chekhov, A.   A tale without a title
    Corvo, F. Baron. About the miraculous fritter of Frat' Agostino of the Cappuccini
    Deutsch, A. H. Bruised reeds
    Deutsch, A. H. Builder of kingdoms
    Deutsch, A. H. Mission to Ghana
    Deutsch, A. H. Obedience without delay
    Deutsch, A. H. The quality of reward
    Deutsch, A. H. Refining fire
    Farmer, P. J. Prometheus
    Farmer, P. J. Sail on! Sail on!
    Gardner, J. The temptation of St Ivo
    Goudge, E. Three men
    Henry, O. The robe of peace
    Hippius, Z. It's all for the worse
    Hippius, Z. The pilgrim
    Hippius, Z. With the star
    La Sale, A. de. The knight, the lady, and the Abbot
    La Sale, A. de. Little Jehan de Saintré
    Margaret of Navarre. A case of sacred and profane love
    Masuccio. Fra Ieronimo and the miraculous arm
    Masuccio. A quick-witted cleric
    Maturin, C. R. The parricide's tale
    Maugham, W. S. Faith
    The Monk of horror
    Moore, B. Catholics
    O'Connor, F. Lost fatherlands
    Parabosco, G. Friar Stefano's resurrection
    Sermini, G. Sister Savina and Brother Girolamo
    Seth, R. The exorcising of the restless monk
    Yeats, W. B. The crucifixion of the outcast
        *See also* Abbots
**MONOLITHS.** *See* Monuments
**MONOLOGS**
    Barthelme, D. Träumerei
    Drake, R. Cousin Hon
    Drake, R. The fifth wheel
    Drake, R. Maiden lady
    Drake, R. The pressure cooker
    Drake, R. The ring-tail tooter
    Drake, R. The wrong element
    Parker, D. Just a little one
    Parker, D. Lady with a lamp
    Parker, D. The little hours
    Parker, D. Sentiment
    Parker, D.   A telephone call
    Quin, A. Motherlogue
    Ruskay, S. Cycles
    Ruskay, S. The indestructible Sarah B. at the age of eighty
    Tindall, G. The visitor
**Monologue** of an old pitcher. Farrell, J. T.
**Monologue** of Isabel watching it rain in Macondo. García Márquez, G.
The **monopoly** story. Locklin, G.
**Monroe, Donald M.**
    Ransome at Sublimity
        New American Review no. 14
The **Monroe** Street monster. Holst, S.
**Monsieur** Charles. Hebel, J. P.
**Monsieur** Maurice. Edwards, A. B.
**Monsoon** Selection Board. Fraser, G. M.
The **monster.** Crane, S.
The **monster.** DeFord, M. A.
The **monster.** Moravia, A.
The **monster** and the maiden. Zelazny, R.
The **monster** of Lakeview. Pentecost, H.
**Monster** of terror. Lovecraft, H. P.
**MONSTERS**
    Aandahl, V. An adventure in the Yolla Bolly Middle Eel Wilderness
    Ballard, J. G. Storm-bird, storm-dreamer
    Biggle, L. The Botticelli horror
    Bradbury, R. The beast from 20,000 fathoms
    Bradbury, R. The Fog Horn
    Chapman, S. Burger Creature
    Coburn, A. The tale of the fourth stranger
    Collier, J. Man overboard
    DeFord, M. A. The monster
    Harrison, M. J. Lamia mutable
    Holly, J. H. The others
    Keller, D. H. The landslide
    Lanier, S. His only safari
    Long, F. B. The man with a thousand legs
    Lovecraft, H. P. The call of Cthulhu
    Matheson, R. Born of man and woman
    Nourse, A. E. Contamination crew
    Pangborn, E. Good neighbors
    Pangborn, E. Longtooth
    Roa Bastos, A. The living tomb
    St Clair, M. Counter charm
    Schmitz, J. H. Greenface
    Smith, C. A. The immeasurable horror
    Valdrwulf
    Wilson, G. [The spot]
    Young, R. F. The ogress
        *See also* Giants; Sea monsters
**Monsters** in the night. Smith, C. A.
**MONSTROSITIES.** *See* Monsters
**MONT ST MICHEL, FRANCE**
    Maxwell, W. The gardens of Mont-Saint-Michel
**Montale, Eugenio**
    The man in pyjamas
        Stevick, P. ed. Anti-story
**Montalvo, Garcia Ordoñes de**
    The Queen of California
        Moskowitz, S. ed. When women rule
**MONTANA**
    Dolson, C. W. Passage to the day

Moore, Raylyn—*Continued*
Trigononomy
  Elwood, R. ed. Showcase
Where have all the followers gone?
  Disch, T. M. ed. Bad moon rising
Moore, William
Voyeur
  The Best little magazine fiction, 1970
MOORS (THE RACE)
  Giraldi, G. B. The Moor of Venice
Moot. Colter, C.
A moral victory. Premchand
MORALITY. *See* Ethics; Political ethics;
  Sexual ethics
Morante, Elsa
The Sicilian soldier
  Decker, C. R. and Angoff, C. eds. Mod-
    ern stories from many lands
Moravia, Alberto
An abject man
  Moravia, A. Bought and sold
Agostino
  Hamalian, L. and Volpe, E. L. eds.
    Eleven modern short novels
Ah, the family!
  Moravia, A. Bought and sold
All-seeing
  Moravia, A. Command, and I will obey
    you
Ambiguities
  Moravia, A. Command, and I will obey
    you
The ashtray
  Moravia, A. Bought and sold
Away with the sun!
  Moravia, A. Bought and sold
Bitter honeymoon
  Johnson, E. W. ed. Short stories inter-
    national
Bores
  Moravia, A. Bought and sold
Bought and sold
  Moravia, A. Bought and sold
A calculated risk
  Moravia, A. Bought and sold
Celestina
  Moravia, A. Command, and I will obey
    you
The chase
  Moravia, A. Command, and I will obey
    you
The chimaera
  Moravia, A. Bought and sold
Cockroaches
  Moravia, A. Bought and sold
Command, and I will obey you
  Moravia, A. Command, and I will obey
    you
Confusion
  Moravia, A. Bought and sold
Consumer goods
  Moravia, A. Bought and sold
Contact with the working class
  Disch, R. and Schwartz, B. eds. Killing
    time
A disengaged conscience
  Moravia, A. Command, and I will obey
    you

Don't let's be dramatic
  Moravia, A. Command, and I will obey
    you
Doubles
  Moravia, A. Command, and I will obey
    you
Down and out
  Moravia, A. Command, and I will obey
    you
Enrica Baile
  Moravia, A. Command, and I will obey
    you
Exactly
  Moravia, A. Command, and I will obey
    you
Finger-nails
  Moravia, A. Bought and sold
A game
  Moravia, A. Bought and sold
He and I
  Thune, E. and Prigozy, R. eds. Short
    stories: a critical anthology
I haven't time
  Moravia, A. Bought and sold
Imagination
  Moravia, A. Bought and sold
Imitation
  Moravia, A. Bought and sold
Invisible woman
  Moravia, A. Bought and sold
The Jack Gang
  Moravia, A. Bought and sold
The Judas tree
  Moravia, A. Command, and I will obey
    you
The leper
  Moravia, A. Bought and sold
Line! Style!
  Moravia, A. Bought and sold
Long live Verdi!
  Moravia, A. Bought and sold
Lovelier than you
  Moravia, A. Bought and sold
Lover of festivals
  Moravia, A. Bought and sold
Man of power
  Moravia, A. Command, and I will obey
    you
A middling type
  Moravia, A. Command, and I will obey
    you
Mistress and mistress
  Moravia, A. Bought and sold
The monster
  Moravia, A. Command, and I will obey
    you
My angel
  Moravia, A. Bought and sold
Orders are orders
  Moravia, A. Bought and sold
The orgy
  Moravia, A. Bought and sold
Paradise
  Moravia, A. Bought and sold
Products
  Moravia, A. Bought and sold
Proto
  Moravia, A. Command, and I will obey
    you

## MUSIC HALLS (VARIETY THEATERS, CABARETS, ETC.)
Bukowski, C. Bop bop against that curtain
Burke, T. The cue
Burke, T. Gina of the Chinatown
The music lover. Drake, R.
The music of the spheres. Patton, F. G.

## MUSIC TEACHERS
Babel, I. The awakening
Biggle, L. Spare the rod
Eisenberg, L. The mighty Matterhorn
Henderson, D. Sylvia
Jhabvala, R. P. The housewife
McCullers, C. Madame Zilensky and the King of Finland
McCullers, C. Wunderkind
Munro, A. Dance of the happy shades
Music to lay eggs by. Bridges, T.
Music when soft voices die . . . Cross, J. K.
Music when soft voices die. O'Connor, F.
Musical boxes. Bichsel, P.
A musical education. Jacobs, H.
A musical enigma. Cranch, C. P.

## MUSICIANS
Emshwiller, C.  Al
Greenberg, J. Orpheus an' Eurydice
Kaplan, B. Mercy
Lowry, M. The forest path to the spring
Marsh, W. Mending wall
    See also Entertainers; Negro musicians

### Bagpipers
The Dance of the Dead
Munro, N. Red hand

### Bass players
Chekhov, A. Love affair with a double-bass

### Cellists
Costello, M. Murphy's misogyny
Gilliatt, P. Staying in bed
McCullers, C. Poldi

### Clarinet players
Brown, F. Eine kleine Nachtmusik

### Composers
Ayrton, M. The pyramid of counterpoint
Beneš, J. Atheism
Biggle, L. The tunesmith
Cather, W. Uncle Valentine
Hoffmann, E. T. A. Ritter Gluck
Kaplan, B. Ben Early is raving
Stern, R. Veni, vidi . . . Wendt
Strong, J. Supperburger

### Conductors
Benét, S. V. The King of the Cats
Burke, T. The cue

### Cornet players
Marsh, W. It always comes out dixie

### Drummers
Petry, A. Solo on the drums

### Flutists
Hesse, H. Flute dream

### Guitarists
Lester, J. Satan on my track
McNair, K. Come blow your horn

Okudzhava, B. Promoxys
Walker, A. To hell with dying

### Mandolin players
Yurick, S. Tarantella

### Organists
Burgess, A. An American organ
Day, J. W. The dead killed him in his own grave
Henderson, D. Caroline and the nuns

### Pianists
Amoury, G. Come into my parlor
Baldwin, J. Sonny's blues
Chopin, K. Wiser than a god
Farrell, J. T. Judith
Hernández, F. The crocodile
L'Heureux, J. Something missing
McCullers, C. Wunderkind
Maddow, B. You, Johann Sebastian Bach
Mann, T. The infant prodigy
May, D. Grace note
Oates, J. C. Nightmusic
Payes, R. C. Half life
Silverberg, R. and Ellison, H. The song the zombie sang
Stewart, N. Chopin
Stewart, N. The critic
Welty, E. Powerhouse
Wilson, A. The wrong set

### Saxophonists
Woolrich, C. One night in Barcelona

### Singers
Aiken, J. The windshield weepers
Baldwin, J. This morning, this evening, so soon
Ballard, J. G. The sound-sweep
Bambara, T. C. Mississippi Ham Rider
Bergé, C. And now, Alexandra . . .
Bontemps, A. Talk to the music
Bontemps, A.  A woman with a mission
Cather, W. Coming, Eden Bower!
Cather, W. The Count of Crow's Nest
Cather, W.  "A death in the desert"
Cather, W. Double birthday
Cather, W. The garden lodge
Cather, W. Nanette: an aside
Cather, W.  A singer's romance
Christie, A. Swan song
Crane, S. The King's favor
DeCles, J. Cruelty
Doctorow, E. L. The songs of Billy Bathgate
Fields, J. Not your singing, dancing spade
Greenberg, J. The Lucero requiem
Griffith, P. B. Nights at O'Rear's
Hemenway, R. The girl who sang with the Beatles
Hoffmann, E. T. A. Councillor Krespel
Hoffmann, E. T. A. The Cremona violin
Kanin, G. Do re mi
Kanin, G. Something to sing about
Kelley, W. M. Cry for me
Leroux, G. Phantom of the Opera
Lester, J. Satan on my track
McCourt, J. Mawrdew Czgowchwz
Madden, D. The singer
Nesvadba, J. The chemical formula of destiny

MUSICIANS—Singers—*Continued*
  Oates, J. C. Happy Onion
  Piercy, M. Love me tonight, God
  Steegmuller, F. The fair singer
  Stevenson, R. L. Providence and the guitar
  Theroux, A. The wife of God
  Wain, J.  I love you, Ricky

**Trumpeters**
  Bankier, W. One clear sweet clue
  Bontemps, A. Lonesome boy, silver trumpet
  Elkin, S. The guest
  Verney, J. The drugged cornet

**Violinists**
  Blavatsky, Madame. The ensouled violin
  Eisenberg, L. The two lives of Ben Coulter
  Goldberg, G. J. The Bach Master
  Hoffmann, E. T. A. Councillor Krespel
  Jäger, F. The devil's instrument
  Targan, B. Harry Belten and the Mendelssohn Violin Concerto

MUSLIMS
  Aidoo, A. A.  A gift from somewhere
  Bowles, P. The time of friendship
  Selimović, M. Death and the dervish

MUSLIMS, BLACK. *See* Black Muslims

MUSSOLINI, BENITO
  Pei, M. The flight that failed

MUSTANGS
  Schaefer, J. The white mustang
The mutant season. Silverberg, R.

MUTANTS. *See* Mutation (Biology)

Mutants for sale. Russell, E. F.

MUTATION (BIOLOGY)
  Anderson, P. The sharing of flesh
  Bayley, B. J. Mutation planet
  Bilker, H. L. Genetic faux pas
  Binder, E. Son of the stars
  Brunner, J. Fifth commandment
  Eklund, G. Free City blues
  Gardner, T. S. The last woman
  Henderson, Z. Ad astra
  Keller, D. H. Chasm of monsters
  Mitchison, N. After the accident
  Mitchison, N. Miss Omega Raven
  Silverberg, R. The mutant season
  Silverberg, R. This is the road
  West, W. G. The last man
  White, T. Stella
  Yarbro, C. Q. False dawn
    *See also* Animal mutation

MUTATION OF ANIMALS. *See* Animal mutation

Mutation planet. Bayley, B. J.

MUTATIONS. *See* Metamorphosis
The mute. Landolfi, T.

MUTES
  Landolfi, T. The mute
  Pangborn, E. Tiger Boy

MUTINY
  Hewat, A. V. Men against the sea
  Mérimée, P. Tamango
  Thomason, J. W. Mutiny
Mutiny. Thomason, J. W.
Mutiny on The Box Cross. Elston, A. V.

Mutterings of a middlewoman. Swenson, M.
Muzhiks. *See* Chekhov, A. Peasants
My angel. Moravia, A.
My apologia. Velsky, V.
My being. Khvylovy, M.
My beloved mafia. Di Donato, P.
My big-assed mother. Bukowski, C.
My big brother. Premchand
My brother down there. Frazee, S.
My brother Leopold. Pangborn, E.
My brother went to college. Yerby, F.
My brother's ghost story. Edwards, A.
My brother's keeper. Pei, M.
My brown friend. Vestdijk, S.
My cats. Lloyd-Jones, B.
My daughter. Orlav, O.
My dear husband. Trevisan, D.
My dear Uncle Sherlock. Pentecost, H.
My enemy. Vaid, K. B.
My expensive leg. Böll, H.
My father decided to plant orchards. Shevchuk, V.
My father sits in the dark. Weidman, J.
My father, the cat. Slesar, H.
My favorite murder. Bierce, A.
My first marriage. Jhabvala, R. P.
My friend Bingham. James, H.
My friend Valentine. Colette
My good ladies. Kotowska, M.
My grandparents. Ayrton, M.
My great-aunt Appearing Day. Prebble, J.
My greatest love. Beneš, J.
My head's in a different place, now. Davis, G.
My heart is broken. Gallant, M.
My Holy City geography book. Elmslie, K.
My house is yours. Marsh, W.
My imaginary father. O'Connor, P. F.
My kinsman, Major Molineaux. Hawthorne, N.
My life. Chekhov, A.
My life with the wave. Paz, O.
My love, my umbrella. McGahern, J.
My Man Bovanne. Bambara, T. C.
My man Closters. Rye, A.
My mother and the roomer. Chu, Yo-sup
My old buddy. Dawson, F.
My old home. Lu, Hsun
My old man. Hemingway, E.
My own true ghost story. Kipling, R.
My own true love. Drake, R.
My pal with the long hair. Böll, H.
My paleface brother. Borchert, W.
My sad face. Böll, H.
My self (Romantica) *See* Khvylovy, M. My being
My sister and me. Baber, A.
My sister Annabelle. De Forbes
My sister's applegarth. Ktorova, A.
My sisters' keeper. Fisher, E.
My son the murderer. Malamud, B.
My son, the physicist. Asimov, I.
My stay in the poet's cottage. Bukowski, C.
My Uncle Jules. Maupassant, G. de
My vocation. Lavin, M.
My wife. Chekhov, A.
My Wonder Horse. Ulibarri, S. R.

Myers, Howard L.
  Out, wit!
    Best SF: 1972

Myers, Walter
  The fare to Crown Point
    Coombs, O. ed. What we must see: young Black storytellers
Myriveles, Strates
  The chronicle of an old rose-tree
    Hall, J. B. ed. The realm of fiction
    Johnson, E. W. ed. Short stories international
Myrtle McAfee Dunlap's concern with culture. Estes, W. M.
Myself and the Tugoman. Elman, R.
The mysterious box. Cottrell, D.
The mysterious death on the Underground Railway. Orczy, Baroness
MYSTERIOUS DISAPPEARANCES. See Disappearances
Mysterious Madame Shanghai. Hughes, L.
The mysterious occurrence in Lambeth. James, G. P. R.

**MYSTERY AND DETECTIVE STORIES**
Allen, G. The episode of the diamond links
Allingham, M. The Allingham Case-book; 18 stories
Allingham, M. The Allingham minibus; 18 stories
Allingham, M. Evidence in camera
Bernkopf, J. F. comp. Boucher's choicest; 24 stories
Best detective stories of the year [1969]-1973
Best of the Best detective stories; 24 stories
Brunner, J. Puzzle for spacemen
DeFord, M. A. Farewell to the Faulkners
Dickinson, S. ed. The drugged cornet, and other mystery stories; 15 stories
Dickson, C. The footprint in the sky
Doyle, Sir A. C. The striped chest
Ellin, S. The house party
Fenner, P. S. comp. Consider the evidence; 10 stories
Fish, R. L. Counter intelligence
Fitzpatrick, R. C. Winkin, Blinkin and $\pi R^2$
Flanagan, T. The cold winds of Adesta
Futrelle, J. Best "Thinking Machine" detective stories; 12 stories
Garrett, R. A stretch of the imagination
Gibson, W. ed. Rogues' gallery; 19 stories
Gilbert, M. The system
Goulart, R. Please stand by
Greene, H. ed. Cosmopolitan crimes; 13 stories
Greene, Sir H. ed. The further rivals of Sherlock Holmes; 13 stories
Greene, H. ed. The rivals of Sherlock Holmes; 13 stories
Henry, O. The theory and the hound
Highsmith, P. The gracious, pleasant life of Mrs Afton
Hitchcock, A. ed. Alfred Hitchcock presents: A month of mystery; 31 stories
Hitchcock, A. ed. Alfred Hitchcock's Daring detectives; 10 stories
Hoch, E. D. Computer cops
Hoch, E. D. The magic bullet
Keating, H. R. F. The old shell collector
Laumer, K. Pime doesn't cray

McComas, J. F. ed. Crimes and misfortunes; 26 stories
McLean, A. C. The case of the vanishing spinster
Manley, S. and Lewis, G. eds. Grande dames of detection; 9 stories
Mystery Writers of America. Crime without murder; 25 stories
Mystery Writers of America. Dear dead days; 15 stories
Mystery Writers of America. Merchants of menace; 20 stories
Mystery Writers of America. Mirror, mirror, fatal mirror; 22 stories
Pentecost, H. Around dark corners
Peyrou, M. Juliet and the magician
Queen, E. Miser's gold
Simenon, G. Stan the killer
Slater, E. The sooey pill
Stout, R. Kings full of aces; 3 stories
Tucker, W. Time exposures
Von Elsner, D. The man who played too well
Walsh, R. J. Gambler's tale
Woolrich, C. Nightwebs; 16 stories
Woolrich, C. The screaming laugh
Yates, D. ed. Latin blood; 17 stories
Zelazny, R. 'Kjwalll'kje'k'koothaïlll'kje'k
  See also Detectives, Private; Murder stories; Poisoning

**Africa, South**
Griffith, G. Five hundred carats

**Algeria**
Bennett, A. In the capital of the Sahara
Bennett, A. A solution of the Algiers mystery

**Argentine Republic**
Ayala Gauna, V. Early morning murder
Domecq, H. B. The twelve figures of the world
Walsh, R. J. Shadow of a bird

**Belgium**
Bennett, A. A bracelet at Bruges
Bennett, A. A comedy on the gold coast

**Canada**
Prichard, H. The murder at the Duck Club

**Chile**
Edwards, A. The case of the travelling corpse
Isla, L. A. The case of the "Southern Arrow"

**Denmark**
Rosenkrantz, P. A sensible course of action

**England**
Allingham, M. The border-line case
Allingham, M. Face value
Allingham, M. Family affair
Allingham, M. Little Miss Know-All
Allingham, M. The man with the sack
Allingham, M. Mr Campion's lucky day
Allingham, M. One morning they'll hang him
Allingham, M. A quarter of a million

## MYSTERY AND DETECTIVE STORIES
### —France—*Continued*

Simenon, G. The fall of the high-flying Dutchman

Simenon, G. Inspector Maigret hesitates

Simenon, G. Maigret and the lazy burglar

Simenon, G. Maigret in society

Simenon, G. Maigret's failure

### Germany

Powell, J. The Altdorf syndrome

### Indonesia, Republic of

Blochman, L. G. Red wine

### Ireland

Orczy, Baroness. The Dublin mystery

### Italy

Segre, A. Justice has no number

### Mexico

Bermúdez, M. E. The puzzle of the broken watch

Boucher, A .The pink caterpillar

De La Vega, P. M. The dead man was a lively one

Halliday, B. Human interest stuff

### Parodies, travesties, etc.

Asimov, I. Author! Author!

### Riviera

Powell, J. Coins in the Frascati Fountain

### Russia

Chekhov, A. The Swedish match

### Scotland

De La Torre, L. The Monbodda ape boy

Innes, M. Comedy of discomfiture

Sayers, D. L. The piscatorial farce of the stolen stomach

### Singapore

Josey, A. Oriental justice

### United States

Anderson, P. and Anderson, K. Dead phone

Armstrong, C. The enemy

Asimov, I. The man who never told a lie

Breen, J. L. The fortune cookie

Breen, J. L. Frank Merriswell's greatest case

Breen, J. L. The Lithuanian eraser mystery

Brennan, J. P. The case of the uncut corpse

Brennan, J. P. The casebook of Lucius Leffing; 17 stories

Brennan, J. P. The enemy unknown

Brennan, J. P. The Mantzen diamond mystery

Brennan, J. P. The strange case of Peddler Phelps

Brennan, J. P. The Walford case

Brittain, W. Mr Strang finds the answers

Brown, F. Witness in the dark

Cain, P. Red 71

Carr, J. D. The gentleman from Paris

Chandler, R. Red wind

Charteris, L. The wicked cousin

Cross, J. The weaker vessel

Davidson, A. The man who killed sailors

Davis, D. S. Backward, turn backward

Eddy, C. M. A solitary solution

Edwards, W. First case for Charlie

Futrelle, J. The flaming phantom

Futrelle, J. The problem of cell 13

Futrelle, J. The superfluous finger

Gallico, P. Hurry, hurry, hurry!

Gardner, E. S. The affair of the reluctant witness

Gardner, E. S. At arm's length

Gardner, E. S. The candy kid

Gardner, E. S. The case of the crimson kiss

Gardner, E. S. The case of the crimson kiss; 5 stories

Gardner, E. S. The case of the crying swallow

Gardner, E. S. The case of the crying swallow; 4 stories

Gardner, E. S. The case of the irate witness

Gardner, E. S. The case of the irate witness; 4 stories

Gardner, E. S. Fingers of Fong

Gardner, E. S. A man is missing

Gardner, E. S. Something like a pelican

Gardner, E. S. The valley of little fears

Gardner, E. S. The vanishing corpse

Gohman, F. The cabinet of Kafru

Gohman, F. The copy boy caper

Gohman, F. The phantom fiddler

Gohman, F. Spider Webb mysteries; 7 stories

Gohman, F. A trunkful of treasure

Gohman, F. Vanishing act

Gores, J. O black and unknown bard

Hammett, D. The Farewell murder

Hammett, D. The scorched face

Henry, O. The adventures of Shamrock Jolnes

Hoch, E. D. The Leopold locked room

Hoch, E. D. Reunion

Hoch, E. D. Whodunit: murder offstage

Jeffrey, W. Shell game

Johnson, E. and Palmer, G. Finger prints can't lie

Kemelman, H. The nine mile walk

Lewis, L. The man who talked with books

McAuliffe, F. The Maltese Falcon Commission

Macdonald, R. Find the woman

Macdonald, R. The singing pigeon

McGerr, P. Selena robs the White House

McKimmey, J. His brother's keeper

Marlowe, S. Drum beat

Palmer, S. Fingerprints don't lie

Palmer, S. Green ice

Parker, P. S. The wineo murder

Patrick, Q. Murder in one scene

Pei, M. The Sparrows of Paris

Pentecost, H. A black eye for Miss Millington

Pentecost, H. The day the children vanished

Pentecost, H. Hunting day

Pentecost, H. Murder throws a curve

Pentecost, H. My dear Uncle Sherlock

Pentecost, H. Room number 23

Queen, E. The adventure of Abraham Lincoln's clue

## MYSTERY AND DETECTIVE STORIES
### —United States—*Continued*

Queen, E. The adventure of the President's half disme

Queen, E. The adventure of the seven black cats

Queen, E. Bride in danger

Queen, E. The Gettysburg bugle

Queen, E. Mystery at the Library of Congress

Queen, E. No parking

Queen, E. The President's half disme

Rice, C. Hard sell

Ritchie, J. By child undone

Sayers, D. L. The abominable history of the man with copper fingers

Stout, R. Bullet for one

Stout, R. The cop-killer

Stout, R. Home to roost

Stout, R. The Squirt and the monkey

Treat, L.   H as in homicide

Treat, L.   T as in threat

Treat, L. The verdict

Walsh, T.   "I killed John Harrington"

Wellman, M. W.   A star for a warrior

Wells, C. Christabel's crystal

Wolson, M. The attacker

Woolrich, C. Dead on her feet

Woolrich, C. Death in the air

Woolrich, C. Murder at the automat

Woolrich, C. One and a half murders

Woolrich, C. One drop of blood

Woolrich, C. You'll never see me again

Yarbro, C. Q. The ghosts at Iron River

Mystery at the Library of Congress. Queen, E.

Mystery in São Cristóvão. Lispector, C.

A mystery of heroism. Crane, S.

The mystery of Myrrh Lane. Brennan, J. P.

The mystery of Room 666. Futrelle, J.

The mystery of the missing cap. Das, M.

The mystery of the poisoned dish of mushrooms. Bramah, E.

The mystery of the vanished Petition Crown. Bramah, E.

## MYSTERY WRITERS OF AMERICA
Deming, R. Bunco game

## MYSTICISM
Beal, M. F. Gold

Cather, W. Lou, the prophet

Hesse, H. Edmund

Hesse, H. Inside and outside

*See also* Supernatural phenomena

**MYTH.** *See* Mythology

The myth of mankind. Lagerkvist, P.

**MYTHICAL ANIMALS.** *See* Animals, Mythical

## MYTHOLOGY
Brown, F. The new one

Corvo, F. Baron. About a vegetable purgatory

Corvo, F. Baron. About the love which is desire and the love which is divine

Pei, M.   A Grecian legend

Silverberg, R. Breckenridge and the continuum

*See also* Amazons; Furies; Legends and folk-tales; and names of mythological characters, e.g. Dionysus

# N

**NASA.** *See* United States. National Aeronautics and Space Administration

The **NRACP.** Elliott, G. P.

**Nabo.** García Márquez, G.

## Nabokov, Vladimir
An affair of honor

Nabokov, V.   A Russian beauty, and other stories

Breaking the news

Nabokov, V.   A Russian beauty, and other stories

The circle

Nabokov, V.   A Russian beauty, and other stories

A dashing fellow

Nabokov, V.   A Russian beauty, and other stories

The Leonardo

Nabokov, V.   A Russian beauty, and other stories

Lips to lips

Nabokov, V.   A Russian beauty, and other stories

Mademoiselle O

Spinner, S. ed. Live and learn

The Potato-Elf

Charyn, J. ed. The single voice

Nabokov, V.   A Russian beauty, and other stories

A Russian beauty

Lish, G. ed. The secret life of our times: new fiction from Esquire

Nabokov, V.   A Russian beauty, and other stories

Solus Rex

Nabokov, V.   A Russian beauty, and other stories

Terra incognita

Nabokov, V.   A Russian beauty, and other stories

"That in Aleppo once . . ."

Davis, R. G. ed. Ten modern masters

Karl, F. R. and Hamalian, L. eds. The naked i

Torpid smoke

Nabokov, V.   A Russian beauty, and other stories

Ultima Thule

Nabokov, V.   A Russian beauty, and other stories

The visit to the museum

Nabokov, V.   A Russian beauty, and other stories

**Nada.** Disch, T. M.

**NADER, RALPH**

Beard, H. The last recall

## Nagibin, Yury
The fourth daddy

Pomorska, K. ed. Fifty years of Russian prose: from Pasternak to Solzhenitsyn v2

The green bird with the red head

Whitney, T. P. ed. The young Russians

**Nagibin, Yury**—*Continued*
A light in the window
Pomorska, K. ed. Fifty years of Russian prose: from Pasternak to Solzhenitsyn v2
The **nail** and the oracle. Sturgeon, T.
**Naipaul, Shiva**
The tenant
Winter's tales 17
**Naipaul, V. S.**
In a free state [novella]
Naipaul, V. S. In a free state.
One out of many
Naipaul, V. S. In a free state.
Tell me who to kill
Naipaul, V. S. In a free state.
**Nair, S.**
Mrs Kimble
Angoff, C. ed. Stories form The Literary Review
Angoff, C. and Povey, J. eds. African writing today
**NAIROBI.** *See* Kenya—Nairobi
The **naked** man. Rodriguez, B.
**Nalkowska, Zofia**
Beside the railroad track
Angoff, C. ed. Stories from The Literary Review
A **name** for the painting. Yashpal
**NAMES**
Herbst, S. An uneven evening
**NAMES, FICTITIOUS.** *See* Pseudonyms
**NAMES, PERSONAL**
Asimov, I. Unto the fourth generation
Barth, J. Ambrose his mark
Clarke, A. C. Sleeping beauty
Maugham, W. S. The choice of Amyntas
Steinbeck, J. Adam and his sons
The **namesake.** Cather, W.
**Namgay** Doola. Kipling, R.
**Nami** and the taffyman. O, Yong-su
The **naming** of names. Bradbury, R.
The **naming** of Rattlesnake Road. Brister, B.
**Nanette:** an aside. Cather, W.
**Nanni** Volpe. Verga, G.
**NANNIES.** *See* Servants—Nursemaids
**NANTUCKET ISLAND.** *See* Massachusetts —Nantucket Island
**Napier** Court. Campbell, R.
The **napkin** ring. Fitzsimmons, P. M.
**NAPLES.** *See* Italy—Naples
**Napoleon** Shave-Tail. Wister, O.
**NAPOLEONIC WARS.** *See* Peninsular War, 1807-1814
**Narayan, R. K.**
Annamalai
Narayan, R. K.   A horse and two goats
A breath of Lucifer
Narayan, R. K.   A horse and two goats
A horse and two goats
Narayan, R. K.   A horse and two goats
Seventh House
Narayan, R. K.   A horse and two goats
Uncle
Narayan, R. K.   A horse and two goats
**NARCOTIC HABIT**
Algren, N. The mad laundress of Ding-dong-Daddyland
Algren, N. Watch out for Daddy

Brown, R.   A letter to Ismael in the grave
Dixon, J. Spike dreams
Elkin, S. The guest
Friedman, B. J. Lady
Howard, V. Let me hang loose
Johnson, M. C. Wild bouquet
Lamb, M. Possession
Leiber, F. The secret songs
Muller-Thym, T.   A word about justice
Myers, W. The fare to Crown Point
Nemerov, H. The native in the world
Oates, J. C. Plot
Olson, D. The blue tambourine
Sanchez, S. After Saturday nite comes Sunday
Schuyler, J. Life, death and other dreams
Stevens, R. L. The physician and the opium fiend
Trevor, W. Kinkies
Wharton, E. Bunner sisters
White, W. Kiss the girls for me
Wilensky, B. On the spike
*See also* Drug abuse; Drugs
**NARCOTICS**
Fisher, R. The city of refuge
Harrison, H. Velvet glove
Lang, A. K. This is a watchbird watching you
Lovecraft, H. P. and Berkeley, E. The crawling chaos
Pei, M. The Sparrows of Paris
Pronzini, B. Cain's mark
Queen, E. Mystery at the Library of Congress
Spinrad, N. The last hurrah of the Golden Horde
*See also* Drugs; Narcotic habit; also names of narcotics; e.g. Hashish; Heroin
**Narokov, Nikolay**
The black something
Angoff, C. ed. Stories from The Literary Review
An inexpensive present for my nephew
Angoff, C. ed. Stories from The Literary Review
Treetops
Angoff, C. ed. Stories from The Literary Review
**Narrow** Valley. Lafferty, R. A.
**NASHVILLE.** *See* Tennesse—Nashville
**Natalie.** Maloney, R.
**NATION OF ISLAM.** *See* Black Muslims
**NATIONAL AERONAUTICS AND SPACE ADMINISTRATION.** *See* United States. National Aeronautics and Space Administration
The **national** pastime. Spinrad, N.
**NATIONAL SOCIALISM**
Borges, J. L. Deutsches requiem
Rothberg, A. The animal trainer
Ruskay, S. The ruby ring
**NATIONALISM**
Bahr, J. The great debate
**NATIONALITY.** *See* Nationalism
The **native** in the world. Nemerov, H.
**Native** innards. Elmslie, K.

NATIVE RACES
Africa, Central
See Africa, Central—Native races
Native's return. Farrell, J. T.
NATURAL DISASTERS. See Disasters
Natural love and affection. Burton, H.
Natural obstacles. Strindberg, A.
NATURAL RESOURCES. See Ecology
The natural talents of Merlin Hancock. Estes, W. M.
NATURALISTS
Clark, A. C. Green fingers
Clement, H. Uncommon sense
Graham, A. Bird of Paradise
Kantor, M. The purple moccasin
Sturgeon, T. Cactus dance
See also Botanists
NATURE
Curley, D. Where you wouldn't want to walk
Ewing, Mrs. Our field
Lowry, M. The forest path to the spring
Rush, N. Closing with nature
Swenson, M. The power and the danger
NATURE CONSERVATION
Wolfe, G. Three million square miles
The nature of the task. Nemerov, H.
The nature of the universe. Dawson, F.
Nature the criminal. Strindberg, A.
The nature Theatre of Oklahoma. Kafka, F.
Naubert, Christiane Benedicte Eugenie. See Von Kramer, Professor
Naughton, Bill
Spit Nolan
Authors' choice
Nausea. Trevisan, D.
NAVAHO INDIANS
Eastlake, W. The death of Sun
Eastlake, W. Portrait of an artist with 26 horses
Eastlake, W. Something big is happening to me
Greenberg, J. L'Olam and White Shell Woman
La Farge, O. All the young men
Price, R. Walking lessons
NAVAL OFFICERS. See subhead Navy— Officers, under names of countries, e.g. Great Britain. Navy—Officers
Naylor, Charles
We are dainty little people
Disch, T. M. ed. Bad moon rising
Naylor, Phyllis Reynolds
The angry heart
Naylor, P. R. Ships in the night
Brief visit back
Naylor, P. R. Ships in the night
The candidate
Naylor, P. R. Ships in the night
Cast the first stone
Naylor, P. R. Dark side of the moon
A change of plans
Naylor, P. R. Ships in the night
A Christmas encounter
Naylor, P. R. Ships in the night
Dark side of the moon
Naylor, P. R. Dark side of the moon

The daughter
Naylor, P. R. Dark side of the moon
Day after tomorrow
Naylor, P. R. Dark side of the moon
Everything today
Naylor, P. R. Ships in the night
Family soliloquy
Naylor, P. R. Ships in the night
Four vignettes from a family tree
Naylor, P. R. Ships in the night
Go tell it on the mountain
Naylor, P. R. Dark side of the moon
I'm the same guy I always was, but—
Naylor, P. R. Ships in the night
Just one small part of living
Naylor, P. R. Ships in the night
Mrs Perry becomes a person
Naylor, P. R. Ships in the night
The nothingness
Naylor, P. R. Dark side of the moon
One of the gang
Naylor, P. R. Ships in the night
Second son
Naylor, P. R. Dark side of the moon
Ships in the night
Naylor, P. R. Ships in the night
Those who think young
Naylor, P. R. Ships in the night
To love mercy
Naylor, P. R. Ships in the night
Too good to last
Naylor, P. R. Dark side of the moon
A triangle has four sides
Naylor, P. R. Dark side of the moon
The Nazi machine. Steinberg, B.
NAZIS. See National socialism
Nazis. Sánta, F.
NEANDERTHAL RACE
Asimov, I. The ugly little boy
Costantini, H. In the beginning
De Camp, L. S. The gnarly man
Del Rey, L. The day is done
Kerr, D. Epiphany for aliens
The nearest cemetery. Hawkes, J.
NEBRASKA
Cather, W. A resurrection
Crane, S. The blue hotel
Farm life
See Farm life—Nebraska
Frontier and pioneer life
See Frontier and pioneer life—Nebraska
NEBULAE. See Stars
The necessary knocking on the door. Petry, A.
The necessity of his condition. Davidson, A.
Necessity's child. Wilson, A.
Necker, Claire
Release from life
Necker, C. ed. Supernatural cats
The necklace of pearls. Sayers, D. L.
NECKLACES
Christie, A. A fruitful Sunday
Christie, A. The manhood of Edward Robinson
Futrelle, J. The missing necklace
Maupassant, G. de. The diamond necklace
The necromancer. Flammenberg, L.

NECROMANCY. *See* Magic; Witchcraft
The **necromantic** tale. Smith, C. A.
**NECROPHILIA**
  Coover, R. The marker
**Nedreaas, Torborg**
  Music from a blue well
    Decker, C. R. and Angoff, C. eds. Modern stories from many lands
The **need.** Bingham, S.
**Needs** must. Strindberg, A.
**Nég** Créol. Chopin, K.
**Negostina.** Ghilia, A. I.
**NEGRESSES.** *See* Negroes
**NEGRO AUTHORS**
  Purdy, J. On the rebound
**NEGRO CHILDREN**
  Boyle, K. Black boy
  Carskadon, T. R. Nigger schoolhouse
  Dumas, H. The crossing
  Edwards, J. Mother Dear and Daddy
  Fair, R. L. We who came after
  O'Connor, F. The lame shall enter first
  O'Connor, P. F. American Gothic
**NEGRO CLERGY.** *See* Clergy, Negro
**NEGRO COWBOYS.** *See* Negroes as cowboys
**NEGRO DIALECT.** *See* Dialect stories—Negro
**NEGRO-JEWISH RELATIONS**
  Neugeboren, J. Elijah
**NEGRO MUSICIANS**
  Bambara, T. C. Mississippi Ham Rider
  Brown, F. L. McDougal
  Dumas, H. Will the circle be unbroken?
  Ferdinand, V. Second line/cutting the body loose
  McCluskey, J. The pilgrims
**NEGRO NATIONALISM.** *See* Black Muslims
**NEGRO SERVANTS.** *See* Negroes as servants
**NEGRO SOLDIERS.** *See* Negroes as soldiers
**NEGRO SONGS**
  Kelley, W. M. Cry for me
**NEGRO STUDENTS**
  Baraka, I. A. The alternative
  Howard, V. Let me hang loose
  Walker, A. We drink the wine in France
**NEGRO WOMEN.** *See* Women, Negro
**NEGROES**
  Bambara, T. C. Basement
  Bambara, T. C. Blues ain't no mockin bird
  Bambara, T. C. Gorilla, my love; 15 stories
  Bambara, T. C. The hammer man
  Bambara, T. C. Happy birthday
  Bambara, T. C. The Johnson girls
  Bambara, T. C. Maggie of the green bottles
  Bambara, T. C. ed. Tales and stories for Black folks; 10 stories
  Bambara, T. C. Talking bout Sonny
  Barker, M. Payday
  Betts, D. Beasts of the southern wild
  Bontemps, A. The cure
  Bradbury, R. June 2003: way in the middle of the air
  Brown, C. The life and loves of Mr Jiveass Nigger (Prologue)

Bullins, E. Dandy
Bullins, E. The enemy
Bullins, E. He couldn't say sex
Bullins, E. The helper
Bullins, E. The hungered one; 21 stories
Bullins, E. In New England winter
Bullins, E. Mister newcomer
Bullins, E. Moonwriter
Bullins, E. The real me
Bullins, E. Support your local police
Bullins, E. Travel from home
Burnett, W. ed. Black hands on a white face; 16 stories
Cady, J. With no breeze
Carter, R. Return of the Kid
Chapman, A. ed. New Black voices; 12 stories
Coombs, O. ed. What we must see; 16 stories
Cottle, T. J. The place between living and dying
Cottrell, D. The mysterious box
Crayton, P. Cotton Alley
Davidson, J. A. The Black sons-of-bitches
DeFord, M. A. Old man Morgan's grave
Drake, R. The cook and the sheriff
Dumas, H. Ark of bones
Dumas, H. Ark of bones, and other stories; 9 stories
Dumas, H. A boll of roses
Dumas, H. Double Nigger
Dumas, H. Echo tree
Dumas, H. A Harlem game
Dumas, H. Rain god
Dumas, H. Strike and fade
Dunbar, P. L. The lynching of Jube Benson
Elliott, G. P. The NRACP
Ellison, R. Cadillac flambé
Ellison, R. Flying home
Ellison, R. King of the bingo game
Ellison, R. W. Mister Toussan
Faulkner, W. Dry September
Faulkner, W. Red leaves
Faulkner, W. Sunset
Fiedler, L. A. The stain
Ford, J. H. The bitter bread
Frazer, C. Zydeco
Friedman, P. The inheritance editor
Fuller, C. H. A love song for seven little boys called Sam
Gaines, E. J. A long day in November
García Márquez, G. Nabo
Giovanni, N. The library
Gores, J. O black and unknown bard
Grau, S. A. Miss Yellow Eyes
Harrison, H. American dead
Hemingway, E. The battler
Herbst, S. Old soul
Hewat, A. V. Men against the sea
Himes, C. All he needs is feet
Himes, C. Black laughter
Himes, C. Black on Black; 17 stories
Himes, C. Da-da-dee
Himes, C. Headwaiter
Himes, C. Heaven has changed
Himes, C. Mama's missionary money
Himes, C. The night's for cryin'
Himes, C. Prediction
Hughes, L. Last whipping

NEGROES—*Continued*

### Race identity
*See* Black nationalism

### Relations with Jews
*See* Negro-Jewish relations

### Religion
Bontemps, A. Let the church roll on
Dunbar, P. L. Jim's probation
Himes, C. Pork chop paradise
Olsen, T.  O yes
Walker, A. The welcome table
*See also* Black Muslims

### San Francisco
Gold, H. Song of the first and last beatnik

### Segregation
Hunter, K. Come out of that corner
Kelley, W. M. The only man on Liberty Street
Schaffer, A. Rabinowitz the fool
Walker, A. The welcome table

### Southern States
Bambara, T. C. Mississippi Ham Rider
Benét, S. V. Freedom's a hard-bought thing
Bennett, H. Dotson Gerber resurrected
Bontemps, A. The Old South; 13 stories
Bontemps, A. Saturday night
Bontemps, A.  A summer tragedy
Brown, W. W. Escape of Clotel
Carskadon, T. R. Nigger schoolhouse
Chesnutt, C. W. The goophered grapevine
Chesnutt, C. W. The gray wolf's ha'nt
Dumas, H. Fon
Dunbar, P. L. Jim's probation
Dunbar, P. L. The wisdom of silence
Gaines, E. J. Just like a tree
Gaines, E. J. The sky is gray
Gaines, E. J. Three men
Hurston, Z. N. Spunk
Kelley, W. M. The only man on Liberty Street
Lester, J. Satan on my track
Lester, J. When freedom came
O'Connor, F. Wildcat
Pettus, R. C. Raining all the time
Phillips, R. Rise up singing
Reeves, D.  A shonuff real man
Thelwell, M. Bright an' mownin' star
Toomer, J. Blood-burning moon
Walker, A. The child who favored Daughter
Walker, A. "Really, doesn't crime pay?"
Walker, A. The revenge of Hannah Kemhuff
Walker, A. Strong horse tea
Wright, R. Almos' a man
Wright, R. Big Boy leaves home
Wright, R. Fire and cloud
Wright, R. The man who was almost a man

### Suffrage
Brown, S. And/or
Edwards, J. Liars don't qualify

### Tennessee
Taylor, P. What you hear from 'em?

### Texas
Brister, B. Moss, mallards and mules
Brister, B. Of perches and pleasures

### Virginia
Bontemps, A. Black thunder; excerpt
Page, T. N. Marse Chan
Page, T. N. Ole 'Stracted
Page, T. N. "Unc' Edinburg's drowndin'"
Styron, W. Hark: 1831, Virginia

### Washington, D.C.
Bahr, J. The burning capital
Fort, K. The coal shoveller
Grover, W. The finer points

## NEGROES AS COWBOYS
Lester, J. The man who was a horse

## NEGROES AS MUSICIANS. *See* Negro musicians

## NEGROES AS SERVANTS
Chesnutt, C. W. Po' Sandy
Colter, C.  A chance meeting
Elman, R. Timmy
Faulkner, W. That evening sun
Ford, J. H. How the mountains are
Hardwick, Michael, and Hardwick, Mollie. Ole rockin' chair
Hughes, L. Cora unashamed
Mabry, T. Lula Borrow
McPherson, J. A.  A solo song: for Doc
Ousmane, S. Black girl
Parker, D. Clothe the naked
Parker, D. Mrs Hofstadter on Josephine Street
Petry, A. Has anybody seen Miss Dora Dean?
Phillips, R. Mealy Marshall and the Whore of Babylon
Rosen, N. What must I say to you?
Rubin, M. Service
Rushmore, R.  A life in the closet
Taylor, P. Cookie
Taylor, P.  A wife of Nashville
Trilling, L. The other Margaret
Williams, J. A. Son in the afternoon

## NEGROES AS SOLDIERS
Algren, N. He couldn't boogie-woogie worth a damn
Anderson, A. Comrade
Davis, G. Ben
Davis, G. Ben [another story]
Gold, I. The nickel misery of George Washington Carver Brown
Shields, J. Candidate
Thomason, J. W. Red pants
Yerby, F. Health card
Yerby, F. The homecoming

## NEGROES AS STUDENTS. *See* Negro students

## NEGROES IN BARBADOS
Marshall, P. To Da-duh, in memoriam
Meriwether, L. M.  A happening in Barbados

## NEGROES IN DENMARK
Wright, R. Big Black good man

## NEGROES IN ECUADOR
Elliott, G. P. Among the Dangs

## NEGROES IN ENGLAND
Golding, W. The Anglo-Saxon
Nevinson, H. Sissero's return
Spark, M. The Black Madonna

**Nesbit, E.**–*Continued*
Man-size in marble
Green, R. L. ed. Thirteen uncanny
tales
Haining, P. ed. Nightfrights
Manley, S. and Lewis, G. eds. Ladies
of horror
**Nesbit, Evelyn**
John Charrington's wedding
Tomlinson, D. ed. Walk in dread
**Nesin, Aziz**
There is a nut on the roof
Decker, C. R. and Angoff, C. eds. Mod-
ern stories from many lands
The **nest** builder. Pritchett, V. S.
A **nest** of boxes. Casper, L.
A **nest** of sparrows on the awning. Cabrera
Infante, G.
**Nesvadba, Josef**
Captain Nemo's last adventure
Rottensteiner, F. ed. View from an-
other shore
The chemical formula of destiny
Nesvadba, J. The lost face: best science
fiction from Czechoslovakia
The death of an apeman
Nesvadba, J. The lost face: best science
fiction from Czechoslovakia
Doctor Moreau's other island
Nesvadba, J. The lost face: best science
fiction from Czechoslovakia
Expedition in the opposite direction
Nesvadba, J. The lost face: best science
fiction from Czechoslovakia
In the footsteps of the Abominable Snow-
man
Nesvadba, J. The lost face: best science
fiction from Czechoslovakia
Inventor of his own undoing
Nesvadba, J. The lost face: best science
fiction from Czechoslovakia
The lost face
Best SF: 1970
Nesvadba, J. The lost face: best science
fiction from Czechoslovakia
The trial nobody ever heard of
Nesvadba, J. The lost face: best science
fiction from Czechoslovakia
Vampire ltd.
Suvin, D. ed. Other worlds, other seas
The **net.** Bullock, M.
**NETHERLANDS**
*See also* Flanders
**16th century**
Hardwick, Michael, and Hardwick, Mollie.
The ruff
**20th century**
Campert, R.    A trip to Zwolle
Krispin, E. ed. Modern stories from Hol-
land and Flanders; 14 stories
**Amsterdam**
Nye, R. The wandering Jew
**Antwerp**
Hardwick, Michael, and Hardwick, Mollie.
The ruff

**Legends and folk tales**
*See* Legends and folk tales—Nether-
lands
**Leyden**
Mitchell, E. P. The clock that went back-
ward
**NETHERLANDS,   PROVINCIAL   AND
RURAL**
Alberts, A. The swamp
Vestdijk, S. My brown friend
**Nettell, Richard**
The way the ladies walk
Hamilton, A. ed. Splinters
**Neugeboren, Jay**
The application
Gulassa, C. M. ed. The fact of fiction
Neugeboren, J. Corky's brother
The campaign of Hector Rodriguez
Neugeboren, J. Corky's brother
The child
Neugeboren, J. Corky's brother
Corky's brother
Neugeboren, J. Corky's brother
Ebbets Field
Neugeboren, J. Corky's brother
Elijah
Neugeboren, J. Corky's brother
A family trip
Neugeboren, J. Corky's brother
Finkel
Neugeboren, J. Corky's brother
Joe
Neugeboren, J. Corky's brother
Luther
Charyn, J. ed. The single voice
Neugeboren, J. Corky's brother
The pass
Neugeboren, J. Corky's brother
Something is rotten in the Borough of
Brooklyn
Neugeboren, J. Corky's brother
The Zodiacs
McCrindle, J. F. ed. Stories from the
Transatlantic Review
Neugeboren, J. Corky's brother
**NEURALGIA**
Mitchell, E. P. The pain epicures
**NEURASTHENIA**
Delany, S. R. High Weir
Du Maurier, D. Not after midnight
Henderson, D. Sylvia
O'Connor, F. The Corkerys
Parker, D. Lady with a lamp
Petrie, G. Sad about Miss Brent
Rollow, D. Dean and Frieda
Roth, P. Eli, the fanatic
**NEUROSES**
Asimov, I. It's such a beautiful day
Brown, F. Aelurophobe
Cather, W. Paul's case
Goff, P. Blind in August
Krleža, M. The cricket beneath the water-
fall
McGivern, W. P. Killer on the turnpike
Oates, J. C. Boy and girl
Rascoe, J. Twice plighted, once removed
**NEUROTICS.** *See* Neuroses
**Neutron** star. Niven, L.

**Neutron** tide. Clarke, A. C.
**NEVADA**

### Las Vegas

Einstein, C. The new deal
Ellison, H. Pretty Maggie Moneyeyes
Gilliatt, P. The position of the planets
Kanin, G. The only game in town
Kranes, D. Dealer
Law, W. Payoff on double zero
**Never** come Monday. Knight, E.
**Never** hit a lady. Tobey, F. S.
**Never** lose your cool. Friedman, P.
**Never** shake a family tree. Westlake, D. E.
**Never** trust a partner. Eckels, R. E.
**Neville, Helen**
The dark unfathomed caves
Women
**Neville, Kris**
Dominant species
Orbit 9
Old Man Henderson
McComas, J. F. ed. Special wonder
*See also* Bretnor, R. jt. auth.; Neville, L. jt. auth.
**Neville, Kris, and O'Donnell, K. M.**
Pacem est
Best SF: 1970
**Neville, Lil, and Neville, Kris**
The quality of the product
Elwood, R. and Kidd, V. eds. Saving worlds
**Nevinson, Henry**
The St George of Rochester
Keating, P. J. ed. Working-class stories of the 1890s
Sissero's return
Keating, P. J. ed. Working-class stories of the 1890s
A **new** attitude toward life. Daskalov, S. T.
**NEW BRUNSWICK.** *See* Canada—New Brunswick
The **new** deal. Einstein, C.
**NEW DELHI.** *See* India—New Delhi
The **new** dress. Woolf, V.
**NEW ENGLAND**
Goodman, P. The architect from New York
James, H. Europe
Westbrook, P. D. ed. Seacoast and upland: a New England anthology; 17 stories

### 17th century

Reynolds, B.   A witch burning

### 19th century

Brown, A. Number five
Heald, H. The horror in the burying ground
James, H.   A landscape painter
Jewett, S. O. The gray man
Jewett, S. O. The gray mills of Farley
Jewett, S. O. The Parshley celebration
Robinson, R. E. The purification of Cornbury

### 20th century

Hawkes, J. The nearest cemetery
Montross, L. Portrait of a worm fisherman
Rushmore, R. The trumpets of Épignon

### Country life

*See* Country life—New England

### Farm life

*See* Farm life—New England
New folks' home. Simak, C. D.
The **new** gardener. Lavin, M.
**NEW GUINEA**
Mulisch, H. What happened to Sergeant Masuro?
**NEW HAMPSHIRE**
Banks, R. With Ché in New Hampshire
McElroy, J. The accident
Marshall, L. The closed door
Marshall, L. Grandfather's nude swim

### Country life

*See* Country life—New Hampshire
**NEW HAVEN.** *See* Connecticut—New Haven
The **new** home. West, J.
The **new** house. Fremlin, C.
**NEW JERSEY**

### Atlantic City

Boyle, K. Black boy
Koch, C. F.   A matter of family
Runyon, D. Dark Dolores

### Newark

Jones, L. The screamers
The **New** Jerusalem, Roberts, R. E.
A **new** life. Bingham, S.
The **new** Melusina. Goethe, J. W. von
The **New** Methuselah. Jewett, S. O.
**NEW MEXICO**
Casper, L. Least common denominator
Price, R. Walking lessons
Ulibarri, S. R. Man without a name
Ulibarri, S. R. Tierra Amarilla; 6 stories

### Picuris

Sabin, E. L. The devil of the Picuris

### Tierra Amarilla

Ulibarri, S. R. The Frater family
Ulibarri, S. R. The stuffing of the Lord
The **new** mirror. Petry, A.
**New** New York New Orleans. Effinger, G. A.
The **new** one. Brown, F.
**NEW ORLEANS.** *See* Louisiana—New Orleans
The **new** people. Beaumont, C.
A **new** place. McPherson, J. A.
The **new** prime. Vance, J.
**New** queens for old. Fielding, G.
**NEW SOUTH WALES.** *See* Australia—New South Wales
The **New** Villa. Chekhov, A.
**NEW YEAR**
Hoch, E. D. Night of the millennium
Wilson, A. Saturnalia
**NEW YEAR'S EVE.** *See* New Year
The **New** Year's sacrifice. Lu, Hsun
**NEW YORK (CITY)**
Bova, B. The sightseers
Brooks, G. Maud Martha and New York
Canzoneri, R. City of heaven
Davidson, A. The Lord of Central Park
Davidson, A. The Sixty-Third Street station
Disch, T. M. Angouleme

NEWSPAPER WORK. *See* Journalists

NEWSPAPERMEN. *See* Journalists

**NEWSPAPERS**
Gohman, F. The copy boy caper
Silverberg, R. What we learned from this
morning's newspaper

**Collectors and collecting**
Brautigan, R. Corporal

NEWSPAPERWOMEN. *See* Women as
journalists

NEWSREEL PHOTOGRAPHY. *See* Photography, Journalistic

**Newton, D. B.**
Chain of command
Western Writers of America. With
Guidons flying
Next door to death. Stern, J.
The next logical step. Bova, B.
Next of kin. Shamir, M.
The next tenants. Clarke, A. C.
Next to a dog. Christie, A.
The next turn of the wheel. Dawson, F.
Neyur. Premchand

**NEZ PERCÉ INDIANS**
Fowler, K. Brothers of the bugle
Henry, W. Lapwai winter

**Neznakomov, Peter**
The Painlevé case
Kirilov, N. and Kirk, F. eds. Introduction to modern Bulgarian literature

**Ngugi, James**
A meeting in the dark
Larson, C. R. ed. African short stories

**NICARAGUA**
Thomason, J. W. Marines see the Revolution
Nice day at school. Trevor, W.
A nice name. Patton, F. G.
A nice quiet place. Fitzgerald, F. S.
Nicholas de Troyes. *See* Nicolas de Troyes
The nickel misery of George Washington
Carver Brown. Gold, I.

**NICKNAMES**
Ulibarri, S. R. The Frater family

**Nicol, Abioseh**
As the night, the day
Larson, C. R. ed. Prejudice: 20 tales of
oppression and liberation
The truly married woman
Katz, N. and Milton, N. eds. Fragment
from a lost diary, and other stories
Larson, C. R. ed. African short stories
Nolen, B. ed. Africa is thunder and
wonder

**Nicolas de Troyes**
The bailiff and the scrupulous curate
Bishop, M. ed. A Renaissance story-
book
The good judge of Troyes
Cholakian, P. F. and Cholakian, R. C.
eds. The early French novella
The spell of the ring
Cholakian, P. F. and Cholakian, R. C.
eds. The early French novella

**Nicolson, Sir Harold**
Lambert Orme
Auchincloss, L. ed. Fables of wit and
elegance

**NIECES**
Fremlin, C. Something evil in the house
Ribnikar, J. She
Rogers, M. A great feeling
*See also* Aunts; Uncles

**Nieh, Hua-ling**
The several blessings of Wang Ta-nien
Hsia, C. T. ed. Twentieth-century Chinese stories

**Nielsen, Helen**
The perfect servant
Ellery Queen's Mystery Magazine. Ellery Queen's Mystery bag

**NIGERIA**
Achebe, C. Akueke
Achebe, C. Chicke's school days
Achebe, C. Dead men's path
Achebe, C. The madman
Achebe, C. Marriage is a private affair
Achebe, C. The sacrificial egg
Achebe, C. Uncle Ben's choice
Achebe, C. Vengeful creditor
Achebe, C. The voter
Freemann, R. A. Indoro Bush College

**Civil War, 1967-1970**
Achebe, C. Civil peace
Achebe, C. Girls at war
Achebe, C. Sugar Baby

**Lagos**
Okara, G. The crooks
A nigger. Himes, C.
Nigger schoolhouse. Carskadon, T. R.
Nigger Sunday. Weaver, G.
Niggertown. Pumilia, J. F.
The night. Agnon, S. Y.
Night. Stuart, D. A.
Night. Wiesel, E.
Night and the loves of Joe Dicostanzo.
Delany, S. R.
A night at Greenway Court. Cather, W.
A night at the fair. Fitzgerald, F. S.
A night at The Millionaire's Club. Crane, S.
Night before battle. Hemingway, E.
The night before Christmas. Zobarskas, S.
Night before landing. Hemingway, E.
Night call, collect. Bradbury, R.
Night club. Brush, K.

**NIGHT CLUBS**
Beneš, J. A rainy night
Brush, K. Night club
Crane, S. The "Tenderloin" as it really is
Dumas, H. Will the circle be unbroken?
Ellison, H. Try a dull knife
Hines, C. Black laughter
McNair, K. The inter-generation communication gap
O'Hara, J. He thinks he owns me
*See also* Restaurants, lunchrooms, etc.
The night-doings at "Deadman's." Bierce, A.
The night driver or an alternative life. Tindall, G.
A night in Acadie. Chopin, K.
A night in '43. Bassani, G.
Night in Funland. Peden, W.
A night in new Arabia. Henry, O.
A night in new Jerusalem. Farrell, J. T.
A night in the grave. Scott, Sir W.

Night meeting. *See* Bradbury, R. August 2002: night meeting
"Night must fall." Landolfi, T.
The night of manhood. Brister, B.
The night of the gar. Ansell, J.
Night of the millennium. Hoch, E. D.
The night of the storm. Heinesen, W.
Night of the twister. Ullman, J. M.
Night out. Ansell, J.
A night out. Carver, R.
Night owls. Leskov, N.
Night piece for Julia. West, J.
Night run to Palestine. Fraser, G. M.
Night scene. Aricha, Y.
NIGHT SCHOOLS. *See* Evening and continuation schools
Night-sea journey. Barth, J.
The night Sea-Maid went down. Lumley, B.
Night stalk. Forester, C. S.
Night streets of madness. Bukowski, C.
Night strike. Tanburn, M.
The night the ghost got in. Thurber, J.
Night vigil. Ellison, H.
A night visitor. Jackson, C.
NIGHT WATCHMEN. *See* Watchmen
Night! Youth! Paris! And the moon! Collier, J.
Nightfall. Asimov, I.
The nightingale. Andersen, H. C.
The nightingale. Boccaccio, G.
The nightingale. Cullinan, E.
The nightingale sings. Borchert, W.
Nightmare in New York. Sweet, J.
NIGHTMARES. *See* Dreams
Nightmusic. Oates, J. C.
Nights at O'Rear's. Griffith, P. B.
The night's for cryin'. Himes, C.
Nights of love in Granada. Trevisan, D.
The nightsong of Dashiki Henry. Welburn, R.
NIGHTWATCHMEN. *See* Watchmen
Nightwings. Silverberg, R.
NIHILISM
    Leskov, N.   A journey with a nihilist
NIHILISTS. *See* Nihilism
NIJINSKY, WASLAW
    Algren, N. Could World War I have been a mistake?
Nil nisi. O'Hara, J.
Niland, D'Arcy
    The sound and the silence
        Burke, J. ed. Tales of unease
Nin, Anaïs
    Nina
        Matthews, J. ed. Archetypal themes in the modern story
    Under a glass bell
        Tytell, J. and Jaffe, H. eds. Affinities
Nina. Nin, A.
The nine. Babel, I.
The nine billion names of God. Clarke, A. C.
Nine lives. Le Guin, U. K.
The nine mile walk. Kemelman, H.
Nine points of the law. Hornung, E. W.
The nine-to-five man. Ellin, S.
1939. Taylor, P.
1962 Cotton Mather newsreel. Brautigan, R.
1976. Pei, M.

The 1980 president. DeFord, M. A.
99.6. West, J.
Ninotchka. Chekhov, A.
The ninth cold day. Weisbrod, R.
Nippy. Kotzwinkle, W.
Nissenson, Hugh
    Charity
        Nissenson, H. In the reign of peace
    The crazy old man
        Nissenson, H. In the reign of peace
    Forcing the end
        Nissenson, H. In the reign of peace
    Going up
        Nissenson, H. In the reign of peace
    Grace
        Nissenson, H. In the reign of peace
    In the reign of peace
        Nissenson, H. In the reign of peace
    Lamentations
        Nissenson, H. In the reign of peace
    The law
        Ribalow, H. U. ed. My name aloud
    The throne of good
        Nissenson, H. In the reign of peace
Nitelife. Deck, J.
NITOCRIS, QUEEN OF EGYPT
    Lumley, B. The Mirror of Nitocris
Niven, Larry
    All the myriad ways
        Silverberg, R. ed. Worlds of maybe
    Becalmed in hell
        Ferman, E. L. and Mills, R. P. eds. Twenty years of The Magazine of Fantasy and Science Fiction
        Knight, D. ed.   A science fiction argosy
    Bird in the hand
        Silverberg, B. ed. Phoenix feathers
    Bordered in black
        SF: authors' choice 3
    Cloak of anarchy
        Del Rey, L. ed. Best science fiction stories of the year [1973]
    Flash crowd
        Three trips in time and space
    Get a horse!
        The Best from Fantasy and Science Fiction; 19th ser.
    Neutron star
        Asimov, I. ed. The Hugo winners v2
        Asimov, I. ed. Where do we go from here?
    Not long before the end
        Knight, D. ed. The golden road
        Nebula award stories 5
    Rammer
        Rel Rey, L. ed. Best science fiction stories of the year [1972]
    There is a wolf in my time machine
        Yolen, J. comp. Zoo 2000
    Wait it out
        Silverberg, R. ed. Tomorrow's worlds
    Wrong way street
        Clement, H. ed. First flights to the moon
Njoku, M. C.
    The python's dilemma
        Angoff, C. and Povey, J. eds. African writing today
A no-account Creole. Chopin, K.

No connection. Asimov, I.
No cumshaw no rickshaw. Algren, N.
No direction home. Spinrad, N.
No feet. Dawson, F.
"No Haid Pawn." Page, T. N.
No Jews or dogs. Glanville, B.
No jokes on Mars. Blish, J.
No justice. O'Hara, J.
No loose ends. DeFord, M. A.
No motive. Mathieson, T.
No neck and bad as hell. Bukowski, C.
No news today. Cartmill, C.
No parking. Queen, E.
No place beneath the rising sun. Beek-
    man, A.
No place for a hawk. Stuart J.
No place for you, my love. Welty, E.
No place like. Gordimer, N.
No rescue. Norman, J.
No ships pass. Smith, Lady E.
No stockings. Bukowski, C.
No story. Schwimmer, W.
No sweetness here. Aidoo, A. A.
No trace. Madden, D.
No truce with kings. Anderson, P.
No 25 to be let or sold. Mackenzie, C.
No war, or battle's sound. Harrison, H.
No way to paradise. Bukowski, C.
**NOAH'S ARK**
    Carpentier, A. The chosen
    Mitchell, E. P. The story of the Deluge
**Noakes, Donald**
    The long silence
        Del Rey, L. ed. Best science fiction
        stories of the year [1973]
**NOBILITY.** See Aristocracy
Nobody ever died from it. Fiedler, L. A.
"Nobody here but—." Asimov, I.
Nobody saw the ship. Leinster, M.
Nobody starves. Goulart, R.
Nobody's fool. De Vries, P.
Nobody's home. Russ, J.
**Nodier, Charles**
    Jean-François Bluestockings
        Bishop, M. ed.   A Romantic storybook
Noire's dialogues. Bullock, M.
**NOISE**
    Noakes, D. The long silence
Noise. Vance, J.
Noise level. Jones, R. F.
Noise of strangers. Garrett, G.
**Nolan, William F.**
    Dark encounter
        Mystery Writers of America. Murder
        most foul
    Death double
        Haining, P. ed. The Hollywood night-
        mare
    Down the long night
        Dickensheet, D. ed. Men and malice
    Happily ever after
        Nolan, W. F. ed.   A wilderness of stars
    He kilt it with a stick
        McComas, J. F. ed. Special wonder
    The strange case of Mr Pruyn
        Hitchcock, A. ed. Alfred Hitchcock pre-
        sents: Stories to be read with the
        lights on

Toe to tip, tip to toe, pip-pop as you go
    Nolan, W. F. ed. The future is now
Violation
    Elwood, R. ed. Future city
**Noma, Hiroshi**
    A red moon in her face
        Decker, C. R. and Angoff, C. eds.
        Modern stories from many lands
Nomad and viper. Oz, A.
**NOMADS**
    Oz, A. Nomad and viper
Nona Vincent. James, H.
**NONCONFORMISTS.** See Conformity; Dis-
    senters
**NONCONFORMITY.** See Conformity
None so blind. Blish, J.
The **Noneatrins.** Varshavsky, I.
Non-horseshit horse advice. Bukowski, C.
**NONSENSE.** See Humor
**NONVIOLENCE**
    Leskov, N. Figúra
Noonday devil. O'Neil, D.
Noone. Just, W.
Nor limestone islands. Lafferty, R. A.
Nora. Just, W.
Nora's friends. See Cullinan, E. Maura's
    friends
**NORFOLK.** See England, Provincial and
    rural—Norfolk
Normal love. Oates, J. C.
**Norman, Charles**
    The smiler
        Mystery Writers of America. Mirror,
        mirror, fatal mirror
    Two muscovy ducks
        Mystery Writers of America. Murder
        most foul
**Norman, James**
    No rescue
        Fenner, P. R. comp. Desperate mo-
        ments
Norman and the killer. Oates, J. C.
A **Normandy** joke. Maupassant, G. de
**NORMANS IN ENGLAND**
    Treece, H. The man on the hill
**Norris, Frank**
    A deal in wheat
        Hall, J. B. ed. The realm of fiction
    Grettir at Thorhall-stead
        Moskowitz, S. ed. Horrors unknown
**NORTH AFRICA.** See Africa, North
A **North** American education. Blaise, C.
**NORTH CAROLINA**
    Chapel Hill
        Cardwell, G. A. Did you once see Shelley?
    Durham
        Patton, F. G.   A friend of the court
**NORTH DAKOTA**
    O'Donnell, M. K.   A celebration of light
The **North** Knoll. Brennan, J. P.
North wind. Oliver, C.
**Norton, André**
    All cats are gray
        Bova, B. ed. The many worlds of sci-
        ence fiction
        Yolen, J. comp. Zoo 2000

Norton, André—*Continued*

Desirable lakeside residence
    Elwood, R. and Kidd, V. eds. Saving worlds

**NORWAY**

Undset, S. Simonsen

**Oslo**

Marshall, J.  A private place

**NORWEGIANS IN THE ARCTIC RE-GIONS**

Lütgen, K. The road to Viton

**NORWEGIANS IN THE UNITED STATES**

Cather, W. Eric Hermannson's soul
Cather, W. On the Divide
Thaxter, C.  A memorable murder
Thurston, J. The cross

**NOSE**

Ditlevsen, T. Modus operandi
The **nose**. Gogol, N.
The **nose** jewel. Rajagopalachari, C.

**NOSTALGIA**

Algren, N. Everything inside is a penny
Dawson, F. The news
Francis, H. E. Don't stay away too long
Greene, G. The innocent
Le Sueur, M. Corn village
Malzberg, B. N. Those wonderful years
Shepherd, J. The return of the smiling Wimpy doll
Sienkiewicz, H. The cranes
Taylor, P. Mrs Billingsby's wine
Vassilikos, V. Jingle Bells
Vassilikos, V. Sarandapikhou Street

Not a very nice story. Lessing, D.
Not after midnight. Du Maurier, D.
Not always. O'Hara, J.
Not final! Asimov, I.
Not for hire. Holmes, E. M.
Not long before the end. Niven, L.
Not my animal. Chernoff, S.
Not snow nor rain. DeFord, M. A.
Not the end of the world. Burton, H.
Not to the swift. Holmes, E. M.
Not we many. Cooper, C. L.
Not with a bang. Fast, H.
Not with a whimper, but . . . Yurick, S.
Not your singing, dancing spade. Fields, J.
A **note** on American literature by my uncle, Monroe Sanderson. Slesar, H.
**Notebook** found in a deserted house. Bloch, R.
**NOTEBOOKS.** *See* Diaries, Stories about
Notes for a case history. Lessing, D.
Notes for a novel about the first ship ever to Venus. Malzberg, B. N.
Notes from a lady at a dinner party. Malamud, B.
Notes just prior to the fall. Malzberg, B. N.
Notes of a potential suicide. Bukowski, C.
Notes on the perception of imaginary differences. Sheckley, R.
Notes on the pest. Bukowski, C.
Notes: what I think pudding says. Deck, J.
**Nothing** but human nature. Waugh, H.
**Nothing** for my noon meal. Ellison, H.
**Nothing** Sirius. Brown, F.

Nothing succeeds like failure. Anderson, P.
The **nothingness.** Naylor, P. R.
**NOTTINGHAM.** *See* England—Nottingham

**Nourse, Alan E.**

Bramble bush
    Nourse, A. E. Rx for tomorrow
The canvas bag
    McComas, J. F. ed. Special wonder
Contamination crew
    Nourse, A. E. Rx for tomorrow
Free Agent
    Nourse, A. E. Rx for tomorrow
A gift for numbers
    Nourse, A. E. Rx for tomorrow
Grand Rounds
    Nourse, A. E. Rx for tomorrow
Heir apparent
    Nourse, A. E. Rx for tomorrow
In sheep's clothing
    Nourse, A. E. Rx for tomorrow
The last house call
    Nourse, A. E. Rx for tomorrow
Plague!
    Nourse, A. E. Rx for tomorrow
Rx
    Nourse, A. E. Rx for tomorrow
Symptomaticus medicus
    Nourse, A. E. Rx for tomorrow

**Nouveaux** riches. Sax, F.

**Nova, Irina**

The grandmother
Women

**NOVA SCOTIA**

MacLeod, A. The boat

**Novás-Calvo, Lino**

As I am . . . as I was
    Howes, B. ed. The eye of the heart

Novel. Bichsel, P.

**NOVELISTS.** *See* Authors; Women as authors

**Novelty** act. Dick, P. K.
**November** dreams. Dawson, F.
**November** night. Hesse, H.
**November** 2002: the fire balloons. Bradbury, R.
**November** 2005: the luggage store. Bradbury, R.
**November** 2005: the off season. Bradbury, R.
**November** 2005: the watchers. Bradbury, R.
**Novice.** Schmitz, J. H.

**NOVICES.** *See* Nuns

**NOVITIATE.** *See* Nuns

Novotny's pain. Roth, P.
Now alone. Berne, S.
Now hear the word of the Lord. Budrys, A.
Now I lay me. Hemingway, E.
Now I'm watching Roger. Panshin, A.
Now is forever. Disch, T. M.
Now wakes the sea. Ballard, J. G.

**Nowakowski, Tadeusz**

The liberty picnic
    Tyrmand, L. ed. Explorations in freedom: prose, narrative, and poetry from Kultura

**Nowlan, Alden**

The coming of age
    Fourteen stories high
The girl who went to Mexico
    Metcalf, J. ed. Sixteen by twelve

# O

**Oates, Joyce Carol**—*Continued*
Wednesday's child
  Oates, J. C. Marriages and infidelities
  Same as: Wednesday
What is the connection between men and
    women?
  Oates, J. C. The wheel of love, and
    other stories
The wheel of love
  Oates, J. C. The wheel of love, and
    other stories
Where are you going, where have you
    been?
  Abrahams, W. ed. Fifty years of the
    American short story v 1
  Kraus, R. and Wiegand, W. eds. Stu-
    dent's choice
  Oates, J. C. The wheel of love, and
    other stories
Where I lived, and what I lived for
  Oates, J. C. Marriages and infidelities
Wild Saturday
  Oates, J. C. The wheel of love, and
    other stories
You
  Oates, J. C. The wheel of love, and
    other stories
**OAXACA.** *See* Mexico, Provincial and rural
  —Oaxaca
The **O'Bannon** blarney file. Gores, J.
**OBEDIENCE**
  Deutsch, A. H. Obedience without delay
**Obedience.** Brown, F.
**Obedience** without delay. Deutsch, A. H.
The **obelisk.** Forster, E. M.
**Ober, Harold**
  Daddy
    New American Review no. 11
**OBESITY.** *See* Corpulence
**OBITUARIES**
  Blish, J. Statistician's Day
  Deutsch, A. H. The quality of reward
**Obituary.** Theridion, P.
**Object** lesson. Queen, E.
The **oblong** box. Poe, E. A.
The **oblong** room. Hoch, E. D.
**O'Brien, Donal C.**
  Pool number 37
    Corodimas, P. ed. In trout country
**O'Brien, Edna**
  Cords
    O'Brien, E. The love object
  How to grow a wisteria
    O'Brien, E. The love object
  Irish revel
    O'Brien, E. The love object
    Spinner, S. ed. Feminine plural
    Same as: Come into the drawing-room,
      Doris, listed in 1959-1963 supple-
      ment
  The love object
    O'Brien, E. The love object
  The mouth of the cave
    O'Brien, E. The love object
  An outing
    O'Brien, E. The love object
  Paradise
    O'Brien, E. The love object

The rug
  O'Brien, E. The love object
**O'Brien, Fitz-James**
  The diamond lens
    Manley, S. and Lewis, G. eds. Shapes
      of the supernatural
  From hand to mouth
    Moskowitz, S. ed. Horrors unknown
**O'Brien, Flann**
  "The little chest"
    Charyn, J. ed. The troubled vision
**OBSCENE LITERATURE.** *See* Pornog-
    raphy
**Observation** of Quadragnes. Andrevon, J. P.
**Obsession.** Phillips, R.
The **obstinate** Finn. Lütgen, K.
**Obudo, Nathaniel**
  They stole our cattle
    Angoff, C. ed. Stories from The Literary
      Review
    Angoff, C. and Povey, J. eds. African
      writing today
**Ocampo, Ricardo**
  The Indian Paulino
    Carpentier, H. and Brof, J. eds. Doors
      and mirrors
**Occam's** razor. Stiles, S.
**Occam's** scalpel. Sturgeon, T.
**OCCULT SCIENCES**
  Bulwer-Lytton, E.  The haunted and the
      haunters
  Crichton, M. The most powerful tailor in
      the world
  Jacobi, C. The random quantity
  Lafferty, R. A. And walk now gently
      through the fire
  Lytton, Lord. The Magician
  Maugham, S. The magician
  Naipaul, S. The tenant
  Pain, B. The grey cat
  Singer, I. B. The bishop's robe
  Smith, C. A. The return of the sorcerer
  Summers, M. The grimoire
  Tarkington, B. The veiled feminists of
      Atlantis
    *See also* Astrology; Cults; Hypno-
      tism; Spiritualism; Supernatural phe-
      nomena; Witchcraft
An **occupational** hazard. Ayrton, M.
**OCCUPATIONS**
  Goulart, R. Joker for hire
  Kafka, F. The nature Theatre of Okla-
      homa
  Naylor, P. R. Second son
  Spielberg, P. The record smasher
    *See also* Employment interviewing
**OCEAN**
  Clarke, A. C. The deep range
  Clarke, A. C. The shining ones
  Delany, S. R. Driftglass
  Hutsalo, Y.  A sea story
  Updike, J. The sea's green sameness
  Warner, S. T. Two children
    *See also* Seashore
      **Economic aspects**
    *See* Marine resources

**O'Donnell, K. M.**—*Continued*
Final war
  The Best from Fantasy and Science Fiction; 18th ser.
  Best SF: 1968
Getting around
  Elwood, R. ed. Tomorrow's alternatives
In the pocket
  Nova 1
Still-life
  Ellison, H. ed. Again, dangerous visions
  *See also* Neville, K. jt. auth.

**O'Donnell, Lawrence**
Clash by night
  The Astounding-Analog reader v 1
Vintage season
  The Astounding-Analog reader v 1
  The Science fiction hall of fame v2A
    *For other stories by this author see*
  Kuttner, Henry; Padgett, Lewis; Vance, Jack

**O'Donnell, Mary Kathleen**
A celebration of light
  American Review 18
**O'Donovan, Michael.** *See* O'Connor, Frank
**Odorous** perfume her harbinger. Boyle, P.
**ODYSSEUS.** *See* Ulysses
**Of** birds and beasts. Kawabata, Y.
**Of** bygone days. Sforim, M. M.
**Of** cabbages and kings. McPherson, J. A.
**Of** death what dreams. Laumer, K.
**Of** mice and men. Steinbeck, J.
**Of** our time. Lelchuk, A.
**Of** perches and pleasures. Brister, B.
**Of** sanctity and whiskey. O'Faolain, S.
**Of** streetcars, drunks, chestnuts and childhood. Rindfleisch, N.
**Of** the people. Dickson, G. R.
**Of** this time, of that place. Trilling, L.
**Of** women and other items. Bernstein, S. E.

**O'Faolain, Julia**
This is my body
  Winter's tales 19

**O'Faolain, Sean**
Brainsy
  O'Faolain, S. The talking trees, and other stories
A dead cert
  O'Faolain, S. The talking trees, and other stories
Feed my lambs
  O'Faolain, S. The talking trees, and other stories
Hymeneal
  O'Faolain, S. The talking trees, and other stories
Innocence
  Tytell, J. and Jaffe, H. eds. Affinities
The kitchen
  O'Faolain, S. The talking trees, and other stories
Of sanctity and whiskey
  O'Faolain, S. The talking trees, and other stories
'Our fearful innocence'
  O'Faolain, S. The talking trees, and other stories

Persecution mania
  Fitz Gerald, G. ed. Modern satiric stories
The planets of the years
  O'Faolain, S. The talking trees, and other stories
The talking trees
  O'Faolain, S. The talking trees, and other stories
Thieves
  O'Faolain, S. The talking trees, and other stories
The time of their lives
  O'Faolain, S. The talking trees, and other stories
The trout
  Hall, J. B ed. The realm of fiction
The **offending** party. Schultz, J.
**OFFENSES AGAINST RELIGION.** *See* Sacrilege
An **offering.** Deck, J.
An **offering** to the moon. Smith, C. A.
The **office.** Munro, A.
**OFFICE EMPLOYEES.** *See* Clerks
**OFFICE WORKERS.** *See* Clerks
**OFFICERS.** *See* subhead Officers, under names of various branches of national armed forces, e.g. France. Army—Officers; Great Britain. Navy—Officers; etc.

**Offord, Carl Ruthven**
So peaceful in the country
  Burnett, W. ed. Black hands on a white face
**Offsey, Sol**
Selection from an unpublished novel
  Voices of Brooklyn
**Offutt, Andrew J.**
For value received
  Ellison, H. ed. Again, dangerous visions
Meanwhile, we eliminate
  Elwood, R. ed. Future city
    *See also* Margroff, R. E. jt. auth.

**O'Flaherty, Liam**
The landing
  Bowman, J. S. ed. A book of islands
The sniper
  Ball, J. E. ed. Designs for reading: short stories
  Stansbury, D. L. ed. Impact
**Ogan, M. G.**
Scent of treason
  Furman, A. L. ed. Teen-age secret agent stories
**Ogden, Maurice**
Freeway to wherever
  Stansbury, D. L. ed. Impact
**Ogot, Grace**
Tekayo
  Nolen, B. ed. Africa is thunder and wonder
**Ogre!** Jesby, E.
**Ogre** in the vly. Davidson, A.
**OGRES.** *See* Monsters
The **ogress.** Young, R. F.
**Oh,** death where is thy sting-aling-aling? Boyle, P.
**Oh,** pity the dwarf's butt. Stone, A.

OLD AGE HOMES—*Continued*
  Davis, O. Irongate
  Drew, W. Homage to Axel Hoeniger
  Goulart, R. Granny
  Hughes, M. G. The foreigner in the blood
  Tyler, A. With all flags flying
      *See also* Almshouses and workhouses
The **old** are valiant. Stuart, J.
**Old** Ben. Stuart, J.
The **old** boys. Graham, W.
The **old** bunch and Dusty Stiggins. DeFord, M. A.
**Old** Carl. Holmes, E. M.
The **old** crawdad. Wylie, P.
**Old** Daniel's treasure. Fremlin, C.
The **old** folks. Gunn, J. E.
**Old** foot forgot. Lafferty, R. A.
The **old** friends. Gallant, M.
The **Old** Glory. Hemenway, R.
**Old** Halgir. Brú, H.
The **Old** Horns. Campbell, R.
**Old** Jackson was my teacher. Stuart, J.
**Old** Joe. Burke, T.
**OLD LADIES.** *See* Old age
The **old** law wasn't strong enough. Stuart, J.
**OLD MAIDS.** *See* Single women
**Old** man. Faulkner, W.
The **old** man. Horn, H.
An **old** man and his hat. Freitag, G. H.
The **old** man and the song. Djilas, M.
**Old** man at the bridge. Hemingway, E.
An **old** man goes wooing. Crane, S.
**Old** man Henderson. Neville, K.
**Old** man Jensen. Rifbjerg, K.
**Old** man Morgan's grave. DeFord, M. A.
The **old** man of the sea. Brennan, M.
The **old** man of the towans. Val Baker, D.
The **old** man of Usumbura and his misery. Liyong, T. L.
**Old** Man Stupidity. Sié, Cheou-kang
**Old** Man Warner. Fisher, D. C.
The **old** man with the bread. Kotowska, M.
An **old** manuscript. Kafka, F.
**Old** Marescot's family. Babel, I.
**OLD MEN.** *See* Old age
**Old** men at Pevensey. Kipling, R.
**Old** men dream dreams, young men see visions. Corrington, J. W.
The **old** nurse's story. Gaskell, E.
**Old** page. *See* Kafka, F. An old manuscript
**OLD PEOPLE.** *See* Old age
The **old** people. Faulkner, W.
The **old** priest. Cullinan, E.
**Old** Raccoon. Munson, G.
**Old** Red. Gordon, C.
The **old** shell collector. Keating, H. R. F.
**Old** soul. Herbst, S.
**Old** Squids and Little Speller. Mitchell, E. P.
An **old** story. Brownstein, M.
An **old**-time March meeting. Robinson, R. E.
The **old**-timer. Farrell, J. T.
**Old** Tom's egg box. Bahr, J.
**Old** Ushitora. Ibuse, M.
**Old** Willie. McGivern, W. P.
The **old** woman. Bingham, S.
The **old** woman. DeFord, M. A.
An **old** woman and her cat. Lessing, D.

**Old** Woman Magoun. Freeman, M. E. W.
**OLD WOMEN.** *See* Old age
**Old** Yotso is watching. Vazov, I.
The **olde** daunce. Sherwin, J. J.
The **older** woman. Gold, H.
**Ole** rockin' chair. Hardwick, Michael, and Hardwick, Mollie
**Ole** 'Stracted. Page, T. N.
**Olesha, Yurii**
  Love
    Minot, S. and Wilson, R. eds. Three stances of modern fiction
**Oliphant, Mrs**
  The library window
    Tomlinson, D. ed. Walk in dread
**Olive** and Camilla. Coppard, A. E.
**Oliver, Chad**
  Blood's a rover
    Silverberg, R. ed. Deep space
  Far from this earth
    Harrison, H. ed. The year 2000
  King of the hill
    Ellison, H. ed. Again, dangerous visions
  North wind
    Nolan, W. F. ed. A wilderness of stars
  Pilgrimage
    McComas, J. F. ed. Special wonder
  Technical adviser
    Haining, P. ed. The Hollywood nightmare
**Oliver, Diane**
  Neighbors
    Adoff, A. ed. Brothers and sisters
    Margolies, E. ed.   A native sons reader
**Oliver, George.** *See* Onions, Oliver
**Ollie** Hopnoodle's haven of bliss. Shepherd, J.
**Olsen, Paul**
  The flag is down
    The Best American short stories, 1970
**Olsen, T. V.**
  A kind of courage
    Western Writers of America. With Guidons flying
  The strange valley
    Hitchcock, A. comp. Alfred Hitchcock's Supernatural tales of terror and suspense
**Olsen, Tillie**
  Hey sailor, what ship?
    Kraus, R. and Wiegand, W. eds. Student's choice
  O yes
    Spinner, S. ed. Feminine plural
  Requa I
    The Best American short stories, 1971
  Tell me a riddle
    Abrahams, W. ed. Fifty years of the American short story v2
    Elkin, S. ed. Stories from the sixties
**Olson, Donald**
  The blue tambourine
    Best detective stories of the year, 1972
**Olwyler, Jay Peter**
  Take your own sweet sorrow
    New Directions in prose and poetry 24
**OLYMPUS, MOUNT**
  Gordon, C. Cloud nine

The **other** place. Borger, R.
The **other** side of the hedge. Forster, E. M.
The **other** times. Taylor, P.
**Other** versions, Aidoo, A. A.
The **other** way. Grau, S. A.
The **other** wife. Colette
The **other** woman. Hall, A.
The **others**. Holly, J. H.
**Others'** dreams. Oates, J. C.
**Otherwise** birds fly in. Gordimer, N.
**OTTAWA.** *See* Canada—Ottawa
**Ottley, Reginald**
  Brumbie running
    Ottley, R. Brumbie dust
  Bush camels
    Ottley, R. Brumbie dust
  Bush secret
    Ottley, R. Brumbie dust
  Dusty deal
    Ottley, R. Brumbie dust
  Epitaph to Jones'y
    Ottley, R. Brumbie dust
  The last of the horsemen
    Ottley, R. Brumbie dust
  Midnight
    Ottley, R. Brumbie dust
  Stampede
    Ottley, R. Brumbie dust
  Yumpin' Yarley
    Ottley, R. Brumbie dust
**Otto** Preminger's strange suspenjers. Algren, N.
An **ounce** of cure. Munro, A.
**Our** oldest friend. Pritchett, V. S.
**Our** father. Stern, J.
**"Our** Father who art in heaven." Katayev, V.
**'Our** fearful innocence'. O'Faolain, S.
**Our** Felix. Rosenberg, E.
**Our** field. Ewing, Mrs
**Our** letters. Maupassant, G. de
**Our** little Mozart. Borchert, W.
**Our** side of the fence and theirs. Gyanranjan
**Our** story of Ah Q. Lusin
**Our** turn to kill. Pentecost, H.
**Our** war with Monaco. Mitchell, E. P.
**Our** Wiff and Daniel Boone. Stuart, J.
**Ousmane, Sembene**
  Black girl
    Larson, C. R. ed. African short stories
An **out**-and-out free gift. O'Connor, F.
**Out** from Ganymede. Malzberg, B. N.
**Out** in the garage. Hill, R.
**Out** of the country. Scott, J.
**Out** of the depths. Agnon, S. Y.
**Out** of the eons. Heald, H.
**Out** of the fountain. Lessing, D.
**Out,** wit! Myers, H. L.
**Out** with the lions. Little, L.
The **outage.** Nemerov, H.
The **outbreeders.** Silverberg, R.
The **outcasts** of Poker Flat. Harte, B.
**OUTDOOR LIFE**
  Crane, S. The holler tree
    *See also* Camping
**OUTDOOR SURVIVAL.** *See* Wilderness survival
**OUTER SPACE**
  Fritch, C. E. The castaway

Nolan, W. F. Happily ever after
Simak, C. D. Lulu
Vance, J. Noise
Vance, J. When the five moons rise
    *See also* Interplanetary voyages
    **Exploration**
Anderson, P. Gypsy
Anderson, P. Lodestar
Blish, J. How beautiful with banners
Clement, H. The foundling stars
Disch, T. M. Things lost
Holly, J. C. The gift of nothing
Lafferty, R. A. Once on Aranea
Lafferty, R. A. World abounding
Le Guin, U. K. Vaster than empires and more slow
Malzberg, B. N. Out from Ganymede
Niven, L. Neutron star
Nourse, A. E. Heir apparent
Sallis, J. Slice of universe
Sheckley, R. Aspects of Langranak
Sheckley, R. The cruel equations
Silverberg, R. Ozymandias
Silverberg, R. Why?
Temple, W. F. The unpicker
Tiptree, J. And I have come upon this place by lost ways
Vinge, V. Long shot
Wolfe, G. Alien stones
    *See also* Interplanetary voyages
The **outgoing** of the tide. Buchan, J.
The **outing.** Baldwin, J.
An **outing.** O'Brien, E.
**OUTLAWS**
  Fox, J. Man-hunting in the Pound
  Hendryx, J. B. The parson
  Henry, O. The passing of Black Eagle
  Midwood, B. The sheriff
  Prebble, J. The regulator
  Spears, R. S. Minding their own business
  Sturgeon, T. and Ward, D. The man who figured everything
    *See also* Brigands and robbers; Fugitives
An **outline** of history. Braly, M.
**Outside** the cave. *See* Hall, J. B. God cares, but waits: Outside the cave
The **Outsider.** Brooks, J.
**Over** insurance. Collier, J.
The **over**-night bag. Greene, G.
**Over** the river. Miller, P. S.
**Over** the river. Peterkin, J.
**Over** the river and through the wood. O'Hara, J.
The **overcoat.** Gogol, N.
**OVERCOATS.** *See* Coats
**Overholser, Wayne D.**
  Beecher Island
    Western Writers of America. With Guidons flying
**OVERLAND JOURNEYS**
  Sienkiewicz, H. Across the plains
  West, J. Heading west
**OVERLAND JOURNEYS TO THE PACIFIC**
  Carr, M. J. Traps of quicksand
  Haycox, E. Into the deep gorge

The **overnight** guest. Di Donato, P.
**Overnight** trip. Colter, C.
**OVERPOPULATION.** *See* Population
**OVERPRODUCTION**
　Pohl, F. The Midas plague
**Overture.** De Vries, P.
**Owen** Wingrave. James, H.
The **owl.** Hawkes, J.
**OWLS**
　West, J. Hunting for hoot owls
**Owners** of Paradise. Khamsing, S.
**OWNERSHIP.** *See* Property
**Oxenhope.** Warner, S. T.
**OXFORD UNIVERSITY**
　Stewart, J. I. M. The men
**OYSTERS**
　Lumley, B. The pearl
**Oz, Amos**
　Nomad and viper
　　Michener, J. A. ed. First fruits
　The Trappist monastery
　　Rabikovitz, D. ed. The new Israeli
　　　writers
**OZARK MOUNTAINS**
　Schultz, J. Visit to my grandfather's grave
　　alone
**Ozick, Cynthia**
　The butterfly and the traffic light
　　Ozick, C. The pagan rabbi, and other
　　　stories
　The dock-witch
　　The Best American short stories, 1972
　　Ozick, C. The pagan rabbi, and other
　　　stories
　The doctor's wife
　　Ozick, C. The pagan rabbi, and other
　　　stories
　Envy; or, Yiddish in America
　　Ozick, C. The pagan rabbi, and other
　　　stories
　The pagan rabbi
　　Best SF: 1971
　　Ozick, C. The pagan rabbi, and other
　　　stories
　　Ribalow, H. U. ed. My name aloud
　The suitcase
　　Ozick, C. The pagan rabbi, and other
　　　stories
　Virility
　　Ozick, C. The pagan rabbi, and other
　　　stories
　Yiddish in America
　　The Best American short stories, 1970
**Ozymandias.** Carr, T.
**Ozymandias.** Silverberg, R.

# P

The **pace** of youth. Crane, S.
**Pacem** est. Neville, K. and O'Donnell, K. M.
**PACIFIC ISLANDS.** *See* Islands of the Pacific
**PACIFISM.** *See* Conscientious objectors;
　Peace
The **pacifist.** Clarke, A. C.

**Packer, Nancy Huddleston**
　Early morning, lonely ride
　　Prize stories, 1969: The O. Henry
　　　Awards
　Oh Jerusalem
　　Lewis, J. D. ed. Tales of our people
**Padgett, Lewis**
　Compliments of the author
　　Necker, C. ed. Supernatural cats
　Mimsy were the borogoves
　　Science fiction hall of fame v 1
　Private eye
　　Silverberg, R. ed. The mirror of infinity
　When the bough breaks
　　Kahn, J. ed. Some things dark and dangerous
　　　　*For other stories by this author see*
　　Kuttner, Henry; O'Donnell, Lawrence;
　　Vance, Jack
**Padgett, Ron, and Gallup, Dick**
　Cold turkey
　　Disch, T. M. ed. Bad moon rising
**Padre** Ignazio. Wister, O.
**PADUA.** *See* Italy—Padua
The **pagan** rabbi. Ozick, C.
**PAGANISM**
　Hauptmann, G. The heretic of Soana
　Lovecraft, H. P. The festival
　Ozick, C. The pagan rabbi
**Page, Thomas Nelson**
　Marse Chan
　　Page, T. N. In Ole Virginia
　Meh Lady: a story of the war
　　Page, T. N. In Ole Virginia
　"No Haid Pawn"
　　Page, T. N. In Ole Virginia
　Ole 'Stracted
　　Page, T. N. In Ole Virginia
　Polly
　　Page, T. N. In Ole Virginia
　"Unc' Edinburg's drowndin'"
　　Page, T. N. In Ole Virginia
**PAGEANTS**
　Malzberg, B. The falcon and the falconeer
**Pages** from Cold Point. Bowles, P.
**Paget, Violet.** *See* Lee, Vernon
**PAGODAS**
　Lafferty, R. A. Nor limestone islands
**Pai, Hsien-yung**
　Li T'ung: a Chinese girl in New York
　　Hsia, C. T. ed. Twentieth-century Chinese stories
A **pail** of air. Leiber, F.
**Pain, Barry**
　The grey cat
　　Parry, M. ed. Beware of the cat
**PAIN**
　Mitchell, E. P. The pain epicures
　　*See also* Suffering
The **pain** epicures. Mitchell, E. P.
A **painful** case. Joyce, J.
The **Painlevé** case. Neznakomov, P.
**PAINTERS**
　Aiken, J. The windshield weepers
　Baldwin, J. Come out the wilderness
　Bullock, M. Two girls and a man coming
　　and going
　Cassill, R. V. The rationing of love

The **passage.** Andersen, B.
The **passage.** Yurick, S.
**Passage** to the day. Dolson, C. W.
**Passenger** to Liverpool. Val Baker, D.
The **passing** of Abraham Shivers. Fox, J.
The **passing** of Big Joe. Jones, J. J.
The **passing** of Black Eagle. Henry, O.
A **passion** in the desert. Balzac, H. de
**Passion** night. Trevisan, D.
The **passion** of upside-down-Emil. Algren, N.

**PASSOVER**
  Agnon, S. J.  A Passover courting
  Fiedler, L. A. The dancing of Reb Hershl
    with the withered hand
  Shapiro, L. Pour out thy wrath
A **Passover** courting. Agnon, S. J.

**PASSPORTS**
  Algren, N.  I know they'll like me in
    Saigon

**Pasternak, Boris**
  Aerial tracks
    Pomorska, K. ed. Fifty years of Russian
      prose: from Pasternak to Solzhenit-
      syn v 1
    Same as: Aerial ways, listed in 1964–
      1968 supplement
  Il tratto di Apelle
    Pomorska, K. ed. Fifty years of Russian
      prose: from Pasternak to Solzhenit-
      syn v 1
The **Pastoral** Symphony. Gide, A.

**PASTORS.** *See* Clergy

**PASTRY**
  Ayrton, M. The surprise pastry
  Horwitz, J. The strudel

**PASTURES.** *See* Grazing
**Pat** Collins. O'Hara, J.
**Pat** Humbert's. Steinbeck, J.
**Patches.** Blum-Alquit, E.
A **patchwork** hog in the petunia world.
  Smith, W.
**Pâté** de foie gras. Asimov, I.

**PATENT MEDICINES.** *See* Medicines,
  Patent, proprietary, etc.
**Patent** pending. Clarke, A. C.

**PATENTS**
  Harness, C. L. An ornament to his pro-
    fession

**Paterson, James Hamilton-** *See* Hamilton-
  Paterson, James
**Pathans.** Linklater, E.
**Paths.** Haitov, N.
The **patient.** Stallman, L.

**PATIENTS.** *See* Illness
**Patients.** Strong, J.

**Paton, Alan**
  The waste land
    Kahn, J. ed. Hanging by a thread
The **patriarch.** Grau, S. A.
**Patricia** Kelly's. Ansell, J.

**PATRICIDE.** *See* Parricide

**Patrick, Q.**
  The fat cat
    Montgomery, J. ed. The world's best
      cat stories
  Murder in one scene
    Best of the Best detective stories

Portrait of a murderer
  Kahn, J. ed. Some things dark and dan-
    gerous

**PATRIOTISM**
  Dorr, L. An act of admiration
  Ostaijen, P. van. Patriotism, inc.
  Parker, D. Song of the shirt, 1941
**Patriotism.** Mishima, Y.
**Patriotism,** inc. Ostaijen, P. van
The **patrol.** Lem, S.
**Patron** of the arts. Rotsler, W.

**PATRONAGE, POLITICAL.** *See* Corrup-
  tion (in politics)
**Pattern** for plunder. Petaja, E.
The **patterns** of Dorne. Sturgeon, T.

**Patterson, Lindsay**
  Miss Nora
    Coombs, O. ed. What we must see:
      young Black storytellers

**Patton, Frances Gray**
  And hearts in heaven
    Patton, F. G. Twenty-eight stories
  Apricot pie
    Patton, F. G. Twenty-eight stories
  As man to man
    Patton, F. G. Twenty-eight stories
  The educated classes
    Patton, F. G. Twenty-eight stories
  Elinor and the normal life
    Patton, F. G. Twenty-eight stories
  The falling leaves
    Patton, F. G. Twenty-eight stories
  The finer things of life
    Patton, F. G. Twenty-eight stories
  First principles
    Patton, F. G. Twenty-eight stories
  A friend of the court
    Patton, F. G. Twenty-eight stories
  The game
    Patton, F. G. Twenty-eight stories
  Grade 5B and the well-fed rat
    Patton, F. G. Twenty-eight stories
  The homunculus
    Patton, F. G. Twenty-eight stories
  An honored guest
    Patton, F. G. Twenty-eight stories
  The house below the street
    Patton, F. G. Twenty-eight stories
  In a Philadelphia park
    Patton, F. G. Twenty-eight stories
  A little obvious
    Patton, F. G. Twenty-eight stories
  Loving hands at home
    Patton, F. G. Twenty-eight stories
  The man Jones
    Patton, F. G. Twenty-eight stories
  The mimosa blight
    Patton, F. G. Twenty-eight stories
  Mothers and daughters
    Patton, F. G. Twenty-eight stories
  The music of the spheres
    Patton, F. G. Twenty-eight stories
  A nice name
    Patton, F. G. Twenty-eight stories
  A piece of luck
    Patton, F. G. Twenty-eight stories
  Remold it nearer
    Patton, F. G. Twenty-eight stories
  Representative ham
    Patton, F. G. Twenty-eight stories

**Pettus, Richard Clyde**
Raining all the time
Alabama prize stories, 1970
**PEYOTE**
Sturgeon, T. Cactus dance
**Peyrou, Manuel**
Juliet and the magician
Yates, D. A. ed. Latin blood
**Pham Van Ky**
Forbidden love
Shimer, D. B. ed. Voices of modern Asia
**Phanishwarnath "Renu"**
The third vow
Roadarmel, G. C. ed. A death in Delhi
**Phantas.** Onions, O.
**PHANTASIES.** See Fantasies
The **phantom** fiddler. Gohman, F.
The **phantom** lover. Delattre, P.
A **phantom** lover. Lee, V.
The **phantom** motor. Futrelle, J.
The **phantom** of Pear Tree Heights. Jones, A.
**Phantom** of the Opera. Leroux, G.
The **Phantom** of the Opera's friend. Barthelme, D.
The **phantom** 'rickshaw. Kipling, R.
The **phantom** setter. Murphy, R.
**PHANTOMS.** See Hallucinations and illusions
**PHARAOHS.** See Egypt—Kings and rulers
The **Pharaohs.** Di Donato, P.
**PHARMACISTS**
Henry, O. The love-philtre of Ikey Schoenstein
O'Connor, F. A life of your own
Trevisan, D. Death on the square
**Pharr, Robert Deane**
The numbers writer
Chapman, A. ed. New Black voices
**Phebe.** Warren, R. P.
**PHILADELPHIA**
**Negroes**
See Negroes—Philadelphia
**PHILANTHROPISTS**
Bierce, A. The applicant
Bontemps, A. A woman with a mission
**Philco** baby. Faust, I.
**Philippe de Vigneulles**
Modicum et bonum
Cholakian, P. F. and Cholakian, R. C. eds. The early French novella
The peddler
Cholakian, P. F. and Cholakian, R. C. eds. The early French novella
**PHILIPPINE ISLANDS**
Arcellana, F. The yellow shawl
Gonzalez, N. V. M. On the ferry
Rivera, A. L. Love in the cornhusks
**Manila**
Buck, P. S. The cockfight
**PHILIPPINE ISLANDS, PROVINCIAL AND RURAL**
Daguio, A. Wedding dance
**Philips, Judson Pentecost.** See Pentecost, Hugh
**Phillifent, John T.**
Aim for the heel
Analog 7

**Phillips, Patricia R.**
Charlotte
Alabama prize stories, 1970
**Phillips, Peter**
Dreams are sacred
The Astounding-Analog reader v2
Manna
Knight, D. ed. A science fiction argosy
**Phillips, Robert**
The angel of the church
Phillips, R. The land of lost content
A boy's tale
Phillips, R. The land of lost content
The death of a good man
Phillips, R. The land of lost content
The dictates of the heart
Phillips, R. The land of lost content
In a country of strangers
Phillips, R. The land of lost content
The kill-joy
Phillips, R. The land of lost content
A lady of fashion
Phillips, R. The land of lost content
The lost and the found
Phillips, R. The land of lost content
The lost child
Phillips, R. The land of lost content
Mealy Marshall and the Whore of Babylon
Phillips, R. The land of lost content
Obsession
Phillips, R. The land of lost content
The quality of feeling
Phillips, R. The land of lost content
Rise up singing
Phillips, R. The land of lost content
Songs of three seasons
Phillips, R. The land of lost content
A teacher's rewards
Phillips, R. The land of lost content
**Phillips, Rog**
Justice, inc.
Bernkopf, J. F. comp. Boucher's choicest
The yellow pill
The Astounding-Analog reader v2
**Phillips, Vic**
Once around the moon
Clement, H. ed. First flights to the moon
**PHILOSOPHERS**
Dilov, L. The stranger
Hesse, H. Inside and outside
Kiš, D. Garden, ashes
Krleža, M. Dr Gregor and the Evil One
Linklater, E. The redundant miracle
Russell, B. The existentialist's nightmare
Russell, B. The metaphysician's nightmare
Sié, Cheou-kang. Illusion
Singer, I. B. The Spinoza of Market Street
See also Scholars
The **philosophy** lesson. Stafford, J.
**PHILOSOPHY OF LIFE.** See Life (Philosophy of life)
**PHOBIAS.** See Neuroses
**PHOENIX (BIRD)**
Nesbit, E. The egg
**Phoenix.** Smith, C. A.
The **phoenix.** Strindberg, A.
**Phog.** Anthony, P.

PLANTS
  Carr, J. The flavor of the tea
  Corvo, F. Baron. About a vegetable purgatory
  Delattre, P. The jewelled garden
  Dickson, G. R. The three
  Gallun, R. Z. Seeds of the dusk
  Lumley, B. The thing from the blasted heath
  Mistral, G. Why reeds are hollow
  Wolfe, G. Morning-glory
      See also Climbing plants; Flowers; and names of specific plants or flowers
A plaque on Via Mazzini. Bassani, G.
PLASTER CASTS
  Bryant, E. Pinup
PLASTIC SURGERY. See Surgery, Plastic
Plath, Sylvia
  Johnny Panic and the Bible of Dreams
      The Best American short stories, 1969
      Karl, F. R. and Hamalian, L. eds. The naked i
      Moss, H. ed. The poet's story
      Winter's tales 15
  Mothers
      The Best American short stories, 1973
PLATONIC LOVE. See Love, Platonic
Platonov, Andrei
  Aphrodite
      Platonov, A. The fierce and beautiful world
  Dzhan
      Platonov, A. The fierce and beautiful world
  The fierce and beautiful world
      Platonov, A. The fierce and beautiful world
  Fro
      Platonov, A. The fierce and beautiful world
      Pomorska, K. ed. Fifty years of Russian prose: from Pasternak to Solzhenitsyn v 1
  Homecoming
      Platonov, A. The fierce and beautiful world
  The Potudan River
      Platonov, A. The fierce and beautiful world
  The third son
      Platonov, A. The fierce and beautiful world
Platt, Charles
  New York Times
  Orbit 11
PLAY
  Brautigan, R. The ghost children of Tacoma
Play. Brodkey, H.
Play like I'm sheriff. Cady, J.
Play up, play up and get tore in. Fraser, G. M.
Playback. Clarke, A. C.
The player at Yellow Silence. Jacobi, C.
The playground. Enright, E.
PLAYGROUNDS
  Niven, L. Cloak of anarchy
Playin with Punjab. Bambara, T. C.

Playing with Mary. Elman, R.
PLAYS. See Amateur theatricals
The play's the thing. Bloch, R.
PLAYWRIGHTS. See Dramatists
Please listen, Aunt Viney. Linn, M. L.
Please no eating no drinking. Bingham, S.
Please stand by. Goulart, R.
PLEASURE. See Pain
A pleasure shared. Aldiss, B.
PLEURISY
  Glanville, B. The dying footballer
  McCullers, C. Breath from the sky
PLEURITIS. See Pleurisy
Pliny the Younger
  The haunted house
      Manley, S. and Lewis, G. eds. A gathering of ghosts
The plot. Manners, M.
Plot. Oates, J. C.
The plot is the thing. Bloch, R.
The plot to save the world. Brownstein, M.
PLOVERS
  Linklater, E.   A sociable plover
Plum Beach. Levy, R.
Plum blossom by night. Ibuse, M.
Plum blossoms. Peterkin, J.
The plumber. Boulle, P.
PLUMBERS
  Boulle, P. The plumber
  Treat, L. Suburban tigress
PLUMBING
  Brautigan, R. Homage to the San Francisco YMCA
  Griffin, S. The sink
Plumbing. Updike, J.
PLUTO (PLANET)
  Niven, L. Wait it out
The Plymouth Express. Christie, A.
PNEUMONIA
  Henry, O. The last leaf
Po' Sandy. Chesnutt, C. W.
POACHERS. See Poaching
POACHING
  Carver, R. Sixty acres
  Holmes, E. M. The day of the hunter
  Holmes, E. M. Hunter's gold
  Maupassant, G. de. The guardian
  Saki. The interlopers
  Winther, M. A. To catch a thief
Podolny, Roman
  Invasion
      Ginsburg, M. ed. The ultimate threshold
Poe, Edgar Allan
  Berenice
      Haining, P. ed. The nightmare reader
  The black cat
      Hale, J. B. ed. The realm of fiction
      Necker, C. ed. Supernatural cats
      Poe, E. A. Tales of terror and fantasy
  The cask of Amontillado
      Haining, P. ed. Gothic tales of terror
      Poe, E. A. Tales of terror and fantasy
      Taylor, J. C. ed. The short story: fiction in transition
  A descent into the maelström
      Poe, E. A. Tales of terror and fantasy
  The facts in the case of M. Valdemar
      Poe, E. A. Tales of terror and fantasy

**Pohl, Frederik—**_Continued_
The Midas plague
  The Science fiction hall of fame v2B
The schematic man
  Best SF: 1969
Shaffery among the immortals
  The Best from Fantasy & Science Fiction; 20th ser.
  Nebula award stories 8
    _For other stories by this author see_
    MacCreigh, James

**Pohl, Frederik, and Kornbluth, C. M.**
The meeting
  Del Rey, L. ed. Best science fiction stories of the year [1973]
Point of conversion. Flythe, S.
Point of focus. Silverberg, R.
A **point** of law. Maugham, W. S.
Point of view. Beekman, A.
**POINT REYES NATIONAL SEASHORE.** See California—Point Reyes National Seashore
**POINTERS (DOGS)** _See_ Bird dogs
**POISON.** _See_ Poisoning
Poison. Dahl, R.
**POISON GASES.** _See_ Gases, Asphyxiating and poisonous
Poison in the cup. Brand, C.
**POISON PEN LETTERS.** _See_ Letters, Stories about
**POISONING**
Amores, A. F.   A scrap of tinfoil
Armstrong, C. The splintered Monday
Barrett, M. Death out of season
Blackhurst, W. E.   A rat's a rat
Bloch, R. Fat chance
Bowen, M. Cambric tea
Brand, C. Poison in the cup
Brunner, J. An elixir for the emperor
Burke, T. Tai Fu and Pansy Greers
Collier, J. Three bears cottage
Cumberland, M. The voice
Donovan, D. The problem of Dead Wood Hall
Manners, M. The plot
Meade, L. T. and Eustace, R. Madame Sara
Mitchell, E. P. The facts in the Ratcliff case
Nye, R. Mary Murder
Phillips, P. R. Charlotte
Queen, E. The adventure of the seven black cats
Sayers, D. L. The leopard lady
Scott, J. Out of the country
Sillitoe, A. Revenge
Smith, C. A. The supernumerary corpse
Smith, C. A. The Venus of Azombeii
Woolrich, C. Murder at the automat
  _See also_ Poisons
**POISONOUS PLANTS**
Hawthorne, N. Rappaccini's daughter
**POISONS**
Brennan, J. P. The intangible threat
**POKER (GAME)**
Aldridge, H. R. Cards with a stranger
Crane, S.   A poker game

Kelley, W. M. The poker party
Landolfi, T. Misdeal
A **poker** game. Crane, S.
The **poker** party. Kelley, W. M.
**POLAND**
Guzy, P. The short life of a positive hero
Stalinski, T. The funeral
Tyrmand, L.   A cocktail party
### Chelm
Blum-Alquit, E. The big light
Blum-Alquit, E.   A highwayman in the woods of Chelm
### Communism
_See_ Communism—Poland
### Warsaw
Singer, I. B. Grandfather and grandson
**POLAND, PROVINCIAL AND RURAL**
Singer, I. B. The blizzard
Singer, I. B.   A dance and a hop
Singer, I. B. The son from America
Poldi. McCullers, C.
**POLES IN ENGLAND**
Tuohy, F. The trap
**POLES IN FRANCE**
Simenon, G. Stan the killer
**POLES IN ISRAEL**
Tammuz, B. Angioxyl, a rare cure
**POLES IN THE UNITED STATES**
Francis, H. E. The fence
Francis, H. E. The man who made people
Gallico, P. Welcome home
O'Connor, F. The displaced person
Shepherd, J. The star-crossed romance of Josephine Cosnowski
Sienkiewicz, H. The cranes
Sienkiewicz, H.   A legionary of Mieroslawski
Singer, I. B.   A day in Coney Island
Targan, B. The clay war
Weidman, J.   I thought about this girl
**POLICE**
Dozios, G. R. Where no sun shines
Goulart, R. Copstate
McCaffrey, A.   Apple
Noakes, D. The long silence
Rathjen, C. H. Touch and blow!
Varshavsky, I.   A raid takes place at midnight
Wilensky, B. On the spike
Woolrich, C. Through a dead man's eye
Wright, R. The man who lived underground
  _See also_ Detectives
### Boston
Sukenick, R. What's your story
### California
Pronzini, B. It's a lousy world
### Czechoslovak Republic
Beneš, J. The problem
### England
Wolfe, G.   A method bit in "B"
### Faeroe Islands
Brú, H.   A summons for the blacksmith
### France
Ionesco, E.   A victim of duty

POLICE—*Continued*

**Germany**

Gallant, M. The old friends
Powell, J. Kleber on murder in 30 volumes

**Ireland**

McGahern, J. Bomb box
O'Connor, F. The majesty of the law

**Italy**

Maltz, A. The cop

**Japan**

Ibuse, M. Tajinko Village

**London**

See London—Police [i.e. Scotland Yard]

**Los Angeles**

Himes, C. One more way to die

**Mexico**

Davidson, A. The power of every root

**New York (City)**

Bambara, T. C. The hammer man
Bova, B. and Ellison, H. Brillo
DeLillo, D. In the men's room of the sixteenth century
Fast, H. The hole in the floor
Fay, W. The conscience of the cop
Henry, O. After twenty years

**Russia**

Dneprov, A. Interview with a traffic policeman
Leskov, N. Singlethought

**South Dakota**

Woods, W. C. The viping hour

**United States**

Barthelme, D. The Policeman's Ball
Cady, J.    I take care of things
Crayton, P. Cotton Alley
Ellin, S. The crime of Ezechiele Coen
Henry, O. The cop and the anthem
Hoch, E. D. End of the day
Montgomery, M. The decline and fall of Officer Fergerson
Rathjen, C. H. Jump job
Ritchie, J. Take another look
Treat, L.    L as in loot
Treat, L.    M as in mugged

**Wisconsin**

Hermann, J. Shebie

**Yugoslavia**

Marinković, R. Badges of rank
Mihajlović, D. When the pumpkins blossomed

POLICE, STATE

McGivern, W. P. Killer on the turnpike
**Police** and Mama-sans get it all. Algren, N.
The **Policemen's** Ball. Barthelme, D.
**Polidori, John William**
The vampyre
    Haining, P. ed. Gothic tales of terror
    Haining, P. ed. Vampires at midnight
POLISH REFUGEES. *See* Refugees, Polish
The **polite** captain. Bahr, J.
**Polite** conversation. Stafford, J.

POLITENESS. *See* Etiquette
POLITICAL CAMPAIGNS

**United States**

*See* Politics—United States
POLITICAL CRIMES AND OFFENSES

Purdy, K. W. In the matter of the assassin Merefirs
Tarasov-Rodyonov, A. Chocolate
    *See also* Assassination; Government, Resistance to
POLITICAL ETHICS

Naylor, P. R. The candidate
POLITICAL PRISONERS. *See* Prisoners, Political
POLITICAL REFUGEES. *See* Refugees
A **political** romance. Theroux, P.
POLITICAL SATIRE. *See* Satire
The **politician**. Khamsing, S.
POLITICIANS. *See* Politics
The **politicians** 1192-1193. Coolidge, O.
POLITICS

Anderson, P. Ramble with a gamblin' man
Bryant, E. Tactics
Eisenberg, L. The chameleon
Farrell, J. T. Dumbroviç
Farrell, J. T. Tom Carroll
Jacobi, C. Exit Mr Smith
Laumer, K. Ballots and bandits
Naylor, P. R. The candidate
Ostaijen, P. van. Patriotism, inc.
Pangborn, E. The world is a sphere
Silverberg, R. Counterpart
Taylor, P. The elect
Wolfe, G. Hour of trust
    *See also* Corruption (in politics); Political ethics

**Africa**

Jones, E. Show me first your penny

**Africa, North**

Reynolds, M. The Cold War . . . continued

**Austria**

Boyle, K. The white horses of Vienna

**Boston**

Mirsky, M. Simcha

**England**

Maugham, W. S. Lord Mountdrago
Maugham, W. S. Pro patria
Purdy, K. W. The Dannold cheque
Wilson, A. The wrong set

**France**

Maugham, W. S. Appearance and reality

**India**

Das, M. The mystery of the missing cap

**Ireland**

Joyce, J. Ivy day in the Committee Room

**Japan**

Kurahashi, Y. Partei

**Latin America**

Bahr, J. Incident on Galiano Street

**Missouri**

Bierce, A. Corrupting the press

POLITICS—*Continued*

**New York (City)**

Weidman, J. Good man, bad man

**Russia**

Leskov, N. Administrative grace

**Texas**

Brister, B. The sand trout seminar

**Thailand**

Khamsing, S. The politician

**United States**

Bukowski, C. Politics is like trying to screw a cat in the ass

Cole, T. Saint John of the Hershey Kisses: 1964

Coover, R. The Cat in the Hat for President

Farrell, J. T. Childhood is not forever

McGerr, P. Campaign fever

Rush, N. Riding

Sladek, J. The great wall of Mexico

Stuart, J.   A pilgrim out in space

Sturgeon, T. The nail and the oracle

Taylor, P. First heat

Wister, O. The Second Missouri Compromise

**Washington, D.C.**

Just, W. The Congressman who loved Flaubert

Just, W.   A guide to the architecture of Washington, D.C.

**Yugoslavia**

Djilas, M.   A Montenegrin jest

Politics. Bukowski, C.

Politics is like trying to screw a cat in the ass. Bukowski, C.

Polluted zone. Ahlin, L.

POLLUTION

Blish, J. We all die naked

Ehrlich, P. Eco-catastrophe!

Lafferty, R. A. Incased in ancient rind

Macfarlane, W. To make a new Neanderthal

Mitchison, N. The factory

Neville, L. and Neville, K. The quality of the product

Sturgeon, T. Occam's scalpel

Zebrowski, G. Parks of rest and culture

POLLUX AND CASTOR. *See* Castor and Pollux

Polly. Page, T. N.

POLO

Kipling, R. The Maltese Cat

POLTERGEISTS. *See* Ghosts

POLYANDRY

Bryant, E. The legend of Cougar Lou Landis

POLYDEUCES. *See* Castor and Pollux

POLYGAMY

Eastlake, W. Something big is happening to me

*See also* Polyandry

POLYNESIANS

Stevenson, R. L. The Isle of Voices

Pomegranate seed. Wharton, E.

The **pomegranate** trees. Saroyan, W.

PONIES

Kipling, R. The Maltese Cat

Ponsonby and the classic cipher. Young, A. K.

Ponsonby and the Shakespeare sonnet. Young, A. K.

The **Ponsonby** case. Pangborn, E.

PONTIUS PILATE. *See* Pilate, Pontius

POOL (GAME) *See* Billiards

Pool number 37. O'Brien, D. C.

The **pool** of the stone god. Fenimore, W.

Pool party. Benedict, A.

The **pool** table caper. Hunter, K.

THE POOR. *See* Poverty

Poor girls of Kowloon. Algren, N.

Poor little Black fellow. Hughes, L.

Poor Liza. Karamzin, N.

Poor man, beggar man. Russ, J.

Poor Margaret. Rees, B.

Poor Richard. James, H.

A **poor** rule. Henry, O.

POORHOUSES. *See* Almhouses and workhouses

The **Pope** 1095. Coolidge, O.

POPES

Eklund, G. The Shrine of Sebastian

Nemerov, H. The Twelve and the one

Silverberg, R. Good news from the Vatican

*See also* names of popes, e.g. Urban II, Pope

POPOCATEPETL (VOLCANO)

Crane, S. The voice of the mountain

Popov, Vassil

This beautiful mankind

Kirilov, N. and Kirk, F. eds. Introduction to modern Bulgarian literature

The **poppy**. Son, S.

A **popular** man. Bukowski, C.

POPULAR MUSIC. *See* Music

POPULAR SINGERS. *See* Musicians—Singers

POPULATION

Ballard, J. G. Billenium

Bunch, D. R. Breakout in Ecol 2

Cogswell, T. R. Probability zero! The population implosion

Harrison, H. Roommates

Laumer, K. Founder's day

Silverberg, R.   A happy day in 2381

Slater, E. The Sooey pill

Winn, P. Right off the map

PORCELAIN. *See* Antiques

Porcelain cups. Cabell, J. B.

Porch fixing. Weaver, G.

Porfiri and Esthalina. Silk, D.

Porges, Arthur

The reason

McComas, J. F. ed. Crimes and misfortunes

A Treasury of modern mysteries v 1

The rescuer

The Astounding-Analog reader v2

Pork chop paradise. Himes, C.

The **pork** chop tree. Schmitz, J. H.

Porkchops with whiskey and ice cream. McGregor, M. W.

PORNOGRAPHY

Bukowski, C. The birth, life and death of an underground newspaper

The **potter's** wheel. Witton, D.

The **Potudan** River. Platonov, A.

**Poulsen, Valdemar**
  The huntsman
    Faroese short stories

**POULTRY**
  Bradbury, R. The Inspired Chicken Motel
  Colette. The fox
  Drake, A. The chicken which became a rat
  Sillitoe, A. Chicken
  Singer, I. B. Cockadoodledoo
  Stuart, J. Powderday's red hen
  Svevo, I. The mother
    *See also* Chickens; Eggs; Roosters

**POULTRY INDUSTRY**
  Stuart, J. Pa's a man's man all right

**Pour** out thy wrath. Shapiro, L.

**POVERTY**
  Ansell, J. Eating out
  Blum-Alquit, E. Patches
  Blum-Alquit, E. Rothschild's relatives
  Böll, H. Business is business
  Böll, H. On the hook
  Carr, J.   A creature was stirring
  Crane, S. An experiment in misery
  Crane, S. The men in the storm
  Deutsch, A. H. Refining fire
  Dumas, H.   A boll of roses
  Enright, E.   A Christmas tree for Lydia
  Fair, R. L. We who came after
  Farrell, J. T. On the Appian Way
  Ford, J. H. The bitter bread
  Gaines, E. J. The sky is gray
  Haldeman, J. W. Counterpoint
  Jewett, S. O.   A dark carpet
  Jewett, S. O. The gray mills of Farley
  Kemal, Y. The baby
  Khamsing, S. The gold-legged frog
  Lee, A. M. Waiting for her train
  Lessing, D. An old woman and her cat
  Linklater, E. The redundant miracle
  Lu, Hsun. The true story of Ah Q
  McCord, J. Bitter is the hawk's path
  Maupassant, G. de. The adoption
  Maupassant, G. de. The horseman
  Moravia, A. You know me, Carlo
  Narayan, R. K.   A horse and two goats
  Peterkin, J. Missie
  Pidmohylny, V. The problem of bread
  Platonov, A. Dzhan
  Purdy, J. Daddy Wolf
  Rostopchin, V. Hard times
  Shahu, M. N. The sun of the blind night
  Shapiro, L. Pals
  Soto, P. J. Scribbles
  Stefanyk, V. The news
  Steinbeck, J. Danny
  Steinbeck, J. Pilon
  Steinbeck, J. The pirate
  Steinbeck, J. The treasure hunt
  Strindberg, A. Bread
  Strindberg, A. Love and the price of grain
  Verga, G. Black bread
  Wu, Tsu-hsiang. Fan village
  Yurick, S. The annealing
  Yurick, S. The siege

Zamyatin, E. The cave
    *See also* Hunger; Starvation; Unemployed

**Powderday's** red hen. Stuart, J.

**Powell, James**
  The Altdorf syndrome
    Ellery Queen's Mystery Magazine. Ellery Queen's Grand slam
  Coins in the Frascati Fountain
    Best detective stories of the year, 1971
  The Gobineau necklace
    Ellery Queen's Mystery Magazine. Ellery Queen's Mystery bag
  Kleber on murder in 30 volumes
    Best detective stories of the year [1969]
  Maze in the elevator
    Ellery Queen's Mystery Magazine. Ellery Queen's Murder menu
  The Stollmeyer sonnets
    Bernkopf, J. F. comp. Boucher's choicest

**Powell, Talmage**
  Murder method
    Best of the Best detective stories

**POWER (SOCIAL SCIENCES)**
  Dam, A. The mandrake
  Just, W.   A guide to the architecture of Washington, D.C.
  Moravia, A. Man of power
  Njoku, M. C. The python's dilemma
  Sturgeon, T. Microcosmic god

The **power** and the danger. Swenson, M.

**POWER FAILURE.** *See* Electric power distribution

The **power** line tapped. Ellison, R.

The **power** of a curse. Premchand

The **power** of every root. Davidson, A.

The **power** of prayer. Cullinan, E.

The **power** of Sergeant Streater. Green, G. F.

The **power** of the nail. Delany, S. R. and Ellison, H.

The **power** of the puppets. Leiber, F.

The **power** of the sentence. Locke, D. M.

The **power** of time. Saxton, J.

**POWER TRANSMISSION, ELECTRIC.**
    *See* Electric power distribution

**Powerhouse.** Welty, E.

**Powers, J. F.**
  The forks
    Thune, E. and Prigozy, R. eds. Short stories: a critical anthology
  Lions, harts, leaping does
    Abrahams, W. ed. Fifty years of the American short story v2
    Taylor, J. C. ed. The short story: fiction in transition
  The valiant woman
    Abrahams, W. ed. Fifty years of the American short story v2
    Fitz Gerald, G. ed. Modern satiric stories

**Powers.** Singer, I. B.

**Powers** being himself. O'Connor, P. F.

The **powers** of observation. Harrison, H.

A **practical** joke. Maupassant, G. de

The **practical** joke. Shannon, D.

**PRACTICAL JOKES.** *See* Humor—Practical jokes

**PREJUDICES AND ANTIPATHIES**—*Continued*
Theroux, A. Three wogs; 3 stories
Theroux, A. The wife of God
Toomer, J.   Becky
Trilling, L. The other Margaret
Wain, J. Down our way
    *See also* Discrimination; Race problems; Segregation
**Preliminary** research. Varshavsky, I.
**PREMATURE BURIAL.** *See* Burial, Premature
The **premature** burial. Poe, E. A.
**Premchand**
A car-splashing
  Premchand. The world of Premchand
A catastrophe
  Premchand. The world of Premchand
A coward
  Premchand. The world of Premchand
  Shimer, D. B. ed. Voices of modern Asia
A day in the life of a debt-collector
  Premchand. The world of Premchand
Deliverance
  Premchand. The world of Premchand
A desperate case
  Premchand. The world of Premchand
A feast for the holy man
  Premchand. The world of Premchand
Intoxication
  Premchand. The world of Premchand
January night
  Premchand. The world of Premchand
A lesson in the holy life
  Premchand. The world of Premchand
A little trick
  Premchand. The world of Premchand
Man's highest duty
  Premchand. The world of Premchand
A moral victory
  Premchand. The world of Premchand
My big brother
  Premchand. The world of Premchand
Neyur
  Premchand. The world of Premchand
Penalty
  Premchand. The world of Premchand
The power of a curse
  Premchand. The world of Premchand
The price of milk
  Premchand. The world of Premchand
The road to hell
  Premchand. The world of Premchand
The road to salvation
  Premchand. The world of Premchand
The shroud
  Premchand. The world of Premchand
The Thakur's well
  Premchand. The world of Premchand
**PREMINGER, OTTO**
Algren, N. Otto Preminger's strange suspenjers
**PREMONITIONS**
Metcalfe, J. 'Beyondaril'
**PREP SCHOOLS.** *See* School life
**PREPARATORY SCHOOLS.** *See* School life
**Present** at a hanging. Bierce, A.

**Present** for Minna. Stern, R. M.
**PRESENTS.** *See* Gifts
**PRESERVATION OF NATURAL SCENERY.** *See* Nature conservation
The **Preserving** Machine. Dick, P. K.
The **President** of the United States, detective. Heard, H. F.
**PRESIDENTS**
**United States**
Bukowski, C. ⚡ [Swastika]
Dick, P. K. Novelty act
Heard, H. F. The President of the United States, detective
Sladek, J. The great wall of Mexico
**United States—Election**
DeFord, M. A. The 1980 president
The **President's** half disme. Queen, E.
**PRESS AGENTS.** *See* Publicity
**Presslie, Robert**
Dial 'O' for operator
  Stern, P. V. ed. The other side of the clock
**Pressure.** Harrison, H.
The **pressure** cooker. Drake, R.
The **pressure** of time. Disch, T. M.
**Prest, Thomas Peckett**
The demon of the Hartz; or, The three charcoal burners
  Haining, P. ed. Gothic tales of terror
The storm visitor
  Haining, P. ed. Vampires at midnight
**PRETENDERS.** *See* Imposters and imposture
**Pretty** boy. Drake, R.
**Pretty** Maggie Moneyeyes. Ellison, H.
The **pretty** office. Brautigan, R.
**Preview.** Long, F. B.
**Previous** days. Algren, N.
**Prévost, Abbé**
The adventure of a desperate man
  Bishop, M. ed.   A Romantic storybook
**Prévost, Antoine François.** *See* Prévost, Abbé
**Prez.** Goulart, R.
**Price, Reynolds**
A dog's death
  Price, R. Permanent errors
Good and bad dreams
  Price, R. Permanent errors
The happiness of others
  Price, R. Permanent errors
Scars
  Price, R. Permanent errors
Truth and lies
  Price, R. Permanent errors
Waiting at Dachau
  Price, R. Permanent errors
  Prize stories, 1971: The O. Henry Awards
Walking lessons
  Price, R. Permanent errors
The **price.** Belcher, C. D.
The **price.** Fast, H.
The **price** of a pintail. Brister, B.
The **price** of pine. Rothschild, M.
The **price** of the harness. Crane, S.
**Prichard, Hesketh**
The murder at the Duck Club
  Greene, H. ed. Cosmopolitan crimes

**Purdy, James**—*Continued*
  Scrap of paper
    New Directions in prose and poetry 20
  Shoot!
    New Directions in prose and poetry 25
  Why can't they tell you why?
    McKenzie, B. ed. The process of fiction
**Purdy, Ken W.**
  A change of plan
    Fenner, P. R. comp. Where speed is
      king
  The Dannold cheque
    Best SF: 1969
  In the matter of the assassin Merefirs
    Best SF: 1972
**Purdy** Robinson's parade. Estes, W. M.
A **pure** accident. Lavin, M.
**PURGATORY.** *See* Hell
The **purification** of Cornbury. Robinson,
  R. E.
The **purification** of Rodney Spelvin. Wode-
  house, P. G.
**Puritan** passions. Hawthorne, N.
**PURITANS**
  Henderson, Z. The walls
**Purple** as an iris. Bukowski, C.
The **purple** envelope. Forster, E. M.
The **purple** is everything. Davis, D. S.
The **purple** moccasin. Kantor, M.
A **purple** rhododendron. Fox, J.
**PUSAN.** *See* Korea—Pusan
**Push** no more. Silverberg, R.
The **push** of a finger. Bester, A.
**Pushkin, Alexander**
  The queen of spades
    Proffer, C. R. ed. From Karamzin to
      Bunin: an anthology of Russian short
      stories
  The shot
    Bishop, M. ed.  A Romantic storybook
  The station master
    Proffer, C. R. ed. From Karamzin to
      Bunin: an anthology of Russian short
      stories
**Puss** in boots. *See* Perrault, C. The Master
  Cat
**Putman, Clay**
  The news from Troy
    Kraus, R. and Wiegand, W. eds. Stu-
      dent's choice
**PUTNAM.** *See* Connecticut—Putnam
**Putois.** France, A.
**Puzzle.** Oates, J. C.
**Puzzle** for spacemen. Brunner, J.
The **puzzle** of the broken watch. Ber-
  múdez, M. E.
**PUZZLES**
  Asimov, I.  A problem of numbers
**PYGMIES**
  Lispector, C. The smallest woman in the
    world
**Pyle, Howard**
  Blueskin the pirate
    Fenner, P. R. comp. Finders keepers
  The dead finger
    Kahn, J. ed. Some things dark and
      dangerous

**Pynchon, Thomas**
  Low-lands
    Fitz Gerald, G. ed. Modern satiric stories
  Under the rose
    Abrahams, W. ed. Fifty years of the
      American short story v2
  V. in love
    Charyn, J. ed. The single voice
**Pyramid.** Abernathy, R.
**Pyramid** Lake. Delattre, P.
The **pyramid** of counterpoint. Ayrton, M.
**PYRAMIDS**
  Cather, W.  A tale of the white pyramid
**PYRÉNÉES.** *See* France, Provincial and
  rural—Pyrénées
The **python's** dilemma. Njoku, M. C.

# Q

**Q.E.D.** Stein, G.
**Q. U. R.** Boucher, A.
**Quack** doctor. Khamsing, S.
**QUACKS AND QUACKERY**
  Defoe, D. The magician
  Fremlin, C. For ever fair
  Joensen, M. To be a dentist
  Khamsing, S. Quack doctor
  Masuccio.  A quick-witted cleric
  Wiser, W.  A soliloquy in tongues
    *See also* Hoaxes
**QUADRUPLETS**
  Gardner, F. The whereabouts of Mr Haber
**QUAILS**
  Stuart, J. Seventy-six days
The **Quaker.** Babel, I.
**QUAKERS.** *See* Friends, Society of
**Quality.** Galsworthy, J.
The **quality** of feeling. Phillips, R.
The **quality** of mercy. Warner, S. T.
The **quality** of reward. Deutsch, A. H.
The **quality** of the product. Neville, L. and
  Neville, K.
The **quarrel.** Witton, D.
**QUARRELING**
  Brodeur, P. The proposal
  Coppard, A. E. Olive and Camilla
  Costello, M. Murphy Agonistes
  Costello, M. Strong is your hold O love
  Foster, B. Brockle-face
  Friedman, P. The inheritance editor
  Lau, S. Grandma takes charge
  Malamud, B. The death of me
  Olsen, T. Tell me a riddle
  Rumaker, M. The pipe
  West, J.  A family argument
  Williams, T. Happy August the 10th
**QUARRIES AND QUARRYING**
  Verga, G. Rosso Malpelo
The **quarry.** Dickson, G. R.
A **quarter** of a million. Allingham, M.
**Que** donn'rez vous? Anderson, P.
**QUEBEC (CITY)** *See* Canada—Quebec
  (City)
**QUEBEC (PROVINCE)** *See* Canada—Que-
  bec (Province)

**Queen, Ellery**
The adventure of Abraham Lincoln's clue
Bernkopf, J. C. comp. Boucher's
choicest
The adventure of the President's half disme
Best of the Best detective stories
Same as: The President's half disme
The adventure of the seven black cats
Hitchcock, A. ed. Alfred Hitchcock's
Daring detectives
Bride in danger
Gibson, W. ed. Rogues' gallery
The Gettysburg bugle
Mystery Writers of America. Dear dead
days
Mind over matter
Mystery Writers of America. Murder
most foul
Miser's gold
Fenner, P. R. comp. Finders keepers
Mystery at the Library of Congress
Mystery Writers of America. Crime
without murder
Same as: Spy dept.: mystery at the
Library of Congress, listed in 1964-
1968 supplement
No parking
McComas, J. F. ed. Crimes and mis-
fortunes
Object lesson
Mystery Writers of America. Mirror,
mirror, fatal mirror
The President's half disme
Mystery Writers of America. Merchants
of menace
Same as: The adventure of the Presi-
dent's half disme
**Parodies, travesties, etc.**
Breen, J. L. The Lithuanian eraser mys-
tery
The **Queen** of Air and Darkness. Ander-
son, P.
The **Queen** of California. Montalvo, G. O. de
The **queen** of moths. Bernard, K.
The **Queen** of Sheba's nightmare. Russell, B.
The **queen** of sleep. Emshwiller, C.
The **queen** of spades. Pushkin, A.
The **queen's** horsekeeper. Boccaccio, G.
The **queen's** jewel. Holding, J.
The **queen's** square. Sayers, D. L.
**Queiroz, Dinah Silveira de**
Tarciso
Howes, B. ed. The eye of the heart
**Quenby** and Ola, Swede and Carl. Coover, R.
The **quest** for "Blank Claveringi". High-
smith, P.
The **quest** for Saint Aquin. Boucher, A.
The **Quest** Sonata. Askeland, L.
The **question.** Ellin, S.
The **question.** Keller, D. H.
The **question** my son asked. See Ellin, S.
The question
A **question** of passports. Orczy, Baroness
**QUEUING**
Laumer, K. In the queue
A **quick**-witted cleric. Masuccio
**Quiet.** Shen, Ts'ung-wen
A **quiet** conversation piece. Bukowski, C.

The **quiet** game. Fremlin, C.
The **quiet** man. Gilbert, A.
**Quiller-Couch, Sir Arthur**
A pair of hands
Dickinson, S. ed. The usurping ghost,
and other encounters and experiences
Green, R. L. ed. Thirteen uncanny tales
**QUILTS.** *See* Coverlets
**Quilty.** Strong, J.
**Quin, Ann**
Motherlogue
Stevick, P. ed. Anti-story
**QUINCE**
Galsworthy, J. The Japanese quince
**Quincey, Thomas de.** *See* De Quincey,
Thomas
**Quinn, Seabury**
Body and soul
Moskowitz, S. ed. Horrows unknown
**Quiroga, Horacio**
The alligator war
Howes, B. ed. The eye of the heart
A **quite** conventional death. Garforth, J.
**QUIZ SHOWS**
Pei, M. Kandyce is the winner
A **quotation** from Klopstock. Singer, I. B.
**QUOTATIONS**
Sheckley, R. The Mnemone
**Quoth** the raven. Russell, R.

# R

**RAF.** *See* Great Britain. Royal Air Force
**R&R.** Karlin, W.
The **Rabbi.** Babel, I.
The **Rabbi.** Currer, B.
The **rabbi** and the rebbetsin. Shapiro, L.
The **Rabbi** had little angels. Deutschman, B.
**RABBIS**
Babel, I. The Rabbi
Barouh, A. Reb Yossl
Boucher, A. Balaam
Buber, M. The prayer book
Deutschman, B. The Rabbi had little
angels
Feldman, A. Living in the sea
Fiedler, L. A. The dancing of Reb Hershl
with the withered hand
Maddow, B. "To hell the rabbis"
Malamud, B. The magic barrel
Malamud, B. The silver crown
Midwood, B. A thief in the temples
Nissenson, H. Forcing the end
Ozick, C. The pagan rabbi
Shapiro, L. The rabbi and the rebbetsin
Singer, I. B. Guests on a winter night
Singer, I. B. The recluse
Singer, I. B. Something is there
*See also* Judaism
The **Rabbi's** son Babel, I.
The **rabbit.** Maupassant, G. de
The **rabbit** census. Mishev, G.
**RABBIT HUNTING**
Blackhurst, W. E. Bringing home the dog
Delapp, T. El Euphoria Gloria Road
The **rabbit** prince. Grubb, D.

Raining all the time. Pettus, R. C.
Rainov, Bogomil
    Rush hour
        Kirilov, N. and Kirk, F. eds. Introduction to modern Bulgarian literature
The rainy day at Big Lost Creek. Stuart, J.
A rainy night. Beneš, J.
The Raja and the tiger. Smith, C. A.
Rajagopalachari, C.
    The nose jewel
        Shimer, D. B. ed. Voices of modern Asia
The Rajah's emerald. Christie, A.
Rake. Goulart, R.
Rakesh, Mohan
    Miss Pall
        Roadarmel, G. C. ed.    A death in Delhi
The Rakshas and the sea market. P'u, Sungling
The rally. Bullins, E.
Rallye ride. Rathjen, C. H.
Rama Rau, Santha
    Who cares?
        Katz, N. and Milton, N. eds. Fragment from a lost diary, and other stories
A ramble in Aphasia, Henry, O.
Ramble with a gamblin' man. Anderson, P.
Ramkumar
    Sailor
        Roadarmel, G. C. ed.    A death in Delhi
Rammer. Niven, L.
RAMS. See Sheep
RANCH LIFE
    Dorr, L. Brindley
    Littke, L. J. The Brand X business
        See also Cowboys; Western stories
        Argentine Republic
    Borges, J. L. The Gospel according to Mark
        Brazil
    Veiga, J. J. Where are the didangos now?
        California
    Steinbeck, J. The gift
    Steinbeck, J. Of mice and men
    Steinbeck, J. The red pony: The great mountains
    Steinbeck, J. The promise
    Steinbeck, J. Tularecito
        Chile
    Coloane, F. A. Cururo . . . sheep dog
        Idaho
    Hayes, A. H.    A sheep crusade
        Montana
    Stegner, W. Carrion spring
        Texas
    Davidson, A. Dr Morris Goldpepper returns
    Green, B. K. Mr Undertaker and the Cleveland Bay horse
    Green, B. K. The Shield mares
    Henry, O. Hearts and crosses
    Henry, O. Hygeia at the Solito
        The West
    Haycox, E. McQuestion rides
    Henry, O. The Last of the Troubadours
    Thompson, T. Son of a King

Randall, Florence Engel
    The watchers
        Stansbury, D. L. ed. Impact
Randall, Margaret
    The impossible film strip; or, History of a marriage
        New Directions in prose and poetry 21
Randolf's party. Lennon, J.
The random quantity. Jacobi, C.
Randy-Tandy man. Rocklynne, R.
RANFAING, ÉLISABETH DE
    Mallet-Joris, F. Elizabeth
The ransacked room. Brennan, J. P.
Ransom, Elmer
    Fishing's just luck
        Lyons, N. ed. Fisherman's bounty
Ransom. Fyfe, H. B.
Ransom demand. Wallmann, J. M.
The ransom of Mack. Henry, O.
The ransom of Red Chief. Henry, O.
Ransome, Arthur
    The tale of the silver saucer and the transparent apple
    Authors' choice
Ransome at Sublimity. Monroe, D. M.
RAPE
    Birkin, C. 'Some new pleasures prove'
    Bukowski, C. The fiend
    Bukowski, C. The killers
    Bukowski, C. Rape! Rape!
    Bukowski, C. Something about a Viet Cong flag
    Burke, T. Old Joe
    Djilas, M. Under the yoke
    Gallant, M. My heart is broken
    Glanville, B. The survivor
    Kemal, Y.    A dirty story
    Kirilov, N. Radiant skies
    Michaels, L. Manikin
    Montross, D. Rape
    Petry, A. The witness
    Simpson, L. The savages
    Trevisan, D. Incident in a store
    Trevisan, D. Under the black bridge
    Verga, G. Temptation
RAPE, ATTEMPTED. See Assault and battery
Rape. Dillon, M.
Rape. Montross, D.
Rape! Rape! Bukowski, C.
Raphael
    The magic watch
        Haining, P. ed. Gothic tales of terror
Rappaccini's daughter. Hawthorne, N.
Rapport. Colter, C.
Rare and stinging days. Kaplan, B.
RARE ANIMALS
    Ferguson, D. The island of the endangered
RARE BOOKS. See Book rarities
A rarity. Vincenz, S.
Rascoe, Judith
    Brief lives, from next door
        Intro #3
        Rascoe, J. Yours, and mine
    Evenings down under
        Rascoe, J. Yours, and mine

**Remizov, Aleksander**
The rat's portion
Tyrmand, L. ed. Explorations in freedom: prose, narrative, and poetry from Kultura
**Remold** it nearer. Patton, F. G.
**RENAISSANCE**
Bishop, M. ed.  A Renaissance storybook; 27 stories
The **renaissance** at Charleroi. Henry, O.
**Rendezvous.** Christopher, J.
**Rendezvous.** Forster, C. S.
**Rendezvous.** Guthrie, A. B.
**Renu, Phanisvaranatha.** See Phanishwarnath "Renu"
**REPAIRING**
Sturgeon, T. Uncle Fremmis
**REPARTEE.** See Conversation
"**Repent,** Harlequin!" said the Ticktockman. Ellison, H.
**REPENTENCE**
Andersen, H. C. The red shoes
Drake, N. The Abbey of Clunedale
**Report.** Barthelme, D.
**Report** on a broken bridge. O'Neil, D.
**Report** on the nature of the lunar surface. Brunner, J.
**Report** on the threatened city. Lessing, D.
A **report** to an Academy. Kafka, F.
A **report** to an Academy: two fragments. Kafka, F.
**REPORTERS.** See Journalists; Women as journalists
**Representative** ham. Patton, F. C.
A **reprieve.** Tuohy, F.
**REPRODUCTION**
Asimov, I. What is this thing called love?
Davidson, A. The tail-tied kings
Harrison, H. Brave newer world
**REPRODUCTION, ASEXUAL**
Bloch, R. Forever and amen
Sargent, P.  A sense of difference
**Requa** I. Olsen, T.
The **request.** Beneš, J.
**Requiem.** Holmes, E. M.
**Requiem.** O'Connor, F.
**Requiem** for a noun. De Vries, P.
**Requiem** for mankind. Wandrei, D.
**Requiescat.** O'Hara, J.
The **rescue.** Colter, C.
The **rescue.** Pritchett, V. S.
The **rescue** of the perishing. Saroyan, W.
**Rescue** operation. Harrison, H.
**RESCUE WORK**
Saroyan, W. The rescue of the perishing
The **rescuer.** Porges, A.
**RESCUES**
Anderson, P. Que donn'rez vous?
Anderson, P. Sunjammer
Asimov, I. The Callistan menace
Bova, B. Fifteen miles
Clarke, A. C. Maelstrom II
Clement, H. Lecture demonstration
Crane, S. The open boat
Dalsgaard, H. Nelson's last stand
Dickson, G. R. The immortal
Forster, E. M. The rock
Laumer, K. Once there was a giant
Maclagan, D.  S.O.S. from a U.F.O.

Macpherson, J. Calthon and Colmal
Reynolds, B.  A witch burning
Schreiber, A. W. The devil's ladder
**RESEARCH.** See Experiments, Scientific
**RESEARCH, MEDICAL.** See Medical research
**RESEARCH, MILITARY.** See Military research
**RESEARCH WORKERS**
Effinger, G. A. $f(x) = (11/15/67)$ $x=$her, $f(x)\neq0$
Gotleib, P. Planetoid idiot
Grekova, I. Beyond the gates
Just, W. Nora
Simak, C. D. Drop dead
Wilhelm, K. The fusion bomb
**Resentment.** Brownstein, M.
**Reservations.** Taylor, P.
**RESERVATIONS, INDIAN.** See Indians of North America—Reservations
**RESIDENCE HALLS.** See Dormitories
**Residue.** Sallis, J.
The **Resin-man.** Bhatty, M.
**RESISTANCE TO GOVERNMENT.** See Government, Resistance to
**RESORTS.** See Summer resorts; Seaside resorts
**RESOURCES, MARINE.** See Marine resources
A **respectable** woman. Chopin, K.
**RESPIRATION, ARTIFICIAL.** See Artificial respiration
**Responsibility.** Clark, E.
**Rest,** heart. Hippius, Z.
**REST HOMES, LABOR.** See Labor rest homes
**RESTAURANTS, LUNCHROOMS, ETC.**
Ansell, J. Eating out
Ansell, J. Patricia Kelly's
Beal, M. F. Survival
Beneš, J. Coming-out party
Bilker, H. L. and Bilker, A. L. All you can eat
Carver, R.  A night out
Chapman, S. Burger Creature
Colette. The other wife
Crane, S. In a Park Row restaurant
Eastlake, W. Portrait of an artist with 26 horses
Greene, G. Brother
Greene, G. The invisible Japanese gentlemen
Hemingway, E. The killers
Henry, O.  A cosmopolite in a café
Himes, C. Headwaiter
Joshi, S. Big brother
McFadden, D. Who can avoid a place?
Marsh, N. The cupid mirror
Millay, E. S. The murder in the Fishing Cat
Osami, D. Villon's wife
Petrakis, H. M. Rosemary
Summers, H. Cafe Nore
See also Hotels, taverns, etc.; Night clubs
**Restitution.** Holmes, E. M.
The **restless** ghost. Garfield, L.
The **restless** ones. Waller, L.

REVOLUTIONISTS—*Continued*
#### Jamaica
West, P. The season of the single women
#### Latin America
Jacobi, C. Exit Mr Smith
#### Mexico
Porter, K. A. Flowering Judas
#### Poland
Singer, I. B. Grandfather and grandson
#### Russia
Shapiro, L. Before the storm
Singer, I. B. The egotist
#### United States
Banks, R. With Ché in New Hampshire
Brunner, J. The inception of the epoch of Mrs Bedonebyasyoudid
Clayton, J. J. Cambridge is sinking
Gores, J. N. Watch for it
Kempton, M. Survivors
Miller, J. Sydney / I am beginning to see
Pechtel, C. Double-cross
Spike, P.   A good revolution
Wolfe, G. Hour of trust
Yglesias, J. The guns in the closet

REVOLUTIONS
Anderson Imbert, E. The General makes a lovely corpse
Babel, I. Gedali
Bova, B. Blood of tyrants
Dozois, G. R. Where no sun shines
Goulart, R. Change over
Goulart, R. The whole round world
Green, J. Let my people go!
Kosinski, J. Steps; excerpt
Le Guin, U. K. The word for world is forest
Reynolds, M. Black sheep astray
Thomason, J. W. Marines see the Revolution
Verga, G. Liberty
Watson, E. The revolution and Mister Wilson
*See also* Coups d'état

The **reward**. Sié, Cheou-kang
The **reward** of virtue. Strindberg, A.

REWARDS (PRIZES, ETC.)
Cobb, I. S. Five hundred dollars reward
*See also* Literary prizes; Prizes

**Rey, Lester del.** *See* Del Rey, Lester

**Reyes, Alfonso**
Major Aranda's hand
Howes, B. ed. The eye of the heart

**Reynold** Stengrow's short story. Katz, E.

**Reynolds, Baillie**
A witch burning
Haining, P.  ed. A circle of witches

**Reynolds, G. W. M.**
The tribunal of the inquisition
Haining, P. ed. Gothic tales of terror

**Reynolds, Mack**
Among the bad baboons
Galaxy Magazine. The eleventh Galaxy reader
Black sheep astray
Astounding

The Cold War . . . continued
Nova 3
Criminal in Utopia
Best SF: 1968
Fiesta brava
Analog 7
Gun for hire
McComas, J. F. ed. Special wonder
Prone
Harrison, H. ed. Worlds of wonder
Utopian
Harrison, H. ed. The year 2000
**Rhapsody** of a hermit. Rothschild, M.

RHEUMATISM
Henry, O. Makes the whole world kin
The **Rhine**. Thomason, J. W.

RHINOCEROS
Kipling, R. How the Rhinoceros got his skin
**Rhinoceros.** Ionesco, E.
**Rhoda** / social disease. Miller, J.

RHODE ISLAND
#### Newport
James, H. Osborne's revenge
#### Providence
Bloch, R. The shadow from the steeple
Lovecraft, H. P. The haunter of the dark
**Rhodes, Eugene Manlove**
The trouble man
Taylor, J. G. ed. Great Western short stories

RHODESIA
Lessing, D. Spies I have known

RHODESIA, NORTHERN. *See* Zambia

RHODODENDRON
Fox, J. A purple rhododendron
The **rhyme** of Lancelot. Sandberg, P. L.
**Rian's** story. Feldman, A.
**Ribalow, Harold U.**
Can you explain love?
Ribalow, H. U. ed. My name aloud
**Ribnikar, Jara**
I
Ribnikar, J.  I and you and she
She
Ribnikar, J.  I and you and she
You
Ribnikar, J.  I and you and she

**Rice, Craig**
Hard sell
Hitchcock, A. ed. Alfred Hitchcock presents: A month of mystery

**Rice, Jane**
The willow tree
Manley, S. and Lewis, G. eds. Mistresses of mystery

RICE
Kemal, Y. The drumming-out
**Rice** water. Lihn, E.
**Rich** in Russia. Updike, J.
RICH MEN. *See* Millionaires; Wealth

RICHARD I, KING OF ENGLAND
Coolidge, O. The politicians 1192-1193
**Richards, Dwynwen**
Traveller's joy
Kahn, J. ed. Some things fierce and fatal

**Ripe** Stilton. Hardwick, Michael, and Hardwick, Mollie

The **ripening** rubies. Pemberton, M.

**Ripped** off. Adams, A.

The **ripper** of Storyville. Hoch, E. D.

**Rise,** my love, rise. Böll, H.

The **rise** of capitalism. Barthelme, D.

**Rise** up singing. Phillips, R.

**Rising** with Surtsey. Lumley, B.

**Ristikivi, Karl**
  The seventh witness
    Decker, C. R. and Angoff, C. eds. Modern stories from many lands

**Ritchie, Jack**
  By child undone
    Bernkopf, J. F. comp. Boucher's choicest
  Dropout
    Best detective stories of the year [1969]
  For all the rude people
    Best of the Best detective stories
  Plan nineteen
    McComas, J. F. ed. Crimes and misfortunes
  Take another look
    Best detective stories of the year, 1972
  A taste for murder
    Hitchcock, A. ed. Alfred Hitchcock presents: A month of mystery
  Ten minutes from now
    Hitchcock, A. ed. Alfred Hitchcock presents: Stories to stay awake by
  Who's got the lady?
    Hitchcock, A. ed. Alfred Hitchcock presents: Stories to be read with the lights on

The **rite** of Latin hips. Deck, J.

**Rite** of spring. Davidson, A.

**RITES AND CEREMONIES**
  Arguedas, J. M. The ayla
  Campbell, R. Potential
  Fouchedjiev, D. The woman who walked about the sky
  Lovecraft, H. P. The festival
  McKenna, R. Mine own ways
  Saxton, C. The day
  Silverberg, R. The Feast of St Dionysus
  Tiptree, J. I'll be waiting for you when the swimming pool is empty

**Rites** fraternal. Barber, J.

**Rites** of passage. Greenberg, J.

**Ritter** Gluck. Hoffmann, E. T. A.

**RITUAL.** *See* Rites and ceremonies

**RITUAL MURDER**
  Bridges, T. Music to lay eggs by

The **ritual** of Ptah-Mes. Pei, M.

The **rivals.** Garrett, G.

**Rive, Richard**
  The bench
    Larson, C. R. ed. Prejudice: 20 tales of oppression and liberation
  Resurrection
    Katz, N. and Milton, N. eds. Fragment from a lost diary, and other stories

**RIVER BOATS**
  Dumas, H. Ark of bones

The **river** god. Pertwee, R.

**RIVER LIFE**
  Stuart, J.   A land beyond the river

**Rivera, Aida L.**
  Love in the cornhusks
    Decker, C. R. and Angoff, C. eds. Modern stories from many lands

**Rivera, Edward**
  Antecedentes
    New American Review no. 13

**RIVERS**
  Brautigan, R. The lost chapters of Trout Fishing in America: "Rembrandt Creek" and "Carthage Sink"
  Dorr, L.   A slow, soft river
  Lafferty, R. A. All pieces of a river shore
  Schneeman, P. American autumn

**Riverworld.** Farmer, P. J.

**RIVIERA**
  Acton, H. The gift horse
  Greene, G. Chagrin in three parts
  Greene, G. May we borror your husband?
  Hippius, Z. You—are you

**Riya's** foundling. Budrys, A.

**Roa Bastos, Augusto**
  Encounter with the traitor
    Howes, B. ed. The eye of the heart
  The living tomb
    Carpentier, H. and Brof, J. eds. Doors and mirrors

**ROACHES.** *See* Cockroaches

The **roaches.** Disch, T. M.

The **road.** Sillitoe, A.

**ROAD ACCIDENTS.** *See* Automobiles—Accidents; Trucks—Accidents

**Road** show. Carpenter, D.

The **road** to anywhere. Savitz, H. M.

The **road** to Damascus. Gilbert, M.

The **road** to hell. Premchand

**Road** to nightfall. Silverberg, R.

The **road** to salvation. Premchand

The **road** to Viton. Lütgen, K.

**ROADS**
  Bradbury, R. Yes, we'll gather at the river
  Cortázar, J. The southern thruway
  Davidson, A. The roads, the roads, the beautiful roads
  Heinlein, R. A. The roads must roll
  Ogden, M. Freeway to wherever
  Spielberg, P. Le carrefour
  Veiga, J. J. The importunate rooster

The **roads** must roll. Heinlein, R. A.

**Roads** of destiny. Henry, O.

The **roads,** the roads, the beautiful roads. Davidson, A.

**Roast** beef: a slice of life. Sukenick, R.

**Robbe-Grillet, Alain**
  In the corridors of the underground: the escalator
    Stevick, P. ed. Anti-story
    Same as: The escalator, listed in 1964-1968 supplement
  The secret room
    Hall, J. B. ed. The realm of fiction
    Johnson, E. W. ed. Short stories international
    Taylor, J. C. ed. The short story: fiction in transition

**ROBBERIES**
  Adams, A. Ripped off
  Allingham, M. The same to us
  Arden, W. The savage

ROBBERIES—*Continued*
Beheaded in error
Bullins, E. In New England winter
Bullins, E. Travel from home
Carr, T. Ozymandias
Clark, W. M. The supermen
Davidson, A. Summon the watch!
Dumonte, E.  A crazy way to make a living
Fox, G. Kessler, the inside man
Francis, H. E. All the carnivals in the world
Gardner, E. S. Something like a pelican
Grau, S. A. The householder
Hughes, L. Why, you reckon?
Kantor, M. The grave grass quivers
Lewis, L. The man who talked with books
Marmer, M. The twelve-hour caper
Morrison, A. The case of Laker, absconded
Osamu, D. Villon's wife
Pirkis, C. L. The Redhill sisterhood
Schoenfeld, H. All of God's children got shoes
Wister, O.  A pilgrim on the Gila
Woolrich, C. Through a dead man's eye
*See also* Theft

ROBBERS. *See* Brigands and robbers; Jewel thieves; Thieves

Robbins, Tod
Freaks
Haining, P. ed. The ghouls
Same as: Spurs
Spurs
Haining, P. ed. The freak show
Same as: Freaks

The robe of peace. Henry, O.

Robert Aghion. Hesse, H.

Roberts, David
The girl on the lake
Burnett, W. ed. That's what happened to me

Roberts, Joseph B.
Ever been to Braden?
Alabama prize stories, 1970

Roberts, Keith
The Lady Margaret
Dozois, G. R. ed.  A day in the life
Timothy
Haining, P. ed. The witchcraft reader
Weihnachtabend
Best SF: 1972

Roberts, Robert E.
The New Jerusalem
Alabama prize stories, 1970

Robertson, Jennie Webb
She went to buy yarn
Alabama prize stories, 1970

ROBES
Delattre, P. The significance of the robe

Robinc. Boucher, A.

Robinson, Frank M.
Dream Street
Santesson, H. S. ed. The days after tomorrow
"East wind, west wind"
Nova 2

Robinson, Rowland Evans
The mole's path
Westbrook, P. D. ed. Seacoast and upland: a New England anthology
An old-time March meeting
Westbrook, P. D. ed. Seacoast and upland: a New England anthology
The purification of Cornbury
Westbrook, P. D. ed. Seacoast and upland: a New England anthology

Robinson Crusoe Liebowitz. Michaels, L.

Robinson Crusoe's Russian rivals. Lütgen, K.

Robot. Davenport, G.

ROBOTS. *See* Automata

Robot's story. Wolfe, G.

Roby, Mary Linn
See and tell
Hitchcock, A. ed. Alfred Hitchcock presents: Stories to stay awake by

ROC
Niven, L. Bird in the hand
Sinbad, the Sailor. The second voyage of Sindbad the Seaman

The rock. Forster, E. M.

The rock and the wind; excerpt. Bretherton, V.

Rock, church. Hughes, L.

ROCK MUSIC
Oates, J. C. Happy Onion
Spinrad, N. The big flash

ROCK MUSICIANS. *See* Entertainers; Rock music

Rock River fugitive. Rinehart, M. R.

ROCKET SHIPS. *See* Space ships

The rocking-horse winner. Lawrence, D. H.

Rocklynne, Ross
Ching witch!
Ellison, H. ed. Again, dangerous visions
Find the face
Galaxy Magazine. The eleventh Galaxy reader
Randy-Tandy man
Universe 3
Time wants a skeleton
The Astounding-Analog reader v 1

ROCKS
Carr, T. Touchstone
Zelazny, R. Collector's fever

RODEOS
Barker, S. O. Champs at the Chuckabug
McCord, J. Sunshine yellow and red
*See also* Cowboys

Rodgers, Carolyn
Blackbird in a cage
Adoff, A. ed. Brothers and sisters

Roditi, Edouard
From rags to riches
New Directions in prose and poetry 27
The Sultan's Little Harum-scarum
New Directions in prose and poetry 26
The vampires of Istanbul: a study in modern communications methods
New Directions in prose and poetry 24

Rodney fails to qualify. Wodehouse, P. G.

Rodney has a relapse. Wodehouse, P. G.

Rodney Parish for hire. Hensley, J. L. and Ellison, H.

**Rodriguez, Bill**
  The naked man
    The Best little magazine fiction, 1970
**Rodyonov, Alexander Tarasov-** *See* Tarasov-
    Rodyonov, Alexander
**Rogers, Michael**
  A great feeling
    Lish, G. ed. The secret life of our
    times: new fiction from Esquire
**Rogoz, Adrian**
  The altar of the random gods
    Rottensteiner, F. ed. View from another
    shore
The **rogue.** Anderson, P.
**Rogue** moon. Budrys, A.
**Rogue** ship. Van Vogt, A. E.
**ROGUES AND VAGABONDS**
  Brown, G. M. The five of spades
  Kipling, R. The man who would be king
**Rohmer, Sax**
  The master of Hollow Grange
    Lamb, H. ed. A tide of terror
  The white hat
    Hitchcock, A. ed. Alfred Hitchcock pre-
    sents: A month of mystery
**Rold, Filippa**
  As it is written
    The Best little magazine fiction, 1971
**Rolland, Romain**
  Pierre and Luce
    Morton, M. ed. Voices from France
**ROLLER SKATING**
  Bukowski, C. Christ on rollerskates
**Rollow, David**
  Dean and Frieda
    Intro #2
**Rolseth, Harold**
  Hey you down there
    Hitchcock, A. ed. Alfred Hitchcock pre-
    sents: Stories to be read with the
    lights on
The **Roman** Candle Affair. Woolgar, J.
The **Roman** kid. Gallico, P.
**ROMAN SOLDIERS.** *See* Soldiers, Roman
**Romance** in the roaring forties. Runyon, D.
**Romance** lingers, adventure lives. Collier, J.
The **romance** of a busy broker. Henry, O.
**Romance** of a horse thief. Opatoshu, J.
The **romance** of certain old clothes. James, H.
The **romance** of Dr Tanner. Goulart, R.
**Romance** of the thin man and the fat lady.
    Coover, R.
**ROMANIA.** *See* Rumania
**ROMANS IN BRITAIN.** *See* England—Ro-
    man period, 55 B.C.-449 A.D.
**ROMANS IN ENGLAND.** *See* England—
    Roman period, 55 B.C.-449 A.D.
**ROME**

### 30 B.C.-476 A.D.

  Brunner, J. An elixir for the emperor
  Cortázar, J. All fires the fire
  Golding, W. Envoy extraordinary
  Molinaro, U. Sweet cheat of freedom
  Tolstoy, A. Amena
**ROME (CITY)** *See* Italy—Rome (City)
**Romeo** and Juliet. Porto, L. da

**Ronild, Peter**
  The man in the cannon
    Holm, S. ed. The Devil's instrument, and
    other Danish stories
The **roof** garden. Davis, O.
**ROOF GARDENS.** *See* Gardens and gar-
    dening
**Roofs** of silver. Dickson, G. R.
**Roog.** Dick, P. K.
**Rook, Clarence**
  Billy the Snide
    Keating, J. P. ed. Working-class stories
    of the 1890s
  Concerning hooligans
    Keating, P. J. ed. Working-class stories
    of the 1890s
  Young Alf
    Keating, P. J. ed. Working-class stories
    of the 1890s
The **room.** Kolpacoff, V.
The **room.** Sartre, J. P.
**Room** no. eleven. Maupassant, G. de
**Room** number 23. Pentecost, H.
**Room** temperature. Kennedy, R.
**ROOMERS.** *See* Boarding houses
The **roomette.** Pei, M.
**ROOMING HOUSES.** *See* Boarding houses
**ROOMMATES**
  McPherson, J. A. Of cabbages and kings
  Madden, D. No trace
**Roommates.** Harrison, H.
**Rooney, Frank**
  Cyclists' raid
    Taylor, J. C. ed. The short story: fiction
    in transition
**Roosevelt, Theodore**
  Bauman's tale
    Howes, B. and Smith, G. J. eds. The
    sea-green horse
**ROOSTERS**
  Neznakomov, P. The Painlevé case
  Peterkin, J. The red rooster
  Stone, A. Oh, pity the dwarf's butt
  Tao Kim Hai. The cock
  Veiga, J. J. The importunate rooster
    *See also* Cock-fighting
**Root, William Pitt**
  That poor man
    Intro #2
The **root** of all evil. Greene, G.
**Rope** enough. Collier, J.
The **rope** trick. Sillitoe, A.
**Rosa, João Guimãres**
  The third bank of the river
    Cohen, J. M. ed. Latin American writ-
    ing today
    Howes, B. ed. The eye of the heart
**Rose, Charles**
  By the waters
    Lytle, A. ed. Craft and vision
**Rose, Christine Brooke-** *See* Brooke-Rose,
    Christine
**Rose:** a Gothick tale. Hardwick, Michael,
    and Hardwick, Mollie
The **Rose** Bowl-Pluto hypothesis. Latham, P.
A **rose** for Ecclesiastes. Zelazny, R.
A **rose** for Emily. Faulkner, W.
"The **Rose** of Dixie." Henry, O.

**Rotsler, William**
Patron of the arts
  Del Rey, L. ed. Best science fiction stories of the year [1973]
  Nebula award stories 8
  Universe 2
**Rottmann, Larry**
Thi Bong Dzu
  Karlin, W.; Paquet, B. T. and Rottmann, L. eds. Free fire zone
**Roueché, Berton**
The lug wrench
  Kahn, J. ed. Trial and terror
**Rough** competition. McNeil, S.
The **rough** stuff. Wodehouse, P. G.
**ROULETTE**
Hunter, E. The last spin
**Round** robin. Jacobi, C.
**Rouse, Mary**
Pigeon pie
Women
**Rout.** Ayrton, M.
The **rout** of the White Hussars. Kipling, R.
**Routine** investigation. Twohy, R.
**ROYAL AIR FORCE.** See Great Britain. Royal Air Force
**ROYAL CANADIAN MOUNTED POLICE.** See Canada. Royal Canadian Mounted Police
The **royal** opera house. Jacobi, C.
**Roz** / beautiful Charlie. Miller, J.
**RUBBER**
Blochman, L. G. Red Wine
**RUBBER PLANTATIONS.** See Rubber
**RUBIES**
Gardner, E. S. The candy kid
**Rubin, Michael**
Service
  Prize stories, 1969: The O. Henry Awards
The **ruby** ring. Ruskay, S.
**Ructions.** Tuohy, F.
The **ruff.** Hardwick, Michael, and Hardwick, Mollie
The **rug.** O'Brien, E.
**Rugel, Miriam**
The flower
  Lewis, J. D. ed. Tales of our people
Paper poppy
  The Best American short stories, 1969
The sweet forever
  Ribalow, H. U. ed. My name aloud
**RUGS**
O'Brien, E. The rug
**RUINS.** See Archeology
**Rukeyser, Muriel**
The club
  Moss, H. ed. The poet's story
**Rule, Jane**
Brother and sister
  New Canadian stories, 72
Theme for diverse instruments
  Stephens, D. ed. Contemporary voices
**RULERS.** See Kings and rulers
**Rulfo, Juan**
The day of the landslide
  Carpentier, H. and Brof, J. eds. Doors and mirrors

Macario
  Howes, B. ed. The eye of the heart
Talpa
  Johnson, E. W. ed. Short stories international
They gave us the land
  Cohen, J. M. ed. Latin American writing today
**Rumaker, Michael**
The pipe
  Taylor, J. C. ed. The short story: fiction in transition
**RUMANIA**
Ghilia, A. I. Negostina
Leskov, N. Deception
Updike, J. Bech in Rumania
**RUMANIANS IN THE UNITED STATES**
Epstein, L. The disciple of Bacon
**Rumfuddle.** Vance, J.
**Rump**-titty-titty-tum-tah-tee. Leiber, F.
**Run** with the wind. McKimmey, J.
**Runaway!** Green, B. K.
**RUNAWAYS (CHILDREN)**
Allen, E. The wrong road
Brownstein, M. Torture: a children's story
Burton, H. The day that went terribly wrong
Crane, S. His new mittens
Hemingway, E. The last good country
Jonas, G. The Shaker revival
Kantor, M. The purple moccasin
Murray, A. Train whistle guitar
Savitz, H. M. The road to anywhere
Veiga, J. J. Where are the didangos now?
West, J. Live life deeply
Wright, R. Almos' a man
Yu, H.  D. M. Z.
**RUNAWAYS (MINORS)** See Runaways (Children)
The **Runenberg.** Tieck, J. L.
**Runesmith.** Sturgeon, T. and Ellison, H.
**Runners** in the park. McKimmey, J.
**RUNNING**
Bambara, T. C. Raymond's run
Crane, S. The wise men: a detail of American life in Mexico
Morrison, A. The loss of Sammy Throckett
Neugeboren, J. Elijah
Sheckley, R. The people trap
Sillitoe, A. The loneliness of the long-distance runner
**Running.** Francis, H. E.
The **running.** Posner, R.
**Runyon, Charles W.**
Dream patrol
  The Best from Fantasy and Science Fiction; 19th ser.
Sweet Helen
  Ferman, E. L. and Mills, R. P. eds. Twenty years of The Magazine of Fantasy and Science Fiction
**Runyon, Damon**
All horse players die broke
  Runyon, D. The best of Damon Runyon
Butch minds the baby
  Runyon, D. The best of Damon Runyon
Dark Dolores
  Runyon, D. The best of Damon Runyon

**Runyon, Damon**—*Continued*
Hold 'em Yale
Runyon, D. The best of Damon Runyon
The hottest guy in the world
Untermeyer, L. ed. Treasury of great humor
A light in France
Runyon, D. The best of Damon Runyon
Lillian
Montgomery, J. ed. The world's best cat stories
The Lily of St Pierre
Runyon, D. The best of Damon Runyon
Little Miss Marker
Runyon, D. The best of Damon Runyon
A piece of pie
Runyon, D. The best of Damon Runyon
Romance in the roaring forties
Runyon, D. The best of Damon Runyon
The snatching of Bookie Bob
Runyon, D. The best of Damon Runyon
A story goes with it
Runyon, D. The best of Damon Runyon
A very honorable guy
Runyon, D. The best of Damon Runyon

**Ruoro, Peter**
End of month
Angoff, C. and Povey, J. eds. African writing today

**RURAL LIFE.** *See* names of foreign countries, with phrase Provincial and rural, e.g. England, Provincial and rural. For the United States *see* Country life; Farm life; Small town life

**Rush, Norman**
Closing with nature
The Best little magazine fiction, 1971
Disch, T. M. ed. The ruins of earth
Fighting fascism
Disch, T. M. ed. Bad moon rising
In late youth
The Best American short stories, 1971
Riding
Disch, T. M. ed. Bad moon rising

**Rush** hour. Rainov, B.

**Rushmore, Robert**
A life in the closet
Rushmore, R.    A life in the closet, and stories
An only child
Rushmore, R.    A life in the closet, and stories
Winter's tales 15
Open water
Rushmore, R.    A life in the closet, and stories
The stopping train
Rushmore, R.    A life in the closet, and stories
The trumpets of Épignon
Rushmore, R.    A life in the closet, and stories
The winning game
Rushmore, R.    A life in the closet, and stories

**Ruskay, Sophie**
Allah will understand
Ruskay, S. The jelly woman

Cycles
Ruskay, S. The jelly woman
The indestructible Sarah B. at the age of eighty
Ruskay, S. The jelly woman
The jack
Ruskay, S. The jelly woman
The jelly woman
Ruskay, S. The jelly woman
Mother Rachel
Ruskay, S. The jelly woman
The portrait
Ruskay, S. The jelly woman
The ruby ring
Ruskay, S. The jelly woman
The scar
Ruskay, S. The jelly woman
A truth to live by
Ruskay, S. The jelly woman
Why bother with Solly?
Ruskay, S. The jelly woman

**Russ, Joanna**
Gleepsite
Orbit 9
The man who could not see devils
McCaffrey, A. ed. Alchemy and academe
Nobody's home
New dimensions 2
Poor man, beggar man
Nebula award stories 7
Universe 1
The second inquisition
Nebula award stories 6
Orbit 6
The soul of a servant
Elwood, R. ed. Showcase
This night, at my fire
Knight, D. ed. A pocketful of stars
Useful phrases for the tourist
Universe 2
When it changed
Ellison, H. ed. Again, dangerous visions
Nebula award stories 8

**Russell, Bertrand**
Benefit of clergy
Russell, B. The collected stories of Bertrand Russell
The Corsican ordeal of Miss X
Russell, B. The collected stories of Bertrand Russell
Dean Acheson's nightmare
Russell, B. The collected stories of Bertrand Russell
Dr Southport Vulpes's nightmare
Russell, B. The collected stories of Bertrand Russell
Eisenhower's nightmare
Russell, B. The collected stories of Bertrand Russell
The existentialist's nightmare
Russell, B. The collected stories of Bertrand Russell
Faith and mountains
Russell, B. The collected stories of Bertrand Russell
The fisherman's nightmare
Russell, B. The collected stories of Bertrand Russell

**RUSSIA, PROVINCIAL AND RURAL**
  *—Continued*
Platonov, A. The fierce and beautiful world
Platonov, A. The third son
Solzhenitsyn, A. Matryona's house
Stefanyk, V. The pious woman
Stefanyk, V.  A stone cross
Tendryakov, V. Creature of a day
Tendryakov, V. Justice
Tolstoy, L. God sees the truth, but waits
Yashin, A. Levers
Zhdanov, N.  A trip home
A **Russian** beauty. Nabokov, V.
**RUSSIAN CHURCH.** *See* Orthodox Eastern Church
**RUSSIAN COMMUNISM.** *See* Communism, Russia
**RUSSIAN ORTHODOX EASTERN CHURCH.** *See* Orthodox Eastern Church
**RUSSIAN REFUGEES.** *See* Refugees, Russian
**RUSSIAN REVOLUTION.** *See* Russia—1917-1945
**RUSSIAN ROULETTE.** *See* Roulette
**RUSSIAN SOLDIERS.** *See* Soldiers, Russian
**RUSSIANS IN CHINA**
McCloy, H. Chinoiserie
Thomason, J. W. Love story of a Marine
Thomason, J. W. The Sergeant and the spy
**RUSSIANS IN ENGLAND**
Bretnor, R.  A matter of equine ballistics
Leskov, N. The steel flea
Linklater, E. The actress Olenina
Litvinov, I. Call it love
Moorcock, M. An apocalypse: some scenes from European life
**RUSSIANS IN FINLAND**
Blum, R. In the blue country
**RUSSIANS IN FRANCE**
Hippius, Z. Metamorphosis
Nabokov, V. The circle
Stewart, N. Sophia, Zoltan, and the postman
**RUSSIANS IN GERMANY**
Nabokov, V. An affair of honor
Nabokov, V. Breaking the news
Nabokov, V. Lips to lips
Nabokov, V.  A Russian beauty
Nabokov, V. Torpid smoke
Narokov, N. Treetops
**RUSSIANS IN ISRAEL**
Silk, D. Porfiri and Esthalina
**RUSSIANS IN MONGOLIA**
Ivanov, V. The child
**RUSSIANS IN SICILY**
Hippius, Z. The pearl-handled cane
**RUSSIANS IN THE ARCTIC REGIONS**
Lütgen, K. Robinson Crusoe's Russian rivals
**RUSSIANS IN THE CZECHOSLOVAK REPUBLIC**
Templeton, E.  A coffeehouse acquaintance
**RUSSIANS IN THE UNITED STATES**
Cather, W. The clemency of the court

Singer, I. B. The egotist
Stewart, N. Grief
**Rust.** Kelleam, J. E.
**RUSTLERS.** *See* Cattle thieves
**Ruyslinck, Ward**
The madonna with the lump
  Krispyn, E. ed. Modern stories from Holland and Flanders
**Rx.** Nourse, A. E.
**Rydell, Forbes.** *See* De Forbes
**Rydell, Helen.** *See* De Forbes
**Rye, Anthony**
My man Closters
  Turner, J. ed. Unlikely ghosts
The **ryebread** trees of spring. Algren, N.
**Ryum, Ulla**
The Siamese cat
  Holm, S. ed. The Devil's instrument, and other Danish stories

# S

**SOMP.** Varshavsky, I.
**S.O.S.** from a U.F.O. Maclagan, D.
**Sabadino degli Arienti**
The jesting inquisitor
  Bishop, M. ed. A Renaissance storybook
**Sabadino degli Arienti, Giovanni.** *See* Sabadino degli Arienti
**Sabah, Victor**
An imaginary journey to the moon
  Best SF: 1972
**SABBATH**
Agnon, S. Y. First kiss
Babel, I. Gedali
Babel, I. The Rabbi
Cohen, F. C. The promise
  *See also* Sunday
**Sabin, Edwin L.**
The devil of the Picuris
  Moskowitz, S. ed. Horrors unknown
**SABOTAGE**
Anderson, P. The rogue
Clement, H. Fireproof
Forester, C. S. December 6th
Harrison, H. Brave newer world
Knox, B. Deerglen Queen
Silverberg, R. Delivery guaranteed
Zelazny, R. The eve of Rumoko
**SABOTEURS.** *See* Sabotage
**SAC INDIANS.** *See* Sauk Indians
**Sachem.** Sienkiewicz, H.
**Sacheverell.** Davidson, A.
**Sackville-West, V.**
Thirty clocks strike the hour
  Auchincloss, L. ed. Fables of wit and elegance
**SACRAMENTO.** *See* California—Sacramento
The **sacred** marriage. Oates, J. C.
The **sacred** skull. Buck, P. S.
The **sacrifice.** Auchincloss, L.
**SACRIFICE, HUMAN**
Blackwood, A. The tarn of sacrifice
Heald, H. The horror in the museum
Robbe-Grillet, A. The secret room
Sabin, E. L. The devil of the Picuris
Smith, C. A. An offering to the moon

Sacrifice spurs. Rathjen, C. H.
Sacrifices. Sassoon, B.
The sacrificial egg. Achebe, C.
SACRILEGE
    Kipling, R. The mark of the beast
Sad about Miss Brent. Petrie, G.
A sad and bloody hour. Gores, J.
A sad fall. Wilson, A.
Saddle marks. Green, B. K.
SADE, DONATIEN ALPHONSE FRAN-
    ÇOIS, COMTE CALLED MAR-
    QUIS DE
    Bloch, R. The skull
SADISM
    Bloch, R.   A toy for Juliette
    Ellison, H. The prowler in the city at the
        edge of the world
    Kaplan, B. Eddie Angel
    Parra, A. Totenbüch
    Woolrich, C. For the rest of her life
        See also Cruelty; Torture
Sadness. Kotowska, M.
Sáenz, Dalmiro A.
    Far South
        Yates, D. A. ed. Latin blood
Safari. Chester, A.
SAFARIS. See Hunting
SAFE-CRACKERS. See Thieves
SAFE-DEPOSIT COMPANIES
    Allingham, M. The lying-in-state
The saffron boat. Berkman, S.
Sāg. Yashpal
The saga of DMM. Eisenberg, L.
The saga of Toby Riddle. Ballard, T.
The sagacious monkey. Des Périers, B.
SAGAS. See Grettis Saga
SAHARA DESERT
    Balzac, H. de. A passion in the desert
Sahoo, Mohapatra Nilamoni. See Shahu,
    Mohapatra Nilamoni
SAIGON. See Vietnam—Saigon
SAIL BOATS. See Boats and boating
Sail on! Sail on! Farmer, P. J.
Sailing day scenes. Crane, S.
SAILING VESSELS. See Ships; Ship-
    wrecks; Sloops
Sailor. Ramkumar
The sailor-boy's tale. Dinesen, I.
SAILORS. See Seamen
Sailors at their mourning: a memory, Deck, J.
The saint. O'Connor, F.
The Saint and the Vicar. Binney, C.
ST BERNARD DOGS
    Boles, P. D. The animal kingdom
St Clair, Margaret
    Brightness falls from the air
        McComas, J. F. ed. Special wonder
    Counter charm
        Elwood, R. and Ghidalia, V. eds. An-
            droids, time machines and blue gi-
            raffes
    Horrer howce
        Haining, P. ed. The freak show
The St George of Rochester. Nevinson, H.
Saint John of the Hershey Kisses: 1964.
    Cole T.

St Joseph's ass. See Verga, G. Story of the
    Saint Joseph donkey; Story of the
    Saint Joseph's ass
ST NICHOLAS. See Santa Claus
Saint Nicolas. Goudge, E.
SAINT PAUL. See Paul, Saint
ST PAUL. See Minnesota—St Paul
Saint Paul and the monkeys. Kelley, W. M.
ST PAUL ISLAND
    Kipling, R. The white seal
SAINT PETER. See Peter, Saint
St Peter right in the eye. Drake, R.
ST PETERSBURG. See Russia—Leningrad
Saint Phalle, Anne de. See De Saint Phalle,
    Anne
The Saint 1298. Coolidge, O.
SAINTS
    Corvo, F. Baron. Stories Toto told me; 18
        stories
    Eklund, G. The Shrine of Sebastian
    Hesse, H. The field devil
    Verga, G. War between saints
    Vondra, V.   A legend of saintly folly
        See also names of individual saints,
        e.g. Agapitus, Saint; Francis of Assisi,
        Saint; George, Saint; etc.
Saki
    The interlopers
        Ball, J. E. ed. Designs for reading: short
            stories
    The lull
        Authors' choice
    The open window
        Untermeyer, L. ed. Treasury of great
            humor
    The reticence of Lady Anne
        Untermeyer, L. ed. Treasury of great
            humor
    The Schartz-Metterklume method
        Fitz Gerald, G. ed. Modern satiric
            stories
    Sredni Vashtar
        Howes, B. and Smith, G. J. eds. The
            sea-green horse
    Tobermory
        Necker, C. ed. Supernatural cats
        Parry, M. ed. Beware of the cat
Salamander. Ibuse, M.
A sale. Maupassant, G. de
SALEM. See Massachusetts—Salem
The Salem horror. Kuttner, H.
The Salem Mass. Hawthorne, N.
SALES CLERKS. See Salesmen and sales-
    manship
SALES PROMOTION
    McIntosh, J. How Boetie came to marry
        a rich lady
Sales reps for the underworld. Khamsing, S.
The salesman from Hong Kong. Weaver, G.
The salesman's son grows older. Blaise, C.
SALESMEN, TRAVELING. See Commer-
    cial travelers
SALESMEN AND SALESMANSHIP
    Allingham, M. He preferred them sad
    Crane, S. Why did the young clerk swear?
    Dawson, F. Double people
    Dawson, F. No feet
    Fiedler, L. A. Nobody ever died from it

Samson and Delilah. Lawrence, D. H.
Samson and Samsoness. Aksyenov, V.
SAMURAI
  Hearn, L. The reconciliation
SANATORIUMS. *See* Hospitals and sanatoriums
Sanchez, Sonia
  After Saturday nite comes Sunday
    Coombs, O. ed. What we must see: young Black storytellers
SANCTUARY (LAW) *See* Asylum, Right of
The sanctuary. Benson, E. F.
Sanctuary. Wharton, E.
The sand castle. Lavin, M.
Sand castles. Brautigan, R.
SAND DUNES
  Bryant, E. Dune's edge
The sand trout seminar. Brister, B.
Sandaval, Jaime
  All the way home
    Mystery Writers of America. Dear dead days
  Art for money's sake
    Mystery Writers of America. Crime without murder
Sandberg, Peter, L.
  The rhyme of Lancelot
    The Best little magazine fiction, 1970
Sandberg-Diment, Erik
  Come away, oh human child
    The Best American short stories, 1973
Sanders, Winston P.
  The word to space
    Mohs, M. ed. Other worlds, other gods
Sandman, John
  One for the road
    New Canadian stories, 72
The sandman. Barthelme, D.
The sandman. Hoffmann, E. T. A.
SAN FRANCISCO. *See* California—San Francisco
A San Francisco woman. O'Connor, P. F.
Sang, Nguyen
  The ivory comb
    Katz, N. and Milton, N. eds. Fragment from a lost diary, and other stories
SANITATION
  Blish, J.  A dusk of idols
  Panshin, A. The destiny of Milton Gomrath
  Schrader, S. The Cohen Dog Exclusion Act
SAN MARTIN, JOSÉ DE
  Borges, J. L. Guayaquil
San Salvador. Bichsel, P.
Sansom, William
  A last word
    Matthews, J. ed. Archetypal themes in the modern story
Sánta, Ferenc
  Nazis
    Simon, J. ed. Fourteen for now
SANTA BARBARA. *See* California—Santa Barbara
SANTA CLARA VALLEY. *See* California—Santa Clara Valley
SANTA CLAUS
  Asimov, I. Christmas on Ganymede

Cather, W. The strategy of the Were-Wolf Dog
  Greene, G. Dear Dr Falkenheim
  Holst, S. The Santa Claus murderer
Santa Claus is a white man. Clarke, J. H.
The Santa Claus murderer. Holst, S.
SANTA MONICA. *See* California—Santa Monica
Santiago, Danny
  The somebody
    The Best American short stories, 1971
Sappho in Wales, Davis, O.
Sara
  So I'm not Lady Chatterley so better I should know it now
    Ribalow, H. U. ed. My name aloud
SARACENS
  Coolidge, O. The possessors 1183
Sarah. Keller, D. H.
Sarandapikhou Street. Vassilikos, V.
SARATOGA. *See* Wyoming—Saratoga
SARDINIA, PROVINCIAL AND RURAL
  Verga, G. Rosso Malpelo
Sarduy, Severo
  From Cuba with a song
    Triple cross
Sargent, Pamela
  Clone sister
    Elder, J. ed. Eros in orbit
  The other perceiver
    Universe 2
  A sense of difference
    Elwood, R. ed. And walk now gently through the fire, and other science fiction stories
Saroyan, William
  The daring young man on the flying trapeze
    Abrahams, W. ed. Fifty years of the American short story v2
  The fifty yard dash
    Foff, A. and Knapp, D. eds. Story
  The pomegranate trees
    Taylor, J. G. ed. Great Western short stories
  The rescue of the perishing
    Brown, E. P. ed. Twice fifteen
  The summer of the beautiful white horse
    Ball, J. E. ed. Designs for reading: short stories
    Insights
  The three swimmers and the educated grocer
    Burnett, W. ed. That's what happened to me
Sarraute, Nathalie
  Tropism XV
    Stevick, P. ed. Anti-story
Sartre, Jean-Paul
  The room
    Johnson, E. W. ed. Short stories international
  The wall
    Hall, J. B. ed. The realm of fiction
    Kahn, J. ed. Trial and terror
    Morton, M. ed. Voices from France
    Thune, E. and Prigozy, R. eds. Short stories: a critical anthology
Sarzan. Diop, B.

SATIRE—*Continued*

Melville, H. The lightning-rod man
Mencken, H. L. The visionary
Mishev, G. The rabbit census
Mitchell, E. P. The pain epicures
Mitchell, E. P. The professor's experiment
Mitchell, E. P. The soul spectroscope
Mitchell, E. P. The story of the Deluge
Monkov, S. Laughter in Ramonia
Moore, G. Home sickness
Nabokov, V. An affair of honor
Nabokov, V. Solus Rex
Nemerov, H. The idea of a university
Nesin, A. There is a nut on the roof
Njoku, M. C. The python's dilemma
Nolan, W. F. Happily ever after
O'Donnell, K. M. Final war
Offutt, A. J. For value received
Oliver, C. King of the hill
Ostaijen, P. van. The city of builders
Ostaijen, P. van. The lost house key
Ostaijen, P. van. Patriotism, inc.
Ostaijen, P. van. Patriotism, inc., and other tales; 11 stories
Ostaijen, P. van. Portrait of a young Maecenas
Ostaijen, P. van. The prison in heaven
Pierce, J. R. The higher things
Pugh, E. The first and last meeting of the M.S.H.D.S.
Rasco, J. Evenings down under
Reed, K. Golden Acres
Reed, K. In behalf of the product
Reed, K. Winston
Ritchie, J. Dropout
Rocklynne, R. Randy-Tandy man
Roditi, E. The vampires of Istanbul: a study in modern communication methods
Russell, B. Benefit of clergy
Russell, B. The Corsican ordeal of Miss X
Russell, B. Dean Acheson's nightmare
Russell, B. Dr Southport Vulpes's nightmare
Russell, B. Eisenhower's nightmare
Russell, B. The existentialist's nightmare
Russell, B. Faith and mountains
Russell, B. The fisherman's nightmare
Russell, B. The guardians of Parnassus
Russell, B. The infra-redioscope
Russell, B. The mathematician's nightmare
Russell, B. Mr Bowdler's nightmare
Russell, B. The psychoanalyst's nightmare
Russell, B. The right will prevail
Russell, B. The theologian's nightmare
Russell, B. Zahatopolk
Russell, E. F. . . . and then there were none
Saki. The interlopers
Saki. The Schartz-Metterklume method
Saki. Tobermory
Sallis, J. At the fitting shop
Saxton, J. Elouise and the doctors of the planet Pergamon
Schrader, S. The Cohen Dog Exclusion Act
Schuyler, G. S. Black no more; excerpt
Shaw, I. The Mannichon solution

Shaw, I. Small Saturday
Shaw, I. Whispers in Bedlam
Sheckley, R. Budget planet
Sheckley, R. Welcome to the standard nightmare
Sheckley, R. Zirn left unguarded, the Jenghik Palace in flames, Jon Westerly dead
Shefner, V. A modest genius
Silverberg, R. A happy day in 2381
Silverberg, R. The Iron Chancellor
Sladek, J. The great wall of Mexico
Sladek, J. The steam-driven boy
Spike, P. The Conference man
Spike, P. A good revolution
Spinrad, N. The national pastime
Stopa, J. Kiddy-Lib
Strindberg, A. Just to be married
Strindberg, A. Love and the price of grain
Sturgeon, T. It was nothing—really!
Sturgeon, T. Microcosmic god
Sturgeon, T. Uncle Fremmis
Twain, M. Extract from Captain Stormfield's visit to heaven
Updike, J. During the Jurassic
Updike, J. Under the microscope
Urquhart, F. The ghostess with the mostest
Vandeloo, J. The day of the dead God
Varshavsky, I. Preliminary research
Vonnegut, K. The big space fuck
Wallach, I. Death opens the mail
Wellen, E. Down by the old maelstrom
West, N. "Shrike and Mrs Shrike"
Wilde, O. The remarkable rocket
Williams, G. The yellow brick road
Wilson, A. Totentanz
Wilson, C. The brief, swinging career of Dan and Judy Smythe
Wilson, S. This is Sylvia
Wolfe, B. The girl with rapid eye movements
Wolfe, G. V. R. T.

See also Fantasy; Humor; Improbable stories; Irony; Parodies

A **satisfactory** settlement. Gordimer, N.
**Saturday** afternoon and Sunday morning. Veiga, J. J.
**Saturday** night. Bontemps, A.
**SATURN (PLANET)**
Harrison, H. Pressure
**Saturnalia.** Wilson, A.
The **satyr** shall cry. Garrett, G.
**SATYRS**
Hesse, H. The field devil
**SAUK INDIANS**
Olsen, T. V. A kind of courage
**Saul Bird** says: Relate! Communicate! Liberate! Oates, J. C.
The **savage.** Arden, W.
**SAVAGES**
Blish, J. And some were savages
The **savages.** Simpson, L.
**Savan** on the roof. Ibuse, M.
**SAVING AND THRIFT**
Sherwin, J. J. A growing economy
**Saving** the world. Carr, T.
A **savior** of the people. Franzos, K. E.
The **saviour.** Bullins, E.

Saviour John. Lagerkvist, P.

**Savitz, Harriet May**
Peter
Savitz, H. M. and Shecktor, M. C. Peter,
and other stories
The road to anywhere
Savitz, H. M. and Shecktor, M. C. Peter,
and other stories
Why, Bo? Why?
Savitz, H. M. and Shecktor, M. C. Peter,
and other stories

Savoir-vivre in a courtesan's parlor. Bandello, M.

**Sax, Fausto**
The crossroads of history
Sax, F. The Icarus to be, and other
observations
Et tu, Uncle Tom
Sax, F. The Icarus to be, and other
observations
Exorcism
Sax, F. The Icarus to be, and other
observations
Nouveaux riches
Sax, F. The Icarus to be, and other
observations
On borrowed time
Sax, F. The Icarus to be, and other
observations
See Naples and die
Sax, F. The Icarus to be, and other
observations

**SAXONS.** *See* Anglo-Saxons

**SAXONY.** *See* Germany, Provincial and rural
—Saxony

**SAXOPHONISTS.** *See* Musicians—Saxophonists

**Saxton, Colin**
The day
Elwood, R. and Kidd, V. eds. Saving
worlds

**Saxton, Josephine**
Elouise and the doctors of the planet Pergamon
Ellison, H. ed. Again, dangerous visions
Heads Africa tails America
Orbit 9
The power of time
New dimensions 1
The triumphant head
McCaffrey, A. ed. Alchemy and academe

Say it with flowers. Anderson, P.

**Saye, Lee**
The morning rush; or, Happy birthday,
dear Leah
Elwood, R. ed. Tomorrow's alternatives

**Sayers, Dorothy L.**
The abominable history of the man with
copper fingers
Sayers, D. L. Lord Peter
Absolutely elsewhere
Sayers, D. L. Lord Peter
The adventurous exploit of the cave of Ali
Baba
Sayers, D. L. Lord Peter
The bibulous business of a matter of taste
Sayers, D. L. Lord Peter

The Cyprian cat
Necker, C. ed. Supernatural cats
The entertaining episode of the article in
question
Sayers, D. L. Lord Peter
The fantastic horror of the cat in the bag
Kahn, J. ed. Some things dark and dangerous
Sayers, D. L. Lord Peter
The fascinating problem of Uncle Meleager's will
Sayers, D. L. Lord Peter
The haunted policeman
Sayers, D. L. Lord Peter
The image in the mirror
Sayers, D. L. Lord Peter
In the teeth of the evidence
Sayers, D. L. Lord Peter
The incredible elopement of Lord Peter
Wimsey
Sayers, D. L. Lord Peter
The inspiration of Mr Budd
Dickinson, S. ed. The drugged cornet,
and other mystery stories
The learned adventure of the Dragon's
Head
Fenner, P. R. comp. Finders keepers
Manley, S. and Lewis, G. eds. Grande
dames of detection
Sayers, D. L. Lord Peter
The leopard lady
Manley, S. and Lewis, G. eds. Mistresses of mystery
The necklace of pearls
Sayers, D. L. Lord Peter
The piscatorial farce of the stolen stomach
Sayers, D. L. Lord Peter
The queen's square
Sayers, D. L. Lord Peter
Striding folly
Sayers, D. L. Lord Peter
The undignified melodrama of the bone of
contention
Sayers, D. L. Lord Peter
The unprincipled affair of the practical
joker
Sayers, D. L. Lord Peter
The unsolved puzzle of the man with no
face
Sayers, D. L. Lord Peter
The vindictive story of the footsteps that
ran
Sayers, D. L. Lord Peter
**Parodies, travesties, etc.**
Bentley, E. C. Greedy night

Sayin good-bye to Tom. Strong, J.

**SAYINGS.** *See* Quotations

Scandal. Hippius, Z.

The scandal detectives. Fitzgerald, F. S.

**SCANDINAVIA**
**Legends and folk tales**
*See* Legends and folk tales—Scandinavia

Scanners live in vain. Smith, C.
The scapegoat. Brand, C.
The scapegoat. Freeman, M.
The scar. Brown, W.
The scar. Ruskay, S.

**SCARABS**
Brennan, J. P. The Keeper of the Dust
Usher, F. The great white bat

**SCARECROWS**
Hawthorne, N. Puritan passions
Roberts, K. Timothy
The **scarlet** thread. Futrelle, J.

**SCARS.** See Face—Abnormities and deformities

**Scars.** Price, R.
**Scars.** Sturgeon, T.

**SCARVES**
Agnon, S. Y. The kerchief
**Scene.** De Vries, P.
**Scene** for "winter". Coover, R.
**Scenes** at Fort Laramie. Parkman, F.
**Scenes** from the big time. Bukowski, C.
**Scenes** of passion and despair. Oates, J. C.
The **scent** of apples. Davis, O.
**Scent** of death. Seth, R.
**Scent** of treason. Ogan, M. G.
**Šćepanović, Bramimir**
The death of Mr Goluža
Angoff, C. ed. Stories from The Literary Review

**SCEPTICISM.** See Skepticism
**Schaefer, Jack**
The white mustang
Fenner, P. R. comp. Desperate moments
**Schaeffer, Robin**
Revolution
Elwood, R. ed. Future city
**Schaffer, Alan**
Rabinowitz the fool
Ribalow, H. U. ed. My name aloud
The **Schartz**-Metterklume method. Saki
The **schematic** man. Pohl, F.
**Schiller, Johann Friedrich von**
The ghost-seer; or, The apparitionist
Haining, P. ed. Gothic tales of terror
**Schiller, Marvin**
Mr Princeton
Ribalow, H. U. ed. My name aloud

**SCHIZOPHRENIA**
Disch, T. M. Thesis on social forms and social controls in the U.S.A.
Val Baker, D. The face in the mirror
**Schloimele.** Singer, I. B.
**Schmitz, James H.**
The end of the line
Silverberg, R. ed. To the stars
Grandpa
The Astounding-Analog reader v2
Silverberg, R. ed. The science fiction bestiary
Greenface
Schmitz, J. H.   A pride of monsters
Lion loose
Schmitz, J. H.   A pride of monsters
Novice
Silverberg, R. ed. Mind to mind
The pork chop tree
Schmitz, J. H.   A pride of monsters
The searcher
Schmitz, J. H.   A pride of monsters
Where the time went
Elwood, R. and Ghidalia, V. eds. Androids, time machines and blue giraffes

The winds of time
Schmitz, J. H.   A pride of monsters
The witches of Karres
The Science fiction hall of fame v2B
**Schneeman, Peter**
American autumn
The Best little magazine fiction, 1971
New American Review no. 8
God of many names
American Review 16
**Schnitzler, Arthur**
Fräulein Else
Steinhauer, H. ed. Ten German novellas
**Schoenfeld, Howard**
All of God's children got shoes
McComas, J. F. ed. Crimes and misfortunes
Built up logically
Knight, D. ed. A science fiction argosy
McComas, J. F. ed. Special wonder

**SCHOLARS**
Brister, B. Professor Tequila Joe
Brodeur, P. The snow in Petrograd
De La Mare, W.   A: B: O.
Dorman, S.   A mess of porridge
Engel, M. Amaryllis
Epstein, L. The disciple of Bacon
Forster, E. M. Ansell
Gilliatt, P. Foreigners
Gilliatt, P. Was I asleep?
Gor, G. The minotaur
Palmer, E. Post-obit
Pei, M. The Devil's Christmas
Pei, M. The Sparrows of Paris
Sheckley, R. The Mnemone
Sherwin, J. J. Unity: an impartial report
Singer, I. B. Pigeons
Summers, H. If you don't go out the way you came in
Uyeda, A. Reunion
Yehoshua, A. B. Facing the forests
See also Teachers

**SCHOOL ATTENDANCE**
Farmer, P. J. Father's in the basement
Joyce, J. An encounter
Stuart, J. Wild plums
Walden, H. T. When all the world is young
Witton, D. The house of the people

**SCHOOL BUILDINGS**
Solzhenitsyn, A. For the good of the cause

**SCHOOL BUSES.** See Buses
**School** days. Dawson, F.
**SCHOOL DROPOUTS.** See Dropouts
**School** for the unspeakable. Wellman, M. W.
The **school** for witches. Thomas, D.
The **school** for wives. O'Connor, F.

**SCHOOL JOURNALISM.** See College and school journalism

**SCHOOL LIFE**
Aandahl, V. Beyond the game
Henderson, Z. The believing child
Henderson, Z. The closest school
Swan, J. The invisible nation
See also Church schools; Students; Teachers

**Africa**
Nicol, A. As the night, the day

**Schultz, John**—*Continued*

Jesse had a wife
Schultz, J. The tongues of men

Morgan
Schultz, J. The tongues of men

The offending party
Schultz, J. The tongues of men

Visit to my grandfather's grave alone
Schultz, J. The tongues of men

Witness
Schultz, J. The tongues of men

**Schuyler, George S.**

Black no more; excerpt
Long, R. A. and Collier, E. W. eds.
Afro-American writing v2

**Schuyler, James**

Life, death and other dreams
Moss, H. ed. The poet's story

**Schwartz, Delmore**

In dreams begin responsibilities
Disch, R. and Schwartz, B. eds. Killing
time
Tytell, J. and Jaffe, H. eds. Affinities

**Schwartz, Eugene**

The interpretation of dreams
Gottesman, L.; Obenzinger, H. and
Senauke, A. eds. A cinch—amazing
works from the Columbia Review

**Schwartz, Jonathan**

Corners
Schwartz, J. Almost home

The deep end
Schwartz, J. Almost home

Dennicker's love story
Schwartz, J. Almost home

Family matters
Schwartz, J. Almost home

Heat
Schwartz, J. Almost home

The immense audience
Schwartz, J. Almost home

The project
Schwartz, J. Almost home

The raconteur
Schwartz, J. Almost home

The shortest vacation ever
Schwartz, J. Almost home

A singular honor
Schwartz, J. Almost home

A trip to Brooklyn
Schwartz, J. Almost home

The voices of the wind
Schwartz, J. Almost home

Waiting
Schwartz, J. Almost home

**Schwimmer, Walter**

Back into the present
Schwimmer, W. It happened on Rush
Street

A bet on marriage
Schwimmer, W. It happened on Rush
Street

Christmas on Rush Street
Schwimmer, W. It happened on Rush
Street

Everything was perfect but. . . .
Schwimmer, W. It happened on Rush
Street

A full and happy life
Schwimmer, W. It happened on Rush
Street

The goodest son in the world
Schwimmer, W. It happened on Rush
Street

Greater love hath no woman
Schwimmer, W. It happened on Rush
Street

Love is a very strange article
Schwimmer, W. It happened on Rush
Street

The luckiest day in history
Schwimmer, W. It happened on Rush
Street

No story
Schwimmer, W. It happened on Rush
Street

The social event of the season for Rush
Street
Schwimmer, W. It happened on Rush
Street

Two brothers
Schwimmer, W. It happened on Rush
Street

Very unique for Rush Street
Schwimmer, W. It happened on Rush
Street

Within the touch of a hand
Schwimmer, W. It happened on Rush
Street

**Science** at heart's desire. Hough, E.

The **Science** Fair. Vinge, V.

**SCIENCE FICTION**

Aldani, L. Good night, Sophie
Aldiss, B. W. The hunter at his ease
Aldiss, B. W. Who can replace a man?
Amis, K. Something strange
Analog 7; 11 stories
Analog 8; 9 stories
Anderson, P. Details
Anderson, P. Escape the morning
Anderson, P. The fatal fulfillment
Anderson, P. Ghetto
Anderson, P. Journeys end
Anderson, P. Kings who die
Anderson, P. License
Anderson, P. The problem of pain
Anderson, P. Seven conquests; 7 stories
Anderson, P. Strange bedfellows
Anderson, P. Tales of the flying moun-
tains; 15 stories
Anderson, P. and Dickson, G. R. The
sheriff of Canyon Gulch
Andrevon, J. P. Observation of Quadrag-
nes
Asimov, I. The dead past
Asimov, I. The early Asimov; 27 stories
Asimov, I. Eyes do more than see
Asimov, I. Half-breed
Asimov, I. ed. The Hugo winners; 14
stories
Asimov, I. The imaginary
Asimov, I. Lenny
Asimov, I. Liar!
Asimov, I. Living space
Asimov, I. The magnificent possession
Asimov, I. Nightfall

## SCIENCE FICTION—*Continued*

**SCIENCE FICTION**—*Continued*

Ellison, H. The beast that shouted love at the heart of the world

Ellison, H. Big Sam was my friend

Ellison, H. Eyes of dust

Ellison, H. I have no mouth, and I must scream

Ellison, H. In lonely lands

Elman, R. Myself and the Tugoman

Elwood, R. ed. And walk now gently through the fire, and other science fiction stories; 10 stories

Elwood, R. ed. Children of infinity; 10 stories

Elwood, R. ed. Future city; 18 stories

Elwood, R. ed. The new mind; 9 stories

Elwood, R. ed. Showcase; 12 stories

Elwood, R. and Ghidalia, V. eds. Androids, time machines and blue giraffes; 24 stories

Elwood, R. and Kidd, V. eds. Saving worlds; 16 stories

Emshwiller, C. Pelt

Farmer, P. J. Down in the black gang, and others; 8 stories

Farmer, P. J. Opening the door

Farmer, P. J. Prometheus

Fast, H. The hoop

Fast, H. The interval

Fast, H. A matter of size

Fast, H. The mouse

Fast, H. The movie house

Fast, H. The vision of Milty Boil

Fast, H. The wound

Finney, J. Such interesting neighbors

Finney, J. The third level

Foray, V. Lost calling

Franke, H. W. Slum

Furman, A. L. ed. Teen-age space adventures; 8 stories

Fyfe, H. B. Ransom

Galaxy Magazine. The eleventh Galaxy reader; 10 stories

Gallun, R. Z. Seeds of the dusk

Gansovski, S. The proving ground

Garrett, R. The muddle of the woad

Ginsburg, M. ed. The ultimate threshold; 13 stories

Glass, D. The ultimate end

Goldin, S. Sweet dreams, Melissa

Gor, G. The minotaur

Gores, J. The Andrech samples

Gotlieb, P. The military hospital

Goulart, R. Broke down engine, and other trouble with machines; 13 stories

Goulart, R. Chameleon

Goulart, R. The Chameleon Corps & other shape changers; 11 stories

Goulart, R. Change over

Goulart, R. Copstate

Goulart, R. Rake

Goulart, R. Sunflower

Goulart, R. What's become of Screwloose? and other inquiries; 10 stories

Grigoriev, V. The horn of plenty

Grinnell, D. Extending the holdings

Gunn, J. E. The cave of night

Gunn, J. E. The listeners

Harrison, H. If

Harrison, H. ed. The light fantastic; 13 stories

Harrison, H. One step from earth; 9 stories

Harrison, H. A tale of the ending

Harrison, H. Waiting place

Harrison, H. ed. Worlds of wonder; 16 stories

Heinlein, R. A. —And he built a crooked house

Heinlein, R. A. The black pits of Luna

Henderson, Z. The effectives

Henderson, Z. Holding wonder; 20 stories

Herbert, F. Murder will in

Highsmith, P. The quest for "Blank Claveringi"

Hoffman, L. and Toomey, R. E. Lost in the marigolds

Jacobi, C. Gentlemen, the scavengers

Jacobi, C. The war of the weeds

Jacobi, C. The white pinnacle

James, M. R. Lost hearts

Kentfield, C. The last one

Keyes, D. Flowers for Algernon

Kneale, N. Minuke

Knight, D. Catch that Martian

Knight, D. comp. Dimensions X; 5 stories

Knight, D. Four in one

Knight, D. Masks

Knight, D. ed. A pocketful of stars; 19 stories

Knight, D. ed. A science fiction argosy; 24 stories

Knight, D. ed. Tomorrow and tomorrow; 10 stories

Kornbluth, C. M. The little black bag

Kornbluth, C. M. The mindworm

Kuttner, H. Dream's end

Kuttner, H. and Moore, C. L. The cure

Lafferty, R. A. Interurban queen

Lafferty, R. A. Narrow Valley

Lafferty, R. A. Nor limestone islands

Lafferty, R. A. Old foot forgot

Lafferty, R. A. Ride a tin can

Lafferty, R. A. World abounding

Langelaan, G. The fly

Lanier, S. The peculiar exploits of Brigadier Ffellowes; 7 stories

Latham, P. The Rose Bowl-Pluto hypothesis

Laumer, K. Of death what dreams

Laumer, K. Once there was a giant; 8 stories

Laumer, K. Retief: ambassador to space; 7 stories

Laumer, K. Retief of the CDT; 5 stories

Laumer, K. Three blind mice

Laumer, K. and Ellison, H. Street scene

LeGuin, U. K. Winter's king

Leiber, F. A pail of air

Lem, S. In hot pursuit of happiness

Lessing, D. Report on the threatened city

Lewis, C. S. The Shoddy Lands

Lindsay, C. Watch your step

London, J. The Red One

Long, F. B. The flame midget

Long, F. B. Green glory

Long, F. B. Humpty Dumpty had a great fall

SCIENCE FICTION—*Continued*

Silverberg, R. Halfway house
Silverberg, R. Hi diddle diddle
Silverberg, R. His head in the clouds
Silverberg, R. ed. Invaders from space; 10 stories
Silverberg, R. ed. Mind to mind; 9 stories
Silverberg, R. ed. The mirror of infinity; 13 stories
Silverberg, R. ed. Other dimensions; 10 stories
Silverberg, R. Parsecs and parables; 10 stories
Silverberg, R. Ringing the changes
Silverberg, R. ed. The science fiction bestiary; 9 stories
Silverberg, R. ed. To the stars; 8 stories
Silverberg, R. ed. Tomorrow's worlds; 10 stories
Silverberg, R. Unfamiliar territory; 13 stories
Silverberg, R. Warm man
Silverberg, R. ed. Worlds of maybe; 7 stories
Simak, C. D. All the traps of earth
Simak, C. D. Best science fiction stories of Clifford D. Simak; 7 stories
Simak, C. D. Crying jag
Simak, C. D. Desertion
Simak, C. D. Drop dead
Simak, C. D. Epilog
Simak, C. D. Founding father
Simak, C. D. Immigrant
Simak, C. D. New folks' home
Simak, C. Shadow show
Sladek, J. The great wall of Mexico
Smith, C. The ballad of lost C'mell
Smith, C. The game of rat and dragon
Smith, C. On the storm planet
Smith, C. A. Phoenix
Smith, G. O. Interlude
Stern, P. V. ed. The other side of the clock; 12 stories
Sternberg, J. Future without future; 5 stories
Stuart, D. A. Who goes there?
Sturgeon, T. And now the news
Sturgeon, T. Baby is three
Sturgeon, T. Brownshoes
Sturgeon, T. Helix the cat
Sturgeon, T. It was nothing—really!
Sturgeon, T. Microcosmic god
Sutton, L. Soul mate
Suvin, D. ed. Other worlds, other seas; 17 stories
Szilard, L. The Mark Gable Foundation
Tenn, W. Child's play
Tenn, W. Party of the two parts
Tevis, W. S. The big bounce
Thomas, T. L. The weather man
Thomas, T. L. The weather on the sun
Three for tomorrow; 3 stories
Three trips in time and space; 3 stories
Tilley, R. J. Something else
Tiptree, J. I'll be waiting for you when the swimming pool is empty
Toman, N. A debate on SF—Moscow 1965
Total Effect. Survival printout; 12 stories

Tucker, W. Time exposures
Universe 1; 12 stories
Universe 2; 13 stories
Universe 3; 7 stories
Vance, J. Eight fantasms and magics; 8 stories
Vance, J. The Howling Bounders
Vance, J. The men return
Vance, J. The new prime
Vance, J. Telek
Vinge, V. The Science Fair
Voiskunsky, Y. and Lukodyanov, I. A farewell
White, J. The conspirators
Wilhelm, K. April Fool's Day forever
Wilhelm, K. A cold dark night with snow
Wilson, R. Deny the slake
Winter, J. A. Expedition Polychrome
Wolfe, G. Beautyland
Wolfe, G. The blue mouse
Wolfe, G. The death of Doctor Island
Wolfe, G. The horars of war
Wolfe, G. Remembrance to come
Wyndham, J. Chronoclasm
Xlebnikov, A. Human frailty
Yolen, J. comp. Zoo 2000; 12 stories
Young, R. F. The ogress
Young, R. F. Starscape with frieze of dreams
Zelazny, R. The doors of his face, the lamps of his mouth, and other stories; 15 stories
Zelazny, R. For a breath I tarry
Zelazny, R. This mortal mountain

*See also* Artificial life; Astronauts; Automata; Earth, Destruction of; Electronic computers; End of the world; Fantasies; Fourth dimension; Future, Stories of the; Gravitation; Imaginary cities; Immortality; Improbable stories; Interplanetary visitors; Interplanetary voyages; Interplanetary wars; Jupiter (Planet); Life on other planets; Manned undersea research stations; Mars (Planet); Martians; Mercury (Planet); Moon; Neptune (Planet); Outer space; Outer space—Exploration; Planets; Pluto (Planet); Saturn (Planet;) Space and time; Space colonies; Space flight; Space flight to the moon; Space flight to the sun; Space flight to Venus; Space probes; Space ships; Space stations; Space travel; Subterranean colonies; Time; Time, Travels in; Time machines; Uranus (Planet); Venus (Planet); Venusians

## SCIENTIFIC EXPEDITIONS

Clarke, A. C. Transit of Earth
Davis, H. To plant a Seed
Delany, S. R. High Weir
Lütgen, K. The road to Viton
Mather, B. The man in the well
Nabokov, V. Terra incognita
Nesvadba, J. The death of an apeman
Nesvadba, J. In the footsteps of the Abominable Snowman
Schmitz, J. H. Grandpa
Silverberg, R. Breckenridge and the continuum

SCIENTIFIC EXPEDITIONS—*Continued*
  Smith, C. A. The amazing planet
  Walsh, D. J. The rings of the Papaloi
SCIENTIFIC EXPERIMENTS. *See* Experiments, Scientific
SCIENTISTS
  Asimov, I. "Breeds there a man . . . ?"
  Asimov, I. Flies
  Asimov, I. Half-breed
  Asimov, I.    A problem of numbers
  Bova, B. The perfect warrior
  Bulgakov, M. The fatal eggs
  Clarke, A. C. The cruel sky
  Clement, H. Sun spot
  Davis, R. L. Teratohippus
  Dneprov, A. When questions are asked
  Du Maurier, D. The breakthrough
  Effinger, G. A. And us, too, I guess
  Eisenberg, L. The irresistible Party Chairman
  Eisenberg, L.    A matter of recordings
  Eisenberg, L.    A matter of time and place
  Eisenberg, L. The open secrets
  Eisenberg, L. The saga of DMM
  Eisenberg, L. The time of his life
  Eisenberg, L. Too many Cooks
  Eisenberg, L. Uncle Sam's children
  Eisenberg, L. The vanishing borough
  Hawthorne, N. The birthmark
  Heinlein, R. A. Universe
  Henderson, Z. Ad astra
  Hippius, Z. The strange law
  Hoffmann, E. T. A. Master Flea
  Holst, S. The language of cats
  Jacobi, C. The war of the weeds
  Just, W. The Congressman who loved Flaubert
  Kerr, D. Epiphany for aliens
  Kersh, G. The unsafe deposit box
  Kevles, B. Mars-station
  Kornbluth, C. M. Gomez
  Lafferty, R. A. Aloys
  Lafferty, R. A. Barnaby's clock
  Landolfi, T. Cancerqueen
  Lightner, A. M. The Mars jar
  Macfarlane, W. The last leaf
  McLaughlin, D. Endorsement, personal
  Mitchell, E. P. The ablest man in the world
  Mitchell, E. P. The crystal man
  Mitchell, E. P. The man without a body
  Mitchell, E. P. The professor's experiment
  Mitchell, E. P. The soul spectroscope
  Mitchell, E. P. The tachypomp
  Mrozek, S. The Ugupu bird
  Nesvadba, J. Expedition in the opposite direction
  Nesvadba, J. The trial nobody ever heard of
  Payes, R. C.  . . . And the power . . .
  Scortia, T. N. Woman's rib
  Shaw, I. The Mannichon solution
  Sheckley, R. Doctor Zombie and his furry little friends
  Sternig, L. Total recall
  Tiptree, J. And I have come upon this place by lost ways
  Varshavsky, I. Preliminary research
  Vinge, V. The Science Fair

Wilhelm, K. Windsong
Williamson, J. With folded hands
  *See also* Anthropologists; Archeologists; Biochemists; Biologists; Chemists; Mathematicians; Naturalists; Physicists; Research workers; Zoologists
Scobie, Stephen
  The white sky
  Fourteen stories high
SCOLDS
  Carr, J. The flavor of the tea
Scones and stones. De Vries, P.
The scorched face. Hammett, D.
Scorner's seat. Lafferty, R. A.
The scorpion. Bowles, P.
The scorpion god. Golding, W.
SCORPIONS
  Chester, A. Safari
Scortia, Thomas N.
  Final exam
    Elwood, R. ed. The other side of tomorrow
  Flowering Narcissus
    Elder, J. ed. Eros in orbit
  The goddess of the cats
    Dickensheet, D. ed. Men and malice
  The icebox blonde
    Scortia, T. N. ed. Strange bedfellows
  Judas fish
    Harrison, H. ed. The year 2000
  The tower
    Elwood, R. ed. Children of infinity
  The weariest river
    Elwood, R. ed. Future city
  When you hear the tone
    Del Rey, L. ed. Best science fiction stories of the year [1972]
  Woman's rib
    Del Rey, L. ed. Best science fiction stories of the year [1973]
SCOTCH DIALECT. *See* Dialect stories—Scotch
SCOTCH IN CANADA
  Scott, D. C. Expiation
SCOTCH IN SPAIN
  Maugham, W. S.    A man from Glasgow
Scotch sour. Shaber, D.
SCOTLAND
  Haining, P. ed. The clans of darkness; 19 stories
            **To 1057**
  Macpherson, J. Calthon and Colmal
            **17th century**
  Linklater, E. The masks of purpose
  Scott, Sir W.    A night in the grave
            **18th century**
  Scott, Sir W. The tale of the mysterious mirror
            **19th century**
  Lathom, F. The water spectre
  Stevenson, R. L. The merry men
            **20th century**
  Cross, J. K. Music when soft voices die . . .
  Hamilton, A. Dead men walk
  Knox, B. Deerglen Queen

SCULPTORS—*Continued*
  Malamud, B. Pictures of Fidelman
  Malamud, B. Rembrandt's hat
  Manov, E. Vanya and the statuette
  Sayers, D. L. The abominable history of the man with copper fingers
  Val Baker, D.   A woman of talent
The sculptor's funeral. Cather, W.
SCULPTURE
  Ayrton, M. The evil head
  Filer, B. K. Eye of the beholder
  Vynnychenko, V.   A strange episode
    *See also* Plaster casts; Statues
SCULPTURE, INDIC
  Harter, E. The stone lovers
SCULPTURE, PRIMITIVE
  Dickson, G. R. Black Charlie
Scut Farkas and the murderous Mariah. Shepherd, J.
Sdeath and Northangerland. Nye, R.
SEA. *See* Ocean
SEA CAPTAINS. *See* Shipmasters
Sea change. Chandler, B.
Sea change. Grau, S. A.
The sea devil. Gordon, A.
The sea girl. Kim, Y. I.
Sea home. Lee, W. M.
The sea-maiden. Campbell, J. F.
SEA MONSTERS
  Bradbury, R. The women
  Engelhardt, F. The Kraken
  Greene, S. The invisible monster
  Lanier, S. The kings of the sea
  Zelazny, R. The doors of his face, the lamps of his mouth
    *See also* Sea-serpents
The sea-raiders. Wells, H. G.
SEA-SERPENTS
  Kipling, R.   A matter of fact
    *See also* Squids
SEA-SHORE. *See* Seashore
SEA STORIES
  Bacon, G. The Gorgon's head
  Ballard, J. G. Now wakes the sea
  Bullins, E. The reluctant voyage
  Clarke, A. C. Cold war
  Coburn, A. The tale of the fourth stranger
  Collins, W. "Blow up with the brig!"
  Conrad, J. The secret sharer
  Crane, S. Flanagan and his short filibustering adventure
  Crane, S. The open boat
  Crane, S. The revenge of the Adolphus
  Day, J. W. The beaked horror which sank a ship
  Dickson, G. R. Home from the shore
  Drake, D. Lord of the depths
  Edmonds, W. D. Tom Whipple
  Hardwick, Michael, and Hardwick, Mollie. The mate of the Squando
  Jesby, E. Sea wrack
  Kipling, R. 'The finest story in the world'
  Kipling, R.   A matter of fact
  Lafferty, R. A. The ugly sea
  Mason, A. E. W. The cruise of the "Willing Mind"

Poe, E. A. MS. found in a bottle
    *See also* Fishermen; Seamen; Ships; Shipwrecks and castaways; United States. Navy; and subdivision Naval operations, under names of wars, e.g. World War, 1939-1945—Naval operations
A sea story. Hutsalo, Y.
SEA VOYAGES. *See* Ocean travel
Sea wrack. Jesby, E.
SEAFARING LIFE. *See* Sea stories
SEAGULLS. *See* Gulls
Seal Tregarthen's cousin. Sharp, M.
SEALS (ANIMALS)
  Kipling, R. The white seal
  Poulsen, V. The huntsman
Sealskin trousers. Linklater, E.
SEAMEN
  Chekhov, A. At sea
  Collins, W. "Blow up with the brig!"
  Crane, S. The auction
  Crane, S. The open boat
  Crawford, F. M. Man overboard
  De La Mare, W. Kismet
  Dinesen, I. The sailor-boy's tale
  Doyle, Sir A. C. The striped chest
  Edmonds, W. D. Tom Whipple
  Engelhardt, F. The Kraken
  Forester, C. S. The boy stood on the burning deck
  Forester, C. S. December 6th
  Hardwick, Michael, and Hardwick, Mollie. The bo'sun's body
  Hoffmann, E. T. A. The mines of Falun
  Irbe, A. Tale of a return
  Jewett, S. O.   A landlocked sailor
  Knight, D. On the wheel
  Lütgen, K. Robinson Crusoe's Russian rivals
  Lütgen, K. Umanarsuak
  Nagibin, Y. The fourth daddy
  Olsen, T. Hey sailor, what ship?
  Petrakis, H. M. The bastards of Thanos
  Sandberg-Diment, E. Come away, oh human child
  Sherwin, J. J. Unity: an impartial report
  The Shipwrecked sailor
  Stoker, B. The watter's mou'
  Strindberg, A. Nature the criminal
  Thompson, E. The header, the rigger, the captain
  Walker, V. S. The long sell
    *See also* Fishermen; United States. Navy
SEAMSTRESSES. *See* Dressmakers
The séance. Singer, I. B.
SÉANCES. *See* Spiritualism
The search. Aleichem, S.
Search and destroy. Karlin, W.
The searcher. Schmitz, J. H.
Searching for summer. Aiken, J.
The sea's green sameness. Updike, J.
SEASHORE
  Ballard, J. G. The drowned giant
  Brautigan, R. Sand castles
  Brennan, M. In and out of never-never land
  Brennan, M.   A large bee

**SEDUCTION**—*Continued*
 Maupassant, G. de. A country excursion
 Oates, J. C. Where are you going, where have you been?
 Ronild, P. The man in the cannon
 Yurick, S. The before and after of Hymie Farbotnik
**See** and tell. Roby, M. L.
**See** Naples and die. Sax, F.
**See** the moon? Barthelme, D.
**See** what tomorrow brings. Thompson, J. W.
**Seeberg, Peter**
 The dent
  Holm, S. ed. The Devil's instrument, and other Danish stories
The **seed** money. Kim, Y. I.
The **seed** of a slum's eternity. Priestley, E.
**Seeds** of the dusk. Gallun, R. Z.
**Seeds** of time. Yates, E. M.
**Segal, Lore**
 Euphoria in the rootcellar
  New American Review no. 10
**Segre, Alfredo**
 Justice has no murder
  Queen, E. ed. Ellery Queen's The golden 13
The **segregated** hearts. Marshall, L.
**SEGREGATION.** *See* Negroes—Segregation
**SEGREGATION IN EDUCATION**
 Naylor, P. R. Go tell it on the mountain
 Oliver, D. Neighbors
 Thompson, J. W. See what tomorrow brings
  *See also* Negroes—Education
**Segregationist.** Asimov, I.
**SEINE RIVER**
 Maupassant, G. de. On the river
**Selection** from an unpublished novel. Offsey, S.
**Selectra** Six-Ten. Davidson, A.
**Selena** robs the White House. McGerr, P.
**SELF.** *See* Individuality
**SELF-CENTERED PEOPLE.** *See* Egoism
The **self**-contained compartment. Goldstein, M.
The **self**-made cuckold
 Cholakian, P. F. and Cholakian, R. C. eds. The early French novella
A **self**-made man. Crane, S.
**SELF-MADE MEN**
 Carpenter, D. Hollywood heart
 Crane, S.   A self-made man
**Self** portrait. Wolfe, B.
**SELF-SACRIFICE**
 Harte, B. The outcasts of Poker Flat
 Kipling, R.   A bank fraud
 Lagerkvist, P.   A hero's death
 Lagerkvist, P. Saviour John
 Silverberg, R. Blaze of glory
 Stoker, B. The invisible giant
**Self**-slaughter. Vassilikos, V.
A **selfish** story. Gold, H.
**Selimović, Meša**
 Death and the dervish
  Johnson, B. ed. New writing in Yugoslavia

**Selph, William**
 The miracle worker
  Andrews, F. E. and Dickens, A. eds. Voices from the big house
**Selzer, Richard A.**
 Fairview
  New American Review no. 13
 A single minute of fear
  Ellery Queen's Mystery Magazine. Ellery Queen's Mystery bag
**SEMANTICS.** *See* Speech
**Semillante.** Maupassant, G. de
**SEMINARIANS**
 Chekhov, A. The student
 Derleth, A. The watcher from the sky
 Deutsch, A. H. Dubious winnings
 Gogol, N. Black Sunday
 Shapiro, L. Eating days
**Senarens, Luis P.**
 Frank Reade Jr's Air wonder
  Elwood, R. and Ghidalia, V. eds. Androids, time machines and blue giraffes
  Same as: Frank Reade, Jr's, Air wonder fights the Klamath Indians, listed in 1964-1968 supplement
**SENATORS.** *See* United States. Congress. Senate
The **senator's** daughter. Mitchell, E. P.
The **Senator's** last trade. Fox, J.
**Sending** the very best. Bryant, E.
**SENILITY.** *See* Old age
**Senka.** Nekrasov, V.
**SENSATION.** *See* Senses and sensation
A **sense** of difference. Sargent, P.
**Sense** of direction. Casper, L.
A **sense** of direction. Panshin, A.
**Sense** of humour. Pritchett, V. S.
A **sense** of ritual. Klein, N.
A **sense** of shelter. Updike, J.
**SENSES AND SENSATION**
 Asimov, I. The secret sense
 Campbell, R. The enchanted fruit
 Eisenberg, L.   A matter of recordings
  *See also* Pain
A **sensible** course of action. Rosenkrantz, P.
**Sentence.** Barthelme, D.
**SENTENCES.** *See* English language—Sentences
**Sentiment.** Parker, D.
A **sentimental** journey. Marsh, W.
The **sentimentality** of William Tavener. Cather, W.
**SENTINELS.** *See* Guard duty
The **Sentinels.** Campbell, R.
**Sentongo, Nuwa**
 Mulyankota
  Larson, C. R. ed. African short stories
**SEPARATION.** *See* Marriage problems
**SEPARATION (LAW)** *See* Divorce
**SEPARATION, MARITAL.** *See* Marriage problems
**September** 2005: the Martian. Bradbury, R.
The **sequel** for Ellen Chester. Hayes, A. H.
**Sequence.** Jacobi, C.
**Sequence** for a seaman. Deck, J.
**SERBIA.** *See* Yugoslavia

SERBIANS IN THE UNITED STATES.
  *See* Yugoslavs in the United States
SERFDOM

### Russia

*See* Peasant life—Russia
The **Sergeant** and the bandits. Thomason, J. W.
The **Sergeant** and the ship. Thomason, J. W.
The **Sergeant** and the siren. Thomason, J. W·
The **Sergeant** and the spy. Thomason, J. W.
**Sergeant** Bridoon of the Horse Marines. Thomason, J. W.
The **Sergeant** runs away. Thomason, J. W.
SERGEANTS. *See* Soldiers, American
The **serjeant's** private mad-house. Crane, S.
**Sermini, Gentile**
  The amorous booklover
    Bishop, M. ed. A Renaissance storybook
  Sister Savina and Brother Girolamo
    Bishop, M. ed. A Renaissance storybook
The **sermon.** Hazaz, H.
SERMONS
  Brown, G. M.   A treading of grapes
  Cady, J. Texts and notes on a sermon preached in Harlan, Ky., Bluefield, West Va., Hamilton, Ohio, and elsewhere
  Joyce, J. Hell fire
  Verga, G. Donna Santa's sin
**Serpent** burning on an altar. Aldiss, B. W.
The **serpent** of Kundalini. Aldiss, B. W.
SERVANTS
  Diego, E. Concerning Señor de la Peña
  Healey, R. M. Guessing game
  Joyce, J. Clay
  Seth, R. The recluse of Kotka Veski
  Wakefield, H. R. The triumph of death
    *See also* Negroes as servants

#### Butlers

  Allingham, M. The perfect butler
  Greene, G. The basement room
  Wodehouse, P. G. High stakes

#### Cleaning women

  Agnon, S. Y. The face and the image
  Ledward, P. Get out of my way
  O'Brien, E. An outing
  Rubin, M. Service

#### Companions

  Lavin, M. The small bequest

#### Cooks

  Collins, W. Mr Policeman and the cook
  Drake, R. The cook and the sheriff
  Maloney, R. Viva Caporetto!
  Marshall, L. The dog
  Sheckley, R. Pas de trois of the chef and the waiter and the customer
  Taylor, P.   A wife of Nashville

#### Hired girls

  Hesse, H. The Latin scholar
  Laurence, M.   A bird in the house
  Maupassant, G. de. The story of a farm-girl
  Mphalele, E. Mrs Plum
  Munro, A. Sunday afternoon
  O, Yŏng-su. Nami and the taffyman
  Purdy, J. Scrap of paper

#### Hired men

  Boyle, P. The betrayers
  Bullins, E. The helper
  Greenberg, J. Rites of passage
  Holmes, E. M.   A part of the main
  O'Connor, F. Greenleaf
  O'Hara, J. The kids
  Rye, A. My man Closters

#### Housekeepers

  Collins, W. Mr Lepel and the housekeeper
  Gilliatt, P. Frank
  Jewett, S. O. The New Methuselah
  Lavin, M. The mock auction
  Marshall, L.   A matter of taste
  Nielsen, H. The perfect servant
  O'Connor, F. Achilles' heel
  O'Connor, F. Public opinion
  Powers, J. F. The valiant woman
  Pritchett, V. S. Blind love
  Steegmuller, F. The fair singer
  Tuohy, F. The license
    *See also* Servants—Maids

#### Laundresses

  Grin, A. The watercolor

#### Maids

  Babel, I. The sin of Jesus
  Boyle, P. The betrayers
  Brush, K. Night club
  Cather, W. Nanette: an aside
  Dilov, L. The stranger
  Elman, R. Timmy
  Flaubert, G.   A simple soul
  Goldreich, G. Z'mira
  Johnson, D. An apple, an orange
  Kanin, G. The lady's maid
  Lavin, M. Sunday brings Sunday
  Lu, Hsün. Benediction
  Lu, Hsün. The New Year's sacrifice
  McCord, J. Images of loss
  Moravia, A. Mistress and mistress
  Nair, S. Mrs Kimble
  Neville, H. The dark unfathomed caves
  O'Faolain, S. The planets of the years
  Offord, C. R. So peaceful in the country
  Parker, D. The custard heart
  Rivera, A. L. Love in the cornhusks
  Sallis, J. 53rd American dream
  Slesinger, T. The Friedmans' Annie
  Stafford, J. The hope chest
  Theroux, P. Dog days
  Thomas, D. The true story
  Trevisan, D. The Marias
  Trevisan, D. Under the black bridge
  Vassilikos, V. The maid and I
  Vassilikos, V. Maids and mistresses
  Wharton, E. All Souls'
  Wharton, E. The lady's maid's bell
    *See also* Servants—Housekeepers

#### Menservants

  Aidoo, A. A. For whom things did not change
  Colette. The judge
  Crane, S. One dash—horses
  Deloney, T. Jack of Newbury and the widow
  Grau, S. A. Stanley
  Ibuse, M. Life at Mr Tange's

SEXUAL PERVERSION—*Continued*
  Bukowski, C. An evil town
  Bukowski, C. Love for $17.50
  Cohen, L.   "A long letter from F."
  Coover, R. Lucky Pierre and the music
    lesson
  Elkin, S. The making of Ashenden
  Kaplan, B. Dear Arthur darling
  Lopate, P. The disciple
  McGahern, J. Lavin
  Mailer, N. The man who studied yoga
  Mishima, Y. Three million yen
  O'Connor, F.   A life of your own
  Rifbjerg, K. Old man Jensen
  Schultz, J. Custom
  Trevor, W.   O fat white woman
  Wolitzer, H. The sex maniac
       *See also* Sodomy; Transvestism
Seymour, William Kean
  A tale in a club
    Turner, J. ed. Unlikely ghosts
Sforim, Mendele Mocher
  Of bygone days
    Wisse, R. R. ed.   A shtetl, and other
      Yiddish novellas
Shaber, David
  Scotch sour
    Prize stories, 1973; The O. Henry
      Awards
Shabos Nahamu. Babel, I.
Shadow. *See* Poe, E. A. Shadow—a parable
Shadow—a parable. Poe, E. A.
The shadow from the steeple. Bloch, R.
The shadow in the rose garden. Law-
  rence, D. H.
The shadow knows. Madden, D.
Shadow of darkness. Casely-Hayford, G. M.
The shadow of death. Canzoneri, R.
The shadow of kindness. Brennan, M.
The shadow of space. Farmer, P. J.
The shadow of wings. Silverberg, R.
The shadow on the Fancher twins. Mitch-
  ell, E. P.
The shadow on the screen. Kuttner, H.
Shadow show. Simak, C.
Shadows. Glaze, E.
Shadows. Landolfi, T.
Shadows on the road. Colby, R.
Shafter, John. *See* Gilchrist, Jack
Shaggai. Carter, L.
Shaham, Nathan
  Coming home
    Michener, J. A. ed. First fruits
  Seven of them
    Rabikovitz, D. ed. The new Israeli
      writers
    Same as: The seven, listed in 1959-
      1963 supplement
Shahu, Mohapatra Nilamoni
  The sun of the blind night
    Shimer, D. B. ed. Voices of modern
      Asia
Shake the dew. Gildner, G.
The Shaker revival. Jonas, G.
SHAKESPEARE, WILLIAM
  Burgess, A. The muse
  Gores, J.   A sad and bloody hour

Characters—Shylock
  Auchincloss, L. Black Shylock
       Macbeth
  Updike, J. Tomorrow and tomorrow and
    so forth
       Parodies, travesties, etc.
  Russell, B. The psychoanalyst's nightmare
       Sonnets
  Wilde, O. The portrait of Mr W. H.
  Young, A. K. Ponsonby and the Shake-
    speare sonnet
Shalamov, Varlam
  A good hand
    Scammell, M. ed. Russia's other writers
Shall the dust praise thee? Knight, D.
The shambler from the stars. Bloch, R.
SHAME
  Himes, C.   A nigger
  Ulibarri, S. R. The Frater family
Shame. Oates, J. C.
A shameful affair. Chopin, K.
Shamir, Moshe
  Mother of the oleanders
    Rabikovitz, D. ed. The new Israeli
      writers
  Next of kin
    Michener, J. A. ed. First fruits
Shandy. Goulart, R.
SHANGHAI. *See* China—Shanghai
Shannon, Dell
  The practical joke
    Burke, J. ed. Tales of unease
Shape. Sheckley, R.
A shape in time. Boucher, A.
The shape of the sword. Borges, J. L.
The shape of things that came. Deming, R.
Shapiro, Lamed
  Before the storm
    Shapiro, L. The Jewish government,
      and other stories
  Children
    Shapiro, L. The Jewish government,
      and other stories
  The cross
    Shapiro, L. The Jewish government,
      and other stories
  Eating days
    Shapiro, L. The Jewish government,
      and other stories
  A guest
    Shapiro, L. The Jewish government,
      and other stories
  Itsikl the mamzer
    Shapiro, L. The Jewish government,
      and other stories
  The Jewish government
    Shapiro, L. The Jewish government,
      and other stories
  The kiss
    Shapiro, L. The Jewish government,
      and other stories
  On guard
    Shapiro, L. The Jewish government,
      and other stories
  Pals
    Shapiro, L. The Jewish government,
      and other stories

**Shapiro, Lamed**—*Continued*

Pour out thy wrath
  Shapiro, L. The Jewish government, and other stories
Principles
  Shapiro, L. The Jewish government, and other stories
The rabbi and the rebbetsin
  Shapiro, L. The Jewish government, and other stories
The smelting furnace and the orchid
  Shapiro, L. The Jewish government, and other stories
Smoke
  Shapiro, L. The Jewish government, and other stories
Tiger
  Shapiro, L. The Jewish government, and other stories
White challa
  Shapiro, L. The Jewish government, and other stories
Wings
  Shapiro, L. The Jewish government, and other stories
With vigor!
  Shapiro, L. The Jewish government, and other stories
**SHARE CROPPERS.** *See* Tenant farming
The **sharing** of flesh. Anderson, P.
**Sharing** time. Henderson, Z.
**Shark.** Bryant, E.
The **shark.** Cady, J.
A **shark**-infested rice pudding. Wright, S.
**SHARKS**
  Brister, B. The sharks
  Bryant, E. Shark
  Cady, J. The sharks
  Clarke, A. C. The deep range
  Patursson, S. Eliesar and the basking shark
  Sambrot, W. Too many sharks
The **sharks.** Brister, B.
**Sharp, Margery**
The amethyst cat
  Montgomery, J. ed. The world's best cat stories
  Sharp, M. The Lost Chapel picnic, and other stories
At the Fort Flag
  Sharp, M. The Lost Chapel picnic, and other stories
Driving home
  Sharp, M. The Lost Chapel picnic, and other stories
George Lambert and Miss P.
  Sharp, M. The Lost Chapel picnic, and other stories
The girl in the grass
  Sharp, M. The Lost Chapel picnic, and other stories
The girl in the leopard-skin pants
  Sharp, M. The Lost Chapel picnic, and other stories
Interlude at Spanish Harbour
  Sharp, M. The Lost Chapel picnic, and other stories
The Lost Chapel picnic
  Sharp, M. The Lost Chapel picnic, and other stories

Mr Hamble's bear
  Sharp, M. The Lost Chapel picnic, and other stories
Seal Tregarthen's cousin
  Sharp, M. The Lost Chapel picnic, and other stories
The snuff-box
  Sharp, M. The Lost Chapel picnic, and other stories
Thief of time
  Sharp, M. The Lost Chapel picnic, and other stories

**SHARPSHOOTERS**
  Brister, B. The London gun
  Brister, B.  A small wager among gentlemen
  Brister, B. Tiro al pichon!
  Walker, E. K. Harlem transfer
**Shaw, Bob**
  Appointment on Prila
    Best SF: 1968
    Harrison, H. ed. Worlds of wonder
  Burden of proof
    Analog 7
  Light of other days
    Knight, D. ed. A science fiction argosy
  Retroactive
    Universe 2

**SHAW, GEORGE BERNARD**
Saint Joan
  Ayrton, M.  A performance of Saint Joan
**Shaw, Irwin**
  Act of faith
    Lewis, J. D. ed. Tales of our people
  God was here but He left early
    Shaw, I. God was here but He left early
  Gunners' passage
    Abrahams, W. ed. Fifty years of the American short story v2
  The Mannichon solution
    Shaw, I. God was here but He left early
  Small Saturday
    Shaw, I. God was here but He left early
  Where all things wise and fair descend
    Shaw, I. God was here but He left early
  Whispers in bedlam
    Shaw, I. God was here but He left early

**SHAWNEE INDIANS**
  Benét, S. V. Jacob and the Indians
**Shcherbakov, Vladimir**
  "We played under your window"
    Ginsburg, M. ed. The ultimate threshold
**She.** Ribnikar, J.
**She** heard it on the radio. Allingham, M.
**She** knew she was right. Litvinov, I.
**She** was strangely affected. Drake, R.
**She** went to buy yarn. Robertson, J. W.
The **she**-wolf. Verga, G.
**Shea, J. Vernon**
  The haunter of the graveyard
    Derleth, A. ed. Tales of Cthulhu Mythos
**Shearing, Joseph**
  The tallow candle
    Kahn, J. ed. Trial and terror
The **shearing** of Samson. Petrakis, H. M.

**SHELLS**
Jacobi, C. The aquarium
Lumley, B. The Cyprus shell
Lumley, B. The deep-sea conch

**Shen, Ts'ung-wen**
Daytime
Hsia, C. T. ed. Twentieth-century Chinese stories
Quiet
Hsia, C. T. ed. Twentieth-century Chinese stories

**Shen, Yen-ping.** *See* Mao, Tun

**Shenhar, Yitzhak**
On Galilean shores
Michener, J. A. ed. First fruits

**Shepherd, Jean**
County fair!
Shepherd, J. Wanda Hickey's night of golden memories, and other disasters
Daphne Bigelow and the spine-chilling saga of the snail-encrusted tinfoil noose
Shepherd, J. Wanda Hickey's night of golden memories, and other disasters
The grandstand passion play of Delbert and the Bumpus hounds
Shepherd, J. Wanda Hickey's night of golden memories, and other disasters
Ollie Hopnoodle's haven of bliss
Shepherd, J. Wanda Hickey's night of golden memories, and other disasters
The return of the smiling Wimpy doll
Shepherd, J. Wanda Hickey's night of golden memories, and other disasters
Scut Farkas and the murderous Mariah
Shepherd, J. Wanda Hickey's night of golden memories, and other disasters
The star-crossed romance of Josephine Cosnowski
Shepherd, J. Wanda Hickey's night of golden memories, and other disasters
Wanda Hickey's night of golden memories
Shepherd, J. Wanda Hickey's night of golden memories, and other disasters

**Shepherd,** show me . . . Wade, R.

The **shepherdess** of the Alps. Marmontel, J. F.

**SHEPHERDESSES**
Marmontel, J. F. The shepherdess of the Alps

**SHEPHERDS**
Bierce, A. Haïta the shepherd
Brodeur, P. The sick fox
Brú, H. Old Halgir
Cady, J. Thermopylae
Coloane, F. A. Cururo . . . sheep dog
Coover, R. Morris in chains
Craven, M. Juan, the Basque shepherd boy
Henry, O. Roads of destiny
Leinster, M. Nobody saw the ship
Meek, F. M. The little shepherd
Patursson, S. The winning of the bounty
Schoonover, S. The star blanket
*See also* Goatherds

The **sheriff.** Midwood, B.

The **sheriff** of Canyon Gulch. Anderson, P. and Dickson, G. R.

The **sheriff** of Chayute. Sturgeon, T.

**SHERIFFS**
Barker, E. Marshal for Las Moras
Chesnutt, C. W. The sheriff's children
Clarke, J. Sheriff's son
Crane, S. The bride comes to Yellow Sky
Crane, S. In a Park Row restaurant
Drake, R. The cook and the sheriff
Garrett, G. Noise of strangers
MacDonald, J. Funny the way things work out
Maltz, A. The way things are
Midwood, B. The sheriff
Oates, J. C. The fine white mist of winter
Prebble, J. The long hate
Rinehart, M. R. Rock River fugitive
Stone, N. B. The long trail
Sturgeon, T. The sheriff of Chayute

The **sheriff's** children. Chesnutt, C. W.

**Sheriff's** son. Clarke, J.

**Sherred, T. L.**
Bounty
Ellison, H. ed. Again, dangerous visions
E for effort
The Science fiction hall of fame v2B

**Sherrel.** Burnett, W.

**Sherwin, Judith Johnson**
Akihi-san: a contemplation
Sherwin, J. J. The life of riot
The fourth annual greater New York revolving-door crisis
Sherwin, J. J. The life of riot
A growing economy
Sherwin, J. J. The life of riot
The life of riot in one Luis Casas
Sherwin, J. J. The life of riot
Love in the human heart
Sherwin, J. J. The life of riot
The machinery of response
Sherwin, J. J. The life of riot
The olde daunce
Sherwin, J. J. The life of riot
These actions shall be held proof
Sherwin, J. J. The life of riot
Unity: an impartial report
Sherwin, J. J. The life of riot
The white paper on sex and technology
Sherwin, J. J. The life of riot

**Shetzline, David**
Country of the painted freaks
The Best American short stories, 1973

**Shevchuk, Valeriy**
The cobbler
Luckyj, G. S. N. ed. Modern Ukrainian short stories
My father decided to plant orchards
Luckyj, G. S. N. ed. Modern Ukrainian short stories

**Shewan, Ida**
Mind is how you go
The Times of London Anthology of detective stories

**Shibil.** Yovkov, Y.

The **Shield** mares. Green, B. K.

**SHIELDING (ELECTRICITY)**
Blish, J. The box

Sladek, John—*Continued*
The steam-driven boy
Nova 2
**SLANDER.** *See* Libel and slander
**SLANG**
Anmar, F. Jenny among the zeebs
**Slater, Elaine**
The Sooey pill
Best detective stories of the year [1969]
Best of the Best detective stories
The **slaughterer.** Singer, I. B.
**SLAUGHTERERS.** *See* Slaughtering and slaughter-houses
**SLAUGHTERING AND SLAUGHTER-HOUSES**
Beal, M. F. The end of days
Dozois, G. R.   A kingdom by the sea
Jews
Singer, I. B. Blood
Singer, I. B. The slaughterer
**SLAVE TRADE**
Davidson, A. The necessity of his condition
DeFord, M. A. The voyage of the "Deborah Pratt"
Mérimée, P. Tamango
**SLAVERY**
Chilson, R. In his image
Clement, H. Halo
Disch, T. M. Thesis on social forms and social controls in the U.S.A.
Le Guin, U. K. The word for world is forest
Molinaro, U. Sweet cheat of freedom
Vance, J. The last castle
*See also* Slavery in the United States
Fugitive slaves
Brown, W. W. Escape of Clotel
Carpentier, A. The fugitives
Lester, J. Louis
Robinson, R. E. The mole's path
**SLAVERY IN CUBA**
Alonso, D. Times gone by
**SLAVERY IN SOUTH AMERICA**
Carpentier, A. The fugitives
**SLAVERY IN THE UNITED STATES**
Benét, S. V. Freedom's a hard-bought thing
Butor, M. Welcome to Utah
Chesnutt, C. W. Po' Sandy
Dunbar, P. L. The ingrate
Lester, J. Ben
Lester, J. Long journey home
Lester, J. When freedom came
Naylor, P. R. Four vignettes from a family tree
Page, T. N. "Unc' Edinburg's drowndin' "
Styron, W. Hark: 1831, Virginia
Warren, R. P. Phebe
West, J. Neighbors
*See also* Negroes
The **slayers** and the slain. Derleth, A.
**Slayton.** Just, W.
**Sled.** Adams, T. E.
**SLEDDING.** *See* Sleighing
**SLEDGEMEN.** *See* Sleighs and sledges

**SLEEP**
Emshwiller, C. The queen of sleep
Spielberg, P. The last day of winter
*See also* Insomnia; Snoring
Experiment
Wolfe, B. The girl with rapid eye movements
**SLEEP, PROLONGED**
Davidson, A. Big Sam
Irving, W. Rip Van Winkle
Szilard, L. The Mark Gable Foundation
**Sleep** is the enemy. Gilbert, A.
**SLEEP-WALKING.** *See* Somnambulism
The **sleeper.** Lynds, S.
**Sleeping** beauty. Clarke, A. C.
**Sleeping** beauty. Collier, J.
**SLEEPLESSNESS.** *See* Insomnia
**Sleepy** time. Wodehouse, P. G.
**SLEIGHING**
Adams, T. E. Sled
Wright, C. Mirror of ice
**SLEIGHS AND SLEDGES**
Chekhov, A. Misery
**Slesar, Henry**
Letter from a very worried man
Mystery Writers of America. Mirror, mirror, fatal mirror
My father, the cat
Necker, C. ed. Supernatural cats
A note on American literature by my uncle, Monroe Sanderson
Mystery Writers of America. Dear dead days
**Slesar, Henry, and Ellison, Harlan**
Survivor #1
Ellison, H. Partners in wonder
**Slesinger, Tess**
After the party
Slesinger, T. On being told that her second husband has taken his first lover, and other stories
The answer on the magnolia tree
Slesinger, T. On being told that her second husband has taken his first lover, and other stories
The Friedman's Annie
Slesinger, T. On being told that her second husband has taken his first lover, and other stories
Jobs in the sky
Slesinger, T. On being told that her second husband has taken his first lover, and other stories
A life in the day of a writer
Slesinger, T. On being told that her second husband has taken his first lover, and other stories
Missis Flinders
Slesinger, T. On being told that her second husband has taken his first lover, and other stories
Mother to dinner
Slesinger, T. On being told that her second husband has taken his first lover, and other stories

SMALL TOWN LIFE—*Continued*
  Taylor, P. Miss Leonora when last seen
  Updike, J. The corner
  Updike, J. When everyone was pregnant
  Welty, E. The demonstrators
  Wilhelm, K. Somerset dreams
  Williams, J. Shorelines
    *See also* Neighbors
Small town taxicab driver. Farrell, J. T.
A small wager among gentlemen. Brister, B.
Small war. MacLean, K.
The smallest woman in the world. Lispector, C.
The smashing of the Dragon King. Wang T'ieh
Smell. Aiken, J.
Smells and the bone. Moravia, A.
The smelting furnace and the orchid. Shapiro, L.
The smeraldina's billet doux. Beckett, S.
The smiler. Norman, C.
Smith, Mrs Castle. *See* Brenda
Smith, Clark Ashton
  An adventure in futurity
    Smith, C. A. Other dimensions
  The amazing planet
    Smith, C. A. Other dimensions
  The Ampoi giant
    Haining, P. ed. The freak show
  The dimension of chance
    Smith, C. A. Other dimensions
  The ghost of Mohammed Din
    Smith, C. A. Other dimensions
  The ghoul
    Smith, C. A. Other dimensions
  The immeasurable horror
    Smith, C. A. Other dimensions
  The invisible city
    Smith, C. A. Other dimensions
  The justice of the elephant
    Smith, C. A. Other dimensions
  The kiss of Zoraida
    Smith, C. A. Other dimensions
  The mahout
    Smith, C. A. Other dimensions
  The Malay krise
    Smith, C. A. Other dimensions
  The mandrakes
    Smith, C. A. Other dimensions
  Marooned in Andromeda
    Smith, C. A. Other dimensions
  The metamorphosis of Earth
    Smith, C. A. Other dimensions
  Monsters in the night
    Smith, C. A. Other dimensions
  The necromantic tale
    Smith, C. A. Other dimensions
  An offering to the moon
    Smith, C. A. Other dimensions
  Phoenix
    Smith, C. A. Other dimensions
  The Raja and the tiger
    Smith, C. A. Other dimensions
  The resurrection of the rattlesnake
    Smith, C. A. Other dimensions
  The return of the sorcerer
    Derleth, A. ed. Tales of the Cthulhu Mythos

  Something new
    Smith, C. A. Other dimensions
  The supernumerary corpse
    Smith, C. A. Other dimensions
  A tale of Sir John Maundeville
    Smith, C. A. Other dimensions
  Thirteen phantasms
    Smith, C. A. Other dimensions
  Told in the desert
    Smith, C. A. Other dimensions
  Ubbo-Sathla
    Derleth, A. ed. Tales of the Cthulhu Mythos
  The uncharted isle
    Manley, S. and Lewis, G. eds. Shapes of the supernatural
  The Venus of Azombeii
    Smith, C. A. Other dimensions
Smith, Cordwainer
  Alpha Ralpha Boulevard
    Silverberg, R. ed. The ends of time
  The ballad of lost C'mell
    The Science fiction hall of fame v2A
  The game of rat and dragon
    Knight, D. ed. A science fiction argosy
    Necker, C. ed. Supernatural cats
    Silverberg, R. ed. The mirror of infinity
  On the storm planet
    Dozois, G. R. ed. A day in the life
  Scanners live in vain
    Science fiction hall of fame v 1
    Total Effect. Survival printout
Smith, Edmund Ware
  The one-eyed poacher's legal salmon
    Lyons, N. ed. Fisherman's bounty
  An underground episode
    Burnett, W. ed. That's what happened to me
    *For another story by this author see* Ware, Edmund
Smith, Lady Eleanor
  No ships pass
    Stern, P. V. ed. The other side of the clock
Smith, Ernest Bramah. *See* Bramah, Ernest
Smith, Evelyn E.
  Calliope and Gherkin and the Yankee Doodle thing
    The Best from Fantasy and Science Fiction; 19th ser.
Smith, George O.
  Interlude
    Astounding
  Lost art
    Hipolito, J. and McNelly, W. E. eds. Mars, we love you
Smith, Jean Wheeler
  Frankie Mae
    King, W. ed. Black short story anthology
Smith, Lee
  The dying of Eunice LeBel
    Alabama prize stories, 1970
Smith, Pauline C.
  Osborn and Sabrina
    Best detective stories of the year, 1972

So I went crazy. Blackhurst, W. E.
So I'm not Lady Chatterley so better I should
    know it now. Sara
So peaceful in the country. Offord, C. R.
So this is called success? Deutschman, B.

**SOAP**
    Lu, Hsun. Soap
**Soap.** Lu, Hsun
**Sober** noises of morning in a marginal land.
    Aldiss, B. W.

**SOCCER**
    Glanville, B. The director's wife
    Glanville, B. The dying footballer
    Glanville, B. Everything laid on
    Glanville, B. Feet of clay
    Glanville, B. The footballers
    Glanville, B. Goalkeepers are crazy
    Glanville, B. Hanger-on
    Glanville, B. If he's good enough, he's big
        enough
    Glanville, B. The king of Hackney Marshes
    Glanville, B. The man behind the goal
    Glanville, B. The prodigy
A **sociable** plover. Linklater, E.

**SOCIAL CLASSES**
    James, H. Daisy Miller
    Jones, R. Cuisine bourgeoise
    Russ, J. The soul of a servant
    Slesinger, T. After the party
    Wilson, A. Saturnalia
        *See also* Class distinction; Social sta-
    tus
**Social** climber. Higgins, R. M.
**SOCIAL CONFORMITY.** *See* Conformity
The **social** event of the season for Rush
    street. Schwimmer, W.
**SOCIAL GROUPS**
    Silverberg, R. In the group
**SOCIAL ISOLATION**
    Mann, T. The clown
        *See also* Alienation (Social psychol-
    ogy)
**SOCIAL SERVICE.** *See* Social workers
**SOCIAL STATUS**
    Auchincloss, L. The prince and the pauper
    Bergé, C. Kou
    Colter, C. The lookout
    Deutschman, B. Society . . . or who says
        they don't have a caste system in
        America
    Di Donato, P. When Willy K. Vanderbilt
        frolicked and I shoveled his snow
    Glanville, B. Roses in burnt oak
    Hubly, E. In Sherwood Forest
    Hunter, K. Debut
    Kipling, R.   A second-rate woman
    Maupassant, G. de. The horseman
    Maupassant, G. de.   A man of influence
    Tuohy, F.   A war of liberation
    Wharton, E. Autres temps
    Wilson, A. Totentanz
        *See also* Class distinction; Snobs and
    snobbishness; Social classes
**SOCIAL WORK.** *See* Public welfare
**SOCIAL WORKERS**
    Bambara, T. C. Playin with Punjab
    Ellison, H. Try a dull knife

Hunter, K. Mom Luby and the social
    worker
Tyre, N. Another turn of the screw
Yurick, S. . . . And a friend to sit by your
    side

**SOCIALISM**
    Bassani, G. The last years of Clelia Trotti
    Lessing, D. Spies I have known
    Pritchett, V. S. The speech
**SOCIALISTS.** *See* Socialism
**SOCIALLY HANDICAPPED CHILDREN**
    Taylor, E. The devastating boys
**SOCIETIES.** *See* Gilds; Secret societies
**SOCIETIES, SECRET.** *See* Secret societies
**SOCIETY.** *See* Social status
**SOCIETY, PRIMITIVE**
    Borges, J. L. Doctor Brodie's report
    Golding, W. Clonk clonk
        *See also* Tribes and tribal system
**SOCIETY OF FRIENDS.** *See* Friends, So-
    ciety of
**Society** . . . or who says they don't have a
    caste system in America. Deutsch-
    man, B.
**Sodom** and Gomorrah, Texas. Lafferty, R. A.
**SODOMY**
    Bukowski, C. Animal crackers in my soup
The **sofa.** Brennan, M.
The **soft** blue bunny rabbit story. Bryant, E.
**SOFTBALL**
    Matthews, C. The dummy
**Sohl, Jerry**
    I am Aleppo
        Elwood, R. ed. The new mind
**SOILS.** *See* Gardens and gardening
**Soirée** à la chandelle. Steegmuller, F.
**SOLAR ENERGY**
    Asimov, I. The last question
    Clarke, A. C. The wind from the sun
**SOLAR POWER.** *See* Solar energy
**Sold** to Satan. Twain, M.
The **soldier** and the census. Meek, F. M.
**Soldier,** ask not. Dickson, G. R.
**Soldier** in the blanket. Kotzwinkle, W.
**Soldier** Key. Lanier, S. E.
**Soldier,** soldier. Rascoe, J.
**SOLDIERS**
    Dickson, G. R. Warrior
    Eisenberg, L. Conqueror
    Harrison, H. No war, or battle's sound
    Neville, K. and O'Donnell, K. M. Pacem
        est
    Wolfe, G. The blue mouse
    Wolfe, G. The horars of war
            **American**
    Adams, C. Hell command
    Aitken, J. Lederer's Legacy
    Anderson, A. Comrade
    Bahr, J. Footnote to a famous peace march
    Ballard, J. G. The killing ground
    Berkson, T. Thirty-day leave
    Bierce, A. The mocking-bird
    Bingham, S. The big day
    Bobrowsky, I. The courier
    Brodeur, P. Behind the moon
    Buck, P. S. Letter home
    Cassill, R. V. Happy marriage

Soul mate. Sutton, L.
The soul of a cat. Benson, M.
The soul of a servant. Russ, J.
The soul spectroscope. Mitchell, E. P.
**SOUND**
 Ballard, J. G. The sound-sweep
 Clarke, A. C. Silence please
 Deck, J. Notes: what I think pudding says
 Hesse, H. An evening with Dr Faust
 Landolfi, T.　A family chat
　　　**Recording and reproducing**
 Kanin, G. The Brahms kick
Sound and fury. Henry, O.
The sound and the silence. Niland, D.
Sound decision. Garrett, R. and Silverberg, R.
The sound of the singing. Laurence, M.
The sound-sweep. Ballard, J. G.
Soundless evening. Hoffman, L.
The sounds of silence. Cady, J.
Soup. Trevisan, D.
Soura Bir. Strashimirov, A.
The source. Dawson, F.
The sources of the Nile. Davidson, A.
**SOUSA, JOHN PHILIP**
 Ayrton, M. The low blow
**THE SOUTH.** See Southern States
**SOUTH AFRICA.** See Africa, South
**SOUTH AFRICANS IN FRANCE**
 Gordimer, N.　A meeting in space
**SOUTH AFRICANS IN THE CONGO**
 Gordimer, N. Rain-queen
**SOUTH AFRICANS IN ZAMBIA**
 Gordimer, N. Abroad
**SOUTH AMERICA**
 Borges, J. L. The intruder
 García Márquez, G. Leaf storm
 García Márquez, G. Monologue of Isabel
　 watching it rain in Macondo
 Güiraldes, R. The gauchos' hearth
 Onetti, J. C. Jacob and the other
 Quiroga, H. The alligator war
 Thomason, J. W. Air Patrol
 Thomason, J. W. The conquest of Mike
 Uslar Pietri, A. The drum dance
 Vos, H. The sons of Pepe Gimenez
　　　See also Amazon River
**SOUTH AMERICANS IN FRANCE**
 Cortázar, J. The other heaven
**SOUTH CAROLINA**
 Marsh, W. On Jordan's stormy banks
 Patton, F. G. The falling leaves
The South Malaysia Pineapple Growers' As-
　 sociation. Theroux, P.
South of Market. Gores, J.
**SOUTH SEA ISLANDS.** See Islands of the
　 Pacific
**SOUTHERN DIALECT.** See Dialect stories
　 —Southern
**SOUTHERN STATES**
 Boles, P. D. Summer candles
 Brent, J.　A little trip through Griffley
 Counselman, M. E. The tree's wife
 Faulkner, W. Dry September
 Fitzgerald, F. S. The dance
 Gaines, E. J. Three men
 Garrett, G. Noise of strangers
 Glaze, E. The embrace
 Gordon, C. Old Red

 Highsmith, P. When the fleet was in at
　 Mobile
 Justice, D. The lady
 Madden, D. Traven
 O'Connor, F. The barber
 O'Connor, F.　A circle in the fire
 O'Connor, F. The displaced person
 O'Connor, F. The geranium
 O'Connor, F. The life you save may be
　 your own
 O'Connor, F. Parker's back
 O'Connor, F. The Partridge festival
 O'Connor, F. Revelation
 O'Connor, F.　A stroke of good fortune
 O'Connor, F.　A Temple of the Holy
　 Ghost
 O'Connor, F. The train
 O'Connor, F. You can't be any poorer than
　 dead
 Phillips, R. Obsession
 Spicehandler, D. Black barbecue
 Taylor, P. Miss Leonora when last seen
 Thelwell, M. Bright an' mownin' star
 Warren, R. P. Phebe
　　　See also Jews in the United States—
　 Southern States; Negroes—Southern
　 States; and names of individual states
　 in this region
　　　**Farm life**
　　　See Farm life—Southern States
The southern thruway. Cortázar, J.
**SOUTHERNERS.** See Southern States
**SOUTHWEST, NEW**
　　　**Frontier and pioneer life**
　　　See Frontier and pioneer life—South-
　 west, New
**SOUTHWEST, OLD.** See states in this re-
　 gion, e.g. Texas
Souvenir. Tavela, J.
Souvenir. See Ballard, J. G. The drowned
　 giant
Sowing asphodel. Litvinov, I.
**SPACE**
　　　**Exploration**
　　　See Outer space—Exploration
**SPACE AND TIME**
 Aldiss, B. W. Man in his time
 Asimov, I. Living space
 Asimov, I. The Red Queen's race
 Asimov, I. The ugly little boy
 Budrys, A. Now hear the word of the Lord
 Curtis, B. The key to out
 DeFord, M. A. Slips take over
 Effinger, G. A. New New York New Or-
　 leans
 Henderson, Z. Three-cornered and secure
 Knight, D. You're another
 Lafferty, R. A. Sky
 Laumer, K. Mind out of time
 Leinster, M. Sidewise in time
 Rocklynne, R. Time wants a skelton
 Stuart, D. A. Forgetfulness
　　　See also Fourth dimension; Time;
　 Time, Travels in; Time machines
**SPACE BIOLOGY**
 Clement, H. Raindrop

SPACE SHIPS—*Continued*
Sheckley, R. Tailpipe to disaster
Van Vogt, A. E. Rogue ship
Van Vogt, A. E. and Ellison, H. The human operators
Wesley, J. Womb to tomb
Wilson, R. Deny the slake
Wolfe, G. Alien stones
　　*See also* Interplanetary voyages
### Pilots
　　*See* Astronauts
SPACE STATIONS
Anderson, P. The rogue
Biggle, L. In his own image
Boulle, P. The heart and the galaxy
Bova, B. Men of good will
Clement, H. Fireproof
Ellison, H. Night vigil
Koontz, D. R. Terra phobia
Long, F. B. The trap
Panshin, A. Now I'm watching Roger
Runyon, C. W. Dream patrol
　　*See also* Space colonies
Space-time for springers. Leiber, F.
Space to move. Green, J.
SPACE TRAVEL
Anderson, P. Nothing succeeds like failure
Asimov, I. Not final!
Asimov, I. Take a match
Asimov, I. Trends
Bova, B. Stars, won't you hide me?
Bova, B. Zero gee
Clement, H. The foundling stars
Clement, H. Sun spot
Clement, H. "Trojan fall"
Earls, W. Jump
Etchison, D. Damechild
Farmer, P. J. The shadow of space
Galouye, D. F. Prometheus rebound
Henderson, Z. Boona on Scancia
Henderson, Z. The indelible kind
Jacobi, C. Sequence
Lem, S. The patrol
Lightner, A. M. Best friend
Malzberg, B. N. Opening fire
Oliver, C. Blood's a rover
Sheckley, R. Tailpipe to disaster
Silverberg, R. Ship-sister, star-sister
Vonnegut, K. The big space fuck
　　*See also* Interplanetary voyages; Space ships
SPACE VOYAGES. *See* Interplanetary voyages; Space travel
SPACEMEN. *See* Astronauts
SPAIN
### 15th century
Bandello, M. Spanish revenge
### 16th century
Alemán, M. Portrait of father
Cervantes. Marriage à la mode
Lopate, P. The disciple
### 18th century
Alarcón, P. A. de. The nun
### 19th century
Balzac, H. de. El Verdugo

### 20th century
Beekman, E. M. Cornada
Sillitoe, A. Guzman, go home
Williams, J. A. A good season
### 20th century—Civil War, 1936-1939
Hemingway, E. The butterfly and the tank
Hemingway, E. The denunciation
Hemingway, E. The fifth column, and four other stories of the Spanish Civil War
Hemingway, E. Night before battle
Hemingway, E. Old man at the bridge
Hemingway, E. Under the ridge
### Andalusia
Maugham, W. S. A man from Glasgow
### Aristocracy
　　*See* Aristocracy—Spain
### Barcelona
Chekhov, A. The sinner from Toledo
Salter, J. Am Strande von Tanger
Weaver, G. Fantastico
### Granada
Alarcón, P. A. de. The nun
Trevisan, D. Nights of love in Granada
### Seville
Roth, H. The surveyor
SPAIN, PROVINCIAL AND RURAL
Fitzsimmons, P. M. The napkin ring
McGahern, J. Peaches
Maugham, W. S. The punctiliousness of Don Sebastian
SPANIARDS IN CUBA
Saltus, E. Fausta
SPANISH-AMERICAN WAR, 1898. *See* United States—19th century—War of 1898
Spanish cholera. Vezhinov, P.
SPANISH CIVIL WAR. *See* Spain—20th century—Civil War, 1936-1939
SPANISH INQUISITION. *See* Inquisition
SPANISH REFUGEES. *See* Refugees, Spanish
Spanish revenge. Bandello, M.
SPANISH SAHARA. *See* Spanish West Africa—Spanish Sahara
SPANISH SOLDIERS. *See* Soldiers, Spanish
Spanish stirrup. Prebble, J.
SPANISH WEST AFRICA
### Spanish Sahara
Davidson, A. Amphora
Spare the rod. Biggle, L.
Spark, Muriel
　Bang-bang you're dead
　　Thune, E. and Prigozy, R. eds. Short stories: a critical anthology
　The Black Madonna
　　Kissin, E. H. ed. Stories in black and white
　Miss Pinkerton's apocalypse
　　Hitchcock, A. comp. Alfred Hitchcock's Supernatural tales of terror and suspense
SPARROWS
Cabrera Infante, G. A nest of sparrows on the awning
The Sparrows of Paris. Pei, M.

Starting from scratch. Sheckley, R.
**STARVATION**
Fox, J. Grayson's baby
Saroyan, W. The daring young man on the flying trapeze
Shiina, R. Midnight banquet
Steinbeck, J. Tortillas and beans
Winther, M. A. Hunger
Yashpal. Two desperate souls
*See also* Hunger
**STATE POLICE.** *See* Police, State
State witness. Beneš, J.
Statement of Ashby Wyndham. Warren, R. P.
The **statement** of Randolph Carter. Lovecraft, H. P.
The **station** master. Pushkin, A.
Station: you are here. Curley, D.
**STATIONS.** *See* Railroads—Stations
**STATISTICIANS**
O'Donnell, K. M. Chronicles of a comer
Tammuz, B. Angioxyl, a rare cure
Statistician's Day. Blish, J.
**STATISTICS**
Böll, H. At the bridge
**STATUES**
Ballard, J. G. The garden of time
Gallico, P. The Roman kid
Hoch, E. D. Whydunit: the Nile cat
Lafferty, R. A. Condillac's statue
McAuliffe, F. The Maltese Falcon Commission
Narayan, R. K. A horse and two goats
Petry, A. Mother Africa
Vestdijk, S. The stone face
Vondra, V. A legend of saintly folly
Wilson, G. M-1
**STATUETTES.** *See* Idols and images
**STATUS, SOCIAL.** *See* Social status
Staying in bed. Gilliatt, P.
**STEALING.** *See* Shoplifting; Theft; Thieves
Stealing cars. Weesner, T.
The **steam**-driven boy. Sladek, J.
**STEAMBOATS**
Gohman, F. Vanishing act
Haycox, E. Long storm; excerpt
The **steamer.** Angoff, C.
**Steegmuller, Francis**
Bella Napoli
Steegmuller, F. Stories and true stories
Ciao Fabrizio
Steegmuller, F. Stories and true stories
The credo
Steegmuller, F. Stories and true stories
The doomed terrapin
Steegmuller, F. Stories and true stories
The fair singer
Steegmuller, F. Stories and true stories
The griffe of the master
Steegmuller, F. Stories and true stories
In the lobby
Steegmuller, F. Stories and true stories
One round trip only
Steegmuller, F. Stories and true stories
A real saint
Steegmuller, F. Stories and true stories
A ride with Ralph
Steegmuller, F. Stories and true stories

Soirée à la chandelle
Steegmuller, F. Stories and true stories
The system
Steegmuller, F. Stories and true stories
Steel brother. Dickson, G. R.
The **steel** cat. Collier, J.
The **steel** flea. Leskov, N.
**Steele, Max**
Color the daydream yellow
Prize stories, 1969: The O. Henry Awards
**Steele, Wilbur Daniel**
The man who saw through heaven
Abrahams, W. ed. Fifty years of the American short story v2
A **steelie** for the King. Carr, J.
**STEERS.** *See* Cattle
Stefano's two sons. Landolfi, T.
**Stefanyk, Vasyl**
The news
Luckyj, G. S. N. ed. Modern Ukrainian short stories
The pious woman
Luckyj, G. S. N. ed. Modern Ukrainian short stories
A stone cross
Luckyj, G. S. N. ed. Modern Ukrainian short stories
**Stegner, Wallace**
Beyond the glass mountain
Abrahams, W. ed. Fifty years of the American short story v2
Carrion spring
Taylor, J. G. ed. Great Western short stories
In the twilight
Satin, J. ed. Reading literature
**Stein, Gertrude**
Fernhurst
Stein, G. Fernhurst, Q.E.D., and other early writings
G. M. P.
Stein, G. Matisse, Picasso and Gertrude Stein
A long gay book
Stein, G. Matisse, Picasso and Gertrude Stein
The making of Americans
Stein, G. Fernhurst, Q.E.D., and other early writings
Many many women
Stein, G. Matisse, Picasso and Gertrude Stein
Q.E.D.
Stein, G. Fernhurst, Q.E.D., and other early writings
**Steinbeck, John**
Adam and his sons
Steinbeck, J. The portable Steinbeck
The Affair at 7 rue de M—
Haining, P. ed. The Lucifer society
Howes, B. and Smith, G. J. eds. The sea-green horse
Steinbeck, J. The portable Steinbeck
Breakfast
Steinbeck, J. The portable Steinbeck
Breakfast and work
Steinbeck, J. The portable Steinbeck

**Stevenson, Robert Louis**—*Continued*

Story of the physician and the Saratoga trunk
  Stevenson, R. L. The complete short stories of Robert Louis Stevenson

Story of the young man in holy orders
  Stevenson, R. L. The complete short stories of Robert Louis Stevenson

Story of the young man with the cream tarts
  Stevenson, R. L. The complete short stories of Robert Louis Stevenson

Strange case of Dr Jekyll and Mr Hyde
  Stevenson, R. L. The complete short stories of Robert Louis Stevenson

Thrawn Janet
  Stevenson, R. L. The complete short stories of Robert Louis Stevenson

Will o' the Mill
  Stevenson, R. L. The complete short stories of Robert Louis Stevenson

    **Parodies, travesties, etc.**

Stevens, R. L. The physician and the opium fiend

The **stewardess.** Vassilikos, V.

**STEWARDS (AIR LINES)** *See* Air lines—Stewards

**STEWARDESSES (AIR LINES)** *See* Air lines—Hostesses

**Stewart, J. I. M.**

A change of heart
  Stewart, J. I. M. Cucumber sandwiches, and other stories

Cucumber sandwiches
  Stewart, J. I. M. Cucumber sandwiches, and other stories

Laon and Cythna
  Stewart, J. I. M. Cucumber sandwiches, and other stories

The men
  Stewart, J. I. M. Cucumber sandwiches, and other stories
    *For another story by this author see* Innes, Michael

**Stewart, John Craig**

The last day
  Alabama prize stories, 1970

**Stewart, Natacha**

Acacias
  Stewart, N. Evil eye, and other stories

By a lake in the Bois
  Stewart, N. Evil eye, and other stories

Chopin
  Stewart, N. Evil eye, and other stories

The critic
  Stewart, N. Evil eye, and other stories

Evil eye
  Stewart, N. Evil eye, and other stories

Grief
  Stewart, N. Evil eye, and other stories

The sin of pride
  Stewart, N. Evil eye, and other stories

Sophia, Zoltan, and the postman
  Stewart, N. Evil eye, and other stories

What sadness
  Stewart, N. Evil eye, and other stories

A **stick** of green candy. Bowles, J.

The **sticking** point. *See* Yurick, S. The before and after of Hymie Farbotnik

**Sticks** and stones. Michaels, L.

The **stigmata** of the Rainy-Day Sun. Hayes, R. E.

**Stiles, George**

Lines from the quick
  Gulassa, C. M. ed. The fact of fiction
  New American Review no. 4

**Stiles, Sean**

Occam's razor
  The Times of London Anthology of detective stories

**Still** life. Helbemäe, G.

**Still**-life. O'Donnell, K. M.

**Still** life composition: woman's clothes. Thompson, K.

**Still** life with fruit. Betts, D.

**Still** life with ice cream. Kotowska, M.

**Still** to the West; excerpt. Jones, N.

**Still** trajectories. Aldiss, B. W.

**STINGINESS.** *See* Misers

**Stinkpot.** Verga, G.

**STOCK BROKERS.** *See* Brokers

The **stocking.** Campbell, R.

**STOCKS**

Fast, H. Tomorrow's "Wall Street Journal"

**Stockton, Frank R.**

The griffin and the Minor Canon
  Silverberg, B. ed. Phoenix feathers

The transferred ghost
  Manley, S. and Lewis, G. eds. A gathering of ghosts

**Stoker, Bram**

The burial of the rats
  Stoker, B. The Bram Stoker Bedside companion

Crooken sands
  Stoker, B. The Bram Stoker Bedside companion

Dracula's daughter
  Haining, P. ed. The ghouls
  Same as: Dracula's guest

Dracula's guest
  Haining, P. ed. Nightfrights
  Kahn, J. ed. Some things strange and sinister
  Same as: Dracula's daughter

The invisible giant
  Stoker, B. The Bram Stoker Bedside companion

The Judge's House
  Stoker, B. The Bram Stoker Bedside companion

The secret of the growing gold
  Stoker, B. The Bram Stoker Bedside companion

The squaw
  Necker, C. ed. Supernatural cats
  Stoker, B. The Bram Stoker Bedside companion

A star trap
  Stoker, B. The Bram Stoker Bedside companion

Three young ladies
  Haining, P. ed. Vampires at midnight

The watter's mou'
  Stoker, B. The Bram Stoker Bedside companion

A **stolen** letter. Collins, W.

**Stolen** pleasures. Jewett, S. O.

The **Stollmeyer** sonnets. Powell, J.
**STOMACH**
    Crane, S. The cry of a huckleberry pud-
        ding: a dim study of camping experi-
        ences
    Greene, G. Alas, poor Maling
**Stone, Alma**
    Oh, pity the dwarf's butt
        Stone, A. The banishment, and three
        stories
    The portrait
        Stone, A. The banishment, and three
        stories
    The traveler
        Stone, A. The banishment, and three
        stories
**Stone, N. B.**
    The long trail
        Lucia, E. ed. This land around us
**Stone, Robert**
    Porque no tiene, porque le falta
        The Best American short stories, 1970
        New American Review no. 6
The **stone** and the violets. Djilas, M.
The **stone** boy. Berriault, G.
A **stone** cross. Stefanyk, V.
The **stone** face. Vestdijk, S.
The **stone** lovers. Harter, E.
The **stone** monster. Lightner, A. M.
The **stone** pigeons. Severnyak, S.
**Stoned** counsel. Hollis, H. H.
**STONEHENGE**
    Zern, E. Something was fishy about Stone-
        henge
**Stonewall** Jackson's Waterloo. Murray A.
**STONYBROOK.** *See* New York (State)—
    Stonybrook
**Stop** me before I tell more. Thurston, R.
**Stop** staring at my tits, mister. Bukowski, C.
**Stopa, Jon**
    Kiddy-Lib
        Elder, J. ed. Eros in orbit
The **stopping** train. Rushmore, R.
**STOREKEEPERS.** *See* Merchants
**STORES**
    O'Hara, J. The hardware man
    Taylor, E. Praises
    Veiga, J. J. The casquemoors
        *See also* Delicatessan stores; Drug-
    stores
**STORES, DEPARTMENT.** *See* Department
    stores
**Stories.** Hemenway, R.
**STORIES ABOUT LETTERS.** *See* Letters,
    Stories about
**Stories** and texts for nothing, III. Beckett, S.
**Stories** from behind the stove. Singer, I. B.
**STORIES IN DIARY FORM.** *See* Diaries
    (Stories in diary form)
**STORIES IN LETTER FORM.** *See* Letters
    (Stories in letter form)
**Stories** of Africa. Brennan, M.
**STORIES OF THE FUTURE.** *See* Future,
    Stories of the
**Stories** told by an artist. Crane, S.
**STORKS**
    Bowles, P. The hyena

**Storm, Theodor**
    Carsten Curator
        Steinhauer, H. ed. Ten German novellas
The **storm.** Van Vogt, A. E.
**Storm**-bird, storm-dreamer. Ballard, J. G.
**Storm** in a teacup. Lu, Hsun
The **Storm**-King. Petaja, E.
The **storm** visitor. Prest, T. P.
**Storm** warning. Wollheim, D. A.
**STORMS**
    Christensen, L. E. The tempest
    Holmes, E. M. Crest of fear
    Holmes, E. M. End of summer
    Jansson, T. The fillyjonk who believed in
        disasters
    O'Flaherty, L. The landing
    Van Vogt, A. E. The storm
    Warner, S. T. Truth in the cup
    Zelazny, R. This moment of the storm
        *See also* Cyclones; Hurricanes; Snow
    storms
"A **story**," by John V. Marsch. Wolfe, G.
A **story** by Maupassant. O'Connor, F.
A **story** goes with it. Runyon, D.
**Story** hour. O'Connor, P. F.
The **story** of a cat. Newlove, J.
The **story** of a commercial venture. Chek-
    hov, A.
The **story** of a conscience. Bierce, A.
The **story** of a good dog. Stephens, J.
The **story** of a lie. Stevenson, R. L.
The **story** of a masterpiece. James, H.
The **story** of a non-marrying man. Lessing, D.
The **story** of a story. Friedman, P.
The **story** of a terribly strange bed. Col-
    lins, W.
The **story** of a year. James, H.
The **story** of an hour. Chopin, K.
The **Story** of Glam
    Green, R. L. ed. Thirteen uncanny tales
A **story** of historical interest. Wilson, A.
A **story** of love, etc. Curley, D.
The **story** of Muhammad Din. Kipling, R.
**Story** of the bandbox. Stevenson, R. L.
The **story** of the Deluge. Mitchell, E. P.
**Story** of the house with the green blinds.
    Stevenson, R. L.
**Story** of the kerchief of my mother. *See*
    Agnon, S. Y. The kerchief
The **story** of the late Mr Elvesham.
    Wells, H. G.
**Story** of the physician and the Saratoga
    trunk. Stevenson, R. L.
**Story** of the Saint Joseph's ass. Verga, G.
**Story** of the young man in holy orders.
    Stevenson, R. L.
**Story** of the young man with the cream tarts.
    Stevenson, R. L.
The **story** of Webster. Wodehouse, P. G.
The **story** of Yemilyan and the empty drum.
    Tolstoy, L.
The **story** teller. Brown, G. M.
**STORY-TELLING.** *See* Storytelling
**STORY WITHIN A STORY**
    Agnon, S. Y. Tehilah
    Aldiss, B. W. The expensive delicate ship
    Asimov, I. The up-to-date sorcerer
    Barlay, K.   A mistake of creation

**Street, Penelope**
  The magic apple
    The Best American short stories, 1972
A **street**. Morrison, A.
**STREET CARS.** *See* Street railroads
**STREET CLEANERS**
  Premchand. Penalty
**STREET PORTERS.** *See* Porters, Street
**STREET RAILROADS**
  Beneš, J. The problem
  Crane, S. The broken-down van
  Elmslie, K. Streetcar
**Street** scene. Laumer, K. and Ellison, H.
**STREET VENDORS.** *See* Vending stands
**STREET WALKERS.** *See* Prostitutes
**Streetcar.** Elmslie, K.
**Streetcorner** man. Borges, J. L.
**STREETS**
  Chesterton, G. K. The angry street
**Strength** of will. Beneš, J.
A **stretch** of the imagination. Garrett, R.
**Streuvels, Stijn**
  October
    Angoff, C. ed. Stories from The Literary
    Review
A **strict** upbringing. Assenov, D.
**Strictly** from the Mississippi. Maxwell, J. A.
**Striding** folly. Sayers, D. L.
**Strike** and fade. Dumas, H.
**Strikebreaker.** Asimov, I.
**STRIKES AND LOCKOUTS**
  Asimov, I. Strikebreaker
  Blum-Alquit, E. Ata Bakhartaunu: thou
    hast chosen us
  Heinlein, R. A. The roads must roll
  Slesinger, T. The mouse-trap
  Steinbeck, J.  A future we can't foresee
  Weissenberg, I. M.  A shtetl
    *See also* Sit-down strikes
**Strindberg, August**
  An attempt at reform
    Strindberg, A. Getting married
  Autumn
    Strindberg, A. Getting married
  Bad luck
    Strindberg, A. Getting married
  Blind faith
    Strindberg, A. Getting married
  Bread
    Strindberg, A. Getting married
  The bread-winner
    Strindberg, A. Getting married
  A business deal
    Strindberg, A. Getting married
  Cheated
    Strindberg, A. Getting married
  The child
    Strindberg, A. Getting married
  Compensation
    Strindberg, A. Getting married
  A doll's house
    Strindberg, A. Getting married
  Duel
    Strindberg, A. Getting married
  For payment
    Strindberg, A. Getting married
  His poem
    Strindberg, A. Getting married

  His servant; or, Debit and credit
    Strindberg, A. Getting married
  Idealistic demands
    Strindberg, A. Getting married
  It's not enough
    Strindberg, A. Getting married
  Just to be married
    Strindberg, A. Getting married
  Like doves
    Strindberg, A. Getting married
  Love and the price of grain
    Strindberg, A. Getting married
  Misfits
    Strindberg, A. Getting married
  Natural obstacles
    Strindberg, A. Getting married
  Nature the criminal
    Strindberg, A. Getting married
  Needs must
    Strindberg, A. Getting married
  The phoenix
    Strindberg, A. Getting married
  The reward of virtue
    Strindberg, A. Getting married
  The stronger
    Strindberg, A. Getting married
  Torn apart
    Strindberg, A. Getting married
  Unnatural selection; or, The origin of the
    race
    Strindberg, A. Getting married
  With or without the ceremony of marriage
    Strindberg, A. Getting married
The **string.** *See* Maupassant, G. de. The piece
  of string
The **striped** chest. Doyle, Sir A. C.
**STROKE.** *See* Paralysis
A **stroke** of good fortune. O'Connor, F.
**Stroke** of good luck. Kotzwinkle, W.
The **stroller** in the air. Ionesco, E.
A **strolling** brink. Glaze, E.
**STROLLING PLAYERS**
  Goudge, E. Saint Nicolas
**Strong, Jonathan**
  Patients
    Prize stories, 1970: The O. Henry
    Awards
    Strong, J. Tike, and five stories
  Quilty
    Strong, J. Tike, and five stories
  Sayin good-bye to Tom
    Strong, J. Tike, and five stories
  Suburban life
    Strong, J. Tike, and five stories
  Supperburger
    Strong, J. Tike, and five stories
  Tike
    Strong, J. Tike, and five stories
  Xavier Fereira's unfinished book: chapter
    one
    The Best American short stories, 1971
**Strong, Paschal N.**
  The airtight case
    Fenner, P. R. comp. Consider the evi-
    dence
**Strong** horse tea. Walker, A.
**Strong** is your hold O love. Costello, M.
**Strong** man. Tucci, N.
The **stronger.** Strindberg, A.

**Strongman, Kenneth**
The speculator
The Times of London Anthology of detective stories
The **strudel.** Horwitz, J.
**Strychnine** in the soup. Wodehouse, P. G.
**Stuart, Dee**
Man's best friend
Hitchcock, A. ed. Alfred Hitchcock presents: Stories to be read with the lights on
**Stuart, Don A.**
Forgetfulness
The Astounding-Analog reader v 1
Night
Asimov, I. ed. Where do we go from here?
Who goes there?
The Science fiction hall of fame v2A
*For other stories by this author see* Campbell, John W.
**Stuart, Jesse**
Appalachian patriarch
Stuart, J. Come back to the farm
The best years of our lives
Stuart, J. Come back to the farm
The blacksnake's operation
Stuart, J. Dawn of remembered spring
The builders and the dream
Stuart, J. Come back to the farm
A Christmas present for Uncle Bob
Stuart, J. Come gentle spring
Come gentle spring
Stuart, J. Come gentle spring
Confrontation
Stuart, J. Dawn of remembered spring
Dawn of remembered spring
Stuart, J. Dawn of remembered spring
Death for two
Stuart, J. Dawn of remembered spring
Disputing warriors
Stuart, J. Dawn of remembered spring
Does the Army always get its man?
Stuart, J. Come gentle spring
Eighty-one summers
Stuart, J. Come back to the farm
Fast-Train Ike
Stuart, J. Come gentle spring
Give Charlie a little time
Stuart, J. Come back to the farm
Grandpa Birdwell's last battle
Stuart, J. Dawn of remembered spring
The highest bidder
Stuart, J. Come back to the farm
Holiday with the Larks
Stuart, J. Come back to the farm
King of the hills
Stuart, J. Come gentle spring
A land beyond the river
Stuart, J. Come gentle spring
The last round up
Stuart, J. Come gentle spring
Little giant
Stuart, J. Come back to the farm
Lost land of youth
Stuart, J. Come back to the farm

Love
Stuart, J. Dawn of remembered spring
Tytell, J. and Jaffe, H. eds. Affinities
Love in the spring
Stuart, J. Come gentle spring
Mad Davids and a mechanical Goliath
Stuart, J. Come gentle spring
Maybelle's first-born
Stuart, J. Come back to the farm
No place for a hawk
Brown, E. P. ed. Twice fifteen
The old are valiant
Stuart, J. Dawn of remembered spring
Old Ben
Stuart, J. Dawn of remembered spring
Old Jackson was my teacher
Stuart, J. Dawn of remembered spring
The old law wasn't strong enough
Stuart, J. Come gentle spring
Our Wiff and Daniel Boone
Stuart, J. Come gentle spring
Pa's a man's man all right
Stuart, J. Come gentle spring
A pilgrim out in space
Stuart, J. Come back to the farm
Powderday's red hen
Stuart, J. Come gentle spring
The rainy day at Big Lost Creek
Stuart, J. Come gentle spring
Seventy-six days
Stuart, J. Come gentle spring
A thousand years is a long time
Stuart, J. Dawn of remembered spring
Time of the cottonmouth winds
Stuart, J. Dawn of remembered spring
The twelve-pole road
Stuart, J. Come back to the farm
Two worlds
Stuart, J. Come gentle spring
Uncle Fonse laughed
Stuart, J. Come gentle spring
Uncle Mel comes to the aid of his clan
Stuart, J. Come back to the farm
The usurper of Beauty Ridge
Stuart, J. Dawn of remembered spring
Victory and the dream
Stuart, J. Come back to the farm
Walk in the moon shadows
Matthews, J. ed. Archetypal themes in the modern story
The war and Cousin Lum
Stuart, J. Come gentle spring
The water penalty
Stuart, J. Come gentle spring
The weakling
Stuart, J. Come gentle spring
Why Menifee wasn't our country
Stuart, J. Come back to the farm
Wild plums
Stuart, J. Come back to the farm
The wind blew east
Brown, E. P. ed. Twice fifteen
Word and the flesh
Stuart, J. Dawn of remembered spring
Yoked for life
Stuart, J. Dawn of remembered spring
**Stubborn** Nadya. Zhurakhovich, S.

Stubbs, Jean
Are you there?
  Turner, J. ed. Unlikely ghosts
Cousin Lewis
  Winter's tales 16
The **student**. Chekhov, A.
**STUDENT HOUSING**. *See* Dormitories
**STUDENT PROTESTS**. *See* Students—Political activity
**STUDENT REVOLT**. *See* Students—Political activity
**STUDENTS**
Aidoo, A. A. Other versions
Alvarez, A. Laughter
Ansky, S. Behind a mask
Asimov, I. The hazing
Barthelme, D. Me and Miss Mandible
Birstein, A. When the wind blew
Brodeur, P. Blue lawns
Bukowski, C. Politics
Bullins, E. Mister newcomer
Carr, A. H. Z. The options of Timothy Merkle
Carrier, J. G. A strangeness of habit, a twist of mind
Chekhov, A. Volodya
Clarke, A. One among them
Dawson, F. Krazy Kat
De Saint Phalle, A. The dismembering of the donkey
Elmslie, K. My Holy City geography book
Emshwiller, C. The institute
Farrell, J. T. An American student in Paris
Fitzgerald, F. S. Basil and Cleopatra
Henderson, Z. The indelible kind
Henderson, Z. Loo Ree
Henderson, Z. Sharing time
Hesse, H. Edmund
Hesse, H. The Latin scholar
Hoffmann, E. T. A. The golden pot
Jacobs, H. Epilogue
Jacobs, H. The girl who drew the gods
Jacobs, H. The lion's share
Knowles, J. A turn with the sun
Larner, J. Oh, the wonder!
Madden, D. No trace
Michaels, L. Finn
Michaels, L. Manikin
Moravia, A. Doubles
Murray, A. Stonewall Jackson's Waterloo
Neugeboren, J. Luther
Oates, J. C. Accomplished desires
Premchand. My big brother
Pritchett, V. S. Creative writing
Ribnikar, J. You
Selzer, R. A. A single minute of fear
Smith, E. E. Calliope and Gherkin and the Yankee Doodle thing
Stafford, J. The echo and the nemesis
Steegmuller, F. The doomed terrapin
Stewart, J. I. M. The men
Theroux, P. A love knot
Tuohy, F. The trap
Updike, J. One of my generation
Weaver, G. Finch the spastic speaks
Yglesias, J. The guns in the closet
Yü, Ta-fu. Sinking

Zobarskas, S. Young love
  *See also* College life; College students; Dropouts; Medical students; Negro students; School life
**Political activity**
Goulart, R. Rake
McNair, K. Sign here. And here
**STUDENTS, MEDICAL**. *See* Medical students
**STUDENTS, NEGRO**. *See* Negro students
**STUDENTS, THEOLOGICAL**. *See* Seminarians
The **stuffing** of the Lord. Ulibarri, S. R.
**STUNT FLYING**. *See* Air pilots
**STUNT MEN**
Algren, N. The passion of upside-down-Emil
The **stupid** Christs. Bukowski, C.
**Sturgeon, Theodore**
And now the news
  Knight, D. ed. Tomorrow and tomorrow
Baby is three
  The Science fiction hall of fame v2A
Brownshoes
  Sturgeon, T. Sturgeon is alive and well . . .
Cactus dance
  Sturgeon, T. and Ward, D. Sturgeon's West
Crate
  Sturgeon, T. Sturgeon is alive and well . . .
Fluffy
  Parry, M. ed. Beware of the cat
The girl who knew what they meant
  Sturgeon, T. Sturgeon is alive and well . . .
Helix the cat
  Astounding
The hurkle is a happy beast
  Silverberg, R. ed. The Science fiction bestiary
  Yolen, J. comp. Zoo 2000
It was nothing—really!
  Sturgeon, T. Sturgeon is alive and well . . .
It's you!
  Sturgeon, T. Sturgeon is alive and well . . .
Jorry's gap
  Sturgeon, T. Sturgeon is alive and well . . .
The man who learned loving
  The Best from Fantasy and Science Fiction; 19th ser.
  Nebula award stories 5
Microcosmic god
  Science fiction hall of fame v 1
The nail and the oracle
  Hitchcock, A. ed. Alfred Hitchcock presents: Stories to stay awake by
Occam's scalpel
  Del Rey, L. ed. Best science fiction stories of the year [1972]
One foot and the grave
  Haining, P. ed. The witchcraft reader

**Sturgeon, Theodore**—*Continued*
  The patterns of Dorne
    Sturgeon, T. Sturgeon is alive and
      well . . .
  Scars
    Sturgeon, T. and Ward, D. Sturgeon's
      West
  The sheriff of Chayute
    Sturgeon, T. and Ward, D. Sturgeon's
      West
  The Silken-swift . . .
    Silverberg, B. ed. Phoenix feathers
  Slow sculpture
    Nebula award stories 6
    Sturgeon, T. Sturgeon is alive and
      well . . .
  Suicide
    Sturgeon, T. Sturgeon is alive and
      well . . .
  Take care of Joey
    Sturgeon, T. Sturgeon is alive and
      well . . .
  Thunder and roses
    The Astounding-Analog reader v2
  To here and the easel
    Sturgeon, T. Sturgeon is alive and
      well . . .
  A touch of strange
    Ferman, E. L. and Mills, R. P. eds.
      Twenty years of The Magazine of
      Fantasy and Science Fiction
  Uncle Fremmis
    Sturgeon, T. Sturgeon is alive and
      well . . .
  Well spiced
    Sturgeon, T. and Ward, D. Sturgeon's
      West
  The world well lost
    Scortia, T. N. ed. Strange bedfellows
**Sturgeon, Theodore, and Ellison, Harlan**
  Runesmith
    Ellison, H. Partners in wonder
**Sturgeon, Theodore, and Ward, Don**
  The man who figured everything
    Sturgeon, T. and Ward, D. Sturgeon's
      West
  Ride in, ride out
    Sturgeon, T. and Ward, D. Sturgeon's
      West
  The waiting thing inside
    Sturgeon, T. and Ward, D. Sturgeon's
      West
A **style** in treason. Blish, J.
**Styron, William**
  Hark: 1831, Virginia
    Burnett, W. ed. Black hands on a white
      face
A **subject** of childhood. Paley, G.
**Subject** to change. Goulart, R.
**Sublimating.** Updike, J.
The **subliminal** man. Ballard, J. G.
The **submarine** boat. Ashdown, C.
**SUBMARINE CABLES.** *See* Cables, Sub-
    marine
**SUBMARINE DIVING.** *See* Diving, Sub-
    marine
**SUBMARINE WARFARE**
  Forester, C. S. Intelligence
  Forester, C. S. Night stalk

**SUBMARINES**
  Engelhardt, F. The Kraken
**Subpoena.** Barthelme, D.
**SUBTEENS.** *See* Children
**SUBTERRANEAN COLONIES**
  Forster, E. M. The machine stops
**SUBTERRANEAN PASSAGES.** *See* Hid-
    ing-places (Secret chambers, etc.)
**Suburban** idyll. Boyle, P.
**SUBURBAN LIFE**
  Blake, G.  A modern development
  Cheever, J. The embarkment for Cythera
  Claiborne, S. The great western civiliza-
    tion caper
  Davis, O. The lodge pin
  Marshall, L. The confrontation
  Munro, A. The shining houses
  Oates, J. C. The children
  Patton, F. G. The music of the spheres
  Roth, P. Eli, the fanatic
  Silverberg, R. What we learned from this
    morning's newspaper
  Whalen, T. Chozen at four a.m.
  Yurick, S. Do they talk about Genêt in
    Larchmont?
**Suburban** life. Strong, J.
**Suburban** tigress. Treat, L.
**SUBVERSIVE ACTIVITIES**
  Bukowski, C. Politics
  Gilbert, M. The African tree beavers
  Gilbert, M. The peaceful people
    *See also* Spies
A **subway** named Mobius. Deutsch, A. J.
**SUBWAYS**
  Asimov, I. and MacCreigh, J. The little
    man on the subway
  Davidson, A. The Sixty-Third Street sta-
    tion
  Deutsch, A. J.  A subway named Mobius
  Fox, R.  A fable
  Michaels, L. Getting lucky
  Peck, R. E. Gantlet
**SUCCESS**
  Aguallo, T. Doing well
  Bodelsen, A. Success
  Deutschman, B. Gittel Branfman the im-
    possible
  Deutschman, B. So this is called success?
  Fitz Gerald, G. The top
  Lafferty, R. A. Slow Tuesday night
    *See also* Self-made men
**Success.** Bodelsen, A.
The **success.** Logan, J.
**Success** of a mission. Arden, W.
**SUCCESSION.** *See* Inheritance and succes-
    sion
**Such** a good idea. Newman, A.
**Such** darling dodos. Wilson, A.
**Such** interesting neighbors. Finney, J.
**Sucker.** McCullers, C.
**SUDAN.** *See* Africa, West
**Sue, Eugene**
  The wandering Jew's sentence
    Haining, P. ed. Gothic tales of terror
**Sue.** O'Connor, F.
**SUFFERING**
  West, J. Night piece for Julia
  Wiesel, E. The accident

**Suffering** women. Jhabvala, R. P.

The **sufferings** of a boy. Meyer, C. F.

**SUFFOLK.** *See* England, Provincial and rural—Suffolk

**SUFFRAGE**

Brown, S. And/or

    *See also* Negroes—Suffrage

**SUGAR**

Achebe, C. Sugar Baby

**Sugar** Baby. Achebe, C.

**SUICIDE**

An, Su-Gil. The green chrysanthemum

Barr, S. The locked house

Betts, D. Hitchhiker

Block, L. Death wish

Bontemps, A.   A summer tragedy

Bowen, M. Cambric tea

Brennan, J. P. Death mask

Brennan, J. P. The way to the attic

Burke, T. The Chink and the child

Carr, C. Inside

Cather, W. Consequences

Cather, W. Paul's case

Cather, W. Peter

Chekhov, A. Volodya

Colette. The landscape

Collier, J. Halfway to Hell

Coover, R. Klee dead

Cronin, A. J. The strange meeting

Dennison, G. On being a son

Dick, P. K. The electric ant

Di Donato, P. In the wide waste

Disch, T. M. The number you have reached

Dozois, G. R. Machines of loving grace

Drake, R. Pretty boy

Edelstein, S. The exhibition

Ellison, H. Lonelyache

Forester, C. S. The man who didn't ask why

Fox, J.   A purple rhododendron

Fremlin, C. The betrayal

Friedman, P. An evening of fun

Friedman, P.   A matter of survival

García Márquez, G. Leaf storm

Gilbert, A. When suns collide

Hamelink, J.   A pause in the thunder

Heard, G. The cat, "I Am"

Henry, O. The furnished room

Hippius, Z. It's all for the worse

Holmes, E. M. Monday through Friday

Holmes, E. M. Not for hire

Hughes, M. G. The Judge

Innes, M. Comedy of discomfiture

James, H. Osborne's revenge

Jepson, E. and Eustace, R. The tea-leaf

Johnson, D. The taking of our own lives

Kafka, F. The judgment

Keller, D. H.   A piece of linoleum

Kelley, W. M.   A good long sidewalk

Kemp, A. The blue of madness

Lagerkvist, P.   A hero's death

Landolfi, T. The calculation of probability

McKern, R. O. When my father died

Madden, D. No trace

Madden, D. The shadow knows

Maddow, B. You, Johann Sebastian Bach

Maloney, R. Natalie

Maltz, A. Sunday morning on Twentieth Street

Marqués, R. There's a body reclining on the stern

Maupassant, G. de. The duel

Maupassant, G. de. A little walk

Maupassant, G. de. Miss Harriet

Maximov, H. The ultimate threshold

Michaels, L. Manikin

Milner, R. The ray

Minot, S. Journey to Ocean Grove

Mishima, Y. Patriotism

Narokov, N. The black something

Naylor, P. R. To love mercy

Niven, L. All the myriad ways

Oates, J. C. Bodies

Oates, J. C. Plot

Oates, J. C. The wheel of love

O'Connor, F. An act of charity

O'Hara, J. Andrea

O'Hara, J. The hardware man

O'Hara, J. He thinks he owns me

O'Hara, J. Nil nisi

O'Hara, J. The O'Hara generation

O'Hara, J. Requiescat

O'Neil, D. Report on a broken bridge

Ousmane, S. Black girl

Ozick, C. The pagan rabbi

Pai, Hsien-yung. Li T'ung: a Chinese girl in New York

Petaja, E. Where is thy sting

Porges, A. The reason

Price, R. Good and bad dreams

Rathjen, C. H. Jump job

Rice, C. Hard sell

Ritchie, J.   A taste for murder

Sambrot, W. That touch of genius

Sargent, P.   A sense of difference

Šćepanović, B. The death of Mr Goluža

Schnitzler, A. Fräulein Else

Singer, I. B. The bishop's robe

Slater, E. The Sooey pill

Sontag, S. Debriefing

Stafford, J. The philosophy lesson

Stevenson, R. L. Story of the young man with the cream tarts

Strongman, K. The speculator

Sturgeon, T. Suicide

Summers, H. The man from Cord's

Tindall, G. Mother Russia

Verga, G. The last day

Warner, S. T. But at the stroke of midnight

West, J. Up a tree

Wilson, A. After the show

Woolrich, C. Too nice a day to die

Yurick, S.   . . . And a friend to sit by your side

Zamyatin, E. The cave

    *See also* Funeral rites and ceremonies

**SUICIDE, ATTEMPTED.** *See* Suicide

**Suicide.** Sturgeon, T.

The **suitable** surroundings. Bierce, A.

The **suitcase.** Mphahlele, E.

The **suitcase.** Ozick, C.

The **suitcase.** Vassilikos, V.

The **suitor.** Woiwode, L.

**SUITS.** *See* Clothing and dress

**Sukenick, Ronald**
The birds
  Sukenick, R. The death of the novel,
    and other stories
The death of the novel
  Sukenick, R. The death of the novel,
    and other stories
The kite
  New American Review no. 1
Momentum
  Sukenick, R. The death of the novel,
    and other stories
The permanent crisis
  Sukenick, R. The death of the novel,
    and other stories
Roast beef: a slice of life
  Sukenick, R. The death of the novel,
    and other stories
What's your story
  Sukenick, R. The death of the novel,
    and other stories
**SUKKOS.** See Sukkoth
**SUKKOTH**
  Shapiro, L. Wings
**Sulak.** Babel, I.
**SULTANS**
  Roditi, E. The Sultan's Little Harum-
    scarum
The **Sultan's** Little Harum-scarum. Roditi, E.
**SUMATRA**
  Saltus, E. A transient guest
The **Sumerian** oath. Farmer, P. J.
**SUMMER**
  Friedman, P. In equal parts
  Hesse, H. Klingsor's last summer
**Summer** by the sea. Aiken, J.
**SUMMER CAMPS.** See Camps, Summer
**Summer** candles. Boles, P. D.
**SUMMER COLONIES.** See Summer resorts
**SUMMER COTTAGES.** See Summer
    homes; Summer resorts
A **summer** day. Stafford, J.
**Summer** eve at "Rockall." Hoydal, K.
**SUMMER HOMES**
  Kanin, G. The grand illumination
  Laurence, M. The loons
  Seth, R. The recluse of Kotka Veski
  Warner, L. Melissa Savage
The **summer** of his discontent. Rindfleisch, N.
The **summer** of the beautiful white horse.
    Saroyan, W.
The **summer** of the Irish Sea. Grant, C. L.
**Summer** people. Greenberg, J.
**Summer** people. Hemingway, E.
**SUMMER RESORTS**
  Barth, J. Lost in the funhouse
  Bingham, S. Rachel's island
  Brennan, J. P. Black thing at midnight
  Carpenter, D. The murder of the frogs
  Chopin, K. The awakening
  Dickinson, M. A murderous slice
  Fitzgerald, F. S. A nice quiet place
  Grau, S. A. The beginning of summer
  Greene, S. The invisible monster
  Hale, L. P. The Peterkins at the farm
  Litvinov, I. Flight from Bright Shores
  Litvinov, I. Portrait of a lady
  Maloney, R. Last stop before the carbarn
  Maloney, R. Yankee go home

  Mann, T. Mario and the magician
  O'Brien, E. Paradise
  Phillips, R. A lady of fashion
  Rush, N. Riding
  Rye, A. My man Closters
  Sherwin, J. J. The olde daunce
  Wain, J. The life guard
    See also Seaside resorts; Vacations
A **summer** tragedy. Bontemps, A.
**SUMMER VACATIONS.** See Vacations
**Summer** voices. Banville, J.
**SUMMER WORK CAMPS.** See Camps,
    Summer
**Summers, Hollis**
  Cafe Nore
    Summers, H. How they chose the dead
  The cardboard screen
    Summers, H. How they chose the dead
  How they chose the dead
    Summers, H. How they chose the dead
  If you don't go out the way you came in
    Summers, H. How they chose the dead
  Love
    Summers, H. How they chose the dead
  The man from Cord's
    Summers, H. How they chose the dead
  Mister Joseph Botts
    Summers, H. How they chose the dead
  The penitent
    Summers, H. How they chose the dead
  The prayer meeting
    Summers, H. How they chose the dead
  The terrible death of Mister Vimont
    Summers, H. How they chose the dead
  The third ocean
    Oates, J. C. ed. Scenes from American
      life
    Summers, H. How they chose the dead
  The woman who loved everybody
    Summers, H. How they chose the dead
**Summers, Merna**
  The blizzard
    New Canadian stories, 73
**Summers, Montague**
  The grimoire
    Haining, P. ed. The nightmare reader
**Summer's** day. O'Hara, J.
**Summon** the watch! Davidson, A.
A **summons** for the blacksmith. Brú, H.
**Sun, Hsi-chen**
  Ah Ao
    Katz, N. and Milton, N. eds. Fragment
      from a lost diary, and other stories
**SUN**
  Clement, H. Proof
  Fast, H. Not with a bang
    See also Space flight to the sun
**Sun.** Filer, B.
**Sun.** Maia, C. V.
The **sun** of the blind night. Shahu, M. N.
**Sun** spot. Clement, H.
The **sun** stood still. Macdougall, A. R.
**Sunburst.** Thorp, R.
**Sundance.** Silverberg, R.
**SUNDAY**
  Knight, E. Never come Monday
  Weaver, G. Nigger Sunday
  Wylie, P. Once on a Sunday

**Supperburger.** Strong, J.

**Support** your local police. Bullins, E.

The **supremacy** of the Hunza. Greenberg, J.

**Surface** tension. Blish, J.

**SURGEONS**
Lang, A. The man in white
Riddell, C. The Banshee's warning
Simak, C. D. Huddling place

**SURGERY**
Beckett, S. Yellow
Breslow, P. Before the operation
Bukowski, C. All the assholes in the world and mine
Cortázar, J. Nurse Cora
Drake, R. They cut her open and then just sewed her back up
Gawsworth, J. The shifting growth
Pilnyak, B. The death of the Army Commander: a tale of the unextinguished moon
Stafford, J. The interior castle

**SURGERY, PLASTIC**
Bukowski, C. ⛨ [Swastika]
Nesvadba, J. The lost face

**SURNAMES.** *See* Names, Personal

The **surprise.** Zobarskas, S.

**SURPRISE ENDINGS**
Anmar, F. Jenny among the zeebs
Baldwin, J. The man child
Beeding, F. Death by judicial hanging
Bloch, R. Untouchable
Bova, B. Stars, won't you hide me?
Bova, B. Test in orbit
Brunner, J. You'll take the high road
Campbell, R. The lost
Cheever, J. Three stories: III
Du Maurier, D. A border-line case
Einstein, C. The new deal
Eisenberg, L. The two lives of Ben Coulter
Fish, R. L. Hijack
Fleming, G. Boomerang
Gloeckner, C. N. Miscount
Graham, W. At the Chalet Lartrec
Graham, W. The basket chair
Graham, W. The Cornish farm
Graham, W. The Medici earring
Gray, L. The little old lady from Cricket Creek
Haldeman, J. W. Counterpoint
Jackson, S. One ordinary day, with peanuts
Jacobi, C. Round Robin
Jacobi, C. Sequence
James, A. The Ohio love sculpture
Jeffrey, W. Shell game
Jones, L. The great clock
Kantor, M. A man who had no eyes
Kennedy, M. Death in the kitchen
O'Flaherty, L. The sniper
Ritchie, J. Ten minutes from now
Saki. The reticence of Lady Anne
Schwimmer, W. Everything was perfect but . . .
Tanburn, M. Night strike
Treat, L. The motive
Waugh, E. Mr Loveday's little outing
Woolrich, C. The penny-a-worder

The **surprise** pastry. Ayrton, M.

**SURREALISM.** *See* Experimental stories; Symbolism

The **surrender** of Forty Fort. Crane, S.

**Sursum** corda (Lift up your hearts). White, E.

**SURTSEY**
Lumley, B. Rising with Surtsey

**SURVEYING**
Carr, T. Hop-friend

The **surveyor.** Roth, H.

**SURVIVAL (AFTER AIRPLANE ACCIDENTS, SHIPWRECKS, ETC.)**
Brown, F. Something green
Bryant, E. Among the dead
Davis, R. L. Teratohippus
Dickson, G. R. Building on the line
Dickson, G. R. On Messenger Mountain
Farmer, P. J. Mother
Forester, C. S. Dr Blanke's first command
Fritch, C. E. The castaway
Goulart R. The Katy dialogues
Hood, H. After the sirens
Hughes, T. Snow
Laumer, K. Three blind mice
London, J. Love of life
Lütgen, K. Robinson Crusoe's Russian rivals
McAllister, B. Prime-time teaser
Price, R. Walking lessons
Reynolds, M. Among the bad baboons
Scott, R. Maybe Jean-Baptiste Pierre Antoine de Monet, Chevalier de Lamarck, was a little bit right
Sturgeon, T. Crate
Thomason, J. W. Air Patrol
Williamson, G. They ate their young shipmate
*See also* Wilderness survival

**Survival.** Beal, M. F.

The **survivor.** Bambara, T. C.

The **survivor.** Glanville, B.

**Survivor #1.** Slesar, H. and Ellison, H.

**Survivors.** Kempton, M.

**SUSPENDED ANIMATION.** *See* Sleep, Prolonged

**SUSPENSE.** *See* Adventure and adventurers; International intrigue; Manhunts; Murder stories; Mystery and detective stories

**Suter, John F.**
Doctor's orders
Hitchcock, A. ed. Alfred Hitchcock presents: Stories to stay awake by

**Sutiasumarga, Rusman**
On the outskirts of the city
Katz, N. and Milton, N. eds. Fragment from a lost diary, and other stories

**SUTOKU, EMPEROR OF JAPAN**
Uyeda, A. Exiled

**Suttee.** Auchincloss, L.

**Sutton, Jeff**
Forerunner
Elwood, R. and Ghidalia, V. eds. Androids, time machines and blue giraffes

**Sutton, Lee**
Soul mate
Mohs, M. ed. Other worlds, other gods

**SWINDLERS AND SWINDLING**—*Continued*

Updike, J.   A gift from the city
> *See also* Fraud; Hoaxes; Imposters and imposture; Quacks and quackery

**SWINDLING.** *See* Swindlers and swindling

**SWISS ALPS.** *See* Alps, Swiss

**SWISS IN ALGERIA**

Bowles, P. The time of friendship

**SWITCHBOARD OPERATORS.** *See* Telephone workers

The **switchman.** Arreola, J. J.

**SWITZERLAND**

Blackwood, A. The attic
Edwards, A. My brother's ghost story
Hauptmann, G. The heretic of Soana
Hemingway, E. Cross-country snow
Hoffmann, E. T. A. The doubles
Rosenberg, E. Our Felix
> *See also* Alps, Swiss

         **Vevey**

James, H. Daisy Miller

**Swoboda, Nancy C.**
Christopher Frame
> Hitchcock, A. ed. Alfred Hitchcock presents: Stories to be read with the lights on

The **sword.** Betts, D.
The **sword.** Landolfi, T.
**Sword** game. Hollis, H. H.

**SWORDS**

Landolfi, T. The sword

**Sydney** / I am beginning to see. Miller, J.

**SYLVESTER II, POPE**

Ayrton, M. The six syllables

**Sylvia.** Henderson, D.

**SYMBIOSIS**

Mrozek, S. The Ugupu bird
Schmitz, J. H. Grandpa
Sheckley, R. Starting from scratch

**SYMBOLISM**

Barth, J. Night-sea journey
Bernard, K. The queen of moths
Carr, C. Inside
Corvo, F. Baron. Why the rose is red
Farmer, P. J. Mother Earth wants you
Fast, H. The pragmatic seed
Fitz Gerald, G. The top
Gansovski, S. The proving ground
Hall, J. B. Us he devours
Jones, L. The eye of the lens
Kafka, F. Blumfeld, an elderly bachelor
Kafka, F.   A dream
Kawabata, Y. One arm
Koolhaas, A.   A hole in the ceiling
Lu, Hsun.   A madman's diary
Merwin, W. S. The locker room
Nemerov, H. The nature of the task
Paz, O. My life with the wave
Schroeder, A. The late man
Schroeder, A. The mill
Schultz, J. The hickory stick rider
Shui, Ching. Hi Lili hi Li . . .
Singh, D. Retaliation
Spielberg, P. The architecture of the city
Stanton, M. The bastard
Thomas, D. Gaspar, Melchoir, Balthasar

Thomas, D. The Holy Six
Thomas, D. Prologue to an adventure
Tieck, J. L. The Runenberg
Walker, A. The diary of an African nun
•Weaver, G. The entombed man of Thule
> *See also* Allegories

**Symons, Julian**
Eight minutes to kill
> Kahn, J. ed. Some things fierce and fatal
Experiment in personality
> Ellery Queen's Mystery Magazine. Ellery Queen's Mystery bag
The impossible theft
> Dickinson, S. ed. The drugged cornet, and other mystery stories
Love affair
> Ellery Queen's Mystery Magazine. Ellery Queen's Grand slam
A theme for Hyacinth
> Ellery Queen's Mystery Magazine. Ellery Queen's Murder menu

**SYMPATHY**

Jacobson, D. The game
Lispector, C. Love
McElroy, J. The accident
> *See also* Empathy

**Symphony** no. 6 in C minor The tragic, by Ludwig van Beethoven II. Jones, L.

**Symptomaticus** medicus. Nourse, A. E.

**SYMPTOMS.** *See* Diagnosis

**SYNAGOGUES**

Ruskay, S. Allah will understand

**SYNTHETIC FOOD.** *See* Food, Artificial

**SYPHILIS.** *See* Venereal diseases

**SYRIA**

         **Damascus**

Smith, C. A. The kiss of Zoraida
The **system.** Gilbert, M.
The **system.** Steegmuller, F.
The **system** of Doctor Tarr and Professor Fether. *See* Poe, E. A. The lunatics

**Szilard, Leo**
Calling all stars
> Kahn, J. ed. Some things dark and dangerous
The Mark Gable Foundation
> Harrison, H. ed. The light fantastic

         **T**

**T** as in threat. Treat, L.
A **table** is a table. Bichsel, P.
**Tablets** of stone. Hufford, L.

**TABOO**

Stevenson, R. L. The beach of Falesá

**Tabori, Paul**
The bridge
> Turner, J. ed. Unlikely ghosts
Janus
> Burke, J. ed. Tales of unease

The **tachypomp.** Mitchell, E. P.
**Tactics.** Bryant, E.
The **tactics** of hunger. Gilliatt, P.
**Ta-fu Yü.** *See* Yü, Ta-fu
**Tai Fu** and Pansy Greers. Burke, T.

**TAIL**
Benét, S. V. The King of the Cats
Carlson, E. Heads you win
The tail-tied kings. Davidson, A.
The tailor who told the truth. Willard, N.

**TAILORS**
Alvarez, A. Laughter
Blum-Alquit, E. Ata Bakhartaunu: thou hast chosen us
Cecil, H. Made to measure
Dorman, S. Harry the tailor
Keller, G. Clothes make the man
Malamud, B. The death of me
Simenon, G. Blessed are the meek
Vincenz, S. A rarity
Willard, N. The tailor who told the truth

**Tailpipe** to disaster. Sheckley, R.

**TAIWAN.** *See* Formosa

**Tajinko** Village. Ibuse, M.

**Take** a match. Asimov, I.

**Take** another look. Ritchie, J.

**Take** care of Joey. Sturgeon, T.

**Take** it easy, Edna. Hemenway, R.

**Take** it or leave it. Masson, D. I.

**Take** Wooden Indians. Davidson, A.

**Take** your own sweet sorrow. Olwyler, J. P.

**Takeda, Taijun**
The bridge
Angoff, C. ed. Stories from The Literary Review

**Taking** chances. Rascoe, J.

The **taking** of our own lives. Johnson, D.

**Tal** Taulai Khan. Lamb, H.

A **tale** for a chimney corner. Hunt, L.

A **tale** in a club. Seymour, W. K.

**Tale** of a return. Irbe, A.

A **tale** of mere chance. Crane, S.

The **tale** of Sir Jeremy Fisher. Carleton, D.

A **tale** of Sir John Maundeville, Smith, C. A.

A **tale** of the ending. Harrison, H.

The **tale** of the fourth stranger. Coburn, A.

The **tale** of the mysterious mirror. Scott, Sir W.

The **tale** of the peasant Osip. Curley, D.

The **tale** of the scribe. Agnon, S. Y.

The **tale** of the silver saucer and the transparent apple. Ransome, A.

The **tale** of the squint-eyed, left-handed Smith of Tula and the steel flea. *See* Leskov, N. The steel flea

A **tale** of the unextinguished moon. *See* Pilnyak, B. The death of the Army Commander: a tale of the unextinguished moon

A **tale** of the white pyramid. Cather, W.

A **tale** without a title. Chekhov, A.

**TALENT.** *See* Genius

The **talent** of Harvey. Fast, H.

**Tales** of Diego. Allen, J. H.

**Talk** to the music. Bontemps, A.

**TALKATIVENESS.** *See* Conversation

**TALKING.** *See* Conversation

**Talking** bout Sonny. Bambara, T. C.

**Talking** horse. Malamud, B.

The **talking** trees. O'Faolain, S.

**Tall, Stephen**
The bear with the knot on his tail
The Best from Fantasy & Science Fiction; 20th ser.

**Tall** boy. Taylor, E.

**Tall** story. Allingham, M.

A **tall** tale. Val Baker, D.

**TALL TALES.** *See* Improbable stories

The **tallow** candle. Shearing, J.

**Talman, Wilfred Blanch**
Two black bottles
Lovecraft, H. P. ed. The horror in the museum, and other revisions

**Talpa.** Rulfo, J.

**Tam** Mackie's trial. MacDiarmid, H.

**TAMALES**
Peirce, J. F. The hot tamales murder case

**Tamango.** Mérimée, P.

**Tammuz, Benjamin**
Angioxyl, a rare cure
Rabikovitz, D. ed. The new Israeli writers
An enigma
Michener, J. A. ed. First fruits

**Tanburn, Miel**
Night strike
Best detective stories of the year [1969]

**Tang.** Himes, C.

**Tangled** hearts. Wodehouse, P. G.

**Tanizaki, Junichiro**
The thief
Shimer, D. B. ed. Voices of modern Asia

The **tank** trapeze. Moorcock, M.

**TANK TRUCKS**
Cady, J. The burning

**TANKS (MILITARY SCIENCE)**
Beneš, J. Expertise
Forester, C. S. An egg for the major

**Tante** Sadie and the matches. Deutschman, B.

**Tanya.** Humphreys, L. G.

**TANZANIA**
Hokororo, A. M.   A day off
Mbilinyi, M. J.   A woman's life

**Tao Kim Hai**
The cock
Shimer, D. B. ed. Voices of modern Asia

**TAPE RECORDINGS**
Auchincloss, L. The double gap
Bradbury, R. Night call, collect

The **tapestried** chamber. Scott, Sir W.

**TAPESTRY**
Delaney, S. R. The unicorn tapestry

**Tarantella.** Yurick, S.

**Tarasov-Rodyonov, Alexander**
Chocolate
Pomorska, K. ed. Fifty years of Russian prose: from Pasternak to Solzhenitsyn v 1

**Tarciso.** Queiroz, D. S. de

**Targan, Barry**
The clay war
American Review 18
Harry Belten and the Mendelssohn Violin Concerto
Elkin, S. ed. Stories from the sixties

**Tarkington, Booth**
The veiled feminists of Atlantis
Moskowitz, S. ed. When women rule

The **tarn** of sacrifice. Blackwood, A.

**TARPON FISHING**
Brister, B. El papa sabalo

**Tartan.** Brown, G. M.

TEACHERS—*Continued*
Moore, R.  A different drummer
Moravia, A. The sister-in-law
Mudrick, M. Cleopatra
Neugeboren, J. Finkel
Neugeboren, J. Luther
Nieh, Hua-ling. The several blessings of Wang Ta-nien
Oates, J. C. Accomplished desires
Oates, J. C. The dead
Oates, J. C. In the region of ice
Oates, J. C. Normal love
Oates, J. C. Saul Bird says: Relate! Communicate! Liberate!
O'Connor, F. The barber
O'Connor, F. The teacher's mass
O'Faolain, S. Brainsy
O'Hara, J. The industry and the Professor
Patton, F. G. The educated classes
Patton, F. G. Grade 5B and the well-fed rat
Patton, F. G. Remold it nearer
Patton, F. G. The second-grade mind
Patton, F. G. The terrible Miss Dove
Phillips, R.  A teacher's rewards
Pei, M. Kandyce is the winner
Petry, A. The necessary knocking on the door
Petry, A. The witness
Pritchett, V. S. Creative writing
Purdy, J. Goodnight, sweetheart
Queen, E. Object lesson
Rees, B. Poor Margaret
Rosenak, M. Behold the dreamer
Rosten, L. Christopher K*A*P*L*A*N
Rothberg, A. The animal trainer
Ruskay, S.  A truth to live by
Ruskay, S. Why bother with Solly?
Sax, F. The crossroads of history
Sax, F. Et tu, Uncle Tom
Sax, F. Nouveaux riches
Shapiro, L. With vigor!
Singer, I. B. The briefcase
Sisskind, M.  A mean teacher
Solzhenitsyn, A. For the good of the cause
Solzhenitsyn, A. Matryona's house
Stafford, J. Caveat emptor
Stafford, J. The liberation
Stein, G. Fernhurst
Stewart, J. I. M. The men
Strindberg, A. Needs must
Sukenick, R. The death of the novel
Sukenick, R. Momentum
Taylor, E. The devastating boys
Taylor, E. Miss A. and Miss M.
Taylor, P. Dean of men
Taylor, P. Miss Leonora when last seen
Telfair, D. In a quart of water
Theroux, P. Dog days
Theroux, P. Memories of a curfew
Theroux, P.  A political romance
Thurston, J. The cross
Trevisan, D.  A visit to the teacher
Trevor, W. Miss Smith
Trilling, L. Of this time, of that place
Tuohy, F. The broken bridge
Tuohy, F. The trap
Updike, J. Tomorrow and tomorrow and so forth

Walker, A. Her sweet Jerome
Walker, A. We drink the wine in France
Walsh, D. J. The rings of the Papaloi
Weaver, G. Elements of the 10th Mountain Infantry reconnoiter
West, J. The condemned librarian
Wilhelm, K. The funeral
Williams, J. A. The figure eight
Wilson, A. Higher standards
Wilson, A. Totentanz
Wilson, C. The brief, swinging career of Dan and Judy Smythe
Wolfe, B. The girl with rapid eye movements
Wolfe, G. Morning-glory
Wolfe, G. Remembrance to come
Wolfe, G. The toy theater
Yashpal. To uphold righteousness
    *See also* Music teachers; Scholars; School life; Tutors
The **teacher's** mass. O'Connor, F.
A **teacher's** rewards. Phillips, R.
**TEACHING**
#### Aids and devices
    *See* Programmed instruction
**Teaching** Jim. Peterkin, J.
**TEACHING MACHINES**
Eisenberg, L. The mighty Matterhorn
**Tear** up the orders! Gulick, B.
**Tears** the world does not see. Chekhov, A.
**Technical** adviser. Oliver, C.
**Technical** slip. Wyndham, J.
**TECHNICAL WRITING**
Harness, C. L. An ornament to his profession
**TECHNOLOGY**
Forster, E. M. The machine stops
**Technology** and a technocrat. Steinbeck, J.
**TECHNOLOGY AND CIVILIZATION**
Ballard, J. G. The subliminal man
Dick, P. K. Autofac
Reynolds, M. Among the bad baboons
**TEDDY BEARS**
Harrison, H.  I always do what Teddy says
**Tedlock, E. W.**
'Tis a fond ambush
Insights
**TEEN-AGERS.** *See* Adolescence
**TEETH**
Dillon, M. "Buttons are made of animal blood"
LeClézio, J. M. G. The day Beaumont became acquainted with his pain
#### Diseases
Stuart, J. Maybelle's first-born
The **teeth.** Fiedler, L. A.
**TEETH, ARTIFICIAL**
Fiedler, L. A. The teeth
Holmes, E. M. Mitch
**TEHERAN.** *See* Iran—Teheran
**Tehilah.** Agnon, S. Y.
**Teichner, Albert**
Christlings
Orbit 10
**Tekayo.** Ogot, G.
**TEL AVIV.** *See* Israel—Tel Aviv

They won't crack it open. Kim, Y. I.
Thi Bong Dzu. Rottmann, L.
. . . thicker than water. Salpeter, S.
The thief. Tanizaki, J.
The thief and his little daughter. Brandão, R.
A thief in the temples. Midwood, B.
Thief of time. Sharp, M.
THIEVES
   Achebe, C. Civil peace
   Acton, H. The gift horse
   Algren, N.   I guess you fellows just don't
      want me
   Andersen, B. The passage
   Barker, S. O. Champs at the Chuckabug
   Bester, A. The Flowered Thundermug
   Borges, J. L. Ibn Hakkan al-Bokhari, dead
      in his labyrinth
   Brandão, R. The thief and his little daugh-
      ter
   Colette. The burglar
   Collins, W. The biter bit
   DeFord, M. A. The eel
   Delattre, P. The decompensator of Lhasa
   Dinesen, I. The ring
   Fejes, E. Engagement
   Fremlin, C. Old Daniel's treasure
   Gorky, M. Chelkash
   Grau, S. A. The thieves
   Helú, A. Piropos at midnight
   Henry, O. Makes the whole world kin
   Henry, O.   A retrieved reformation
   Higgins, R. M. Social climber
   Hoch, E. D. The theft of the laughing
      lions
   Holding, J. The queen's jewel
   Holmes, E. M.   A little sweetening
   Law, W. The Harry Hastings Method
   Leiber, F. Ill met in Lankhmar
   Lumley, B. De Marigny's clock
   MacDonald, J. Funny the way things
      work out
   McPhee, J. The fair of San Gennaro
   Marsh, R. The man who cut off my hair
   Maupassant, G. de. The rabbit
   Midwood, B. The burglars
   Midwood, B.   A thief in the temples
   Miller, H. D. Johnny Dio and the sugar
      plum burglars
   Moravia, A. Contact with the working
      class
   Moravia, A. The Jack Gang
   Pemberton, M. The ripening rubies
   Pentecost, H. The monster of Lakeview
   Powell, J. The Altdorf syndrome
   Runyon, D. Butch minds the baby
   Schmitz, J. H. The searcher
   Steinbeck, J. The treasure hunt
   Stevenson, R. L.   A lodging for the night
   Tanizaki, J. The thief
   Treat, L. The cautious man
   Wyndham, J. Close behind him
      See also Automobile thieves; Brigands
      and robbers; Cattle thieves; Jewel
      thieves
Thieves. Chekhov, A.
The thieves. Grau, S. A.
Thieves. O'Faolain, S.
The thin thread. James, D.

Thine alabaster cities gleam. Janifer, L. M.
A thing about cars! Lumley, B.
The thing about Mrs Slezinger. Lane, M.
The thing at Nolan. Bierce, A.
The thing from the blasted heath. Lumley, B.
The thing in the cellar. Keller, D. H.
A thing is a thing. Moravia, A.
Things go better. Effinger, G. A.
Things lost. Disch, T. M.
The things that grow. Moravia, A.
Things which are Caesar's. Dickson, G. R.
THINKING MACHINES. See Cybernetics
Thiotimoline to the stars. Asimov, I.
The third bank of the river. Rosa, J. G.
The third hill. Bosem, H.
The third level. Finney, J.
The third ocean. Summers, H.
The third one. Singer, I. B.
The third person. James, H.
A third presence. Gordimer, N.
The third son. Platonov, A.
The third vow. Phanishwarnath "Renu"
Thirteen for Centaurus. Ballard, J. G.
Thirteen phantasms. Smith, C. A.
The thirteenth journey of Ion Tichy. Lem, S.
Thirty clocks strike the hour. Sackville-
   West, V.
Thirty-day leave. Berkson, T.
Thirty-seven nights of passion. Trevisan, D.
This beautiful mankind. Popov, V.
This bed which is mine which is thine.
   Trevisan, D.
This bighearted business. Blackhurst, W. E.
This certainly day. Glaze, E.
This is a watchbird watching you. Lang,
   A, K.
This is Moscow speaking. Daniel, Y.
This is my body. O'Faolain, J.
This is Sylvia. Wilson, S.
This is the road. Silverberg, R.
This is what killed Dylan Thomas. Bukow-
   ski, C.
This majestic lie. Crane, S.
This moment of the storm. Zelazny, R.
This morning, this evening, so soon. Bald-
   win, J.
This mortal mountain. Zelazny, R.
This night, at my fire. Russ, J.
This one's a beauty. McGerr, P.
This time. O'Hara, J.
This way for the gas, ladies and gentlemen.
   Borowski, T.
This year at the Arabian Nights Hotel.
   Richler, M.
Thithyphuth. Borchert, W.
THOMAS AQUINAS, SAINT
         Summa theologica
   Corvo, F. Baron. About Sodom, Gomor-
      rah, and the two admirable Jesuits
THOMAS, OF ERCELDOUNE, CALLED
      THE RHYMER
   Thomas the Rhymer
Thomas, Audrey
   Aquarius
      Stephens, D. ed. Contemporary voices

Thompson, J. C.
  The right man for the right job
    Bernkopf, J. F. comp. Boucher's choic-
      est
Thompson, James W.
  See what tomorrow brings
    King, W. ed. Black short story anthology
Thompson, Kent
  The complicated camera: Jeremy & Greta
    The Best little magazine fiction, 1971
  Still life composition: woman's clothes
    Fourteen stories high
Thompson, Marilyn
  A woman's story
    The Best little magazine fiction, 1971
Thompson, Robert
  Day and night
    Intro #2
Thompson, Thomas
  Memento
    Western Writers of America. With
      Guidons flying
  Son of a King
    Lucia, E. ed. This land around us
Thórdarson, Agnar
  If your sword is short
    Johnson, E. W. ed. Short stories inter-
      national
THOREAU, HENRY DAVID
  West, J. Like visitant of air
THOROUGHBRED HORSES. See Horses
Thorp, Roderick
  Sunburst
    Orbit 6
Those in peril on the tee. Wodehouse, P. G.
Those who think young. Naylor, P. R.
Those who walk the streets. Beekman, A.
Those wonderful years. Malzberg, B. N.
Thought of love on a summer afternoon.
  Ansell, J.
THOUGHT-TRANSFERENCE
  Aldiss, B. W. Psyclops
  Anderson, P. Call me Joe
  Anderson, P. Journeys end
  Bauer, G. M. From all of us
  Bixby, J. It's a good life
  Bloch, R. Space-born
  Bova, B. The perfect warrior
  Crowley, A. The Testament of Magdalen
    Blair
  Delany, S. R. Corona
  Eklund, G. Free City blues
  Fitzpatrick, R. C. Winkin, Blinkin and
    $\pi R^2$
  Henderson, Z. The indelible kind
  Henderson, Z. Sharing time
  Jacobi, C. The royal opera house
  Koontz, D. R.  A mouse in the walls of
    the Global Village
  Lafferty, R. A.  A special condition in
    Summit City
  Lewis, C. S. The Shoddy Lands
  Pangborn, E. Angel's egg
  Phillips, P. Dreams are sacred
  Schmitz, J. H. Novice
  Sheckley, R. Carrier
  Sheckley, R. Potential
  Silverberg, R. Ship-sister, star-sister
  Silverberg, R. Something wild is loose

  Silverberg, R. Translation error
  Smith, C. The ballad of lost C'mell
  Smith, C. The game of rat and dragon
  Stover, L. E. What we have here is too
    much communication
  Sutton, J. Forerunner
  Sutton, L. Soul mate
  Vance, J. The miracle workers
  White, J. The conspirators
  Wilhelm, K. The infinity box
  Wilson, R. S. Gone fishin'
  Yep, L. Looking-glass sea
  Zelazny, R. 'Kjwalll'kje'k'koothaïlll'kje'k
      See also Mind reading
A thousand years is a long time. Stuart, J.
Thrawn Janet. Stevenson, R. L.
Thread. Dawson, F.
Threat. Ayrton, M.
The three. Dickson, G. R.
3. Francis, H. E.
Three. Grau, S. A.
Three and one are one. Bierce, A.
Three Annas. See Chekhov, A. Anna on the
    neck
Three bears cottage. Collier, J.
Three blind mice. Laumer, K.
3 chickens. Bukowski, C.
Three-cornered and secure. Henderson, Z.
The three dark kings. See Borchert, W. The
    three dark magi
The three dark magi. Borchert, W.
The three-day blow. Hemingway, E.
Three days and a child. Yehoshua, A. B.
Three falling stars. Maclagan, D.
Three ghost stories. Yüan, Mei
Three is a lucky number. Allingham, M.
Three men. Gaines, E. J.
Three men. Goudge, E.
Three million square miles. Wolfe, G.
Three million yen. Mishima, Y.
Three miraculous soldiers. Crane, S.
Three o'clock in the morning. Trevisan, D.
3-part puzzle. Dickson, G. R.
3 pennies for luck. Bontemps, A.
The three poets. Linklater, E.
Three, seven, ace. Tendryakov, V.
Three shots. Hemingway, E.
Three stories: I. Cheever, J.
Three stories: II. Cheever, J.
Three stories: III. Cheever, J.
The three swimmers and the educated gro-
    cer. Saroyan, W.
Three Washington stories: Noone. Just, W.
Three Washington stories: Slayton. Just, W.
Three Washington stories: The brigadier
    general and the columnist's wife.
    Just, W.
Three ways to rob a bank. Daniels, H. R.
Three who ate. Frishman, D.
THREE WISE MEN. See Magi
3 women. Bukowski, C.
Three years. Chekhov, A.
Three young ladies. Stoker, B.
The throne of good. Nissenson, H.
Through a dead man's eye. Woolrich, C.
Through a glass—darkly. Henderson, Z.
Through other eyes. Lafferty, R. A.
Through the Gap. Fox, J.

**Tolstoi, Lev Nikolaevich, Graf.** *See* Tolstoy, Leo
**Tolstoy, Alexis**
  Amena
    Tolstoy, A. Vampires
  The family of a Vourdalak
    Tolstoy, A. Vampires
  The reunion after three hundred years
    Hitchcock, A. comp. Alfred Hitchcock's Supernatural tales of terror and suspense
    Tolstoy, A. Vampires
  The vampire
    Tolstoy, A. Vampires
**Tolstoy, Leo**
  After the ball
    Davis, R. G. ed. Ten modern masters
    Foff, A. and Knapp, D. eds. Story
  The death of Iván Ilých
    Hamalian, L. and Volpe, E. L. eds. Eleven modern short novels
    Proffer, C. R. ed. From Karamzin to Bunin: an anthology of Russian short stories
  God sees the truth, but waits
    Proffer, C. R. ed. From Karamzin to Bunin: an anthology of Russian short stories
    Same as: God sees the truth but is in no hurry to reveal it, listed in 1964-1968 supplement
  The story of Yemilyan and the empty drum
    Hall, J. B. ed. The realm of fiction
      **About**
    Barthelme, D. At the Tolstoy Museum
**Tom** Carroll. Farrell, J. T.
**Tom** Whipple. Edmonds, W. D.
**Toman, Nikolay**
  A debate on SF—Moscow 1965
    Suvin, D. ed. Other worlds, other seas
**Tomb** of an ancestor. Lavin, M.
The **Tombling** day. Bradbury, R.
**TOMBOYS.** *See* Girls
**TOMBS**
  Carr, T. Ozymandias
  Ibuse, M. Yosaku the settler
**TOMBSTONES**
  De La Mare, W. De mortuis
  Hawthorne, N. Chippings with a chisel
**Tommaso Guardato.** *See* Masuccio
**Tommy,** the unsentimental. Cather, W.
**Tomorrow.** Lu, Hsun
**Tomorrow** and tomorrow and so forth. Updike, J.
**Tomorrow** and tomorrow and tomorrow. Vonnegut, K.
The **tomorrow**-tamer. Laurence, M.
**Tomorrow's** child. Bradbury, R.
**Tomorrow's** "Wall Street Journal." Fast, H.
**TONGUE TWISTING.** *See* Speech, Disorders of
The **tongueless** woman of Glamis Castle. Day, J. W.
**Tonight** at nine thirty-six. Gillespie, A.
The **tonsured** husband. Marguerite de Navarre
**Too** bad. Parker, D.

The **too** clever fox. Des Périers, B.
**Too** good to last. Naylor, P. R.
**Too** many Cooks. Eisenberg, L.
**Too** many sharks. Sambrot, W.
**Too** nice a day to die. Woolrich, C.
**Too** poor. Moravia, A.
**Too** sensitive. Bukowski, C.
**Toole, Wyc**
  A matter of need
    Best detective stories of the year, 1973
**Toomer, Jean**
  Avey
    Long, R. A. and Collier, E. W. eds. Afro-American writing v2
  Becky
    Larson, C. R. ed. Prejudice: 20 tales of oppression and liberation
  Blood-burning moon
    James, C. L. ed. From the roots
  Fern
    Turner, D. T. ed. Black American literature
**Toomey, Robert E.** *See* Hoffman, L. jt. auth.
**Toonder, Jan Gerhard**
  The spider
    Karl, F. R. and Hamalian, L. eds. The naked i
**TOOTHACHE.** *See* Teeth; Teeth—Diseases
A **toothbrush** from the sweet-gum tree. Reid, J. G.
**TOP (TOY)**
  Shepherd, J. Scut Farkas and the murderous Mariah
The **top.** Fitz Gerald, G.
**Top** man. Ullman, J. R.
**Torn** apart. Strindberg, A.
**TORNADOES**
  Ullman, J. M. Night of the twister
    *See also* Cyclones
**Torpid** smoke. Nabokov, V.
The **torque.** Forster, E. M.
**Torre, Lillian de la.** *See* De la Torre, Lillian
**Tortillas** and beans. Steinbeck, J.
The **tortoise** and the hair. Gohman, F.
**TORTURE**
  Aldiss, B. W. Sober noises of morning in a marginal land
  Bullins, E. The saviour
  Burke, T. The paw
  Ellison, H. I have no mouth, and I must scream
  Huddle, D. The interrogation of the prisoner Bung by Mister Hawkins and Sergeant Tree
  Nabokov, V. The Leonardo
  Poe, E. A. The pit and the pendulum
    *See also* Cruelty; Sadism
**Torture:** a children's story. Brownstein, M.
The **total** portrait. Peirce, J. F.
**Total** recall. Helvick, J.
**Total** recall. Sternig, L.
**Total** stranger. Cozzens, J. G.
**TOTALITARIANISM**
  Aldiss, B. W. Sober noises of morning in a marginal land
  Böll, H. My sad face
  Ćosić, D. Freedom
  Goulart, R. Copstate

**Trevor, William**—*Continued*

The grass widows
> Trevor, W. The ballroom of romance, and other stories

A happy family
> Trevor, W. The ballroom of romance, and other stories

Kinkies
> Trevor, W. The ballroom of romance, and other stories

The Mark-2 wife
> Trevor, W. The ballroom of romance, and other stories

A meeting in middle age
> McCrindle, J. F. ed. Stories from the Transatlantic Review

Miss Smith
> Hamilton, A. ed. Splinters

Nice day at school
> Trevor, W. The ballroom of romance, and other stories

O fat white woman
> Trevor, W. The ballroom of romance, and other stories

**Trial** by summer. McCord, J.

The **trial** nobody ever heard of. Nesvadba, J.

The **trial** of Job. Brister, B.

**TRIALS**
> Asimov, I. Legal rites
> Barth, J. The law
> Beneš, J. The class enemy
> Benét, S. V. All that money can buy
> Benét, S. V. The Devil and Daniel Webster
> Camus, A. The stranger
> Čapek, K. The last judgment
> Cecil, H. Brief tales from the bench; 8 stories
> Cecil, H. Chef's special
> Cecil, H. Contempt of court
> Cecil, H. Free for all
> Cecil, H. Made to measure
> Cecil, H. Operation enticement
> Cecil, H. Perjury
> Chekhov, A. The culprit
> Chesnutt, C. W. The web of circumstance
> Corvo, F. Baron. About the heresy of Fra Serafico
> Crane, S. An eloquence of grief
> DeFord, M. A. The eel
> De La Torre, L. A fool for a client
> Dickson, G. R. Zeepsday
> Dillon, M. Rape
> Duodu, C. The tax dodger
> Fleming, G. Boomerang
> Greene, G. The case for the defence
> Harte, B. Tennessee's partner
> Jepson, E. and Eustace, R. The tea-leaf
> McGerr, P. Justice has a high price
> McKimmey, J. The man who danced
> McPherson, J. A. An act of prostitution
> Masur, H. Q. The $2,000,000 defense
> Maupassant, G. de. A sale
> Meinhold, W. The amber witch
> Miller, H. D. Johnny Dio and the sugar plum burglars
> Oates, J. C. Did you ever slip on red blood?
> Pangborn, E. My brother Leopold

> Patton, F. G. A friend of the court
> Pentecost, H. Hector is willin'
> Pierce, J. Miss Paisley on a diet
> Porges, A. The rescuer
> Purdy, K. W. In the matter of the assassin Merefirs
> Ristikivi, K. The seventh witness
> Son, S. The poppy
> Starrett, V. The eleventh juror
> Strong, P. N. The airtight case
> Tendryakov, V. Justice
> Warren, S. The March assize
> Wister, O. A pilgrim on the Gila
>> *See also* Courts-martial and courts of inquiry; Justice; Witnesses

**TRIALS (FRAUD)**
> Cecil, H. The hidden money
> Cecil, H. The truth

**TRIALS (LARCENY)**
> Cecil, H. Retrial

A **triangle** has four sides. Naylor, P. R.

The **triangle** on the jungle wall. Dawson, F.

**TRIBES AND TRIBAL SYSTEM**
> Elliott, G. P. Among the Dangs
> Platonov, A. Dzhan

The **tribunal** of the inquisition. Reynolds, G. W. M.

The **trick**. Chekhov, A.

A **trick** o' trade. Fox, J.

**TRICK** or treaty. Laumer, K.

**TRICKERY.** *See* Fraud; Hoaxes

**Tricky** tonnage. Jameson, M.

**TRICYCLES.** *See* Bicycles and bycycling

**Trifle** from life. *See* Chekhov, A. A trifle from real life

A **trifle** from real life. Chekhov, A.

**Trifling** occurrence. *See* Chekhov, A. A trifle from real life

**Trigononomy.** Moore, R.

**Trilling, Lionel**

Of this time, of that place
> Tytell, J. and Jaffe, H. eds. Affinities

The other Margaret
> Larson, C. R. ed. Prejudice: 20 tales of oppression and liberation

**TRILOBITES**
> Thomas, T. The intruder

The **trimmed** lamp. Henry, O.

The **trip**. Fielding, G.

A **trip** home. Zhdanov, N.

A **trip** to Brooklyn. Schwartz, J.

A **trip** to the coast. Munro, A.

A **trip** to Zwolle. Campert, R.

**Tripout.** Sheckley, R.

The **triumph** of death. Wakefield, H. R.

The **triumph** of night. Wharton, E.

**Triumph** of the Boon. Forester, C. S.

**Triumph** of the Omophagists. Hall, J. B.

The **triumphant** head. Saxton, J.

"**Trojan** fall." Clement, H.

The **troll**. Cady, J.

**TROLLEY BUSES**
> Borchert, W. There are voices in the air—at night
> Lafferty, R. A. Interurban queen

**TROLLEY CARS.** *See* Street railroads; Trolley buses

**TROLLS**
Redd, D. Sundown
**Troop** withdrawal—the initial step. Parker, T.
**Tropic** of Cuba. Di Donato, P.
**TROPICAL FISH**
Hermann, J. The Piranha
**Tropism** XV. Sarraute, N.
**TROUBADOURS**
Henry, O. The Last of the Troubadours
Hesse, H. Chagrin d'amour
Linklater, E. The Crusader's key
Walsh, J. P. and Crossley-Holland, K. Leof's leavetaking
The **trouble** I see. Brunner, J.
The **trouble** man. Rhodes, E. M.
**Trouble** on Tantalus. Miller, P. S.
**Trouble** with a battery. Bukowski, C.
The **trouble** with machines. Goulart, R.
The **trouble** with the past. Eisenstein, A. and Eisenstein, P.
**TROUT**
Carrighar, S. The cutthroat trout
O'Faolain, S. The trout
Peterson, E. L. The King
The **trout**. Ford, J. H.
The **trout**. O'Faolain, S.
**TROUT FISHING**
Blackhurst, W. E. So help me—it's the truth
Blackhurst, W. E. This bighearted business
Blackmore, R. D. Crocker's Hole
Bonner, J. H. John Monahan
Brautigan, R. The hunchback trout
Brautigan, R. The lost chapters of trout fishing in America
Corodimas, P. ed. In trout country; 21 stories
Foote, J. T. A wedding gift
Gilchrist, J. Opening day
Hemingway, E. Big two-hearted river
Hemingway, E. Big two-hearted river: part II
Lamb, D. S. Perfidia
Macdougall, A. R. The sun stood still
Manning, R. Don't fish while I'm talking
O'Brien, D. C. Pool number 37
**Trout** fishing in America terrorists. Brautigan, R.
"A **trout** fishing sampler." Brautigan, R.
**Trout** widows. Ford, C.
**Troyes, Nicolas de.** See Nicolas de Troyes
**TRUANCY (SCHOOL)** See School attendance
**Truce** or consequences. Laumer, K.
**TRUCK DRIVERS**
Cady, J. The burning
Cady, J. The forest ranger
Cady, J. Ride the thunder
Farrell, J. T. The old-timer
Ford, R. Chicken catchers
González León, A. The rainbow
Jameson, M. Tricky tonnage
Lavin, M. The cemetery in the demesne
Matheson, R. Duel
Mitchell, D. Diesel
**TRUCKING.** See Truck drivers

**TRUCKS**
See also Tank trucks
**Accidents**
Cady, J. The burning
Coover, R. A pedestrian accident
**True** confessions story. Holst, S.
A **true** story. Levine, N.
The **true** story. Thomas, D.
A **true** story. Tindall, G.
The **true** story of Ah Q. Lu, Hsun
The **true** story of Chicken Licken. Holmes, L.
The **truly** married woman. Nicol, A.
**TRUMPETERS.** See Musicians—Trumpeters
The **trumpets** of Épignon. Rushmore, R.
A **trunkful** of treasure. Gohman, F.
**TRUTH**
Boucher, A. We print the truth
Cecil, H. The truth
See also Truthfulness and falsehood
The **truth**. Cecil, H.
**Truth** and lies. Price, R.
**Truth** in the cup. Warner, S. T.
A **truth** to live by. Ruskay, S.
**TRUTHFULNESS AND FALSEHOOD**
Asimov, I. Super-neutron
Beerbohm, M. A. V. Laider
Chekhov, A. A trifle from real life
Crane, S. The knife
Dickson, G. R. Lulungomeena
Forster, E. M. The obelisk
Kotzwinkle, W. The great liar
Nicol, A. As the night, the day
Price, R. Truth and lies
Roby, M. L. See and tell
Stevenson, R. L. The story of a lie
Strong, P. N. The airtight case
Treece, H. I cannot go hunting tomorrow
Vonnegut, K. The lie
Wain, J. I love you, Ricky
Willard, N. The tailor who told the truth
See also Perjury; Truth
**Try** a dull knife. Ellison, H.
**Trying** to lick the licks. McCord, J.
**Tso** Ying Tie. Sié, Cheou-kang
**Tsonev, Vassil**
Let's go vacationing
Kirilov, N. and Kirk, F. eds. Introduction to modern Bulgarian literature
**Tsu-hsiang Wu.** See Wu, Tsu-hsiang
**Ts'ung-wen Shen.** See Shen, Ts'ung-wen
**TUBERCULOSIS**
Arlt, R. Esther Primavera
Henry, O. Hygeia at the Solito
McCullers, C. Breath from the sky
McKenna, R. Casey Agonistes
Verga, G. Consolation
West, J. The condemned librarian
West, J. I'll ask him to come sooner
West, J. 99.6
**TÜBINGEN.** See Germany—Tübingen
**Tucci, Niccolò**
Strong man
Insights
**Tucker, Wilson**
Time exposures
Universe 1
**TUCSON.** See Arizona—Tucson

**TUGBOATS**
Forester, C. S. The dumb Dutchman

**Tularecito.** Steinbeck, J.

**Tulip.** De Vries, P.

**Tumas, Juozas.** *See* Vaižgantas

The **tumbler.** Casper, L.

**TUMORS.** *See* Brain—Tumors

The **tune.** Val Baker, D.

The **tunesmith.** Biggle, L.

**TUNISIA**
Algren, N. Brave bulls of Sidi Yahya
Taylor, E. Crêpes flambées

**TUNNELS**
Maltz, A. Man on a road
Williamson, G. Trapped in a flooded tunnel

**Tuohy, Frank**
At home with the Colonel
  McCrindle, J. F. ed. Stories from the Transatlantic Review
The broken bridge
  Winter's tales 17
Discontinued lines
  Tuohy, F. Fingers in the door, and other stories
Fingers in the door
  Tuohy, F. Fingers in the door, and other stories
A floral tribute
  Tuohy, F. Fingers in the door, and other stories
The licence
  Tuohy, F. Fingers in the door, and other stories
A life membership
  Tuohy, F. Fingers in the door, and other stories
Love to Patsy
  Winter's tales 18
The Palladian Bridge
  Tuohy, F. Fingers in the door, and other stories
A reprieve
  Tuohy, F. Fingers in the door, and other stories
Ructions
  Tuohy, F. Fingers in the door, and other stories
A special relationship
  Tuohy, F. Fingers in the door, and other stories
Thunderbolt
  Tuohy, F. Fingers in the door, and other stories
  Winter's tales 15
The trap
  Tuohy, F. Fingers in the door, and other stories
A war of liberation
  Tuohy, F. Fingers in the door, and other stories
Windows
  Winter's tales 19

**Tur, Pramudya Ananta.** *See* Toer, Pramoedya Ananta

The **turf** and the dirt. Watkins, R. H.

**Turgenev, Ivan**
Bezhin Meadow
  Proffer, C. R. ed. From Karamzin to Bunin: an anthology of Russian short stories
The country doctor
  Tytell, J. and Jaffe, H. eds. Affinities
  Same as: District doctor, listed in earlier volumes
The inn
  Turgenev, I. Three novellas: Punin and Baburin, The inn, The watch
Punin and Baburin
  Turgenev, I. Three novellas: Punin and Baburin, The inn, The watch
The watch
  Turgenev, I. Three novellas: Punin and Baburin, The inn, The watch

**TURIN.** *See* Italy—Turin

**TURKEY**

### Istanbul
Disch, T. M. The Asian shore
Roditi, E. From rags to riches
Roditi, E. The vampires of Istanbul: a study in modern communications methods

### Peasant life
*See* Peasant life—Turkey

**TURKEY, PROVINCIAL AND RURAL**
Kemal, Y. A dirty story
Kemal, Y. The drumming-out
Kemal, Y. On the road
Kemal, Y. The shopkeeper
Kemal, Y. The white trousers
The **turkey.** O'Connor, F.

**TURKEYS**
Brister, B. The wrong-way ambush
McWhirter, G. The harbinger
O'Connor, F. The turkey

**TURKS**
Kotsyubynsky, M. On the rock

**TURKS IN BULGARIA**
Strashimirov, A. Soura Bir
Yovkov, Y. Heroes' heads

The **turn** of the screw. James, H.
The **turn** of the screw. Oates, J. C.
The **turn** of the tide. Forester, C. S.
**Turn** on Guatemala. Elman, R.
A **turn** with the sun. Knowles, J.

**Turner, Charles E.**
The beginning of tomorrow
  Brown, E. P. ed. Twice fifteen

**Turning** point. Kotzwinkle, W.
The **turtle.** Brodeur, P.
The **turtle.** Steinbeck, J.
The **turtle** hunt. Fogel, A.

**TURTLES**
Brodeur, P. The turtle
Dickens, C. Lively turtle
Highsmith, P. The terrapin
Sargent, P. The other perceiver
Steinbeck, J. The turtle

**Tushnet, Leonard**
Gifts from the universe
  The Best from Fantasy and Science Fiction; 18th ser.
In re Glover
  Ellison, H. ed. Again, dangerous visions

Twohy, Robert—*Continued*
  Routine investigation
    Best of the Best detective stories
Two's enough of a crowd. Hunter, K.
Tyler, Anne
  The common courtesies
    Prize stories, 1969: The O. Henry Awards
  With all flags flying
    Prize stories, 1972: The O. Henry Awards
Tyme. Goldberg, G. J.
Tynianov, I. N. *See* Tynyanov, Yury
Tynyanov, Yuri Nicholaievich. *See* Tynyanov, Yury
Tynyanov, Yury
  Second Lieutenant Likewise
    Pomorska, K. ed. Fifty years of Russian prose: from Pasternak to Solzhenitsyn v 1
    Same as: Second Lieutenant Asfor, listed in 1964-1968 supplement
TYPE-SETTERS
  Hesse, H. Tragic
TYPEWRITERS
  Swenson, M. Mutterings of a middle-woman
TYPISTS
  Brautigan, R. 1/3, 1/3, 1/3
  Henry, O. The enchanted profile
  Henry, O. Springtime à la carte
  Litvinov, I. Call it love
  Moravia, A. Command, and I will obey you
  Swenson, M. Mutterings of a middle-woman
TYRANNY. *See* Dictators
The tyrant. Greenberg, J.
Tyre, Nedra
  Another turn of the screw
    Ellery Queen's Mystery Magazine. Ellery Queen's Grand Slam
Tyrmand, Leopold
  A cocktail party
    Tyrmand, L. ed. Explorations in freedom: prose, narrative, and poetry from Kultura

# U

UFO. Fast, H.
UNIVAC. *See* Electronic computers
U.S.S. Cornucopia. Forester, C. S.
Ubbo-sathla. Smith, C. A.
Ueda, Akinari. *See* Uyeda, Akinari
UGANDA
  Kimenye, B. The winner
  Obudo, N. They stole our cattle
The ugliest pilgrim. Betts, D.
The ugliest white woman you ever saw in your life. Drake, R.
UGLINESS
  Betts, D. The ugliest pilgrim
  Maupassant, G. de. Ugly
  Silverberg, R. Caliban
Ugly. Maupassant, G. de
The ugly devils. Kurahashi, Y.
The ugly little boy. Asimov, I.

The ugly sea. Lafferty, R. A.
The Ugupu bird. Mrozek, S.
UKRAINE. *See* Russia—Ukraine
UKRAINIANS IN CANADA
  Kreisel, H. The broken globe
ULCERS
  Nourse, A. E.    A gift for numbers
Ulibarri, Sabine R.
  Forge without fire
    Ulibarri, S. R. Tierra Amarilla
  The Frater family
    Ulibarri, S. R. Tierra Amarilla
  Get that straight
    Ulibarri, S. R. Tierra Amarilla
  Man without a name
    Ulibarri, S. R. Tierra Amarilla
  My Wonder Horse
    Ulibarri, S. R. Tierra Amarilla
  The stuffing of the Lord
    Ulibarri, S. R. Tierra Amarilla
Ullian, Robert
  A snag in the harp
    Lish, G. ed. The secret life of our times: new fiction from Esquire
Ullman, James Michael
  Night of the twister
    Fenner, P. R. comp. Consider the evidence
Ullman, James Ramsey
  Mountains of the axis
    Fenner, P. R. comp. Perilous ascent
  Top man
    Fenner, P. R. comp. Perilous ascent
Ultima Thule. Nabokov, V.
The ultimate end. Glass, D.
The ultimate melody. Clarke, A. C.
The ultimate threshold. Maximov, H.
Ultimatum. Laumer, K.
Ulyansky, Anton
  The fleecy jacket
    Scammell, M. ed. Russia's other writers
Ulyatt, Kenneth
  Ghost riders of the Sioux
    Dickinson, S. ed. The usurping ghost, and other encounters and experiences
ULYSSES
  Welty, E. Circe
Umanarsuak. Lütgen, K.
UMBRELLAS
  Colter, C. The beach umbrella
Unamuno y Jugo, Miguel de
  Abel Sanchez
    Hamalian, L. and Volpe, E. L. eds. Eleven modern short novels
The unattached smile. Crews, H.
Unbelievable characters. Nemerov, H.
The unbeliever. Johnson, D. M.
The unborn. Dawson, F.
"Unc' Edinburg's drowndin'." Page, T. N.
The uncertain hours of Willie Post People. Dillon, M.
The uncharted isle. Smith, C. A.
Uncle. Narayan, R. K.
Uncle Benny. Blum-Alquit, E.
Uncle Ben's choice. Achebe, C.
Uncle Ben's whale. Edmonds, W. D.
Uncle Donato's death. Kovač, M.
Uncle Fonse laughed. Stuart, J.
Uncle Fremmis. Sturgeon, T.

**UNICORNS**
Delany, S. R. The unicorn tapestry
Lehrman, H. The ancient last
Niven, L. Get a horse!
Sturgeon, T. The Silken-swift . . .

**UNIFORMS, MILITARY**
Hemingway, E. A way you'll never be

The **uninhabited** house. Riddell, Mrs J. H.

The **union** forever. Malzberg, B. N.

**Union** reunion. Wilson, A.

**UNION SQUARE.** *See* New York (City)—
Union Square

**Union** Street changing. Wardwell, P.

**UNIONS.** *See* Labor unions

**Unique.** Bakhnov, V.

**UNITED STATES**
  *See also* regions of the country, e.g.
  Gulf States; New England; The West;
  etc.

**18th century—French and Indian War**
Edmonds, W. D. The matchlock gun

**18th century—Revolution**
Edmonds, W. D. Wilderness clearing
Fast, H. The afternoon
  *See also* Wyoming Massacre, 1778

**19th century**
Graham, W. Jacka's fight
Slesar, H. A note on American literature
  by my uncle, Monroe Sanderson

**19th century—Civil War**
Bierce, A. The affair at Coulter's Notch
Bierce, A. An affair of outposts
Bierce, A. A baffled ambuscade
Bierce, A. The coup de grâce
Bierce, A. George Thurston
Bierce, A. A horseman in the sky
Bierce, A. Incident at Owl Creek
Bierce, A. Jupiter Doke, Brigadier-General
Bierce, A. Killed at Resaca
Bierce, A. The major's tale
Bierce, A. A man with two lives
Bierce, A. The mocking-bird
Bierce, A. Parker Adderson, philosopher
Bierce, A. A resumed identity
Bierce, A. The story of a conscience
Bierce, A. Three and one are one
Bierce, A. A tough tussle
Bierce, A. Two military executions
Crane, S. A grey sleeve
Crane, S. The little regiment
Crane, S. A mystery of heroism
Crane, S. The red badge of courage
Crane, S. Three miraculous soldiers
Edmonds, W. D. Cadmus Henry
Jewett, S. O. Peach-tree Joe
Page, T. N. Meh Lady: a story of the war
Roberts, R. E. The New Jerusalem
Stuart, J. Two worlds
West, J. After the battle

**19th century—Civil War—Casualties**
James, H. The story of a year

**19th century—1865-1898**
Wister, O. The Second Missouri Compromise

**19th century—War of 1898**
Crane, S. The clan of no-name
Crane, S. An episode of war
Crane, S. "God rest ye, merry gentlemen"
Crane, S. The lone charge of William B.
  Perkins
Crane, S. Marines signaling under fire at
  Guantanamo
Crane, S. The price of the harness
Crane, S. The revenge of the Adolphus
Crane, S. The second generation
Crane, S. The serjeant's private mad-house
Crane, S. This majestic lie
Crane, S. Virtue in war
Crane, S. War memories

**20th century**
Butor, M. Welcome to Utah
Zahn, C. A view from the sky

**Air Force**
Bahr, J. Flagged

**Air Force—Bases**
*See* Military bases, American

**Air Force—Officers**
Gerald, J. B. Blood letting

**Army**
Chatain, R. The adventure of the mantises
Disch, T. M. 1-A
Gold, I. The nickel misery of George
  Washington Carver Brown
Goodwin, S. Sole surviving son
Litwak, L. E. The solitary life of man
Roth, P. Defender of the faith
Roth, P. Novotny's pain
  *See also* Soldiers, American

**Army—Bases**
*See* Military bases, American

**Army—Cavalry**
Adams, C. Hell command
Fowler, K. Brothers of the bugle
Green, B. K. Saddle marks
Grove, F. War path
Gulick, B. Tear up the orders!
Newton, D. B. Chain of command
Remington F. When a document is official
Western Writers of America. With Guidons flying; 12 stories

**Army—Medical Corps**
Paquet, B. T. Warren
Pitts, O. R. Temporary duty

**Army—Officers**
Bahr, J. The polite captain
Bierce, A. The affair at Coulter's Notch
Bierce, A. An affair of outposts
Bierce, A. George Thurston
Bierce, A. Jupiter Doke, Brigadier-General
Bierce, A. Killed at Resaca
Bierce, A. The major's tale
Bierce, A. One officer, one man
Bierce, A. A son of the Gods
Bierce, A. The story of a conscience
Brodeur, P. The sick fox
Crane, S. Virtue in war
Currer, B. The Rabbi
Dorris, J. R. The accident
Grinstead, D. A day in operations

**Updike, John—***Continued*
The pro
  Updike, J. Museums and women, and
    other stories
Rich in Russia
  Updike, J. Bech: a book
The sea's green sameness
  Updike, J. Museums and women, and
    other stories
A sense of shelter
  Minot, S. and Wilson, R. eds. Three
    stances of modern fiction
  Roecker, W. A. ed. Stories that count
The slump
  Updike, J. Museums and women, and
    other stories
Solitaire
  Updike, J. Museums and women, and
    other stories
Sublimating
  Updike, J. Museums and women, and
    other stories
The taste of metal
  Updike, J. Museums and women, and
    other stories
Tomorrow and tomorrow and so forth
  Spinner, S. ed. Live and learn
  Zolotow, C. ed. An overpraised season
Under the microscope
  Updike, J. Museums and women, and
    other stories
When everyone was pregnant
  Updike, J. Museums and women, and
    other stories
Wife-wooing
  Elkin, S. ed. Stories from the sixties
  Insights
  12 short story writers
The witnesses
  Updike, J. Museums and women, and
    other stories
Your lover just called
  Updike, J. Museums and women, and
    other stories
Upon the waters. Greenberg, J.
**UPRISINGS.** *See* Revolutions
Uprooted. O'Connor, F.
Ups and downs. Malzberg, B. N.
The upturned face. Crane, S.
**URANUS (PLANET)**
  Weinbaum, S. G. The planet of doubt
**URBAN II, POPE**
  Coolidge, O. The Pope 1095
**URBAN TRAFFIC.** *See* Traffic engineering
Urbana, Illinois. Dawson, F.
Uri and Rachel. Rabikovitz, D.
**URNS.** *See* Vases
**Urquhart, Fred**
  The ghostess with the mostest
    Turner, J. ed. Unlikely ghosts
**URUGUAY**
  Borges, J. L. The end of the duel
  Somers, A. Madness
**URUGUAYANS IN THE UNITED STATES**
  Maloney, R.   A bird of gaudy plumage
Us he devours. Hall, J. B.
The use of force. Williams, W. C.
The used-boy raisers. Paley, G.
**USED CARS.** *See* Automobiles—Used cars

Useful phrases for the tourist. Russ, J.
Useless beauty. Maupassant, G. de
The **useless** planet. Larionova, O.
The **uses** of intelligence. Gant, M.
**Usher, Frank**
  Amazonian horrors
    Canning, J. ed. 50 great horror stories
  The bath of acid
    Canning, J. ed. 50 great horror stories
  The Black Dahlia
    Canning, J. ed. 50 great horror stories
  The great white bat
    Canning, J. ed. 50 great horror stories
  The walking dead
    Canning, J. ed. 50 great horror stories
**Uslar Pietri, Arturo**
  The drum dance
    Howes, B. ed. The eye of the heart
**USURERS.** *See* Pawnbrokers
The **usurer's** will. *See* Straparola. The will of
  the wicked usurer
The **usurper** of Beauty Ridge. Stuart, J.
The **usurping** ghost. Garfield, L.
**Utopian.** Reynolds, M.
**UTOPIAS**
  Barthelme, D. Paraguay
  Davis, G. My head's in a different place,
    now
  Reynolds, M. Utopian
  Russell, E. F.  . . . and then there were
    none
  Shelley, P. B. The Assassins
**Uyeda, Akinari**
  Bewitched
    Uyeda, A. Tales of moonlight and rain
  Birdcall
    Uyeda, A. Tales of moonlight and rain
  Daydream
    Uyeda, A. Tales of moonlight and rain
  Demon
    Uyeda, A. Tales of moonlight and rain
  Exiled
    Uyeda, A. Tales of moonlight and rain
  Homecoming
    Uyeda, A. Tales of moonlight and rain
  Prophesy
    Uyeda, A. Tales of moonlight and rain
  Reunion
    Uyeda, A. Tales of moonlight and rain
  Wealth
    Uyeda, A. Tales of moonlight and rain

# V

V. in love. Pynchon, T.
V. R. T. Wolfe, G.
Vaarlem and Tripp. Garfield, L.
The **vacation.** Porter, J. A.
Vacation. Posner, R.
Vacation. Sternberg, J.
**VACATIONS**
  Aandahl, V. An adventure in the Yolla
    Bolly Middle Eel Wilderness
  Aldiss, B. W. When I was very Jung
  Bahr, J. Incident on Galiano Street
  Bingham, S. August ninth at Natural
    Bridge

VAMPIRES—*Continued*

Matheson, R. Drink my blood
Miller, P. S. Over the river
Norris, F. Grettir at Thorhall-stead
Polidori, J. The vampyre
Prest, T. P. The storm visitor
Quinn, S. Body and soul
Roditi, E. The vampires of Istanbul: a study in modern communications methods
Seth, R. Visit from a vampire
Stoker, B. Three young ladies
Tieck, J. L. The bride of the grave
Tolstoy, A. The family of a Vourdalak
Tolstoy, A. The vampire
Wellman, M. W. When it was moonlight
Wyndham, J. Close behind him

The **vampires** of Istanbul: a study in modern communications methods. Roditi, E.

The **vampyre**. Polidori, J.

**Vance, Jack**
Cil
   Vance, J. Eight fantasms and magics
The Dragon masters
   Asimov, I. ed. The Hugo winners v2
Green magic
   McComas, J. F. ed. Special wonder
Guyal of Sfere
   Silverberg, R. ed. The ends of time
   Vance, J. Eight fantasms and magics
The Howling Bounders
   Harrison, H. ed. Worlds of wonder
The last castle
   Asimov, I. ed. The Hugo winners v2
The men return
   Vance, J. Eight fantasms and magics
The miracle workers
   Vance, J. Eight fantasms and magics
The moon moth
   The Science fiction hall of fame v2B
The new prime
   Vance, J. Eight fantasms and magics
Noise
   Silverberg, R. ed. Deep space
   Vance, J. Eight fantasms and magics
Rumfuddle
   Three trips in time and space
Telek
   Vance, J. Eight fantasms and magics
When the five moons rise
   Vance, J. Eight fantasms and magics
   *For other stories by this author see* Kuttner, Henry; O'Donnell, Lawrence; Padgett, Lewis

**VANCE, PHILO**
Breen, J. L. The Austin murder case

**VANDALISM.** *See* Malicious mischief

**Vandeloo, Jos**
The day of the dead God
   Krispyn, E. ed. Modern stories from Holland and Flanders

**Vanderbilt, William Kissam**
Di Donato, P. When Willy K. Vanderbilt frolicked and I shoveled his snow

**Van Duyn, Mona**
The bell
   Moss, H. ed. The poet's story

**Van Dyke, Henry**
A fatal success
   Lyons, N. ed. Fisherman's bounty

**VANES**
Mitchell, E. P. The flying weathercock

**Van het Reve, Gerard Kornelis.** *See* Reve, Gerard Kornelis van het

The **vanished** crown. *See* Bramah, E. The mystery of the vanished Petition Crown

**Vanishing** act. Gohman, F.

**VANISHING ANIMALS.** *See* Rare animals

The **vanishing** borough. Eisenberg, L.

The **vanishing** corpse. Gardner, E. S.

The **vanishing** point. Ayrton, M.

**Van Itallie, Jean-Claude**
François-Yattend
   McCrindle, J. F. ed. Stories from the Transatlantic Review

**VANITY.** *See* Pride and vanity

**Van Ostaijen, Paul.** *See* Ostaijen, Paul van

**Van Peebles, Melvin**
A bear for the F.B.I.; excerpt
   Adoff, A. ed. Brothers and sisters

**Van Vogt, A. E.**
Don't hold your breath
   Elwood, R. and Kidd, V. eds. Saving worlds
Far Centaurus
   Clareson, T. D. ed. A spectrum of worlds
   Silverberg, R. ed. Deep space
Resurrection
   Silverberg, R. ed. Invaders from space
Rogue ship
   Knight, D. ed. Tomorrow and tomorrow
The storm
   The Astounding-Analog reader v 1
The weapon shop
   Science fiction hall of fame v 1
The witch
   Haining, P. ed. The witchcraft reader
   *See also* Ellison, H. jt. auth.

**Van Vogt, A. E. and Ellison, Harlan**
The human operators
   Ellison, H. Partners in wonder

**Vanya** and the statuette. Manov, E.

**Vargas Llosa, Mario**
Sunday, Sunday
   Howes, B. ed. The eye of the heart

**VARIATION (BIOLOGY)** *See* Mutation (Biology)

**Variation** on a theme. Collier, J.

**Variations** on a theme. *See* O'Connor, F. A set of variations on a borrowed theme

**Varma, Shrikant**
His cross
   Roadarmel, G. C. ed. A death in Delhi

**Varshavsky, Ilya**
Biocurrents, biocurrents . . .
   Suvin, D. ed. Other worlds, other seas
Lectures on parapsychology
   Suvin, D. ed. Other worlds, other seas
The Noneatrins
   Suvin, D. ed. Other worlds, other seas
Preliminary research
   Ginsburg, M. ed. The ultimate threshold

Varshavsky, Ilya—*Continued*
  A raid takes place at midnight
    Magidoff, R. ed. Russian science fiction,
      1969
  SOMP
    Suvin, D. ed. Other worlds, other seas
Vasconcelos, José
  The boar hunt
    Hall, J. B. ed. The realm of fiction
VASES, GREEK
  Davidson, A. Amphora
Vassilev, Orlin
  Null with a capital letter
    Kirilov, N. and Kirk, F. eds. Introduc-
      tion to modern Bulgarian literature
Vassilikos, Vassilis
  "Ça ne peut pas durer"
    Vassilikos, V. The harpoon gun
  Departure
    Vassilikos, V. The harpoon gun
  The dinner party
    Vassilikos, V. The harpoon gun
  The harpoon gun
    Vassilikos, V. The harpoon gun
  Jingle Bells
    Vassilikos, V. The harpoon gun
  The maid and I
    Vassilikos, V. The harpoon gun
  Maids and mistresses
    Vassilikos, V. The harpoon gun
  Parallel lives
    Vassilikos, V. The harpoon gun
  The reason why
    Vassilikos, V. The harpoon gun
  Sarandapikhou Street
    Vassilikos, V. The harpoon gun
  Self-slaughter
    Vassilikos, V. The harpoon gun
  The stewardess
    Vassilikos, V. The harpoon gun
  The suitcase
    Vassilikos, V. The harpoon gun
  There and back
    Vassilikos, V. The harpoon gun
  The vegetable garden
    Vassilikos, V. The harpoon gun
Vaster than empires and more slow. Le
    Guin, U. K.
The vat. Davidson, A.
VAUDEVILLE
  Moyano, D. Vaudeville artists
Vaudeville artists. Moyano, D.
VAULTS (SEPULCHRAL) *See* Tombs
Vazov, Ivan
  Old Yotso is watching
    Kirilov, N. and Kirk, F. eds. Introduc-
      tion to modern Bulgarian literature
Vega, Pepe Martínez de la. *See* De la Vega,
    Pepe Martínez
The vegetable garden. Vassilikos, V.
Veiga, José J.
  The canine cannibal
    Veiga, J. J. The misplaced machine,
      and other stories
  The casquemoors
    Veiga, J. J. The misplaced machine,
      and other stories

The courting couple
    Veiga, J. J. The misplaced machine,
      and other stories
Dialogue on relativity
    Veiga, J. J. The misplaced machine,
      and other stories
Holiday Sunday
    Veiga, J. J. The misplaced machine,
      and other stories
The importunate rooster
    Veiga, J. J. The misplaced machine,
      and other stories
Incident at Sumauma
    Veiga, J. J. The misplaced machine,
      and other stories
The misplaced machine
    Veiga, J. J. The misplaced machine,
      and other stories
On the road to Daybreak
    Veiga, J. J. The misplaced machine,
      and other stories
A pebble on the bridge
    Veiga, J. J. The misplaced machine,
      and other stories
Saturday afternoon and Sunday morning
    Veiga, J. J. The misplaced machine,
      and other stories
The ten-league journey
    Veiga, J. J. The misplaced machine,
      and other stories
Twentymaster Square
    Veiga, J. J. The misplaced machine,
      and other stories
Where are the didangos now?
    Veiga, J. J. The misplaced machine,
      and other stories
The veiled feminists of Atlantis. Tarking-
    ton, B.
VEILS
  Hawthorne, N. The minister's Black Veil
Veitch, Tom
  Beads of brains
    Gottesman, L.; Obenzinger, H. and
      Senauke, A. eds. A cinch
VELOCITY. *See* Speed
Velsky, Victor
  My apologia
    Scammell, M. ed. Russia's other writers
Velvet glove. Harrison, H.
VENANTIUS, SAINT
  Corvo, F. Baron. About doubles in gen-
    eral: and Sanvenanzio and Santaga-
    pito, in particular
  Corvo, F. Baron. About Sanvenanzio, San-
    tagapito, and Padre Dotto Vagheg-
    gino, S. J.
The vendetta. *See* Maupassant, G. de.
    Semittante
VENDING STANDS
  Crane, S.   A great mistake
  Soto, P. J. Bayaminiña
VENEREAL DISEASES
  Michaels, L.   A green thought
  Miller, J. Rhoda/social disease
  Ostaijen, P. van. The lost house key
    *See also* Gonorrhea
Venetian dialogue. Landolfi, T.

**VENEZUELA**
    **Caracas**
  Gallegos, R. The Devil's twilight
**VENGEANCE.** *See* Revenge
**Vengeance** is mine. Blackhurst, W. E.
**Vengeful** creditor. Achebe, C.
The **vengeful** vision. Eddy, C. M.
**Veni,** vidi . . . Wendt. Stern, R.
**VENICE.** *See* Italy—Venice
**VENTRILOQUISTS**
  Brown, C. B. Memoirs of Carwin, the bilo-
    quist
  Collier, J. Spring fever
**Venture** to the moon. Clarke, A. C.
**VENUS (PLANET)**
  Asimov, I. Half-breeds on Venus
  Asimov, I. The weapon too dreadful to use
  Clarke, A. C. Before Eden
  Dickens, A. Let there be light
  Disch, T. M. Come to Venus melancholy
  Jacobi, C. The gentleman is an Epwa
  Long, F. B. The critters
  O'Donnell, L. Clash by night
  Smith, G. O. Interlude
  Zelazny, R. The doors of his face, the
    lamps of his mouth
    *See also* Space flight to Venus; Venu-
  sians
**Venus,** Cupid, Folly and Time. Taylor, P.
The **Venus** of Azombeii. Smith, C. A.
**Venusian** invader. Sternig, L.
**VENUSIANS**
  Asimov, I. The weapon too dreadful to use
  Brackett, L. and Bradbury, R. Lorelei of
    the red mist
  Dickens, A. Let there be light
  Smith, C. A. An adventure in futurity
  Sternig, L. Venusian invader
  Tushnet, L. Gifts from the universe
    *See also* Interplanetary visitors
**VERBOSITY**
  Andrews, F. E. Ynnel eht naitram
The **verdict.** Treat, L.
**El Verdugo.** Balzac, H. de
**VERDUN.** *See* France—Verdun
**Verga, Giovanni**
  Black bread
    Verga, G. The She-wolf, and other stories
  Buddies
    Verga, G. The She-wolf, and other stories
  Cavalleria rusticana
    Verga, G. The She-wolf, and other stories
  Consolation
    Hall, J. B. ed. The realm of fiction
    Verga, G. The She-wolf, and other stories
  Donna Santa's sin
    Verga, G. The She-wolf, and other stories
  Freedom
    Verga, G. The She-wolf, and other stories
  Gramigna's mistress
    Verga, G. The She-wolf, and other stories
  Ieli
    Verga, G. The She-wolf, and other stories
  The last day
    Verga, G. The She-wolf, and other stories
  Liberty
    Kraus, R. and Wiegand, W. eds. Stu-
    dent's choice

  Malaria
    Verga, G. The She-wolf, and other stories
  The mark X
    Verga, G. The She-wolf, and other stories
  Nanni Volpe
    Verga, G. The She-wolf, and other stories
  The orphans
    Verga, G. The She-wolf, and other stories
  Property
    Bowman, J. S. ed. A book of islands
    Verga, G. The She-wolf, and other stories
  Rosso malpelo
    Verga, G. The She-wolf, and other stories
  The She-wolf
    Taylor, J. C. ed. The short story: fiction
    in transition
    Verga, G. The She-wolf, and other stories
  Stinkpot
    Verga, G. The She-wolf, and other stories
  Story of the Saint Joseph's ass
    Kraus, R. and Wiegand, W. eds. Stu-
    dent's choice
    Same as: St Joseph's ass, entered in ear-
    lier volumes; Story of the Saint Joseph
    donkey
  Story of the Saint Joseph donkey
    Verga, G. The She-wolf, and other stories
    Same as: St Joseph's ass, entered in ear-
    lier volumes; Story of the Saint Jo-
    seph's ass
  Temptation
    Verga, G. The She-wolf, and other stories
  War between saints
    Verga, G. The She-wolf, and other stories
**Verma, Nirmal**
  A difference
    Roadarmel, G. C. ed. A death in Delhi
**VERMONT**
  Brodeur, P. The spoiler
  Green, B. K. Texas cow horses and the
    Vermont maid
  Robinson, R. E. The mole's path
  Robinson, R. E. An old-time March meet-
    ing
      **Country life**
    *See* Country life—Vermont
**Verne, Jules**
  The Begum's fortune
    Elwood, R. and Ghidalia, V. eds. An-
    droids, time machines and blue gi-
    raffes
**Verney, John**
  The drugged cornet
    Dickinson, S. ed. The drugged cornet,
    and other mystery stories
A **verray** parfit gentil knight. Boles, P. D.
The **vertical** fields. Dawson, F.
A **very** fine deal. Mergendahl, C.
A **very** honorable guy. Runyon, D.
The **very** last day of a good woman. Elli-
  son, H.
A **very** old man with enormous wings. Gar-
  cía Márquez, G.
A **very** pretty girl. Canzoneri, R.
**Very** sincerely yours. Sternberg, J.
A **very** small grove. Curley, D.
The **very** special dead people. Jones, A.
**Very** unique for Rush Street. Schwimmer, W.
The **vest.** Thomas, D.

The **visit**. Bingham, S.
The **visit**. Lynch, J.
**Visit** from a vampire. Seth, R.
A **visit** in bad taste. Wilson, A.
A **visit** next door. Jewett, S. O.
A **visit** of charity. Welty, E.
A **visit** to a mine. Kafka, F.
A **visit** to Avoyelles. Chopin, K.
A **visit** to grandmother. Kelley, W. M.
A **visit** to Morin. Greene, G.
**Visit** to my grandfather's grave alone.
    Schultz, J.
A **visit** to the cemetery. Lavin, M.
A **visit** to the doctor's wife. Spielberg, P.
The **visit** to the museum. Nabokov, V.
A **visit** to the teacher. Trevisan, D.
The **visitation** of Aunt Clara. Barlay, K.
**VISITING**
    Bingham, S. The visit
    Oates, J. C. Problems of adjustment in sur-
        vivors of natural/unnatural disasters
    Rascoe, J. When you go away
    Stuart, J. The twelve-pole road
    Taylor, P. Mrs Billingsby's wine
    Welty, E.    A visit of charity
A **visitor**. Stanev, L.
The **visitor**. Tindall, G.
**VISITORS**. *See* Guests; Visiting
**VISITORS, FOREIGN**
    Naipaul, V. S. One out of many
    Naipaul, V. S. Tell me who to kill
    Sorensen, V. In strange country
**VISITORS, INTERPLANETARY**. *See* In-
    terplanetary visitors
**VISITORS FROM OTHER PLANETS**. *See*
    Interplanetary visitors
**VISITORS FROM OUTER SPACE**. *See* In-
    terplanetary visitors
The **Vitanuls**. Brunner, J.
**Viva** Caporetto! Maloney, R.
**Vive** le roi. Graham, W.
**Vivian** thanks God. Farrell, J. T.
The **Viy**. *See* Gogol, N. Black Sunday
**Voelker, John Donaldson**. *See* Traver, R.
**Vogt, A. E. van**. *See* Van Vogt, A. E.
The **voice**. Cumberland, M.
The **Voice** from on high
    Cholakian, P. F. and Cholakain, R. C.
        eds. The early French novella
**Voice** from the past. Val Baker, D.
The **voice** of the mountain. Crane, S.
**Voice** of the town. Harnack, C.
The **voices** of the picture. Trevisan, D.
The **voices** of the wind. Schwartz, J.
The **voices** of time. Ballard, J. G.
The **voices** of women at the back of my
    mind. Drake, R.
**Voiskunsky, Yevgeny, and Lukodyanov, Isai**
    A farewell on the shore
        Magidoff, R. ed. Russian science fiction,
        1969
**VOLCANOES**
    Lafferty, R. A. World abounding
    Laumer, K. Crime and punishment
    Zelazny, R. The eve of Rumoko
**Volen, Iliya**
    Groudka
        Kirilov, N. and Kirk, F. eds. Introduc-
        tion to modern Bulgarian literature

**Volodya**. Chekhov, A.
**Von Arnim, Achim**. *See* Arnim, Achim von
**Von Chamisso, Adelbert**. *See* Chamisso,
    Adelbert von
**Von Doderer, Heimito**. *See* Doderer, Heim-
    ito von
**Vondra, Vladimir**
    A legend of saintly folly
        Decker, C. R. and Angoff, C. eds. Mod-
        ern stories from many lands
**Von Elsner, Don**
    The man who played too well
        Mystery Writers of America. Merchants
        of menace
**Von Goethe, Johann Wolfgang**. *See* Goethe,
    Johann Wolfgang von
**Von Kleist, Heinrich**. *See* Kleist, Heinrich
    von
**Von Kramer, Professor**
    The Hall of Blood
        Haining, P. ed. Gothic tales of terror
**Vonnegut, Kurt**
    The big space fuck
        Ellison, H. ed. Again, dangerous visions
    Deer in the works
        Disch, T. M. ed. The ruins of earth
    EPICAC
        Minot, S. and Wilson, R. eds. Three
        stances of modern fiction
    The lie
        Zolotow, C. ed. An overpraised season
    Tomorrow and tomorrow and tomorrow
        Schulman, L. M. ed. The cracked look-
        ing glass
**Von Schiller, Johann Friedrich**. *See* Schil-
    ler, Johann Friedrich von
**VOODOOISM**
    Brennan, J. P. Zombique
    Cross, J. Pin money
    Goulart, R. Junior partner
    Lupoff, R. A. With the Bentfin Boomer
        Boys on little old New Alabama
    Matheson, R. From shadowed places
    Usher, F. The walking dead
    Walsh, D. J. The rings of the Papaloi
    Yurick, S. The Child-God dance
**Vos, Herman**
    The sons of Pepe Gimenez
        Krispyn, E. ed. Modern stories from
        Holland and Flanders
The **voter**. Achebe, C.
**VOTING**. *See* Elections; Suffrage
The **voyage** inside the shell. Kotowska, M.
The **voyage** of the "Deborah Pratt." DeFord,
    M. A.
The **voyage** of the peanut. Jacobs, H.
**VOYAGES, INTERPLANETARY**. *See* In-
    terplanetary voyages
**VOYAGES, OCEAN**. *See* Ocean travel
**VOYAGES AND TRAVELS**
    Buck, P. S. The green sari
    DeFord, M. A. The voyage of the "De-
        borah Pratt"
    Kipling, R. The knights of the joyous ven-
        ture

VOYAGES AND TRAVELS—*Continued*
Mitchell, E. P. The terrible voyage of the Toad
*See also* Interplanetary voyages; Pilgrims and pilgrimages; Travel; Travelers
Voyeur. Moore, W.
VOYEURS
James, P. D. Moment of power
VULTURES
Hawkes, J.   A song outside
Vuyk, Beb
All our yesterdays
Decker, C. R. and Angoff, C. eds. Modern stories from many lands
Vynnychenko, Volodymyr
A strange episode
Luckyj, G. S. N. ed. Modern Ukrainian short stories

# W

Waddell, M. S.
Love me, love me, love me
Hitchcock, A. ed. Alfred Hitchcock presents: A month of mystery
Wade, James
The deep ones
Derleth, A. ed. Tales of Cthulhu Mythos
The elevator
Derleth, A. ed. Dark things
Wade, Rosalind
Shepherd, show me . . .
Turner, J. ed. Unlikely ghosts
The wager. Singer, I. B.
WAGERS
Brister, B. The London gun
Brister, B.   A small wager among gentlemen
Bukowski, C. Pittsburgh Phil & Co.
Clarke, A. Griff!
Crane, S. The wise men: a detail of American life in Mexico
Ellin, S. The payoff
Graham, W. Jacka's fight
Knight, W. E. The way we went
Lamb, H. Khlit
Morrison, A. The case of Janissary
Runyon, D.   A piece of pie
Sallis, J. Winner
Schwimmer, W.   A bet on marriage
Schwimmer, W. The goodest son in the world
Schwimmer, W. The luckiest day in history
Singer, I. B. The wager
Stuart, J. Seventy-six days
Thackeray, W. M. The Devil's wager
Twain, M. The celebrated jumping frog of Calaveras County
*See also* Gambling
The wages of good. Diop, B.
A Wagner matinee. Cather, W.
WAGON TRAINS
Farrell, C. Westward—to blood and glory
Fisher, C. The skinning of black coyote
Sienkiewicz, H. Across the plains

WAGONS
Ottley, R. The last of the horsemen
Wah-Tis-Kee—Little Flame. Hayes, A. H.
Waiguru, Joseph
The untilled field
Nolen, B. ed. Africa is thunder and wonder
Wain, John
Down our way
Larson, C. R. ed. Prejudice: 20 tales of oppression and liberation
I love you, Ricky
Wain, J. The life guard
The innocent
Wain, J. The life guard
The life guard
Wain, J. The life guard
A man in a million
Wain, J. The life guard
Master Richard
Fitz Gerald, G. ed. Modern satiric stories
Matthews, J. ed. Archetypal themes in the modern story
A sample of the ocean
Wain, J. The life guard
While the sun shines
Wain, J. The life guard
You could have fooled me
Wain, J. The life guard
Wait it out. Niven, L.
The Waitabits. Russell, E. F.
Waiter, a bock! Maupassant, G. de
WAITERS. *See* Servants—Waiters
Waiting. Schwartz, J.
Waiting. Weaver, G.
Waiting at Dachau. Price, R.
Waiting for her train. Lee, A. M.
Waiting for the Forty-one Union. Gold, H.
Waiting place. Harrison, H.
The waiting thing inside. Sturgeon, T. and Ward, D.
WAITRESSES. *See* Servants—Waitresses
The waiver. Auchincloss, L.
The wake. Trevisan, D.
Wake up! Moravia, A.
Wake up to Thunder. Koontz, D. R.
Wakefield, H. Russell
Appointment with fire
Derleth, A. ed. Dark things
Lucky's Grove
Dickinson, S. ed. The usurping ghost, and other encounters and experiences
Mr Ash's studio
Hitchcock, A. comp. Alfred Hitchcock's Supernatural tales of terror and suspense
The Red Lodge
Lamb, H. ed. A tide of terror
The triumph of death
Hitchcock, A. comp. Alfred Hitchcock's Supernatural tales of terror and suspense
WAKES. *See* Funeral rites and ceremonies
Waking up. Elmslie, K.
Walden, Howard T.
When all the world is young
Lyons, N. ed. Fisherman's bounty

**Waldo, Edward Hamilton.** *See* Sturgeon, Theodore

**WALES**

Anne of Swansea. The unknown!
Davis, O. Sappho in Wales
Johnson, B. S. Sheela-na-gig
Thomas, D. The Holy Six
Thomas, D. The school for witches

**WALES, PROVINCIAL AND RURAL**

Davies, R. The chosen one
Richards, D. Traveller's joy
Stubbs, J. Cousin Lewis
Warner, S. T.   A visionary gleam
Wyndham, J. Chinese puzzle

The **Walford** case. Brennan, J. P.
The **walk** before supper. Bassani, G.
A **walk** in the country. De Vries, P.
A **walk** in the dark. Clarke, A. C.
**Walk** in the moon shadows. Stuart, J.
A **walk** in the rain. Mayer, T.
A **walk** with Raschid. Jacobsen, J.

**Walker, Alice**

The child who favored Daughter
    Walker, A. In love & trouble
The diary of an African nun
    Walker, A. In love & trouble
Entertaining God
    Walker, A. In love & trouble
Everday use
    Walker, A. In love & trouble
The flowers
    Walker, A. In love & trouble
Her sweet Jerome
    Walker, A. In love & trouble
"Really, doesn't crime pay?"
    Walker, A. In love & trouble
The revenge of Hannah Kemhuff
    Walker, A. In love & trouble
Roselily
    Walker, A. In love & trouble
Strong horse tea
    King, W. ed. Black short story anthology
    Walker, A. In love & trouble
To hell with dying
    Bambara, T. C. ed. Tales and stories for Black folks
    Walker, A. In love & trouble
We drink the wine in France
    Walker, A. In love & trouble
The welcome table
    Walker, A. In love & trouble

**Walker, Evan K.**

Harlem transfer
    Coombs, O. ed. What we must see: young Black storytellers
    King, W. ed. Black short story anthology

**Walker, Victor Steven**

The long sell
    Chapman, A. ed. New Black voices

**Walker** Brothers cowboy. Munro, A.

**WALKING**

Blackmon, W. D. Walking to Ft. Worth
De Vries, P.   A walk in the country
    *See also* Backpacking

The **walking** dead. Usher, F.

**Walking** lessons. Price, R.

**Walking** out. Beckett, S.

**Walking** to Ft. Worth. Blackmon, W. D.

**Walking** wounded. Gerald, J. B.

The **wall** around the world. Cogswell, T. R.

**Wall** of darkness. Clarke, A. C.

**Wallace, Edgar**

The treasure hunt
    Kahn, J. ed. Trial and terror

**Wallach, Ira**

Death opens the mail
    Fitz Gerald, G. ed. Modern satiric stories

**Waller, Leslie**

The restless ones
    Brown, E. P. ed. Twice fifteen

**Wallmann, Jeffrey M.**

Ransom demand
    Hitchcock, A. ed. Alfred Hitchcock presents: Stories to be read with the lights on

**WALLS**

Keene, D. Homicide house

The **walls.** Henderson, Z.

**Walpole, Horace**

Maddalena; or, The fate of the Florentines
    Haining, P. ed. Gothic tales of terror

**Walpole, Sir Hugh**

Mrs Lunt
    Lamb, H. ed. A tide of terror

**Walrond, Eric**

The yellow one
    James, C. L. ed. From the roots

**Walsh, Donald J.**

The rings of the Papaloi
    Derleth, A. ed. Dark things

**Walsh, Jill Paton, and Crossley-Holland, Kevin**

Asser's book
    Walsh, J. P. and Crossley-Holland, K. Wordhoard
Cædmon
    Walsh, J. P. and Crossley-Holland, K. Wordhoard
The childmaster
    Walsh, J. P. and Crossley-Holland, K. Wordhoard
The eye of the hurricane
    Walsh, J. P. and Crossley-Holland, K. Wordhoard
The horseman
    Walsh, J. P. and Crossley-Holland, K. Wordhoard
Leof's leavetaking
    Walsh, J. P. and Crossley-Holland, K. Wordhoard
Thurkell the Tall
    Walsh, J. P. and Crossley-Holland, K. Wordhoard
The woodwose
    Walsh, J. P. and Crossley-Holland, K. Wordhoard

**Walsh, Rodolfo J.**

Gambler's tale
    Yates, D. A. ed. Latin blood
Shadow of a bird
    Yates, D. A. ed. Latin blood

**Walsh, Thomas**

Enemy agent
    Fenner, P. R. comp. Stories of escapes and hurried journeys

Ware, Edmund
  A lady comes to Paradise
    Collier, N. ed. Great stories of the West
    *For other stories by this author see*
    Smith, Edmund Ware
WARFARE. *See* War
The warlock. Leiber, F.
WARLOCKS. *See* Witchcraft
Warm man. Silverberg, R.
Warm simplicity. Dawson, F.
Warma kuyay. Arguedas, J. M.
Warner, Lucy
  A born homemaker
    Warner, L. Mirrors
  Breakthrough
    Warner, L. Mirrors
  Every girl has a mother somewhere
    Warner, L. Mirrors
  The expectancy of my survival
    Warner, L. Mirrors
  The girl who liked Communists
    Warner, L. Mirrors
  How sweet my daughter, how deep my
    anger
    Warner, L. Mirrors
  An insubstantial father
    Warner, L. Mirrors
  Melissa Savage
    Warner, L. Mirrors
  The minor repairs of life
    Warner, L. Mirrors
  Sky in winter
    Warner, L. Mirrors
Warner, Sylvia Townsend
  Bruno
    Warner, S. T. The innocent and the
      guilty
  But at the stroke of midnight
    Warner, S. T. The innocent and the
      guilty
  The green torso
    Warner, S. T. The innocent and the
      guilty
  Oxenhope
    Warner, S. T. The innocent and the
      guilty
  The perfect setting
    Warner, S. T. The innocent and the
      guilty
  The quality of mercy
    Warner, S. T. The innocent and the
      guilty
  Truth in the cup
    Warner, S. T. The innocent and the
      guilty
  Two children
    Warner, S. T. The innocent and the
      guilty
  A visionary gleam
    Warner, S. T. The innocent and the
      guilty
A warning to sceptics. Hardwick, Michael,
  and Hardwick, Mollie
A warning to the curious. James, M. R.
Warren, Robert Penn
  Goodwood comes back
    Howes, B. and Smith, G. J. eds. The
      sea-green horse

Meet me in the green glen
    The Best American short stories, 1972
  Phebe
    Burnett, W. ed. Black hands on a white
      face
  Statement of Ashby Wyndham
    Lytle, A. ed. Craft and vision
Warren, Samuel
  The March assize
    Kahn, J. ed. Trial and terror
Warren. Paquet, B. T.
Warrior. Dickson, G. R.
The warrior. Harrison, W.
WARS, INTERPLANETARY. *See* Inter-
    planetary wars
WARSAW. *See* Poland—Warsaw
WARSHIPS. *See* Destroyers (Warships)
Was I asleep? Gilliatt, P.
Wash. Faulkner, W.
Wash us and comb us. Deming, B.
WASHINGTON, GEORGE, PRESIDENT
    U.S.
  The Ghost of Washington
  Queen, E. The adventure of the Presi-
      dent's half disme
Washington, Irving
  Rip Van Winkle
    Haining, P. ed. Gothic tales of terror
Washington, James
  It only happens once
    Andrews, F. E. and Dickens, A. eds.
      Voices from the big house
WASHINGTON, D.C.
  Bates, H. Farewell to the master
  Davis, O. The roof garden
  Hubbard, L. R. He didn't like cats
  Just, W. The brigadier general and the
      columnist's wife
  Just, W. The congressman who loved Flau-
      bert, and other Washington stories;
      9 stories
  Just, W. Nora
  Just, W. Simpson's wife
  Mazor, J. The skylark
  Naipaul, V. S. One out of many
  Tiptree, J. Filomena & Greg & Rikki-Tikki
      & Barlow & the alien
WASHINGTON (STATE)
  Jones, N. Still to the West; excerpt
        Seattle
  Dolson, C. W. Passage to the day
  Ross, Z. When Seattle burned
WASTE DISPOSAL. *See* Refuse and refuse
    disposal
The waste land. Paton, A.
Wasted on the young. Brunner, J.
The watch. Turgenev, I.
Watch for it. Gores, J. N.
Watch out for Daddy. Algren, N.
Watch your step. Lindsay, C.
Watchdøg. Haldeman, J. C.
The watcher. Calvino, I.
A watcher by the dead. Bierce, A.
The watcher from the sky. Derleth, A.
The watchers. Randall, F. E.
WATCHES. *See* Clocks and watches
The watching. McCord, J.
WATCHMAKING. *See* Clocks and watches

**WATCHMEN**
Brennan, J. P. Death of a derelict
Charnock, G. The Chinese boxes
Ellison, H. Night vigil
Midwood, B. What of it?
O'Connor, F. The party
Wright, R. Big Black good man
The **watchtowers**. Ballard, J. G.
**WATER**
Barash, A. Hai's well
Carr, T. Hop-friend
Kassam, S. The child and the water-tap
Paz, O. My life with the wave

#### Pollution
Brister, B. The sand trout seminar
Howard, H. Oil-mad bug-eyed monsters
Jacobi, C. Mr Iper of Hamilton
The **water** ceremony. Bergé, C.
**Water** never hurt a man. Edmonds, W. D.
The **water** penalty. Stuart, J.
**WATER POLLUTION.** *See* Water—Pollution
The **water** spectre. Lathom, F.
**Water** treatment and the sore-tailed bronc. Green, B. K.
A **water** witch. Everett, Mrs H. D.
The **watercolor**. Grin, A.
**WATERFALLS**
Harrison, H. By the Falls
The **waterfowl** tree. Kittredge, W. A.
**Watermelon** hauler's mule. Green, B. K.
**WATERMELONS**
Crane, S. The knife
**Watkins, Richard Howells**
The turf and the dirt
Fenner, P. R. comp. Where speed is king
**Watson, Ethel Marriott-** *See* Marriott-Watson, Ethel
**Watson, Eugene**
The dropouts
Andrews, F. E. and Dickens, A. eds. Voices from the big house
The revolution and Mister Watson
Andrews, F. E. and Dickens, A. eds. Voices from the big house
The **watter's** mou'. Stoker, B.
**Waugh, Evelyn**
Cruise
Fitz Gerald, G. ed. Modern satiric stories
Incident in Azania
Auchincloss, L. ed. Fables of wit and elegance
Mr Loveday's little outing
Kahn, J. ed. Some things dark and dangerous

#### Parodies, travesties, etc.
De Vries, P. The man who read Waugh
**Waugh, Hillary**
Nothing but human nature
Mystery Writers of America. Murder most foul
The **waves** of night. Petrakis, H. M.
**WAX MUSEUMS.** *See* Waxworks
**WAXWORKS**
Nesbit, E. The head
Thomas, D. Jarley's

The **way** back. Grau, S. A.
The **way** it all comes loose. Maloney, R.
The **way** it is now. Bingham, S.
The **way** of life of Don Clintock. Holmes, E. M.
The **Way** of the Cross. Du Maurier, D.
The **way** of the world. Cather, W.
A **way** station. Jewett, S. O.
The **way** the dead love. Bukowski, C.
The **way** the ladies walk. Nettell, R.
The **way** the wind blows. Deck, J.
The **way** things are. Maltz, A.
The **way** to the attic. Brennan, J. P.
The **way** up to heaven. Dahl, R.
The **way** we went. Knight, W. E.
The **way** you'll never be. Hemingway, E.
The **wayfarer**. Coover, R.
**WAYLAND THE SMITH**
Kipling, R. Weland's sword
**We** all die naked. Blish, J.
**We** are dainty little people. Naylor, C.
**We** can remember it for you wholesale. Dick, P. K.
**We** didn't do anything wrong, hardly. Kuykendall, R.
**We** drink the wine in France. Walker, A.
**We** have not lived the right life. Gass, W. H.
**We**, in some strange power's employ, move on a rigorous line. Delany, S. R.
"**We** played under your window." Shcherbakov, V.
**We** print the truth. Boucher, A.
**We** spy. Howard, C.
**We** who came after. Fair, R. L.
The **weaker** sex. Blackhurst, W. E.
The **weaker** vessel. Cross, J.
The **weakling**. Stuart, J.
**WEALTH**
Bingham, S. Conversations
Cheever, J. The jewels of the Cabots
Chopin, K. Miss McEnders
Christie, A. The call of wings
Crane, S. A night at The Millionaire's Club
Di Donato, P. Tropic of Cuba
Elkin, S. The making of Ashenden
Gordimer, N. Otherwise birds fly in
Haldeman, J. W. Counterpoint
Henry, O. Mammon and the archer
Henry, O. The trimmed lamp
Maine, C. E. Short circuit
Marshall, L. Dialogue on a cliff
O'Hara, J. Mrs Stratton of Oak Knoll
Parker, D. The bolt behind the blue
Parker, D. The custard heart
Parker, D. The standard of living
Purdy, J. I am Elijah Thrush
Saxton, J. The power of time
Spike, P. The diary of Noel Wells
Uyeda, A. Wealth
Vonnegut, K. The lie
*See also* Millionaires; Property
The **weapon** shop. Van Vogt, A. E.
The **weapon** too dreadful to use. Asimov, I.
**WEAPONS.** *See* Arms and armor; Firearms; Ordnance
The **weary** Falcon. Mayer, T.

**Weinbaum, Stanley G.**
A Martian odyssey
   Asimov, I. ed. Where do we go from here?
   De Camp, L. S. and De Camp, C. C. eds. 3000 years of fantasy and science fiction
   Hipolito, J. and McNelly, W. E. eds. Mars, we love you
   Science fiction hall of fame, v 1
   Silverberg, R. ed. The science fiction bestiary
The planet of doubt
   Silverberg, R. ed. Tomorrow's worlds
The worlds of if
   Silverberg, R. ed. Other dimensions
**Weiner, Andrew**
Empire of the sun
   Ellison, H. ed. Again, dangerous visions
**Weisbrod, Rosine**
The ninth cold day
   The Best American short stories, 1970
**Weissenberg, I. M.**
A shtetl
   Wisse, R. R. ed. A shtetl, and other Yiddish novellas
**WELAND THE SMITH.** See Wayland the Smith
Weland's sword. Kipling, R.
**Welburn, Ron**
The nightsong of Dashiki Henry
   Intro #3
Welcome home. Gallico, P.
The welcome table. Walker, A.
Welcome to the standard nightmare. Sheckley, R.
Welcome to Utah. Butor, M.
**WELFARE.** See Public welfare
**WELL DRILLERS**
Cheever, J. Artemis, the honest well digger
Well of the deep wish. Biggle, L.
Well spiced. Sturgeon, T. and Ward, D.
**Wellen, Edward**
Down by the old maelstrom
   Orbit 11
**Wellman, Manly Wade**
School for the unspeakable
   Dickinson, S. ed. The usurping ghost, and other encounters and experiences
A star for a warrior
   Queen, E. ed. Ellery Queen's The golden 13
When it was moonlight
   Haining, P. ed. Vampires at midnight
**Wells, Carolyn**
Christabel's crystal
   Manley, S. and Lewis, G. eds. Grande dames of detection
**Wells, H. G.**
Aepyornis island
   Bowman, J. S. ed. A book of islands
Chronic Argonaut
   Elwood, R. and Ghidalia, V. eds. Androids, time machines and blue giraffes
The Country of the Blind
   Schulman, L. M. ed. The cracked looking glass

The door in the wall
   Green, R. L. ed. Thirteen uncanny tales
A dream of Armageddon
   Haining, P. ed. The nightmare reader
The flowering of the strange orchid
   Manley, S. and Lewis, G. eds. Shapes of the supernatural
   Same as: The strange orchid, listed in earlier volumes
The inexperienced ghost
   Manley, S. and Lewis, G. eds. A gathering of ghosts
The Lord of the Dynamos
   Hall, J. B. ed. The realm of fiction
The magic shop
   Kahn, J. ed. Some things fierce and fatal
The new accelerator
   De Camp, L. S. and De Camp, C. C. eds. 3000 years of fantasy and science fiction
The red room
   Dickinson, S. ed. The usurping ghost, and other encounters and experiences
The sea raiders
   Clareson, T. D. ed. A spectrum of worlds
   Kahn, J. ed. Hanging by a thread
The star
   Silverberg, R. ed. The mirror of infinity
The story of the late Mr Elvesham
   Kahn, J. ed. Some things strange and sinister
   Stern, P. V. ed. The other side of the clock
The time machine
   The Science fiction hall of fame v2A
The truth about Pyecraft
   Knight, D. ed. The golden road
Under the knife
   Knight, D. ed. Perchance to dream
The valley of the spiders
   Haining, P. ed. Nightfrights
War of the worlds
   Hipolito, J. and McNelly, W. E. eds. Mars, we love you
**WELLS**
Barash, A. Hai's well
Brodeur, P. The siphon
Nedreaas, T. Music from a blue well
Rolseth, H. Hey you down there
Sturgeon, T. Well spiced
   See also Well drillers
**Welty, Eudora**
Circe
   Matthews, J. ed. Archetypal themes in the modern story
Death of a traveling salesman
   Thune, E. and Prigozy, R. eds. Short stories: a critical anthology
The demonstrators
   Abrahams, W. ed. Fifty years of the American short story v2
   Davis, R. G. ed. Ten modern masters
   Gulassa, C. M. ed. The fact of fiction
   McKenzie, B. ed. The process of fiction
   Oates, J. C. ed. Scenes from American life

Welty, Eudora—*Continued*
The hitch-hikers
  12 short story writers
Livvie is back
  Abrahams, W. ed. Fifty years of the American short story v2
  Same as: Livvie, listed in earlier volumes
Moon Lake
  Lytle, A. ed. Craft and vision
No place for you, my love
  McKenzie, B. ed. The process of fiction
Petrified man
  Davis, R. G. ed. Ten modern masters
A piece of news
  12 short story writers
Powerhouse
  12 short story writers
A visit of charity
  Fitz Gerald, G. ed. Modern satiric stories
The wide net
  Foff, A. and Knapp, D. eds. Story
A worn path
  Davis, R. G. ed. Ten modern masters
The **werewolf.** Housman, C.
The **werewolf.** Lamb, D. S.
The **werewolf.** Marryat, H. B.
The **werewolf** of St-Claude. Seth, R.
**WEREWOLVES.** *See* Werwolves
**Werewoman.** Moore, C. L.
**Wertheim, Joan**
C'mon you
  Voices of Brooklyn
**WERWOLVES**
Aiken, J. Furry night
Aiken, J. The green flash
Boucher, A. The compleat werewolf
Case, D. The cell
Christensen, L. E. The tempest
Day, J. W. The dog-man horror of the valley
Eddy, C. M. The ghost-eater
Greene, L. Bound by a spell; excerpt
Housman, C. The werewolf
Kipling, R. The mark of the beast
Lamb, D. S. The werewolf
Marryat, H. B. The werewolf
Menzies, S. Hugues, the wer-wolf
Seth, R. The werewolf of St-Claude
Smith, C. A. Monsters in the night
**Wescott, Glenway**
Prohibition
  Abrahams, W. ed. Fifty years of the American short story v2
**Wesley, Joseph**
Womb to tomb
  Analog 8
  Best SF: 1969
**West, Anne**
The conversion
  Intro 4
**West, Jessamyn**
After the battle
  West, J. Except for me and thee
Alive and real
  West, J. Crimson Ramblers of the world, farewell

Child of the century
  West, J. Crimson Ramblers of the world, farewell
The condemned librarian
  West, J. Crimson Ramblers of the world, farewell
Cress Delahanty
  Ball, J. E. ed. Designs for reading: short stories
Crimson Ramblers of the world, farewell
  West, J. Crimson Ramblers of the world, farewell
  Zolotow, C. ed. An overpraised season
The day of the hawk
  West, J. Crimson Ramblers of the world, farewell
A family argument
  West, J. Except for me and thee
Fast horseflesh
  West, J. Except for me and thee
First loss
  West, J. Except for me and thee
Gallup Poll
  West, J. Crimson Ramblers of the world, farewell
Growing up
  West, J. Except for me and thee
Heading west
  West, J. Except for me and thee
The heavy stone
  West, J. Crimson Ramblers of the world, farewell
Home for Christmas
  West, J. Except for me and thee
Hunting for hoot owls
  West, J. Crimson Ramblers of the world, farewell
I'll ask him to come sooner
  West, J. Crimson Ramblers of the world, farewell
Like visitant of air
  West, J. Crimson Ramblers of the world, farewell
Live life deeply
  West, J. Crimson Ramblers of the world, farewell
Mother of three
  West, J. Except for me and thee
Mother's Day
  West, J. Crimson Ramblers of the world, farewell
Neighbors
  West, J. Except for me and thee
The new home
  West, J. Except for me and thee
Night piece for Julia
  West, J. Crimson Ramblers of the world, farewell
99.6
  West, J. Crimson Ramblers of the world, farewell
There ought to be a judge
  West, J. Crimson Ramblers of the world, farewell
Up a tree
  Dickensheet, D. ed. Men and malice
  West, J. Crimson Ramblers of the world, farewell

White challa. Shapiro, L.
The white church. Brú, H.
The white city. Keller, D. H.
The white city. Megged, A.
White days and red nights. Conroy, F.
White flowers. Vinhranovsky, M.
The white hat. Rohmer, S.
The white horses of Vienna. Boyle, K.
The White Khan. Lamb, H.
The white line. Ferguson, J.
The white mustang. Schaefer, J.
White on black. Slesinger, T.
The white paper on sex and technology.
    Sherwin, J. J.
The white people. Machen, A.
The white pinnacle. Jacobi, C.
A white pussy. Bukowski, C.
The white seal. Kipling, R.
The white sky. Scobie, S.
White summer in Memphis. Eklund, G.
The white swallow. Yovkov, Y.
The white trousers. Kemal, Y.
**Whitechurch, Victor L.**
    The affair of the German Dispatch-Box
        Greene, Sir H. ed. The further rivals of
        Sherlock Holmes
Whitewash. Macauley, R.
The whitewing snow job. Brister, B.
Who can avoid a place? McFadden, D.
Who can replace a man? Aldiss, B. W.
Who cares? Rama Rau, S.
Who cares about an old woman? Gilbert, A.
Who goes there? Stuart, D. A.
Who has seen the wind? McCullers, C.
Who killed Charlie Winpole? Bramah, E.
Who killed Pretty Brilliant? Elman, R.
Who knows where the time goes? Brown-
    stein, M.
Who to who. Kanin, G.
Whodunit: murder offstage. Hoch, E. D.
A whole loaf. Agnon, S. Y.
The whole round world. Goulart, R.
The whole truth. Anthony, P.
**WHORES.** *See* Prostitutes
Who's got the lady? Ritchie, J.
"Whose children?" Peterkin, J.
Why? Silverberg, R.
Why Atlantis sank. Donev, A.
Why, Bo? Why? Savitz, H.
Why bother with Solly? Ruskay, S.
Why can't they tell you why? Purdy, J.
Why did the young clerk swear? Crane, S.
Why do the heathen rage? O'Connor, F.
Why haven't you written? Gordimer, N.
Why Herbert killed his mother. Holtby, W.
Why I am not editing "The Stinger."
    Bierce, A.
Why Menifee wasn't our country. Stuart, J.
Why reeds are hollow. Mistral, G.
Why the rose is red. Corvo, F. Baron
Why we're here. McGahern, J.
Why, who said so? Moravia, A.
Why, you reckon? Hughes, L.
Whydunit: the Nile cat. Hoch, E. D.
Wicked Captain Walshawe. Le Fanu, J. S.
The wicked cousin. Charteris, L.
The wicked flee. Harrison, H.
The wicked ghost. Brand, C.
The wide net. Welty, E.

Wide O-. Gardner, E. A.
The widening circle. McCloud, R.
The widow. Babel, I.
The widow. Trevisan, D.
The widow, bereft. Blake, J.
The widow Ching, lady pirate. Borges, J. L.
The widower Turmore. Bierce, A.
**WIDOWERS**
    Agnon, S. J.   A Passover courting
    Bar-Yosef, Y. The window
    Bierce, A. The widower Turmore
    Blake, G.   A modern development
    Brennan, M. The drowned man
    Carr, A. H. Z. The black kitten
    Cather, W. Eleanor's house
    Chute, B. J. The legacy
    Colter, C. Girl friend
    Colter, C. Rapport
    Goldin, S. and Hensel, C. F.   Harriet
    Lavin, M. Heart of gold
    Lavin, M. In the middle of the fields
    Matthews, J. On the shore of Chad Creek
    Moravia, A. Don't let's be dramatic
    Nabokov, V. Ultima Thule
    Oates, J. C. The wheel of love
    Onetti, J. C. Dreaded hell
    Pelin, E. All Souls' Day
    Ramkumar. Sailor
    Ruskay, S. The portrait
    Steegmuller, F.   A real saint
    Taylor, E. Flesh
    Tuohy, F. The licence
    Verga, G. The orphans
    Wolfe, G. Sonya, Crane Wessleman, and
        Kittee
    Young, R. F. The years
    Zobarskas, S.   A woman's laugh
**WIDOWS**
    Agnon, S. J.   A Passover courting
    Ansell, J. Love, Mother
    Auchincloss, L. Suttee
    Beckett, S. Draff
    Betts, D. The glory of his nostrils
    Blythe, R. Everything a man needs
    Brown, R.   A letter to Ismael in the grave
    Buck, P. S. The green sari
    Calisher, H. The scream on 57th Street
    Capote, T.   Miriam
    Cheever, J. Three stories: II
    Chopin, K. The story of an hour
    Chu, Yo-sup. My mother and the roomer
    Deloney, T. Jack of Newbury and the
        widow
    Drake, R. The fifth wheel
    Francis, H. E. The fence
    Gillespie, A. Tonight at nine thirty-six
    Gilliatt, P. As we have learnt from Freud,
        there are no jokes
    Goldberg, G. J. The Bach Master
    Grau, S. A. Three
    Harvor, B. Countries
    James, D. The thin thread
    James, H. The abasement of the North-
        mores
    Kanin, G. The dog act
    Lane, M. The thing about Mrs Slezinger
    Lavin, M. The cuckoo-spit
    Lavin, M. In the middle of the fields
    Lavin, M. The long ago

Wilhelm, Kate—*Continued*
  On the road to Honeyville
    Orbit 11
  The planners
    Nebula award stories 4
  The red canary
    Orbit 12
  Somerset dreams
    Knight, D. ed. A science fiction argosy
    Orbit 5
  The village
    Disch, T. M. ed. Bad moon rising
  Windsong
    Knight, D. ed. A pocketful of stars
Will o' the Mill. Stevenson, R. L.
The will of the wicked usurer. Straparola
Will the circle be unbroken? Dumas, H.
Will the merchant prince's son come down
  the sawdust trail? Drake, R.
Will you wait? Bester, A.
Willard, Nancy
  The tailor who told the truth
    New Directions in prose and poetry 24
  Theo's girl
    Prize stories, 1970: The O. Henry
    Awards
WILLIAM I, THE CONQUEROR, KING
  OF ENGLAND
  Graham, W. Vive le roi
  Treece, H. The man on the hill
WILLIAM III, KING OF GREAT BRIT-
  AIN
  Linklater, E. The masks of purpose
WILLIAM OF ORANGE. *See* William III,
  King of Great Britain
William Wilson. Poe, E. A.
Williams, Gene
  The yellow brick road
    Best of the Best detective stories
Williams, Jay
  Somebody to play with
    Howes, B. and Smith, G. J. eds. The
    sea-green horse
Williams, John A.
  The figure eight
    Adoff, A. ed. Brothers and sisters
  A good season
    King, W. ed. Black short story anthol-
    ogy
  Son in the afternoon
    Disch, R. and Schwartz, B. eds. Killing
    time
    Gulassa, C. M. ed. The fact of fiction
    Margolies, E. ed. A native sons reader
Williams, Joy
  The lover
    Lish, G. ed. The secret life of our times:
    new fiction from Esquire
  Shorelines
    Lish, G. ed. The secret life of our times:
    new fiction from Esquire
Williams, Tennessee
  Happy August the 10th
    The Best American short stories, 1973
Williams, William Carlos
  The use of force
    Minot, S. and Wilson, R. eds. Three
    stances of modern fiction
    Tytell, J. and Jaffe, H. eds. Affinities

Williamson, Geoffrey
  Accusing eyes of vengeance
    Canning, J. ed. 50 great horror stories
  They ate their young shipmate
    Canning, J. ed. 50 great horror stories
  Trapped in a flooded tunnel
    Canning, J. ed. 50 great horror stories
Williamson, J. N.
  They never even see me
    Ellery Queen's Mystery Magazine. El-
    lery Queen's Headliners
Williamson, Jack
  The metal man
    Clareson, T. D. ed. A spectrum of
    worlds
    Elwood, R. and Ghidalia, V. eds. An-
    droids, time machines and blue
    giraffes
  With folded hands
    The Science fiction hall of fame v2A
The willing muse. Cather, W.
Willing victim. Hershman, M.
Willis Shumaker's resignation. Estes, W. M.
The Willow tree. Rice, J.
WILLS
  Barth, J. The law
  Bierce, A. The famous Gilson bequest
  Carr, J. D. The gentleman from Paris
  Cather, W. Her boss
  Colette. Green sealing-wax
  Collins, W. Mr Lepel and the housekeeper
  Di Donato, P. When Willy K. Vanderbilt
    frolicked and I shoveled his snow
  Eddy, C. M. A solitary solution
  Gilbert, M. Accessories after the fact
  Maugham, W. S. A point of law
  Orczy, Baroness. The Dublin mystery
  Petaja, E. Hunger
  Sayers, D. L. The fascinating problem of
    Uncle Meleager's will
  Sayers, D. L. The undignified melodrama
    of the bone of contention
  Straparola. The will of the wicked usurer
  Verga, G. Nanni Volpe
    *See also* Inheritance and succession
Willumsen, Dorrit
  Complication
    Holm, S. ed. The Devil's instrument,
    and other Danish stories
Willy-nilly. Friedman, A.
Wilson, Angus
  After the show
    Wilson, A. Death dance
  Animals or human beings
    Haining, P. ed. The Lucifer society
  A bit off the map
    Wilson, A. Death dance
  Christmas Day in the workhouse
    Wilson, A. Death dance
  Crazy crowd
    Wilson, A. Death dance
  Et Dona Ferentes
    Wilson, A. Death dance
  A flat country Christmas
    Wilson, A. Death dance

**Winslow, Joyce Madelon**
Benjamin burning
The Best American short stories, 1969
**Winston, Daoma**
Circles in the sky
Mystery Writers of America. Mirror,
mirror, fatal mirror
**Winston.** Reed, K.
**Winter, J. A.**
Expedition Polychrome
Norton, A. and Donaldy, E. eds. Gates
to tomorrow
**WINTER**
Clark, W. V. The wind and the snow of
winter
Coover, R. Scene for "winter"
**Winter.** Reed, K.
A **winter** day. Leskov, N.
A **winter** evening. Bromhead, F.
The **winter** flies. Leiber, F.
**Winter** is here. Kesey, K.
**Winter** northwester. Holmes, E. M.
**Winter** rug. Brautigan, R.
The **winter** soldiers. Kobak, D.
**WINTER SPORTS.** *See* Coasting; Skating
**Winters, Emmanuel**
God's agents have beards
Lewis, J. D. ed. Tales of our people
**Winter's** king. LeGuin, U. K.
A **winter's** tale. Eustis, H.
A **winter's** tale. James, B. P.
A **winter's** tale. Marsh, W.
**Winther, M. A.**
The battle of Klandurskot
Faroese short stories
Hunger
Faroese short stories
To catch a thief
Faroese short stories
**Wintle, William**
The black cat
Parry, M. ed. Beware of the cat
A **wireless** message. Bierce, A.
The **wireless** set. Brown, G. M.
**WISCONSIN**
Derleth, A. The dweller in darkness
McNear, R. Death's door
**Green Bay**
Shaw, I. Whispers in Bedlam
**Police**
*See* Police—Wisconsin
The **wisdom** of silence. Dunbar, P. L.
The **wise** and foolish ladies. Marguerite de
Navarre
**WISE MEN.** *See* Magi
The **wise** men: a detail of American life in
Mexico. Crane, S.
**Wiser, William**
A soliloquy in tongues
Bernkopf, J. F. comp. Boucher's choic-
est
**Wiser** than a god. Chopin, K.
The **wisest** oracle. Delattre, P.
The **wish.** Zobarskas, S.
**WISHES**
Aiken, J. All you've ever wanted
Beckford, W. The Nymph of the Fountain
Hesse, H. Faldum

Holst, S. The man who was always wish-
ing
Jan Schalken's three wishes
Pyle, H. The dead finger
Schwimmer, W.   A full and happy life
Sheckley, R. The same to you doubled
Stern, P. V. The greatest gift
Stevenson, R. L. The bottle imp
**Wister, Owen**
Hank's woman
Wister, O. The West of Owen Wister
Little Big Horn medicine
Wister, O. The West of Owen Wister
Napoleon Shave-Tail
Wister, O. The West of Owen Wister
Padre Ignazio
Wister, O. The West of Owen Wister
A pilgrim on the Gila
Wister, O. The West of Owen Wister
The Second Missouri Compromise
Wister, O. The West of Owen Wister
The winning of the biscuit-shooter
Taylor, J. G. ed. Great Western short
stories
The **witch.** Chekhov, A.
The **witch.** Gold, H.
The **witch.** Jackson, S.
The **witch.** Van Vogt, A. E.
The **witch** baiter. Anthony, R.
A **witch** burning. Reynolds, B.
**WITCH DOCTORS.** *See* Witchcraft
The **Witch** of Eye. D'Arnaud, F. B.
The **witch** of the marsh. Marriott-Watson, E.
The **Witch** spectre
Haining, P. ed. A circle of witches
**Witch** wood. Dunsany, Lord
**WITCHCRAFT**
Ainsworth, W. H. The midnight assembly
Anthony, R. The witch baiter
Beaumont, C. The new people
Benson, E. F. Gavon's Eve
Blackwood, A. Ancient sorceries
Bloch, R. Broomstick ride
Bradbury, R. Invisible boy
Bradbury, R. The mad wizards of Mars
Brennan, J. P. Canavan's back yard
Brennan, J. P. The seventh incantation
Brunner, J. All the devils in hell
Bukowski, C. Six inches
Carter, L. Shaggai
Chekhov, A. The sinner from Toledo
Cloete, S. The second nail
Collier, J. The lady on the gray
D'Arnaud, F. B. The Witch of Eye
Davidson, A. The power of every root
Dickinson, W. C. The witch's bone
Di Donato, P. La Smorfia
Eddy, C. M. Deaf, dumb and blind
Eisenstein, P. Born to exile
Ellison, R.   A coupla scalped Indians
Fraser, Mrs H. The Satanist
Gilbert, A. Door to a different world
Gogol, N. Black Sunday
Green, W. C. Secrets of Cabalism
Greene, L. Bound by a spell; excerpt
Haining, P. ed. A circle of witches; 11
stories
Haining, P. ed. The necromancers; 10
stories

**Wright, Richard**
  Almos' a man
    James, C. L. ed. From the roots
    Same as: The man who was almost a
      man
  Big Black good man
    Kissin, E. H. ed. Stories in black and
      white
  Big Boy leaves home
    James, C. L. ed. From the roots
    Margolies, E. ed. A native sons reader
  Bright and morning star
    Long, R. A. and Collier, E. W. eds.
      Afro-American writing v2
    Thune, E. and Prigozy, R. eds. Short
      stories: a critical anthology
    Tytell, J. and Jaffe, H. eds. Affinities
  Fire and cloud
    Abrahams, W. ed. Fifty years of the
      American short story v2
  The man who killed a shadow
    Gulassa, C. M. ed. The fact of fiction
  The man who lived underground
    Hamalian, L. and Volpe, E. L. eds.
      Eleven modern short novels
  The man who was almost a man
    Adoff, A. ed. Brothers and sisters
    Turner, D. T. ed. Black American liter-
      ature
    Same as: Almos' a man
  The man who went to Chicago
    Karl, F. R. and Hamalian, L. eds. The
      naked i
    Margolies, E. ed. A native sons reader
**Wright, S. Fowler**
  The better choice
    Necker, C. ed. Supernatural cats
**Wright, Sylvia**
  Dans le vrai
    Wright, S.  A shark-infested rice pud-
      ding
  Fathers and mothers
    Wright, S.  A shark-infested rice pud-
      ding
  A shark-infested rice pudding
    Wright, S.  A shark-infested rice pud-
      ding
**Wright, Waldo Carlton**
  The green fly and the box
    Hitchcock, A. ed. Alfred Hitchcock pre-
      sents: Stories to be read with the
      lights on
**WRIGHT, WILLARD HUNTINGTON**
    **Parodies, travesties, etc.**
  Breen, J. L. The Austin murder case
The **writer** in the garret. Lumley, B.
**WRITERS.** *See* Authors; and special classes
    of writers, e.g. Dramatists
**WRITERS' CONFERENCES.** *See* Authors'
    conferences
**WRITERS' WORKSHOPS.** *See* Authors'
    conferences
**WRITING.** *See* Picture writing, Indian
**WRITING (AUTHORSHIP)** *See* Author-
    ship
**Writing** of the rat. Blish, J.
The **wrong** element. Drake, R.
The **wrong** order. Taylor, E.

The **wrong** road. Allen, E.
The **wrong** set. Wilson, A.
The **wrong** sword. Gulik, R. van
The **wrong**-way ambush. Brister, B.
**Wrong** way street. Niven, L.
**Wu, Ch'eng-en**
  The temptation of Saint Pigsy
    Birch, C. ed. Anthology of Chinese
      literature v2
**Wu, Tsu-hsiang**
  Fan village
    Hsia, C. T. ed. Twentieth-century Chi-
      nese stories
**Wulffson, Don**
  You too can be a floorwax that even your
      husband could apply
    New Directions in prose and poetry 23
**Wunderkind.** McCullers, C.
**Wyal, Pg**
  The castle on the crag
    Best SF: 1969
**Wylie, Philip**
  The old crawdad
    Corodimas, P. ed. In trout country
  Once on a Sunday
    Lyons, N. ed. Fisherman's bounty
**Wyndham, John**
  Chinese puzzle
    Silverberg, B. ed. Phoenix feathers
  Chronoclasm
    Stern, P. V. ed. The other side of the
      clock
  Close behind him
    Haining, P. ed. Nightfrights
  Consider her ways
    Knight, D. ed. A science fiction argosy
  Jizzle
    Haining, P. ed. The freak show
  Technical slip
    Carr, T. ed. Into the unknown
**WYOMING**
    **Frontier and pioneer life**
    *See* Frontier and pioneer life—Wyo-
    ming

    **Saratoga**
  Hayes, A. H. The last laugh
**WYOMING MASSACRE, 1778**
  Crane, S. The battle of Forty Fort
  Crane, S. "Ol' Bennet" and the Indians
  Crane, S. The surrender of Forty Fort

# X

**Xavier** Fereira's unfinished book: chapter
    one. Strong, J.
**Xlebnikov, A.**
  Human frailty
    Magidoff, R. ed. Russian science fiction,
      1969

# Y

**Yaari, Yehuda**
  The wanderer and the blind man
    Michener, J. A. ed. First fruit

**YACHT RACING**
Clarke, A. C. Sunjammer
Clarke, A. C. The wind from the sun
**YACHTS AND YACHTING**
Collier, J. Man overboard
Ellin, S. The payoff
  *See also* Yacht racing
**Yadav, Rajendra**
A reminder
  Roadarmel, G. C. ed. A death in Delhi
**Yamamoto, Mitsu**
The blue rug
  Hitchcock, A. ed. Alfred Hitchcock presents: Stories to be read with the lights on
Miss Kemper comes home in the dark
  Best detective stories of the year, 1973
**Yang, P'ing.** *See* Shih, Ming
**Yang, Yi.** *See* Shui, Ching
**Yankee** go home. Maloney, R.
**Yanovsky, Yuriy**
A boat in the sea
  Luckyj, G. S. N. ed. Modern Ukrainian short stories
**Yarbro, Chelsea Quinn**
False dawn
  Scortia, T. N. ed. Strange bedfellows
The ghosts at Iron River
  Dickensheet, D. ed. Men and malice
**YARDS**
Brautigan, R. Revenge of the lawn
**Yarov, Romain**
The founding of civilization
  Suvin, D. ed. Other worlds, other seas
**Yashin, Alexander**
Levers
  Pomorska, K. ed. Fifty years of Russian prose: from Pasternak to Solzhenitsyn v2
**Yashpal**
The book of experience
  Yashpal. Short stories of Yashpal
The Emperor's justice
  Yashpal. Short stories of Yashpal
The essence of love
  Yashpal. Short stories of Yashpal
A name for the painting
  Yashpal. Short stories of Yashpal
One cigarette
  Yashpal. Short stories of Yashpal
Purchased happiness
  Yashpal. Short stories of Yashpal
Sāg
  Yashpal. Short stories of Yashpal
To uphold righteousness
  Yashpal. Short stories of Yashpal
Two desperate souls
  Yashpal. Short stories of Yashpal
**Yates, Ethel M.**
Seeds of time
  Alabama prize stories, 1970
**Yates, Richard**
The best of everything
  Matthews, J. ed. Archetypal themes in the modern story
Builders
  Johnson, E. W. ed. Short stories international

Jody rolled the bones
  Roecker, W. A. ed. Stories that count
**Yatskiv, Mykhaylo**
Cedar wood will grow
  Luckyj, G. S. N. ed. Modern Ukrainian short stories
**Ye** lyttle Salem maide; excerpt. Mackie, P.
The **year.** Keeling, N.
A **year** in Regent's Park. Lessing, D.
**Year** nine. Connolly, C.
The **years.** Young, R. F.
**Yeats, W. B.**
The crucifixion of the outcast
  Haining, P. ed. The wild night company: Irish stories of fantasy and horror
**Yehoshua, A. B.**
Facing the forests
  Lish, G. ed. The secret life of our times: new fiction from Esquire
  Yehoshua, A. B. Three days and a child
Flood tide
  Yehoshua, A. B. Three days and a child
A long hot day
  Michener, J. A. ed. First fruits
  Same as: A long hot day, his despair, his wife and daughter
A long hot day, his despair, his wife and his daughter
  Yehoshua, A. B. Three days and a child
  Same as: A long hot day
A poet's continuing silence
  Yehoshua, A. B. Three days and a child
Three days and a child
  Yehoshua, A. B. Three days and a child
**Yellen, Samuel**
The four sides of a triangle
  Ribalow, H. U. ed. My name aloud
**Yellow.** Beckett, S.
The **yellow** brick road. Williams, G.
The **yellow** cat. Mordaunt, E.
The **yellow** one. Walrond, E.
The **yellow** pill. Phillips, R.
The **yellow** shawl. Arcellana, F.
The **yellow** sweater. Garner, H.
The **yellow** teapot. Hayes, A. H.
The **yellow** wall paper. Gilman, C. P.
**Yemtsev, Mikhail, and Parnov, Yeremey**
He who leaves no trace
  Ginsburg, M. ed. The ultimate threshold
**Yen-Hock** Bill and his sweetheart. Crane, S.
**Yentl** the Yeshiva boy. Singer, I. B.
**Yep, Laurence**
Looking-glass sea
  Scortia, T. N. ed. Strange bedfellows
**Yerby, Frank**
Health card
  Kissin, E. H. ed. Stories in black and white
The homecoming
  James, C. L. ed. From the roots
My brother went to college
  Turner, D. T. ed. Black American literature
The **yes**-men of Venus. Goulart, R.
**Yes,** we have no Ritchard. Friedman, B. J.
**Yes,** we'll gather at the river. Bradbury, R.
**YESHIVA.** *See* Religious education, Jewish

**YOUTH—**Continued

  Blackmon, W. D. Walking to Ft. Worth
  Brister, B. Of perches and pleasures
  Brister, B. Tiro al pichon!
  Brunner, J. Wasted on the young
  Buchan, P. It's cold out there
  Charyn, J. Sing, Shaindele, sing
  DeVries, P. Afternoon of a faun
  Di Donato, P. The broken scaffold
  Di Donato, P. The overnight guest
  Drake, R. My own true love
  Dubus, A. If they knew Yvonne
  Dumas, H. Double Nigger
  Duodu, C. The tax dodger
  Fitzgerald, F. S. Emotional bankruptcy
  Fitzgerald, F. S. Forging ahead
  Flythe, S. Point of conversion
  Griffith, P. B. Nights at O'Rear's
  Hesse, H. The cyclone
  Hesse, H. The island dream
  Hunter, E. Terminal misunderstanding
  Jewett, S. O. An every-day girl
  Knowlton, D. Murderer on the mountain
  Lamb, D. S. Perfidia
  Laurence, M. Horses of the night
  Lavender, D. High victory
  Lavin, M. The young girls
  Levy, R. Plum Beach
  Lindholm, C.   A California novel
  Litvinov, I. Pru girl
  Muller, E. The Irish sixpence
  Munro, A. Sunday afternoon
  Munro, A. Thanks for the ride
  Naylor, P. R. Everything today
  Naylor, P. R. The nothingness
  Olsen, T. Requa I
  Petrakis, H. M. The sweet life
  Rolland, R. Pierre and Luce
  Sargent, P.   A sense of difference
  Schulman, L. M. ed. The loners; 10 stories
  Shenhar, Y. On Galilean shores
  Shetzline, D. Country of the painted
    freaks
  Silverberg, R. Caught in the organ draft
  Spike, P. Specks saga
  Stewart, N. Evil eye
  Strong, J. Supperburger
  Strong, J. Tike
  Stuart, J. The highest bidder
  Stuart, J. Victory and the dream
  Thomas, D. One warm Saturday
  Tiptree, J. Filomena & Greg & Rikki-Tikki
    & Barlow & the alien
  Trevor, W. Kinkies
  Tuohy, F. Thunderbolt
  Updike, J. The hillies
  Weston, J. Goat songs
  White, E. Sursum corda (Lift up your
    hearts)
  Willard, N. Theo's girl
  Yates, E. M. Seeds of time
  Zolotow, C. ed. An overpraised season; 10
    stories
      *See also* Adolescence; College students

**Employment**

  Mayer, T. The feel of it

Youth. Stanev, L.

**YOUTH EMPLOYMENT.** *See* Youth—Employment

Youth from Vienna. Collier, J.

**YOUTH MOVEMENT.** *See* Students—Political activity

**Yovkov, Yordan**
  Heroes' heads
    Kirilov, N. and Kirk, F. eds. Introduction to modern Bulgarian literature
  Shibil
    Kirilov, N. and Kirk, F. eds. Introduction to modern Bulgarian literature
  The white swallow
    Kirilov, N. and Kirk, F. eds. Introduction to modern Bulgarian literature

**Yu, Hyŏn-jong**
  D. M. Z.
    Shimer, D. B. ed. Voices of modern Asia

**Yü, Ta-fu**
  Sinking
    Hsia, C. T. ed. Twentieth-century Chinese stories

**Yüan, Mei**
  Three ghost stories
    Birch, C. ed. Anthology of Chinese literature v2

**YUGOSLAVIA**
  Ćosić, B. The king of the poets
  Djilas, M. The brothers and the girl
  Harrison, H. The powers of observation
  Harrison, H. Rescue operation
  Johnson, B. ed. New writing in Yugoslavia; 17 stories
  Mihajlović, D. When the pumpkins blossomed
    *See also* Croatia

**Belgrade**
  Ribnikar, J. You

**Bosnia and Herzegovina**
  Kovač, M. Uncle Donato's death

**Collective farms**
  *See* Collective farms—Yugoslavia

**Dubrovnik**
  Symons, J.   A theme for Hyacinth

**Montenegro**
  Djilas, M.   A Montenegrin jest
  Djilas, M. The old man and the song
  Djilas, M. The stone and the violets; 11 stories

**YUGOSLAVIA, PROVINCIAL AND RURAL**
  Koš, E. The man who knew where the north was and where the south
  Šćepanović, B. The death of Mr Goluža
  Tolstoy, A. The family of a Vourdalak

**YUGOSLAVS IN FRANCE**
  Krleža, M. Hodorlahomor the Great

**YUGOSLAVS IN HUNGARY**
  Djilas, M. An eye for an eye

**YUGOSLAVS IN THE UNITED STATES**
  Collins, M. Freedom fighter
  Stern, R. Milius and Melanie

**Yukio Mishima.** *See* Mishima, Yukio

# PART II

# List of Collections Indexed

An author and title list of collections indexed, with their various editions.

**Abrahams, William**
*808.83* (ed.) Fifty years of the Ameri-
*ABR* can short story; from The O.
Henry Awards, 1919-1970; ed.
and with an introduction by
William Abrahams. Doubleday
1970 2v
*Fic.* ISBN 0-385-07452-2
*PRI* (ed.) Prize stories, 1969-1973:
*70,71,72,* The O. Henry Awards. *See*
*73* Prize stories, 1969-1973: The
O. Henry Awards

**Achebe, Chinua**
Girls at war, and other stories.
Doubleday 1973 129p
ISBN 0-385-00852-X

**Adoff, Arnold**
(ed.) Brothers and sisters; modern stories by Black Americans.
Macmillan (N Y) 1970 237p

**Adventures** into unknowns. Maclagan, D.

**Affinities.** Tytell, J. and Jaffe, H.
eds.

**Africa** is thunder and wonder. Nolen, B. ed.

**African** short stories. Larson, C. R.
ed.

**African** writing today. Angoff, C.
and Povey, J. eds.

**Afro-American** writing. Long, R. A.
and Collier, E. W. eds.

**Afterglow.** Blackhurst, W. E.

**Afternoon** in the jungle. Maltz, A.

*Fic* **Again,** dangerous visions. Ellison, H.
*ELL* ed.
*sci.Fi.*

**Agnon, S. Y.**
Twenty-one stories; ed. by Na-
hum N. Glatzer. Schocken
1970 287p
ISBN 0-8052-3020-3

An **agreement** between us. Hermann, J.

**Aidoo, Ama Ata**
No sweetness here. Doubleday
1971 [1970] 156p
ISBN 0-385-03233-1

**Aiken, Joan**
The green flash, and other tales
of horror, suspense, and fantasy. Holt 1971 163p
ISBN 0-03-080288-1

**Alabama** prize stories, 1970; ed. and
with an introduction by O. B.
Emerson. Strode 1970 342p
illus
ISBN 0-87397-014-4

**Alchemy** and academe. McCaffrey, A. ed.

The **Aleph,** and other stories, 1933-
1969. Borges, J. L.

*808.83* **Alfred** Hitchcock presents: A month
*HIT* of mystery. Hitchcock, A. ed.

**Alfred** Hitchcock presents: Stories
*808.83* to be read with the lights on.
*HIT* Hitchcock, A. ed.

**Alfred** Hitchcock presents: Stories
*808.83* to stay awake by. Hitchcock,
*HIT* A. ed.

**Alfred** Hitchcock's Daring detectives. Htichcock, A. ed.

**Alfred** Hitchcock's Supernatural
tales of terror and suspense.
Hitchcock, A. comp.

**Algren, Nelson**
The last carousel. Putnam 1973
435p
SBN 399-11131-X
Analyzed for short stories
only

**All** fires the fire, and other stories.
Cortázar, J.

**Allingham, Margery**
The Allingham Case-book. Mor-
row 1969 221p
The Allingham minibus. Morrow
1973 240p
ISBN 0-688-00178-5

The **Allingham** Case-book. Allingham, M.

The **Allingham** minibus. Allingham, M.

**Almost** home. Schwartz, J.

**Alone** against tomorrow. Ellison, H.

**Alquit, Eliezer Blum-** *See* Blum-
Alquit, Eliezer

**American** Review. *See also* New
American Review v 1-15

**American** Review, 16-18; the magazine of new writing. [Editor:
Theodore Solotaroff]. Bantam
1973 3v
Analyzed for short stories
only

# B

**Babel, Isaac**
Benya Krik, the gangster, and other stories; ed. by Avrahm Yarmolinsky. Schocken 1969 128p
ISBN 0-8052-0244-7
You must know everything; stories, 1915-1937; tr. from the Russian by Max Hayward; ed. and with notes, by Nathalie Babel. Farrar, Straus 1969 283p
    Analyzed for short stories only

**Baby** Perpetua, and other stories. Dillon, M.

**Bad** moon rising. Disch, T. M. ed.

**Bad** news. Spike, P.

**Bahr, Jerome**
The perishing republic. Trempealeau Press 1971 148p
ISBN 0-912540-01-X

**Baker, Denys Val.** *See* Val Baker, Denys

**Ball, Jane Eklund**
(ed.) Designs for reading: short stories. Houghton 1969 250p (Houghton Bks. in literature)

FIC BAL Sci.Fic
**Ballard, J. G.**
Chronopolis, and other stories. Putnam 1971 319p
ISBN 0-399-10141-1

**Ballard, Todhunter**
(ed.) Western Writers of America. A Western bonanza

The **ballroom** of romance, and other stories. Trevor, W.

FIC BAM
**Bambara, Toni Cade**
Gorilla, my love. Random House 1972 177p
ISBN 0-394-48201-8
(ed.) Tales and stories for Black folks. Doubleday 1971 164p (Zenith bks)
ISBN 0-385-06598-1
    Partially analyzed

The **banishment,** and three stories. Stone, A.

**Barbed** wire, and other stories. Canzoneri, R.

**Barthelme, Donald**
City life. Farrar, Straus 1970 168p illus
ISBN 0-374-12408-6
Sadness. Farrar, Straus 1972 183p illus
ISBN 0-374-25333-1

The **Basil** and Josephine stories. Fitzgerald, F. S.

**Bassani, Giorgio**
Five stories of Ferrara; tr. from the Italian by William Weaver. Harcourt 1971 203p (A Helen and Kurt Wolff bk)
ISBN-0-15-131400-4

The **beach** umbrella. Colter, C.

**Beacham, Walton**
(ed.) Intro 4. *See* Intro 4

**Beachhead** in Bohemia. Marsh, W.

**Beasts** of the southern wild, and other stories. Betts, D.

**Because** it is absurd. Boulle, P.

**Bech:** a book. Updike, J.

**Beckett, Samuel**
More pricks than kicks. Grove 1970 191p
ISBN 0-394-47516-X

**Bedrock.** Spielberg, P.

**Beecroft, John**
(ed.) Kipling, R. A selection of his stories and poems

**Beekman, Allan**
Hawaiian tales. Harlo 1970 112p

**Beneš, Jan**
The blind mirror; stories; tr. from the Czech by Jan Herzfeld. Grossman Pubs. 1971 247p (An Orion Press book)
ISBN 0-670-17430-0

**Bennett, Arnold**
The loot of cities; being the adventures of a millionaire in search of joy. A fantasia. O. Train 1972 156p

**Benya** Krik, the gangster, and other stories. Babel, I.

**Bergé, Carol**
A couple called Moebius; eleven sensual stories. Bobbs 1972 270p
ISBN 0-672-51676-4

**Berne, Stanley**
The unconscious victorious, and other stories; with the correspondence of Sir Herbert Read. Woodcuts by Herman Zaage. Wittenborn 1969 308p illus
ISBN 0-8151-0016-2
    Analyzed for short stories only

**Bernkopf, Jeanne F.**
(comp.) Boucher's choicest; a collection of Anthony Boucher's favorites from Best Detective Stories of the Year; introduction by Allen J. Hubin. Dutton 1969 320p

The **Best** American short stories, 1969-1973; & the Yearbook of the American short story; ed. by Martha Foley and David Burnett. Houghton 1969-1973 5v

*FIC BES*

> Volumes for 1972-1973 edited by Martha Foley alone
> ISBN 1970 (0-395-10940-X); 1971 (0-395-12709-2); 1972 (0-395-13950-3); 1973 (0-395-17119-9)

**Best** detective stories of the year [1969, i.e. 1970]-1973; 24th-27th annual collection; ed. by Allen J. Hubin. Dutton 1970-1973 4v

*We have 21st-23rd*
*FIC BES Mystery*

> ISBN [1969 i.e. 1970] (0-525-06429-X); 1971 (0-525-06430-3); 1972 (0-525-06431-1); 1973 (0-525-06432-X)

The **Best** from Fantasy and Science Fiction; 18th-20th series; ed. by Edward L. Ferman. Doubleday 1969-1973 3v illus (Doubleday Science fiction)

*We have 19th 20th, 22nd*
*FIC MAG Sci-Fic.*

> ISBN 20th series (0-385-07816-1)

The **best** laid schemes. Eisenberg, L.

The **Best** little magazine fiction, 1970-1971; ed. by Curt Johnson. N.Y. Univ. Press 1970-1971 2v illus

> Volume for 1971 edited by Curt Johnson and Alvin Greenberg
> ISBN 1970 (0-8147-4150-9); 1971 (0-8147-4152-5)

**Best** Max Carrados detective stories. Bramah, E.

The **best** of Damon Runyon. Runyon, D.

**Best** of the Best detective stories; 25th anniversary collection; ed. by Allen J. Hubin. Dutton 1971 380p

> ISBN 0-525-06450-8

**Best** SF: 1968-1972; ed. by Harry Harrison and Brian W. Aldiss. Putnam 1969-1973 5v

*FIC BES Sci-Fic.*

> Analyzed for short stories only
> Earlier volumes entered in 1964-1968 supplement under the editors
> ISBN 1969 (0-399-10082-2); 1970 (0-399-10083-0); 1971 (0-399-10984-6); 1972 (0-399-11112-3)

**Best** science fiction stories of Clifford D. Simak. Simak, C. D.

**Best** science fiction stories of the year. Del Rey, L. ed.

**Best** "Thinking Machine" detective stories, Futrelle, J.

The **Bethlehem** Inn, and other Christmas stories. Meek, F. M.

A **betting** man, and other stories. Glanville, B.

**Betts, Doris**
Beasts of the southern wild, and other stories. Harper 1973 192p
ISBN 0-06-010321-3

**Beware** of the cat. Parry, M. ed.

**Beyond** control. Silverberg, R. ed.

**Bichsel, Peter**
And really Frau Blum would very much like to meet the milkman; 21 short stories; tr. from the German by Michael Hamburger. Delacorte Press 1968 88p (A Seymour Lawrence bk)
> Partially analyzed
There is no such place as America; stories; tr. from the German by Michael Hamburger. Delacorte Press [1971 c1970] 85p (A Seymour Lawrence bk)

The **bicycle** rider & six short stories. Keefe, F. L.

**Bierce, Ambrose**
The complete short stories of Ambrose Bierce; comp. with commentary by Ernest Jerome Hopkins. Doubleday 1970 496p

*FIC BIE*

**Biggle, Lloyd**
The metallic muse; a collection of science fiction stories, by Lloyd Biggle, Jr. Doubleday 1972 228p (Doubleday Science fiction)
> ISBN 0-385-03830-5

*Fic BIG SF*

(ed.) Nebula award stories 7. *See* Nebula award stories 7

*FIC NEB Sci-Fic.*

**Bingham, Sallie**
The way it is now; stories. Viking 1972 182p
SBN 670-75195-2

**Birch, Cyril**
(ed.) Anthology of Chinese literature v2; from the 14th century to the present day; ed. and with an introduction. Grove 1972 xxxi, 476p illus
ISBN 0-394-48014-7
> Analyzed for short stories only

A **bird** in the house. Laurence, M.

**Birstein, Ann**
Summer situations. Coward, McCann & Geoghegan 1972 191p

**Bishop, Morris**
(ed.) A Renaissance storybook; selected and ed. by Morris Bishop; drawings by Alison Mason Kingsbury. Cornell Univ. Press 1971 304p illus
ISBN 0-8014-0592-0
> Partially analyzed

**Bradbury, Ray**—*Continued*

*FIC BRA Sci.Fic.*

The Martian chronicles; biographical sketch and bibliography of Ray Bradbury's books and stories by William F. Nolan; illus. by Karel Thole. Doubleday [1973 c1958] 298p illus
ISBN 0-385-03862-3
Earlier edition analyzed in 1955-1958 supplement

**Brainstorms.** Brownstein, M.

The **Bram Stoker** Bedside companion. Stoker, B.

**Bramah, Ernest**
Best Max Carrados detective stories; selected with an introduction by E. F. Bleiler. Dover 1972 244p
ISBN 0-486-20064-7

**Brautigan, Richard**
Revenge of the lawn; stories, 1962-1970. Simon & Schuster 1971 174p
ISBN 0-671-78209
Partially analyzed

**Brennan, Joseph Payne**
The casebook of Lucius Leffing; illus. by Neal Macdonald. Macabre House [distributed by Donald M. Grant] 1973 [c1972] 191p front
Stories of darkness and dread. Arkham House 1973 173p

**Brennan, Maeve**
In and out of never-never land; 22 stories. Scribner 1969 274p

The **bridge** to the other side. Kotowska, M.

**Brief** tales from the bench. Cecil, H.

*Fic BRI*

**Brister, Bob**
Moss, mallards and mules, and other hunting and fishing stories; illus. by Stanley Farnham. Winchester Press 1973 216p illus
ISBN 0-87691-113-0

**Brodeur, Paul**
Downstream. Atheneum Pubs. 1972 206p
ISBN 0-689-10453-7

**Brof, Janet.** *See* Carpentier, H. jt. ed.

**Broke** down engine, and other troubles with machines. Goulart, R.

**Bronner, Hedin**
(ed.) Faroese short stories. *See* Faroese short stories

**Brothers** and sisters. Adoff, A. ed.

**Brown, Estelle Paige**
(ed.) Twice fifteen; an anthology. John C. Schweitzer, consulting editor. Drawings by Marilyn Miller. Scribner 1970 300p illus
ISBN 0-684-51504-0
Analyzed for short stories only

**Brown, Fredric**
Paradox lost, and twelve other great science fiction stories. Random House 1973 210p
ISBN 0-394-48448-7

**Brown, George Mackay**
A time to keep, and other stories. Harcourt 1969 181p
ISBN 0-15-190469-3

**Brownstein, Michael**
Brainstorms; stories; drawings by Donna Dennis. Bobbs 1971 87p illus
ISBN 0-672-51554-7
Analyzed for short stories only

**Bruised** reeds, and other stories. Deutsch, A. H.

**Brumbie** dust. Ottley, R.

*FIC BRU Sci.Fic.*

**Brunner, John**
From this day forward. Doubleday 1972 238p (Doubleday Science fiction)
ISBN 0-385-07105-1
Analyzed for short stories only

**Bryant, Edward**
Among the dead, and other events leading up to the Apocalypse. Macmillan (N Y) 1973 210p

**Buck, Pearl S.**
*FIC BUC*
The good deed, and other stories of Asia, past and present. Day 1969 254p
ISBN 0-381-98032-4

**Buckskin** and smoke. Hayes, A. H.

**Bukowski, Charles**
Erections, ejaculations, exhibitions and general tales of ordinary madness; ed. by Gail Chiarrello. City Lights Bks. 1972 478p
ISBN 0-87286-061-2
South of no north; stories of the buried life. Black Sparrow Press 1973 189p
ISBN 0-87685-190-1

**Bulgakov, Mikhail**
Diaboliad, and other stories; ed. by Ellendea Proffer & Carl R. Proffer; tr. by Carl R. Proffer. Ind. Univ. Press 1972 xx, 236p
ISBN 0-253-11605-8

**Bullins, Ed**
The hungered one; early writings. Morrow 1971 149p
ISBN 0-688-06040-4

**Bullock, Michael**
Sixteen stories as they happened. Sono Nis Press 1969 116p

**Burke, John**
*808.83 BUR*
(ed.) Tales of unease. Doubleday 1969 229p

**Burke, Thomas**
Limehouse nights; introduction by Alfred Kazin. Horizon Press 1973 304p
ISBN 0-8180-0619-6

**Burnett, Whit**
(ed.) Black hands on a white face; a timepiece of experiences in a Black and white America; an anthology. Dodd 1971 392p
ISBN 0-396-06374-8
   Analyzed for short stories only
(ed.) Story: the yearbook of discovery/1969. *See* Story: the yearbook of discovery/1969
(ed.) That's what happened to me. Four Winds 1969 224p

The **burning**, & other stories. Cady, J.

**Burton, Hester**
The Henchmans at home; illus. by Victor G. Ambrus. Crowell [1972 c1970] 182p
ISBN 0-690-37706-1

A **butterfly's** dream & other Chinese tales. Sié, Cheou-Kang

# C

**Cady, Jack**
The burning, & other stories. Univ. of Iowa Press 1972 157p
ISBN 0-87745-030-7

The **calibrated** alligator, and other science fiction stories. Silverberg, R.

The **caller** of The Black. Lumley, B.

**Calvino, Italo**
The watcher & other stories. Harcourt 1971 181p (A Helen and Kurt Wolff bk)
ISBN 0-15-194880-1

**Camp, Catherine Crook de.** *See* De Camp, Catherine Crook

**Camp, L. Sprague de.** *See* De Camp, L. Sprague

**Campbell, John W.**
*analog 8*
*FIC*
*CAM sci.fic*
(ed.) Analog 7-8. *See* Analog 7-8

**Campbell, Ramsey**
Demons by daylight. Arkham House 1973 153p

**Can** you feel anything when I do this? Sheckley, R.

**Cancerqueen,** and other stories. Landolfi, T.

**Canning, John**
(ed.) 50 great horror stories. Taplinger 1969 494p

**Canzoneri, Robert**
Barbed wire, and other stories. Dial Press 1970 182p

**Carpenter, Don**
The murder of the frogs, and other stories. Harcourt 1969 242p

**Carpentier, Alejo**
War of time; tr. from the Spanish by Frances Partridge. Knopf 1970 179p
ISBN 0-394-45100-7

**Carpentier, Hortense, and Brof, Janet**
(eds.) Doors and mirrors; fiction and poetry from Spanish America, 1920-1970; selected and ed. by Hortense Carpentier and Janet Brof. Grossman Pubs. 1972 454p
SBN 670-28042-9
   Analyzed for short stories only

**Carr, Jess**
A creature was stirring, and other stories. Commonwealth Press 1970 125p

**Carr, Terry**
*FIC*
*CAR*
*S.F.*
(ed.) An exaltation of stars; transcendental adventures in science fiction; comp. and ed. by Terry Carr. Simon & Schuster 1973 191p
SBN 671-21469-1
(ed.) Into the unknown; eleven tales of imagination. Nelson 1973 192p
ISBN 0-8407-6342-5
(ed.) Universe 1-3. *See* Universe 1-3

**Case, David**
The cell; three tales of horror. Hill & Wang 1969 269p
ISBN 0-8090-3383-6

The **case** of the crimson kiss. Gardner, E. S.

The **case** of the crying swallow. Gardner, E. S.

The **case** of the irate witness. Gardner, E. S.

The **casebook** of Lucius Leffing. Brennan, J. P.

**Casey** Agonistes, and other science fiction and fantasy stories. McKenna, R.

**Casper, Leonard**
A lion unannounced; twelve stories and a fable; illus. by Vicky C. Olmos. Southern Methodist Univ. Press 1971 218p illus (A National Council of the Arts selection)
ISBN 0-87074-028-8

**Cassill, R. V.**
(ed.) Intro #2-3. *See* Intro #2-3

**Cast** of characters. Kanin, G.

**Cather, Willa**
Uncle Valentine, and other stories; Willa Cather's Uncollected short fiction, 1915-1929; ed. with an introduction by Bernice Slote. Univ. of Neb. Press 1973 xxx, 183p
ISBN 0-8032-0820-0
Willa Cather's Collected short fiction, 1892-1912; ed. by Virginia Faulkner; introduction by Mildred R. Bennett. [Rev. ed] Univ. of Neb. Press 1970 3v in 1 (xli, 600p)
ISBN 0-8032-0770-0
Earlier edition listed in 1964-1968 supplement
Contents: v 1 The Bohemian girl; v2 The troll garden; v3 On the Divide
Analyzed for short stories only

**Cecil, Henry**
Brief tales from the bench; eight courtroom vignettes. Simon & Schuster [1972 c1968] 180p (An Inner Sanctum mystery special)
ISBN 0-671-21145-5

The **cell.** Case, D.

**Chains** of the sea; three original novellas of science fiction, by Geo. Alec Effinger, Gardner R. Dozois [and] Gordon Eklund; ed. and with an introduction by Robert Silverberg. Nelson 1973 221p
ISBN 0-8407-6314-X

The **Chameleon** Corps & other shape changers. Goulart, R.

**Chapman, Abraham**
(ed.) New Black voices; an anthology of contemporary Afro-American literature; ed. with an introduction and biographical notes, by Abraham Chapman. New Am. Lib. 1972 606p (A Mentor bk)
Analyzed for short stories only

**Charyn, Jerome**
(ed.) The single voice; an anthology of contemporary fiction. Collier Bks. 1969 516p
Analyzed for short stories only
(ed.) The troubled vision; an anthology of contemporary short novels and passages. Collier Bks. 1970 510p

**Cheever, John**
The world of apples. Knopf 1973 174p
ISBN 0-394-48346-4

**Chekhov, Anton**
The Oxford Chekhov; stories. Tr. and ed. by Ronald Hingley. v5 1889-1891; v6 1892-1893. Oxford 1970-1971 2v
ISBN v5 (0-19-211353-4); v6 (0-19-211363-1)
Partially analyzed
Seven short novels; tr. by Barbara Makanowitzky; with an introduction and prefaces by Gleb Struve. Norton [1971 c1963] 440p (The Norton lib)
SBN 393-00552-6
The sinner from Toledo, and other stories; tr. by Arnold Hinchliffe. Fairleigh Dickinson Univ. Press 1972 168p
ISBN 0-8386-7890-4

**Child Study Association of America**
Insights. *See* Insights

**Childhood** is not forever. Farrell, J. T.

**Children** are civilians too. Böll, H.

**Children** of infinity. Elwood, R. ed.

**Cholakian, Patricia Francis, and Cholakian, Rouben Charles**
(eds.) The early French novella; an anthology of fifteenth- and sixteenth-century tales; ed. and tr. by Patricia Francis Cholakian and Rouben Charles Cholakian. State Univ. of N.Y. Press 1972 244p illus
ISBN 0-87395-090-9
Partially analyzed

**Cholakian, Rouben Charles.** *See* Cholakian, P. F. jt. ed.

**Chopin, Kate**
The awakening, and other stories; ed. with an introduction by Lewis Leary. Holt 1970 xxi, 341p
ISBN 03-078395-X

**Christie, Agatha**
The golden ball, and other stories. Dodd 1971 280p
ISBN 0-396-06293-X

**Chronopolis,** and other stories. Ballard, J. G.

A **cinch.** Gottesman, L.; Obenzinger, H. and Senauke, A. eds.

A **circle** of witches. Haining, P. ed.

**City** life. Barthelme, D.

The **clans** of darkness. Haining, P. ed.

**Clareson, Thomas D.**
808.83 (ed.) A spectrum of worlds; ed. CLA with an introduction and notes by Thomas D. Clareson. Doubleday 1972 311p (Doubleday Science fiction)
ISBN 0-385-01657-3
Analyzed for short stories only

Clarke, Arthur C.
Tales from the White Hart. Harcourt 1970 179p
ISBN 0-15-187979-6

The wind from the sun; stories of the space age. Harcourt 1972 193p
ISBN 0-15-196810-1

Clarke, Austin
When he was free and young and he used to wear silks; stories. Little 1973 243p
ISBN 0-316-14694-3

The **classic** short story. Konigsberg, I. ed.

Clement, Hal
(ed.) First flights to the moon; with an introduction by Isaac Asimov. Doubleday 1970 xx, 217p
ISBN 0-385-06863-8

Small changes. Doubleday 1969 230p (Doubleday Science fiction)
ISBN 0-385-09087-0

The **cocotte** (Boule de suif) and three other stories. Maupassant, G. de

Cohen, J. M.
(ed.) Latin American writing today. Penguin 1967 267p
ISBN 0-8446-1876-4
Analyzed for short stories only

Colette
The other woman; tr. from the French and with an introduction by Margaret Crosland. Bobbs 1972 140p

**Collected** short stories of Julia Peterkin. Peterkin, J.

**Collected** stories. Greene, G.

**Collected** stories. Lavin, M.

The **collected** stories of Bertrand Russell. Bertrand, R.

The **collected** stories of Jean Stafford. Stafford, J.

The **collected** stories of Peter Taylor. Taylor, P.

Collier, Eugenia W. *See* Long, R. A. jt. ed.

Collier, John
The John Collier reader. Knopf 1972 571p
ISBN 0-394-46186-X
Analyzed for short stories only

Collier, Ned
(ed.) Great stories of the West. Doubleday 1971 346p
ISBN 0-385-01274-8

Collins, Wilkie
Tales of terror and the supernatural; selected and introduced by Herbert van Thal. Dover 1972 294p
ISBN 0-486-20307-7

The **colonel's** photograph. Ionesco, E.

Colter, Cyrus
The beach umbrella. Univ. of Iowa Press 1970 225p
ISBN 0-87745-005-6

Columbia Review
Gottesman, L.; Obenzinger, H. and Senauke, A. eds. A cinch

**Come** back if it doesn't get better. Gilliatt, P.

**Come** back to the farm. Stuart, J.

**Come** gentle spring. Stuart, J.

**Command,** and I will obey you. Moravia, A.

The **compleat** werewolf, and other stories of fantasy and science fiction. Boucher, A.

The **complete** short stories of Ambrose Bierce. Bierce, A.

The **complete** short stories of Robert Louis Stevenson. Stevenson, R. L.

The **complete** stories. Kafka, F.

The **complete** stories. O'Connor, F.

The **confrontation,** and other stories. Marshall, L.

The **Congressman** who loved Flaubert, and other Washington stories. Just, W.

**Consider** the evidence. Fenner, P. R. comp.

**Contemporary** voices. Stephens, D. ed.

Coolidge, Olivia
Tales of the Crusades. Houghton 1970 225p
ISBN 0-395-06720-0

Coombs, Orde
(ed.) What we must see: young Black storytellers; an anthology ed. with an introduction. Dodd 1971 210p
ISBN 0-396-06357-8

Coover, Robert
Pricksongs & descants; fictions. Dutton 1969 256p
ISBN 0-525-18363-9

**Corky's** brother. Neugeboren, J.

**Corn** village. Le Sueur, M.

**Corodimas, Peter**
(ed.) In trout country; ed. and with an introduction; illus. by Leslie Morrill. Little 1971 300p illus (A Sports Illustrated bk)
ISBN 0-316-15743-0
Analyzed for short stories only

**Cortázar, Julio**
All fires the fire, and other stories; tr. from the Spanish by Suzanne Jill Levine. Pantheon Bks. 1973 152p
ISBN 0-394-46821-X

**Corvo, Baron.** *See* Corvo, Frederick, Baron

**Corvo, Frederick, Baron**
Stories Toto told me; with a preface by Christopher Sykes. St Martins [1971 c1969] 254p

**Cosmopolitan** crimes. Greene, H. ed.

**Costello, Mark**
The Murphy stories. Univ. of Ill. Press 1973 120p
ISBN 0-252-00303-9

A **couple** called Moebius. Bergé, C.

**Covici, Pascal**
(ed.) Steinbeck, J. The portable Steinbeck

The **cracked** looking glass. Schulman, L. M. ed.

**Craft** and vision. Lytle, A. ed.

**Crane, Stephen**
The portable Stephen Crane; ed. with an introduction and notes, by Joseph Katz. Viking 1969 xxvi, 550p (The Viking Portable lib)
ISBN 0-670-67041-3
Analyzed for short stories only
The red badge of courage, and other stories; with a critical and biographical profile of Stephen Crane. Watts, F. [1969] 356p (A Watts Ultratype ed)
ISBN 0-531-00422-8
Tales of adventure; ed. by Fredson Bowers; with an introduction by J. C. Levenson. Univ. Press of Va. 1970 cxcv, 242p illus (The Univ. of Va. Ed. of The works of Stephen Crane v5)
SBN 8139-0302-5
Tales of war . . . ed. by Fredson Bowers; with an introduction by James B. Colvert. Univ. Press of Va. [1970] cxci, 400p illus (Univ. of Va. Ed. of the works of Stephen Crane, v6)
SBN 8139-0294-0

Tales, sketches, and reports; ed. by Fredson Bowers; with an introduction by Edwin H. Cady. Univ. Press of Va. 1973 xli, 1183p front (Univ. of Va. Ed. of the works of Stephen Crane, v8)
ISBN 0-8139-0405-6
Analyzed for short stories only

A **creature** was stirring, and other stories. Carr, J.

The **credo.** Steegmuller, F.

The **cricket** beneath the waterfall, and other stories. Krleža, M.

**Crime** prevention in the 30th century. Santesson, H. S. ed.

**Crime** without murder. Mystery Writers of America

**Crimes** and misfortunes. McComas, J. F. ed.

**Crimson** Ramblers of the world, farewell. West, J.

**Crossing** over, and other tales. Elman, R.

**Crossley-Holland, Kevin.** *See* Walsh, J. P. jt. auth.

A **crown** of feathers, and other stories. Singer, I. B.

The **crystal** man. Mitchell, E. P.

The **cube** root of uncertainty. Silverberg, R.

**Cucumber** sandwiches, and other stories. Stewart, J. I. M.

**Cullinan, Elizabeth**
The time of Adam; stories. Houghton 1971 178p
ISBN 0-395-12041-1

**Cuomo, George**
Sing, choirs of angels. Doubleday 1969 214p

**Curley, Daniel**
In the hands of our enemies. Univ. of Ill. Press 1970 207p
ISBN 0-252-00141-9

# D

**Damon** Knight's Orbit 5-12. *See* Orbit 5-12

**Dance** of the happy shades, and other stories. Munro, A.

**Dances** of death. Tindall, G.

**Danger**—human. Dickson, G. R.

**Daniel, Yuli**
This is Moscow speaking, and other stories [by] Yuli Daniel (Nikolai Arzhak) Tr. by Stuart Hood, Harold Shukman [and] John Richardson; with a foreword by Max Hayward. Dutton 1969 [c1968] 159p front

Daring detectives, Alfred Hitchcock's. Hitchcock, A. ed.

Dark side of the moon. Naylor, P. R.

Dark things. Derleth, A. ed.

Daughters of Earth. Merril, J.

Davidson, Avram
*FIC DAV sci. fic·*
Strange seas and shores; a collection of short stories. Doubleday 1971 219p (Doubleday Science fiction)
ISBN 0-385-03985-9

Davis, Dorothy Salisbury
(ed.) Mystery writers of America. Crime without murder

Davis, Olivia
The scent of apples; stories. Houghton 1972 224p
ISBN 0-395-14009-9

Davis, Robert Gorham
(ed.) Ten modern masters; an anthology of the short story. 3d ed. Harcourt 1972 583p
ISBN 0-15-590281-4

Dawn of remembered spring. Stuart, J.

Dawson, Fielding
Krazy Kat/ The unveiling & other stories. Black Sparrow Press 1969 186p
Partially analyzed

A day in the life. Dozois, G. R. ed.

The Day the sun stood still; three original novellas of science fiction, by Poul Anderson, Gordon R. Dickson [and] Robert Silverberg; with a foreword by Lester del Rey. Nelson 1972 240p
ISBN 0-8407-6206-2

The days after tomorrow. Santesson, H. S. ed.

Dear dead days. Mystery Writers of America

Death dance. Wilson, A.

A death in Delhi. Roadarmel, G. C. ed.

The death of the novel, and other stories. Sukenick, R.

De Camp, Catherine Crook. *See* De Camp, L. S. jt. ed.

De Camp, L. Sprague, and De Camp, Catherine Crook
*808.83 DEC*
(eds.) 3000 years of fantasy and science fiction; foreword by Isaac Asimov. Lothrop 1972 256p
Analyzed for short stories only

Deck, John
Greased Samba, and other stories. Harcourt 1970 247p
ISBN 0-15-136875-9

Decker, Clarence R. and Angoff, Charles
(eds.) Modern stories from many lands; 2d enl. ed. selected and ed. by Clarence R. Decker [and] Charles Angoff; rev. ed. edited by Charles Angoff. Manyland Bks. 1972 434p
ISBN 0-87141-040-0
Earlier edition listed in 1959-1963 supplement, entered under: The Literary Review

Deep space. Silverberg, R. ed.

DeFord, Miriam Allen
Elsewhere, elsewhen, elsehow; collected stories. Walker & Co. 1971 180p
ISBN 0-8027-5540-2

De La Mare, Walter
Eight tales; with an introduction by Edward Wagenknecht. Arkham House 1971 xx, 108p

Delany, Samuel R.
*FIC DEL SF*
Driftglass. Doubleday 1971 274p

Delapp, Terry
El Euphoria Gloria Road. New Am. Press [distributed by Ward Ritchie] 1968 163p

Delattre, Pierre
Tales of a Dalai Lama; drawings by the author. Houghton 1971 142p illus
ISBN 0-395-12707-6
Partially analyzed

Del Rey, Lester
*FIC DEL sci. fic·*
(ed.) Best science fiction stories of the year; [first]- second annual collection. Dutton 1972-1973 2v
ISBN v 1 (0-525-06490-7); v2 (0-523-06491-5)

De Maupassant, Guy. *See* Maupassant, Guy de

Deming, Barbara
Wash us and comb us; stories. Drawings by Jane Watrous. Grossman Pubs. 1972 162p illus
SBN 670-75003-4
Analyzed for short stories only

Demons by daylight. Campbell, R.

Derleth, August
(ed.) Dark things. Arkham House 1971 330p
*FIC TAL SF*
(ed.) Tales of the Cthulhu Mythos; collected by August Derleth. Arkham House 1969 407p

Designs for reading: short stories. Ball, J. E. ed.

Desperate moments. Fenner, P. R. comp.

Deutsch, Alfred H.
Bruised reeds, and other stories. St Johns Univ. Press 1971 213p

**Deutschman, Ben**
In a small town a kid went to shul, and other stories. Aurora Pubs. 1971 183p
SBN 87695-139-6
Partially analyzed

The **devastating** boys, and other stories. Taylor, E.

The **Devil's** instrument, and other Danish stories. Holm, S. ed.

**De Vries, Peter**
Without a stitch in time; a selection of the best humorous short pieces. Little 1972 328p
ISBN 0-316-18186-2
Analyzed for short stories only

**Diaboliad,** and other stories. Bulgakov, M.

**Dickens, Albert.** *See* Andrews, F. E. jt. ed.

**Dickensheet, Dean**
(ed.) Men and malice; an anthology of mystery and suspense by West Coast authors. Doubleday 1973 248p
ISBN 0-385-02779-6

**Dickinson, Susan**
(ed.) The drugged cornet, and other mystery stories; chosen by Susan Dickinson; illus. by Robert Micklewright. Dutton [1973 c1972] 230p illus
ISBN 0-525-28928-3
(ed.) The usurping ghost, and other encounters and experiences; chosen by Susan Dickinson; illus. by Antony Maitland. Dutton [1971 c1970] 318p illus
SBN 0-525-41902-0

**Dickson, Gordon R.**
Danger—human. Doubleday 1970 228p (Doubleday Science fiction)
ISBN 0-385-01037-0
Mutants; a science fiction adventure. Macmillan (N Y) 1970 250p
The star road. Doubleday 1973 229p (Doubleday Science fiction)
ISBN 0-385-06811-5

**Di Donato, Pietro**
Naked author. Phaedra Pubs. 1970 311p
ISBN 0-87366-018-8

**Dillon, Millicent**
Baby Perpetua, and other stories. Viking 1971 147p
SBN 670-14376-6

**Dimension** X. Knight, D. comp.

**Disch, Robert, and Schwartz, Barry**
(eds.) Killing time; a guide to life in the happy valley. Prentice-Hall 1972 501p
ISBN 0-13-515189-9
Analyzed for short stories only

**Disch, Thomas M.**
(ed.) Bad moon rising. Harper 1973 302p
SBN 06-011046-5
Analyzed for short stories only
Fun with your new head. Doubleday 1971 [c1968] 207 p (Doubleday Science fiction)
ISBN 0-385-09490-6
(ed.) The ruins of earth; an anthology of stories of the immediate future. Putnam 1971 318p
ISBN 0-399-10712-6

**Disclosures** in scarlet. Jacobi, C.

**Ditch** Valley. Henderson, D.

**Djilas, Milovan**
The stone and the violets; tr. by Lovett F. Edwards. Harcourt 1972 238p
ISBN 0-15-185100-X
Partially analyzed

**Doctor** Brodie's report. Borges, J. L.

**Donovan, Michael.** *See* O'Connor, Frank

**Donaldy, Ernestine.** *See* Norton, A. jt. ed.

**Donato, Pietro di.** *See* Di Donato, Pietro

**Don't** go to sleep in the dark. Fremlin, C.

**Don't** look now. Du Maurier, D.

**Doors** and mirrors. Carpentier, H. and Brof, J. eds.

The **doors** of his face, the lamps of his mouth, and other stories. Zelazny, R.

**Dorr, Lawrence**
A slow, soft river; seven stories; ed. and introduced by Corbin Scott Carnell. Eerdmans 1973 127p
ISBN 0-8028-1498-0

**Down** in the black gang, and others. Farmer, P. J.

**Downstream.** Brodeur, P.

**Dozois, Gardner R.**
(ed.) A day in the life; a science fiction anthology; ed. with introduction & commentary. Harper 1972 288p
SBN 06-011076-7

**Drake, Robert**
 The single heart. Aurora Pubs. 1971 171p
 SBN 87695-142-6

*FIC DEL SF*

-Driftglass. Delany, S. R.

The **drugged** cornet, and other mystery stories. Dickinson, S. ed.

**Dumas, Henry**
 Ark of bones, and other stories; ed. by Hale Chatfield and Eugene Redmond. Southern Ill. Univ. Press [1971 c1970] 116p
 ISBN 0-8093-0442-2

**Du Maurier, Daphne**
 Don't look now. Doubleday 1971 303p
 ISBN 0-385-08733-0

*FIC DUM*

# E

**EQMM** Annual v24-27. *See* various titles under Ellery Queen's Mystery magazine

The **early** Asimov. Asimov, I.

The **early** French novella. Cholakian, P. F. and Cholakian, R. C. eds.

**Early** prose writings. Thomas D.

The **Easter** man (a play) and six stories. Hunter, E.

**Eddy, C. M.**
 Exit into eternity; tales of the bizarre and supernatural, by C. M. Eddy, Jr. With an introduction by Muriel E. Eddy. Oxford Press 1973 121p

**Edmonds, Walter D.**
 Seven American stories; illus. by William Sauts Bock. Little 1970 400p illus
 ISBN 0-316-21150-8

The **egg** of the Glak, and other stories. Jacobs, H.

**Eight** fantasms and magics. Vance, J.

**Eight** tales. De La Mare, W.

**Eisenberg, Larry**
 The best laid schemes. Macmillan (N Y) 1971 191p

**Elder, Joseph**
 (ed.) Eros in orbit; a collection of all new science fiction stories about sex. Trident Press 1973 189p
 ISBN 0-671-27102-4

**Elephant** bangs train. Kotzwinkle, W.

**Eleven** modern short novels. Hamalian, L. and Volpe, E. L. eds.

The **eleventh** Galaxy reader. Galaxy Magazine

**Elkin, Stanley**
 Searches and seizures. Random House 1973 304p
 ISBN 0-394-48329-4

*808.83 ELK*

 (ed.) Stories from the sixties; ed. with a preface by Stanley Elkin. Doubleday 1971 400p
 ISBN 0-385-04431-3

**Ellery** Queen's Grand slam. Ellery Queen's Mystery Magazine

**Ellery** Queen's Headliners. Ellery Queen's Mystery Magazine

**Ellery** Queen's Murder menu. Ellery Queen's Mystery Magazine

**Ellery** Queen's Mystery bag. Ellery Queen's Mystery Magazine

**Ellery Queen's Mystery Magazine**
 Ellery Queen's Grand slam; 25th anniversary annual of the EQMM; 25 stories from Ellery Queen's Mystery Magazine; ed. by Ellery Queen. World Pub. 1970 316p

 Ellery Queen's Headliners; 26th mystery annual; 20 stories from Ellery Queen's Mystery Magazine; ed. by Ellery Queen. World Pub. 1971 315p

 Ellery Queen's Murder menu; 24th EQMM annual; 22 stories from Ellery Queen's Mystery Magazine; ed. by Ellery Queen. World Pub. 1969 333p

 Ellery Queen's Mystery bag; 27th mystery annual; 25 stories from Ellery Queen's Mystery Magazine; ed. by Ellery Queen. World Pub. 1972 358p
 ISBN 0-529-04562-1

**Ellery** Queen's The golden 13. Queen, E. ed.

**Ellison, Harlan**
 (ed.) Again, dangerous visions; 46 original stories; illus. by Ed Emshwiller. Doubleday 1972 xxiii, 760p illus (Doubleday Science fiction)
 ISBN 0-385-07953-2
 Analyzed for short stories only

*FIC ELL Sci-Fic*

 Alone against tomorrow; stories of alienation in speculative fiction. Macmillan (N Y) 1971 312p

 Partners in wonder, by Harlan Ellison in collaboration with Robert Bloch [and others]. Walker & Co. 1971 471p illus
 ISBN 0-8027-5527-5
 Analyzed for short stories only

**Elman, Richard**
 Crossing over, and other tales. Scribner 1973 176p
 ISBN 0-684-13021-1
 Partially analyzed

**Elmslie, Kenward**
The orchid stories. Doubleday 1973 247p (Paris Review Editions)
ISBN 0-385-07365-8
Analyzed for short stories only

**Elsewhere,** elsewhen, elsehow. De-Ford, M. A.

**Elwood, Roger**
(ed.) And walk now gently through the fire, and other science fiction stories. Chilton Bk. Co. 1972 185p
ISBN 0-8019-5701-X

(ed.) Children of infinity; original science fiction stories for young readers; illus. by Jacqui Morgan. Watts, F. 1973 178p illus
ISBN 0-531-02599-3

(ed.) Future city. Trident Press 1973 256p
ISBN 0-671-27103-2
Analyzed for short story only

(ed.) The new mind; original science fiction. Macmillan Pub. Co. 1973 180p (Frontiers 2)

(ed.) The other side of tomorrow; original science fiction stories about young people of the future; illus. by Herbert Danska. Random House 1973 207p illus
ISBN 0-394-82468-7

(ed.) Showcase. Harper 1973 191p
ISBN 0-06-011177-1

(ed.) Tomorrow's alternatives; original science fiction. Macmillan Pub. Co. 1973 198p (Frontiers 1)

**Elwood, Roger, and Ghidalia, Vic**
(eds.) Androids, time machines and blue giraffes; a panorama of science fiction; jacket design by Franz Altschuler. Follett 1973 381p
ISBN 0-695-80369-7

**Elwood, Roger, and Kidd, Virginia**
(eds.) Saving worlds; a collection of original science fiction stories; with an introduction by Frank Herbert. Doubleday 1973 237p (Doubleday Science fiction)
ISBN 0-385-05409-2
Analyzed for short stories only

The **embrace,** and stories. Glaze, E.

**Emerson, O. B.**
(ed.) Alabama prize stories, 1970. See Alabama prize stories, 1970

The **ends** of time. Silverberg, R. ed.

The **entombed** man of Thule. Weaver, G.

**Erections,** ejaculations, exhibitions and general tales of ordinary madness. Bukowski, C.

**Eros** in orbit. Elder, J. ed.

**Esquire**
Lish, G. ed. The secret life of our times: new fiction from Esquire

**Estes, Winston M.**
A streetful of people. Lippincott 1972 276p
ISBN 0-397-00768-X

The **eternal** smile. Lagerkvist, P.

El **Euphoria** Gloria Road. Delapp, T.

**Evil** eye, and other stories. Stewart, N.

An **exaltation** of stars. Carr, T. ed.

**Except** for me and thee. West, J.

**Exit** into eternity. Eddy, C. M.

An **experience** of India. Jhabvala, R. P.

**Explorations** in freedom: prose, narrative, and poetry from Kultura. Tyrmand, L. ed.

The **eye** of the heart. Howes, B. ed.

The **eye** of the lens. Jones, L.

# F

**Fables** of wit and elegance. Auchincloss, L. ed.

**Fabrications.** Ayrton, M.

The **face** in the mirror. Val Baker, D.

The **fact** of fiction. Gulassa, C. M. ed.

**Fairy** tales for computers, by E. M. Forster [and others]. Eakins Press 1969 163p
Analyzed for short stories only

**Family** ties. Lispector, C.

**Fantasy and Science Fiction**
The Best from Fantasy and Science Fiction. See the Best from Fantasy and Science Fiction

**Farmer, Philip José**
Down in the black gang, and others; a story collection. Doubleday 1971 215p

**Faroese** short stories; tr. from the Faroese and the Danish with introduction and notes by Hedin Brønner. Twayne & Am-Scandinavian Foundation 1972 267p (The Lib. of Scandinavian literature)

**Farrell, James T.**

*Fic FAR* Childhood is not forever. Doubleday 1969 300p

*Fic FAR* Judith, and other stories. Doubleday 1973 363p
ISBN 0-385-04819-X

**Fast, Howard**
The general zapped an angel; new stories of fantasy and science fiction. Morrow 1970 159p

A touch of infinity; thirteen new stories of fantasy and science fiction. Morrow 1973 182p
ISBN 0-688-00180-7

**Feminine** plural. Spinner, S. ed.

**Fenner, Phyllis R.**
(comp.) Consider the evidence; stories of mystery and suspense. Illus. by Charles Geer. Morrow 1973 192p illus
ISBN 0-688-20080-X

(comp.) Desperate moments; stories of escapes and hurried journeys; illus. by Charles Geer. Morrow 1971 191p

(comp.) Finders keepers; stories of treasure seekers; illus. by Charles Geer. Morrow 1969 222p illus

(comp.) Perilous ascent; stories of mountain climbing; illus. by Charles Geer. Morrow 1970 190p illus

(comp.) Where speed is king; stories of racing adventure; illus. by Charles Geer. Morrow 1972 192p illus

**Ferman, Edward L.**
(ed.) The Best from Fantasy and Science Fiction. *See* The Best from Fantasy and Science Fiction

**Ferman, Edward L. and Mills, Robert P.**
(eds.) Twenty years of The Magazine of Fantasy and Science Fiction. Putnam 1970 264p
ISBN 0-425-01923-3

**Fernhurst**, Q.E.D., and other early writings. Stein, G.

A **few** last words. Sallis, J.

**Fiedler, Leslie A.**
Nude croquet; the stories of Leslie A. Fiedler. Stein & Day 1969 288p
SBN 8128-1244-1

**Fielding, Gabriel**
New queens for old; a novella and nine stories. Morrow 1972 224p

The **fierce** and beautiful world. Platonov, A.

**Fifteen** by Maupassant. Maupassant, G. de

The **fifth** column, and four stories of the Spanish Civil War. Hemingway, E.

The **fifth** head of Cerberus. Wolfe, G.

**50** great horror stories. Canning, J. ed.

**Fifty** years of Russian prose: from Pasternak to Solzhenitsyn. Pomorska, K. ed.

**Fifty** years of the American short story. Abrahams, W. ed.

**Finders** keepers. Fenner, P. R. comp.

**Fingers** in the door, and other stories. Tuohy, F.

**First** flights to the moon. Clement, H. ed.

**First** fruits. Michener, J. A. ed.

**Fish** in a stream in a cave. Maloney, R.

**Fisherman's** bounty. Lyons, N. ed.

**Fitzgerald, F. Scott**
The Basil and Josephine stories; ed. with an introduction by Jackson R. Bryer and John Kuehl. [Scribner 1973] xxix, 287p
SBN 684-13398-9

**Fitz Gerald, Gregory**
(ed.) Modern satiric stories; the impropriety principle. Scott 1971 472p
ISBN 0-673-07576-1

*Fic LAU Sci.Fic* **Five** fates, by Keith Laumer [and others]. Doubleday 1970 256p (Doubleday Science Fiction)

**Five** stories of Ferrara. Bassani, G.

**Five** Victorian ghost novels. Bleiler, E. F. ed.

**Fix** bayonets! And other stories. Thomason, J. W.

**Foff, Arthur, and Knapp, Daniel**
(eds.) Story; an introduction to prose fiction. 2d ed. Wadsworth Pub. 1971 521p

**Foley, Martha**
(ed.) The Best American short stories. *See* The Best American short stories

The **Folsom** flint, and other curious tales. Keller, D. H.

**Ford, Miriam Allen de.** *See* DeFord, Miriam Allen

**Forester, C. S.**
*Fic FOR* Gold from Crete; ten stories. Little 1970 263p
ISBN 0-316-28919-1

*Fic FOR* The man in the yellow raft. Little 1969 190p
ISBN 0-316-28918-3

**Forster, E. M.**
(ed.) Fairy tales for computers.
*See* Fairy tales for computers

The life to come, and other short
stories. Norton [1973 c1972]
xxi, 240p
ISBN 0-393-08381-0
Partially analyzed

FIC
BOV
S/F
**Forward** in time. Bova, B.

**Four** futures; four original novellas
of science fiction, by R. A. Lafferty [and others] with a foreword by Isaac Asimov. Hawthorn Bks. 1971 195p

**Fourteen** for now. Simon, J. ed.

**Fourteen** stories high, ed. by David
Helwig and Tom Marshall.
Oberon Press 1971 172p
ISBN 0-88750-047-1
1972-1973 editions are entered under: New Canadian
stories

**Fox, John**
A purple rhododendron, and other
stories, by John Fox, Jr. Young
Publications [1972 c1967]
151p

**Fragment** from a lost diary, and
other stories. Katz, N. and Milton, N. eds.

**Francis, H. E.**
The itinerary of beggars. Univ. of
Iowa Press 1973 278p
ISBN 0-87745-039-0

**Fraser, George MacDonald**
The general danced at dawn, and
other stories. Knopf 1973
[c1970] 205p
ISBN 0-394-47435-X

The **freak** show. Haining, P. ed.

**Free** fire zone. Karlin, W.; Paquet,
B. T. and Rottmann, L. eds.

**Fremlin, Celia**
Don't go to sleep in the dark; short
stories. Lippincott 1970 158p
ISBN 0-397-00643-8

**French** tales of love and passion.
Maupassant, G. de

**Friedman, Paul**
And if defeated allege fraud; stories. Univ. of Ill. Press 1971
146p
ISBN 0-252-00159-1

A **friend** of Kafka, and other stories.
Singer, I. B.

**From** Karamzin to Bunin: an anthology of Russian short stories.
Proffer, C. R. ed.

**From** the roots. James, C. L. ed.

**From** this day forward. Brunner, J.

**Fun** with your new head.
Disch, T. M.

**Furman, A. L.**
(ed.) Teen-age secret agent stories; stories by Jack Woolgar
[and others]. Lantern Press
(N Y) 1970 191p
(ed.) Teen-age space adventures.
Lantern Press (N Y) 1972 192p

The **further** rivals of Sherlock
Holmes. Greene, Sir H. ed.

**Futrelle, Jacques**
Best "Thinking Machine" detec-
tive stories; ed. by E. F. Bleiler.
Dover 1973 241p
ISBN 0-0486-20537-1

**Future** city. Elwood, R. ed.

The **future** is now. Nolan, W. F. ed.

**Future** without future. Sternberg, J.

# G

**G.M.P.** *See* Stein, G. Matisse, Picasso and Gertrude Stein

**Galaxy Magazine**
The eleventh Galaxy reader; ed.
by Frederik Pohl. Doubleday
1969 254p (Doubleday Sci-
ence fiction)

**Gallant, Mavis**
The Pegnitz Junction; a novella
and five short stories. Random
House 1973 193p
ISBN 0-394-48348-7

**García Márquez, Gabriel**
Leaf storm, and other stories; tr.
from the Spanish by Gregory
Rabassa. Harper 1972 146p
ISBN 0-06-012779-1

**Gardner, Erle Stanley**
FIC
GAR
Mystery
The case of the crimson kiss; a
Perry Mason novelette, and
other stories. Morrow [1972]
189p

The case of the crying swallow;
a Perry Mason novelette, and
other stories. Morrow 1971
192p

FIC
GAR
Mystery
The case of the irate witness; a
Perry Mason mystery, and other
stories. Morrow 1972 192p

**Garfield, Leon**
The restless ghost; three stories;
with illus. by Saul Lambert.
Pantheon Bks. 1969 132p illus
ISBN 0-394-80784-7

**Garrett, George**
The magic striptease. Doubleday
1973 272p
ISBN 0-385-05034-8

FIC
GAT
SciFic
**Gates** to tomorrow. Norton, A. and
Donaldy, E. eds.

A **gathering** of ghosts. Manley, S. and Lewis, G. eds.

The **general** danced at dawn, and other stories. Fraser, G. M.

The **general** zapped an angel. Fast, H.

**Gerald, Gregory Fitz.** *See* Fitz Gerald, Gregory

**Getting** married. Strindberg, A.

**Ghidalia, Vic.** *See* Elwood, R. jt. ed.

The **ghost** stories of Edith Wharton. Wharton, E.

The **ghostly** tales of Henry James. *See* James, H. Henry James: stories of the supernatural

The **ghouls.** Haining, P. ed.

**Gibson, Walter**
(ed.) Rogues' gallery; a variety of mystery stories: illus. by Paul Spina. Doubleday 1969 398p illus
ISBN 0-385-09371-3

**Gill, Brendan**
(ed.) Parker, D. The portable Dorothy Parker

**Gilliatt, Penelope**
Come back if it doesn't get better. Random House 1969 212p
First published in London 1968 with title: What's it like out?
ISBN 0-394-41984-7
Nobody's business; stories. Viking 1972 185p
ISBN 0-670-51497-7
Analyzed for short stories only

**Ginsburg, Mirra**
(ed.) The ultimate threshold; a collection of the finest in Soviet science fiction; ed. and tr. by Mirra Ginsburg. Holt 1970 244p
SBN 03-081847-8

The **girl** who sang with the Beatles, and other stories. Hemenway, R.

**Girls** at war, and other stories. Achebe, C.

**Glanville, Brian**
A betting man, and other stories. Coward-McCann 1969 223p
ISBN 0-698-10033-6

**Glaze, Eleanor**
The embrace, and stories. Bobbs 1970 277p

The **go-between,** and other stories. Shiina, R.

**Goat** songs. Weston, J.

**God** was here but He left early. Shaw, I.

**Gohman, Fred**
Spider Webb mysteries. Lantern Press (N Y) 1969 185p illus

**Going** places. Michaels, L.

**Gold, Herbert**
The magic will; stories and essays of a decade. Random House 1971 304p
ISBN 0-394-46018-9
Analyzed for short stories only

**Gold** from Crete. Forester, C. S.

**Goldberg, Gerald Jay**
126 days of continuous sunshine. Dial Press 1972 215p

The **golden** ball, and other stories. Christie, A.

The **golden** road. Knight, D. ed.

The **golden** 13, Ellery Queen's. Queen, E. ed.

**Golding, William**
The scorpion god; three short novels. Harcourt Brace Jovanovich [1972 c1971] 178p
ISBN 0-15-136410-9

The **golf** omnibus. Wodehouse, P. G.

The **good** deed, and other stories of Asia, past and present. Buck, P. S.

**Good** neighbors, and other strangers. Pangborn, E.

**Goodman, Philip**
(ed.) The Yom Kippur anthology. Jewish Pub. 1971 xxix, 399p illus
Analyzed for short stories only

**Gordimer, Nadine**
Livingstone's companions; stories. Viking 1971 248p
SBN 670-43570-8

**Gorilla,** my love. Bambara, T. C.

**Gothic** tales of terror. Haining, P. ed.

**Gottesman, Leslie; Obenzinger, Hilton, and Senauke, Alan**
(eds.) A cinch—amazing works from the Columbia Review. Columbia Univ. Press 1969 339p illus
SBN 231-0-3382-6
Analyzed for short stories only

**Goudge, Elizabeth**
The lost angel. Coward, McCann & Geoghegan 1971 144p illus
ISBN 0-698-10220-7

**Goulart, Ron**
Broke down engine, and other troubles with machines. Macmillan (N Y) 1971 192p

The Chameleon Corps & other shape changers. Macmillan (N Y) 1972 216p

What's become of Screwloose? And other inquiries. Scribner 1971 184p
SBN 684-12338-X

**Graham, Winston**
*FIC GRA*
The Japanese girl. Doubleday [1972 c1971] 250p
ISBN 0-385-00483-4

**Grand** slam, Ellery Queen's. Ellery Queen's Mystery Magazine

**Grande** dames of detection. Manley, S. and Lewis, G. eds.

**Grau, Shirley Ann**
The wind shifting west. Knopf 1973 247p
ISBN 0-394-48890-3

**Greased** Samba, and other stories. Deck, J.

**Great** stories of the West. Collier, N. ed.

**Great** Western short stories. Taylor, J. G. ed.

**Green, Ben K.**
Some more horse tradin'; illus. by Joe Beeler. Knopf 1972 255p illus
ISBN 0-394-46123-1

**Green, Roger Lancelyn**
(ed.) Ten tales of adventure; chosen and ed. by Roger Lancelyn Green; with colour frontispiece and line drawings by Philip Gough. Dutton 1972 188p illus
ISBN 0-525-40875-4
(ed.) Thirteen uncanny tales; chosen and ed. by Roger Lancelyn Green; with colour frontispiece and line drawings in the text by Ray Ogden. Dutton 1970 201p illus
ISBN 0-525-41080-5

The **green** flash, and other tales of horror, suspense, and fantasy. Aiken, J.

**Green** grass, blue sky, white house. Morris, W.

**Greenberg, Joanne**
Rites of passage. Holt 1972 197p
ISBN 0-03-086617-0

**Greene, Graham**
Collected stories; including May we borrow your husband? A sense of reality [and] Twenty-one stories. Viking [1973 c1972] 561p
SBN 670-22911-3

The portable Graham Greene; ed. by Philip Stratford. Viking 1973 xxiii, 610p (The Viking Portable lib)
SBN 670-56566-0
Analyzed for short stories only

**Greene, Sir Hugh**
(ed.) Cosmopolitan crimes; foreign rivals of Sherlock Holmes; collected & introduced by Hugh Greene. Pantheon Bks. 1971 347p
ISBN 0-394-47340-X
(ed.) The further rivals of Sherlock Holmes. Pantheon Bks. 1973 317p
ISBN 0-394-48827-X
(ed.) The rivals of Sherlock Holmes; early detective stories; ed. and introduced by Hugh Greene. Pantheon Bks. 1970 351p map
ISBN 0-394-41330-X

**Guests** in the promised land. Hunter, K.

**Gulassa, Cyril M.**
(ed.) The fact of fiction; social relevance in the short story. Canfield Press 1972 395p
ISBN 0-06-383497-3

**Gulik, Robert van**
Judge Dee at work; eight Chinese detective stories; with illus. drawn by the author in Chinese style. Scribner [1973 c1967] 174p illus
SBN 684-13027-0

**Guzman**, go home, and other stories. Sillitoe, A.

# H

**Haining, Peter**
(ed.) A circle of witches; an anthology of Victorian witchcraft stories; selected and introduced by Peter Haining. Taplinger 1971 235p illus
ISBN 0-8008-1590-4
Analyzed for short stories only
(ed.) The clans of darkness; Scottish stories of fantasy and horror; foreword by Angus Wilson. Taplinger 1971 272p
ISBN 0-8008-1621-8
Analyzed for short stories only
(ed.) The freak show; freaks, monsters, ghouls, etc. Nelson 1972 239p
ISBN 0-8407-6244-5

**Haining, Peter—***Continued*

808.83
HAI

(ed.) The ghouls; introduced by Vincent Price; with an afterword by Christopher Lee. Stein & Day 1971 383p

SBN 8138-1365-0

(ed.) Gothic tales of terror; classic horror stories from Great Britain, Europe and the United States, 1765-1840. Taplinger 1972 928p illus

ISBN 0-8008-3590-5

Analyzed for short stories only

(ed.) The Hollywood nightmare; tales of fantasy and horror from the film world; introduced by Christopher Lee. Taplinger [1971 c1970] 276p

ISBN 0-8008-3921-8

Analyzed for short stories only

808.83
HAI

(ed.) The Lucifer society; macabre tales by great modern writers; with a foreword by Kingsley Amis. Taplinger 1972 256p

ISBN 0-8008-5042-4

(ed.) The necromancers; the best of black magic and witchcraft; introduction by Robert Bloch. Morrow 1972 [c1971] 255p illus

Analyzed for short stories only

(ed.) Nightfrights; occult stories for all ages; with illus. by David Smee. Taplinger 1972 254p

ISBN 0-8008-5556-6

(ed.) The nightmare reader. Doubleday 1973 340p (Doubleday Science fiction)

ISBN 0-385-02215-8

Analyzed for short stories only

(ed.) The Satanists. Taplinger [1970 c1969] 249p

ISBN 0-8008-6995-8

Analyzed for short stories only

(ed.) Vampires at midnight; formerly titled The midnight people. Seventeen brilliant and chilling tales of the ghastly blood-sucking undead. Grosset 1970 255p

Analyzed for short stories only

(ed.) The wild night company: Irish stories of fantasy and horror; foreword by Ray Bradbury. Taplinger [1971 c1970] 287p

ISBN 0-8008-8335-7

Analyzed for short stories only

808.83
HAI

(ed.) The witchcraft reader. Doubleday 1970 [c1969] 204p

ISBN 0-385-06959-6

**Hall, James B.**

(ed.) The realm of fiction; 65 short stories. 2d ed. McGraw 1970 528p

ISBN 0-07-025593-8

**Hamalian, Leo.** *See* Karl, F. R. jt. ed.

**Hamalian, Leo, and Volpe, Edmond L.**

(eds.) Eleven modern short novels. 2d ed. edited and with commentaries by Leo Hamalian and Edmond L. Volpe. Putnam 1970 754p

ISBN 0-399-30004-X

1958 edition with title: Ten modern novels, listed in 1955-1958 supplement

**Hamilton, Alex**

(ed.) Splinters; a new anthology of modern macabre fiction. Walker & Co. 1969 237p

**Hanging** by a thread. Kahn, J. ed.

**Happiness,** and other stories, Lavin, M.

The **harpoon** gun. Vassilikos, V.

**Harrison, Harry**

Fic
HAR
Sci.Fic.

(ed.) Astounding. *See* Astounding

Fic.
AST
Sci.Fic

(ed.) The Astounding-Analog reader. *See* The Astounding-Analog reader

Fic
BES
Sci.Fic

(ed.) Best SF: 1968-1972. *See* Best SF: 1968-1972

(ed.) The light fantastic; science fiction classics from the mainstream; introduction by James Blish. Scribner 1971 216p

SBN 684-10228-5

Nova 2
Fic
HAR
Sci.Fic.

(ed.) Nova 1-3. *See* Nova 1-3

One step from earth. Macmillan (N Y) 1970 210p

Fic
HAR
Sci.Fic

(ed.) SF: authors' choice 3. *See* SF: authors' choice 3

(ed.) Worlds of wonder; sixteen tales of science fiction. Doubleday 1969 287p

ISBN 0-385-07027-6

(ed.) The year 2000; an anthology. Doubleday 1970 288p

**Hawaiian** tales. Beekman, A.

**Hawkes, John**

Lunar landscapes; stories & short novels, 1949-1963: Charivari; The owl; The goose on the grave. New Directions 1969 275p

**Hayes, Anna Hansen**

Buckskin and smoke. Naylor 1971 119p

ISBN 0-8111-0427-3

**Heckelmann, Charles N.**
(ed.) Western Writers of America. With Guidons flying

**Helwig, David**
(ed.) Fourteen stories high. *See* Fourteen stories high
(ed.) New Canadian stories, 72-73. *See* New Canadian stories, 72-73.

**Hemenway, Robert**
The girl who sang with the Beatles, and other stories. Knopf 1970 209p
ISBN 0-394-42636-3

**Hemingway, Ernest**
The fifth column, and four stories of the Spanish Civil War. Scribner 1969 151p
ISBN 0-684-10238-2
Analyzed for short stories only

*Fic HEM* The Nick Adams stories; preface by Philip Young. Scribner 1972 268p
SBN 684-12485-8
Partially analyzed

The **Henchmans** at home. Burton, H.

**Henderson, Daryl**
Ditch Valley. Scribner 1972 117p
SBN 684-12995-7

**Henderson, Zenna**
Holding wonder. Doubleday 1971 302p (Doubleday Science fiction)

**Henry, O.**
Tales of O Henry. Doubleday 1969 565p
ISBN 0-385-02877-6

**Henry** James: stories of the supernatural. James H.

**Hermann, John**
An agreement between us; stories. Univ. of Mo. Press 1973 113p (A Breakthrough bk)
ISBN 0-8262-0141-5

**Hesse, Hermann**
*Fic HES* Klingsor's last summer; tr. by Richard and Clara Winston. Farrar, Straus 1970 217p
SBN 374-1-8166-7
Stories of five decades; ed. and with an introduction, by Theodore Ziolkowski; tr. by Ralph Manheim; with two stories tr. by Denver Lindley. Farrar, Straus [1973 c1972] xx, 328p
ISBN 0-374-27050-3
Strange news from another star, and other tales; tr. by Denver Lindley. Farrar, Straus 1972 145p
*Fic HES*

**Highsmith, Patricia**
*Fic HIG* The snail-watcher, and other stories. Doubleday 1970 177p

**Himes, Chester**
Black on Black; Baby sister, and selected writings. Doubleday 1973 287p
ISBN 0-385-02526-2
Analyzed for short stories only

**Hippius, Zinaida**
Selected works of Zinaida Hippius; tr. and ed. by Temira Pachmuss. Univ. of Ill. Press 1972 315p front
ISBN 0-252-00260-1

**Hipolito, Jane, and McNelly, Willis E.**
(ed.) Mars, we love you; tales of Mars, men and Martians. With an introduction by Isaac Asimov. Doubleday 1971 xx, 332p (Doubleday Science fiction)

**Hitchcock, Alfred**
*80883 HIT* (ed.) Alfred Hitchcock presents: A month of mystery. Random House 1969 428p
*808.83 HIT* (ed.) Alfred Hitchcock presents: Stories to be read with the lights on. Random House 1973 433p
ISBN 0-394-48720-6
*808.83 HIT* (ed.) Alfred Hitchcock presents: Stories to stay awake by. Random House 1971 466p
ISBN 0-394-47303-5
(ed.) Alfred Hitchcock's Daring detectives; illus. by Arthur Shilstone. Random House 1969 208p illus
ISBN 0-394-81490-8
(comp.) Alfred Hitchcock's Supernatural tales of terror and suspense; illus. by Robert Shore. Random House [1973] 172p illus
ISBN 0-394-92676-5

**Hobhouse, Caroline**
(ed.) Winter's tales 17. *See* Winter's tales 17

**Hoch, Edward D.**
(ed.) Mystery Writers of America. Dear dead days

**Hoffmann, E. T. A.**
Selected writings of E. T. A. Hoffmann; ed. and tr. by Leonard J. Kent and Elizabeth C. Knight; illus. by Jacob Landau. The tales, v 1. Univ. of Chicago Press 1969 315p illus
SBN 226-34788-3
Three Märchen of E. T. A. Hoffmann; tr. and with an introduction by Charles E. Passage. Univ. of S.C. Press 1971 xxvii, 402p illus
ISBN 0-87249-188-9

Holding wonder. Henderson, Z.

Holland, Kevin Crossley- *See* Crossley-Holland, Kevin

The Hollywood nightmare. Haining, P. ed.

Holm, Sven
(ed.) The Devil's instrument, and other Danish stories; tr. from the Danish by Paula Hostrup-Jessen and ed. by Sven Holm; with an introduction by Elias Bredsdorff. Dufour 1971 266p (UNESCO Collection of contemporary works)
ISBN 0-8023-1251-9

Holmes, Edward M.
A part of the main; short stories of the Maine coast; with drawings by Arline K. Thomson. Univ. of Me. Press 1973 177p illus (Maine studies no. 95)

Holst, Spencer
The language of cats, and other stories. McCall Pub. Co. 1971 86p
SBN 8415-0079-7

Hope should always. Jones, A.

The horror in the museum, and other revisions. Lovecraft, H. P. ed.

Horrors unknown. Moskowitz, S. ed.

A horse and two goats. Narayan, R. K.

House of the sleeping beauties, and other stories. Kawabata, Y.

How they chose the dead. Summers, H.

Howes, Barbara
(ed.) The eye of the heart; short stories from Latin America. Bobbs 1973 415p
ISBN 0-672-51637-3

Howes, Barbara, and Smith, Gregory Jay
(eds.) The sea-green horse; a collection of short stories. Macmillan (N Y) 1970 274p

Hsia, C. T.
(ed.) Twentieth-century Chinese stories; ed. by C. T. Hsia with the assistance of Joseph S. M. Lau. Columbia Univ. Press 1971 239p
ISBN 0-231-03589-6

Hsun, Lu. *See* Lu, Hsun

Hubin, Allen J.
(ed.) Best detective stories of the year [1969]-1973. *See* Best detective stories of the year [1969]-1973

(ed.) Best of the Best detective stories. *See* Best of the Best detective stories

Hue and cry. McPherson, J. A.

The Hugo winners. Asimov, I. ed.

The human equation. Nolan, W. F. ed.

The hungered one. Bullins, E.

Hunter, Evan
The Easter Man (a play) and six stories. Doubleday 1972 253p
ISBN 0-385-01413-9
Analyzed for short stories only

Hunter, Kristin
Guests in the promised land; stories. Scribner 1973 133p
SBN 684-13227-3

# I

I and you and she. Ribnikar, J.

I sing the Body Electric! Bradbury, R.

I thought you were a unicorn, and other stories. Boles, P. D.

Ibuse, Masuji
Lieutenant Lookeast, and other stories; tr. by John Bester. Kodansha 1971 247p
SBN 87011-147-7

The Icarus to be, and other observations. Sax, F.

Ik, Kim Yong. *See* Kim, Yong Ik

Impact. Stansbury, D. L. ed.

In a free state. Naipaul, V. S.

In a small town a kid went to shul, and other stories. Deutschman, B.

In and out of never-never land. Brennan, M.

In love & trouble. Walker, A.

In loveless clarity, and other stories. Rindfleisch, N.

In Ole Virginia. Page, T. N.

In the hands of our enemies. Curley, D.

In the middle of the fields, and other stories. Lavin, M.

In the reign of peace. Nissenson, H.

In trout country. Corodimas, P. ed.

Innes, Michael. *See* Stewart, J. I. M.

The **innocent** and the guilty. Warner, S. T.

**Insights;** a selection of creative literature about childhood; selected and ed. by the Child Study Association of America; with an introduction and comment by Anna W. M. Wolf. Aronson, J. 1973 462p
ISBN 0-87668-116-X
Analyzed for short stories only

**Into** the unknown. Carr, T. ed.

**Intro #2;** ed. with an introduction by R. V. Cassill. McCall Pub. Co. 1970 [c1969] 269p
SBN 8415-0015-0
Analyzed for short stories only
Intro #1, first published 1968 by Bantam Books in paper only, was unavailable for analyzing

**Intro #3;** ed. with an introduction by R. V. Cassill. McCall Pub. Co. 1970 239p
SBN 8415-0044-4
Analyzed for short stories only

**Intro #4;** ed. by Walton Beacham and R. V. Cassill. Published for Va. Commonwealth University by Univ. Press of Va. 1972 207p
ISBN 0-8139-0387-4
Analyzed for short stories only

**Introduction** to modern Bulgarian literature. Kirilov, N. and Kirk, F. eds.

The **invaders.** Treece, H.

**Invaders** from space. Silverberg, R. ed.

**Ionesco, Eugene**
The colonel's photograph; tr. by Jean Stewart with the exception of "The stroller in the air" tr. by John Russell. Grove [1969 c1967] 177p
ISBN 0-394-17300-7

An **Isaac** Bashevis Singer reader. Singer, I. B.

**It** happened on Rush Street. Schwimmer, W.

The **itinerary** of beggars. Francis, H. E.

# J

**Jacobi, Carl**
Disclosures in scarlet. Arkham House 1972 181p

**Jacobs, Harvey**
The egg of the Glak, and other stories. Harper 1969 276p

**Jaffe, Harold.** *See* Tytell, J. jt. ed.

**James, Charles, L.**
(ed.) From the roots; short stories by Black Americans. Dodd 1970 370p
ISBN 0-396-06112-5

**James, Henry,** 1843-1916
Henry James: stories of the supernatural; ed. with a new introduction and headnotes by Leon Edel. Taplinger [1970 c1949] 762p
ISBN 0-8008-3830-0
Analyzed in basic Short story index with title: The ghostly tales of Henry James

The spoils of Poynton, and other stories; introduction by Louis Auchincloss. Doubleday 1971 593p
ISBN 0-385-08036-0
Analyzed for short stories only

The tales of Henry James; v 1, 1864-1869; ed. by Maqbool Aziz. Oxford 1973 516p illus (Clarendon Press Bk)

The **Japanese** girl. Graham. W.

The **jelly** woman. Ruskay, S.

**Jewett, Sarah Orne**
The uncollected short stories of Sarah Orne Jewett; ed. with an introduction, by Richard Cary. Colby College Press 1971 394p

The **Jewish** government, and other stories. Shapiro, L.

**Jhabvala, R. Prawer**
An experience of India. Norton 1972 220p
SBN 393-0-8659-3

The **John** Collier reader. Collier, J.

**Johnson, Bernard**
(ed.) New writing in Yugoslavia. Penguin 1970 342p (The Writing today ser)
ISBN 0-14-003114-6
Analyzed for short stories only

**Johnson, Curt**
(ed.) The Best little magazine fiction, 1970-1971. *See* The Best little magazine fiction, 1970-1971

**Johnson, E. W.**
(ed.) Short stories international. Houghton 1969 406p

**Kidd, Virginia.** *See* Elwood, R. jt. ed.

**Killing** time. Disch, R. and Schwartz, B. eds.

**Kim, Yong Ik**
Love in winter; decorations by Park, Minja. Doubleday 1969 206p
ISBN 0-385-06523-x

**King, Woodie**
*808.83 KIN* (ed.) Black short story anthology. Columbia Univ. Press 1972 381p
ISBN 0-231-03711-2

**Kings** full of aces. Stout, R.

**Kipling, Rudyard**
A selection of his stories and poems, by John Beecroft; illus. by Richard M. Powers. Doubleday [1969 c1956] 2v illus
Analyzed for short stories only

**Kirilov, Nikolai, and Kirk, Frank**
(eds.) Introduction to modern Bulgarian literature; an anthology of short stories. Twayne 1969 480p (Twayne's Introduction to world literature ser)

**Kirk, Frank.** *See* Kirilov, N. jt. ed.

**Kissin, Eva H.**
*808.83 KIS* (ed.) Stories in black and white; collected and ed. by Eva H. Kissin. Lippincott 1970 315p
ISBN 0-397-31114-1

**Klein, Norma**
Love and other euphemisms. Putnam 1972 255p
ISBN 0-399-11009-7

**Klingsor's** last summer. Hesse, H.

**Knapp, Daniel.** *See* Foff, A. jt. ed.

**Knight, Damon**
(comp.) Dimension X; 5 science fiction novellas. Simon & Schuster 1970 351p
SBN 671-65129-3

(ed.) The golden road; great tales of fantasy and the supernatural. Simon & Schuster 1973 447p
*Wehave Orbit 10,11,12 Fic Orb.Fic. Sci.* SBN 671-21554-X

(ed.) Orbit 5-12. *See* Orbit 5-12

*808.83 KNI* (ed.) Perchance to dream. Doubleday 1972 208p (Doubleday Science fiction)
ISBN 0-385-08378-5

*Fic KNI Sci.Fic* (ed.) A pocketful of stars. Doubleday 1971 294p (Doubleday Science fiction)
ISBN 0-385-01917-3

(ed.) A science fiction argosy. Simon & Schuster 1972 828p
SBN 671-21126-9
Analyzed for short stories only

*808.83 KNI* (ed.) Tomorrow and tomorrow; ten tales of the future. Simon & Schuster 1973 253p
SBN 671-65210-9

**Konigsberg, Ira**
(ed.) The classic short story. Harper 1971 446p
SBN 06-043748-0

**Kotowska, Monika**
The bridge to the other side; tr. by Maia Wojciechowska. Doubleday 1970 164p
ISBN 0-385-03412-1

**Kotzwinkle, William**
Elephant bangs train. Pantheon Bks. 1971 148p
ISBN 0-394-46047-2

**Kraus, Richard, and Wiegand, William**
(eds.) Student's choice; an anthology of short stories; ed. and with an introduction by Richard Kraus and William Wiegand. Merrill 1970 222p
ISBN 0-675-09342-9

**Krazy** Kat/The unveiling & other stories. Dawson, F.

**Krispyn, Egbert**
(ed.) Modern stories from Holland and Flanders; an anthology. Twayne 1973 283p (The Lib. of Netherlandic literature v2)

**Krleža, Miroslav**
The cricket beneath the waterfall, and other stories; ed. by Branko Lenski. Vanguard 1972 269p
SBN 8149-0699-0

# L

**Ladies** of horror. Manley, S. and Lewis, G. eds.

**Lafferty, R. A.**
Four futures. *See* Four futures
Strange doing; stories. Scribner 1972 276p
SBN 684-12530-7

**Lagerkvist, Pär**
The eternal smile; three stories. Hill & Wang 1971 206p
ISBN 0-8090-4309-2
The marriage feast. Hill & Wang [1973 c1954] 222p
ISBN 0-8090-6786-2
Partially analyzed

**Lamb, Harold**
The mighty manslayer. Doubleday 1969 230p

**Lamb, Hugh**
(ed.) A tide of terror; an anthology of rare horror stories; introduction by Peter Haining. Taplinger [1973 c1972] 243p
ISBN 0-8008-7695-4
Analyzed for short stories only

The **land** of lost content. Phillips, R.

**Landolfi, Tommaso**
Cancerqueen, and other stories; tr. by Raymond Rosenthal. Dial Press 1971 276p

The **language** of cats, and other stories. Holst, S.

**Lanier, Sterling**
The peculiar exploits of Brigadier Ffellowes. Walker & Co. 1972 159p
ISBN 0-8027-5548-8

**Larson, Charles R.**
(ed.) African short stories; a collection of contemporary African writing; ed. and with an introduction. Collier Bks. 1970 210p
(ed.) Prejudice; 20 tales of oppression and liberation; ed. and with an introduction. New Am. Lib. 1971 302p (A Mentor bk)

The **last** carousel. Algren, N.

**Latin** American writing today. Cohen, J. M. ed.

**Laughlin, J.**
(ed.) New Directions in prose and poetry 19-27. *See* New Directions in prose and poetry 19-27

**Latin** blood. Yates, D. A. ed.

**Laumer, Keith**
Five fates. *See* Five fates
Once there was a giant. Doubleday 1971 252p (Doubleday Science fiction)
ISBN 0-385-07029-2
Retief: ambassador to space; seven incidents of the Corps Diplomatique Terrestrienne. Doubleday 1969 216p (Doubleday Science fiction)
Retief of the CDT. Doubleday 1971 172p (Doubleday Science fiction)

**Laurence, Margaret**
A bird in the house; stories. Knopf 1970 207p
ISBN 0-394-41696-1

**Lavin, Mary**
Collected stories; with an introduction by V. S. Pritchett. Houghton 1971 425p
ISBN 0-395-12099-3

Happiness, and other stories. Houghton 1970 [c1969] 152p
ISBN 0-395-07903-9
In the middle of the fields, and other stories. Macmillan (N Y) 1969 215p
A memory, and other stories. Houghton 1973 [c1972] 223p
ISBN 0-395-17122-9

**Leaf** storm, and other stories. García Márquez, G.

**Leskov, Nikolai**
Satirical stories of Nikolai Leskov; tr. and ed. by William B. Edgerton. Pegasus (N Y) 1969 411p
ISBN 0-672-53589-0

**Lessing, Doris**
The temptation of Jack Orkney, and other stories. Knopf 1972 308p
ISBN 0-394-48244-1

**Lester, Julius**
Long journey home; stories from Black history. Dial Press 1972 147p

**Le Sueur, Meridel**
Corn village; a selection. Stanton & Lee 1970 74p
Analyzed for short stories only

**Lewis, Gogo.** *See* Manley, S. jt. ed.

**Lewis, Jerry D.**
(ed.) Tales of our people; great stories of the Jew in America; introduction by Harry Golden. Geis 1969 332p illus

**Lieutenant** Lookeast, and other stories. Ibuse, M.

The **life** guard. Wain, J.

A **life** in the closet, and stories. Rushmore, R.

The **life** of riot. Sherwin, J. J.

The **life** to come, and other short stories. Forster, E. M.

The **light** fantastic. Harrison, H. ed.

**Limehouse** nights. Burke, T.

**Linklater, Eric**
The stories of Eric Linklater. Horizon Press [1969 c1968] 377p
ISBN 0-8180-0605-6

A **lion** unannounced. Casper, L.

**Lish, Gordon**
(ed.) The secret life of our times: new fiction from Esquire; introduction by Tom Wolfe. Doubleday 1973 xxviii, 641p
ISBN 0-385-06215-X

**Lispector, Clarice**
Family ties; tr. with an introduction by Giovanni Pontiero. Univ. of Tex. Press 1972 156p (Tex. Pan-Am. ser)
ISBN 0-292-72404-7

**The Literary Review**
Angoff, C. ed. Stories from The Literary Review
Decker, C. R. and Angoff, C. eds. Modern stories from many lands

**Litvinov, Ivy**
She knew she was right; stories. Viking [1971] 247p
SBN 670-63947-8

**Live** and learn. Spinner, S. ed.

**Livingstone's** companions. Gordimer, N.

The **loners.** Schulman, L. M. ed.

**Long, Frank Belknap**
The rim of the unknown. Arkham House 1972 291p

**Long, Richard A. and Collier, Eugenia W.**
(eds.) Afro-American writing; an anthology of prose and poetry. N.Y. Univ. Press 1972 2v (794p)
ISBN 8147-4954-2
Analyzed for short stories only
**Long** journey home. Lester, J.

The **loot** of cities. Bennett, A.

**Lord** Peter. Sayers, D. L.

The **lost** angel. Goudge, E.

The **Lost** Chapel picnic, and other stories. Sharp, M.

The **lost** face: best science fiction from Czechoslovakia. Nesvadba, J.

**Love** and other euphemisms. Klein, N.

**Love** in winter. Kim, Y. I.

The **love** object. O'Brien, E.

**Lovecraft, H. P.**
(ed.) The horror in the museum, and other revisions. Arkham House 1970 383p

**Lu, Hsun**
Selected stories of Lu Hsun. [Tr. by Yang-Hsien-yi and Gladys Yang] Oriole Eds. [1972?] 306p
ISBN 0-88211-042-X

**Lucia, Ellis**
(ed.) This land around us; a treasury of Pacific Northwest writing; ed. and with commentary by Ellis Lucia; illus. by Mel Klapholz. Doubleday 1969 xxiv, 981p illus
ISBN 0-385-04109-8
Analyzed for short stories only

The **Lucifer** society. Haining, P. ed.

**Luckyj, George S. N.**
(ed.) Modern Ukrainian short stories; parallel text ed. Edited with a preface. Ukrainian Academic Press 1973 228p
ISBN 0-87287-061-8

**Lumley, Brian**
The caller of The Black. Arkham House 1971 235p

**Lunar** landscapes. Hawkes, J.

**Lütgen, Kurt**
Next to the north wind; tr. by Maria Pelikan. Doubleday 1973 223p illus
ISBN 0-385-05714-8

**Lyons, Nick**
(ed.) Fisherman's bounty; a treasury of fascinating lore and the finest stories from the world of angling. Crown 1970 352p illus
Analyzed for short stories only

**Lytle, Andrew**
(ed.) Craft and vision; the best fiction from the Sewanee Review. Delacorte Press 1971 457p (A Seymour Lawrence book)
Analyzed for short stories only

# M

**McCaffrey, Anne**
(ed.) Alchemy and academe; a collection of original stories concerning themselves with transmutations, mental and elemental, alchemical and academic. Doubleday 1970 239p (Doubleday Science fiction)
ISBN 0-385-08188-X

**McComas, J. Francis**
(ed.) Crimes and misfortunes; the Anthony Boucher Memorial anthology of mysteries. Random House 1970 459p
Analyzed for short stories only
(ed.) Special wonder; the Anthony Boucher Memorial anthology of fantasy and science fiction. Random House 1970 410p

**McCord, Jean**
Bitter is the hawk's path. Atheneum Pubs. 1971 149p
ISBN 0-689-20682-8

**McCrindle, Joseph F.**
(ed.) Stories from the Transatlantic Review. Holt 1970 304p
SBN 03-084524-6

Fic
MAL

Mars, we love you. Hipolito, J. and McNelly, W. E. eds.

**Marsh, Willard**
Beachhead in Bohemia; stories. La. State Univ. Press [1970 c1969] 202p
SBN 8071-0914-2

**Marshall, Lenore**
The confrontation, and other stories; with a foreword by Alfred Kazin. Norton 1972 158p
ISBN 0-393-08448-5

The **Martian** chronicles. Bradbury, R.

**Marx, Paul**
(ed.) 12 short story writers. *See* 12 short story writers

**Masur, Harold Q.**
(ed.) Mystery Writers of America. Murder most foul

**Matisse,** Picasso and Gertrude Stein. Stein, G.

**Matthews, Jack**
(ed.) Archetypal themes in the modern story. St Martins 1973 385p
Analyzed for short stories only

**Maugham, W. Somerset**
Seventeen lost stories. Comp. and with an introduction by Craig V. Showalter. Doubleday 1969 273p

*Fic MAU*

**Maupassant, Guy de**
The cocotte (Boule de suif) and three other stories; illus. by Howard Baer. Watts, F. [1972 c1971] 80p illus
SBN 85166-154-8
Fifteen by Maupassant; a collection of short stories by the great French writer; selected and tr. by Mariam Morton. Doubleday 1972 190p
ISBN 0-385-07085-3
French tales of love and passion. Young Publications 1968 262p
Selected short stories; with a critical and biographical profile of Guy de Maupassant by Jean-Albert Bédé. Watts, F. [1969] 312p (A Watts Ultratype ed)
ISBN 0-531-00423-6

**Mayer, Tom**
The weary Falcon. Houghton 1971 174p
ISBN 0-395-12045-4

**Meek, Frederick M.**
The Bethlehem Inn, and other Christmas stories. Decorations by Marian Ebert. Westminster Press 1972 126p
ISBN 0-664-20943-2

A **memory,** and other stories. Lavin, M.

**Men** and malice. Dickensheet, D. ed.

**Merchants** of menace. Mystery Writers of America

**Merril, Judith**
Daughters of Earth; three novels. Doubleday 1969 [c1968] 255p (Doubleday Science fiction)

*Fic BIG SF* —The **metallic** muse. Biggle, L.

**Metcalf, John**
(ed.) Sixteen by twelve; short stories by Canadian writers. McGraw 1970 224p illus
ISBN 0-7700-3214-1

**Michaels, Leonard**
Going places. Farrar, Straus 1969 191p
ISBN 0-374-16496-7

**Michener, James A.**
(ed.) First fruits; a harvest of 25 years of Israeli writing; with a foreword by Chaim Potok; ed. and with an introduction by James A. Michener. Jewish Pub. 1973 xxv, 346p
ISBN 0-8276-0018-6

**Midwood, Barton**
Phantoms; a collection of stories. Dutton 1970 191p
ISBN 0-525-17870-8

The **mighty** manslayer. Lamb, H.

**Miller, Jimmy**
Some parts in the single life. Knopf 1970 242p
ISBN 0-394-44617-8

**Mills, Robert P.** *See* Ferman, E. L. jt. ed.

**Milton, Nancy.** *See* Katz, N. jt. ed.

**Mind** to mind. Silverberg, R. ed.

**Minot, Stephen, and Wilson, Robley**
(eds.) Three stances of modern fiction; a critical anthology of the short story; ed. by Stephen Minot [and] Robley Wilson, Jr. Winthrop Pubs. 1972 307p
ISBN 0-87626-875-0

**Mirror,** mirror, fatal mirror. Mystery Writers of America

The **mirror** of infinity. Silverberg, R. ed.

**Mirrors.** Warner, L.

The **misplaced** machine, and other stories. Veiga, J. J.

**Miss** Muriel, and other stories. Petry, A.

**Mistresses** of mystery. Manley, S. and Lewis, G. eds.

**Mitchell, Edward Page**
The crystal man; landmark science fiction; collected and with a biographical perspective by Sam Moskowitz. Doubleday 1973 lxxii 358p (Doubleday Science fiction)
ISBN 0-385-03139-4

**Modern** satiric stories. Fitz Gerald, G. ed.

**Modern** stories from Holland and Flanders. Krispyn, E. ed.

**Modern** stories from many lands. Decker, C. R. and Angoff, C. eds.

**Modern** Ukrainian short stories. Luckyj, G. S. N. ed.

**Mohs, Mayo**
(ed.) Other worlds, other gods; adventures in religious science fiction. Doubleday 1971 264p
ISBN 0-385-00664-0

**Montgomery, John**
(ed.) The world's best cat stories; illus. by Janet and Anne Grahame-Johnstone. McGraw [1970 c1969] 217p illus
ISBN 0-07-042855-7
Analyzed for short stories only

**Moravia, Alberto**
Bought and sold; tr. by Angus Davidson. Farrar, Strauss [1973 c1971] 221p
ISBN 0-374-1555-9
Published in England 1971 with title: Paradise

Command, and I will obey you; tr. from the Italian by Angus Davidson. Farrar, Straus 1969 190p
ISBN 0-374-12660-7

**More** pricks than kicks. Beckett, S.

**Morris, Wright**
Green grass, blue sky, white house. Black Sparrow Press 1970 67p

The **mortgaged** heart. McCullers, C.

**Morton, Miriam**
(ed.) Voices from France; ten stories by French Nobel Prize winners; selected and ed. by Miriam Morton. Doubleday 1969 212p
ISBN 0-385-04348-1

**Moskowitz, Sam**
(ed.) Horrors unknown; ed. with an introduction and notes. Newly discovered masterpieces by great names in fantastic terror. Walker & Co. 1971 214p
ISBN 0-8027-5534-8

(ed.) When women rule; ed. with an introductory essay. Walker & Co. 1972 221p
ISBN 0-8027-5547-X

**Moss, Howard**
(ed.) The poet's story. Macmillan Pub. Co. 1973 xx, 268p

**Moss,** mallards and mules, and other hunting and fishing stories. Brister, B.

**Munro, Alice**
Dance of the happy shades, and other stories. McGraw [1973 c1968] 224p
ISBN 0-07-044048-4

**Murder** most foul. Mystery Writers of America

The **murder** of the frogs, and other stories. Carpenter, D.

The **Murphy** stories. Costello, M.

**Museums** and women, and other stories. Updike, J.

**Mutants.** Dickson, G. R.

**My** name aloud. Ribalow, H. U. ed.

**Mystery Writers of America**
Crime without murder; an anthology of stories by the Mystery Writers of America; ed. by Dorothy Salisbury Davis. Scribner 1970 301p
ISBN 0-684-10101-7

Dear dead days; the 1972 Mystery Writers of America anthology; ed. by Edward D. Hoch. Walker & Co. 1972 243p
ISBN 0-8027-5267-5

Merchants of menace; an anthology of mystery stories, by the Mystery Writers of America; ed. by Hillary Waugh. Doubleday 1969 298p

Mirror, mirror, fatal mirror; an anthology of mystery stories; ed. by Hans Stefan Santesson. Doubleday 1973 254p
ISBN 0-385-05073-9

Murder most foul; the 1971 Mystery Writers of America anthology; ed. by Harold Q. Masur. Walker & Co. 1971 167p
ISBN 0-8027-5238-1

# N

**Nabokov, Vladimir**
A Russian beauty, and other stories. McGraw 1973 268p
ISBN 0-07-045735-2

**Naipaul, V. S.**
In a free state. Knopf 1971 256p
ISBN 0-394-47185-7

**Naked** author. Di Donato, P.

The **naked** i. Karl, F. R. and Hamalian, L. eds.

**Narayan, R. K.**
*Fic NAR*
A horse and two goats; stories. With decorations by R. K. Laxman. Viking 1970 148p illus
ISBN 0-670-37885-2

A **native** sons reader. Margolies, E. ed.

**Naylor, Phyllis Reynolds**
Dark side of the moon; stories; drawings by Joseph Papin. Fortress Press 1969 124p illus
ISBN 0-8006-0193-9
Ships in the night. Fortress Press [1971 c1970] 121p illus
ISBN 0-8006-0142-4
Analyzed for short stories only

**Nebula** award stories 4; ed. by Poul Anderson. Doubleday 1969 236p (Doubleday Science fiction)

*Fic NEB Sci.Fic*
**Nebula** award stories 5; ed. by James Blish. Doubleday 1970 215p (Doubleday Science fiction)
ISBN 0-385-03851-8

**Nebula** award stories 6; ed. by Clifford D. Simak. Doubleday 1971 204p

*Fic NEB Sci.Fic*
**Nebula** award stories 7; ed. by Lloyd Biggle, Jr. Harper 1973 xx, 289p
SBN 06-010328-0
Analyzed for short stories only

*Fic NEB Sci.Fic*
**Nebula** award stories 8; ed. by Isaac Asimov. Harper 1973 xx, 248p
ISBN 0-06-010151-2

**Necker, Claire**
*808.83 NEC*
(ed.) Supernatural cats; an anthology. Doubleday 1972 439p
ISBN 0-385-07561-8
Partially analyzed

The **necromancers.** Haining, P. ed.

**Nemerov, Howard**
Stories, fables & other diversions. David R. Godine 1971 121p
ISBN 0-87923-030-4

**Nesvadba, Josef**
The lost face: best science fiction from Czechoslovakia. Taplinger 1971 215p
ISBN 0-8008-5020-3

**Neugeboren, Jay**
Corky's brother. Farrar, Straus 1969 261p
ISBN 0-317-12968-1

**New** American Review, no. 1-15. [Ed. by Theodore Solotaroff] Analyzed for short stories only
Numbers 1-10 published by New American Library; Numbers 11-15 published by Simon & Schuster; Numbers 16-18 published by Bantam Books with title: American Review
Numbers 13-15 published by Simon & Schuster in the Touchstone books series
*See also* American Review v16-18

**New** Black voices. Chapman, A. ed.

**New** Canadian stories 72-73; ed. by David Helwig & Joan Harcourt. Oberon Press 1972-1973 2v
ISBN 1972 (0-88750-066-8); 1973 (0-88750-088-9)
The 1971 compilation of this annual was published under title: Fourteen stories high

*Fic NEW Sci.Fic*
**New** dimensions 1; fourteen original science fiction stories; ed. by Robert Silverberg. Doubleday 1971 246p (Doubleday Science fiction)
ISBN 0-385-07016-0

*Fic NEW Sci.Fic*
**New** dimensions 2; eleven original science fiction stories; ed. by Robert Silverberg. Doubleday 1972 229p (Doubleday Science fiction)
ISBN 0-385-09141-9

**New** Directions in prose and poetry 19-27; ed. by J. Laughlin. New Directions 1966-1973 9v illus (New Directions bks)
Analyzed for short stories only
ISBN v26 (0-8112-0476-6; v27 (0-8112-0484-7)
Volumes 25-27 are edited by J. Laughlin with Peter Glassgold and Frederick R. Martin

The **new** Israeli writers. Rabikovitz, D. ed.

The **new** mind. Elwood, R. ed.

**New** queens for old. Fielding, G.

**New** writing in Yugoslavia. Johnson, B. ed.

**Next** to the north wind. Lütgen, K.

*Fic HEM*
The **Nick** Adams stories. Hemingway, E.

**Night,** Dawn, The accident. Wiesel, E.

**Nightfall,** and other stories. Asimov, I.

**Nightfrights.** Haining, P. ed.

**Nightlines.** McGahern, J.

The **nightmare** reader. Haining, P. ed.

**Nightwebs.** Woolrich, C.

**1968.** Stern, R.

**Nissenson, Hugh**
In the reign of peace. Farrar, Straus 1972 157p
ISBN 0-374-17657-4

**No** mind of man; three original novellas of science fiction, by Terry Carr, Richard A. Lupoff [and] Robert Silverberg. Hawthorn Bks. 1973 182p

**No** sweetness here. Aidoo, A. A.

**Nobody's** business. Gilliatt, P.

**Nolan, William F.**
(ed.) The future is now; all-new all-star science fiction stories; comp. and ed. by William F. Nolan. Sherbourne 1970 248p
ISBN 0-8202-0056-5
(ed.) The human equation; four science fiction novels of tomorrow; ed. and with biographical prefaces. Sherbourne 1971 254p
(ed.) A wilderness of stars; stories of man in conflict with space; introduction by Shelly Lowenkopf. Sherbourne 1969 276p
ISBN 0-8202-0111-1

**Nolen, Barbara**
(ed.) Africa is thunder and wonder; contemporary voices from African literature; with an introduction by Abioseh Nicol; illus. by African artists. Scribner 1972 272p illus
SBN 684-12726-1
Analyzed for short stories only

A **North** American education. Blaise, C.

**Norton, Andre, and Donaldy, Ernestine**
(eds.) Gates to tomorrow; an introduction to science fiction; selected and ed. by Andre Norton & Ernestine Donaldy. Atheneum Pubs. 1973 264p (A Margaret K. McElderry bk)
ISBN 0-689-30321-1

**Nourse, Alan E.**
Rx for tomorrow; tales of science fiction, fantasy and medicine. McKay 1971 216p

**Nova** 1; an anthology of original science fiction stories; ed. by Harry Harrison. Delacorte Press 1970 222p

**Nova** 2-3; ed. by Harry Harrison. Walker & Co. 1972-1973 2v
ISBN v2 (0-8027-5550-X); v3 (0-8027-5558-5)

**Nude** croquet. Fiedler, L. A.

**Nye, Robert**
Tales I told my mother. Hill & Wang 1969 172p
ISBN 0-8090-9106-2

# O

The **O.** Henry Awards. *See* Prize stories, 1969-1973: The O. Henry Awards

**Oates, Joyce Carol**
Marriages and infidelities; short stories. Vanguard 1972 497p
SBN 8149-0718-0
(ed.) Scenes from American life; contemporary short fiction. Vanguard 1973 271p
SBN 8149-0750-4
The wheel of love, and other stories. Vanguard 1970 440p
SBN 8149-0676-1

**Obenzinger, Hilton.** *See* Gottesman, L. jt. ed.

**O'Brien, Edna**
The love object; stories. Knopf 1969 [c1968] 172p
ISBN 0-394-43435-8

**O'Connor, Flannery**
The complete stories. Farrar, Straus 1971 555p
ISBN 0-374-12752-2

**O'Connor, Frank**
A set of variations; twenty-seven stories. Knopf 1969 338p
ISBN 0-394-44486-8

**O'Connor, Philip F.**
Old morals, small continents, darker times. Univ. of Iowa Press 1971 186p
ISBN 0-87745-023-4

**O'Donovan, Michael.** *See* O'Connor, Frank

**O'Faolain, Sean**
The talking trees, and other stories. Little 1970 279p (An Atlantic Monthly Press book)

**O'Hara, John**
The O'Hara generation. Random House 1969 491p
ISBN 0-394-43126-X
The time element, and other stories. Random House 1972 244p
ISBN 0-394-48211-5

The **O'Hara** generation. O'Hara, J.

**Old** morals, small continents, darker times. O'Connor, P. F.

The **Old** South. Bontemps, A.

**On** being told that her second husband has taken his first lover, and other stories. Slesinger, T.

**Once** there was a giant. Laumer, K.

**126** days of continuous sunshine. Goldberg, G. J.

**One** step from earth. Harrison, H.

**Orbit** 5-12; an anthology of new science fiction stories [ed. by Damon Knight]. Putnam 1970-1973 8v
   ISBN v6 (0-399-10605-7); v7 (0-399-10606-5); v8 (0-399-10607-3); v9 (0-399-10608-1); v10 (0-399-10609-X); v11 (0-399-10981-1); v12 (0-399-11101-8)
    Subtitle of volume 5 varies

The **orchid** stories. Elmslie, K.

**Ostaijen, Paul van**
   Patriotism, inc. and other tales; ed. & tr. by E. M. Beekman. Univ. of Mass. Press 1971 170p
   ISBN 0-87023-084-0

**Ostayen, Paul van.** *See* Ostaijen, Paul van

**Other** dimensions. Silverberg, R. ed.

**Other** dimensions. Smith, C. A.

The **other** side of the clock. Stern, P. V. ed.

The **other** side of tomorrow, Elwood, R. ed.

The **other** woman. Colette

**Other** worlds, other gods. Mohs, M. ed.

**Other** worlds, other seas. Suvin, D. ed.

**Ottley, Reginald**
   Brumbie dust; a selection of stories. Harcourt 1969 143p
   ISBN 0-15-212658-9

On **overpraised** season. Zolotow, C. ed.

The **Oxford** Chekhov. Chekhov, A.

**Ozick, Cynthia**
   The pagan rabbi, and other stories. Knopf 1971 270p
   ISBN 0-394-46970-4

# P

The **pagan** rabbi, and other stories. Ozick, C.

**Page, Thomas Nelson**
   In Ole Virginia; or, Marse Chan and other stories; with an introduction by Kimball King. Univ. of N.C. Press 1969 xxxvi, 230p (Southern literary classics ser)
   ISBN 0-8078-1100-9

**Pangborn, Edgar**
   Good neighbors, and other strangers. Macmillan (N Y) 1972 195p

**Paquet, Basil T.** *See* Karlin, W. jt. ed.

**Paradise.** *See* Moravia, A. Bought and sold

**Paradox** lost, and twelve other great science fiction stories. Brown, F.

**Parker, Dorothy**
   The portable Dorothy Parker. Rev. and enl. ed. With a new introduction by Brendan Gill. Viking 1973 xxvii, 610p
   SBN 670-54016-1
    Analyzed for short stories only
    Earlier edition analyzed in basic Short Story Index with title: Dorothy Parker

**Parry, Michel**
   (ed.) Beware of the cat; stories of feline fantasy and horror. Taplinger [1973 c1972] 192p illus
   ISBN 0-8008-0730-8

**Parsecs** and parables. Silverberg, R.

A **part** of the main. Holmes, E. M.

**Partners** in wonder. Ellison, H.

**Patriotism,** inc., and other tales. Ostaijen, P. van

**Patton, Frances Gray**
   Twenty-eight stories. Dodd 1969 375p
   ISBN 0-396-05890-6

The **peculiar** exploits of Brigadier Ffellowes. Lanier, S.

The **Pegnitz** Junction. Gallant, M.

**Pei, Mario**
   Tales of the natural and supernatural; designs by Laura Torbet. Devin-Adair 1971 310p illus

**Pentecost, Hugh**
   Around dark corners; a collection of mystery stories. Dodd 1970 182p

**Perchance** to dream. Knight, D. ed.

**Perilous** ascent. Fenner, P. R. comp.

The **perishing** republic. Bahr, J.

**Permanent** errors. Price, R.

**Petaja, Emil**
Stardrift, and other fantastic flotsam. Fantasy Pub. Co. 1971 220p

**Peter,** and other stories. Savitz, H. M. and Shecktor, M. C.

**Peterkin, Julia**
Collected short stories of Julia Peterkin; selected and ed. and with an introduction by Frank Durham. Univ. of S.C. Press 1970 384p
SBN 87249-184-6
Partially analyzed

**Petrakis, Harry Mark**
The waves of night, and other stories. McKay 1969 230p

*[handwritten: Fic PET]*

**Petry, Ann**
Miss Muriel, and other stories. Houghton 1971 305p
ISBN 0-395-12671-1

**Phantoms.** Midwood, B.

**Philips, Judson.** *See* Pentecost, Hugh

**Phillips, Robert**
The land of lost content. Vanguard 1970 189p
ISBN 0-8149-0674-5

**Phoenix** feathers. Silverberg, B. ed.

**Pincherle, Alberto.** *See* Moravia, Alberto

**Platonov, Andrei**
The fierce and beautiful world; stories; introduction by Yevgeny Yevtushenko; tr. by Joseph Barnes. Dutton 1970 252p
ISBN 0-525-10475-5

A **pocketful** of stars. Knight, D. ed.

**Poe, Edgar Allan**
Tales of terror and fantasy; ten stories from Tales of mystery and imagination; chosen and ed. by Roger Lancelyn Green; with colour plate and line drawings by Arthur Rackham. Dutton 1971 150p illus (Children's illustrated classics)
ISBN 0-460-05091-5

The **poet's** story. Moss, H. ed.

**Pohl, Frederik**
(ed.) The eleventh Galaxy reader. *See* Galaxy Magazine. The eleventh Galaxy reader

The **politician,** and other stories. Khamsing S.

**Pomorska, Krystyna**
(ed.) Fifty years of Russian prose: from Pasternak to Solzhenitsyn. MIT Press 1971 2v
ISBN v1 (0-262-16037-4); v2 0-262-16038-2)
Analyzed for short stories only

The **portable** Dorothy Parker. Parker, D.

The **portable** Graham Greene. Greene, G.

The **portable** Steinbeck. Steinbeck J.

The **portable** Stephen Crane. Crane, S.

**Porter, William Sydney.** *See* Henry, O.

**Povey, John.** *See* Angoff, C. jt. ed.

**Prebble, John**
Spanish stirrup, and other stories. Holt 1973 260p
ISBN 0-03-001461-1

**Prejudice:** 20 tales of oppression and liberation. Larson, C. R. ed.

**Premchand**
The world of Premchand; selected stories of Premchand; tr. by David Rubin. Ind. Univ. Press 1969 215p
SBN 253-19500-4

**Price, Reynolds**
Permanent errors. Atheneum Pubs. 1970 253p
ISBN 0-689-10357-3
Analyzed for short stories only

**Pricksongs** & descants. Coover, R.

A **pride** of monsters. Schmitz, J. H.

**Prigozy, Ruth.** *See* Thune, E. jt. ed.

**Prisoners** of this world. Kaplan, B.

**Pritchett, V. S.**
Blind love, and other stories. Random House 1969 246p
ISBN 0-394-41714-3

*[handwritten: Fic PRI]*

**Prize** stories, 1969-1973: The O. Henry Awards; ed. and with an introduction by William Abrahams. Doubleday 1969-1973 5v
ISBN 1970 (0-385-07984-2); 1971 (0-385-06666-X); 1972 (0-385-04176-4); 1973 (0-385-06693-7)

*[handwritten: Fic PRI]*

The **process** of fiction. McKenzie, B. ed.

**Proffer, Carl R.**
(ed.) From Karamzin to Bunin: an anthology of Russian short stories; ed. with a critical commentary and eleven new translations. Ind. Univ. Press 1969 468p
ISBN 0-253-32505-6

A **purple** rhododendron, and other stories. Fox, J.

# Q

**Queen, Ellery**
(ed.) Ellery Queen's Mystery Magazine. Ellery Queen's Grand slam

*Fic QUE mystery*
(ed.) Ellery Queen's Mystery Magazine. Ellery Queen's Headliners

*Fic QUE mystery*
(ed.) Ellery Queen's Mystery Magazine. Ellery Queen's Murder menu

(ed.) Ellery Queen's Mystery Magazine. Ellery Queen's Mystery bag

(ed.) Ellery Queen's The golden 13. World Pub. [1971 c1970] 347p

# R

**Rx** for tomorrow. Nourse, A. E.

**Rabikovitz, Dalia**
(ed.) The new Israeli writers; short stories of the first generation. Funk 1969 319p
SBN 87631-006

**Rascoe, Judith**
*Fic RAS*
Yours, and mine; novella and stories. Little 1973 204p (An Atlantic Monthly Press book)
ISBN 0-316-75634-2

**Reading** literature. Satin, J. ed.

The **realm** of fiction. Hall, J. B. ed.

The **red** badge of courage, and other stories. Crane, S.

**Red** Dust 2: new writing; Babette Sassoon: Sacrifices and Green; Simon Vestdijk: My brown friend; Alan Burns: Buster. Red Dust 1972 139p
SBN 87376-019-0

**Rees, Barbara**
Try another country; three short novels. Harcourt 1969 178p

**Rembrandt's** hat. Malamud, B.

A **Renaissance** storybook. Bishop, M. ed.

The **restless** ghost. Garfield, L.

**Retief:** ambassador to space. Laumer, K.

**Retief** of the CDT. Laumer, K.

**Revenge** of the lawn. Brautigan, R.

**Revolt** of the apprentices, and other stories. Blum-Alquit, E.

**Rey, Lester del.** *See* Del Rey, Lester

**Rhapsody** of a hermit, and three tales. Rothschild, M.

**Ribalow, Harold U.**
(ed.) My name aloud; Jewish stories by Jewish writers. Yoseloff 1969 560p
SBN 498-06763-7

**Ribnikar, Jara**
I and you and she; tr. by Eva Tucker. McGraw 1972 207p
ISBN 0-07-052144-1

The **rim** of the unknown. Long, F. B.

**Rindfleisch, Norval**
In loveless clarity, and other stories. Ithaca House 1972 141p (An Ithaca House bk)
ISBN 0-87886-017-7

**Rites** of passage. Greenberg, J.

The **rivals** of Sherlock Holmes. Greene, H. ed.

**Roadarmel, Gordon C.**
(ed.) A death in Delhi; modern Hindi short stories; tr. and ed. by Gordon C. Roadarmel. Univ. of Calif. Press 1972 211p
ISBN 0-520-02220-3

**Roecker, William A.**
(ed.) Stories that count. Holt 1971 214p

**Rogues'** gallery. Gibson, W. ed.

**Rolfe, Father.** *See* Corvo, Frederick, Baron

**Rolfe, Frederick William.** *See* Corvo, Frederick, Baron

A **Romantic** storybook. Bishop, M. ed.

**Rosmond, Babette**
*808.83 ROS*
(comp.) Today's stories from Seventeen; a fiction anthology. Macmillan (NY) 1971 271p
Analyzed for short stories only

**Rothschild, Michael**
Rhapsody of a hermit, and three tales. Viking 1973 183p
ISBN 0-670-59725-2

**Rottensteiner, Franz**
(ed.) View from another shore; European science fiction; ed. and with an introduction. Seabury 1973 234p (A Continuum bk)
ISBN 0-8164-9151-8

**Rottmann, Larry,** ed. *See* Karlin, W. jt. ed.

The **ruins** of earth. Disch, T. M. ed.

**Runyon, Damon**
The best of Damon Runyon; with an introduction by Damon Runyon, Jr. Hart 1966 252p

**Rushmore, Robert**
A life in the closet, and stories. Bobbs 1973 175p
ISBN 0-672-51775-2

**Ruskay, Sophie**
The jelly woman; short stories and
selected pieces. Barnes, A. S.
[1970 c1969] 169p
SBN 498-07563-X
Analyzed for short stories
only

**Russell, Bertrand**
The collected stories of Bertrand
Russell; comp. and ed. by Barry
Feinberg. Simon & Schuster
[1973 c1972] 349p illus
SBN 671-21489-6
Analyzed for short stories
only

A **Russian** beauty, and other stories.
Nabokov, V.

**Russian** science fiction, 1969. Magidoff, R. ed.

**Russia's** other writers. Scammell, M.
ed.

# S

**SF**: authors' choice 3; ed. by Harry
Harrison. Putnam 1971 222p
ISBN 0-399-10730-4

**Sadness.** Barthelme, D.

**Sallis, James**
A few last words. Macmillan
(NY) 1970 226p
Analyzed for short stories
only

**Saltus, Edgar**
A transient guest and other epi-
sodes. AMS Press 1970 199p
ISBN 0-404-05509-5

**Sanders, Winston, P.** *See* Anderson,
Poul

**Santesson, Hans Stefan**
(ed.) Crime prevention in the
30th century; ed. with an introduction by Hans Stefan Santesson. Walker & Co. 1969
175p
ISBN 0-8027-5506-2
(ed.) The days after tomorrow;
science fiction stories by Isaac
Asimov [and others]. Little
1971 261p
ISBN 0-316-77065-5
—(ed.) Mystery Writers of America. Mirror, mirror, fatal mirror

**Satan** on my track. Lester, J.

The **Satanists.** Haining, P. ed.

**Satin, Joseph**
(ed.) Reading literature; stories,
plays, and poems. Houghton
1968 xx, 683p
Analyzed for short stories
only

**Satirical** stories of Nikolai Leskov.
Leskov, N.

**Saving** worlds. Elwood, R. and
Kidd, V. eds.

**Savitz, Harriet May, and Shecktor,
M. Caporale**
Peter, and other stories. Day 1969
93p
ISBN 0-381-99714-6

**Sax, Fausto**
The Icarus to be, and other observations. Pulse-Finger Press
1971 199p
ISBN 0-912282-01-0
Analyzed for short stories
only

**Sayers, Dorothy L.**
Lord Peter; a collection of all the
Lord Peter Wimsey stories;
comp. and with an introduction
by James Sandoe; coda by
Carolyn Heilbrun; codetta by
E. C. Bentley. Harper 1972
464p map
ISBN 0-06-013787-8

**Scammell, Michael**
(ed.) Russia's other writers; se-
lections from Samizdat literature; selected and introduced
by Michael Scammell; foreword by Max Hayward. Praeger 1971 216p

**Scenes** from American life. Oates,
J. C. ed.

The **scent** of apples. Davis, O.

**Schmitz, James H.**
A pride of monsters. Macmillan
(N Y) 1970 248p

**Schulman, L. M.**
(ed.) The cracked looking glass;
stories of other realities. Macmillan (N Y) 1971 254p
(ed.) The loners; short stories
about the young and alienated.
Macmillan (N Y) 1970 279p
(ed.) Travelers; stories of Americans abroad. Macmillan (N Y)
1972 286p

**Schultz, John**
The tongues of men. Big Table
Pub. Co. 1969 352p

**Schwartz, Barry.** *See* Disch, R. jt.
ed.

**Schwartz, Jonathan**
Almost home; collected stories.
Doubleday 1970 225p

**Schwimmer, Walter**
It happened on Rush Street; a
group of short stories and vi-
gnettes. Fell 1971 235p
SBN 8119-0205-6
Partially analyzed

A **science** fiction argosy. Knight, D. ed.

The **science** fiction bestiary. Silverberg, R. ed.

*Fic SCI Sci.Fic.*
**Science** fiction hall of fame, v 1; the greatest science fiction stories of all time; chosen by the members of the Science Fiction Writers of Amercia. Ed. by Robert Silverberg. Doubleday 1970 558p
ISBN 0-385-01958-0

*Fic SCI Sci.Fic*
The **Science** fiction hall of fame, v2A-2B; the greatest science fiction novellas of all time chosen by the members of the Science Fiction Writers of America. Ed. by Ben Bova. Doubleday 1973 2v
ISBN 0-385-04576-X; 0-385-05788-1

**Science Fiction Writers of America**
The Science fiction hall of fame, v 1, v2A-2B. *See* The Science fiction hall of fame, v 1, v2A-2B

The **scorpion** god. Golding, W.

**Scortia, Thomas N.**
(ed.) Strange bedfellows; sex and science fiction. Random House [1973 c1972] 273p
ISBN 0-394-48155-0
Partially analyzed

**Scott, Duncan Campbell**
Selected stories of Duncan Campbell Scott; ed. and with an introduction by Glenn Clever. Univ. of Ottawa Press 1972 135p (Canadian Short stories ser)

The **sea**-green horse. Howes, B. and Smith, G. J. eds.

**Seacoast** and upland: a New England anthology. Westbrook, P. D. ed.

**Searches** and seizures. Elkin, S.

**Second** chance. Auchincloss, L.

The **secret** life of our times: new fiction from Esquire. Lish, G. ed.

**Selected** short stories. Maupassant, G. de

**Selected** stories of Duncan Campbell Scott. Scott, D. C.

**Selected** stories of Lu Hsun. Lu, Hsun

**Selected** works of Zinaida Hippius. Hippius, Z.

**Selected** writings of E. T. A. Hoffmann. Hoffmann, E. T. A.

A **selection** of his stories and poems. Kipling, R.

**Senauke, Alan.** *See* Gottesman, L. jt. ed.

A **set** of variations. O' Connor, F.

**Seven** American stories. Edmonds, W. D.

**Seven** conquests. Anderson, P.

**Seven** short novels. Chekhov, A.

**Seventeen** lost stories. Maugham, W. S.

**Sewanee Review**
Lytle, A. ed. Craft and vision.

The **shadow** knows. Madden, D.

**Shapes** of the supernatural. Manley, S. and Lewis, G. eds.

**Shapiro, Lamed**
The Jewish government, and other stories; ed. and tr. with an introduction by Curt Leviant. Twayne 1971 186p

A **shark**-infested rice pudding. Wright, S.

**Sharp, Margery**
The Lost Chapel picnic, and other stories. Little 1973 201p
ISBN 0-316-782939

**Shaw, Irwin**
God was here but He left early; short fiction. Arbor House 1973 268p
ISBN 0-87795-055-5

**She** knew she was right. Litvinov, I.

The **She**-wolf, and other stories. Verga, G.

**Sheckley, Robert**
*Fic SHE Sci.Fic*
Can you feel anything when I do this? Doubleday 1971 191p (Doubleday Science fiction)
ISBN 0-385-03495-4

**Shecktor, M. Caporale.** *See* Savitz, H. M. jt. auth.

**Shepherd, Jean**
*Fic SHE*
Wanda Hickey's night of golden memories, and other disasters. Doubleday 1971 350p
ISBN 0-385-04870-X

**Sherwin, Judith Johnson**
The life of riot; stories. Atheneum Pubs. 1970 242p
ISBN 0-689-10326-3

**Shiina, Rinzo**
*Fic SHI*
The go-between, and other stories; tr. by Noah S. Brannen. Judson Press 1970 128p
ISBN 0-8170-0490-4

Fic
SIL
Sci. Fic.

Fic
SIL
Sci. Fic

Fic
SIM
Sci. Fic.

Fic
SIL
Sci. Fic.

**Simon, John**
(ed.) Fourteen for now; a collection of contemporary stories; ed. and with commentaries by John Simon. Harper 1969 316p
ISBN 0-06-080258-8

Sin at Easter, and other stories. Vaižgantas

Sing, choirs of angels. Cuomo, G.

**Singer, Isaac Bashevis**
*Fic SIN*
A crown of feathers, and other stories. Farrar, Straus 1973 342p
ISBN 0-374-13217-8
A friend of Kafka, and other stories. Farrar, Straus 1970 311p
ISBN 0-374-15880-0
An Isaac Bashevis Singer reader. Farrar, Straus 1971 560p
ISBN 0-374-17747-3
Analyzed for short stories only

The single heart. Drake, R.

The single voice. Charyn, J. ed.

The sinner from Toledo, and other stories. Chekhov, A.

Sinning with Annie, and other stories. Theroux, P.

Sixteen by twelve. Metcalf, J.

Sixteen stories as they happened. Bullock, M.

**Slesinger, Tess**
On being told that her second husband has taken his first lover, and other stories. Quadrangle Bks. 1971 396p
SBN 8129-0176-2
A slow, soft river. Dorr, L.

Small changes. Clement, H.

**Smith, Clark Ashton**
Other dimensions. Arkham House 1970 329p

**Smith, Gregory Jay.** See Howes, B. jt. ed.

The snail-watcher, and stories. Highsmith, P.

**Solotaroff, Theodore**
(ed.) American Review, 16-18. See American Review, 16-18.
(ed.) New American Review, no. 1-15. See New American Review, no. 1-15

**Solzhenitsyn, Alexander**
Stories and prose poems; tr. by Michael Glenny. Farrar, Straus 1971 267p
ISBN 0-374-27033-3
Analyzed for short stories only

Some more horse tradin'. Green, B. K.

Some parts in the single life. Miller, J.

Some things dark and dangerous. Kahn, J. ed.

Some things fierce and fatal. Kahn, J. ed.

Some things strange and sinister. Kahn, J. ed.

Someone just like you. Yurick, S.

Something soft, and other stories. Starke, R.

**Soto, Pedro Juan**
Spiks; stories; tr. and with an introduction by Victoria Ortiz. Monthly Review 1973 92p
ISBN 0-85345-299-7
Partially analyzed

South of no north. Bukowski, C.

Spanish stirrup, and other stories. Prebble, J.

Special wonder. McComas, J. F. ed.

A spectrum of worlds. Clareson, T. D. ed.

Spider Webb mysteries. Gohman, F.

**Spielberg, Peter**
Bedrock; a work of fiction composed of fifteen scenes from my life. Crossing Press 1973 198p
ISBN 0-912278-39-0

**Spike, Paul**
Bad news. Holt 1971 152p
SBN 03-085970-0

Spiks. Soto, P. J.

**Spinner, Stephanie**
(ed.) Feminine plural; stories by women about growing up. Macmillan (N Y) 1972 240p
(ed.) Live and learn; stories about students and their teachers. Macmillan Pub. Co. 1973 265p
ISBN 0-02-786020-5
Partially analyzed

Splinters. Hamilton, A. ed.
The spoils of Poynton, and other stories. James, H.

**Srivastava, Dhanpat Rai.** See Premchand

**Stafford, Jean**
*Fic STA*
The collected stories of Jean Stafford. Farrar, Straus 1969 463p
ISBN 0-374-60850-4

**Stansbury, Donald L.**
(ed.) Impact; short stories for pleasure. Prentice-Hall 1971 377p
ISBN 0-13-451724-5

The star road. Dickson, G. R.

**Stardrift,** and other fantastic flotsam. Petaja, E.

**Starke, Roland**
Something soft, and other stories. Doubleday 1969 213p

**Steegmuller, Francis**
Stories and true stories. Little 1972 276p (An Atlantic Monthly Press book)
ISBN 0-316-81221-8
Analyzed for short stories only

**Stein, Gertrude**
Fernhurst, Q.E.D., and other early writings. Liveright 1971 xxxiv, 214p
SBN 87140-532-6

Matisse, Picasso and Gertrude Stein; with two shorter stories. Something Else 1972 278p
ISBN 0-87110-085-1

**Steinbeck, John**
The portable Steinbeck; rev. selected, and introduced by Pascal Covici, Jr. Viking 1971 xlii, 692p
SBN 670-66960-1
Analyzed for short stories only

**Steinhauer, Harry**
(ed.) Ten German novellas; tr. and ed. by Harry Steinhauer. Doubleday 1969 xxv, 570p (Anchor bks)

**Stephens, Donald**
(ed.) Contemporary voices; the short story in Canada. Prentice-Hall 1972 182p
ISBN 13-171314-0

**Stern, James**
The stories of James Stern. Harcourt 1968 270p
Partially analyzed

**Stern, Philip Van Doren**
(ed.) The other side of the clock; stories out of time, out of place; collected and with an introduction by Philip Van Doren Stern. Van Nostrand 1969 192p
ISBN 0-442-37977-3

**Stern, Richard**
1968; a short novel, an urban idyll, five stories, and two trade notes. Holt 1970 209p
SBN 03-084529-7
Analyzed for short stories only

**Sternberg, Jacques**
Future without future. Seabury 1973 210p (A Continuum bk)
ISBN 0-8164-9170-4

**Stevenson, Robert Louis**
*Fic STE*
The complete short stories of Robert Louis Stevenson; with a selection of the best short novels; ed. and with an introduction by Charles Neider. Doubleday 1969 xxx, 678p
ISBN 0-385-07875-7

**Stevick, Philip**
(ed.) Anti-story; an anthology of experimental fiction. Free Press 1971 xxiii, 319p
Partially analyzed

**Stewart, J. I. M.**
Cucumber sandwiches, and other stories. Norton [1970 c1969] 255p
SBN 393-08600-3

**Stewart, Natacha**
Evil eye, and other stories. Houghton 1972 212p
ISBN 0-395-13693-8

**Stoker, Bram**
The Bram Stoker Bedside companion; 10 stories by the author of Dracula; ed. and with an introduction by Charles Osborne. Taplinger 1973 224p
ISBN 0-8008-0963-7
Analyzed for short stories only

**Stone, Alma**
*Fic STO*
The banishment, and three stories; The portrait, The traveler [and] Oh, pity the dwarf's butt. Doubleday 1973 279p
ISBN 0-385-03899-2
Analyzed for short stories only

The **stone** and the violets. Djilas, M.

**Stories** and prose poems. Solzhenitsyn, A.

**Stories** and true stories. Steegmuller, F.

**Stories,** fables & other diversions. Nemerov, H.

**Stories** from The Literary Review. Angoff, C. ed.

**Stories** from the sixties. Elkin, S. ed.

**Stories** from the Transatlantic Review. McCrindle, J. F. ed.

**Stories** in black and white. Kissin, E. H. ed.

**Stories** of darkness and dread. Brennan, J. P.

The **stories** of Eric Linklater. Linklater, E.

**Stories** of five decades. Hesse, H.

The **stories** of James Stern. Stern, J.

**Stories** that count. Roecker, W. A. ed.

**Stories** Toto told me. Corvo, F. Baron

**Story.** Foff, A. and Knapp, D. eds.

**Story:** the yearbook discovery/1969; the best creative work from the universities and colleges of the United States & Canada as judged by Louise Bogan [and others] cooperating in the Story College Creative Awards contest of 1968-1969; ed. by Whit and Hallie Burnett. Four Winds 1969 416p

**Stout, Rex**
Kings full of aces; a Nero Wolfe omnibus. Viking [1969] 472p
Analyzed for short stories only

**Strange** bedfellows. Scortia, T. N. ed.

**Strange** doings. Lafferty, R. A.

**Strange** news from another star, and other tales. Hesse, H.

**Strange** seas and shores. Davidson, A.

**Stratford, Philip**
(ed.) Greene, G. The portable Graham Greene

A **streetful** of people. Estes, W. M.

**Strindberg, August**
Getting married; tr. from the Swedish, ed. and introduced by Mary Sandbach. Viking 1972 384p
SBN 670-33760-9

**Strong, Jonathan**
Tike, and five stories. Little 1969 210p (An Atlantic Monthly Press bk)
ISBN 0-316-81920-4

**Stuart, Jesse**
*Fic STU* —Come back to the farm. McGraw 1971 246p
ISBN 0-07-062239-6
*Fic STU* —Come gentle spring. McGraw 1969 282p
ISBN 0-07-062243-4
*Fic STU* —Dawn of remembered spring. McGraw 1972 179p
ISBN 0-07-062240-X

**Student's** choice. Kraus, R. and Wiegand, W. eds.

**Sturgeon, Theodore**
Sturgeon is alive and well . . . A collection of short stories. Putnam 1971 221p
ISBN 0-399-10775-4

**Sturgeon, Theodore, and Ward, Don**
*Fic WAL Western* Sturgeon's West. Doubleday 1973 186p
ISBN 0-385-05393-2

**Sturgeon** is alive and well . . . Sturgeon, T.

*Fic WAL Western* **Sturgeon's** West. Sturgeon, T. and Ward, D.

**Sukenick, Ronald**
The death of the novel, and other stories. Dial Press 1969 175p

**Summer.** Ansell, J.

**Summer** situations. Birstein, A.

**Summers, Hollis**
How they chose the dead; stories. La. State Univ. Press, 1973 182p
ISBN 0-8071-0221-0

**Supernatural** cats. Necker, C. ed.

**Supernatural** tales of terror and suspense, Alfred Hitchcock's. Hitchcock, A. comp.

**Survival** printout. Total Effect

**Suvin, Darko**
(ed.) Other worlds, other seas; science-fiction stories from socialist countries; selected, ed. and with a preface. Random House 1970 xxxiii, 217p
ISBN 0-394-43951-1

# T

**Tales** and stories for Black folks. Bambara, T. C. ed.

**Tales** from the White Hart. Clarke, A. C.

**Tales** I told my mother. Nye, R.

**Tales** of a Dalai Lama. Delattre, P.

**Tales** of adventure. Crane, S.

The **tales** of Henry James v 1. James, H.

**Tales** of moonlight and rain. Uyeda, A.

**Tales** of O. Henry. Henry, O.

**Tales** of our people. Lewis, J. D. ed.

**Tales** of terror and fantasy. Poe, E. A.

**Tales** of terror and the supernatural. Collins, W.

**Tales** of the Crusades. Coolidge, O.

*Fic TAL* **Tales** of the Cthulhu Mythos. Derleth, A. ed.

**Tales** of the flying mountains. Anderson, P.

**Tales** of the natural and supernatural. Pei, M.

**Tales** of unease. Burke, J. ed.

**Tales** of war. Crane, S.

Tales, sketches, and reports. Crane, S.

The talking trees, and other stories. O'Faolain, S.

Taylor, Elizabeth
The devastating boys, and other stories. Viking 1972 179p
ISBN 0-670-27067-9

Taylor, J. Chesley
(ed.) The short story: fiction in transition. Scribner 1969 638p
ISBN 0-684-13046-7

Taylor, J. Golden
(ed.) Great Western short stories; with an introduction by Wallace Stegner. Am. West 1967 572p

Taylor, Peter
The collected stories of Peter Taylor. Farrar, Straus 1969 535p
ISBN 0-374-12548-1

Teen-age Mexican stories. Witton, D.

Teen-age secret agent stories. Furman, A. L. ed.

Teen-age space adventures. Furman, A. L. ed.

The temptation of Jack Orkney, and other stories. Lessing, D.

Ten German novellas. Steinhauer, H. ed.

Ten modern masters. Davis, R. G. ed.

Ten modern short novels. *See* Hamalian, L. and Volpe, E. L. eds. Eleven modern short novels

Ten tales of adventure. Green, R. L. ed.

Tendryakov, Vladimir
Three, seven, ace & other stories; tr. from the Russian by David Alger, Olive Stevens, Paul Falla; with a foreword by Max Hayward. Harper 1973 252p
ISBN 0-06-014242-1

That's what happened to me. Burnett, W. ed.

There is no such place as America. Bichsel, P.

Theroux, Alexander
Three wogs. Gambit 1972 216p
ISBN 0-87645-055-9

Theroux, Paul
Sinning with Annie, and other stories. Houghton 1972 210p
ISBN 0-395-13996-1

Thirteen uncanny tales. Green, R. L. ed.

This is Moscow speaking, and other stories. Daniel, Y.

This land around us. Lucia, E. ed.

Thomas, Dylan
Early prose writings; ed. with an introduction by Walford Davies. New Directions [1972 c1971] 204p
Analyzed for short stories only

Thomason, John W.
Fix bayonets! And other stories; illus. by the author. Scribner 1970 523p illus

Three days and a child. Yehoshua, A. B.

Three for tomorrow; three original novellas of science fiction, by Robert Silverberg, Roger Zelazny [and] James Blish; with a foreword by Arthur C. Clarke. Meredith 1969 204p

Three Märchen of E. T. A. Hoffmann. Hoffmann, E. T. A.

Three: 1971; The good professor, who murdered the bad little girl, by Arthur Gould; The last one, by Calvin Kenfield; A coffeehouse acquaintance, by Edith Templeton. Random House 1971 208p
ISBN 0-394-46219-X

Three novellas: Punin and Baburin, The inn, The watch. Turgenev, I.

Three, seven, ace & other stories. Tendryakov, V.

Three stances of modern fiction. Minot, S. and Wilson, R. eds.

3000 years of fantasy and science fiction. De Camp, L. S. and De Camp, C. C. eds.

Three trips in time and space; original novellas of science fiction, by Larry Niven, John Brunner, and Jack Vance. Foreword by Robert Silverberg. Hawthorn Bks. 1973 193p

Three wogs. Theroux, A.

Thune, Ensaf, and Prigozy, Ruth
(eds.) Short stories: a critical anthology [ed. by] Ensaf Thune [and] Ruth Prigozy. Macmillan (N Y) 1973 615p

Tibbets, Albert B.
(ed.) Boys are boys; stories from around the world. Little 1969 210p
ISBN 0-316-84498-5

A tide of terror. Lamb, H.

Tierra Amarilla. Ulibarri, S. R.

Tike, and five stories. Strong, J.

The time element, and other stories. O'Hara, J.

The **time** of Adam. Cullinan, E.

A **time** to keep, and other stories. Brown, G. M.

The **Times** of London Anthology of detective stories. Day [1973 c1972] 251p
ISBN 0-381-98254-8

**Tindall, Gillian**
Dances of death; short stories on a theme. Walker & Co. 1973 221p
ISBN 0-8027-0426-3

To the stars. Silverberg, R. ed.

**Today's** stories from Seventeen. Rosmond, B. comp.

**Tolstoĭ, Alekseĭ Konstantinovich, Graf.** *See* Tolstoy, Alexis

**Tolstoy, Alexis**
*[handwritten: FIC TOL]*
Vampires; stories of the supernatural. Tr. by Fedor Nikanov; ed. by Linda Kuehl; illus. by Mel Fowler. Hawthorn Bks. 1969 183p illus

**Tomlinson, Dorothy**
(ed.) Walk in dread; twelve classic eerie tales; ed. and with an an introduction. Taplinger 1972 287p
ISBN 0-8008-8037-4

**Tomorrow** and tomorrow. Knight, D. ed.

**Tomorrow's** alternatives. Elwood, R. ed.

**Tomorrow's** worlds. Silverberg, R. ed.

The **tongues** of men. Schultz, J.

**Total Effect**
Survival printout [ed. by] Leonard Allison, Leonard Jenkin [and] Robert Perrault. Vintage 1973 332p
ISBN 0-394-71857-7
Analyzed for short stories only

A **touch** of infinity. Fast, H.

**Transatlantic Review**
McCrindle, J. F. ed. Stories from the Transatlantic Review

A **transient** guest and other episodes. Saltus, E.

**Travelers.** Schulman, L. M. ed.

**Treasury** of great humor. Untermeyer, L. ed.

*[handwritten: 808.83 TRE v.1+2]*
A **Treasury** of modern mysteries [by] Agatha Christie [and others]. Doubleday 1973 2v
Analyzed for short stories only

**Treece, Henry**
The invaders; three stories; introduced by Margery Fisher; illus. by Charles Keeping. Crowell 1972 120p illus
ISBN 0-690-44993-3

**Trevisan, Dalton**
The vampire of Curitiba, and other stories; tr. from the Portuguese by Gregory Rabassa. Knopf 1972 267p
ISBN 0-394-46645-4

**Trevor, William**
The ballroom of romance, and other stories. Viking 1972 269p
SBN 670-14681-1

**Trial** and terror. Kahn, J. ed.

**Triple** cross; Carlos Fuentes: Holy place; José Donoso: Hell has no limits; Servero Sarduy: From Cuba with a song. Dutton 1972 329p
ISBN 0-525-22280-4

The **troubled** vision. Charyn, J. ed.

**Try** another country. Rees, B.

**Tuohy, Frank**
Fingers in the door, and other stories. Scribner 1970 157p

**Turgenev, Ivan**
Three novellas: Punin and Baburin, The inn, The watch. Farrar, Straus [1969 c1968] 208 p
ISBN 0-374-27672-2

**Turner, Darwin T.**
(ed.) Black American literature; essays, poetry, fiction, drama. Merrill 1970 610p (Charles E. Merrill Literary texts)
ISBN 0-675-09279-5
Analyzed for short stories only

**Turner, James**
(ed.) Unlikely ghosts. Taplinger 1969 218p
SBN 8008-7940-6

**12** short story writers; Guy de Maupassant [and others] ed. by Paul Marx. Holt 1970 451p
ISBN 0-03-081332-8

**Twentieth**-century Chinese stories. Hsia, C. T. ed.

**Twenty-eight** stories. Patton, F. G.

**Twenty-one** stories. Agnon, S. Y.

**Twenty** years of The Magazine of Fantasy and Science Fiction. Ferman, E. L. and Mills, R. P. eds.

**Twice** fifteen. Brown, E. P. ed.

**Tyrmand, Leopold**
(ed.) Explorations in freedom: prose, narrative, and poetry from Kultura. Free Press 1970 442p
   Analyzed for short stories only

**Tytell, John, and Jaffe, Harold**
(eds.) Affinities; a short story anthology. Crowell 1970 468p
ISBN 0-690-05248-0
   Analyzed for short stories only

# U

**Ulibarri, Sabine R.**
Tierra Amarilla; stories of New Mexico (Cuentos de Nuevo Mexico) tr. from the Spanish by Thelma Campbell Nason; illus. by Kercheville. Univ. of N. Mex. Press 1971 167p illus
ISBN 0-8263-0211-4

The **ultimate** threshold. Ginsburg, M. ed.

**Uncle** Valentine, and other stories. Cather, W.

The **uncollected** short stories of Sarah Orne Jewett. Jewett, S. O.

The **unconscious** victorious, and other stories. Berne, S.

**Unfamiliar** territory. Silverberg, R.

**Universe** 1; ed. by Terry Carr. Ace Bks. 1971 250p illus

**Universe** 2; an original collection of all-new science fiction; ed. by Terry Carr. Ace Bks. [1972] 255p

**Universe** 3; ed. by Terry Carr. Random House 1973 209p
ISBN 0-394-48181-X

**Unlikely** ghosts. Turner, J. ed.

**Untermeyer, Louis**
(ed.) Treasury of great humor; including wit, whimsy, and satire from the remote past to the present; ed. with a running commentary, by Louis Untermeyer. McGraw 1972 683p
ISBN 0-07-065939-7
   Analyzed for short stories only

**Updike, John**
Bech: a book. Knopf 1970 206p
ISBN 0-394-41638-4
Museums and women, and other stories. Knopf 1972 282p illus
ISBN 0-394-48173-9

The **usurping** ghost, and other encounters and experiences. Dickinson, S. ed.

**Uyeda, Akinari**
Tales of moonlight and rain; Japanese gothic tales; tr. by Kengi Hamada. Columbia Univ. Press 1972 [c1971] xxix, 150p illus
ISBN 0-231-03631-0

# V

**Vaižgantas**
Sin at Easter, and other stories; tr. from the Lithuanian by Danguolé Sealey [and others]; biographical outline by Antanas Vaičiulaitis; ed. by Nola M. Zobarskas; introduction by Charles Angoff. Manyland Bks. 1971 131p
ISBN 0-87141-038-9

**Val Baker, Denys**
The face in the mirror. Arkham House 1971 113p

The **vampire** of Curitiba, and other stories. Trevisan, D.

**Vampires.** Tolstoy, A.

**Vampires** at midnight. Haining, P. ed.

**Vance, Jack**
Eight fantasms and magics; a science fiction adventure. Macmillan (N Y) 1969 288p

**Van Ostaijen, Paul.** *See* Ostaijen, Paul van

**Vassilikos, Vassilis**
The harpoon gun; tr. by Barbara Bray. Harcourt 1973 246p
ISBN 0-15-138800-8

**Veiga, José J.**
The misplaced machine, and other stories; tr. from the Portuguese by Pamela G. Bird. Knopf 1970 141p
ISBN 0-394-43651-2

**Verga, Giovanni**
The She-wolf, and other stories; 2d ed. rev. and enl. Tr. with an introduction by Giovanni Cecchetti. Univ. of Calif. Press 1973 xxiv, 299p
ISBN 0-520-02153-3

**Victorian** doll stories, by Brenda, Mrs Gatty [and] Frances Hodgson Burnett; with an introduction by Gillian Avery. Schocken [1969] 141p illus (Victorian revivals)
ISBN 0-8052-3275-3

**View** from another shore. Rottensteiner, F. ed.

Voices from France. Morton, M. ed.

Voices from the big house. Andrews, F. E. and Dickens, A. eds.

Voices of Brooklyn; an anthology; ed. by Sol Yurick; sponsored by Brooklyn Public Library. A.L.A. 1973 xxiii, 278p
ISBN 0-8389-0140-9
    Analyzed for short stories only

Voices of modern Asia. Shimer, D. B. ed.

Volpe, Edmond L. *See* Hamalian, jt. ed.

Vries, Peter de. *See* De Vries, Peter

# W

Wain, John
    The life guard; stories. Viking [1972 c1971] 172p
    SBN 670-42800-0

Waldo, Edward Hamilton. *See* Sturgeon, Theodore

Walk in dread. Tomlinson, D. ed.

Walker, Alice
    In love & trouble; stories of Black women. Harcourt 1973 138p
    ISBN 0-15-144405-6

Walsh, Jill Paton, and Crossley-Holland, Kevin
    Wordhoard; Anglo-Saxon stories. Farrar, Straus 1969 122p
    ISBN 0-374-38514-9

Wanda Hickey's night of golden memories, and other disasters. Shepherd, J.

War of time. Carpentier, A.

Ward, Don. *See* Sturgeon, T. jt. auth.

Warner, Lucy
    Mirrors; stories. Knopf 1969 181p
    ISBN 0-394-43636-9

Warner, Sylvia Townsend
    The innocent and the guilty; stories. Viking 1971 135p
    ISBN 0-670-39837-3

Wash us and comb us. Deming, B.

The watcher & other stories. Calvino, I.

Waugh, Hillary
    (ed.) Mystery Writers of America. Merchants of menace

The waves of night, and other stories. Petrakis, H. M.

The way it is now. Bingham, S.

The weary Falcon. Mayer, T.

Weaver, Gordon
    The entombed man of Thule; stories. La. State Univ. Press 1972 185p
    ISBN 0-8071-0245-8

West, Jessamyn
    Crimson Ramblers of the world, farewell. Harcourt 1970 247p
    ISBN 0-15-123086-2

    Except for me and thee; a companion to The friendly persuasion. Harcourt 1969 309p
    ISBN 0-15-129454-2

The West of Owen Wister. Wister, O.

Westbrook, Perry D.
    (ed.) Seacoast and upland: a New England anthology. Barnes, A. S. 1972 381p
    ISBN 0-498-01032-5
        Analyzed for short stories only

A Western bonanza. Western Writers of America

Western septet. Sienkiewicz, H.

Western Writers of America
    A Western bonanza; eight short novels of the West, by members of the Western Writers of America; ed. by Todhunter Ballard. Doubleday 1969 419p

    With Guidons flying; tales of the U.S. cavalry in the Old West, by members of the Western Writers of America; ed. by Charles N. Heckelmann. Doubleday 1970

Weston, John
    Goat songs. Atheneum Pubs. 1971 242p
    ISBN 0-689-10471-5

Wharton, Edith
    The ghost stories of Edith Wharton; illus. by Laszlo Kubinyi. Scribner 1973 276p illus
    SBN 684-13338-5

    Madame de Treymes, and others: four novelettes. Scribner 1970 314p
    ISBN 0-684-13235-4

What we must see: young Black storytellers. Coombs, O. ed.

What's become of Screwloose? And other inquiries. Goulart, R.

What's it like out? *See* Gilliatt, P. Come back if it doesn't get better

The wheel of love, and other stories. Oates, J. C.

When he was free and young and he used to wear silks. Clarke, A.

When women rule. Moskowitz, S. ed.

**Yolen, Jane**
(comp.) Zoo 2000; twelve stories of science fiction and fantasy beasts; comp. and introduced by Jane Yolen. Seabury 1972 224p
ISBN 0-8164-3103-5

The **Yom** Kippur anthology. Goodman, P. ed.

**You** must know everything. Babel, I.

**Young** love, and other infidelities. Zobarskas, S.

The **young** Russians. Whitney, T. P. ed.

**Yours,** and mine. Rascoe, J.

**Yurick, Sol**
Someone just like you. Harper 1972 253p
SBN 06-014783-0

(ed.) Voices of Brooklyn. *See* Voices of Brooklyn

# Z

**Zelazny, Roger**
The doors of his face, the lamps of his mouth, and other stories. Doubleday 1971 229p
ISBN 0-385-08216-9

**Zobarskas, Stepas**
Young love, and other infidelities; introduction by Charles Angoff. Manyland Bks. 1971 115p
ISBN 0-87141-035-4

**Zolotow, Charlotte**
(ed.) An overpraised season; 10 stories of youth; selected by Charlotte Zolotow. Harper 1973 188p
ISBN 0-06-026953-7

**Zoo** 2000. Yolen, J. comp.

# Directory of Publishers and Distributors

A. L. A. American Library Association, 50 E Huron St, Chicago, Ill. 60611

AMS Press. AMS Press, 56 E 13th St. New York, N.Y. 10003

Ace Bks. Ace Books, 1120 Av. of the Americas, New York, N.Y. 10036

Am-Scandinavian Foundation. American-Scandinavian Foundation, 127 E 73d St, New York, N.Y. 10017

Am. West. American West Publishing Company, 599 College Av, Palo Alto, Calif. 94306

Arbor House. Arbor House Publishing Company, Inc, 757 3d Av, New York, N.Y. 10017

Arkham House. Arkham House, Sauk City, Wis. 53583

Aronson, J. Jason Aronson, Inc, 59 4th Av, New York, N.Y. 10003

Atheneum Pubs. Atheneum Publishers, 122 E 42d St, New York, N.Y. 10017

Aurora Pubs. Aurora Publishers, Inc, 118 16th Av, S, Nashville, Tenn. 37219

Bantam. Bantam Books, Inc, 666 5th Av, New York, N.Y. 10019

Barnes, A. S.   A. S. Barnes & Company, Inc. Forsgate Dr, Cranbury, N.J. 08512

Barnes & Noble. *See* Harper

Behrman. Behrman House, Inc. 1261 Broadway, New York, N.Y. 10001

Big Table Pub. Co. Big Table Publishing Company, 1010 W Washington Blvd, Chicago, Ill. 60607

Black Sparrow Press. Black Sparrow Press, Box 25603, Los Angeles, Calif. 90025

Bobbs. The Bobbs-Merrill Company, Inc. 4300 W 62d St, Indianapolis, Ind. 46268

Braziller. George Braziller, Inc, 1 Park Av, New York, N.Y. 10016

Canfield Press. Canfield Press, 850 Montgomery St, San Francisco, Calif. 04133

Cherry Hill Bks. Cherry Hill Books, 202 Highland Av, Cheshire, Conn. 06410

Chilton Bk. Co. Chilton Book Company, Chilton Way, Radnor, Pa. 19089

City Lights Bks. City Lights Books, Inc, 1562 Grant Av, San Francisco, Calif. 94133

Colby College Press. Colby College Press, Waterville, Me. 04910

Collier Bks. Collier Books, 866 3d Av, New York, N.Y. 10022

Columbia Univ. Press. Columbia University Press, 562 W 113th St, New York, N.Y. 10025

Commonwealth Press. Commonwealth Press, Inc, 1st & Berkeley Sts, Radford, Va. 24141

Cornell Univ. Press, Cornell University Press, 124 Roberts Pl, Ithaca, N.Y. 14850

Coward-McCann. *See* Coward, McCann & Geoghegan

Coward, McCann & Geoghegan. Coward, McCann & Geoghegan, Inc, 200 Madison Av, New York, N.Y. 10016

Crossing Press. The Crossing Press, R.D. 3, Trumansburg, N.Y. 14886

Crowell. Thomas Y. Crowell Company, 666 5th Av, New York, N.Y. 10019

Crown. Crown Publishers, Inc, 419 Park Av, S, New York, N.Y. 10016

Day. The John Day Company, Inc, 257 Park Av, S, New York, N.Y. 10010

Delacorte Press. *See* Dell

Dell. Dell Publishing Company, Inc, Dag Hammarskjold Plaza, 245 E 47th St, New York, N.Y. 10017

Devin-Adair. The Devin-Adair Company, 1 Park Av, Old Greenwich, Conn. 06870

Dial Press. The Dial Press, 1 Dag Hammarskjold Plaza, 245 E 47th St, New York, N.Y. 10017

Dodd. Dodd, Mead & Company, 79 Madison Av, New York, N.Y. 10016

Doubleday. Doubleday & Company, Inc, 277 Park Av, New York, N.Y. 10017

Dover. Dover Publications, Inc, 180 Varick St, New York, N.Y. 10014

Dufour. Dufour Editions, Inc, Chester Springs, Pa. 19425

Dutton. E. P. Dutton & Company, Inc, 201 Park Av, S, New York, N.Y. 10003

Eakins Press. The Eakins Press, 155 E 42d St, New York, N.Y. 10017

Eerdmans. William B. Eerdmans Publishing Company, 255 Jefferson Av, S. E., Grand Rapids, Mich. 49502

Fairleigh Dickinson Univ. Press. Fairleigh Dickinson University Press, Rutherford, N.J. 07070

Fantasy Pub. Co. Fantasy Publishing Company, Alhambra, Calif. 91802

Farrar, Straus. Farrar, Straus & Giroux, Inc, 19 Union Sq, W, New York, N.Y. 10003

Fawcett. Fawcett Publications, Inc, Fawcett Bldg, Fawcett Pl, Greenwich, Conn. 06830

Fell. Frederick Fell Publishers, Inc, 386 Park Av, S, New York, N.Y. 10016

Follett. Follett Publishing Company, 1010 W Washington Blvd, Chicago, Ill. 60607

Fortress Press. Fortress Press, 2900 Queen La, Philadelphia, Pa. 19129

Four Winds. The Four Winds Press, 50 W 44th St, New York, N.Y. 10036

Free Press. The Free Press, 866 3d Av, New York, N.Y. 10022

Funk. Funk & Wagnalls Publishing Company, 666 5th Av, New York, N.Y. 10019

Gambit. Gambit, Inc, 53 Beacon St, Boston, Mass. 02108

Geis. Bernard Geis Associates, Inc, 128 E 56th St, New York, N.Y. 10022

Godine, David R. David R. Godine, Publisher, 282 Newton St, Brookline, Mass. 02146

Grant, Donald M. Donald M. Grant, West Kingston, R. I. 02892

Grosset. Grosset & Dunlap, Inc, 51 Madison Av, New York, N.Y. 10010

Grossman Pubs. Grossman Publishers, 625 Madison Av, New York, N.Y. 10022

Grove. Grove Press, Inc, 53 E 11th St, New York, N.Y. 10003

Harcourt. Harcourt Brace Jovanovich, Inc, 757 3d Av, New York, N.Y. 10017

Harlo. Harlo Press, 16721 Hamilton Av, Detroit, Mich. 48203

Harper. Harper & Row, Publishers, 10 E 53d St, New York, N.Y. 10022

Hart. Hart Publishing Company, Inc, 719 Broadway, New York, N.Y. 10003

Hawthorn Bks. Hawthorn Books, Inc, 260 Madison Av, New York, N.Y. 10016

Herder & Herder. See Seabury

Hill & Wang. Hill & Wang, 19 Union Sq, W, New York, N.Y. 10003

Holt. Holt, Rinehart and Winston, Inc, 383 Madison Av, New York, N.Y. 10017

Horizon Press. Horizon Press, 156 5th Av, New York, N.Y. 10010

Houghton. Houghton Mifflin Company, 2 Park St, Boston, Mass. 02107

Ind. Univ. Press. Indiana University Press, 10th & Morton Sts, Bloomington, Ind. 47401

Ithaca House. Ithaca House, 108 N Plain St, Ithaca, N.Y. 14850

Jewish Pub. Jewish Publication Society of America, 222 N. 15th St, Philadelphia, Pa. 19102

Judson Press. Judson Press, Valley Forge, Pa. 19481

Knopf. Alfred A. Knopf, Inc, 201 E 50th St, New York, N.Y. 10022

Kodansha. Kodansha International/USA, 10 E 53d St, New York, N.Y. 10022

La. State Univ. Press. Louisiana State University Press, Baton Rouge, La. 70803

Lantern Press (N Y) Lantern Press, Inc, 354 Hussey Rd, Mt. Vernon, N.Y. 10552

Lippincott. J. B. Lippincott Company, E. Washington Sq, Philadelphia, Pa. 19105

Little. Little, Brown and Company, 34 Beacon St, Boston, Mass. 02106

Liveright. Liveright, 386 Park Av, S, New York, N.Y. 10016

Lothrop. Lothrop, Lee & Shepard Company, 105 Madison Av, New York, N.Y. 10016

MIT Press. Massachusetts Institute of Technology Press, 28 Carleton St, Cambridge, Mass. 02142

McCall Pub. Co. See Saturday Review Press

McClain. McClain Printing Company, 212 Main St, Parsons, W. Va. 26287

McGraw. McGraw-Hill Book Company, Inc, 1221 Av. of the Americas, New York, N.Y. 10020

McKay. David McKay Company, Inc, 750 3d Av, New York, N.Y. 10017

Macmillan (N Y) See Macmillan Pub. Co.

Macmillan Pub. Co., Macmillan Publishing Company, Inc, 866 3d Av, New York, N.Y. 10022

Manyland Bks. Manyland Books, Inc, Box 266, Wall St Sta., New York, N.Y. 10005

Meredith. Meredith Corporation, 1716 Locust St, Des Moines, Iowa 50336

Merrill. Charles E. Merrill Publishing Company, 1300 Alum Creek Dr, Columbus, Ohio 43216

Monthly Review. Monthly Review Press, 116 W 14th St, New York, N.Y. 10011

Morrow. William Morrow & Company, Inc, 105 Madison Av, New York, N.Y. 10016

N. Y. Univ. Press. New York University Press, Washington Sq, New York, N.Y. 10003

Naylor. Naylor Company, 1015 Culebra Av, San Antonio, Tex. 78201

Nelson. Thomas Nelson, Inc, 407 7th Av, S, Nashville, Tenn. 37203

New Am. Lib. The New American Library, Inc, 1301 Av. of the Americas, New York, N.Y. 10019

New Directions. New Directions Publishing Corporation, 333 Av. of the Americas, New York, N.Y. 10014

Norton. W. W. Norton & Company, Inc, 55 5th Av, New York, N.Y. 10003

Oberon Press. Oberon Press, 555 Maple La, Ottawa K1M, Ontario 7, Canada

Oriole Eds, Oriole Editions, 19 W 44th St, New York, N.Y. 10036

Oxford. Oxford University Press, Inc, 200 Madison Av, New York, N.Y. 10016

Oxford Press. Oxford Press, P.O. Box 728, Providence, R. I. 02901

Pantheon Bks. Pantheon Books, Inc, 201 E 50th St, New York, N.Y. 10022

Pegasus (N Y) See Bobbs

Penguin. Penguin Books, Inc, 7110 Ambassador Rd, Baltimore, Md. 21207

Phaedra Pubs. Phaedra Publishers, Inc, 49 Park Av, New York, N.Y. 10016

Praeger. Praeger Publishers, Inc, 111 4th Av, New York, N.Y. 10003

Prentice-Hall. Prentice-Hall, Inc, Route 9W, Englewood Cliffs, N.J. 07632

Pulse-Finger Press. Pulse-Finger Press, Box 16697, Philadelphia, Pa. 19139

Putnam. G. P. Putnam's Sons, 200 Madison Av, New York, N.Y. 10016

Quadrangle Bks. See Quadrangle/The N.Y. Times Bk. Co.

Quadrangle/The N.Y. Times Bk. Co. Quadrangle/The New York Times Book Company, 10 E 53d St, New York, N.Y. 10022

Random House. Random House, Inc, 201 E 50th St, New York, N.Y. 10022

Red Dust. Red Dust, Inc, 218 E 81st, New York, N.Y. 10028

Saturday Review Press. Saturday Review Press, 380 Madison Av, New York, N.Y. 10017